The Federal Courts

The Federal Courts

An Essential History

PETER CHARLES HOFFER
WILLIAMJAMES HULL HOFFER
N. E. H. HULL

OXFORD
UNIVERSITY PRESS

OXFORD
UNIVERSITY PRESS

Oxford University Press is a department of the University of Oxford. It furthers
the University's objective of excellence in research, scholarship, and education
by publishing worldwide.Oxford is a registered trade mark of Oxford University
Press in the UK and certain other countries.

Published in the United States of America by Oxford University Press
198 Madison Avenue, New York, NY 10016, United States of America.

© Supreme Court Historical Society 2016

Library of Congress Cataloging-in-Publication Data
Names: Hoffer, Peter Charles, 1944– author. | Hoffer, Williamjames, author. |
Hull, N. E. H., 1949– author.
Title: The federal courts : an essential history / Peter Charles Hoffer,
Williamjames Hull Hoffer, N. E. H. Hull.
Description: New York : Oxford University Press, 2016. | Includes
bibliographical references and index.
Identifiers: LCCN 2015040625 (print) | LCCN 2015040760 (ebook) |
ISBN 978–0–19–938790–8 (hardcover : alk. paper) | ISBN 978–0–19–938791–5 (E-book) |
ISBN 978–0–19–938792–2 (E-book)
Subjects: LCSH: Courts—United States—History.
Classification: LCC KF8719. H64 2016 (print) | LCC KF8719 (ebook) |
DDC 347.73/209—dc23
LC record available at http://lccn.loc.gov/2015040625

1 3 5 7 9 8 6 4 2
Printed by Sheridan, USA

The Federal Courts: An Essential History is sponsored by the Supreme Court Historical Society in partnership with the Federal Judicial Center.

This book is dedicated to Ralph I. Lancaster, Jr.

THE SUPREME COURT HISTORICAL
SOCIETY GRATEFULLY ACKNOWLEDGES
THE FINANCIAL SUPPORT FOR THIS BOOK
FROM THE FOLLOWING INSTITUTIONS
AND INDIVIDUALS

Benefactors

Katherine L. Adams
American College of Trial Lawyers
Peter G. Angelos
Boies Schiller & Flexner LLP
The Clark-Winchcole Foundation
Cleary Gottlieb Steen & Hamilton
    LLP
Clifford Law Offices, P.C.
Cohen & Gresser LLP
Cornerstone Research
Cravath, Swaine & Moore LLP
Gibson, Dunn & Crutcher LLP
Gregory P. Joseph Law Offices LLC
Paul and Josefin Hilal
Honeywell

Joseph Hage Aaronson LLC
Kirkland & Ellis LLP
McDermott Will & Emery LLP
McGuire Woods LLP
O'Melveny Myers LLP
Paul, Weiss, Rifkind, Wharton &
    Garrison LLP
Price Philanthropies Foundation
Sidley Austin LLP
Skadden, Arps, Slate, Meagher &
    Flom LLP
Sullivan & Cromwell LLP
Talmer Bank and Trust
Wachtell, Lipton Rosen & Katz
David C. Weinstein

Patrons

Debevoise & Plimpton LLP
Ford Motor Company Fund
Kramer Levin Naftalis & Frankel LLP

Liberty Institute
Merck & Co.
Morgan Lewis & Bockius LLP

Sponsors

Christopher T. Handman
William J. Haynes, II
Benjamin W. Heineman, Jr.
Paul C. Hilal
A. E. Dick Howard
Christy D. Jones
Robb M. Jones
Brad S. Karp
Neal Katyal
Judith S. Kaye
August P. Klein
Daniel F. Kolb
Philip Allen Lacovara
Christopher Landau
Thomas C. Leighton
David G. Leitch
Alan Levine
Robert A. Long
Joan A. Lukey
Thurgood Marshall, Jr.
Deanne E. Maynard
Teri P. McClure
William G. McGuinness
Lee I. Miller
Patricia A. Millett
Jeffrey P. Minear
Theodore N. Mirvis
Steven F. Molo
Michael E. Mone
Lucas E. Morel
James W. Morris, III
Gary P. Naftalis
John M. Nannes
Rick D. Nydegger
James B. O'Hara
Ronald L. Olson
Theodore B. Olson
Barry R. Ostrager

Michael H. Park
R. Hewitt Pate
Leon B. Polsky
Robert E. Price
James W. Quinn
John B. Quinn
Harry M. Reasoner
Abraham C. Reich
Teresa Wynn Roseborough
Jonathan D. Schiller
Richard A. Schneider
Jay A. Sekulow
Kelly J. Shackelford
Pratik A. Shah
Steven R. Shapiro
John S. Siffert
Paul M. Smith
Kenneth W. Starr
Mathew D. Staver
Cathleen Douglas Stone
Jeffrey E. Stone
Stephen D. Susman
Theodore W. Ullyot
Anton R. Valukas
Paul R. Verkuil
Alan B. Vickery
James L. Volling
Seth P. Waxman
Dan K. Webb
Tal M. Weberg
David C. Weinstein
W. Foster Wollen
Bruce E. Yannett
Dean A. Ziehl
Robert E. Juceam, General Counsel
David T. Pride, Executive Director
Kathleen Shurtleff, Assistant Director

SUPREME COURT HISTORICAL SOCIETY'S ACKNOWLEDGMENTS:

Editors: Clare Cushman, Bruce A. Ragsdale

Authors: Peter Charles Hoffer, Williamjames Hull Hoffer, N.E.H. Hull

Afterword Authors: John S. Cooke, Russell R. Wheeler, with Daniel S. Holt and Jake Kobrick

Historical Research Assistance from: Daniel S. Holt, Associate Historian Federal Judicial Center; Jake Kobrick, Associate Historian Federal Judicial Center; Louis Hoffer, Consultant

Editorial Research: Isabel Dorval, Louis Hoffer, Joanna Labor, Laura Frank Shaw, Dana John Stefanelli

Illustrations: Clare Cushman, Peter Charles Hoffer

Development Consultant: Janet Tramonte

Technology Consultant: Sean Burchett

CONTENTS

PART III   NO LONGER THE WEAKEST BRANCH,
THE COURTS FROM 1929 TO 1986

FOREWORD

One of the missions of the Federal Judicial Center, in addition to overseeing research and education for the federal judiciary, is to conduct, coordinate, and encourage programs related to the history of the judicial branch of the federal government. When the Supreme Court Historical Society suggested that we collaborate on a one-volume history of the federal courts, we immediately and enthusiastically agreed. We were pleased to find and work with three eminent historians—Peter Charles Hoffer, Williamjames Hull Hoffer, and N. E. H. Hull—to produce this magnificent history.

Works that explore political, economic, social, and cultural currents in the history of our country too often exclude the federal courts. At the same time, historical writing about the federal courts too often has failed to situate their development in a broader context.

This book endeavors to explain the role of the federal courts in our broader national history: both how the courts helped to shape it and how they were shaped by it. Federal courts often make decisions that affect not only the parties before them but also political, social, and economic issues of local, regional, national, and even international importance. The evolution of the federal courts, and even their existence, was not preordained. How and why did they develop as they have? Who were the men and women whose thought and efforts contributed to making the courts the unique institution they have come to be?

It has been our pleasure at the Federal Judicial Center to collaborate with the Supreme Court Historical Society, particularly David Pride and Clare Cushman, and with the authors on this ambitious and valuable project. We hope that this book will enhance understanding of the rich story of the federal courts and spur additional interest in the study and exposition of the third branch.

Jeremy Fogel
Director, Federal Judicial Center
November 2015

PREFACE

At first it seemed that the Supreme Court Historical Society had asked us to perform an impossible task: write the history of the entire federal court system, its personnel, procedures, achievements, output, and failures, for both general audiences and legal professionals, in the space of a single volume. It was only with great humility and trepidation that we agreed to try.

We adopted and have tried to follow a number of housekeeping rules to structure our research and writing. While much of what we needed to cover required technical language, we knew that general readers were unlikely to understand such explanations without help. We determined to simplify as much as possible without sacrificing accuracy. The best known members of the federal court system are the justices of the U.S. Supreme Court, and the "rule of recognition" gives their jurisprudence pride of place in any account of the federal judiciary because it is the template for lower courts' decisions in cases involving similar issues. At the same time, the lower courts are in many ways even more important institutions, for they are the face of the federal judiciary for the vast majority of litigants and litigators who seek redress in federal courts. A history of the federal courts is a history of people who serve, but there have been too many members of the federal judiciary to provide even capsule biographies of every federal judge in a work such as this. This volume profiles those judges and justices who we believe played the most important part in the story of the courts. The Federal Judicial Center website, fjc.gov, has biographies of all Article III federal judges at http://www.fjc.gov/history/home.nsf/page/judges.html.

There is a vast array of secondary literature on the federal courts, most of it law review pieces; some of it in books, administrative government reports, and other sources. Including more than a small portion of these in the notes would overwhelm the narrative and unnecessarily puff up the citations. Where portions of these secondary sources are especially relevant or the source for an argument or quotation, they appear in the endnotes.

A bibliographical note at the end of the work is a very brief guide to research in the primary sources, for we recognized that sound historical scholarship rests on primary source research. Judicial opinions and other public records are in print and online, as are the texts of statutes. The Library of Congress, the National Archives, and the National Archives and Record Administration regional depositories are treasure troves for unpublished (manuscript) materials. One could spend years in the archives and never do full justice either to their holdings or to a book project like this. Self-imposed selectivity was necessary in using all of these sources. So, too, the newspapers, the correspondence of the judges, and other traditional historical primary sources had to be mined, but only a small selection could be included here.

Selectivity also demanded that we determine criteria for the inclusion of cases, institutional information, content of statutes, congressional debates, judicial biographies, and other materials. We adopted four rules. Contemporary significance was the first criterion for inclusion. If it mattered to men and women at the time, it belongs in this volume. Second, subsequent or lasting impact on the development of the law or the institutions of the federal judiciary weighed in our calculations. The third criterion was how clearly the judicial event illustrated or reflected a time and place in history. Finally, we selected anecdotes about cases that we hope will especially enhance readers' understanding of the work of the federal courts. We give more space to these than to other cases because in our thinking they are what law professor Karl Llewellyn called "cases of trouble"— cases wherein basic values or customs are at stake.

The narrative is divided in three parts according to the expertise and interests of the authors. Peter Charles Hoffer is largely responsible for the first part; Williamjames Hull Hoffer for the second part; and N. E. H. Hull for the third part, although the authors collaborated throughout the course of the research and writing. All read and commented on each part, and the final version bears the imprint of all three authors.

It is rare treat for readers and authors of histories when they can tap the expertise of those who had inside knowledge of the story and, even more important, helped frame it. Russell Wheeler is a former deputy director of the FJC, a post that John S. Cooke now holds. Both were in a unique position to observe the evolution of the federal courts from the 1980s to the present. The authors are delighted and honored that John and Russell have contributed an afterword to this history covering that period.

Finally, a due humility imposes a warranty of use. Writing books is always a learning experience for authors. In the course of learning more about the federal courts, we discussed among ourselves two ways that we might present our story. The first envisioned a great panorama, full of people, places, and events, a vast still life thorough which we would lead the reader. Textbooks and narratives of long period of time often take this form. We opted instead for a second kind of depiction, a view of a world in motion, constantly changing, unfinished, which authors and readers together watch unfold. Nothing in this landscape stays the same and nothing is predetermined. To paraphrase Felix Frankfurter, this sort of assay would be as "tentative, reflective, suggestive, contradictory, and incomplete" as "the perversities and complexities" of our nation's history itself.

AUTHORS' ACKNOWLEDGMENTS

Executive director David Pride and editorial director Clare Cushman of the Supreme Court Historical Society, co-editor of the volume, invited us to participate as authors in this project. For that honor, and the many courtesies that followed, we are deeply grateful. Cushman read the manuscript many times and shared in the burden of finding an academic publisher. Robert Juceam, pro bono legal counsel for the Society, worked over the contracts with the authors and the presses.

Judge Jeremy D. Fogel, director of the Federal Judicial Center, supported the project from its inception. We gratefully acknowledge his good offices. At the History Office of the Federal Judicial Center, former director Bruce A. Ragsdale and his associates Daniel S. Holt and Jake Kobrick were not only graciously accommodating with the results of their own research, they were an unflagging source of encouragement during the entire process of research and writing and gave special assistance to FJC Deputy Director John S. Cooke in the preparation of the afterword. Bruce read portions of the manuscript four times and ably chaired the Board of Editors, John stepped in to help with the final chapters of the book, and his assistance was greatly appreciated.

At the University of Georgia, department heads John Morrow and Claudio Saunt supported the research and writing with assigned research duty. At Rutgers Law School–Camden, Dean Rayman Solomon provided essential resources and access to his own research. Law students Mana Ameri, Jared Dorfman, Barbara Previ, and Rachel Savicki read and commented on early drafts of chapters 1–10. At Seton Hall University, Dean Michael Zavada was a strong supporter of the project and provided funding for travel. To all of these folks, we offer our sincere thanks.

Against the threat of flood, fire, mildew, and funding exigency, the archivists at the regional National Archives and Records Administration have preserved the records of the courts and, more important, made research in them a joy. Among them with whom we worked most closely, we thank Joan Gearin and Nathaniel Wiltzen at NARA Boston; Charles Miller at NARA San Francisco; Jefferson Moak and Gail Farr at NARA Philadelphia; Lori Cox-Paul and Jake Ersland at NARA Kansas City, Missouri; Shane Bell, Nathan Jordan, and Arlene Royer at NARA Atlanta; Katie Dishman at NARA Chicago; Rodney Krajka and Barbara Rust at NARA Ft. Worth; and Gregory J. Plunges at NARA New York City. At the National Archives in Washington, D.C., Robert Ellis helped our research in the D.C. Circuit records. Louis Hoffer joined the team of authors to research NARA manuscript court records, traversing the country in search of tales from the archives. He also served as a fact checker. His contribution to the project was invaluable.

Many fellow students of the courts graciously read portions of the manuscript and offered helpful comments or provided insights on the project along the way. They include Michal Belknap, Michael Les Benedict, Steven Berry, Barry Cushman, Carol Emberton, Paul Finkelman, Daniel Hulsebosch, Paul Kens, Jonathan Lurie, Pauline Maier, William Nelson, Judith Resnik, Michael Ross, Michael Wells, and William Wiecek. They put aside their work to help us with ours, one of the most admirable traditions of collegiate academia.

We are grateful as well to the fact checkers whose thoroughness improved the manuscript. In addition to Louis Hoffer, they were Laura Rachel Shaw Frank, Joanna Kathleen Labor, and Dana John Stefanelli.

Our advisory board, the Honorable J. Harvie Wilkinson, the Honorable Diane Wood, the Honorable Laura Taylor Swain, Professors Daniel Ernst, Laura Kalman, Edward Purcell, and Russell Wheeler of the Brookings Institution read and critiqued the manuscript at a crucial moment in its development. It was a pleasure and an honor to have them as our advisors. A special "call out" to Russell Wheeler is appropriate. His devotion of time and energy to the revision of the manuscript far exceeded the call of duty. We are grateful to him for his expertise and his patience and for joining John S. Cooke in preparing the afterword.

We acknowledge permission from Charles Myers, director of the University Press of Kansas, to recast in close paraphrase without quotation marks portions of Peter Charles Hoffer, Williamjames Hull Hoffer, and N. E. H. Hull, *The Supreme Court: An Essential History* (2007); Brian Wheel, senior editor at Oxford University Press, to adapt portions of Peter Charles Hoffer, *For Ourselves and Our Posterity: The Preamble to the Federal Constitution in American History* (2013); and Robert J. Brugger, senior editor emeritus at the Johns Hopkins University Press, to reuse portions of Peter Charles Hoffer, *Law and People in Colonial America* (2nd ed., 1998) in the present work. Citations in the notes indicate when the authors relied on these three works. Senior editor

David McBride of Oxford University Press kept faith with the project from its inception to its fruition. A special word about David: Everyone who has worked with him has had the same experience as we had, making their books, like this one, a joy to see through production. David's assistant, Katie Weaver, was a wonderful and skilled hand at moving the project from the editorial to the production stage.

Introduction

Most often the story of the federal judiciary is simply a tale of hard work—of sometimes numbing caseloads and unpleasant travel, of finding order in the chaotic system of state and federal law, local custom, and contentious lawyering. Then again, there are moments in American history when all eyes are focused on what is happening in a federal court; when its bench speaks for millions of Americans; when its decisions change the course of events. Ours is a story of these courts and the judges who served on them, but even more important, first and foremost, overall and throughout, a story of the courts' vital part in our history.

Our retelling of that history is framed by the location of the courts in the center of what may be visualized as three concentric rings. These three rings are themes that shape the narrative in the following pages. The first and smallest of the rings is the system of separation of powers, monitored by checks and balances among the various branches of the federal government. The federal courts are one of three independent yet interlocking parts of the federal government. The fundamental though sometimes contentious relationship among the executive branch, the courts, and Congress, in particular, the "precise limits of Congress's authority" to confer and restrict jurisdiction, to create and modify the structure of the lower courts, make housekeeping rules for all the courts, and at times to engage in direct confrontation with the judiciary shaped the evolution of the federal judiciary. Most of the time, it appears that the checks and balances system is weighted heavily in favor of the other two branches of the federal government. The president nominates and the Senate confirms appointments to the federal bench, after which the president signs the commissions. Congress can create new kinds of federal courts and add or subtract jurisdiction from all the federal courts except what the Constitution gives to the Supreme Court as its original jurisdiction. By contrast, the courts' check on the presidency and the Congress is far weaker and less direct. The power of the federal courts to declare legislation or executive action unconstitutional is a check employed only with great caution, although courts sometimes call on Congress to revise legislation.[1]

1

A second, wider, circle is the federal system itself, in which both the national and the state governments are sovereign. This seemingly awkward design of dual federalism was necessary to secure ratification of the Constitution in the states, but it had the potential to pit federal courts against state courts and legislatures. Alexander Hamilton, an astute and successful practitioner in the New York courts, recognized the potential for this kind of conflict in his Federalist No. 82. To allay suspicions that federal courts would subordinate the states' courts, he told readers "the states will retain all pre-existing" jurisdiction over civil suits, save "where an exclusive authority is in express terms granted to the union," or when "the exercise of a like authority is prohibited to the states," or if overlapping jurisdiction "would be utterly incompatible." Hamilton made the same points in defense of the federal courts later at the New York ratification convention.[2]

This judicial federalism sometimes brought state statute law and court decisions into federal courts, for the federal Constitution and the Judiciary Act of 1789 and subsequent congressional statutes provided review of state law by the federal courts. (State courts could and do use federal law to settle suits as well.) Sometimes the overlapping boundaries of judicial federalism brought state and federal judicial authorities into conflict. More often, state and federal courts worked in close accord.[3]

The first and second circles are the two prongs of what is now termed the "Madisonian Compromise," in reality a series of compromises that Madison and others brokered at the Constitutional Convention of 1787 and the first session of the U.S. Congress in 1789. The framers of these compromises could not, of course, predict how they would work in the long term, but both checks and balances and judicial federalism have proven durable, workable systems.[4]

The widest, third, circle in which the federal courts operate is the democratic-republican system of American self-government. The federal judiciary is not elective, and its principal judges serve during good behavior rather than at the pleasure of Congress, the president, or the electorate. But the independence that lifetime tenure theoretically confers did not and does not isolate the judiciary from political currents, partisan quarrels, and public opinion. Many vital political issues came to the federal courts, and the courts' decisions in turn shaped American politics.[5]

Although the Constitution nowhere mentions political parties, and the framers of the Constitution regarded political factions as something on a spectrum between dangerous cabals and self-interested coteries, parties and politics—and the partisanships they engender—have been a fact of national American political life from the moment that the Constitution went into effect. We are an especially political people, and our public arena demonstrates "a conflict, limited and regularized, but nonetheless relentless, among groups . . . who have contradictory interests and more or less mutually exclusive hopes of securing them." In such a public arena, the courts could isolate themselves from these controversies and conflicts if they tried, but no serious observer believes that the courts are entirely insulated from the currents of political opinion. In the words of turn-of-the-century journalist Finley Peter Dunne's immensely popular alter ego, "Mr. Dooley," "No matther whether th' constitution follows th' flag or not, th' Supreme Coort follows th' illiction returns."[6]

At the same time, the impact of political ideologies and partisanships on the courts should not be overstated. Many years ago, law professor Alexander Bickel, one of the most astute observers of the federal courts, made the same point. "It is never altogether realistic to conclude that behind all judicial dialectic there was personal preference and personal power and nothing else . . . if it be true . . . then their authority over us is totally intolerable and totally irreconcilable with the theory and practice of political democracy." In fact, the judges themselves are the people most concerned that it not be true. As Chief Justice John G. Roberts Jr., writing for the Court in *Lanell Yulee-Williams v. Florida Bar* (2015), put the matter, "Judges are not politicians, even when they come to the bench by way of the ballot." The restraints posed on judges by precedent, the judicial code, and norms of ethical conduct also moderate any partisan tendencies. Today, the vast majority of federal judges' background and professional experience leans them toward more moderate stances on public issues than the more partisan players in the political arena would advocate.[7]

Operating within these three circles, the federal courts, the least democratic branch in theory, have proved in some ways and at various times to be the most democratic: open to ordinary people seeking redress for example. Litigation in the federal courts reflects the changing aspirations and values of America's many peoples. As Massachusetts Supreme Judicial Court judge and scholar Oliver Wendell Holmes Jr. told the Suffolk Massachusetts Bar Association in 1885, judge-made law was "a magic mirror, wherein we see reflected our own lives." To this one should add that the decisions of the judges of the federal courts changed those lives. It was a reciprocal arrangement, magic mirrors facing one another, the reflections in each repeated over and over through time.[8]

Within the three circles one also finds epicycles of continuity and discontinuity. The most obvious continuity consists in the overall growth and elaboration of the function of the federal courts. Similarly, one cannot miss the growing administrative apparatus of the courts, including the Administrative Office of the United States Courts, Federal Judicial Center, and United States Sentencing Commission among other judicial branch agencies. Institutional bodies, like the Conference of Senior Circuit Court Judges (in 1948 retitled the Judicial Conference of the United States), provide counsel to the judicial branch and, under a statutory framework, abet the administration of the courts.

This growth was not linear—the number of judges and variety of courts adapting to the demands on the court system in a simple upward progression. Instead, the growth was punctuated, long periods of increasing caseloads behind which lagged the courts' carrying capacity, followed by sudden spurts of activity in which additional judgeships were authorized. Often Congress did not want to spend more on the courts, or political divisions in Congress, or friction between Congress and the president delayed necessary remedies.[9]

The increasing flow of cases the federal courts faced over time is another continuity that accompanied their growth. Since the 1830s the system periodically was overloaded with civil litigation and criminal matters. The growth of the court system did not accommodate the flood. Overloaded dockets have long concerned students of the federal court system. In 1927, Harvard Law School professors Felix Frankfurter and James Landis published a seminal tract entitled *The Business of the Supreme Court of the United States: A Study in the Federal Judicial System*. While they lauded the operation of the courts, they worried that "the great increase in prosecutions for petty offenses in the federal courts, for which Prohibition is largely but not exclusively responsible, has cast burdens upon the federal courts that to no small degree transform their traditional place in our federal system." Forty-five years later, federal Court of Appeals Judge Henry J. Friendly dedicated his Carpentier Lectures at Columbia University to the same subject. He found the federal courts faced with "a breakdown." The civil rights revolution, a spate of habeas corpus appeals, the war on drugs, and economic and environmental regulatory initiatives threatened to overwhelm the lower courts. Congress was heaping more and more on the courts' plate. More judges, more (specialized) courts, and legislation that gave the Supreme Court almost entire discretion over its docket did not relieve the courts' burdens or reduce the danger of a breakdown. As Judge Richard A. Posner of the U.S. Court of Appeals for the Seventh Circuit wrote in 1999, the increase in the district courts' cases from the 1970s to 1999, though "dramatic" in itself, was "dwarfed" by a rising tide of appeals. He feared that the system was staggering, and the palliative reforms proposed, much less those assayed, did not get to the root of the matter.[10]

The discontinuities in the history of the federal courts are perhaps even more striking than the continuities. Three of them dictate the tripartite structure of this book. The first was the decision the framers made to create a system of lower federal courts. This expanded the federal court system into every state. At the Constitutional Convention and later during debates over the Judiciary Act of 1789 in the first federal Congress, many of the framers opposed the creation of lower federal courts. Part I of our story follows the elaboration of this system from one end of the country to the other, ending in 1860, by which time the nation was truly continental. The second great watershed was the Civil War and

Reconstruction. As a result of wartime and postwar legislation in Congress, the scope, size, and jurisdiction of the federal courts expanded dramatically, ending with the creation of an entirely new tier of appellate tribunals. The expansion of the courts accompanied the shift from a largely rural, agricultural nation with a relatively small federal government to a largely urban and industrial giant. The rise of administrative forms of organization also reshaped the structure and everyday operation of the federal courts into something like their modern form. Part II traces this story. Part III begins with the Great Depression, a time when federal courts faced some of the most critical challenges. New kinds of litigation and litigants reflected sea changes in social and cultural ideas, and these once again remade the place of the federal courts in our history. The boundaries of the parts and the chapters could have been placed differently, but as presently arrayed, the three parts conform to the conventional narrative arcs, that is, the scholarly periodization of American history textbooks. Each chapter surveys a portion of that narrative.

As is apparent from the preceding, we do not see the courts as insulated from larger historical forces. The contrary is true. The judiciary operates in the context of national and local politics, economic developments, and intellectual currents, and changes with them. The first of these contexts is geographical. The rapid territorial expansion of the nation was soon followed by the expansion of the lower courts' into the newly settled areas, first as territorial courts, then as district and circuit courts. The courts' accommodation to territorial expansion over time ensured that litigants in the West had access to the same judicial remedies as litigants in the more settled portions of the country. To be sure, diversity in the sorts of cases and varied ethnic makeup of the litigants coming to federal courts in different parts of the country were reflected in the varied handling of cases in the districts.[11]

Such a "federalism of outcomes," to coin a phrase, promoted local attachment to the federal system in its infancy and continues to accommodate the social and cultural differences of different parts of the country. With one early exception (the District of Maine) and one current exception (Wyoming and those portions of Yellowstone National Park situated in Montana and Idaho constitute one judicial district), the boundaries of the districts coincide with the boundaries of states in which the district court sits. After holding hearings in ten cities throughout the nation, Congress's Commission on Revision of the Federal Court Appellate System in 1973 conceded that regional attachment to the various circuits was too strong to recommend reorganizing the boundaries of the existing circuits as a means of adjusting the geographical jurisdiction of their courts of appeals. Members of the bar gave "eloquent testimony" to the sense of community within the circuit and the "loyalty" that lawyers had to the existing bench and the law of the circuit. Twenty-five years later, a different statutory commission concluded that the Court of Appeals for the Ninth Circuit was too large to function effectively, but that the remedy to the situation was not to divide the circuit but to reorganize its Court of Appeals. (In any event, Congress declined to do anything.) As Court of Appeals for the Second Circuit Judge Irving Kaufman wrote when he introduced a historical exhibit about his circuit in 1977, "each of the circuits retains its regional character." At the same time, the hierarchical system of appeals and the fact that judges in one circuit take notice of decisions in other circuits ensured that there would be some degree of finality and uniformity, in turn fostering national unity.[12]

Second, cycles of economic boom and bust, in particular periods of economic distress, turned the eyes of debtors and creditors to the courts. Rapid commercial expansion fueled by speculation followed by rapid contraction, due to domestic tight-money policy and overseas staple market fluctuations, was a regular feature of the nation's commercial and working life in the nineteenth century and to some extent remain so. Federal bankruptcy statutes made the courts into miniature managers of personal and company distress. In times of economic trouble, the business of the courts boomed, causing a crisis of its own as dockets crowded and caseloads exploded.[13]

Third, national political controversies and pivotal elections, including scandals involving officers of the federal government, often landed in the federal courts. From the battles over the Second Bank of the United States in the first decades of the nineteenth century to the Watergate scandal of 1972–1974 to the controversial handling of suspected terrorists in the first years of the twenty-first century, federal courts acted as referees in contests over power begun in the other branches. Quarrels and scandals brought a flurry of congressional enactments, for example, regulation of political contributions that federal courts had to interpret.

The pivotal elections that most entangled the federal courts included the election of Thomas Jefferson, in 1801, with its consequent struggle between Jeffersonian Republicans and Federalists for control of the judiciary; the election of Andrew Jackson, in 1828, leading to both federalism and separation of powers tests of federal courts' authority; the election of 1860, with the ensuing secession of the southern states and the closing of all but two southern federal courts; the disputed Tilden-Hayes contest of 1876, settled by a fifteen-member commission that included five Supreme Court justices, with consequences for the judicial enforcement of the Civil Rights Acts; the election of 1936 followed by Franklin D. Roosevelt's "Court-packing plan"; and the election of 2000, in which the Supreme Court played a decisive role in determining the outcome of the presidential race.

Fourth, alterations in the larger aims and activity of the federal government profoundly changed patterns of litigation and the expectations that litigants had about the relief available from the federal courts. These shifts were not a straightforward progression from a weak to a strong federal government, but multiformal, as the commitment of the federal government to play its part in American life shifted, sometimes within an administration. Larger swings in government policy included eras of regulatory innovation in the Progressive and New Deal eras followed by conservative reactions. In more recent times, as the concept of public rights shifted from an almost exclusive emphasis on property rights to a far broader ideal of both property rights and personal dignity, the federal courts became arbiters of a wide range of civil rights. Then a period of retrenchment and retreat constrained the reformist role of courts. Changing definitions of federal crimes, in particular Prohibition in the 1920s and the war on drugs from the 1970s to the 1990s, and, most recently, immigration law enforcement, increased criminal cases on the docket significantly. On top of the spurt in prosecution of drug, weapons, and white-collar crimes in federal courts, a shift in federal sentencing rules in 1984 increased the population of federal prisons eightfold— 25,000 in 1980 to 219,000 in 2012.[14]

Fifth, changes in the values of American culture and society, for example, shifting attitudes toward race relations, women's rights, alcohol and drug use, the civil rights of gay men, lesbians, bisexuals, and transgendered individuals have impressed themselves on the federal courts. In turn, the revised concepts of law changed how Americans related to one another. A study of history shows that the old adage "law cannot change society" is wrong. As Martin Luther King Jr. put it, "while it may be true that morality cannot be legislated, behavior can be regulated. It may be true that the law cannot change the heart but it can restrain the heartless."[15]

Finally, the growing importance of managerial skills in business and education applied to the judiciary as well. After the adoption of the Federal Rules of Civil Procedure in 1938, federal courts sitting in equity have become managers of school systems and pollution-abatement cases. Complex litigation over mass torts joined as class actions have required federal district court judges to oversee diverse and ongoing settlement plans. The modern federal judge must have the administrative skills of a CEO and be learned in the law.[16]

The afterword surveys the modern courts from a different vantage point than the first thirteen chapters. Our perspective as historians means we look back from the present. John S. Cooke and Russell R. Wheeler's intimate and informed engagement with the administration of the courts allowed them to consider recent events in light of ongoing developments. We believe that the afterword thus gives this study a unique authority and freshness.

PART I

COURTS IN THE FORMATIVE
ERA, 1776–1860

In the first years of the federal courts, the nation's independence, won at great cost after a seven-year war against Britain, was still insecure. Imperial powers on its borders and their Indian allies posed grave threats to peace and growth. In debt from the war and a postwar buying spree, the nation wallowed in a recession and the confederation government proved unable to pay what it owed. A new and unproven federal political system based on a Constitution that many (perhaps a majority) of Americans opposed, opened its doors in the temporary capital of New York City.[1]

Yet from these small and uncertain beginnings a great nation would come. The American multiplication table that Benjamin Franklin described, its population doubling every twenty-five years, allowed native born and newcomers to spread through the Northwest and Southwest Territories. The acquisition in 1803 from France of a vast land mass called the Louisiana Territory, stretching from the Mississippi to the Rocky Mountains and by the 1840s to the Pacific Ocean, spurred westward movement. New lands for family farming and ranching meant opportunity for cultivators from older, less productive farming regions, and for land speculators. With the introduction of canals and railroads, the produce of the farms supported the advance of commerce and industry in the cities.[2]

From an unpromising start—what Alexander Hamilton called the "least dangerous" and what was the least busy branch of an unproven constitutional system—federal courts' dockets grew in fits and starts. Initially, the largest portion of the docket was suits brought by the federal government, diversity cases (in which the vying parties resided in different states), admiralty cases (maritime contracts, torts, crimes, and injuries), and cases arising from the Constitution or treaties.

Despite the relative paucity of cases, federal judges were aware that they were under close scrutiny from state authorities and local communities of law practitioners. Reading their eulogies would lead one to believe that their personal qualities and professional reputation among the members of its bar shielded them from all criticism, but this was not true. The job demanded a tough skin, great tact, and learning in the law. Some of the judges in this period rose above even these exacting standards to contribute to the body of the law. It is thus tempting to see these first judges representing a golden age of the bench, though not all of them deserve that accolade.

Throughout this formative period, the federal judiciary's role was not limited to convening sessions of the courts and deciding cases. The judges and justices were often major political figures with ambitions that extended beyond the bench. Most had served in other branches of state and federal government. There was no professional canon that barred such extrajudicial political roles. Judges were also asked at times to perform ex officio functions. At the same time, controversies spurred by opposing nationalist and states' rights' ideologies found their way to the courts.

The district and circuit courts created by the Judiciary Act of 1789 did not have appellate supervision over the state courts in criminal or civil matters. That was reserved for the U.S. Supreme Court; although, the Habeas Corpus Act of 1867 allowing counsel for those held in state custody to seek habeas corpus aid in federal courts was and remains a species of federal supervision of state court criminal proceedings. State courts were far more important in civil litigation than federal courts. The vast majority of suits then, as now, began and were resolved in state courts. But in areas of law crucial to the economic development and political condition of the nation, for example admiralty, territorial land use, and slavery, federal courts had the final say.[3]

As chattel slavery (in which slaves were personal property) went west from its outposts in the Carolina Lowcountry and the Chesapeake to the rich bottom lands of the Mississippi Delta and the Southwest, federal courts and federal law followed. Slavery's value—providing able labor in the cotton, sugar, and tobacco cultivation, along with the profits of the internal slave trade and the increased value of the new generations of slaves—was a vital factor in the economic growth of the nation, but it alienated free labor and isolated the southern slave states. The stage was set for a legal clash over slavery, for without legal sanction, slavery could not exist. That legal clash erupted as early as the debate over the slave trade at the Philadelphia Constitutional Convention, continued into the crisis over the admission of Missouri as a slave state in 1819–1821, worsened during the disputed annexation of Texas in 1836–1845, and paralyzed Congress repeatedly in acerbic duels over California's admission as a free state in 1850 and the opening of the Kansas Territory to slavery in 1854.[4]

Congress was not the only branch of the federal government that had to deal with slavery. Slave cases were not the most frequent types of federal court hearings, but they were often the most snarled. Some judges found themselves caught between statutes and precedents that protected slavery and their own conscientious revulsion at the institution. A series of slavery cases in the federal courts concluding with *Dred Scott v. Sanford* in 1857 and *Ableman v. Booth* two years later moved the federal courts front and center to the crisis. With Congress stalemated and courts struggling over the slavery question, the election of the first free soil president, Republican Abraham Lincoln in 1860, proved the last straw for die-hard defenders of the South's "peculiar institution." South Carolina's radical response was secession, and federal judges in the South resigned their commissions some to take up judicial office in the newly established Confederate States of America.[5]

Founding the Federal Courts, 1776–1789

The elaboration of the federal courts as a system from its inception to the present was never inevitable or predetermined. It resulted instead from a myriad of choices and contingencies that sometimes had unexpected and unplanned consequences. That said, there were foretastes of the evolution of the federal courts in the first years of the new nation; the powerful themes that run through the long history of the federal courts showed themselves early in our tale. The first of these themes is the close connection between national politics and the federal judiciary. The second is the concern that some state leaders exhibited about any threat to their state's sovereignty and the countervailing desire of a cadre of nationalists to expand the powers of the federal government. The third theme is that of the judiciary's contested role, autonomy, and discretion in a three-branch system of checks and balances. These themes first appeared in the Revolutionary era, framed the debate over the inclusion of federal courts in the Constitution, and shaped the Judiciary Act and the Process Act of 1789.[1]

Courts for Revolutionaries

The American Revolution was a political and military upheaval, transforming thirteen colonies of the British crown into a confederation of thirteen independent republics and then defending that transformation through seven years of war. Though both organized and spontaneous violence was an integral part of this transformation, the American Revolution is distinguished from others in that age of revolutions by the attention that our Revolutionary leaders gave to legal matters. The writing of state constitutions was among their first tasks. They inverted English legal theory, wherein the constitution was the compilation of the acts of the existing government. Revolutionary constitutions stood apart from and marked the foundation of the new American republics. Those constitutions featured innovations like bills of rights, guarantees of the sovereignty of the people, and, perhaps most important, an entirely new practice unlike any in either British domestic law or its imperial system—separation of powers. In turn, the separation of powers doctrine afforded the new nation's courts an independence not seen in Britain or its colonies.[2]

British colonial government in the eighteenth century was marked by overlapping and multiple office holding. Assemblies and councils (the upper houses of the legislatures) were both legislative bodies and courts. The governors were executive heads and judges. For example, during much of the 1760s, Thomas Hutchinson of Massachusetts was the lieutenant governor of the colony, the chief judge of its Superior Court of Judicature, and a voting member of the council. Multiple office holding facilitated English political allegiances and patronage control of the colonies. This was particularly true for the judiciary. Under the Act of Settlement of 1701, judges in England served during good behavior and could only be removed by Parliament. By contrast, the judges in the colonies served at the monarch's pleasure and could be removed by him whenever he chose—one of the grievances cited in the Declaration of Independence.[3]

Revolutionary lawgivers rejected multiple office holding and the holding of judicial office at pleasure. Their new republics must be safe from the corruptive effects of such political practices. Out of this concern came the foundational notion of republican jurisprudence—a concept of the independence of the judicial "branch" of government from the legislative and executive branches. This separation of powers would be monitored and maintained by checks and balances each branch of government exercised against the others.[4]

The phrase "separation of powers" was common in English political discourse as early as the pamphlet wars of the mid-seventeenth century. John Locke employed the term, as did other advocates of constitutional reform. Eighteenth-century French political writer Montesquieu saw separation of the monarchical from the legislative and judicial branches as a guarantor of liberty. These early formulations gained precision and power in John Adams's *Thoughts on Government* (1776), a short tract written to influence the shaping of a new constitution for Massachusetts. In it he asked, rhetorically, "As good government is an empire of laws, how shall your laws be made?" He hated multiple office holding and advised that no official should be allowed to hold more than one.[5]

Adams, a lawyer by trade who played a vital role in challenging multiple office holding in Massachusetts during the crisis, insisted that the independence of the judiciary was essential to prevent its capture by the legislature or its domination by the executive. "The dignity and stability of government in all its branches, the morals of the people, and every blessing of society depend so much upon an upright and skillful administration of justice that the judicial power ought to be distinct from both the legislative and executive, and independent upon both, that so it may be a check upon both, as both should be checks upon that."[6]

Adams's formulation of the idea of an independent judiciary became a hallmark of revolutionary constitutionalism. He wrote it into the Massachusetts state constitution. Other states followed the same course. In the new republican regime, the independent judiciary was supposed to be safe from the grasp (if not the reach) of the elective executive and legislative offices, away from the influence of the mob, influence peddlers, and the potential tyrant—at least in theory.[7]

Adams's notion of the independence of the judiciary imposed strict standards on appointment to and performance in that branch of government. He insisted that judges, particularly supreme court judges, must embody the authority of the law. "The judges, therefore, should be always men of learning and experience in the laws, of exemplary morals, great patience, calmness, coolness, and attention. Their minds should not be distracted with jarring interests; they should not be dependent upon any man, or body of men." In short, they should have a judicial temperament. Alexander Hamilton, also a lawyer, made the same point in 1788: "The benefits of the integrity and moderation of the judiciary have already been felt in more states than one . . . Considerate men of every description ought to prize whatever will tend to beget or fortify that temper in the courts." John Jay, the first chief justice of the Supreme Court (the title was changed in 1866 to Chief Justice of the United States) explained these matters to a New York grand jury in 1790: "wise and virtuous men . . . have at length unanimously agreed" that the powers of government "should be divided into three distinct, independent departments, the executive, legislative, and judicial." A system of checks and balances would "keep each within its proper limits."[8]

With royal judges gone, the theoretical quarrel the revolutionaries had with the judiciary dissipated. Because the new states' judges all had Revolutionary credentials, Adams's call for judicial tenure during good behavior (as opposed to colonial system of tenure during the pleasure of the crown) would immediately become the rule in eight of the new states. For example, Massachusetts's new constitution expressly stated that "it is essential to the preservation of the rights of every individual, his life, liberty, property, and character, that there be an impartial interpretation of the laws, and administration of justice . . . the judges of the supreme court should hold their offices as long as they behave themselves well." Pennsylvania's supreme court judges were barred by its constitution from "holding any other office, civil or military, not to take or receive fees or perquisites of any kind" but on good behavior could be reappointed to office every seven years and were to have a fixed salary. [9]

Republican jurisprudence elevated the status of the republican judge above the virulent politics of the Revolutionary era in part because courts would be called upon to protect the procedural and civil rights gained in the Revolution and enumerated in the state constitutions. These included freedom of speech and assembly, jury trial, the right to counsel, prohibitions on illegal searches and seizures, and the right to own and bear arms. Defending these provisions sometimes brought judges into direct conflict with legislatures, but in the main the prestige and independence of the judiciary survived the challenges. Only in North Carolina and Pennsylvania did state supreme court judges face impeachment in this period, and in neither case was the judge removed. The New Hampshire framers even included a provision to prevent "too numerous impeachments."[10]

Though jealous of their own judicial branches' independence, in one area of law the first states had to concede a modicum of jurisdiction to other tribunals. Even before independence was declared, the Continental Congress established a tribunal to hear cases of confiscations at sea. It was an appellate body to which parties in Revolutionary state courts could appeal those courts' determination of cases. In 1780, again before the adoption of the Articles of Confederation officially created the United States, the Confederation Congress fashioned a three-judge court of its own to hear cases of admiralty, including who got to keep the proceeds of "prize" ships and cargoes taken by Revolutionary privateers, and "appointing courts" for the trial of cases of piracy on the high seas. In keeping with the principle of separation of powers, "no member of Congress" was to be appointed to these courts. Overall, over 1,500 cases of prize captures were heard by the states, of which sixty-nine were appealed to Congress's tribunal. They were not standing courts with fixed judicial officers, but ad hoc courts, created and dissolved as needed. The work was episodic: in 1782 two cases, in 1784, twelve, then nothing for two years. Enforcement of its decisions was left to the states in whose ports the captured ships and cargos arrived, however. Such obstacles to even a limited national judiciary were necessary to satisfy a jealous state sovereignty but portended rivalry between state and national courts should the latter ever be established.[11]

The Articles also provided for commissions to ad hoc tribunals to settle disputes among the states on contested land grants and boundaries. While a number of these bodies met, primarily to hear disputes over the Wyoming land grants in Pennsylvania, the commissioners had no means of enforcing their decisions, Congress having no police force and the commissions having no marshals of their own. The preference of state governments for their own courts dictated the weakness of the commissions—despite the fact that the settlement of the western territory and the resolution of disputes at sea were major concerns of land speculators and overseas merchants.[12]

Chaffing at the restraints on effective and uniform courts among problems of confederation government, nationalists like New York's Hamilton and James Madison of Virginia argued for replacement of the confederation of the states by a genuinely federal body. Led by the two men, the Annapolis "Commissioners to Remedy Defects of the Federal Government" met for four days, from September 11 to 14, 1786. Hamilton and Madison drafted its report to the Confederation Congress: "there are important defects in the system of the Federal Government is acknowledged by the Acts of all those States, which have concurred in the present Meeting ... from the embarrassments which characterize the present State of our national affairs, foreign and domestic." One bulwark of that reformed government system would have been a comprehensive national system of courts owing allegiance not to the states but to the United States.[13]

State courts were hardly safe places to adjudicate interstate matters as the closing of state courts by angry Massachusetts farmers in 1786 and 1787 demonstrated. The lawlessness of these tax rebellions persuaded George Washington to attend a constitutional convention in Philadelphia, in the spring of 1787. As he wrote to fellow planter and Revolutionary War officer Henry "Light-horse Harry" Lee, "The picture which you have exhibited, and the accounts which are published of the commotions, and temper of numerous bodies in the Eastern States, are equally to be lamented and deprecated ... I am mortified beyond expression when I view the clouds that have spread over the brightest morn that ever dawned upon any Country." [14]

Figure 1.1 Restored interior of Independence Hall, 1787, where the constitutional convention met. Courtesy of the National Park Service.

On the eve of the meeting in Philadelphia, the absence of a national court was keenly felt by lawyers and litigants. As Hamilton would later write at the beginning of Federalist No. 78, "In unfolding the defects of the existing confederation, the utility and necessity of a federal judicature have been clearly pointed out." There was no national court to handle disputes arising on the high seas (vitally important for a nation dependent on its overseas trade), disputes over the finances of the confederation (in particular the laxness of some states in providing their share of funding for the confederation), and disputes in which foreigners sued American citizens (in particular English merchants owed money by Americans).[15]

Courts Become Part of the Federal Constitution

When the Constitutional Convention was called to order at the end of May, 1787, the Virginia delegation proposed a plan to create a national government. Although the Confederation Congress had asked states to name delegates to the meeting to prepare amendments to the Articles of Confederation, most of the delegates at least tacitly agreed that they would be going beyond these instructions to formulate an entirely new government. In line with this, the so-called Virginia Plan included a national judiciary. Its judges would serve during good behavior for a fixed salary so that the court would be independent of the other branches. Its jurisdiction would include those cases that only a national judiciary could hear, cases that had especially vexed the old confederation—piracy and other crimes on the seas, disputes over ships captured from the enemy, cases in which foreigners were suing Americans or citizens of one state were suing citizens of another, cases touching the national revenue, and cases of impeachment of federal officers. Although Governor Edmund Randolph, who introduced the plan, and James Madison, who largely composed it, could not have realized, their plan began a conversation about federalism that continues to this day.[16]

The impeachment provision in the Virginia Plan offers a clue to where the Virginians' idea for a national supreme court originated. It came from the Virginia Constitution of 1776. Under it, any officeholder could be impeached on the vote of the legislature that the official had violated his public trust or committed a crime in office. The penalty for impeachment was removal from office and disqualification from holding office again. So, too, the provisions for a national supreme court were modeled on the state's constitution. The combination of necessity arising from the absence of a judicial arm of the confederation and familiarity with the provisions of its state constitution shaped the Virginia delegation's vision of national judiciary. Much in the final version of the Constitution exemplified this "corresponding powers" approach.[17]

Delegates from New Jersey were not happy with the Virginia Plan. They did not care for the idea that both branches of the national legislature would be based on the "free population" of each state. Virginia, a larger state with a larger population than New Jersey, would automatically have more weight in the proposed national legislature. But the so-called New Jersey Plan, formally presented in the second week of June, also included a national judiciary. It was very similar to that in the Virginia Plan for a simple reason: the New Jersey delegation framed its plan in response to the same dismay over the weakness of the confederation and relied on the same kind of corresponding or analogous borrowing from state law as did the Virginians'. According to the New Jersey Plan, the federal judiciary was to be appointed by the executive; to hold office during good behavior at a fixed salary; and to hear and determine all cases of impeachment, disputes over ambassadors, cases of captures of enemy shipping, cases in which foreigners were parties, and federal laws regarding the revenue or trade.[18]

While the New Jersey delegation was preparing its plan, discussion of the national judiciary opened on the convention floor. Randolph's resolution was taken off the table and debated. The first part was no longer controversial— "resolved that a national judiciary be established" easily passed. That this major revision of the Articles of Confederation passed so quickly and easily is evidence that the observation in Hamilton's Federalist No. 78 was right—lawyers throughout the nation had wanted a national court. The second clause was more controversial because it introduced the concept of a hierarchy of federal courts parallel to and modeled on the state's system. "It was then moved and seconded to add these words to the first clause of the ninth resolution namely 'to consist of one supreme tribunal, and of one or more inferior tribunals.'" It too passed the next day. A clarification followed, to delete "one or more." That passed. Next, appointment by "the national legislature" was deleted. If not appointed by the legislative branch, was the national judiciary to be the creature of the executive? Was the Congress thus to have no further part in checking the federal judiciary? Pennsylvania's James Wilson, one of the foremost legal thinkers in the nation and a proponent of a strong, independent national judiciary, had anticipated opposition to lower federal courts and announced "that he should at a future day move for a reconsideration of that clause which respects 'inferior tribunals.'" Charles Pinckney of South Carolina had a different concern and added "that when the clause which respects the appointment of the Judiciary came before the Committee he should move to restore the words 'the national legislature.'"[19]

The tenure clause of the Virginia Plan's judiciary was easily adopted, a rejection of the colonial tenure at pleasure of the crown. But the lower courts provision rankled the southern and small state delegations; to the latter it promised a further diminution of their sovereignty and to the former it foretold an even more dire eventuality—that somehow federal judges unsympathetic to slavery would rule against slaveholders' interests. On June 5, by a five to four vote, they succeeded in deleting it; Edmund Rutledge of South Carolina "arguing that the State Tribunals might and ought to be left in all cases to decide in the first instance[;] the right of appeal to the supreme national tribunal being sufficient to secure the national rights & uniformity of Judgmts: that [inferior federal courts were] . . . an unnecessary encroachment on the jurisdiction of the States, and creating unnecessary obstacles to their adoption of the new system." Rutledge sounded the battle cry of what would later be called states' rights—the forerunner of many constitutional and political contests over the boundary between federal and state power.[20]

Madison's notes indicated that he replied immediately: "Mr. Madison observed that unless inferior tribunals were dispersed throughout the Republic with final jurisdiction in many cases, appeals [to a supreme court] would be multiplied to a most oppressive degree; that besides, an appeal would not in many cases be a remedy. What was to be done after improper Verdicts in State tribunals obtained under the biased directions of a dependent Judge, or the local prejudices of an undirected jury?" This was the defense of a comprehensive federal court system in a nutshell. Behind it lay case after case of state courts refusing to honor the provisions of the Peace Treaty of 1783. British creditors, led to expect relief in state courts by the treaty ending the War for Independence, had found none.[21]

Madison understood that the third branch of any national government must have the same reach and authority as the legislative and executive in order to protect itself against the other branches—Adams's point exactly. Madison: "An effective Judiciary establishment commensurate to the legislative authority, was essential. A Government without a proper Executive & Judiciary would be the mere trunk of a body without arms or legs to act or move." Madison had allies. "Mr. Wilson opposed the [Rutledge] motion on like grounds. He said the admiralty jurisdiction ought to be given wholly to the national Government, as it related to cases not within the jurisdiction of particular states, & to a scene in which controversies with foreigners would be most likely to happen."[22]

Then the delegates returned to the appointment of judges. Wilson wanted the executive branch to appoint them. Madison wanted the Senate to name them. On June 13, Alexander Hamilton offered a compromise. He suggested that the executive branch nominate and the Senate confirm the nominations. It was a winning proposal.[23]

On July 18, the shape of the new federal judiciary seemed decided, but not for long. The question to agree "That a national Judiciary be established" passed unanimously; so did the resolution "To consist of One supreme Tribunal," but the motion to replace nomination of the judges by the "second branch of the national Legislature" with nomination by the "national executive" failed, "Ayes—2; noes—6."[24]

Who was to choose federal judges remained a sticking point. The states had various methods: appointment, election, or some mixture of the two. Nathaniel Gorham of Massachusetts was a judge and legislator there, and much attached to its institutions. Madison reported, "Mr. Ghorum [sic], wd. prefer an appointment by the 2d branch [i.e., the Senate] to an appointmt. by the whole Legislature; but he thought even that branch too numerous, and too little personally responsible, to ensure a good choice." Massachusetts judges were appointed by the governor. Gorham liked that system, having taken a part in constructing it and serving in its judiciary. Thus he seconded Hamilton's idea that "the Judges be appointed by the Executive with the advice & consent of the 2d branch, in the mode pre-scribed by the constitution of Massachusetts. This mode had been long prac-tised in that country, & was found to answer perfectly well." Wilson conceded the point, though he would have preferred executive appointment. Gouverneur Morris agreed. Sensing a lingering division of opinion in the nationalist camp, Luther Martin of Maryland "was strenuous for an appt. by the 2d. branch." Martin, an able lawyer and something of an eccentric, would eventually depart the Convention in high dudgeon and work hard to defeat ratification of the Constitution in his native Maryland.[25]

George Mason tried a different tack to argue against executive appointment. He worried that the judges would be too beholden to the president for their appointment. Gorham thought that comment a slur on the impartiality of the chief executive. Both men expected that first president would be Washington, and both held him in high esteem, but it was the judges' impartiality rather than the president's that was at issue. Neither man mentioned the danger of party, that is, that the president would be the head of one party and choose only its members for the bench, excluding equally capable individuals who happened to belong to other parties. In fact, that is exactly what would happen in the years to come, and confirmation by the Senate, itself a politicized body, sometimes aided and abetted such partisanship. But Gorham warned against regionalism in the legislative branch. "The Senators will . . . likely to form their attachments at the seat of Govt where they reside . . . If they can not get the man of the particular State to which they may respectively belong, they will be indifferent to the rest." Worse still was the danger of "intrigue and cabal" in the legislative branch. He did not cite his own state in this regard, but a New England neighbor. "Rh[ode] Island is a full illustration of the insensibility to character produced by a par-ticipation of numbers, in dishonorable measures, and of the length to which a public body may carry wickedness & cabal." As Rhode Island had sent no one to the convention, its reputation was not defended by anyone in the chamber— perhaps the reason why Gorham felt free to sully it.[26]

Madison had more to say about appointment of the judiciary. Short, slight of build, and conservatively dressed, Madison might seem lost as he moved about the floor of the Philadelphia assembly hall. He was no orator and spoke quietly. Nor was he as a penman the equal of Morris or Hamilton. His authority derived from his mastery of any subject on which he spoke. In committee meetings he was a driving force. In open debate he preferred the circular to the direct argument, in this case to second the position Hamilton and Gouverneur Morris proposed. "Mr. Madison, suggested that the Judges might be appointed by the Executives with the concurrence of 1/3 at least of the 2d. branch. This would unite the advantage of responsibility in the Executive with the security afforded in the 2d. branch agst. any incautious or corrupt nomination by the Executive."[27]

Madison was still pressing for a system of lower federal courts. It seemed that he would lose this fight, as only Pennsylvania(led by Wilson), Delaware, Maryland, and Virginia supported his views. But Madison was clever, and citing an idea that lawyer and Revolutionary leader John Dickinson, representing Delaware at the Convention, first mentioned, Madison proposed to give to Congress discretion to create, or not to create, lower tribunals. By postponing the creation of these until the federal Constitution was ratified and the new government installed (hoping with some reason that the new Congress would be more amenable to lower federal courts than the delegates at the convention), Madison was offering a compromise, later known somewhat inelegantly as part of the Madisonian Compromise (even though part of the credit should go to Dickinson, the author of the Articles of Confederation).

Pierce Butler of South Carolina, repeating Rutledge's objection to lower federal courts, refused to budge: "The people will not bear such innovations. The States will revolt at such encroachments." But Rufus King of New York, a lawyer and politician who was a member of the nationalist coalition, "remarked as to the comparative expence that the establishment of inferior tribunals wd. cost infinitely less than the appeals that would be prevented by them." Randolph was on board. "Mr. Randolph observed that the Courts of the States can not be trusted with the administration of the National laws. The objects of jurisdiction are such as will often place the General & local policy at variance." Gouverneur Morris, already a trustworthy defender of a strong national government, lent his weight to the compromise. Now the ayes had it, Massachusetts, New Jersey, North Carolina, and Georgia joining the original four who voted to allow lower federal tribunals. South Carolina and Connecticut alone objected to the compromise motion. When a final vote was taken, however, it was agreed to with no objections. Madison had carried the day.[28]

The debate over who was to appoint the judges resumed on July 21. Randolph joined Madison, Hamilton, Morris, Wilson, and Gorham. "Mr. Randolph wd. have preferred the mode of appointmt. proposed formerly by Mr Ghorum [sic], as adopted in the Constitution of Massts. but thought the motion depending [Madison's version] so great an improvement of the clause as it stands, that he anxiously wished it success." But Mason, the third Virginia delegate, was already showing what would become his staunch opposition to the new Constitution. "He considered the appointment by the Executive as a dangerous prerogative. It might even give him an influence over the Judiciary department itself." Mason did not carry Virginia's vote, but the smaller states still wanted the "second branch," as they called the Senate, to have sole charge of choosing the judges. The Madison motion failed, six states voting nay, and only Virginia, Pennsylvania, and Massachusetts voting aye. But Madison would eventually win this one too, outlasting his opponents and gaining in the Committee of Detail nomination by the president and confirmation by a majority of the Senate.[29]

When the judiciary article was presented in full to the Convention, on August 27, there was more debate, and one significant alteration of the text. The Maryland Constitution's provision for removal of judges based on a legislative request to the executive was voted down. Impeachment would remain the only way to remove a sitting judge. Now the last major insertion came. William Samuel Johnson "suggested that the judicial power ought to extend to equity as well as law—and moved to insert the words 'both in law and equity.' " Connecticut, his state, had long allowed equitable remedies in its courts rather than having a separate court of chancery. Johnson won his suit, six votes to two.[30]

Near the end of the Convention, a dispute over the removal of judges again erupted, with Elbridge Gerry of Massachusetts insisting that they should be removable by the legislature, to which Gouverneur Morris rejoined that "it is a contradiction in terms to say that the Judges should hold their offices during good behavior, and yet be removable without a trial. Besides it was fundamentally wrong to subject Judges to so arbitrary an authority." Roger Sherman of Connecticut, one of the drafters of the Declaration of Independence, "saw no contradiction or impropriety if this were made part of the Constitutional regulation of the Judiciary establishment. He observed that a like provision was contained in the British Statutes." Wilson "considered such a provision in the British Government as less dangerous than here, the House of Lords & House of Commons being less likely to concur on the same occasions." Whether that was so or not, were removal so easy, "The Judges would be in a bad situation if made to depend on every gust of faction which might prevail in the two branches of our Govt." Randolph opposed the motion because it would undercut the independence of the judges. It failed, seven states to one. The concept of good behavior tenure—and with it the relative (not absolute) independence of the judiciary from the other branches—had withstood the challenge.[31]

Madison was pleased with the outcome of the deliberations. As he later wrote to his confidant Thomas Jefferson, then serving as a diplomat in France, "It may be said that the Judicial authority under our new system will keep the States within their proper limits, and supply the place of a negative on their laws." In the proposed language (not yet called Article III—that was the work of the Committee of Style and Arrangement, and, within it, of Gouverneur Morris), the entire judicial function of the new federal government was vested in the Supreme Court and such inferior courts as might be created by act of Congress.[32]

Article III, as it emerged from the Committee of Style on September 12, read:

> Sec. 1: The judicial power of the United States, shall be vested in one Supreme Court, and in such inferior courts as the Congress may from time to time ordain and establish. The judges, both of the supreme and inferior courts, shall hold their offices during good behaviour, and shall, at stated times, receive for their services, a compensation, which shall not be diminished during their continuance in office.

> Sec. 2: The judicial power shall extend to all cases, in law and equity, arising under this Constitution, the laws of the United States, and treaties made, or which shall be made, under their authority;—to all cases affecting ambassadors, other public ministers and consuls;—to all cases of admiralty and maritime jurisdiction;—to controversies to which the United States shall be a party;—to controversies between two or more states;—between a state and citizens of another state;—between citizens of different states;—between citizens of the same state claiming lands under grants of different states, and between a state, or the citizens thereof, and foreign states, citizens or subjects. In all cases affecting ambassadors, other public ministers and consuls, and those in which a state shall be party, the Supreme Court shall have original jurisdiction. In all the other cases before mentioned, the Supreme Court shall have appellate jurisdiction, both as to law and fact, with such exceptions, and under such regulations as the Congress shall make.

At the heart of the article stood key parts of the Madisonian Compromise—in reality two compromises—first, involving both the executive and the legislative in the choice of judges, and second, to leave to Congress the creation and jurisdiction of lower courts. The first sounded in checks and balances; the second in federalism. Both left much to be determined when the new government met—if state ratifying conventions approved the Constitution. The language of Article III, Section 1 was still Madison's in concept, and he sat on the Committee of Style, but it was Gouverneur Morris who fashioned the language of Article III. Done so swiftly in the closing days of the convention, giving the judicial branch its own article was a triumph for the party in favor of a strong central government and a strong judiciary. By according the courts nominal equality with the Congress (Article I) and the presidency (Article II), Morris protected the independence of the judiciary. One notes that although the terminology of Article III was far vaguer than Articles I and II, it had within it language permitting growth of an expansive federal judicial system.[33]

Article III did not comprise the entirety of the framers thoughts on the judiciary. Article I, Section 8, Clause 9 allowed Congress to "constitute tribunals inferior to the Supreme Court." The relationship between this provision and the first clause of Article III's "such inferior courts" is not entirely clear. Was a court different from a tribunal? In any case, from Article I would come a variety of judicial bodies, including territorial courts, the courts of claims, bankruptcy courts, magistrate courts, and others. The distinction was that Article I judges did not have life tenure.[34]

All in all, advocates for a system of national courts in Philadelphia had fashioned a system fully attuned to the ideal of separation of powers, with checks and balances on federal courts coming from the executive and legislative branches. Out of deliberation, conciliation, and compromise the framers fashioned what hopefully would be a substantial improvement on the juridical ineptitude of the confederation.

Judicial Review?

There was a wrinkle in the fabric of the proposed new Supreme Court, a kind of jurisdiction not enumerated in Article III. The objects of the new Supreme Court's purview were clear. These included its original jurisdiction and its authority to review state court decisions and lower federal court decisions (should these courts be established). But was the Court to have sole or even primary authority to rule on the meaning of the new Constitution's provisions? William Samuel Johnson offered an amendment to the Committee of Detail report adding "all cases arising under this Constitution" to the jurisdiction of the new court. Madison worried aloud that this might give the Supreme Court the power to issue advisory opinions, that is, to interpret the Constitution when it did not have a case or controversy before it. Such a provision in Article III might encourage the justices to meddle in the operations of the other branches, the exact opposite of separation of powers. A proposal for this was debated in the Committee of Detail but not reported out of it.[35]

Elbridge Gerry, a Massachusetts delegate, argued that the judiciary should only rule on the constitutionality of laws pertaining to judicial matters although he did not attempt to define what these might be. The problem, unexamined in the brief debates in the convention on the new Supreme Court, was that any matter might be deemed "judicial" by the court once it sat, even purely political issues best left to the elected branches. In fact, at least eight times during the debates over the federal judiciary, members of the Convention said that some government institution must have the final say on the meaning of the Constitution and implied that it would lie with the Supreme Court. Among these speakers, Rufus King, Madison, and Gouverneur Morris served on the Committee of Style, but it left the matter open.[36]

Contrariwise, did the framers suppose that Congress, without a constitutional amendment, could restrict the jurisdiction of the Supreme Court? Congress can set the number of members of the Court, and since 1789 has changed that number from six to seven to nine, to ten, down to seven (by barring President Andrew Johnson from naming someone to replace Justices John Catron and James Wayne after they died), and back to nine. Congress can also prescribe rules of procedure for the Supreme Court's appellate jurisdiction—"under such regulations as the Congress shall make"—knowing full well that procedural rules may restrict jurisdiction and even dictate outcomes of cases. In the end, it was the Supreme Court itself that established judicial review, which we discuss in chapters 2 and 3.

Article III during the Ratification Debates

Ratification of the new Constitution was not assured, although its supporters, self-styled federalists, were confident that they would prevail. The major obstacle was the absence in the draft Constitution of some of the guarantees of individual rights that already existed in the state constitutions. When Madison returned to the Confederation Congress in New York City after the Constitutional Convention sent the draft document to the Congress, he cleverly defended sending it to the states by turning the absence of a bill of rights on its head. Madison expressed his views with diffident modesty. Not only was this Madison's preferred form of speaking, he knew that the opposition was led by Richard Henry Lee, a friend and a fellow Virginia planter. To offend the powerful Lee clan, particularly in view of Madison's hope to be elected to the federal Congress under the new Constitution, would be political suicide. New York's Melancton Smith took notes on Madison's address. Smith recorded that Madison "should feel delicacy if he had not assented in Convention though he did not approve it." The notes that Smith took of the rest of Madison's comments are equally impenetrable because Madison's speeches, like his writings, were full of intricately looped clauses related to one another. Madison's habit was to qualify everything he said, sometimes before he had finished saying it. But the gist of his argument was clear. There was "[n]o probability of Congress agreeing in alterations. Those who disagree, differ in their opinions. A bill of rights [is] unnecessary because the powers are enumerated and only extend to certain cases, and the people who are to agree to it are to establish this." In other words, the Constitution had to be first

ratified and the new government put into operation before amendments, including something like a bill of rights, could be proposed.[37]

Article III was a serious object of criticism for some opponents of the
Constitution. Mason, who returned home without signing the Constitution
and opposed its ratification, put the objection succinctly: "The Judiciary of
the United States is so constructed and extended, as to absorb and destroy the
judiciaries of the several States; thereby rendering law as tedious, intricate and
expensive, and justice as unattainable, by a great part of the community, as in
England, and enabling the rich to oppress and ruin the poor." Writing under
the pseudonym Brutus, either Smith, or his fellow New Yorker Robert Yates,
returned home before the conclusion of the meeting and opposed ratification,
listing the entire project of federal courts as a grievance. Brutus feared consolidation of sovereign states "under the direction of one executive and judicial"
branch, meeting far from most people's homes, proceeding under rules, and
enforcing laws foreign to those of the respective states. Even absent lower federal courts, the Supremacy Clause of the Constitution's claim that it would be
"the supreme law of the land; and the judges in every state shall be bound thereby,
anything in the constitution, or law of any state to the contrary notwithstanding"
rendered every state judge and state court inferior to the U.S. Supreme Court.[38]

The longest lever the opponents of ratification had to raise opposition to
Article III and the judicial arrangements of the new Constitution was the absence
of a guarantee of jury trial in civil suits. As "A Farmer" wrote to Maryland readers, "Without then the check of the *democratic* branch—*the jury*, to ascertain
those facts . . . the latitude of judicial power, combined with the various and
uncertain nature of evidence, will render it impossible to convict a judge of corruption, and ascertain his guilt." The blanket authorization that Congress under
Article I could establish lower courts, coupled with the enumerated power that
Congress had to enact laws on bankruptcy, caused antifederalists even more
sleepless nights. As the Federal Farmer complained, "By giving this [bankruptcy]
power to the union, we greatly extend the jurisdiction of the federal judiciary . . .
and I think it may be shewn, that by the help of these laws, actions between citizens of different states, and the laws of the federal city, aided by no overstrained
judicial fictions, almost all civil causes may be drawn into those courts."[39]

Article III received considerable attention in the Virginia ratification convention meeting in Richmond. There Madison and Mason renewed their debate over
the creation of lower federal courts. At the opening session, on June 24, 1788,
Edmund Pendleton, perhaps the state's leading lawyer and one of its judges, tried
to allay Mason's fear of an intrusive, overbearing federal court system. Pendleton
predicted that Congress would never create courts to take business away from
the state courts. The proposed Supreme Court's appellate jurisdiction would
ensure suitable general rules of law. Given his reputation, his assurances had

to be taken seriously, but Mason's suspicions were not quieted: Pendleton's "mere hope" was not sufficient. Mason worried that the prospect of federal courts sitting side by side with state courts would "destroy the dearest rights" of property holders. Madison, characteristically diffident and conciliatory, replied as he had in Philadelphia. Defending the compromises there (which he had brokered), he told Mason that state courts would have full dockets and litigants need not fear that federal courts would ignore their substantive or procedural rights— a hint of the "Rules of Decision" provisions of the Judiciary Act to come in 1789. He even promised that members of the Supreme Court would travel the land, making its members available to local counsel, again a foretoken of the circuit courts provisions of the Judiciary Act. Patrick Henry, a lawyer whose appeals to local juries had no peer, countered that the absence of a guarantee of jury trial undermined the entire Constitution. John Marshall, whose legal practice in Richmond was gaining momentum, replied directly to Henry, lawyer to lawyer, in a striking preview of his view of judicial review in *Marbury v. Madison* (1803) many years later: if Congress gave too much authority to any federal court, the Supreme Court would declare those legislative acts unconstitutional.[40]

Prior to the state convention, Randolph, who had left the Philadelphia Convention without signing the draft, had changed sides once again. He joined Madison in calling for ratification first and amendments later. As Randolph explained, with eight states already having ratified, Virginia's vote would determine "union or no union," and he did not want to be the one blamed for the latter event. A day later, the federalists knew that victory was within their grasp. On June 26, after three days of remarkably able and learned debate, the Convention resolved to send its affirmation of the proposed Constitution to the Congress, along with a resolution—the concession to the dissenters—that the Constitution be soon amended to include basic guarantees of rights, a course Massachusetts and other states had already followed.

The fullest defense of the proposed federal judiciary appeared in New York newspapers in the year before that state met in convention to debate ratification. In response to New York opponents of the new Constitution, Hamilton and John Jay, both from New York, and Madison, set about to defend it in a series of newspaper articles. Later enshrined by scholars as the Federalist Papers, these serialized essays explained the need for checks and balances in language that would become a part of the American political heritage. The *Federalist* articles regarded the separation of the judiciary from the other branches as a vital safeguard in republican governance. Madison wrote in Federalist No. 47, "The accumulation of all powers legislative, executive, and judiciary in the same hands, whether of one, a few, or many, and whether hereditary, self appointed, or elective, may justly be pronounced the very definition of tyranny." How to avoid it? Madison returned to the topic in No. 51, "by so contriving the interior structure of the government, as that its several constituent parts may, by their mutual relations, be the means of keeping each other in their proper places."[41]

The news of Virginia's ratification came just in time to New York, where Hamilton was holding the antifederalist majority at bay by explaining every clause in the Constitution in detail. There is no verbatim account of his speeches, though they did run for hours. No doubt he insisted, as he had on December 14, 1787, in Federalist No. 22, that "[a] circumstance, which crowns the defects of the confederation, remains yet to be mentioned—the want of a judiciary power. Laws are a dead letter without courts to expound and define their true meaning and operation." In particular, he cited the problems arising from the treaty that ended the Revolutionary War. "The treaties of the United States to have any force at all, must be considered as part of the law of the land. Their true import as far as respects individuals, must, like all other laws, be ascertained by judicial determinations. To produce uniformity in these determinations, they ought to be submitted in the last resort, to one SUPREME TRIBUNAL." Without a national supreme court whose decisions would be final, there was no protection from "the bias of local views and prejudices, and from the interference of local regulations."[42]

Then he turned to the guarantee of jury trial in federal courts. Not to worry—trust Congress's power to create lower courts and regulate them. "A power to constitute courts, is a power to prescribe the mode of trial; and consequently, if nothing was said in the constitution on the subject of juries, the legislature would be at liberty either to adopt that institution, or to let it alone." The people had nothing to fear from these courts, for "according to the plan of the convention, all the judges who may be appointed by the United States are to hold their offices during good behaviour, which is conformable to the most approved of the state constitutions; and among the rest, to that of this state" (i.e., New York). The final argument was directed at the separation of powers question.[43]

> Whoever attentively considers the different departments of power must perceive, that in a government in which they are separated from each other, the judiciary, from the nature of its functions, will always be the least dangerous to the political rights of the constitution . . . The judiciary . . . has no influence over either the sword or the purse, no direction either of the strength or of the wealth of the society, and can take no active resolution whatever. It may truly be said to have neither Force nor Will, but merely judgment; and must ultimately depend upon the aid of the executive arm even for the efficacy of its judgments.

The judiciary was the weakest department of government the federalists had created.

When news came on June 24 that Virginia was likely to ratify, the New York federalists were dealt a trump card. By early July, with the heat taking its toll, the delegates knew that Virginia and New Hampshire had ratified. Ten states now belonged to the new federal Union. Was New York in or out? It was the same question that Edmund Randolph had asked himself. Hamilton warned of the evils of staying out of the Union, and Jay moved that the Constitution be accepted without conditions. By the middle of July, antifederalist leader Melancton Smith, like Randolph, answered the question in the affirmative—New York should ratify. His was the first defection from the antifederalist camp but not the last. On July 26, by a vote of thirty to twenty-seven, New York joined the Union. The ratification was unconditional, but the convention proposed amendments to the body of the Constitution. Among these amendments was a proposal that Congress not be allowed to create lower federal courts of general jurisdiction.[44]

A Judiciary Act...

The language of Article III was a triumph of political compromise, but as the ratification debates proved, it was open to all three of the areas of controversy that had plagued courts in the new nation. Political partisanship, interbranch rivalries within governments, and now, competition with state courts might hamstring federal courts. Much depended on the way in which the Congress handled the question of lower courts' structure and jurisdiction. What members of the new federal Congress carried with them from Philadelphia in the summer of 1787 to New York City in the spring of 1789 remains a subject of great interest among historians, law professors, and judges, because in effect, debate over the lower courts in the coming session of the Congress would amount to a reconvening of the Constitutional Convention to settle the terms of Article III. [45]

When the newly established Congress met, some members still expressed strong resistance to the creation of a system of lower courts. The New York convention's resolution that lower courts' jurisdiction be limited was not attached to its ratification, but Virginia's ratification resolution asked that the first clause of Article III be revised to read: "That the judicial power of the United States shall be vested in one supreme Court, and in such courts of Admiralty as Congress may from time to time ordain and establish in any of the different States." This was the work of Mason, Lee, and the other critics of lower federal courts, and along with the demand for jury trials, had been the core of the Virginia antifederalists' complaint against lower federal courts.[46]

Deliberations over a judiciary act began in the Senate then went to the House. As Madison, by then a member of the lower house, wrote to a private correspondent on July 31, 1789, "The Judiciary system has been sent from the Senate

Figure 1.2 Federal Hall, New York City, seat of Congress 1789–1790, where the Judiciary Act of 1789 and the proposed amendments to the Constitution were drafted and passed. Hand-colored engraving by Amos Doolittle, depicting Washington's April 30, 1789, inauguration. Credit: Library of Congress.

and will probably be taken up to day in the House of Rep's. It is pregnant with difficulties, not only as relating to a part of the constitution which has been most criticised, but being in its own nature peculiarly complicated & embarrassing ... The Senate have proceeded on the idea that the federal Gov't ought not to depend on the State Courts any more than on the State Legislatures." Madison's concerns proved warranted when the Senate version arrived in the House. Samuel Livermore of New Hampshire told his fellow representatives,

"I fear this principle of establishing judges of a supreme court will lead to an entire new system of jurisprudence, and fill every state in the union with two kinds of courts for the trial of many causes, a thing so heterogeneous, must give great disgust: Sir, it will be establishing a government within a government, and one must prevail upon the ruin of the other." Another member of Congress floated the idea that the state supreme courts ought to double as federal district courts. Another answered, "I do not see how our state courts can execute the laws of the general government." The reason, he opined, was that the state courts were entirely independent of the federal establishment. Clearly, neither members of Congress who opposed lower federal courts nor members who favored such courts had mastered the complications of federalism.[47]

Oliver Ellsworth, who had much to say about framing courts at the Convention and led the Judiciary Act ad hoc drafting committee in the Senate, spoke often and earnestly when House and Senate versions went to a conference committee. Senator William Maclay of Pennsylvania recorded one exchange in his journal during the debates over the bill, "I made a remark where Ellsworth in his diction [on the bill] had varied from the Constitution. This vile bill is a child of his, and he defends it with the care of a parent, even with wrath and anger. He kindled, as he always does, when it is meddled with." But others who worked closely with Ellsworth portrayed a different man. William Vans Murray of Maryland, who shared a diplomatic mission with Ellsworth, wrote to John Quincy Adams, "I greatly admired the neatness and accuracy of [Ellsworth's] mind." That neatness and accuracy were no doubt needed throughout the debates on the Judiciary Act in the Senate. In any case, the judiciary bill was batted back and forth between House and Senate over a course of weeks in the conference.[48]

With Ellsworth at its head, the Senate committee to write the Judiciary Act first met on April 7, and by early June was circulating its draft widely to constituents. That draft was printed on June 12, but Madison had surely seen it before that time. While the Senate was pruning the draft of a judiciary act, Madison was writing notes for his June 8 speech on amendments to the Constitution. The heart of his proposal was the Virginia Resolutions—absent the article that would have limited lower federal courts to equity, maritime, and admiralty jurisdiction. In fact, that restriction on lower federal courts was the only major omission from the Virginia Resolutions in Madison's proposal, suggesting that Madison was working in accord with the bill's sponsors in the Senate.[49]

When they took up the proposed amendments, members of the upper house understood that certain proposals responded to the antifederalists' criticism of the Constitution, including opposition to a comprehensive system of lower federal courts. Ellsworth and his allies made further concessions in the drafts of the Judiciary Act and the Process Act to allay former antifederalists' fears of a federal judiciary. The Judiciary Act's Section 34 (later termed the "Rules of

Figure 1.3 Senator Oliver Ellsworth of Connecticut, chief draftsman of the Judiciary Act of 1789 and future chief justice of the Supreme Court, with his wife, Abigail. Portrait by Ralph Earl, 1792. Credit: Wadsworth Atheneum, Hartford, CT. Gift of the Ellsworth heirs.

Decision Act") reassured antifederalists that the substantive laws of the states would be the rules governing civil suits in federal courts sitting in that state, and the Process Act made civil process in the states the rule in federal courts, except as congressional acts, treaties, or the Constitution provided otherwise. [50]

Opponents of the lower courts plan continued to grumble. As Maclay noted in his journal, "Mr. Lee, after some time, rose and urged that the State judges would be all sworn to support the Constitution; that they must obey their oath and, of course, execute the Federal laws. He varied this idea in sundry shapes." Lee had been an author of the Virginia Resolutions and had supported their limitation on the jurisdiction of lower courts (and Congress's authority to create additional federal courts). By the end of the debate, Lee conceded the battle, though he had hardly reconciled himself to the new judiciary system. He wrote to Governor Patrick Henry of Virginia, the chief of the antifederalist faction there, on September 14, 1789: "I have endeavored successfully in the bill to remedy, in so far as a law can remedy, the defects of the constitution." However, it was seen by contemporaries, in the long perspective that one must agree that the Judiciary Act absorbed and burnished the Madisonian Compromise.[51]

Though they had compromised on the point in Philadelphia, in 1789 Ellsworth and Madison felt confident that Article III commanded Congress to establish lower courts. If admiralty and piracy cases were part of federal jurisdiction, and no one in 1789 doubted that they were, and if federal courts were charged with the exclusive handling of these cases, as they were, and if these cases were not included in the original jurisdiction of the Supreme Court, as they were not, then what federal court was going to resolve them? James Madison made the point in his characteristically elliptical fashion on the floor of the House. He asked: Can "the judicial power be placed elsewhere, unless the Constitution has made an exception [to the admiralty jurisdiction]?" The language of Article III, by inference and indirection (two of Madison's favored rhetorical devices), implied that there must be lower federal trial courts.[52]

As Maclay conceded on the Senate floor, "the Constitution expressly extended it to all cases, in law and equity, under the Constitution and laws of the United States; treaties made or to be made, etc. We already had existing treaties, and were about making many laws. These must be executed by the Federal judiciary." Watching from his new post as secretary of the treasury, Hamilton could only think back to his arguments in Federalist No. 82: "The evident aim of the plan of the convention is that all the causes of the specified classes, shall for weighty public reasons, receive their original or final determination in the courts of the union." If Article III mandated such courts, who was to create them? The Article's very next clause imposed this duty, no longer an option, on Congress. In other words, although the Article said that Congress may establish lower courts, its internal logic required the establishment of such courts, if only to hear and decide admiralty and piracy cases.[53]

The act that emerged from the debates was a compromise between a fully autonomous federal court system and one sharing power with the state courts. As adopted on September 24, the Judiciary Act's provisions included section 25, in which the U.S. Supreme Court gained appellate jurisdiction over decisions of the lower federal and decisions by state courts holding invalid any statute or treaty of the United States; or holding valid any state law or practice that was challenged as inconsistent with the federal Constitution, treaties, or laws; or rejecting any claim made by a party under a provision of the federal constitution, treaties, or laws.[54]

The Supreme Court bench was set at six justices including a chief justice. The reason for a six justices on the Supreme Court was the division of the country into three circuits, the eastern, middle, and southern, and the provision that two justices were to sit in each of the circuit courts (ride circuit) along with the district judge. The country was divided into thirteen judicial districts, each district coincident with the boundaries of the (then eleven) states in which they sat (with the addition of Kentucky, not yet a state, and Maine, a province of Massachusetts), and each district having a single district judge. In Kentucky and Maine, district court judges heard cases that would have gone to circuit court sessions. Rhode Island and North Carolina had not yet ratified the federal Constitution. Anticipating their ratification of the Constitution and entry into the Union, they were assigned district courts and became part of the eastern and southern circuits, respectively. Like the district courts, the circuit courts were primarily trial courts whose original jurisdiction included serious crimes and civil cases of at least $500 where the parties were domiciled in different states (diversity jurisdiction) or the United States was plaintiff, and a limited appellate role in equity and admiralty cases. The single-judge district courts had jurisdiction primarily over admiralty cases, petty crimes, and suits by the United States for at least $100.

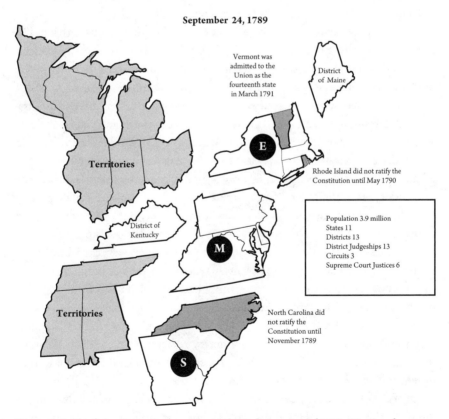

September 24, 1789

Vermont was admitted to the Union as the fourteenth state in March 1791

District of Maine

Territories

Rhode Island did not ratify the Constitution until May 1790

District of Kentucky

Population 3.9 million
States 11
Districts 13
District Judgeships 13
Circuits 3
Supreme Court Justices 6

Territories

North Carolina did not ratify the Constitution until November 1789

Figure 1.4 The federal circuits according to the Judiciary Act of 1789. Diagram from Cynthia E. Harrison and Russell R. Wheeler, *Creating the Federal Judicial System,* courtesy of the Federal Judicial Center.

The Act did not give further detail to the Article III provision for jurisdiction over all civil suits "arising under" federal law. In this case, Congress elected not to fulfill the broad grant of judicial powers in the Constitution. In later years, proponents of such a grant would attempt by statute (the Judiciary Act of 1801) and by dicta (Chief Justice John Marshall in *McCulloch v. Maryland* [1819]) to arrogate this authority to the federal courts. It was not until the Judiciary Act of 1875, however, that Congress explicitly conferred this jurisdiction on the circuit courts. By contrast, state courts remained free to determine civil cases on the basis of federal law, the federal Constitution, and state law.[55]

As in the refusal to grant to the federal courts the full measure of what the Constitution allowed, the Judiciary Act of 1789 and subsequent acts of Congress demonstrated that the federal legislative branch could not only create lower federal courts, it could also apportion jurisdiction among them. There was nothing in the Judiciary Act that forbade Congress from future elaboration of the system of lower courts under Article I, Section 8 "to constitute tribunals lower to the Supreme Court" and Congress did just that over the years. As Justice Peter V. Daniel wrote for the Court in *Cary v. Curtis* (1845): "the doctrine so often ruled in this court, that the judicial power of the United States, although it has its origin in the Constitution, is (except in enumerated instances, applicable exclusively to this court) dependent for its distribution and organization, and for the modes of its exercise, entirely upon the action of Congress."[56]

Federal courts were to use the laws of the state in which they sat as the rules of decision in civil cases. Whether that meant states' judicial precedents as well as states' statutes remained an open question. The rules for evidence in "admiralty and maritime" cases was to be uniform in all the federal courts, as admiralty and maritime cases could only be brought in federal courts. Procedure in equity cases in the federal courts was also to be uniform, which meant that federal courts could develop equity rules at variance with the equity rules used in the states where the federal court sat. Appeals from the decisions of the district courts sitting in equity could be taken to the Supreme Court. A borrowing from equity rules that applied to all suits in federal court, mistakes in the form of the pleadings in civil cases were not to result in dismissal of the cases but were to be read in light "of the right of the cause."[57]

The act separated the equity and law dockets. This proved a considerable inconvenience to suitors seeking a monetary remedy at law who also wanted the judge to issue temporary restraining orders or temporary injunctions or seek other equitable remedies. The first formal objection to this separation came from Secretary of the Treasury Alexander Hamilton. Rather than sue each defaulter in a separate legal action, Hamilton wanted federal courts to have the authority to join different plaintiffs and different defendants in a common suit when the issue or complaint was common to all parties (so-called joinder). As he wrote to William Rawle, U.S. attorney for the District of Pennsylvania, "I wish it to be considered whether a proceeding cannot be instituted in some Court of the United States on behalf of the United States in the nature of a Bill of Interpleader, bringing all the parties interested before the Court to contest their respective rights and consequently the validity of the attachment. It would seem to me that this course can be pursued, and if it can I should prefer it." This kind of joinder of parties was permissible in an equity suit. A partial reform came in the Judiciary Act of 1911, allowing litigants in a lawsuit to take depositions instead of presenting all the facts at trial. Merger of the two dockets came in the Federal Rules of Civil Procedure in 1938.[58]

Federal circuit courts had jurisdiction over diversity cases in which the parties were citizens of different states. Defendants in the suit could remove such suit to the federal court in their own state from the state court where it was brought if the case entailed a minimum financial stake (which would be raised periodically). Diversity jurisdiction was another controversial provision of the Act, in part because its defenders did not spell out their concerns. It still is. Hints at the time, however, like the concern that Madison raised at the Constitutional Convention about bias in state legal proceedings, have led later commentators to argue that fear of state judges, state court juries, and even state legislatures' prejudice against foreign (both nonnative and out of state) plaintiffs would unduly bias the decisions of state courts. In any case, the provision, with revisions, has withstood repeated attacks.[59]

Federal courts had jurisdiction over suits by noncitizens when the complaint alleged a violation of the law of nations (the precepts of law regulating the conduct of nations and the relations among different nations—today called international law) or a U.S. treaty. While the Constitution itself did not incorporate the law of nations, it asserted that Congress "define and punish" offenses that violated "the law of nations." Presumably this was directed to piracy and other violations of neutrality by individuals within the jurisdiction of federal courts, and the Judiciary Act simply spelled this out. At the same time, the provision was a reminder that federal courts operated in a world arena and that the foreign wars, foreign trade, and foreign affairs that had played a role in the creation of the new nation would remain a part of its judicial life.[60]

The Act created the office of the Attorney General of the United States and provided for federal attorneys and marshals for each district; gave the federal courts exclusive jurisdiction over federal crimes; and gave the federal courts the authority to issue all the writs (commands of the court and requests to the court for action), including habeas corpus, "which may be necessary" for the operation of the courts. These included orders to produce documentary evidence and take testimony usually reserved to courts of equity. A more precise and "unequivocal" instruction that the procedures used in civil cases in federal district and circuit courts would conform to the procedures of states in which they sat came in the Process Act of 1789. This was further evidence of the Madisonian Compromise—the assurance that suitors in federal courts would not face unfamiliar rules when bringing suits and gaining execution of verdicts in their cases. [61]

The reason for the circuits was clear to contemporaries. As Ellsworth, its author, explained: "One federal Judge at least, resident in each State, appears unavoidable. And without creating any more, or much enhancing the expence, there may be circuit courts, which would give system to the department, uniformity to the proceedings, settle many cases in the States that would otherwise go to the Supreme Court, & provide for the higher grade of offences." By dividing the trial business, the circuit court spread the docket a little more evenly. In addition, Ellsworth argued that if only district courts were created, the burden of hearing appeals would fall directly on the Supreme Court. Its meetings were to be but a few weeks twice a year in duration, and it would be swamped with appeals (along with its original jurisdiction cases) were there no circuit courts. Of course, the district judge had to attend his own court and the circuit court, but when he sat in the latter, more often than not, he could defer to the two Supreme Court justices sitting with him.[62]

Advocates of the newly-established system of federal courts defended the justices' circuit riding duties as the best way for local lawyers' to become acquainted with the justices. Indeed, as news of the passage of the Act spread throughout the states, lawyers began to advertise their availability to litigants in the new courts. For example, Andrew Ronald of Richmond took out ads in a number of newspapers in New York and Philadelphia to tell their subscribers that "it is his intention to practice in the federal courts of this state" (i.e., Virginia). Many of these lawyers would never argue a case in the nation's capital, but they still wanted to see and hear the Supreme Court justices at work. The local bar doubled as the catch pond for state politicians. They too wanted to get a closer look at the justices. The best defense of the system came in 1802, during a debate over the repeal of the Judiciary Act of 1801. Senator David Stone of North Carolina told his fellow senators, "the judges of the Supreme Court, whose power controls all the other tribunals . . . should, by riding the circuit, render themselves practically acquainted with" the laws of the states, according to the Rules of Decision provisions of the Judiciary Act.[63]

There were critics of the two-tiered system and of circuit riding. William Davie, governor of North Carolina and a lawyer himself, wrote to Justice James Iredell that the Act seemed "so defective in point of arrangement, and so obscurely drawn . . . that it would disgrace the meanest legislature of the states." The division of the workload in the federal courts between district and circuit courts saw criticism from another source: the justices themselves. The most often repeated criticism regarded circuit riding. The burden of circuit riding that the division of courts placed on the justices was so irksome that many nominees refused to serve and those who accepted appointment complained about dangerous roads, uncomfortable accommodations, and backbreaking travel schedules. Justice Samuel Chase, notorious for his frankness on and off the bench, would call riding circuit an "unmerited abuse" of his mind and body, while Justice James Iredell, ordinarily more circumspect in his language, would complain that riding the southern circuit demanded "1800 miles" of severe discomfort. Iredell was the instigator of a letter to President George Washington: "we . . . find the burdens laid upon us so excessive that we cannot forbear representing them in strong and explicit language." Sharing beds in inns with strangers seemed to be the most obnoxious of these burdens. Congress responded in 1793 by reducing the number of justices to one per circuit court and allowing a two-year cycle in the circuit. [64]

Key portions of the Judiciary Act inform Title 28 of the U.S. Code, although, among other changes, the minimum amount for filing in diversity has risen exponentially, the circuit trial courts have disappeared, and more formal rules for process have appeared. The Madisonian Compromise struck in Philadelphia was a sound basis for the compromise struck in the new nation's first capital, New York City, and has remained a centerpiece of federal courts throughout their existence. Modern jurists have claimed that the first judiciary act was "a transcendent achievement" with at least "three claims to greatness." The first is that it overcame the resistance of the most stubborn states' rights advocates. Second, because it has lasted, more or less intact, over two centuries. And third, because it allowed for appeal of both state and federal cases to the U.S. Supreme Court the Act had a nationalizing influence at a time when national attachments were still weak. If, as some historians believe, the Judiciary Act was flawed by the compromises to the antifederalists and advocates of states' rights, the Act itself, read alongside the "from time to time" clause in Article III, hinted that Congress could and would return to the subject periodically. In fact, since 1789 Congress has passed legislation that either directly (in judiciary acts) or indirectly (in regulatory, criminal, and other legislation) tinkered with, added to, and limited the jurisdiction and duties of the federal courts to overcome the infelicities in the 1789 Act. The framers of the Act expected this—or the Constitution had expressed confidence in "the discretion of the legislature" to amend the structure and procedure of the federal courts.[65]

Further evidence of the deal struck by nationalists and states' rights advocates in the Congress, a kind of extension of the federalism prong of the Madisonian Compromise after the Judiciary Act, lay in the Process Act of September 29,

1789, in which civil process of the federal courts was to conform to the procedures used in the state supreme court where the federal court sat, except as Congress expressly provided and except for the fees and fines provided by federal law. (Once again excluded were procedures in admiralty, equity, and criminal matters.) It continued with the Judiciary Act of 1793 (Anti-Injunction Act): federal courts were not allowed to enjoin state court proceedings unless the state court was hearing a suit about federal lands, the state court interfered in an ongoing federal suit, or a suit was brought in state court to undo a federal court decision. Last but not least, the Act formally and forcefully barred the judges from accepting fees.[66]

Some modern commentators argue that the Process Act of 1789 was poorly drafted. That is a somewhat unfair judgment for a number of reasons. In the first place, the Act was supposed to be a stopgap measure. In the second place, its author was Ellsworth, the primary author of the Judiciary Act, who knew that the questions it addressed were novel at the time and fraught with complexities. Third, the act was as subject to state-federal rivalry as the Judiciary Act and had thus to leave wiggle room for individual judges to work with local counsel. Finally, as with criminal, admiralty, equity, and international law questions, local rules were subject to the rule-making powers of the U.S. Supreme Court because appeal to it was readily available in civil cases. In any case, it was pragmatic rather than normative or formal rule making that underlay the statute and its successors.[67]

... And A Bill of Rights

The Judiciary Act was not be the only courts bill making its way through Congress in the months from May to September 1789. Running parallel to it was James Madison's proposal that the Constitution be amended to include all but one of the Virginia Resolutions. He omitted the resolution's limitation on the jurisdiction of lower federal courts. Combined, the two judicial enactments enabled Congress to complete the Madisonian Compromise. For as Madison wrote to Edmund Pendleton near the end of the first session of the Congress, a bill of rights would take from the antifederalists their most potent objection to lower courts, while a Judiciary Act that went beyond the limitations on lower federal courts in the Virginia Resolutions would fulfill the hope of the federalists for a comprehensive system of lower courts.[68]

By 1787, most states had some enumerations of rights either preceding or embedded in their state constitutions. The delegates in Philadelphia included some of these rights, for example a bar on ex post facto prosecutions, bills of attainder, and suspension of the writ of habeas corpus in Article I, Section 9 of the Constitution. These applied to the states and to the federal government. Thus, like the bar to states' violation of contract, they were evidence that the Constitution empowered Congress to limit what states could do with their sovereignty. An effort to include a more extensive list (for example protecting free speech, the press, the right of assembly, the right to a jury trial, and the right to counsel) failed after a relatively brief debate at the Convention.

After his election to the House of Representatives in 1788, having promised to introduce the Virginia Resolutions at his first opportunity, Madison prepared notes on potential amendments to the new Constitution. On May 4, 1789, Madison rose and announced that in three weeks he would propose amendments to the Constitution. On May 25, the proposal was delayed by other business. Madison used the time to polish his remarks. On June 8, he read to the House of Representatives his proposed amendments and immediately encountered opposition. It was too soon, some said, while others simply opposed the idea of changing what the federalists had so arduously framed. Madison turned to the device that had served him so well at the Constitutional Convention. He moved that the amendments be sent to a committee of which he was named a member. Throughout the committee sessions and certainly throughout the debates in the House of Representatives, Madison was the driving force behind the amendments, pressing for consideration and ultimately gaining the necessary support in the House. On July 28 that committee reported favorably, and in August the entire House debated the proposal. There is no record of the Senate debates, as the upper house sat behind closed doors. But the Senate began its deliberations on August 25, and after a conference with a committee from the House to iron out differences, the Senate agreed to the final version of twelve amendments on September 25. On October 2, President Washington sent copies of the twelve amendments to the states in the Union (as well as Rhode Island and North Carolina although they had not yet ratified the Constitution). In the winter of 1791, Washington informed Congress that ten of the amendments had been ratified.[69]

Of these amendments, five would directly affect the operation of federal courts. The Fourth Amendment's application to federal courts applied as well to Congress. "The right of the people to be secure in their persons, houses, papers, and effects, against unreasonable searches and seizures, shall not be violated, and no Warrants shall issue, but upon probable cause, supported by Oath or affirmation, and particularly describing the place to be searched, and the persons or things to be seized" limited the discretion of federal prosecutors acting under federal law. Insofar as Congress did not yet have before it any crime bills, the amendment seemed to harken back to hated imperial criminal law. The extension of the procedural guarantees in state constitutions to federal prosecutors suggested that federal trial courts should follow the lead of state trial courts, but the Judiciary Act of 1789 and the Process Act of 1789 did not require federal courts to follow state criminal procedure.

The Fifth Amendment was far broader in scope.

> No person shall be held to answer for a capital, or otherwise infamous crime, unless on a presentment or indictment of a Grand Jury, except in cases arising in the land or naval forces, or in the Militia, when in actual service in time of War or public danger; nor shall any person be subject for the same offence to be twice put in jeopardy of life or limb; nor shall be compelled in any criminal case to be a witness against himself, nor be deprived of life, liberty, or property, without due process of law; nor shall private property be taken for public use, without just compensation.

The Due Process Clause of the Fifth Amendment interacted with Article III in a subtle fashion. Read in its broadest sense, the clause hinted that Congress did not have entire and untrammeled discretion over the jurisdiction of the lower federal courts and the appellate jurisdiction of the Supreme Court. Were Congress to violate due process rights of individuals in an act limiting the kinds of issues the federal courts could hear, the courts might respond that the act of Congress violated the Fifth Amendment. Such a finding required courts to deploy the doctrine of judicial review of an act of Congress, an issue that might not have been apparent to the framers of the Bill of Rights. The amendment also imported the concept of compensation for "takings" by federal officials. The first Congresses would pass new kinds of "excise" taxes on the sale of certain goods. Did the collection of these taxes violate the Takings Clause? The answer at the time was no.

The Sixth Amendment, the third of the procedural guarantee amendments, asserted:

> In all criminal prosecutions, the accused shall enjoy the right to a speedy and public trial, by an impartial jury of the State and district wherein the crime shall have been committed, which district shall have been previously ascertained by law, and to be informed of the nature and cause of the accusation; to be confronted with the witnesses against him; to have compulsory process for obtaining witnesses in his favor, and to have the Assistance of Counsel for his defence.

The great trial amendment ensured that trials would take place as close to home as possible and gave compulsory process to defendants, including the right to cross-examine witnesses and have counsel present at all stages of the defense, which were rights that state law already ensured for most defendants (the most glaring exception being trials of slaves by inquisition rather than by juries). It answered the most potent of Mason's objections to Article III courts—that no provision was made for jury trials in criminal cases.

The Seventh and the Eighth Amendments, respectively, provided for jury trial. "In Suits at common law, where the value in controversy shall exceed twenty dollars, the right of trial by jury shall be preserved, and no fact tried by a jury, shall be otherwise re-examined in any Court of the United States, than according to the rules of the common law," and that "excessive bail shall not be required, nor excessive fines imposed, nor cruel and unusual punishments inflicted." Again, these were part of the proposed amendments that Virginia sent with its ratification. Along with the provision for jury trials in criminal cases in the vicinage in the Sixth Amendment, the first clause of the Seventh fully replied to the antifederalist quarrel with the lack of juries in federal courts. The jury trial guarantee did not apply to proceedings in equity, where the court proceeded by pretrial depositions and interrogatories.

The Judiciary Act and the Bill of Rights proceeded through the Congress alongside each other. The precise means by which that concordance came to fruition will remain hidden from historical inquiry, for there is no record of the conversations between the main authors writing the Judiciary Act, principally Ellsworth and Madison, but strong inferences are possible. Recall, for example, that Madison had told the Philadelphia Convention that the Supreme Court justices would tour the nation—and the circuit courts' bench included the justices. True, Madison and Ellsworth were not intimates, at least according to Madison's recollection, but they had worked together when Ellsworth and Madison were in the Confederation Congress. Madison and Ellsworth lived in proximity to one another in a New York City small enough to walk from one end to another in an hour. "Housing was hard to come by," though the city fathers did their best to accommodate the personnel of the new government. Out of town members boarded with those who had residences in New York City and conversation surely included rival plans for the judiciary.[70]

The Judiciary Act of 1789, combined with the Bill of Rights, not only fulfilled the promise of the Madisonian Compromise of 1787, locating the lower federal courts within the structure of separation of powers, the Act also extended the compromise to judicial federalism. With the rules of decision and the allotment of district courts by states, the Act fashioned a working relationship between the new courts and the states. Nonetheless, if the compromises that created the lower federal court system fulfilled the promise of Article III, no one could predict how well those compromises would work in practice in the new government system. Would the same sort of passionate politics that contested ratification find their way to the new federal courts? Would rivalry with the state courts poison the wells for the federal courts? Would the courts—"the least dangerous branch" in Hamilton's words—survive in competition with the far more power-ful executive and legislative branches? In framing and ratification of Article III and the Judiciary and Process Acts of 1789, the party of hope for the new federal system had won a round over the party of fear of a central government. The next round would come when President Washington had to fill the district courts' and Supreme Court's seats.

2

Open for Business, 1789–1801

No sooner were the federal courts open for business, than issues involving partisan politics, federalism, and separation of powers reappeared. In the appointments process, the day-to-day operation of the courts, and the courts' handling of a series of highly charged cases from 1789 to 1801, the strengths and weaknesses of the Madisonian Compromise became apparent to friends and critics of the new institution.

Complicating the first decade of the first federal courts was the rise of a national two-party system, a rivalry between Hamiltonian Federalists and Jeffersonian Republicans that had major repercussions for the federal judicial system. Disputes over domestic and foreign policy, and the very nature of constitutional republicanism, separated the two parties. Federal courts were thrust into the maelstrom of political passions that the framers perhaps should have but did not anticipate.

Appointments and Disappointments: Funding

In September 1789, after the passage of the Judiciary Act, Congress and President George Washington faced the practical matters of setting compensation for the judges and other officers of the courts and filling the slots. Patronage and clientage were constants of eighteenth-century office holding. The appointments provision of the Constitution and the Judiciary Act did not prevent those in office from rewarding their loyal followers with judicial posts. But outright repayment of favors was not the primary concern of President Washington or members of the Senate in the selection of the judges and justices. The political affiliation of the candidate (that is, was he a federalist or antifederalist), the geographical alignment of the candidate with the judicial seat, and the reputation of the candidate among his peers in the bar were more important considerations.

Actually, placing the appointment process in the hands of the executive with confirmation in the power of the Senate worked against the bargain and sale of judgeships. When the president and the majority of the Senate were in accord, as in September and October of 1789, confirmation occurred smoothly. In later years, when the president and the majority of the Senate were at loggerheads, the process could take months, and some nominees went away empty-handed. The dynamics of this coordinate mechanism are one more proof that the checks and balances system was designed to prevent corruption.[1]

The states' rights objections to the creation of a lower federal judiciary reappeared in the debates over reimbursement of the judges and justices. When, in late September 1789, the House of Representatives debated the question of salaries for Supreme Court justices, for example, members suggested that the justices should not be paid more than their counterparts in the states. Members wondered aloud if higher salaries for the federal bench would debase service on the state courts. Not suspicion or envy per se, but certainly a tender concern for the reputations and the self-image of state officials slowed agreement on the justices' recompense.[2]

Article III provided that the members of the Supreme Court and "inferior" courts that Congress might create "at stated times, receive for their services, a compensation, which shall not be diminished during their continuance in office." This was an alternative to the fee-based system that characterized colonial and some state courts. During the ratification debate, antifederalist Melancton Smith had lamented that "the judicial department alone with its concomitant train of judges, justices, chancellors, clerks, sheriffs [the state equivalent of marshals] . . . etc. in every state and in every county in each state, will be a burden beyond the limits of the people to bear." The framers of the Judiciary Act were well aware of such complaints. Consequently the salaries that Congress provided for the new judges were low compared with the income of a successful private practitioner. The federal government was already in debt, and in any case congressmen believed that expensive government was an open door to corruption.[3]

The funds allotted to the new Supreme Court under the Compensation Act of 1789 was $21,500, all for salaries. No provision was made for reimbursement of travel expenses. Salaries for associate justices were set at $3,500 a year (the chief justice was budgeted an additional $500 for his administrative duties). The pay scale for the district judges varied according to the anticipated caseload of the court, from $800 to $1,800 a year, a calculation based on the anticipated amount of business in the district court. Judge Henry Marchant of Rhode Island was as committed to the new nation and its courts as anyone in the judiciary, writing in 1792 to Chief Justice John Jay that "our country has a claim to the highest exertions of all its sons," but he was furious that his post paid only $800 and the North Carolina judgeship would be worth $1,500. It was "degrading to myself, and to the honor and interest of the state." The total appropriation for the federal courts in 1793 was $59,460. This included the $1,500 salary of the attorney general. By 1800, the appropriation had risen to $78,900. Congress in 1822 increased the disbursement to $122,450, as salaries had been modestly raised in 1820 to a range of $1,000–$3,000 for the district judges and $4,000 for the justices ($4,500 for the chief justice). In 1860 those figures again rose, to $2,000–$5,000 dollars for the judges and $6,000 for the justices. In 1861, the appropriation (ignoring the fact that all but two southern federal judges defected to the Confederacy), reached $1,275,100. On the one hand, throughout the period federal judges earned about as much in salary as members of Congress, hinting that the judicial branch was a respected part of the federal system. On the other hand, federal judges made far less money than the leading members of the bar, and men like Marchant knew it. The low salaries created the very situation that they were supposed to avoid. Judges had to retain their legal practices or engage in other business enterprises to make ends meet, an open door to conflict of interest at best and corruption at worst until an act of Congress in 1812 forbade the judges from engaging in private practice. Given this, it is a tribute to the personal integrity of the appointees that so few cases of corrupt practice are documented.[4]

Appointments and Disappointments

The first appointments to the U.S. Supreme Court and the district courts displayed the influence of partisanship that has, in one form or another, characterized federal judicial appointments throughout their history. There were no well-organized, standing national parties in 1789 when President George Washington submitted the first slate of nominees to the Senate at the end of September 1789, but the division between the loose coalitions of federalists and antifederalists was still fresh. Members of both factions sought seats in the new government and pledged to make it work. But all the nominees for the first courts as well as their successors in the 1790s, with one exception, had been federalists. In fact, Washington made support for the Constitution along with character, Revolutionary credentials, and local reputation explicit criteria for nominees. All the nominees were also well-known lawyers. Almost all had played a prominent role in the Revolution, and many had some hand in drafting the Constitution and the Judiciary Act. Some had served as state court judges, but others, like Supreme Court Justice James Wilson, had no experience on the bench. Still, as South Carolina federalist Ralph Izard wrote when he learned that his friend John Rutledge had been chosen, "the judges of both the Supreme Court and the district courts are chosen from among the most eminent and distinguished characters in America, and I do not believe that any Judiciary in the world is better filled."[5]

Washington sought the advice of people he trusted in making the appointments, but likely candidates were not shy about petitioning him for his support. Wilson, lobbying for an appointment, wrote the president: "But how shall I now precede? Shall I enumerate reasons in justification of my high pretensions . . . and inform you that my aim rises to the important office of chief justice?" Wilson stopped there, knowing that the Pennsylvania delegation in Congress would sing his praises and that Washington, who presided at the Constitutional Convention, would know of Wilson's contributions to the framing and ratification of the document.[6]

Pennsylvania lawyer and judge Edward Shippen had to promote himself, and he was not shy about it. "I promise you to execute the Trust with assiduity and fidelity and according to the best of my abilities" he told Washington. The salary would also help him support his eight children. Washington did not choose him. Virginia lawyer Arthur Lee also offered his services—as one Virginia gentleman to another, "it is not without great apprehension of presuming too much on the favor you have always shown me, that I offer you my services, as a judge of the Supreme Court." Washington agonized over this offer, but in the end declined it because Lee was an antifederalist and known to be testy.[7]

The process of solicitation and choice of the first justices and judges set a number of lasting precedents. Because the Senate had to confirm the nomination, many of those who expected to serve asked their states' U.S. senators to put in a good word with Washington or with John Adams, the new vice president and presiding officer of the Senate. Although there were exceptions, senators from the potential appointee's state were consulted about the appointment, in what would later be known as "senatorial courtesy."

The barrage of letters and personal pleas also set a precedent, turning the chief executive into what today would compare with the hiring partner in a large law firm. Before the Civil Service Act of 1886, just about every federal "office" was a patronage post appointed by the president, and judgeships were among these. Sifting through these recommendations and offers of service, Washington selected those men whose views were substantially in accord with his own. He did not appoint men known for contentiousness either, assuming that the federal judges should have a judicial temperament. In a pattern that set precedent, President Washington included geographical considerations in his choices. When a justice from one region left the court or a district judge stepped down, Washington and subsequent presidents selected a successor from the same region or state. A collateral benefit was the reinforcement of judicial federalism. Justices and judges from the locality could be expected to share its values, for federal judges' background and family connections would not be very different from state judges'.

The average age of the first courts' members was a little over fifty. At a time when the average life expectancy of white males was under forty, the appointees were exceptional for their longevity. In a sad proof of this fact, shortly after their nomination two of the six justices became too ill to serve. As rule, justices and judges from the Tidewater lasted a shorter time than those from New England— the brackish marshland of the Chesapeake was home to malaria and typhoid. There were even outbreaks of yellow fever as far north as Philadelphia, New York City, and Boston in 1798.[8]

Figure 2.1 Chief Justice John Jay, in 1794, before he was called to lead a diplomatic mission to England. Portrait by Gregory Stepko after Gilbert Stuart, Collection of the Supreme Court of the United States.

Washington wanted to consult members of the federal bench on a regular basis, making such consultation a part of their judicial duties. While judges and justices did perform ex officio assignments as individuals, had they complied with his requests in their roles as judges, it would have set a precedent profoundly revising the checks and balances system. In a response that preserved separation of powers, Chief Justice John Jay consistently refused to allow his judicial office to be used in this way. For example, in 1793 Secretary of State Thomas Jefferson, at the behest of President Washington, asked the members of the U.S. Supreme Court to advise the president on questions of international law. A list of twenty-nine interrogatories was prepared and transmitted to Chief Justice Jay, but he replied that "the lines of separation drawn by the Constitution between the three departments" prohibited the Court from giving such opinions. Jay and other judges did take on tasks away from the bench. For example, shortly before refusing to give official opinions on international law, Jay prepared a draft of the Declaration of Neutrality for the president, who wished to keep the country out of the wars of the French Revolution. As a leading Revolutionary era diplomat, Jay was an expert on such matters and prepared the document. A year later Jay would travel to England, at the president's behest, to negotiate a treaty mitigating the troubles between the two nations. He did not travel as the chief justice, although he still held that office.[9]

Appointments and Disappointments: The Justices and Judges

Just as George Washington was chosen president of the United States in part for his accomplishments and in part for his demeanor—truly acting and appearing to fit the part of father of his country—the first chief justice set the tone for that office. Jay came from one of New York's most wealthy families and had a significant law practice when not in public service. He was a moderate during the Revolution, not an advocate of the breach but strongly supporting independence after July 1776. His caution and wide experience of law made him a natural diplomat, and his mission to Spain during the war was, if not entirely successful, proof that he could perform his job in the most trying of circumstances. (He would repeat the performance as head of the U.S. delegation to Britain, in 1795, to negotiate a treaty resolving differences between the two countries.) He had attended the New York State ratification convention and joined with Hamilton and Madison to write the Federalist Papers explaining the new Constitution. His was the first name submitted by Washington to the Congress and two days later, on September 26, 1789, Jay was confirmed by the Senate. Jay would serve until 1795, when he resigned to accept his election as governor of New York. He stepped down from that post in 1801, refused President John Adams's nomination and the Senate confirmation to the chief justiceship, and lived twenty-eight more years in retirement on his Westchester, New York, estate. "Reliable, rather than inspirational, solid and admirable without rising to the heroic," his judicial legacy as chief justice expanded the purview of the court and the power of the federal government. In some areas of law, for example criminal punishment, he was a reformer. He also urged the gradual abolition of slavery, serving as the first president of the New York Manumission Society and signing the act that provided for the eventual end of slavery in the state.[10]

Not every appointment proved so wise. Washington's second appointment to the Supreme Court was an embarrassment to him. John Rutledge of South Carolina had a distinguished career as a South Carolina judge and Revolutionary governor, and a huge law practice. What was more, he had strongly supported the Constitution. But there was a mercurial streak in him. Although he did ride the Southern Circuit once, he resigned his post on the Supreme Court without ever having sat on it. William Cushing's route to the Court was even more troubled that Rutledge's, but not because of Cushing's temperament. Instead, he had a rival from Massachusetts who, in effect, ran against him for the post. Vice President John Adams favored John Lowell, with whom he had close ties, but Cushing won out. He was hardly the patrician that Jay and Rutledge were, instead coming from an upwardly mobile middle-class family. He was also, typical of some Americans of that day, a man on the make—ambitious and eager for personal and financial advancement. His talents and opportunism took him from rural Massachusetts to rural Maine (then a province of Massachusetts) and back, finally to a place on the colonial supreme court (while not abandoning any of his private law practice). He served the crown, then the new state, with equal ability. In financial and legal matters he was a conservative, with no affection for the farmers of his birth region. But he was the jurist who struck down slavery as incompatible with the state's constitution. Always "careful and pragmatic," he served on the Supreme Court until his death in 1810.[11]

James Wilson seemed an obvious choice for the Supreme Court bench. Though outspoken, fulsome, and egocentric, Wilson was brilliant in defense of the Constitution in Philadelphia and helped ensure its ratification in Pennsylvania. Born in Scotland and educated for the ministry, he came to Pennsylvania to make his fortune. Reading law in John Dickinson's law office was a superb step in that direction—Dickinson was one of the colony's leading practitioners. Alongside Dickinson, Wilson became an avid Revolutionary politician and propagandist. He understood that the safety of a republican government lay in wise laws. As he told a Philadelphia audience in his lectures on the law, "it

Figure 2.2 Justice William Cushing of Massachusetts's carriage, used while riding circuit, 1789–1810; although the poor conditions of the roads sometimes forced him to travel on horseback. Credit: Rudolph Mitchell/Scituate Historical Society.

is the right, and generally it is the duty, of a state, to form a constitution, and to institute civil government, and to establish laws" for the good of the people.[12]

At the same time as his political career flourished, his law practice grew, including clients like Robert Morris, the leading financier of the confederation period. Unfortunately, he engaged in a number of highly speculative land deals (along with Morris, who joined them enthusiastically) and was deeply in debt by 1789, when his appointment to the Court was confirmed. Although he had some income from his appointment as the College of Philadelphia's first professor of law, it hardly slaked his appetite for speculation or the avidity of his creditors. He was hounded on circuit by lawyers representing his creditors, sometimes missed sessions to rush back to Philadelphia to refinance his debts, and in 1797 was briefly jailed for nonpayment of nearly $200,000. His friends feared that he would be "disgraced by a conviction on an impeachment." Mute witness to Wilson's incapacity was his absence from the circuit court in Charleston, where Judge Thomas Bee continued to adjourn the fall sessions of the court in hope, vain as it proved, that Wilson would appear. In broken health and dire poverty, this flawed framer died in 1798.[13]

When Maryland's Robert Harrison was too ill to serve, Washington chose James Iredell of North Carolina for the slot. Iredell came from Bristol, England, in 1768 to serve as a customs collector in North Carolina. His brother was a minister in the Church of England and his family was well off but not gentry. He read for the bar in North Carolina and began practicing law there in 1773. By the next year, he was writing antiparliamentary pamphlets, but he was not in favor of independence (like many of the Carolina professional and merchant class) until it was declared. He served his new state's government as attorney general and judge, and continued his private practice. He strongly supported the right to private property against almost all comers, and he saw the new Constitution as a bulwark of that right. A strong and outspoken federalist, he nevertheless was an early proponent of states' rights. He sat on the Court until his death in 1799, at the age of forty-seven. Iredell was a close friend of Wilson's. When Wilson begged the younger man to ride the Southern Circuit in his stead, Iredell declined, but after the 1793 Judiciary Act reduced the number of justices sitting with each circuit court from two to one, in effect easing the burden of riding circuit for individual justices, Iredell rode circuit in the South, as it included his North Carolina home.[14]

Other newcomers to the Court included Thomas Johnson of Maryland, William Paterson of New Jersey, Samuel Chase of Maryland, and Oliver Ellsworth of Connecticut. Samuel Chase was the first justice whose conduct in court was controversial. Chase came from relative obscurity to high office. His father was a clergyman, and the family always had trouble making ends meet (even when Chase's law practice was going well). He did not marry into wealth and never felt comfortable around the rich. He did find friends in the Revolutionary crowd however, and he was as close to a rabble-rouser as any of Washington's appointees. He was most at home in the legislature of his own Maryland, and he was the only former antifederalist whom Washington tabbed, although by 1788 he had changed course and became a staunch federalist. His support for the Jay Treaty brought him to Washington's attention, and Chase, one step ahead of bankruptcy, was happy for the salaried position. He served from 1796 to 1811 and was involved in many of the most politically divisive cases coming to the circuit courts over which he presided. He died while serving.[15]

The last of Washington's appointments to the Supreme Court was Ellsworth as chief justice. When the Senate rejected John Rutledge as chief justice, in all likelihood because of his strenuous opposition to the Jay Treaty (the first of thirty presidential nominations to the Supreme Court formally rejected by the Senate thus far), and Cushing declined (at sixty-three-years old feeling his age), Washington turned to the Connecticut lawyer and legislator. Ellsworth attended Yale and Princeton, and, unlike Chase, married well (the daughter of a former governor). He preferred farming and legal practice to hobnobbing with the rich, however, and walked to the nearby county court rather than ride a horse or drive a chaise. He mastered detail, learned how to work well with others, and gained the respect of people of all parties. He was a federalist during the ratification debates, was selected for the U.S. Senate in 1789, and played a major role (described earlier) in the crafting of the Judiciary Act of 1789. During his service as chief justice, from 1796 to 1800, he worked for unity on the Court. Journeying to France in 1799 as President John Adams's spokesman (not as the chief justice), Ellsworth helped heal the rupture of relations with a former ally and prevent war, a feat for which arch-federalist politicians like Alexander Hamilton never forgave him.[16]

Each of these justices wore three judicial hats. On circuit they were trial court judges. They and their successors spent more time traveling to and from the two sessions of the circuit court each year than they did sitting on the Supreme Court bench. When cases were appealed from the district to the circuit courts, for example suits in equity, the justices were appeal court judges. Then they sat together as the U.S. Supreme Court.

At first the Court met for winter and summer terms, each no more than a few weeks at most. Pursuant to the Judiciary Act of 1802, they began sitting for a single term, commencing in February (after 1827 in January), that rarely lasted through March. These were men who had already devoted much of their adult lives to the public weal in peace and war. Circuit riding was a burden but, for most of them, service on the Court was the capstone of their careers.[17]

Figure 2.3 Supreme Court courtroom, housed in the Philadelphia City Hall annex, restored to its 1790s appearance. Credit: National Park Service.

When the justices held circuit court, they sat with the district court judges. Appointments to the district courts were not as prestigious as those to the Supreme Court, but the nominees were experienced and respected members of their local bar. Washington did not spend as much time choosing them as he did on the Supreme Court justices, and he did not know the judges as well as he knew the justices, but he chose according to the same criteria: federalists of good character.

Each state had one judicial district, as did the "province of Maine" (then part of Massachusetts) and the Kentucky Territory. Reviewing the nominees' backgrounds and achievements suggests that the district judges' credentials elevated the new courts' status. Some of the district judges had prominent careers before they came to the federal bench. Some distinguished themselves once on it. Others left little mark on the law or the courts they served. All represented their states in a way comparable to the members of Congress. Though not directly chosen by their states' electorate, they were virtual representatives of their states. In this way the appointment process reinforced judicial federalism. Attorney General Edmund Randolph wryly acknowledged as much in a letter to Washington: "At this instant too it is possible that the federal judges may not be so far forgetful of their connection with the state governments as to be indifferent about the continuance of their old interest there."[18]

Capsule biographies of some of these first district court judges reveal their status and their local connections. For example, James Duane's service during the Revolution, at the Continental Congress, in the New York State legislature, where he helped draft the state's first constitution, his support for the ratification of the federal Constitution (while mayor of New York City), all connected him to the powerful Livingston and Schuyler clans in the state. Hamilton persuaded Washington to select Duane, and the Senate confirmed the choice. Duane expected to continue his legal practice while on the bench, a fairly common though erroneous supposition among the new judges. He served until 1794 and died three years later. An appointment like this one, typical of the first district judges, could only promote judicial federalism.[19]

Richard Peters, nominated, confirmed, and commissioned in 1792 for the District of Pennsylvania, would become the best known and perhaps the most respected of the district court bench, in part because his court sat in Philadelphia (from 1790 to 1800 the nation's capital), and in part because of his superb handling of the trials following the Whiskey Rebellion and Fries Rebellion in Pennsylvania. His family owned an estate in what is now Fairmont Park, and he never lost his interest in improving agricultural methods. A graduate of the College of Philadelphia (later incorporated as the University of Pennsylvania), he read law, gained entrance to the bar, and practiced in the city. A supporter of the Revolutionary protests, he was named to the Continental Congress and during the confederation served in the state assembly, becoming speaker of the upper house in 1791. When in the next year the city was stricken with the worst yellow fever epidemic in its history, Peters retired to his country house above the Schuylkill River to the west of the city, and the court did not meet. After the state was divided into two districts, he remained judge in the Eastern District until his death in 1828. A sober-minded and learned man with a jovial sense of humor and genuine thoughtfulness, he never indulged in the histrionics of some of his fellow judges on the bench, remaining on good terms with political leaders on both sides of the Federalist-Republican controversies of the 1790s. Peters's career was another example of the way that the state credentials of the men appointed to the district courts ensured harmony among state and federal bars.[20]

A final example of this point: David Brearley, formerly the chief justice of the New Jersey Supreme Court and a signer of the Constitution, was an obvious choice for the New Jersey post. Yet failing health afforded him but one

Figure 2.4 Judge Richard Peters of Pennsylvania, artist unknown. Peters was, arguably, the most respected member of the district court bench in its formative era. Courtesy of The Historical Society of Pennsylvania, Simon Gratz Collection.

opportunity to hold court, and he died five months after receiving his commission. He was succeeded by Robert Morris, who served in the post until his death in 1815. Morris's ties to the state were as strong as Brearley's—Morris had preceded Brearley as chief justice of New Jersey. Like his predecessor, Morris was regarded as "a judicious lawyer" and considered a man of "integrity" by both his fellow New Jersey lawyers and members of Congress.[21]

Although the new district judges became a human chain holding together judicial federalism, not every district judge demonstrated a judicial temperament. Harry Innes, judge of the Kentucky district court, was never regarded as a paragon of judiciousness. Innes came from a middle-class Virginia family, studied law at William and Mary under George Wythe (Thomas Jefferson's and John Marshall's mentor), and after the Revolution migrated to Kentucky when it was still part of Virginia. There he practiced law, traded slaves and horses, speculated in Indian land (after driving the native peoples off it), and joined the Kentucky independence movement. He sat for a short time on the superior court, resigned to practice before it (the fees were better for a lawyer than a judge), and opposed ratification of the Constitution. Washington appointed him to the federal bench in 1789. Innes continued to practice law on the side, seeing no contradiction and much profit in it. Although personally close to Jefferson, Innes became a little more circumspect in his politics after his appointment. He wrote in 1791 to Jefferson, "[T]he Peasantry are perfectly mad. Extraordinary prejudices and without foundation have arisen against the present officers of government, the lawyers and the men of fortune" all of which he had become. He served until 1816.[22]

Sometimes long service to the state left the nominee to the federal bench unable to perform his duties. In North Carolina, District Judge John Stokes died from the lingering effects of his Revolutionary War wounds shortly after receiving his commission. Other judges, for example Brearley and William Drayton of South Carolina, succumbed to their debilities shortly after accepting their commissions. The disability or death of district judges constituted a continuing dilemma for lawyers, clerks, marshals, and others who waited, sometimes for weeks, for the judge to appear and open court. According to Simeon Baldwin, clerk of the court for the District of Connecticut, day-to-day adjournments caused "serious difficulties for counsel." The newspapers reported the inconvenience to suitors and their counsel when either the justice (most often) or the judge (less often) failed to attend and the court had to be adjourned. Congress finally provided a time limit for the sessions of the circuit courts, after which the court would automatically adjourn until the next scheduled session.[23]

Along with the failing health of some of the judges, a few exhibited a lack of financial probity. One example was Nathaniel Pendleton. He came from the Virginia aristocracy. His uncle Edmund Pendleton was the foremost judge in

Virginia. Like a number of this generation of Virginia gentry, Nathaniel moved to Georgia to seek his fortune in land speculation. He was the attorney general of Georgia from 1785 to 1786 and was elected to the Constitutional Convention and the first federal Congress but attended neither. He did accept the post of federal judge and held it in Savannah until his resignation in 1796. In a clear example of questionable ethics, while on the federal bench he was deeply involved in the Yazoo land purchase scandal that led to a veritable political upheaval in the state, duels, and the infamous case of *Fletcher v. Peck* (1810). After he resigned he relocated to Dutchess County, about 100 miles north of New York City, and died there in 1804. Before his death, he performed one last service for the federalists, acting as Alexander Hamilton's "second" in the infamous Hamilton-Aaron Burr duel. Pendleton knew and respected both men, and to his credit tried unsuccessfully to prevent the final, fatal encounter.[24]

Some of the district court judges gained notoriety for their fierce partisanship. Vermont gained statehood in 1791. Its first federal judge, Nathaniel Chipman, was an early recruit to Alexander Hamilton's Federalist Party and one of the strongest proponents of Vermont statehood. A feisty lawyer, his conservative views led to an exchange of blows with another of Vermont's future state leaders, Matthew Lyon—Chipman wielding his cane, Lyon a fireplace poker. Chipman served Vermont as attorney general and chief justice of the supreme court. His stint on the federal bench was short, ending with his return to private practice in 1793. There he practiced what he preached in his *Sketches of the Principles of Government* (1793): the goal of all good government was "to regulate the mode of acquiring, and to secure the acquisition of property . . . and to restrain and punish those crimes, which attack private property."[25]

Officers in but Not of the Federal Courts

Although the early federal bench members stoutly resisted encroachment on their independence, until 1939 the system of lower federal courts was administered by a succession of executive branch officers and agencies, including those in the departments of State, Interior, and Justice. These offices decided how much to ask Congress to appropriate for the courts and then supervised the disbursement. Congress assigned these tasks to the newly created Administrative Office of United State Courts in 1939.[26]

The location of administrative authority for the courts outside the judicial branch notwithstanding, the Judiciary Act of 1789 provided for three officers for each court—a clerk, a marshal, and a federal attorney. The clerks' duties, explained a little more carefully in the Process Act of 1789, including issuing summonses and other official orders by the judge, keeping the minute book and dockets (the schedule of hearings and trials), and dealing with the lawyers who came to court to file suits and represent clients. The clerk was the internal administrator of his court and its secretary, handling naturalization petitions, conducting auction sales of seized goods, handling the funds gathered from fines and fees, and registering copyrights (until this duty passed to the Library of Congress in 1870). The District Court for the District of New Hampshire, for example, registered the first copyright in 1791 for minister and former Harvard College president Samuel Langdon's *Observations on the Revelation of Jesus Christ to St. John*. Clerks also handled applications for naturalization; the fees were an important addition to their income. The clerk was also, in effect, the chief financial officer for the court, recording funds paid to witnesses, jurors, the marshals, and other expenses. (The marshals were responsible for delivering the funds.) Clerks like Simeon Baldwin supplemented their income by holding other jobs, in his case collector of revenue and clerk of New Haven, on whose board of alderman he also served. Baldwin resigned his clerkship and ran successfully for Congress in 1803. He attempted to return to his clerkship in 1805 but discovered to his dismay that the appointment was a patronage post entirely in the control of the judge after Federalist Richard Law died in 1806, and Jeffersonian Republican Pierpont Edwards dismissed Baldwin He had to find other uses for his considerable talents—on the state court's bench.[27]

Despite some notorious cases of mismanagement of funds and clerks' neglectfulness in reporting their fees, there was little congressional regulation of the clerk's office until 1841, when Congress imposed stricter supervision of the collection of fees; in 1842, when the clerks had to report all their business to the secretary of the treasury (in 1849 to the secretary of the interior); and in 1853, when a uniform fee schedule (much like that already in existence in state courts) was imposed. In 1870, as part of the reform establishing the Department of Justice, supervision of the clerks passed from the Department of the Interior to the new department. Still, the clerks were compensated by fees until Congress replaced the fee system with a salary in 1919.[28]

Under the Judiciary Act of 1789, marshals were nominated by the president and confirmed by the Senate. They kept order in the courts, served and returned summons and subpoenas, and, to a limited extent, enforced federal law. Like the clerks, they were paid on a fee system until Congress, in 1896, provided salaries. Patronage sometimes played a role in their appointment. For example, the marshal of the district court in New York when James Duane served was his old friend William S. Smith.[29]

Attorneys for the United States, often referred to as "federal attorneys for the district" were far better known than the clerks and marshals because the post was often a stepping stone to the judgeship or other federal and state offices. According to the Judiciary Act, the district's attorney was to be "learned in the law," to prosecute federal crimes, and to represent the United States in all civil actions to which it was a party. These officers did not have to abandon their private practices, unlike the federal judges. William Rawle, for example, took time from his duties as U.S. attorney for the District of Pennsylvania to represent clients in just about all the equity cases coming before the circuit court from 1792 to 1800.

In effect, the post of federal attorney was a part-time one, as was the U.S. attorney general. Caleb Cushing in 1853 was the first to dedicate himself full time to the office. Some of the appointees, like Joseph Daveiss in Kentucky, would play important roles in the early history of the nation. Daveiss was one of the first federal officials to denounce Aaron Burr as a traitor to his country. He brought charges against the ex-vice president in federal court for the District of Kentucky. Burr, defended by young attorney Henry Clay, was preparing to face a Frankfort grand jury when Daveiss backed down. [30]

Appointment rewarded the appointee's political connections. For example, Richard Harison, the first New York federal attorney, was a Federalist and Alexander Hamilton's law partner. Harison continued his law practice during his service as a federal attorney. When Harison resigned, in 1801, his place was taken by a Republican, Edward Livingston, whose family connections were almost unequaled. "Boss Ned" continued to serve as mayor of New York until President Thomas Jefferson persuaded him to resign two years later. The length of the terms of federal attorneys was undetermined until 1820, when Congress prescribed a four-year tenure for the attorneys, although it also provided for their removal at the pleasure of the president.[31]

Federal attorneys did not at first answer for their conduct directly to the attorney general of the United States. As early as 1791 Attorney General Edmund Randolph complained to President Washington that he had no authority over or communication from the federal attorneys, who received from the secretary of state what little direction they had. During debate on a bill in 1792, the House of Representatives refused to give the attorney general supervisory authority. Until 1861 the U.S. attorneys reported to the man who sent them their commissions— the secretary of state. An act of 1861 finally granted the attorney general authority to supervise and direct the U.S. attorneys and required the attorneys to report their official proceedings to the attorney general. When the Department of Justice was established in 1870, Congress gave the attorney general supervisory authority over the accounts of the U.S. attorneys—ironic in the light of fact that Ulysses S. Grant's new attorney general, Amos Akerman, had been a colonel in the Confederate army. After the war, however, Akerman became a strong advocate of the rights of the freedmen and women and a staunch Republican.[32]

There was a fair amount of nepotism, or at least lineal relationships, in these appointments with judges naming relatives as clerks of the court (the appointment of which lay wholly in the discretion of the judges). For example, David

Sewall, named judge of the District of Maine in 1789, immediately appointed his nephew, Henry, as his court's clerk. So, too, federal judicial office might pass down, like an estate, through the male line of the family—for example among the Draytons in South Carolina and the Cushings in Massachusetts. This was particularly true in the parts of the country where prominent families had established a tradition of service in public office.[33]

The Business of the First Federal Courts

At their first sessions, the federal courts had little or no substantive business. When it first convened, in New York City, even the Supreme Court did not have an official seal for its documents and no one to swear in its officers. Chief Justice Jay made do. He announced a design of the seals and asked the state court of appeals chief judge to swear in the federal officers—after all, they had all practiced for years in New York courts. After the swearing in, Jay ended the first session of the Supreme Court for lack of a case or controversy. The circuit court met in the city on April 5 and 12, 1790, where Jay reminded the charged the grand jury of the vital importance of the checks and balances system. "The Constitution of the United States has accordingly instituted these three departments, and much pains have been taken so to form and define them as that they may operate as checks one upon the other, and keep each within its proper limits." After Jay charged the grand jury, the court "adjourned to the following term."[34]

In Richmond, District Judge Cyrus Griffin opened court and "there being no business, soon closed it." But business picked up in the next few years. The District Court for the District of Rhode Island sat five times in 1791, and heard six admiralty cases and three cases of debt. In these, and in all but six of the 101 cases that went to a verdict over the next decade, plaintiffs won nearly 90 percent of the time. The plaintiff won by default if the defendant did not show up in court—suggesting that the court was acting as a debt collection agency of a sort. Defendants fared much better at the circuit court, winning about 40 percent of the time, though most of the time one or the other party failed to appear. The District Court for the District of Maine (recall that it had jurisdiction of both district and circuit courts) had the dubious distinction of hearing and deciding the first capital case in the federal system. Judge David Sewall presided over the 1790 trial of Thomas Bird, and Englishman, and the Norwegian Hans Hanson for piracy and murder. A jury found Bird guilty and he was hanged. Hanson was acquitted. Justices Rutledge and Iredell arrived in Charleston to hold the circuit court in 1789 and learned that District Judge William Drayton was too ill to attend. They named Thomas Hall clerk of the court, Isaac Huger read his commission as federal marshal (both men from respected families), everyone took oaths to preserve and defend the Constitution, then the justices admitted "practitioners" including Charles Cotesworth Pinckney and Jacob Drayton (men of the highest social and economic strata in the state), and departed, for the docket was empty. While the circuit courts were open for two days each term, the justices had good reason to complain that their travel to the distant Southern Circuit was largely a waste of time. In disgust, Rutledge resigned his federal post to accept a place on the South Carolina Supreme Court. Nathaniel Pendleton opened the District Court for the District of Georgia in Savannah, admitted U.S. Congressman James Jackson among others to practice, and heard a salvage case. At the next session, convening in Augusta, the court had no business. It was not, overall, an auspicious beginning for the federal courts.[35]

Bit by bit, the district courts grew a little busier with seamen's claims for unpaid wages and other maritime contractual matters and suits in admiralty for the seizure and sale of goods on board ships brought into harbor as prizes by combatants in the wars of the French Revolution or by violators of the customs laws. Importers and shippers could appeal the verdict in these cases directly to the district court. So, too, could diplomats representing foreign shipowners. In the District of New York, for example, there were twenty-six recorded petitions for remission of fines. These, added to civil suits and a trickle of appeals from the district courts to the circuit courts in the first decade of the federal courts, built the caseload into the hundreds in New York and South Carolina. Even Rhode Island's courts grew busier by the end of the decade, the district court hearing and deciding an average of twelve suits a year by the end of the decade, and the circuit court averaging over twenty suits in the same years. Much of that load in the latter jurisdiction concerned repeated or return suits like *Higginson v. Greenwood*, dragging on session after session in Charleston, as Greenwood's counsel tried to fend off Higginson's estate's demands for repayment of a pre-war debt. The circuit court handled a mini crime-wave in October 1794, when the grand jury indicted fourteen men for piracy. Two were discharged after the grand jurors found "no bill" in their cases. Fortunately for the remaining defendants, all were found not guilty by a trial jury (whose foreman, T. J. Brown, may or may not have been related to the leader of the crew, Joseph Brown). In any case, a jury from Charleston where the circuit court sat would surely have known most of the crew of the suspected pirate brig *Betty*. Overall, the Southern Circuit courts heard more than 3,200 cases in the period 1789–1800.[36]

Federal courts had exclusive jurisdiction over federal crimes. Some of these cases fell under the Federal Crimes Act of 1790, including treason, counterfeiting, forgery, and felonies on federal property. More often, assault and affray at sea filled out the criminal docket. Federal criminal cases never amounted to more than a small portion of the docket during the early years of the courts, however. In Maryland, for example, the circuit court did not hear a criminal case until 1793, when Samuel Monroe of Baltimore was prosecuted for stealing a letter from the post office. The federal offense was the theft of a stamp (one cent), but inside the letter was a bill of exchange for $1,500. The circuit courts would hear all manner of criminal cases involving the post, including robbery of the post carrier, forging an endorsement on a postal bank note, and interfering with the delivery of mail.[37]

In their first decade, federal courts' criminal and civil caseload did not expand in linear fashion. Instead, there were slack times followed by sudden surges in business. In the New Haven sessions of the Circuit Court for the District of Connecticut from 1790 to 1797, for example, the court handled twenty-nine civil cases in 1790, thirty-six in 1791, forty-two in 1792, but only sixteen in 1794 and eleven in 1795. The Circuit Court for the District of North Carolina heard nine cases in 1791, twenty-five in 1792, fifty-eight in 1793, thirty-eight in 1794, and only two in 1795. In the Circuit Court for the District of Pennsylvania, criminal cases were few (a total of thirty before 1794), and then exploded in 1794 and 1795 to over 100, as "the insurgents" in the western Pennsylvania counties of Washington and Allegheny, rebelling against the excise tax on distilled spirits, were hauled into court. So numerous were the defendants in these cases that the courts introduced the first printed forms for grand jury indictments and summons for witnesses. In 1797 the criminal docket was back to normal—merely two cases. Then Fries's Rebellion in eastern Pennsylvania in 1798–1799 bloated the criminal dockets again, with nearly seventy defendants, the indictments coming under the conspiracy provisions of the Sedition Act of 1798 discussed below.[38]

Private suits dominated the Kentucky docket, starting slowly (nothing for the first two years) then varying from an average of six per year to a high of forty-nine in 1800. As in the other federal courts, only a handful of cases involved alleged crimes, until the end of the decade brought a spate of prosecutions for revenue violations and attacks on federal revenue collectors. New Jersey's district court heard over 100 revenue cases, but only a handful went to trial (the federal attorney allowed violators to plead out and pay the fine). Apparently, as in colonial times and later, during Prohibition, the long Jersey coastline invited customs duty violators. In New York, the district court disposed of 269 cases, and neighboring Connecticut's district court heard and decided 101. "Prize" cases involving ships taken by privateers in the war between Britain and France took up many sittings of the courts' time. Circuit courts did have a feature the district courts lacked even when business was slow. Because the justices were present, they addressed the grand jury the marshal had summoned. These "charges," often hours in the reciting, made the justices of the Supreme Court very visible to counsel and jurors, a positive contribution to judicial federalism and part of the administration's plan to show the flag of the national government throughout the land.[39]

Over the course of the period from 1790 to 1797, there were only 191 suits in equity in the circuit courts. This relatively small number of equity cases appealed from the district does not truly reflect the time and trouble these suits entailed. To handle the extensive depositions and documents equity suits brought to court, district judges named masters in equity to take depositions and present them in court, saving the judges' immense time and effort. Of the forty suits in equity docketed between 1792 and the end of 1800 in the Philadelphia sessions of the Circuit Court for the District of Pennsylvania, almost all required two or three returns to court before they were ended with a "rule" for production of documents or other evidence. Some featured years of filings and replies. Leading Philadelphia attorneys like the Alexander James Dallas (a future reporter of Supreme Court cases and secretary of the treasury in James Madison's first administration), Jared Ingersoll, William Lewis, and William Tilghman, along with Rawle, appeared for their clients, sometimes joining together in various configurations of counsel. Following equity practice, the party structure of these suits could be complex, with various individuals and occurrences liberally joined together. The complainants included the United States, the State of Maryland, and various foreign dignitaries including John Penn, formerly the proprietor of the colony of Pennsylvania. In one remarkable suit, Rawle, acting for the United States, filed a bill in equity against Edmund Randolph, former attorney general of the United States. Although both men had private practices and routinely sought the aid of federal courts to compel the production of documents in private suits, Rawle here was acting in his official capacity. A month later Rawle sought permission from the court to discharge the subpoena. Apparently Randolph had complied. Robert Morris, the debt-ridden former financier of the Revolution, also appeared as a defendant in suits instituted by the United States.[40]

If in black letter law the rules for equity, criminal prosecutions, and admiralty "libels" (the original complaints) were supposed to be uniform, and not derived from precedent or statute of states where the courts sat, judges almost reflexively employed state practices with which they were familiar. For example, in Pennsylvania, District Judge Francis Hopkinson used familiar state forms of subpoena in criminal cases, and in Maryland, Judge William Paca allowed sureties to put up bonds for the defendants' good behavior according to his state's practice. (The first printed forms used in federal courts were in Maryland—receipts for the "recognizances" of these sureties). Maryland's federal judges' attachment to its state formulary went further—even when indicting for piracy and other federally defined crimes, the grand jurors "of the U.S. for the *State of* Maryland" rather than for the *District of* Maryland [italics added] indicted or did not indict suspects. At the same time, Judge Paca departed from state procedure when he allowed a slave, one "Negro Jack," to testify "before the court" in *U.S. v. Francis Pratt*, a case of robbery on the high seas. Maryland criminal law barred slaves' testimony. Those counsel who practiced in the federal courts brought with them extensive experience in the state courts and expected state customs would be followed. Thus Egbert Benson, whose law practice spanned the colonial era, early national period, and early nineteenth century, asked that the District Court for the District of New York use state law "to protect" the interests of his client, the widow Thompkins. He told Judge James Duane, long a colleague of his at the bar, that "according to the laws of New York" the administrator of the estate had acted entirely properly. As it happened, he was the administrator of the estate and counsel for the widow. Also noteworthy was the fact that the circuit court was sitting in chancery, whose rules did not automatically follow those of the state in which the court sat.[41]

Some of the business of the courts in these first years was marked by occurrences that modern readers will find unethical or worse. There was no set rule telling a judge when his personal "interest" in a matter before the court requiring him to recuse himself or disqualifying him on motion of a party in the case. With only one district judge per district, strict recusal and disqualification rules would have been a considerable hardship on litigants. Judges were not supposed to act as counsel in their own causes either—an obvious grounds for disqualification. Insofar as the judges not so long ago had practices in the states where they now held court, there were plenty of occasions where recusal or disqualification might apply. But over time and particularly in the first years of the courts, rules ensuring the impartiality of judges "have been a work in progress." In 1792, Congress enacted a standard, but there was no enforcement mechanism. [42]

Admonitions did not prevent abuses. In 1794, the putative heirs to a large parcel of New Jersey land hired Richard Stockton to represent their interests before the circuit court; on the bench sat former New Jersey real estate lawyer Robert Morris (no relation to the financier). Morris had an interest in the parcel and refused to respond to the bill in equity when it was presented. The suit was finally argued in 1799, when Morris literally left the circuit bench to argue the case before his colleague Justice Bushrod Washington. Morris wanted the suit quashed for laches (delay in filing) but lost and decided to appeal to the Supreme Court. Morris's co-counsel could not catch up to Justice Washington as he left Trenton, however. In the meantime, Morris, ill and worried, consulted with Robert Livingston, New York's chancellor, looking for a loophole in Justice Washington's decree allowing the suit to go forward. Next Morris turned to his in-law, Justice William Paterson. The case reached the Supreme Court in 1800 but disappeared from the record until 1830, fifteen years after Morris had died—another example of the often voiced complaint against the dilatory nature of equity suits.[43]

Hayburn's Case (1792) and Chisholm
v. Georgia (1793)

Two of these early cases raised fundamental questions of separation of powers and judicial federalism. The first, *Hayburn's Case*, came in the circuit court sessions of 1792 as a consequence of the Invalid Pensions Act of 1792. The statute would have turned the circuit courts into pension commissions, with the justices hearing and recommending action to the secretary of war on applications for veterans' pensions. Moreover, under the Act, Congress could review and revise the secretary of war's decisions about the circuit courts' recommendations. It was an unwieldy system at best, crisscrossing all three branches of government, but that was not what concerned the justices. When U.S. Attorney General Edmund Randolph sought a writ of mandamus from the Circuit Court of the District of Pennsylvania putting William Hayburn on the pension list, the response of the justices sitting on circuit was swift and unanimous. Justice Wilson wrote a letter to President Washington for himself, Justice Blair, and Judge Peters, "Upon due consideration, we have been unanimously of opinion that under this act, the circuit court held for the Pennsylvania District could not proceed . . . Because the business directed by this act is not of a judicial nature. It forms no part of the power vested by the Constitution in the courts of the United States." Any judgment the court might make of Hayburn's petition "might, under the same act, have been revised and controlled by the legislature, and by an officer in the executive department. Such revision and control we deemed radically inconsistent with the independence of that judicial power which is vested in the courts."

Written at the Circuit Court for the District of New York , Chief Justice Jay's letter to the president was more diplomatic than Wilson's, not surprising given the former's diplomatic service during the Revolutionary War. "Neither the Legislative nor the Executive branches, can constitutionally assign to the Judicial any duties, but such as are properly judicial, and to be performed in a judicial manner. That the duties assigned to the Circuit courts, by this act [of Congress], are not of that description" nor were the other branches "authorized to sit as a court of errors on the judicial acts or opinions of this court." Justice Iredell, riding the Southern Circuit, sent a similar letter to President Washington.[44]

Almost as important as the justices' refusal to perform the duties assigned them by the statute as part of their duties as judges was the language of their refusal. All the judges were acting "in the belief that the . . . Act was unconstitutional." Wilson said as much to Attorney General Randolph when they happened upon one another on a Philadelphia street in front of the courthouse, or so Randolph later reported to President Washington. Randolph persisted, asking the justices at the August session of the Supreme Court to order the circuit courts to comply with the Act, in effect asking them to reverse the opinions they expressed to President Washington. There is no report of exactly what the members of the Supreme Court replied, but some evidence comes from a Randolph letter to James Madison and from Iredell's notes on the Court's deliberation. At first the Court would not hear Randolph, unsure if he was representing the government or acting in his private capacity as counsel for Hayburn. He reappeared later that day with Hayburn in tow, and this time the Court allowed him to make his points. The Court then took the case under advisement, deferring an opinion until the next session.[45]

At least one member of Congress in 1792 reproached the judges for finding the Act unconstitutional, and early nineteenth-century commentators like New York's chancellor James Kent agreed that the judges had found the law an "unconstitutional" violation of separation of powers, although Alexander James Dallas's report of the case did not contain the word unconstitutional. It was not, thus, the first instance of federal judicial review, but the clear and definitive exposition of separation of powers doctrine that makes the case so important. All the judges understood, and wanted the president and Congress to understand, that the judicial branch was not an agency of the other two branches of the federal government.[46]

The subsequent history of the case, with the passage of a revised Act and Randolph's second appearance either on behalf of Hayburn or the president, or Congress, or his own recognizance (the record on this matter is unclear), is clouded by the fact that there is no report of what the Court actually decided. Randolph withdrew his petition. The striking informality of Wilson's revelation to Randolph, combined with the sketchy reporting of the case by Dallas, is best understood in its context. Although larger than the first capital of New York City, Philadelphia was still geographically small by modern standards, the center of the city about eighteen blocks square north and south along the Delaware and perhaps as much to the west beyond the Statehouse. Randolph and Wilson were virtually neighbors. On Chestnut Street and Sixth Street, Congress met in the remodeled county courthouse; the House in the lower chamber, the Senate on the upper floor. "Congress Hall" as it was called lay next to the Pennsylvania Statehouse (Independence Hall). On the other side of the Statehouse, the U.S. Supreme Court, the circuit court, and district court met in the old City Hall building. Along this portion of Chestnut Street members of the federal judiciary, Congress, and the "heads" of the departments of state, treasury, and war passed one another on their way to work and back to their homes or boarding houses. Hayburn could petition the circuit court in person and then appear alongside Randolph at the Supreme Court without leaving the city. It was a sometimes unwanted intimacy, particularly after the rise of the rival political factions Hamilton and Madison led. [47]

The judges' refusal to turn the federal courts into administrative agencies under the Act notwithstanding, Jay opined in a dictum (a statement unnecessary to the disposition of the case) that Congress could name anyone it wanted to act as commissioners to hear petitions under the Act, and if that was the will of Congress, "the judges of this court will, as usual, during the session thereof, adjourn the court from day to day or other short periods as circumstances may render proper, and that they will regularly, between the adjournments, proceed as commissioners to execute the business of this act in the same courtroom or chamber." We cannot find evidence that petitioners took advantage of this offer, although one member of Congress told the lower house that he had a list of pensions approved by one of the circuit courts. Congress amended the Act to provide for review of the petitions by district judges or anyone they named as commissioners. Federal courts routinely named commissioners to take inventories and testimony in admiralty, and Congress assigned to the judges, as judges, to make determinations on naturalization, tax abatements, the health and welfare of sailors, and other nonjudicial administrative activities. The difference between these assignments and the commissioning of the circuit court members under the Act was that in the latter the other branches of federal government would have the power to overrule the courts.[48]

A second early case raised serious federalism questions, pitting a state's government against the federal courts. In *Chisholm v. Georgia* (1793) the Court heard a suit by the executor of a South Carolina citizen's estate against the State of Georgia to collect a wartime debt the state supposedly owed. Alexander Chisholm could have gone to the Georgia courts to seek payment, but he brought the suit in federal circuit court instead under Article III's provision for federal courts hearing the suit of a citizen of one state against another state. Chisholm probably assumed that the state court would rule in favor of the state, a fear that Georgia's later conduct proved grounded. At the circuit session, Justice Iredell ruled that his court had no jurisdiction in the case and dismissed it. Chisholm then filed the suit in the Supreme Court.[49]

Georgia, claiming state sovereignty, refused to participate in oral argument. The Supreme Court found for Chisolm in a 4–1 vote. On the jurisdictional issue, Chief Justice Jay reasoned that if one state could sue another in the Supreme Court, then a citizen of one state could sue another state. Georgia's sovereignty, which the Constitution guaranteed and Jay conceded, did not protect it from a lawsuit. He went on to suggest that the purpose of the federal court system was to protect litigants from the "errors" of state courts, a strong version of the federalist position. Justice Wilson agreed.[50]

Justices Cushing and Blair did not press as hard for a "national court's" total supremacy over state courts (this would have crushed the sovereignty of the states) but found grounds for jurisdiction in the plain language of Article III.

If the Supreme Court had original jurisdiction in suits to which a state was a party, and Chisholm was suing the State of Georgia, then the Supreme Court had to hear the case. Iredell dissented. The Judiciary Act did not spell out jurisdiction when a private citizen sued a state and since the Act came after the drafting of the Constitution, it should control or provide the meaning of the grant of original jurisdiction in Article III.[51]

When the ruling reached the members of the Georgia state legislature, they resolved "that any federal marshal, or any other person or persons levying or attempting to levy on the territory of this state . . . or any of the people thereof, under and by virtue of any execution or other compulsory process issuing out of, or by authority of the supreme court of the United States . . . on behalf of the aforementioned Alexander Chisholm . . . are hereby declared guilty of felony, and shall suffer death." In hindsight, one might argue that the imposition of a criminal sentence without a criminal trial was a bill of attainder outlawed by the federal Constitution; the imposition of such a sentence on an officer of the United States doing his duty was an act of treason as defined by the federal Constitution and the Federal Crimes Act of 1790; and the assertion of Georgia's right to disobey a decision of the U.S. Supreme Court was a violation of the Supremacy Clause of the federal Constitution, a document that the Georgia constitutional convention had ratified in a single day. In hindsight, it is clear that such a violently phrased assertion of states' rights was a harbinger of Georgia's refusal to obey the Supreme Court on future occasions, for example in the state's refusal to recognize the treaty rights of its Native American inhabitants. It was certainly not a good omen for the survival of the "More Perfect Union" described in the Preamble to the Constitution. On this occasion, however, Georgia's resistance to federal authority echoed throughout the country and resulted in the congressional passage, in 1794, and ratification by three-fourths of the states, in 1795, of the Eleventh Amendment: "The Judicial power of the United States shall not be construed to extend to any suit in law or equity, commenced or prosecuted against one of the United States by Citizens of another State, or by Citizens or Subjects of any Foreign State." The ratification was reported by Secretary of State Timothy Pickering in 1798 and thereby became part of the Constitution.[52]

A Testing Time for the Federal Courts

Although by the early 1790s most of the nation's voters conceded the authority of the new federal government, the political unity of the country remained fragile. More than 90 percent of the population of four million lived in rural areas. Roads connected only a small portion of these localities, and travel along rivers, the major highways in the country, was dangerous in spring because of flooding.

Rapid expansion to the west created a desire for a "providential nationalism," that justified conquest and settlement, but most Americans still thought of themselves first as members of their village, town, parish, church, or state before they thought of themselves as citizens of the United States. Such nationalistic feeling as existed was contested among different interest groups and political parties.[53]

The partisanships of the confederation period continued into the 1790s. In the states, eastern creditors and western farmers still contested control of legislatures. Creditors and debtors vied over fiscal policy. In the nation, "sectional" (large-scale regional) differences between the North and the South over slavery and the expansion of the nation to the west simmered. No matter what Madison wrote in defense of the new Constitution in Federalist No. 10, it did not curb factionalism.[54]

The fierce partisanship that marked this era affected the federal judiciary. Supposed by the independence that life tenure conferred to be above party rancor, federal judges found themselves the arbiters of what was permissible political dissent and what crossed the line into criminal activity. That task began when Pennsylvania and Maryland farmers objected to the federal excise taxes in 1791 and 1792 on distilled spirits that Federalist Party leader and Secretary of the Treasury Alexander Hamilton proposed and Congress enacted. Farmers attacked tax collectors sent west from the capital in Philadelphia. President Washington responded sternly, "[I] have issued a proclamation warning against all unlawful combinations and proceedings having for their object or tending to obstruct the operation of the law in question." But the Whiskey Rebellion in western Pennsylvania only grew more violent.[55]

On August 11, 1794, Washington read the riot act to the tax resisters. Their threats now encompassed the federal bench. Washington reported, "The judiciary was pronounced to be stripped of its capacity to enforce the laws; crimes which reached the very existence of social order were perpetrated without control." To William Rawle, federal attorney for the District of Pennsylvania, fell the duty of prosecuting the rebels in circuit court in 1795. Sitting in Philadelphia were District Judge Richard Peters and Justice William Paterson. The marshal was David Lenox, who had taken the job but a year previously and found himself fired upon as he tried to deliver warrants in western Pennsylvania. The entire process of trying so many men for treason, assembling so many witnesses, and producing so much paperwork (including the new printed forms for indictments and summonses), so strained the circuit court's slender manpower and fiscal resources that it did not sit to hear a criminal case the next year.[56]

A jury convicted twenty-four men of unlawful assembly with the purpose of obstructing the operation of a federal law. Two other defendants were found guilty of treason. Rawle had argued that "if any of the conspirators actually levy war, it is treason in all the persons that conspired," a broad reading of the constitutional definition of levying war that included conspiracy and actual acts of levying war. Rawle believed to the end of his life that treason "may be complete before any force is actually used." William Tilghman, counsel for the defendants, replied that Rawle was incorporating the English notion of a constructive treason into the courtroom. "Take, then, the distinction of treason by levying war, as laid down by the Attorney of the District, and it is a constructive, or interpretative, weapon, which is calculated to annul all distinctions heretofore wisely established in the grades and punishments of crimes; and by whose magic power a mob may easily be converted into a conspiracy; and a riot aggravated into High Treason." He viewed Rawle's definition of treason at variance with Section 3 of Article III and the Federal Crimes Act of 1790, which was "a shield from oppression with which the Constitution furnishes the prisoner."[57]

Justice Paterson's "bench notes," including the charge he gave to the jury in the case of *U.S. v. Barnet*, indicated that he agreed with Tilghman. American treason law was distinct from England's. Treason was defined in the Constitution as levying war against the United States and required an act witnessed by two people. There was no such thing as "constructive treason"—a crime that one found in English law. Paterson told the jury:

> This brings us to consider the particular case of the p[risone]r. at the bar; and to examine how far he was traitorously concerned—The traitorous purpose is a necessary ingredient—The mind of the prisoner must be manifested by some . . . overt act, and it is your province, gen[tleme]n., to collect or infer the intention from the testimony said before you. A person may be present from curiosity or from accident, but if he does not . . . by his conduct indicate a traitorous spirit or intention, he is not to be criminated.[58]

The honor of the nation and the ordinary process of justice restored, Washington pardoned the convicts. He had seen over a long military career the effects of real violence and had no desire to add to it. What is more, "he knew the western country," the temper of its people, the hardships they faced, and he wished no "insult" to them. Perhaps the most important fact about the indictments and trials was that the prisoners were represented by counsel. The prisoners' rights under the Fourth, Fifth, and Sixth Amendments and a jury verdict according to law marked all the proceedings.[59]

If one could say that the federal judiciary had passed its first major test with flying colors, demonstrating that the Madisonian Compromise led to fair trials in federal lower courts, a sterner test was on its way. The partisanship of the early 1790s stirred by Hamilton's program of domestic finance to which Madison, Jefferson, and others objected, ripened into full-blown national division over diplomatic relations between the federal government and the government of France. In 1789, French revolutionaries created a constitutional monarchy. In 1792, they adopted a republican form of government. The next year leaders of that government executed the king and queen and found themselves enmeshed in a war with Great Britain and a coalition of European powers. War brought a reign of terror to French domestic politics, horrifying Hamilton and his Federalist allies. They regarded amity with Britain as essential to American domestic order and national security. This was made difficult by Britain's impressment of sailors on the high seas and occupation of forts on the Great Lakes. The Jeffersonian party, by contrast, believed that the success of the French Revolution should be the first priority of American foreign policy. A diplomatic mission to England led by John Jay did not resolve all points of difference between the United States and Great Britain. Even before Jay returned with his draft treaty, whiffs of dissent had spread over the land. As James Iredell, riding circuit in New York, told the federal grand jury: "It has been, I believe, as generally as justly thought, that the mischiefs of disunion, however lightly contemplated at a distance, would upon an unhappy experience be felt in a manner we should have eternal reason to regret. To prevent so great a calamity . . . the present constitution of the United States was formed." Iredell knew that a grand jury in Pennsylvania had already faced the prospect of severing western portions of the Union from the whole. He hoped that the rule of law and respect for the federal courts would prevent a recurrence of such divisions. But the newspaper that published his charge at the request of the grand jurors, summoned to court by the marshal, was a Federalist stalwart.[60]

Convinced that Republican partisans posed a real danger to public order and worried about the outcome of the election of 1800 on their party's near monopoly of federal offices, the Federalists decided to silence the most vituperative of the Republican newspaper publishers and editors. The test case of this kind came in 1798, in the indictment of William Bache, a heavy-handed Republican publicist, for seditious libel (publication calling a public official into disrepute) of President John Adams. Rawle convinced the grand jury that the federal government could try Bache for criminal libel based on English law. (Note that the jury was selected by the marshal, and he was a Federalist, as were they.)

There was no federal law against seditious libel, however, a point that became crucial when Bache was brought to trial in the circuit court. Alexander James Dallas and Moses Levy, co-counsel for Bache, had just represented Robert Worrall, a craftsman accused of trying to bribe a federal revenue commissioner, in the same court. In that case, the two lawyers argued the indictment was faulty because Worrall had not violated any federal law. Dallas told the court, Justice Samuel Chase and District Judge Peters presiding, "The judicial authority of the Federal Courts, must be derived, either from the Constitution of the United States, or from the Acts of Congress, made in pursuance of that Constitution.

It is, therefore, incumbent upon the Prosecutor to shew, that an offer to bribe the Commissioner of the Revenue, is a violation of some Constitutional, or Legislative, prohibition." Chase then asked the prosecutor, Rawle, "Do you mean . . . to support this indictment solely at [English] common law? If you do, I have no difficulty upon the subject: The indictment cannot be maintained in this Court." Rawle said that he intended a common law prosecution, having brought that indictment before the grand jury. Chase lectured Rawle, "This is an indictment for an offence highly injurious to morals, and deserving the severest punishment" but an attempt "to supply the silence of the Constitution and Statutes of the Union, by resorting to the Common law, for a definition and punishment of the offence which has been committed" was not sustainable. "The United States, as a Federal government, have no common law; and, consequently, no indictment can be maintained in their Courts, for offences merely at the common law." The federal government had no power to bring indictments under English criminal law without an enabling statute from Congress. On these same grounds, the case against Bache was dismissed.[61]

The lesson was plain: if the Federalists wanted help from the federal courts to muzzle their opposition, they must have an act of Congress on which to base the prosecutions. The Sedition Act of 1798's seditious libel provisions did the trick. Rammed through both houses of Congress by Federalist majorities and signed into law on July 14, 1798, it provided that "if any person shall write, print, utter or publish, or shall cause or procure to be written, printed, uttered or published . . . any false, scandalous and malicious writing or writings against the government of the United States . . . with intent to defame the said government, or either house of the said Congress, or the said President . . . or to excite any unlawful combinations" to suborn such a libel, the violator would face a fine not exceeding $3,000, and imprisonment not exceeding two years. Truth was a defense, but who could prove that political opinion, especially opinion expressed in the vitriolic language of the eighteenth-century partisan, was true? Another section of the Act prohibited conspiracies to undermine the government or to aid and abet the defamation of the government or its officials. Justice Paterson, addressing the circuit court grand jury at Rutland, Vermont, in 1798 explained that the danger was the evil tendency of such publications. "False, scandalous, and malicious" attacks on the government would lead the "rude and ill-informed part of the community, who delight in irregularity, sedition, and licentiousness" to think that sedition was freedom.[62]

Despite his strong aversion to such libels, Paterson was not the most avid in their prosecution. That dubious prize went to Justice Chase. He proved to be the most intrusive and unyielding of the circuit judges during these trials, again and again overstepping the line of neutral trial management to aid the prosecution. Whether his rulings in matters of law were correct, they were often delivered in an overbearing, even sneering, manner. He was abusive to defendants, disrespectful to their counsel, and he bullied jurors. In the trial of Thomas Cooper, for example, Chase heckled the defendant openly saying that even though Cooper was not a lawyer, he would be allowed some latitude in defending himself. In fact, Cooper's training as a lawyer at the Inns of Court in England and his practice in central Pennsylvania qualified him to defend himself. Chase went farther when instructing the jury: "All governments which I have ever read or heard of punish libels against themselves. If a man attempts to destroy the confidence of the people in their officers, their supreme magistrate, and their legislature, he effectually saps the foundation of the government." Chase not only concluded the prosecution summation, he made the jury aware of Cooper's political aims (and not incidentally his own). Chase would campaign for Adams in the 1800 presidential election.[63]

Twenty-five Republican editors, political writers, and a congressman were arrested, seventeen indictments were handed down by grand juries (the grand juries did not find true bills in the other cases), fourteen of which came under the Sedition Act. Eleven actually were tried, and all convicted. With Cooper's travail before their eyes, Republican writers like the Scottish immigrant James Callender ran for cover. Though Callender thought himself safe in Jefferson's Virginia, federal attorney Thomas Nelson summoned a grand jury there to indict Callender for writing that the "reign of Mr. Adams has hitherto been one continued tempest of malignant passions. As president, he has never opened his lips, or lifted his pen, without threatening and scolding. The grand object of his administration has been to exasperate the rage of contending parties, to calumniate and destroy every man who differs from his opinions." The handpicked Federalist members of the grand jury found a true bill on May 24, 1800; trial began on June 3; and after the jury found Callender guilty, on June 4 Justice Chase sentenced Callender to nine months in jail. Callender's writings had so infuriated Justice Chase that he insisted the jury find Callender guilty.[64]

In the course of their defense of Callender, George Hay and Philip Nicholas (both of whom would gain office when Thomas Jefferson won the presidency in 1801), tried to argue that Callender should be allowed to present evidence that his words were true. Chase demanded to see the evidence, in writing, before he would allow it in open court. When he saw it, he ruled that it was too prejudicial—that is, that it would "deceive and mislead the jury." When a third counsel, William Wirt, a leading Richmond lawyer, asked permission to address the jury on the constitutionality of the sedition law, Chase squelched Wirt. Chase's rulings were so abusively rendered that the three lawyers left the court and their client to the not so tender mercies of the bench. The jury convicted Callender, and Chase sentenced him to a $200 fine and prison. He was released on the last day of Adams's incumbency. Incoming President Thomas Jefferson pardoned him.[65]

The Judiciary Act of 1801

John Adams was angered by the Republican attack on his administration and signed the Sedition Act willingly, but he was never as virulent a partisan as Chase. His administration adopted the same views of fitness for judicial office as prevailed in the Washington administration. He and his advisors celebrated the federal courts and the judges as exemplars of "an upright intelligent and patriotic administration." Adams, in his presidential message of 1800, then called for the reform of the courts to ensure the quality of the bench.[66]

As framed and defended, the Judiciary Act of 1801, passed by a lame-duck (the new Congress did not assemble until December of that year) Federalist majority in Congress, would "provide for the more convenient organization of the Courts of the United States." The act reduced the size of the Supreme Court from six justices to five and eliminated the justices' circuit-riding duties. To replace the justices on circuit, the Act created sixteen judgeships for six judicial circuits, instead of the three established in the Judiciary Act of 1789. The new courts were trial courts, although they retained the appellate jurisdiction in equity and admiralty that the first circuit courts exercised. The first of the six new circuits included Maine, New Hampshire, Massachusetts, and Rhode Island. The states of New York, Vermont, and Connecticut comprised the second circuit. The two Districts of New Jersey, the District of Pennsylvania, and the state of Delaware were in the new third circuit. Maryland and the three districts of Virginia composed the fourth circuit. The fifth circuit included North and South Carolina and Georgia, and the sixth circuit encompassed Tennessee, Kentucky, and the Ohio and Indiana portions of the Northwest Territory. The Act gave to the new circuit courts jurisdiction over federal questions ("arising under the Constitution and laws of the United States"), a jurisdiction that the Federalists perhaps hoped would create greater uniformity of law throughout the nation (such questions hitherto being the province of state courts). The statute also made it easier to get a suit to federal court by eliminating the minimum dollar amount required for diversity suits about land sales and reducing the amount in other categories of lawsuits.

One might regard the Act as a response to a decade of complaints the justices lodged about their circuit-riding duties; as a sop to the Federalists defeated at the polls in 1800; an attempt to curb the unwonted populist impulse of the Republican Party; or as an attempt to marginalize state courts. Before one attributes the passage of the Act to partisan motives, one must concede that the idea for further reform of the circuits was discussed before the election of 1800, when Adams might well have believed that he would retain the presidency and the Federalists would continue to control Congress. While on its face, the Act seemed to shift business away from state courts toward federal courts, a fundamental change in the structure of judicial federalism, many Federalist lawyers, including Alexander Hamilton, had a substantial practice in the state courts, and influential jurists like Francis Dana, chief justice of the Massachusetts Supreme Judicial Court, were diehard Federalists. [67]

The removal of minimum financial requirements for diversity suits involving land and the reduction of the minimum amount in controversy in other suits might divert them as well from state to federal courts, but the extent and the impact of such diversion could not be predicted. Nevertheless, Republicans feared that this part of the measure was a deliberate attempt to undercut state courts by denying them business. Even if such fears were well founded in Federalist motives for the Act, there was no reason to assume that the outcomes of the cases would undermine state law. Federal courts hearing such cases were still bound by the Rules of Decision Act.[68]

Whether the Act changed key portions of the Madisonian Compromise or not, in the context of the Sedition Act controversy, the trials of Republican editors in federal court, and the election of 1800, the debate over the bill in Congress and its public reception showed that the courts and partisan politics were so closely linked that one could not propose any alteration of the Judiciary Act of 1789 without it becoming part of partisan debate. Insofar as such animus took the form of defense of national government on the one hand and a defense of states' rights on the other, it might be argued that the controversy was simply a continuation of the antifederalists' objections to the creation of lower federal courts, but in 1789 Madison and other future Republicans favored that step.

After the Sedition Act prosecutions, Republicans, with good reason, did not trust the federal courts. Republican members of Congress claimed that the new federal courts would "increase, instead of diminishing, the present inconvenience" that parties experienced when they sought remedies in federal courts. Out of doors, the Republican *Aurora* blasted the bill as the last gasp of a "failing aristocratic party."[69]

Federalist members of Congress replied that the measure was a necessary, nonpartisan reform. For example, Maryland's Robert Goodloe Harper wrote:

> The new system relieves the justices from this intolerable labour, reduces their number to five, and assigns them no other duty but that of holding the supreme court at the seat of government. The post will now become so eligible as to be accepted and retained by the most eminent characters in the nation; which will gradually render the supreme court of the United States what it ought to be, and what surely the pride of every American must induce him to wish that it may be, one of the first tribunals in the world, for the ability learning and dignity of its members.[70]

Fighting against the repeal of the Act at the opening of the next session of the Senate, Federalists like Gouverneur Morris, who had more to do with the Constitution's drafting that anyone else in the Senate, argued for the end of circuit riding on practical grounds: "Can it be possible that men advanced in years . . . men who from their habits of life must have more strength of mind than of body . . . that such men can be running from one end of the continent to the other? . . . I have been told by men of eminence on the bench, that they could not hold their offices" under the circuit-riding system. If hindsight is any judge, the Federalists had the better of the argument.[71]

Following the signing of the bill into law, on February 13, outgoing President Adams and Secretary of State John Marshall prepared 217 commissions for judges, magistrates, collectors of customs, military officers, and other officials of the federal government. Ninety-three of these were court-related appointments. The Senate confirmed all of them. As of February 20, 1801, appointments to the new circuit courts had been sent to and returned from a roster of well-respected and able men, but all were Federalists. Appointees like Massachusetts's John Lowell, New York's Egbert Benson, Maryland's Philip Barton Key, Connecticut's Oliver Wolcott, and Pennsylvania's William Tilghman were highly qualified for their new posts.

While some of the Jeffersonians viewed the federal courts as genuine enemies to states' rights and state courts, the essential disagreement between Federalists and Republicans was not about the necessity of federal courts. It was not a reprise of the federalist–antifederalist quarrel during ratification. The essential disagreement was partisan: the Republicans regarding the Federalist appointments as part of a Federalist Party plot. One indirect proof of the partisan tone of these early appointments came when the Republicans had the chance to fill vacancies—and did with loyal Republicans—before the Judiciary Act of 1801 was repealed on March 8, 1802. After the Act was repealed and the posts disappeared, newly elected President Jefferson arranged for his appointees to take other places in the federal judiciary. For example, Jefferson asked Henry Potter, whom he had appointed to the short-lived circuit courts, to sit in the District Court for the District of North Carolina. Potter would serve in it from 1802 until his death in 1857. Dominick Hall's Fifth Circuit Court duties ended with the repeal of the Act, but Jefferson named him territorial judge for the District of Orleans in 1804, and when that post was abolished in 1812, President James Madison asked the Senate to confirm Hall as district judge for the District of Louisiana. The point is this: Jefferson, as a lawyer, recognized the need for reform of the courts. Had Adams nominated and the Senate confirmed Republicans to some of the new circuit courts, perhaps the Act would have survived the Republican majorities in the new Congress.[72]

The Federalists also created the D.C. circuit by a separate Act on February 27, 1801. Hence the repeal of the Judiciary Act of 1801, Act did not affect the

D.C. judges. William Cranch was named to preside. Cranch nearly matched Potter's longevity on the bench, falling one year short (1801–1855). Cranch, also the reporter of the Supreme Court, thus was, like Alexander James Dallas in the previous decade, something like an unofficial court historian. Unfortunately, he and his brethren had to hold court in taverns, boarding houses, and establishments of less repute, until a place was found for the court in the unfinished city hall. On the plus side, travel within the district gradually improved. By 1808, "a fine turnpike was laid out from Alexandria to the Potomac. The four mile run was bridged and the Long Bridge constructed across the Potomac. Hence Judge Cranch could leave his Alexandria home and drive or ride in less than an hour to the foot of Maryland Avenue or the commons over which 14th Street was laid out." Perhaps the convenience of his office contributed to Cranch's longevity in it.[73]

The federal courts' reputation had suffered during the last years of the Federalist era, as the judiciary seemed to be the Federalists' chosen engine of political repression. So, too, a facially reasonable reform of the court system seemed in the harsh light of partisanship one more offense against the ideal of impartial federal courts. The implications of all this for the federal courts were plain. The fear and animosity against a system of lower courts that the antifederalists had expressed a decade earlier was stoked to great heat by the seditious libel prosecutions and the Judiciary Act of 1801. Could the federal courts recover their prestige and, more important, reestablish the legitimacy of the federal judicial system in the face of party politics, states' rights impulses, and the antagonism of the Republican ascendency in the other branches of the federal government? If so, leadership in this effort would have to come from the federal judiciary itself. Fortunately, it did.

3

A New Beginning, 1801–1835

The Sedition Act lapsed in 1801, but Samuel Chase's malignity on the bench in the Sedition Act prosecutions became the public face of the federal courts for their critics. The Jeffersonian majority in both houses of Congress would not arrive until December 1801, but the fate of the Judiciary Act of 1801 would surely be sealed when the new Congress convened. Perhaps a repeal of the Judiciary Act of 1789 would follow? Would federal courts whose conduct in the Sedition Act trials were so suspect be able to survive the antagonism of the Republican Party majority? At the time, answers to these questions were not clear at all. A president and congressional majority hostile to the lower courts; state judicial officials angered by a federal judiciary sitting in their midst; and volatile politics could have undone this portion of the Madisonian Compromise.[1]

The election of 1800 has been called the "Jeffersonian Revolution," and in truth the triumph of an organized opposition to an incumbent administration was an essential step toward truly democratic government in the United States. On March 4, 1801, Jefferson's inaugural bromide—"we are all republicans, we are all federalists"—could not hide what everyone in earshot of his speech knew: Jefferson was no friend to the federal courts as they stood in 1801. They were sure to face a storm when Republican majorities took control of Congress. No one recognized that likelihood more than the newly confirmed Chief Justice of the Supreme Court, John Marshall. While few historians today subscribe to the "great man" theory of historical explanation, Marshall succeeded in the task of piloting the federal courts system and the idea of a national jurisprudence to a safe harbor.[2]

The Great Chief Justice

As difficult as it is to contend that any one man could have restored trust in the judiciary, one can argue that Chief Justice John Marshall played a vital, perhaps crucial, role in reviving the reputation and efficacy of the federal courts. While it would be a mistake to see in the newly-appointed chief the elder statesman of 1835, no one can doubt that Marshall played a key role at a critical period in helping make the federal court system "a major force in American life." Obviously, he could not end the rivalry between the judiciary and the other branches of the federal government nor fully resolve the tensions inherent in separation of powers and federalism, but he averted the most serious partisan assaults of the Jeffersonians. Ironically, it was Marshall's good sense and management skills that saved the Madisonian Compromise from the more extreme members of Madison's own party.[3]

In person Marshall was a remarkable combination of entrepreneur and speculator (he had a huge law practice and invested in land), deep thinker, principled believer in the prospects of the new nation, and political opportunist. In short, he embodied many of the contradictions and ironies of early national America. He was born to the gentry and inherited a plantation, but preferred to live and work in Richmond. He saw combat as a young officer in the Revolution; and served as a diplomat, in Congress, and later as secretary of state. Though briefly a member of the House of Representatives, he never sought high elective office. Simple in dress and manner, he rarely stood on ceremony and had little attachment to the aristocratic pretensions of the great Virginia Tidewater aristocracy. Not bookish or pedantic, he had a great store of common sense and personal charisma. When he passed away, the judges of the district court and the Maryland state courts gathered in Baltimore to honor him. They resolved "to wear the badge of mourning for two months." Missouri Senator Thomas H. Benton wrote of Marshall, "he was supremely fitted for high judicial station—a solid judgment, great reasoning powers, acute and penetrating mind . . . attentive, patient, laborious . . . grave on the bench, social in the intercourse of life, simple in his tastes, and inexorably just."[4]

Marshall gave little clue to his personal or political beliefs when he wrote for the Court. He opined as though the law dictated the course of his pen, worked hard for consensus on the Court, based his writing on the broadest possible grounds, and pioneered in switching the Court from "seriatim" opinions, in which every justice read his own, to "Opinions for the Court," in which justices "signed on" to one another's opinions. In this, and in many other ways, he worked to ensure harmony, if not uniformity of opinion, on his court. But as much as Marshall wanted to take the federal courts out of partisan politics, or at least defend their independence by appearing to take them out of partisan politics, President Thomas Jefferson's efforts to purge the courts of Federalists posed an almost insuperable obstacle.[5]

The Jeffersonians and the Federal Courts

In almost its first action concerning the federal courts, repealing the Judiciary Act of 1801, the Jeffersonian majority in Congress seemed bent on disabling this last Federalist stronghold. The Judiciary Act of April 29, 1802: "An Act to amend the Judicial System of the United States" perpetuated the Federalists' plan of six regional circuits, returned to the old system of circuit courts held by the district court judge and a Supreme Court justice riding circuit, but denied the now restored old circuit courts the broad federal question jurisdiction given the federal courts in the 1801 Act. The 1802 Act reduced New Jersey's two districts to one and Virginia's three districts to one. Congress also eliminated the Supreme Court's summer session and provided for one annual session to begin on the first Monday in February.[6]

In response, the ousted judges sought reinstatement, publishing their case widely, petitioning Congress for redress, and finally bringing test cases arguing that the repeal of the 1801 Act denied them constitutionally protected property rights in the offices. Hearing one of these suits, *Stuart v. Laird* (1802), in the Circuit Court for the District of Virginia at the end of 1802, Marshall dismissed the argument that a Supreme Court justice could not hear a case in the circuit court without a commission as a circuit court judge. When the Supreme Court took the case on appeal, Justice William Paterson's opinion for a unanimous Court (Marshall taking no part in the decision) found that Congress could arrange, or rearrange, the lower courts in any manner it chose. While appearing to be a concession to reality, if not to the Jeffersonians, in fact Paterson's rationale legitimated Congress's authority to pass the 1801 Act and its repeal.[7]

Jefferson then ordered his party managers to bring impeachment proceedings against the most vulnerable of the Federalist federal judges. John Pickering of the District of New Hampshire was low-hanging fruit—his discordant rambles in court and his frequent absence from sessions led to his impeachment and removal by the Senate on March 12, 1804.[8]

Pickering's malfeasance stemmed from alcoholism. Samuel Chase's alleged offense was extreme partisanship in grand jury charges and the conduct of trials. On February 26, 1805, the next-to-the-last day of Chase's impeachment trial, Representative Caesar Rodney of Delaware, one of the lower house "managers" (prosecutors) of the impeachment, told the Senate, "No man can seriously say that for a judge to continue in the exercise of his authority and the receipt of his salary, after any acts of misbehaviour, is not a violation of this essential provision of the Constitution. He holds his office explicitly and expressly during good behaviour . . . The people have leased out the authority upon certain specified terms." Rodney proposed a democratic-republican basis for tenure, a type of virtual elective federal judiciary. Although a majority of the Senate voted against Chase on a number of the impeachment counts, on none did the vote reach the required two-thirds for removal. A chastened Chase pulled in his horns and died in office six years later. Jefferson, who had hoped to follow the conviction of Chase with a thoroughgoing campaign against the

Supreme Court bench, in his mind a form of "recall" of the justices, abandoned the impeachment initiative.[9]

The Jeffersonians never intended to demolish the federal judiciary. They were intent on "cracking the Federalist hold" on the courts and wanted to "pack them with Republicans." Republicans in the Congress and Jefferson knew that to the victors in the congressional and presidential elections of 1800 would go the spoils of federal office—among which were patronage appointments to the federal bench. The Jeffersonians filled vacancies in the federal courts with party loyalists, more proof, if it were needed, of the close tie between partisan politics and federal judicial office then (and now).[10]

For example, when Ohio became a state in 1803, the newly-appointed district court judge was Charles Willing Byrd, scion of a well-to-do Virginia clan. He had practiced law in Ohio, lobbied for statehood, and aligned himself with the Jeffersonians—a wise choice as the election results of 1800 demonstrated. Joining him as federal marshal was David Ziegler, a Revolutionary War veteran and an early supporter of Jefferson's party. The U.S. attorney was Connecticut-born Michael Baldwin, brother of Abraham Baldwin, a Georgia senator and founder of the University in Athens, and half brother of Henry Baldwin, whom President Andrew Jackson named to the Supreme Court in 1830.[11]

Jefferson appointed Republicans William Johnson of South Carolina, Henry Brockholst Livingston of New York, and Thomas Todd of Virginia and Kentucky to the Supreme Court. Todd and Livingston came from their states' supreme courts. Johnson was confirmed on the Supreme Court in 1804 and fulfilled Jefferson's not so secret desire to have a member of the Court dissenting from some of Marshall's opinions. Livingston and Todd followed Johnson onto the Court in 1807; Todd taking a new (seventh) seat created by Congress in 1807. Todd and Livingston generally voted with Marshall.[12]

The same partisan pattern prevailed in appointments to the district courts. In New Jersey, for example, the Jeffersonians chose William S. Pennington and then William Rossell. Both Pennington and Rossell were well qualified. Peninngton had been a state supreme court judge and a governor of New Jersey when President Madison tapped him to replace Morris as district judge, throughout which tenure he was a stalwart Republican. Rossell had followed Pennington on to the state supreme court and was there when John Quincy Adams named him to replace Pennington, who had died. In a memo he wrote to himself about one candidate for the District of South Carolina, Jefferson noted with approval the man's "Republican connections." Indeed, it was essential in his mind for all nominees to "be known as a Republican in politics." What the Federalists could do, so could the Republicans.[13]

Jefferson was aware that the federal courts must keep up with the expansion of the nation. His ideal of a yeoman republic spreading across the continent to the Pacific demanded that he satisfy the juridical needs of the western portion of the country. After consulting with Republican members of Congress, Jefferson pressed for the establishment of a Seventh Circuit comprising Tennessee, Kentucky, and Ohio, and thus a seventh seat on the Supreme Court. The resulting legislation passed through Congress almost unanimously, Federalists joining in the vote.[14]

The view that most of the Jeffersonian judges took of judicial federalism, in particular the jurisdictional boundary between federal and state courts and the larger question of the relationship of federal government to state government, differed sharply from some of the Federalists. But not every Republican appointee was an advocate of states' rights just as not every Federalist incumbent was a devotee of strong central government. There were ideological differences on the bench mirroring the ideological divide between the two parties, but the Republican-appointed federal judges unhesitatingly exercised the powers given them by the Constitution and congressional acts.[15]

Party-based appointments not only reflected both national and local party allegiances but also personal alliances. Take for example the first of the Alabama federal judges, Charles Tait. A youth during the great Virginia planters' migration to Georgia's rich Broad River lands, Tait grew to manhood in the rough and tumble of the locality's politics. The insecure gentility of the southern planter aristocracy in the first years of the new nation churned the state's politics, with ideological differences of the Tait family's Republicanism and their rivals' Federalism far less important than personal connections and personal animosities. As the newspaper publisher Hezekiah Niles observed of these combinations and feuds, "we know not what they differ about—but they violently differ." Tait read law, taught school, and after a campaign that resembled a brawl more than an election, gained office as a superior court judge in Georgia and then as one of the state's U.S. senators. When he left Congress he moved to Alabama, where his family ties and wealth brought him a cotton plantation of thousands of acres and over 115 slaves. But President James Monroe remembered Tait from their days in the District of Columbia, and named him Alabama's first federal judge. A conservative, law-and-order Jeffersonian (he prefaced every one of his grand jury charges "We should never forget that patriotism consists in devotion to our constitutions, and the laws that emanate from them. There is no true liberty without security"), he served until 1826, when exhausted with travel in a buggy up and down the entire state, he returned to more pastoral occupations. For Tait, like so many others in the federal judiciary at the time, was never just a judge. He was a planter, a teacher, a practicing lawyer, and a political figure on the local, state, and national stage. [16]

As the Tait appointment demonstrates, when Jefferson retired, the outline of his appointments process was retained by his successors. In particular, President

Figure 3.1 Judge Charles Tait of Alabama. Tait served in both the state and the federal legislative branches and on the district court bench. Courtesy of the Alabama Department of Archives and History.

Andrew Jackson surpassed Jefferson in rewarding supporters with offices, including judicial appointments. During his two terms in the White House, from 1829 to 1837, he appointed eighteen district judges, all of them Jacksonian Democrats, of whom seventeen were confirmed. Two of them, Philip Barbour and Peter V. Daniel, would later serve on the Supreme Court. Jackson's idea of the right sort of candidate was a man of sound constitutional principles, by which he meant principles of states' rights akin to his own. He also consulted state Jacksonian leaders, a recognition of their role in his party's electoral victories.[17]

Above all, Jackson's nominees were men who did not question his actions. Florida, for example, not yet a state but acquired by the 1819 Adams-Onis treaty, needed territorial judges, and President James Monroe had named author and bon vivant Henry Marie Brackenridge to the western post. The judge at first got along well with the new territorial governor, none other than Jackson, but then Brackenridge spoke publicly against Jackson's unauthorized filibuster (a military adventure) in Florida, and Jackson never forgot or forgave an insult. When Jackson became president, he did not reappoint Brackenridge (territorial judges were and are still appointed by the president), after which the feisty judge published a condemnation of the president calling for his impeachment. Brackenridge protested "those who were enemies to me were chiefly in the politics of the territory, in which I took no active part." Instead, despite endemic disease and lack of facilities, "during ten years, I never missed a court, although over an extensive district, thinly inhabited, I had to travel hundreds of miles regardless of flood and tempest." Jackson's choice to replace Brackenridge, John Cameron, was a loyal Jacksonian Democrat.[18]

To summarize: the Jeffersonians and Jacksonians in power completely changed the political cast of the federal bench, rendering its composition strikingly different from its composition when Marshall first occupied the center chair of the Supreme Court in 1801. But the transformation did not fundamentally change the operation of the federal judiciary. Although the Federalist Party was gone, mortally wounded by Federalist opposition to the War of 1812, and Federalists no longer dominated the federal bench, Federalist instincts for orderly society and strong national government animated the conservative wing of the postwar Republican Party. Led by converts from Federalism, like Joseph Story of Massachusetts, these men would find places on the bench alongside the Jacksonians.[19]

John Marshall and Tests of the Madisonian Compromise

While Jefferson and his successors were changing the political composition of the federal judiciary, John Marshall was reasserting the centrality of the federal courts in the interpretation of federal law. Once one sees that, apart from Jefferson's personal animosity against Marshall, the Jeffersonians and their successors did not pose a fundamental threat to the operation of federal courts, one can view Marshall's contributions to the federal courts' story in a new light. Rather than battling against the Jeffersonians, he was carrying on the efforts of the framers. [20]

In four seminal cases, he and his Court faced and passed critical tests of separation of powers and judicial federalism. The first of these cases, *Marbury v. Madison* (1803), allowed Marshall to define the relationship between the federal courts and Congress with more precision, giving new meaning to the concept of judicial independence in a checks and balances system. The second case, the first of two treason prosecutions of Aaron Burr (1807), again raised separation of powers questions, this time the courts' relations with the president. The third and fourth cases, *McCulloch v. Maryland* (1819) and *Osborn v. Bank of the U.S.* (1824), surveyed the boundaries of judicial federalism. It is true that all of these cases entailed some partisan consequences, but one should see them primarily as a running commentary on the Madisonian Compromise, a continuation of the debates over the federal courts system at the Constitutional Convention and in the first Congress.

Because it came in the midst of the controversy over the Judiciary Acts of 1801 and 1802, and because Federalists suspected Jefferson of seeking to destroy the federal court system in order to undermine their party, *Marbury* was seen by some politicians and jurists then (and now) as a test of the independence of the judiciary. As framed by Marshall, it was a much narrower matter—whether Congress could confer on the Supreme Court a procedural authority not included in Section 2 of Article III. But on that narrow foundation, Marshall's opinion built a great edifice. He used the case to explain the role of the Supreme Court in constitutional interpretation. In so doing, he established in the Court a check on Congress.[21]

The facts of the case are relatively simple: William Marbury, an Annapolis financier, Federalist supporter, and tax collector for the state of Maryland, was supposed to receive a commission as a justice of the peace for the District of Columbia. Marshall, still performing the secretary of state's duties, failed to send it on and incoming Secretary of State Madison, with the assent of President Jefferson, did not remedy Marshall's oversight. When he did not get the commission, Marbury filed suit with the clerk of the Supreme Court under the provisions of the Judiciary Act of 1789. Its Section 13 authorized the Supreme Court to issue a writ (a judicial command) "of mandamus, in cases warranted by the principles and usages of law, to any courts appointed, or persons holding office under the authority of the United States," to perform some act—in this case requiring Secretary of State Madison to send the commission to Marbury. Thus the case went directly to the Court. Over the long course of the Marshall Court, less than 1 percent of its cases were based on its original jurisdiction under Article III, Section 2.[22]

The issue before the Court, as Marshall framed it, was whether the Court had jurisdiction over the case. He intentionally ignored the political context of the suit. In a very long opinion for that day (twenty-six pages), Marshall wrote for a unanimous Court. He ruled that the justices could not issue the writ because it was not one of the kinds of original jurisdiction given the Court in Article III of the Constitution. The Constitution controlled or limited what Congress could do and in particular prohibited the Congress from expanding the original jurisdiction of the Court. Congress had violated the Constitution by giving this authority to the Court. Marshall struck down that part of the Judiciary Act of 1789 as unconstitutional. The power that Marshall assumed in the Court to find acts of Congress unconstitutional, and thus null and void, was immensely important. First, it protected the independence of the Court from Congress. Second, Marshall implied that the Court was the final arbiter of the meaning of the Constitution. This vital pronouncement of judicial supremacy would be elaborated and extended in the coming years to include state legislation and state court judgments. The other branches of the federal government might engage in some sort of constitutional self-scrutiny when they acted, asking if they had exceeded their power, but the final voice in contested cases must be the Supreme Court's. Finally, Marshall reminded everyone that the Constitution was the supreme law and that every act of Congress had to be measured against it. To be sure, the Court had no intention of involving itself in the everyday details of the other branches' operation, for example how the secretary of state ran his office, and giving the Supreme Court the power to do this through writs of mandamus would violate basic tenets of the separation of powers.[23]

Marshall knew that his opinion would be viewed as a slap at Jefferson. Jefferson certainly felt it to be. But Marshall had covered this base as well. In what seemed at the time almost an aside, he wrote that "questions in their nature political" would be rejected by his court "without hesitation." He then qualified that blanket denial of jurisdiction by adding, "but where" an official of an elected branch of government acted outside the law or did not perform an act that the law commanded, it was the duty of the courts to intervene. To fail to do so would ignore the legal rights of a complainant. Marshall's dictum would in the fullness of time become both the basis for the abstention of the Court from political questions and the intervention of the Court in matters of voting law and redistricting.[24]

The second case in which Marshall's jurisprudence defined the boundaries of separation of powers found him at the circuit court meeting in Richmond, Virginia, in the spring of 1807. To the circuit court what amounted to a federal posse comitatus had brought Aaron Burr, and there he was charged by Jefferson's handpicked team of prosecutors with treason. In February 1807 Burr had been arrested in Mississippi by order of the territorial governor General James Wilkinson, and without a grand jury indictment or the chance to defend himself was hustled back to Richmond. Earlier in Burr's travels through the West, similar charges were brought, and he was not indicted on them. But Jefferson was convinced that his former vice president had intended to sever the trans–Appalachian West from the rest of the nation and had told Congress that Burr was guilty.[25]

In the course of the trial, Burr, a fine attorney himself, assisted by Luther Martin, turned the tables on Jefferson and left Marshall in a quandary: could he subpoena Jefferson commanding the production of Wilkinson's letters about the alleged Burr conspiracy and Jefferson's replies? If Wilkinson's correspondence with Jefferson might be material in Burr's defense, could Marshall deny the motion? For four days, counsel for both sides argued the permissibility of Burr's motion. Finally, on June 13, 1807, Marshall ruled on the request for the papers. "When this subject was suddenly introduced, the court felt some doubt concerning the propriety of directing a subpoena to the chief magistrate, and some doubt also concerning the propriety of directing any paper in his possession, not public in its nature, to be exhibited in court." But as in *Marbury*, Marshall claimed his hands were tied. "The practice in this country has been, to permit any individual, who was charged with any crime, to prepare for his defense, and to obtain the process of the court, for the purpose of enabling him so to do." Was the president subject to such process? No man was above the law, Marshall determined, and the "Constitution and laws of the United States" made plain the president's duty to the Court.

According to Marshall, neither Congress nor the president could rescind the rights so precisely laid out in the Federal Crimes Act of 1790 and the Sixth Amendment: "'every such person or persons accused or indicted of the crimes aforesaid, [including treason] shall be allowed and admitted in his said defense to make any proof that he or they can produce by lawful witness or witnesses, and shall have the like process of the court where he or they shall be tried, to compel his or their witnesses to appear at his or their trial as is usually granted to compel witnesses to appear on the prosecution against them." The 1790 Act placed both sides at trial "on equal ground." Marshall continued: "A subpoena duces tecum, then, may issue to any person to whom an ordinary subpoena may issue, directing him to bring any paper of which the party praying it has a right to avail himself as testimony." Marshall promised that all such evidence from the president would be handled with the care and decorum that Jefferson's high station required, but he must comply with the subpoena.[26]

Marshall was firm but not unaware of the delicate nature of this subpoena. "Much has been said about the disrespect to the chief magistrate, which is implied by this motion . . . These observations will be very truly answered by the declaration that this court feels many, perhaps, peculiar motives for manifesting as guarded a respect for the chief magistrate of the Union as is compatible with its official duties." Jefferson's reply was frostily formal, but he bowed to the court's order. "In answering your [Marshall's] letter . . . I informed you . . . that I had delivered [Wilkinson's letter], with all other papers respecting the charges against Aaron Burr, to the attorney general [Caesar Rodney] when he went to Richmond." Jefferson assumed that Rodney would share them with the Court, but Rodney was no longer in Richmond, and Jefferson promised to write Rodney "to forward that particular letter without delay." Jefferson instructed the heads of his departments to send to Richmond "two letters from the secretary at war, which appeared to be within the description expressed in your letter."[27]

At stake in *McCulloch v. Maryland* was the jurisdiction of federal courts when state statutes appeared to violate provisions of an act of Congress. The case raised the federalism issue directly. By rooting the jurisdiction of the federal courts in the Constitution and reminding the states that the Constitution was the supreme law of the land, Marshall not only protected a congressional act from a state's interference, but he also reasserted the privileged role of the federal courts in interpreting the relationship between his court and state statutes.

In 1819 the United States was mired in one of its worst economic panics. Land speculation had overheated the economy, and banks all over were failing. The Second Bank of the United States, chartered in 1816 after the federal government's financial troubles during the War of 1812, was supposed to prevent such collapses before they occurred, but the overseers of the bank were speculators, and many of the bank's practices were both inefficient and corrupt. A number of states, including Maryland, passed laws regulating the bank branches in the state. James McCulloch was the cashier of the Maryland branch of the Bank of the United States, and he was fined for trying to do its business without paying the licensing fee of $15,000 to the state. When his conviction was upheld by the state's highest court he appealed to the U.S. Supreme Court.[28]

There was an ominous hint of something more than states' rights in the arguments that Maryland's counsel made. Joseph Hopkinson and Walter Jones, appearing for the state, proposed that the Constitution was "a compact between the States, and all the powers which are not expressly relinquished by it, are reserved to the States." While one might conclude that Hopkinson and Jones were simply repeating James Madison's Virginia Resolutions' incautious reference to a "compact" theory of the Constitution, in the chamber above the Supreme Court's courtroom, members of Congress were furiously debating whether Missouri could enter the Union as a slave state. Neither of the Maryland lawyers mentioned slavery, but everyone in the courtroom was aware that Maryland was a slave state, and its congressional delegation supported the admission of Missouri. If antislavery forces prevented the admission of Missouri, could the compact theory be redeployed as the basis for severing the Union? The case had already generated "great excitement," and Marshall's decision for the Court would become a landmark defense of constitutional nationalism.[29]

The decision of the Court was unanimous. Writing for the Court, Marshall rejected the compact theory of the Constitution. Instead, he found that it reflected the will of an entire people. It followed that the federal government spoke for that people, not for the concurrent will of the independent states. The federal government could not be bound by the narrowest confines of strict construction of the Constitution because it could not respond to exigency nor take advantage of opportunity. The Bank of the United States was constitutional; it enabled the federal government to tax, to borrow, and to carry out other economic policies;

it fit the very definition of "necessary and proper" (the clause in Article I, Section 8, authorizing Congress to enact legislation to effectuate its enumerated powers). Insofar as "the power to tax involves the power to destroy," and the state licensing fee would "annihilate" the Bank, Marshall had no choice but to strike down the Maryland law. Not to do so would be to subject the whole of the Constitution to the whims of state legislatures. The power to strike down a state statute expanded the jurisdiction of the federal courts to the full extent prescribed in the Constitution's Supremacy Clause, attaching it to Article III, Section 2's opening words: "The judicial power shall extend to all cases, in law and equity, arising under this Constitution" now firmly belonging to the federal courts.[30]

In a reaction to the Court's pronouncement, defenders of strong states' rights sought to revise the Judiciary Act of 1789. Led by jurists like Virginia Court of Appeals Judge Spencer Roane, they found the line of decisions beginning with *McCulloch* and continuing with *Cohens v. Virginia* (1821) "disastrous in its consequences," as violating the "boundaries between the powers of two sovereign and independent governments." Advocates of revising Section 25 of the Judiciary Act of 1789, which gave the Court jurisdiction over appeals from the state supreme courts, made their case in Congress from 1820 to 1831 when the House of Representatives voted down the last of the proposals, 138 to 51. Nevertheless, the gap between Marshall's vision of the role of the federal courts in the federal system and his critics' views would not be easily bridged. The effect of the criticism of his opinions, however, was to make Marshall appear to be an advocate of a central government so strong it would engulf state sovereignty. That was not Marshall's intent.[31]

Article III gave to the federal courts jurisdiction over those causes arising under the Constitution and federal law. Just what did that mean for federalism? The question gained urgency in the closing years of the Panic of 1819 when holders of the Second Bank of the United States' commercial paper sought to gain repayment due them on the face of the notes. In two cases with a common nexus of fact and law, one from Ohio, *Osborn v. Bank of the United States,* and the other from Georgia, *Bank of the United States v. Planters Bank of Georgia,* the Supreme Court had to decide the reach of the "arising under" clause of Article III and its decision was as important to federalism questions as *McCulloch.*

In 1819 the Ohio legislature authorized Ralph Osborn, the state treasurer, to collect a tax on the state branch of the Second Bank of the United States. The tax would relieve the state banks of some of their own indebtedness to the tune of some $100,000. In effect it was a state-mandated transfer of funds from a federal bank to the local banks. The Bank asked the circuit court to enjoin the collection of the tax. The Circuit Court for the District of Ohio, in 1819, refused the request. The Bank then sued for recovery of the taxes from the state in the circuit court, and it found in favor of the Bank. The state appealed to the Supreme

Court. In the Georgia case, the Bank went after a local bank that owed it money. In both cases, defendants pleaded that the federal courts in which the suits were brought lacked jurisdiction to hear the cases, despite the fact that the enabling act creating the Bank allowed such suits in federal court.

Marshall went directly to the jurisdictional questions. The statute rechartering the Bank of the United States allowed suits against it in state and federal courts. "These words seem to the Court to admit of but one interpretation." To be sued meant the capacity to bring a suit. The decision of the circuit court should have prevented collection of the tax. The more important point was that the jurisdiction of the circuit court was not that conferred by the Act creating the Bank. It was the jurisdiction conferred by the Constitution itself. "The 3d article . . . declares 'that the judicial power shall extend to all cases in law and equity arising under this constitution, the laws of the United States, and treaties made, or which shall be made, under their authority.' This clause enables the judicial department to receive jurisdiction to the full extent of the constitution, laws, and treaties of the United States." The Constitution conferred the jurisdiction on the circuit court whenever a federal law was at issue. If the Bank could sue officers

Figure 3.2 Although federal courts protected the Second Bank of the United States as a constitutional exercise of congressional power, it remained a political target after *McCulloch v. Maryland* (1819). Here President Andrew Jackson attempts to slay a many-headed monster that symbolizes the national bank. Credit: Library of Congress.

of Ohio in federal court, it could sue the officers of a bank chartered by the state of Georgia.[32]

The Business of the Federal Courts in the Age of Jefferson and Jackson

One of Chief Justice Marshall's great accomplishments lay in the way that the Supreme Court supported the lower courts' decisions. In very few cases was the lower court opinion overturned. In one sense, this was predictable—the justices sat with the district judges in the circuit courts and two men worked closely together. Even as Jefferson and his successors and Marshall feuded and fussed with one another, the lower federal courts in the period 1801–1835 continued handling cases in uninterrupted fashion.

Unfortunately, the settings in which these courts met did not match the seriousness of their business or the competence of their personnel. There were no federal district or circuit courthouses at first. State courthouses, for example in New Castle, Delaware, served the new federal district and circuit courts, the federal government renting space from the state. If a suitable site was not available in the state court buildings, other facilities were found. While leaders of the business community were building palaces of commerce like the New York Stock Exchange and temples of finance like the Philadelphia Bank of the United States, and states were erecting grand statehouses, the Supreme Court sat in hand-me-down chambers. As the federal government moved its operations to the new capital in the District of Columbia, where the president occupied a mansion and Congress convened in an imposing three-story, federal-style office building, the Supreme Court met in what was hardly more than a cloakroom in the Capitol. The space was described by one contemporary as "meanly furnished and very inconvenient." More permanent housing came in 1810, with a Benjamin Latrobe–designed chamber in the basement of remodeled Capitol. That did not last long, as the British invasion of Washington, D.C. in 1814 left the Capitol in flames. In 1819, the space was restored, and the Court sat there until it moved above ground into the old Senate Chamber in 1860.[33]

Despite the lack of suitable quarters for the courts in the first decades of the new century, the business of the courts was rapidly growing. Much of this was due to new congressional legislation. For example, cases arising under the first federal Bankruptcy Act demonstrated that the federal courts could play a vital role in the nation's business. The act not only offered managed relief to creditors, it enabled commercial debtors a way out of debtors prison. The District Court for the District of Maryland listed fifty-five debtors for the period 1800–1803 during which the Act was in operation. The district court sitting in New York

City recorded 131 debtors against whom creditors filed in the period 1801–1803. The District of Pennsylvania records show that 208 cases were filed under the statute. Speculation in land was rampant in the new nation, and no more so than among its "better sort." The debtors included men like James Greenleaf, one of the District of Columbia's earliest, foremost, and most unlucky land speculators (he landed in debtors prison for a year before the debt was discharged); Jacob Cuyler, one of Albany's foremost Revolutionary leaders; Peter Livingston, a scion of the most important political family in New York and later in life acting speaker of his state's legislature; and Charles Biddle of Pennsylvania, a banker, friend to Aaron Burr, and father of Nicholas Biddle, an even more famous banker.[34]

Location and historical circumstances also set the dockets of the lower federal courts. For example, the district of South Carolina faced important international questions when the Haitian Revolution of 1795 had sent hundreds of French-speaking planters fleeing to the United States. Some, finding refuge with the descendants of the Huguenot exiles in South Carolina, sought citizenship there under the Naturalization Act of 1798 (requiring fourteen years residence). Thus one "John Joseph Riondel a native of Savoy in France appeared and presented a petition praying to be admitted a citizen of the United States, which being read, and the proofs adduced and considered satisfactory, ordered the petitioner to be admitted and sworn."[35]

During the War of 1812, federal judges faced a multitude of admiralty and prize cases. Although the Royal Navy tried to blockade American ports, prize ships taken by privateers slipped through the blockade. The 118 prize cases the Southern District of New York courts heard resembled equity cases: no jury, evidence taken as affidavit or deposition, and final decrees never final because one side or the other could appeal from the district court to the circuit court and then to the U.S. Supreme Court (just as in equity). So, too, the courts appointed commissioners (much like the master in equity) to take evidence, supervise the masters of ports as they examined cargoes, prepare lists of costs, and ensure that the cargoes went to the customs houses instead of disappearing into private warehouses. Such commissioners were not new to federal courts. They first appeared in criminal bail hearings, replacing local magistrates. In 1812, Congress enlarged the powers of the commissioners, enabling them to take depositions and gather evidence in civil and criminal cases. In effect, these provisions created a miniature bureaucracy, during the war facilitating the handling of prize cases, another example of the way in which federal courts acted as administrative agencies of the federal government. Despite accusations of corruption, the customs officials were not sympathetic to the privateers. Juries, however, and public sentiment generally, were sympathetic, and more often than not the accused were acquitted.[36]

Figure 3.3 Busy East Coast port cities were the setting for the many maritime and admiralty cases that came before the federal courts, including those involving prize ships and their cargoes. Image of the port of Boston, engraved by W. J. Bennett in 1833. Credit: Library of Congress.

The case of the owners of the letter of marque (a government-issued document authorizing the holder to capture enemy vessels at sea in time of war) of the Baltimore registry brig *Expedition* versus the schooner *Adeline* was hardly typical, but its many convolutions illustrated how complex and daunting such cases could be for crews, merchants, lawyers, and the courts. It began with an American privateer (privateers had letters of marque; pirates did not), the 147-ton schooner *Adeline*, sailing from a French port. Its cargo was "owned in part by citizens of the United States, and in part by French subjects." On the 14 of March 14, 1814, Royal Navy vessels ran her down in the Bay of Biscay and sent her to Gibraltar. On the way to the British base there, the American brig *Expedition*, sailing with its own letter of marque out of Baltimore, mistook the schooner for a British merchant vessel and seized her.[37]

On April 28, 1814, a prize ship's crew brought the *Adeline* to the port of New York. There, commissioners Matthew Davis and Ogden Edwards interviewed the crew of the captured schooner and the master of the schooner. The formal set of forty interrogatories used in these inquiries included thorough review of when and where the prize ship was taken; the details of its papers, its crew members, and its cargo; and the events preceding, during, and after its capture. As the picture of capture and recapture emerged, the court contest began. Counsel for the libellants (the term in admiralty law for the party who brought the suit), William Harris, wanted the entire ship and cargo sold at auction for the holders of the letter of marque, but Peter Augustus Jay, son of the former chief justice, and other counsel for merchants in Boston, New York, Philadelphia, and Baltimore claimed that the cargo was not owned by British subjects at all. The ship and its cargo were American! The ownership of every piece of merchandise, every cask of wine and barrel of prunes was disputed. In the meantime, the cases of wine were beginning to leak and the court ordered them sold by the marshal and the money held in escrow by the court.

After reviewing 271 pages of evidence over eight months from May through the end of the year, the district court found that the captors were entitled to all property on the vessel not belonging to the American merchants and the value of one-sixth of the American goods "for salvage" costs. But the case was not over. At stake was a cargo valued at over $120,000. Both sides appealed to the circuit court, and then carried its affirmation of the district court decree to the U.S. Supreme Court. There, after voluminous presentations by counsel for all the parties, Justice Story affirmed the circuit court ruling.[38]

The War of 1812 brought a slew of criminal cases. New England federal courts heard prosecutions of trading with the enemy in time of war. Federal marshals were handed the unenviable task of identifying "enemy aliens" under the hitherto dormant 1798 Enemy Aliens Act. They found 7,000 British citizens in the states, but few were ordered to leave. Some found federal judges helpful in securing their release under habeas corpus writs. Federal judges also sorted out the facts in prosecutions of merchants deemed by federal attorneys too friendly to Britain. Hearings on piracy charges were even more confused, as different federal courts read the 1790 federal statute differently. In two 1813 cases Justice Bushrod Washington, sitting in one circuit court, found that robbery at sea amounted to piracy, while Justice Joseph Story, holding court in another circuit, denied that federal law encompassed the offense. Congress tried to bridge the difference of opinion in the 1817 Piracy Act, but able local counsel and friendly juries still helped accused win acquittals.[39]

The coming of peace in North America opened a season of Latin American revolts against Spain, aided by Americans' "filibustering" activities. These private freebooters hoped to profit from the rebellions. Intervention by foreign diplomatic services complicated trial of these freebooters, and in the end, they were freed. Apparently the admiralty jurisdiction of the federal courts did not reach the shores of foreign countries. Sometimes the filibusterers at sea became merchants once they reached American ports. Customs officials were then wont to seize the filibusterers' ships and cargoes for violation of U.S. customs laws. Ship captains then turned to the federal circuit courts for relief against the customs officials. Chief Justice Marshall, sitting in the Circuit Court for the District of Virginia, explained why some of the seizures were wrong: "I think, then, that our revenue laws do not apply to privateers, unless they take up the character of merchant-men, by attempting to import goods. When they do so, they attempt, under the garb of their military character, to conceal real commercial transactions. This would be fraud on the revenue laws, which no nation will or ought to tolerate. The privateer, which acts as a merchant vessel, must be treated and considered as a merchant vessel. In this case, there is no evidence, that any goods were landed, or that more were brought in, than were intended to be carried out."[40]

Throughout the period from 1816–1824, cases of filibusterers continued to find their way into the federal courts because President James Monroe declined to seek a comprehensive diplomatic solution to American ships preying on Spanish vessels in international waters. It was only through the medium of the admiralty jurisdiction of the federal courts, that the "endemic violence of the high seas" was transformed into "private claims over the legal status of captured persons, vessels and goods." Spanish or Portuguese claimants often regained the ships and goods taken by the privateers. When the power of the federal government was impressed on the privateers, it was the federal judge, not the customs agent, who was responsible for securing a just solution. [41]

Many of these cases, particularly those for which the penalty was a fine and confiscation, ended in a presidential pardon or a remission of the fines. As far as the emerging republics of Latin America were concerned, the filibusters at sea were privateers. But the United States was not at war, and ships sailing out of U.S. ports to engage in such martial ventures, then returning to U.S. ports with their prizes, were tried as pirates under U.S. law. But even pirates, like the five convicted in South Carolina in 1820, were more likely to be pardoned than executed—only two of the five were hanged after a conference between Justice William Johnson, hearing the cases on his circuit rounds, and Secretary of State John Quincy Adams. President Monroe pardoned over 400 convicted felons during his two terms in office, an episode of executive clemency unparalleled in American history until the pardons of former Confederate officers after the Civil War. (Washington pardoned sixteen people and John Adams twenty-one, almost all in cases arising from the Whiskey and Fries Rebellions; Jefferson had pardoned 119, including those editors convicted of violating the Sedition Act of 1798; and Madison pardoned 198, including those convicted by courts martial for dereliction of duty during the War of 1812.)[42]

Secretary of State John Quincy Adams abhorred the filibusterers in principal, but he was enchanted by one Joseph Almeida, a "jovial jack tar" who became a scourge of Spanish shipping in the Caribbean. The fact that Almeida was a U.S. citizen waging a private war against a nation with which the United States was, nominally at least, at peace made the legal issues almost impossible to disentangle. Given the commonness of mitigation of punishment, one may conclude that some of the prosecutions were spurred by an animus external to the law, while other prosecutions were meant to be exemplary rather than punitive. Defendants who were found not guilty faced the payment of court costs, but taken all together, the amount of money collected in fines was scarcely equal to what the government spent on the cases. Unlike the fees and fines levied by medieval English courts, the federal courts were not a source of revenue for the federal government. Indeed, the expense of the courts was a subject of concern to the members of Congress, and pay scales were altered episodically rather than regularly. As Ellsworth wrote in 1800, "tho our country pays badly, it is the only one in the world worth working for."[43]

Most of the prize cases and criminal prosecutions from the War of 1812 had been resolved when in 1819 Secretary of State Adams reported to the Senate on the cases pending ("depending" was the term used in the report) in the various districts as of October 1819. His count showed that Maine had eighteen cases waiting determination, only one-third of which were held over from earlier sessions. Rhode Island had but thirteen cases on its docket, only one of which was filed before 1818. The Connecticut docket was similarly empty, only eight cases and all filed within a year of the Adams report. By contrast, in Massachusetts the total was twenty-nine, of which all but two were filed in years prior to 1819. Vermont had sixteen, the majority of which had already lasted over three years. Obviously, uniformity of handling was not a characteristic of the New England districts. The Northern District of New York's docket was far more crowded, some ninety-seven cases of which all but twenty-one were held over from previous years. In part this was due to the court's combined district and circuit jurisdiction. The Southern New York District court clerk reported forty-nine cases, all of long duration, but both districts of New York only reported cases from 1817, 1818, and 1819. In the Eastern Pennsylvania federal courts there were 134 cases pending, in the Western District, ninety-three.[44]

The variation in the information in the reports to Adams reflected also variation in ways that the original records were kept. Clerks labeled the manuscript docket and minute books variously, indexed the case files variously, and entered the information in bound ledgers variously. The variety of recording practices matched the variety of housekeeping rules each district promulgated for practitioners, for summoning grand and petty jurors, and for other administrative operations. On top of the clerks' exercise of their own discretion, the Judiciary and Process Acts instructed the clerks to use the formularies of the state courts in which the district lay, and state courts' processes varied. There was an exception to this rule as well—in criminal, admiralty, and equity cases, the federal courts were to employ the uniform practices of the other federal courts—as if the clerks knew precisely what these were.

The returns Adams reported thus show a patchwork quality. Some of the evidence for this must be attributed to the various districts' clerks' varying styles of reporting cases. Some clerks did not report at all. Some reported for the entire decade. Some clerks only had the years 1818's and 1819's records on hand. Although the circuit courts had a broader jurisdiction than the district courts, in general they had fewer cases "depending" on their dockets than the district courts. They did have another category of case that did not appear in district courts—appeals. Of the twenty-six cases pending in Massachusetts in 1819, four had come on appeal. Six were criminal cases, and twelve were civil. [45]

As might be expected, in ports like New York City and Philadelphia, admiralty suits made up a good fourth of the docket. In more frontier districts, however, like the Northern District of New York, the Western District of Pennsylvania, and the District of Mississippi, (the latter two, like the Northern District of New York, exercising both district and circuit court jurisdiction), there were no admiralty cases, but disputes over civil matters like land sales were prominent. In the years immediately after the War of 1812, suits brought by the United States filled the dockets. These dropped by 1819. Federal circuit courts sitting in the older states heard few diversity suits. In newer states like Louisiana, suits based on diversity of state citizenship amounted to thirty-three of the 114 pending. Once again, local conditions and national events determined who would sue and who would be sued.[46]

Diversity suits in the circuit courts comprised the bulk of suits reported as pending. All but three of Rhode Island's sixteen circuit court pending suits were diversity cases, as were eight of ten cases awaiting resolution on the Connecticut docket, and sixteen of the thirty-three cases pending in Vermont. As in the district courts, New York pending suits were but two of ninety-one, but suits to which the United States was a party numbered thirty-seven. Pennsylvania had a total of 197 suits pending, but the clerk had not sorted them by year of filing. Virginia's circuit courts had a comparable number of pending suits for the years 1811–1819. The District of Columbia court, which served as both federal and local court, counted a whopping 3,997 pending suits, almost all from the years immediately preceding 1820 and almost all on the civil side of the docket.[47]

On the criminal docket side, with the exception of the occasional arrest at sea or in port for piracy, cases involving more than one individual were rare but noteworthy. For example, in 1827 the Circuit Court for the Eastern District of Pennsylvania tried the Moses clan's counterfeiting ring. The trial entailed many appearances of various malefactors—from the female "shovers," whose ladylike dress and manner concealed their criminal acts, to the tough boss of the gang— and consumed much of the session. Otherwise, there was no real pattern to the Eastern District's criminal business, with a high of twenty-seven cases in 1820 (the result of the economic hard times) and a low of four in 1836. Most often the offense was a violation of the customs, excise, or other fiscal laws, the occasional trespass on federal property, and a few of the felonies that happened to be committed on federal property or the high seas.[48]

The length of time that any given civil or criminal case remained unfinished might depend on a number of variables—the nature of the litigation itself, the conduct of the case by counsel, the appearance or nonappearance of parties, and the backlog of cases. Some litigation involved the production of documents, and this required a bill in equity rather than the suit at law. Federal courts could do both, but the two kinds of civil litigation were usually heard on different days at sessions of the court. Federal courts of law followed the procedural rules of the state in which they sat, but when the court sat in equity or heard an admiralty case, it followed the somewhat complicated rule laid down in the Process Act of 1792: "in those of equity and in those of admiralty and maritime jurisdiction, according to the principles, rules and usages which belong to courts of equity and to courts of admiralty respectively, as contradistinguished from courts of common law." Then came the list of exceptions, in effect creating a distinct federal body of law. Note that this body of law was a mixture of statute, common law precedent, and judicial rule-making: "except so far as may have been provided for by the act to establish the judicial courts of the United States, subject however to such alterations and additions as the said courts respectively shall in their discretion deem expedient, or to such regulations as the supreme court of the United States shall think proper." Supplemental rules for the federal courts sitting in equity appeared in 1822, the former largely restating the common practice, and in 1842, requiring the taking of depositions. When parties to a common law or admiralty case asked the court to order an equitable remedy, such as the taking of depositions, clerks docketed the equity claim as if it were a separate case. Equitable process thus delayed a decision in the original suit.[49]

Because the Judiciary Acts of 1792, 1822, and 1842 allowed appeal of equity suits directly to the U.S. Supreme Court, the Supreme Court found itself poring over the same often voluminous records as the lower courts sitting in equity. One typical case was *Alexander v. Pendleton* (1814). The dispute, like so many in equity, went back many years, here nearly ninety, as heirs to a disputed parcel of Virginia land sought to quiet (settle) title (ownership). Through the generations, various heirs brought suit to oust one another. In 1796, Charles Alexander turned to the Virginia Court of Chancery, over which George Wythe presided, for assistance in partitioning the land. Ironically, the land in question was well known to Chief Justice Marshall, as he had been counsel to one of the parties in a suit over the same lands. As well, his law teacher was Wythe. Petitioners turned to the federal court and when they lost in the circuit court, they brought an appeal to the Supreme Court. The Judiciary Acts had imposed on the Supreme Court the final adjudication of what amounted to a private spat between two of

Virginia's leading families. The question was then whether the original deeds created a trust, and the present owners were trustees for the petitioners. Marshall ruled that the petitioners' use of the land over the long course of time did not constitute a constructive trust, for the legal owners had brought suit after suit to regain possession. Eighty-two times between 1790 and 1815 the Supreme Court had to deal with such and similar questions involving trusts and trustees. Between 1816 and 1836, the number had grown to 203. In some of the cases, the trust or trusteeship was a minor consideration. In others, it was the central concern. [50]

In the end, a few generalizations, and only a few, can be derived from this schematic report of cases in the federal courts. The number of cases filed varied according to external forces and local conditions—the War of 1812, the Panic of 1819, the opening of a particular parcel of the national domain, or new regulations on customs duties or excise tax collections, rather than a simple upward trend. Some courts were slow while others were more expeditious in handling cases. Some pressed for resolution before trial, a process that might actually lengthen the time a case sat on the docket. The federal court for the District of New Hampshire was so unsettled that its clerk never did return the information Secretary of State Adams requested. Despite the irregularities in the reports, the overall conclusion is unquestionable: whatever might have been the politics of appointment and jurisdiction, private litigants and the United States were bringing an increasing number of cases to the lower courts.[51]

The Impeachment and Acquittal of a Feisty Judge

If one were to compare the checks and balances arrangement to medieval hand-to-hand combat, congressional revision of the Judiciary Act would be a mace, members of Congress swinging it over the heads of all the judges. Impeachment and trial would be a rapier, members of Congress piercing one judge at a time. Judge James H. Peck of the Missouri district court felt the sharpened point of congressional rebuke when he not only published his criticism of a local lawyer, but he also held the counselor in contempt of court and barred him from practice in the federal court for a year and a half.

Peck was a self-made man, "a typical product of the frontier environment." A duelist, a land speculator and politician, self-styled gentleman, and one of the state's hundred odd (some more odd than others) lawyers in 1822, when President Monroe named him to the bench. To his court came a tangled web of land claims based on various sources, including grants allegedly made during the period of Spanish rule. Problems of competing claims made under much earlier Spanish imperial rule would tie federal territorial and district courts in knots, particularly in Arkansas, Florida, Texas, California, and New Mexico, just as similar claims made under British imperial governance earlier roiled courts in New Jersey, New York, and Pennsylvania. Local commentators and lawyers were not happy when the courts awarded title based on the foreign claims. When Peck published one of his decisions, one of the losing counselors, Luke Lawless, responded in the press, anonymously, in a dry and generally respectful manner save for one telling passage: "The judge's recollection of the argument of the counsel for this petitioner, as delivered at the bar, differs materially from what I can remember, who also heard it." In other words, Lawless was implying that Peck had misquoted him. That was a more serious charge than Peck getting the law wrong.[52]

When Lawless's authorship was revealed, Peck found Lawless guilty of contempt of court, for "intent to impair the public confidence in the upright intentions of the said court, and to bring odium upon the court, and especially with intent to impress the public mind, and particularly many litigants in this court, that they are not to expect justice in the causes now pending therein." Lawless had his own friends in high places, including Pennsylvania congressman James Buchanan. In 1830 the House overwhelmingly voted one article of impeachment. George McDuffie of South Carolina, one of the managers of the impeachment, told the Senate, "If any public functionary ought to be held responsible to the press, which was the organ, the only true organ, of the people, it was the judges, who alone held their offices during good behavior." The Senate was not persuaded, and voted 22–21 on January 31, 1831, to acquit the judge. Congress then passed legislation limiting the contempt power to proceedings in and around the courthouse. One notes in passing that the South Carolina congressional delegation was united in its effort to suppress the freedom of the press when it came to abolitionist literature.[53]

"A Wolf by the Ear": Slavery in the Federal Courts, 1801–1836

Slavery suits in the federal courts did not pit federal versus state courts or set the other branches of the federal government versus the judiciary. In fact, the reverse was true, the federal courts were in step with state law and state court decisions, the majority in Congress, and the president in protecting the institution of slavery where it existed by law. The efficacy of adjudication of slave suits was an ironic proof that the Madisonian Compromises worked well—so long as slavery was not a divisive national issue. But wary statesmen like Thomas Jefferson knew that dealing with the slavery issue was like grasping a "wolf by the ear."[54]

In 1787, the issue of chattel slavery roiled the debates at the Constitutional Convention, but the controversy ended with a whimper. The fact of the matter was that the issue of slavery had early on divided the country into free and slave states. Prompted by revolutionary rhetoric and local reform movements, all northern states either ended slavery or provided by law for its gradual disappearance by the early nineteenth century. The Confederation Congress had barred slavery from the Northwest Territory in 1787. Southern states did not end slavery. Instead, their slaveholders extended their peculiar institution into the rich "black bottom" lands of central Alabama and western Mississippi. When these states entered the Union, they came as slave states. If some southern politicians expected slavery to die of its own accord, the demand for the newly developed cotton crop outweighed any liberal sentiment.[55]

The law of slavery followed a similar course. The Constitutional Convention compromised on the slavery question. Though some would call it a pact with death, and scholars today debate whether it was a proslavery document, in fact the framers accepted slavery's existence rather than advocating it. The Constitution did not use the word slave or refer directly to slavery, but in three places acknowledged slavery's influence. First, in the "three-fifths compromise," it permitted states to include three-fifths of the total of "other persons" in its population counts for apportionment purposes. Second, Congress could make no law ending the international slave trade until 1808. Finally, under the so-called Rendition Clause of Article IV ("no person held to service or labor in one state, under the laws thereof, escaping into another, shall, in consequence of any law or regulation therein, be discharged from such service or labor, but shall be delivered up upon claim of the party to whom such service or labor may be due") runaway slaves could be recaptured in free states and returned to their masters.

The slave trade provisions of the Constitution brought slavery to the federal courts. Congress barred American shippers from engaging in overseas slave trading in a series of acts, beginning in 1794 (Americans not to supply slave ships); 1800 (forfeiture of the vessel violating the 1794 act); 1807 (expanding the 1800 Act to cover any vessel engaging in the trade in American waters); 1818 (forbidding any participation in the international slave trade by American vessels); 1819 (empowering the president to use the U.S. Navy to interdict vessels violating the 1818 Act); and finally 1820 (making violation of the earlier Acts the capital offense of piracy). All of these violations of federal law were tried exclusively in federal courts. South Carolina district Judge Thomas Bee read the statutes so strictly that defendants got off easily. South Carolina's economy depended on the external and internal slave trade, as well as the labor of slaves. As Bee wrote in *U.S. v. Kitty* (1808), dismissing the charges against a slaver for violating the 1807 ban on importation of slaves, "especially as the act of congress upon which the suit is grounded expressly gives the court a discretionary power in extreme cases, of which this is surely one" the court could show leniency. The slaves were sold on the Charleston auction block. In the meantime, the burden in time and effort of these slave trade cases induced Bee to write to the South Carolina congressional delegation seeking additional pay.[56]

Slavery had also become the business of the federal courts with the Fugitive Slave Law of 1793, passed to provide an enforcement mechanism for the Rendition Clause. It provided that any federal court could hold a hearing on a detained person of color and find, on the basis of evidence presented to the judge, that the person was a runaway from service in a slave state. In fact, few fugitive slave cases trickled into the federal courts during the period 1801–1836. Those that did taxed the creativity of the bench. In Ohio, Judge Byrd resolved a suit that George Jackson brought against Moses and Jacob Ayers for abetting the escape of his slave Alice. Jackson had owned Alice in Virginia and summoned her to join his family when they relocated to Ohio. After six months of taking care of his children, she ran away. Unable to gain the assistance of local justice in recapturing her, Jackson sued the Ayers brothers under the terms of the 1793 Fugitive Slave Act for her value. Byrd heard the case in 1817, and when jurors asked him to explain the law, he took two years to answer. He found that the Ayers brothers had not violated federal law: Ohio was a free state, Alice lived in Ohio, and thus she did not run away from a slave state to Ohio. In effect, Jackson had freed her by domiciling her in Ohio.[57]

In Re Susan (1818) turned out quite differently. John Chasteen of Kentucky had chased his runaway slave Susan across the Ohio River to Indiana and brought her before a justice of the peace to regain possession. The evidence he presented of ownership satisfied the magistrate, but Susan had found a legal "next friend" who gained a temporary injunction against her recaption and filed a motion in the federal court for the District of Indiana that evidence of ownership must be decided at a jury trial. If Susan were a citizen, she had a right to a jury trial under the Sixth Amendment. If she were property (a runaway horse, for example, or a bale of cotton), she could claim no such right. Judge Benjamin Parke was but one year on the bench after having served the territorial government in a variety of capacities. He ruled against the motion: "By the law of congress, a judge or magistrate is competent to decide, finally, the service of the owner." He conceded that counsel for Susan would have had a colorable case had the question arisen under the law of the state, but "[i]t is unnecessary to inquire whether one or the other is best calculated to promote the ends of justice. It is sufficient that congress have prescribed the mode, and the motion must, therefore, be overruled."[58]

Slavery cases did not draw sharp lines between the jurisdiction of the state and the federal courts. Even those northern federal judges who found slavery repellant had to concede its legality where it existed in the United States. Such contradictions bedeviled jurists like Massachusetts's Joseph Story, who served on the Supreme Court from 1811 to his death in 1845. Story came from a large family and found his way to Harvard and the law by diligent study. His frequent illnesses and the tragic deaths of his father and his first wife drove him further into his books and his law practice (and, to make ends meet, a bank presidency). A man of great personal honesty and conscience, he was an independent-minded Republican in state politics and his brief term in Congress saw him oppose Jefferson's foreign policy, an opposition that many New Englanders shared. President Madison would not have named him to the Court had his first three choices not declined. Marshall came to respect greatly Story's learn-ing, and Story came to greatly admire the chief justice. Story loved the law and exalted the role of judge, believing that law was capable of "being improved, and expanded, and modified, to meet the exigencies of society by the gradual appli-cation of its principles in courts of justice to new cases."[59]

As Dane Professor at Harvard Law School from 1829 until his death, Story published his lectures in his various commentaries, the most respected, reprinted, and influential of which was his three-volume *Commentaries on the Constitution* (1833). He thought that an authoritative exposition of the Constitution would "best enable the reader to estimate for himself the true value" of the Union and the Constitution. "In this way (as it is hoped) his judgment as well as his affections will be enlisted on the side of the Constitution, as the truest security of the Union, and the only solid basis, on which to rest the private rights, the public liberties, and the substantial prosperity of the people composing the American Republic."[60]

But as legal scholar Robert Cover wrote, "the judicial conscience is an artful dodger, and rightfully so." In the matter of slavery, Story's strong moral sensibili-ties ran headlong into his even stronger unionism. Story knew that slavery had brought the government of the nation to its knees during the Missouri statehood crisis of 1819–1821, and members of Congress justified their opposing views of admitting Missouri as a slave state on widely varying interpretations of the Constitution. That controversy literally went on in the chambers of the Capitol just above the room where the Supreme Court met. He knew how vituperative the debates had become and how close Henry Clay's compromise had come to failure. Both sides threatened disunion, but the loudest voices were southerners, and they seemed to speak as one. Attack slavery frontally and the South might secede. It was the nightmare hovering over antebellum federalism.[61]

Story's *Commentaries* afforded slavery little space, and when he did, he made clear his personal dislike of the institution. Of the Rendition Clause, the Constitution's most obvious concession to slavery, he wrote, "This clause was introduced into the constitution solely for the benefit of the slave-holding states, to enable them to reclaim their fugitive slaves, who should have escaped into other states, where slavery was not tolerated. . . . In fact, it cannot escape the attention of every intelligent reader, that many sacrifices of opinion and feeling are to be found made by the Eastern and Middle states to the peculiar interests of the south," his own opinions and feelings included. Given this, the South and its slave interest should never contemplate leaving the Union.[62]

Recognizing that slavery was a legal minefield, the federal courts' slavery jurisprudence avoided the kind of sweeping language that it favored in other cases involving private property. The personal aversion or at least unease with slavery that many of the judges shared may have dictated this course of action. If the domestic law of the state in which the case arose treated slaves as property, then the federal courts had to follow suit. If international law gave possession of slaves to foreign claimants, the federal courts could not deny those claimants their rights. At first, with states willing to respect one another's judicial pronouncements under the Full Faith and Credit (Comity) Clause of the Constitution, the issues seemed similar to cases regarding interstate commerce. In the later antebellum years, however, adjudication of slavery cases would prove anything but easy. For federal common law and congressional statute made slavery "national rather than sectional." Slavery in the federal courts would transform and intensify all three of the challenges—political partisanship, federal-state intercourse, and interbranch relations—the antebellum judges faced.[63]

Slavery cases to one side, the federal courts in the first three decades of the new century had weathered the shifting winds of partisan politics, kept faith with their part in the Madisonian Compromise, and fulfilled the original purpose of the Judiciary Acts. They provided forums for diversity suits, handled federal criminal prosecutions, and adjudicated admiralty and equity matters with relative efficiency, if not always consistently. The quality of the bench was remarkably high, given the partisan winds that blew through the often drafty federal courtrooms.

4

The Antebellum Courts, 1836–1860

The years from 1836 through 1860 were not quiet ones for the federal courts. The federal court system had to expand to keep pace with the rapid, somewhat unplanned, and often controversial expansion of the nation. Economic "panics" in 1837–1843 and 1857–1858 inundated federal courts' dockets with bankruptcy suits. Congress continued to tinker with jurisdiction and procedure and on occasion refused to accept presidents' nominees for judicial service.

Judges, for their part, did not hesitate to advise members of Congress and presidents on matters of law (and politics). For example, while sitting on the U.S. Supreme Court, Justice Joseph Story authored two bankruptcy statutes that he passed on to confidants in Congress. Neither was enacted into law. Story also advised president John Quincy Adams on measures of diplomacy. The boundaries of separation of powers in these years were semipermeable membranes, not well-mortised stone walls. With controversy over the Fugitive Slave Laws boiling, the admission of Texas and California causing convulsions in Congress, and the donnybrook of "Bleeding Kansas" bringing the national legislature to its knees, politicians turned to the federal courts to resolve public policy. As a result, the jurisdictional tug of war between state and federal courts worsened during the sectional crisis. In the last years before secession and Civil War, all eyes turned to the federal courts in the hope that somehow the judges could find a formula to prevent catastrophe.

The federal courts surmounted all but the last of these challenges. Replication of the district court/circuit court system from the East Coast to the Pacific promoted attachment to the national government throughout the land. Although the courts were now spread over great distances, the introduction of cheap rotary-press newspapers and the invention of the telegraph allowed lawyers and litigants in one part of the country to follow cases in other parts of the country as they were decided. Published reports of cases found their way to lawyers' and judges' bookshelves. If the continuing lack of central direction of the U.S. attorneys and the diverseness of outcomes from district to district because of the Rules of Decision Act and the Process Act undermined the ideal of a truly uniform national law, local elites preferred regional variation anyhow. The result was not chaos, but a kind of controlled disorder.[1]

Continuity on the bench and the close tie between state and federal judicial service facilitated the work of the federal courts. Of the forty-eight district judges commissioned between the beginning of 1837 and the end of November, 1860, twenty-two served in their state legislature, seventeen held judicial posts in their states, and ten held other high state offices. All had practiced in state courts. Thus they were known to the "local legal fraternity." Indeed, the assemblage of lawyers and judges was much like a fraternity, sharing lodgings on the circuit and engaging in common social activities. These activities and attachments muted state-federal court rivalry.[2]

Another source of stability for the federal courts was the growing professionalism of the federal bar. Most still "read law" in a practicing attorney's office, but lawyers who practiced in federal courts increasingly had some years of formal legal education in hand. The result was that lawyers admitted to practice in the federal courts shared a common body of technical knowledge. The appearance of reliable court reports, including the arguments of counsel and the opinions of the judges, added to this common body of legal knowledge. When in the course of litigation lawyers cited and judges listened to the same case law (precedent) it created intellectual bonds and resulted in greater uniformity in judicial decisions.[3]

A third source of stability was that although many of the foremost members of the legal fraternity, for example Henry Clay and Daniel Webster, were also members of Congress, they did not bring the coruscating clamor of stump speaking at polling time and rhetorical fustian of congressional debate into the courtroom. The federal courts' sessions were islands of old-fashioned courtesy often elevated by counselors' elegant oral argument, quite distinct from the conduct of the same lawyers on the floor of the House and Senate. (For example, the debate over the "gag rule" in Congress, whether to forbid the reading of abolitionist pamphlets on the floor of the House or Senate, was hardly civil, despite the legal training of the two protagonists, Representative John Quincy Adams and Senator John C. Calhoun.)[4]

The Antebellum Federal Judiciary

It is a maxim of classical political philosophy that an age of gold will be followed by an age of lesser value. Certainly the lawyers of the antebellum years (1836–1860) would have been hard pressed to measure up to the generation that wrote the Constitution and the Judiciary Act of 1789. But neither were the leaders of that later period a "blundering generation" of greedy and thoughtless bumblers stumbling into a Civil War. Perhaps no group of legal thinkers and practitioners could have closed the yawning chasm that slavery cut through the republic.[5]

On the contrary, antebellum lawyers and judges in the federal courts wove ties binding sections and interests together. Lawyers and judges accompanied the great migration west, as the nation grew rapidly in population and territory, from almost thirteen million inhabitants in 1829 to thirty-one million inhabitants in 1859, and added Texas, Arizona, New Mexico, parts of Colorado, California, the Oregon Territory (including what would become Washington state). Also, border disputes with Britain on all lands south of the 49th parallel (including the future states of Idaho, North Dakota, and Montana) were settled. Lawyers and judges ensured that a nation preoccupied with expansion did not break itself into pieces—though ironically it was the issue of the expansion of slavery into the western territories that would set politics afire, bring Congress to a halt, and draw the federal courts into the middle of the political storm.[6]

It cannot be denied, however, that under the weight of rapid geographic and demographic growth, the district/circuit system creaked and groaned. As President Abraham Lincoln told Congress in December 1861, surveying the entire antebellum period, "the country generally has outgrown our present judicial system. If uniformity was at all intended, the system requires that all the States shall be accommodated with circuit courts, attended by Supreme judges, while, in fact, Wisconsin, Minnesota, Iowa, Kansas, Florida, Texas, California, and Oregon have never had any such courts." Lincoln, a man of that West, knew that part of the problem was the inability of members of Congress to agree on the boundaries of new circuits. From 1823 until 1837, Congress had periodically debated the question of how to reconfigure old and create new circuits but could not resolve it. As Representative James Buchanan of Pennsylvania fumed on the floor of the House in 1826, while the existing federal courts "had the entire confidence of the people" they labored under an almost intolerable burden—"the complaints of the entire western portion of the country" grew with each addition to the nation's boundaries. The vast extent of the circuit-riding duties of the present Court required that "a man must be more than mortal" to accomplish his duties. Echoing Buchanan's plaint, Daniel Webster who had once ridden the circuit as a lawyer but lately confined his practice to the Supreme Court, wrote to Joseph Story, "My object, in short, would be to provide, that all the judges of the supreme court should perform some circuit duty; and as much as they could conveniently; that there should be circuit judges enough to perform the rest; and that such arrangements should be made in this respect, as, when vacancies occur on your bench, giving the opportunity, two supreme judges should be allotted to the West; in other words, that the West should have two judges on the supreme bench." Story was a conscientious circuit rider, and much respected for his circuit opinions, "even though he often complained about the arduous demands of circuit riding" and generally agreed with Webster's ideas.[7]

With Congress dithering and fussing, President Jackson, who as a Tennessee Supreme Court justice had ridden circuit in his state, repeatedly urged Congress to create new federal circuits. In December 1829, in his first annual message, Jackson reminded Congress that one-fourth of the nation was without access to a circuit court.[8]

Three solutions to the problem of expanding the federal courts system vied for acceptance in Congress: extend the present system by creating new circuits and naming additional judges; create a new layer of circuit courts with exclusive appellate jurisdiction; or close the circuit courts entirely (effectually leaving all jury trials to the district courts and all appeals to the Supreme Court). Congress selected the first. The second would become the heart of the Evarts Act of 1891, and the third was the core of the Judiciary Act of 1911, ending the operations of the circuit trial courts. As early as January 5, 1826, James Buchanan defended the first option, to "extend to other parts of the Union the benefits of a system the wisdom of which has already been tested by the experience of all the Atlantic States . . . a prosperous and happy judicial course." It took ten years for Buchanan's words to work their way through Congress. In 1836 and 1837, two more states entered the Union without being included within a circuit—Arkansas and Michigan. If the provisions of the Judiciary Acts of 1793 and 1802 were to be observed, Congress would have to establish new seats of the Supreme Court to service these states, which in turn mandated an increase in the number of circuits and some revision of their boundaries. While prior attempts at such a reform had failed in Congress, Jackson's party's political savvy and the growing necessity of federal jurisdiction over the new territories eventually overcame the Whig Party's opposition (based on the well-founded assumption that all new judges would be Jacksonians).[9]

More circuits meant more justices to ride circuit. The Whigs were right: they would be Jackson loyalists. Jackson's nominees for the Supreme Court's new seats and vacated slots might be delayed by Jackson's enemies in the Senate, but they were not blocked. In the winter of 1837, after the electors had chosen Jackson's vice president, Martin Van Buren, as his successor, the lame duck Congress approved the last of Jackson's choices for the Supreme Court—John Catron of Tennessee and John McKinley of Alabama—and established two additional circuits and two new seats on the Supreme Court. Congress increased the size of the Supreme Court to support the circuit court system rather than in response to the caseload of the Supreme Court itself.[10]

The creation of the Eighth and Ninth Circuits in the Judiciary Act of 1837 was the first adjustment of the circuits since 1820, when Maine, newly admitted to the Union, was added to the First Circuit. District courts in the new states doubling as circuit courts were replaced with distinct district and circuit courts. Some members of Congress still furiously opposed realignment. Thomas Hart Benton of Missouri had called one version of a new Eighth Circuit a monstrosity, tying the frigid regions of the North to the torrid regions of the South. The bill's sponsor, Theodore Frelinghuysen of New Jersey, took offense at Benton's jab at the judiciary committee's long labors (over which he presided) and explained that the Mississippi River touched every state in the new circuit. Surely riverboat travel along the "mother of waters" unified the new circuit. In any case, a new bill followed.[11]

In the Act creating what were then the Eighth and Ninth Circuits, Congress reorganized the Seventh Circuit to include Illinois, Indiana, Michigan, and Ohio; Kentucky, Tennessee, and Missouri formed the Eighth Circuit; and the Ninth Circuit consisted of Alabama, Arkansas, Louisiana, and Mississippi. Although the Act had not imposed a residency requirement on the new justices, both appointees, Catron of Tennessee and McKinley of Alabama, lived in the circuits to which they were assigned. The Act made certain exceptions for the travel requirements of the justices by excluding one district and two distant meeting places from the circuit system that otherwise incorporated every state. The U.S. District Court for the Western District of Louisiana, the District Court for the Northern District of New York when meeting at Utica, and the District Court for the Western District of Pennsylvania when meeting in Williamsport—all at the far edge of their districts—continued also to exercise the jurisdiction of the circuit courts. In the following years, Congress allowed further exceptions as some justices found it difficult to travel twice a year to all the districts within their assigned circuits.[12]

The district judges of the antebellum period were drawn from all over the eastern part of the country but by law resided in the state where they held court. Their backgrounds were more uniform than their geographical dispersion would suggest. All the new appointees were white Protestant males from propertied families. Although, unlike the first generation of federal judges, the antebellum judges had not held high political office prior to going on the bench, they were very well-educated jurists. For example, John Davis, named district judge for Massachusetts in 1801, had attended Harvard College, read law in Boston, and served as U.S. attorney when he went on the bench. He resigned in 1841. Peleg Sprague, Davis's successor, went to Harvard, studied at the Litchfield (Connecticut) Law School, and practiced in Maine. He represented the new state in Congress and resigned in 1865.

From 1812 to 1826, William Peter Van Ness presided over New York's Southern District. Ness was a Columbia College graduate who read law with Edward Livingston and Aaron Burr (for whom he served as second in the duel with Alexander Hamilton). He was followed by Samuel Rossiter Betts, who went to Williams College, read law in New York, represented the state in Congress, and was a judge on the state supreme court. Betts was the country's foremost admiralty law expert, writing the treatise on the subject in 1838.

St. George Tucker, named to the District of Virginia in 1813 and reassigned to the Eastern District of Virginia when it was created in 1816, was a much respected legal scholar. His *Commentaries on Blackstone* was essential reading for every well-schooled young lawyer. He resigned in 1825 and was replaced in office by George Hay, one of the state's leading practitioners and formerly the U.S. attorney. When Hay died in 1830, his successor was Philip Barbour, who served until 1836, at which time President Andrew Jackson picked him for the U.S. Supreme Court. Barbour, as it happened, was the second appointee to the Supreme Court with lower federal court experience.[13]

The first four judges of the district court of Alabama, from 1820 to 1859, Charles Tait, William Crawford, John Gayle, and William Jones, all came from prominent families in either Virginia or South Carolina. All had extensive elective political experience and had practiced law. Though they came from different political parties, the choice was less partisan than geographic—whether to appoint men from southern or northern Alabama. The pattern in these appointments is clear: although the country was becoming more democratic and the antebellum politicians often did not have the educational or family connections the founders had, the succession of federal judges from the early nineteenth century to its middle years continued a tradition of learning, experience, and talent.[14]

After the Mexican-American War (1846–1848) and the cession California to the United States as part of the peace treaty of 1848, Congress faced the immediate problem of how to extend federal justice to the Pacific shore. At first, with wagon travel along the Overland Trail or ship travel around Cape Horn the only means for a justice to service the California federal circuit courts, California's northern and southern district courts were allowed to exercise the jurisdiction of district and circuit courts. But after a flood of appeals of a commission's rulings on land grants dating from the Spanish and Mexican government periods of California history, Congress established a circuit judgeship and a circuit court without a Supreme Court justice presiding.[15]

The Act authorized an annual salary of $4,500 for the circuit judge for the U.S. Circuit Court for the Districts of California. The organizing statute repealed the circuit court jurisdiction of the California district courts, although those two courts continued to hear appeals from the board of commissioners established to confirm private land claims. The new circuit court was to meet once a year in San Francisco and once in Los Angeles, and the circuit judge could hold special sessions of the courts as necessary. The circuit judge might also preside with the district judges in order to expedite appeals from the board of commissioners.

Only one judge, Matthew McAllister, ever served on this California circuit court, and soon after he resigned in 1863. Congress then abolished the court and established a Tenth Circuit comprising the two districts.[16]

Antebellum Courts' Business

Following the creation of the new circuits, John Forsyth of Georgia, President Van Buren's secretary of state, reported the caseloads of the circuits to the Senate. As with the returns that Secretary of State John Quincy Adams ordered from the clerks and shared with Congress, the 1838 returns' variety and inaccuracy make impossible any but the most rudimentary quantitative analysis. One conclusion from the clerks' reports is obvious, however. No sooner were new circuits created than their courts were busy with cases. The District of Illinois, for example, had sixty-seven cases filed between 1836 and 1837; the District of Missouri had the same number over those years. Territorial courts, functioning as both local and federal tribunals, were swamped. Wisconsin's had 345 cases in a single session in 1837, almost all of these reflecting complicated disputes over the sale of federal lands.[17]

Figure 4.1 Bankruptcy cases in diversity were a mainstay of the federal courts. The Panic of 1837 caused widespread unemployment and bankruptcy, and this 1837 cartoon depicts those hard times. The Customs House, carrying a sign "All Bonds must be paid in Specie" is idle. In contrast, the Mechanics Bank next door, which displays a sign "No specie payments made here" is mobbed by frantic customers. Credit: Library of Congress.

With economic hardship stalking the land, lawsuits increased. In times of prosperity, the caseload leveled off. In other words, the pattern of caseloads was dictated by the business cycle. But even during boom times, the unlucky and the unwise in this largely unregulated financial and commercial system faced bankruptcy. A rough estimate of early national bankruptcy suggests that one in ten creditors would himself face bankruptcy in the course of trying to collect from his debtors. State laws provided a bewildering variety of voluntary and involuntary means of repayment. In all the states, the courts became the final collection agencies for the creditors. Many famous lawyers, for example Daniel Webster, started their legal careers as little more than debt collection agents. The first efforts at a uniform federal law, the Act of 1800, repealed in 1803, was not a success.[18]

As the Wisconsin filings hint, the Panic of 1837 hit the upper Midwestern states especially hard, as overheated land speculation, suddenly curbed by the Specie Circular of 1836 (requiring hard currency for the purchase of federal lands), caused widespread financial distress the next year. Their federal circuit courts' dockets reflected the sharp increase in diversity debt suits. The economy did not recover until the early 1840s. This made bankruptcy the number one concern of the Congress and the federal courts. The Bankruptcy Act of 1841 marked the first time debtors were able to voluntarily file for bankruptcy and receive a discharge of their debts. Under Article I, the federal government could supersede all state bankruptcy laws, providing for uniform national handling of bankruptcy in the wake of the Panic of 1837. The Act continued, "All persons whatsoever, residing in any State, District or Territory of the United States, owing debts" could provide a list of all their creditors, with the address and amount due to each, and after swearing or affirming that they could not pay the debts, would be considered bankrupt under the Act.[19]

Although the Act was repealed eighteen months later, thousands of insolvent businessmen were able to gain court decrees wiping their indebtedness clean. For example, from 1842 to 1844, petitions poured into the Southern District of Georgia Court sitting in Savannah. They came from all over the state, the propertied and the poor. Among the 302 petitioners, William Roberts was a merchant, Ami Sherwood was a carpenter, Drury Cox was a railroad contractor, Frederick Lewis was a tailor, Gabriel Roberts was a coach painter, and Eldridge Jones was a planter. The Southern District of New York was especially active in resolving these matters, serving as an administrative agency as much as an adjudicative body. Judges in these courts required that creditors' claims of debtor fraud be backed with the "strictest proof." The Act "shifted" the balance of power in court, through the mechanism of the voluntary confession of bankruptcy, from the creditor to the debtor, a shift that has characterized the federal law to this day.[20]

After 1848, with California gold certificates pouring into the coffers of banks, a new round of speculative mania swept the nation. The resulting Panic of 1857 was a short-term but severe bust, in which a new element was added to the economy. In addition to overseas staple trade and land speculation, the rapid and unregulated expansion of the railroad lines and the trading in railroad stocks and bonds made the national economy especially volatile. The planned rails would connect the East Coast to the California market, but long before that, members of Congress fought fiercely to have the right of way go through or benefit their states. This was one of Stephen Douglas's aims in the Kansas-Nebraska act. Rail line lobbyists spent freely to gain this support, a herald of the corruption that would dominate the Gilded Age Congresses.[21]

In 1856, a series of midwestern bank failures, though not uncommon in themselves, were tied to a decline in demand for American exports and corrupt local and state practices in issuing railroad bonds. This triggered the bankruptcy of railroad companies which had a falling domino-like effect on other commercial enterprises. As in 1819 and 1837, widespread unemployment, the disappearance of investment credit, and political panic ensued. Federal court dockets reflected the collapse. The Circuit Court for the Southern District of New York, for example, experienced a rise in civil filings of nearly 100 percent. In the Eastern District of Missouri, circuit court caseloads that had averaged about 55 per year before the panic, in 1857 zoomed to 105 and in 1858 rose further to 125. St. Louis was a busy river port, and the panic hit it hard.[22]

The Panic of 1857 brought another surfeit of creditors to the federal courts. A report by Secretary of the Interior Jacob Thompson listed the cases handled by the district and circuit courts in the single year 1857. Massachusetts had "disposed" of 241; New York's Southern District closed 519; Philadelphia's Eastern District 148; Virginia's Western District 102, Georgia 229; Michigan 444; Illinois 624; and Ohio 589. The cases filed that year roughly equaled or slightly exceeded those closed. Even California's gold rush did not deflect the panic. A special term of the circuit court in and for the North District logged twenty-eight cases "in common law" on the first day of its meeting, and each sitting for the next three months brought cases in double figures. The bulk of these were attempts by merchants to recoup their losses from purchasers who did not pay. Typically, the common law debt cases were delayed—"no one appearing," "pleading amended," or simply adjourned from session to session. By the end of the special term, however, most were terminated. Not so the equity cases, whose depositions were almost invariably incomplete and whose adjudication was postponed until the next regular term. Only one of the ten led to a decree, typically, a temporary injunction.[23]

The minutes for the Northern District of Georgia 1857 March session, when the Panic of 1857 had begun and out-of-state companies were rushing to sue

Georgians for nonpayment of debts and other civil obligations, noted 54 cases (mostly in assumpsit–goods had but not paid for), seven in equity, and three federal criminal suits for opening the mails, counterfeiting, and failure to pay taxes. In March 1859, the number of civil filings had grown modestly, to seventy-eight, with three equity suits, all of them carried over from earlier sessions. The economy righted itself by 1859, but rapid expansion of slavery into the Southwest posed the prospect of future busts. The spread of slavery also raised the prospect of sectional discord so serious that a portion of the country once more weighed the option of departing the Union.[24]

The panic may have played a part in one of the most audacious violations of public trust in antebellum America. A special session of the California circuit court in 1857 spent many days sorting out the "refiner's trial." The smelter and refiner at the federal mint at San Francisco, one Agoston Haraszthy, had found a unique way to make his own fortune in those hard times. A Hungarian-American of good family and formerly the high sheriff of San Diego, he relocated to the north of the state and found a position of trust at the federal mint. Accused of graft in his former office (he was paid over $12,000 to build a city jail that wasn't worth anything), in San Francisco he kept a portion of the clippings of

Figure 4.2 Federal courthouse in Windsor, Vermont, built in 1858, which also served as a post office. Multiple use was common in the eighteenth and nineteenth centuries and into the twentieth century. Credit: National Archives.

the gold coins he was supposed to be minting—a theft from the federal government amounting to over $150,000. After all, the gold shavings were just lying
around. He and an ally named William Bain were indicted, tried, and convicted
of embezzlement, with a sentence of hard labor and a fine of $20,000.[25]

In these hard times, Americans had become comfortable with a federal court
system running in parallel to the state courts. In part this was due to the success
of the Madisonian Compromise, in particular the section of the Judiciary Act of
1789 requiring the federal courts in civil matters to follow the substantive law of
the state (except in equity, admiralty, and federal crimes), and the Process Acts,
requiring the federal courts to use state procedure (except in equity or as federal
law otherwise prescribed).

One mark of this growing accommodation to federal jurisprudence could be
seen in brick and mortar. In the antebellum years, the physical facilities of the
federal court system were hardly imposing. For example, the federal circuit court
that heard *Dred Scott v. Sanford* in 1854 met in the top floor of a store in St. Louis.
In the 1850s, Judge Thomas Drummond of the District of Illinois held court
in George Meeker's vacant shop. Meeker was the clerk of the court. If a case
was likely to attract a crowd, it was removed to the Cook County Courthouse,
a far grander site. On May 19, 1851, the first session of the District Court for
the District of California met in the alderman's chamber of the San Francisco
City Hall, smoke from the most recent of downtown fires seeping through the
open windows. Recognizing these debilities, in 1852, the federal government
employed architect Amni B. Young as supervising architect of the Treasury
Department. Among his works for the government were Italian Renaissance-
style courthouses in Rutland, Vermont, and Indianapolis, Indiana, featuring
wrought-iron staircases, heavy masonry foundations, marble floors, and fire-
proof interiors. The federal courts were beginning to get facilities of which they
could be proud.[26]

Fraud and the Federal Courts

Viewing the economic dealings of a people through the lens of its courts' records,
one inevitably sees the underside of human conduct. Not all of them were criminal trials. Cases of fraud may give us an atypical, even jaundiced, picture of the
world of business, but the historian of law finds such cases especially valuable.
They throw light on the disparity between contemporary ideals of fiscal probity
and actual commercial practices.

Federal courts heard a wide variety of fraud cases in the antebellum years,
and the courts played a vital role in preventing scoundrels from escaping justice
by crossing state borders or carrying their misdeed across state lines. In these,

there was always the potential for friction between competing state and federal courts. *Swift v. Tyson* (1842) was one such case of interstate fraud demonstrating judicial federalism.[27]

One of the most important sectors of antebellum commerce was the exploitation of natural resources. Forest products were an important export in the colonial period, and domestic demand for wood for building materials, paper, furniture, and firewood grew apace with the new nation. Sale of the bounty of the forests to foreign countries and the domestic market made the lumber industry one of the most profitable in the antebellum period. With the lure of profits came swindlers. As Bangor, Maine, emerged as a major center of the lumber industry, unscrupulous speculators in Maine along with conspirators in commercial entrepôts like New York City and Boston engaged in fast and loose deals selling timber land to which they had no title.[28]

In earlier years, Maine land shenanigans had led to gunplay, but by the 1830s, the lumber merchants' schemes had become more sophisticated. They used commercial paper (in this case "bills of exchange") that were endorsed (a promise to pay, like endorsing a bank check) and circulated far beyond the circle of original entrepreneurs to kite their speculation. The problem came when a creditor received an endorsed bill of exchange, without notice of the underlying fraud, and tried to pass it on for payment. If the original drawer "dishonored" it, that is, refused to accept it and pay it, the entire chain of transactions could come under the scrutiny of the courts. That is what happened with increasing frequency after the Panic of 1837 brought banks crashing down and spurred creditors to demand payment on notes.[29]

George W. Tyson, a New York resident, had given the bill as payment for land in Maine. Unbeknownst to him, the sellers did not have title to the land. He had been duped. The bill of exchange passed through a series of hands until it arrived in Swift hands, and when he demanded payment on it, Tyson refused. Tyson removed the suit from the state court to the federal circuit court in the Southern District of New York, where under New York law, Tyson could (and did) offer proof of the original fraud as a defense to Swift's demand for payment. Presumably, as the federal court was bound by the Rules of Decision Act to use the law of the state in which it sat, that would end the matter.[30]

Hearing the case at the beginning of May 1836, District Judge Samuel Betts and Justice Smith Thompson disagreed, however, and on the division of opinion, the case automatically went to the U.S. Supreme Court. There it changed character and significance. From a pretty typical and straightforward (in law, if not in its facts) case of fraud, it became the basis of the doctrine of federal common law. Justice Story, writing for a unanimous court, knew all about these frauds from his travels on the New England circuit. He also knew that the negotiability (legal circulation) of commercial paper was vital for business dealings.

"It is for the benefit and convenience of the commercial world to give as wide an extent as practicable to the credit and circulation of negotiable paper."

How then to promote the flow of business across the land without violating the strictures of the Judiciary Act of 1789? Story found a way to get around the New York law imposed by its courts, and with it, the vagaries that state court interpretations of state law imposed on interstate commerce. "It is, however, con-tended, the . . . judiciary act of 1789 . . . furnishes a rule obligatory upon this Court to follow the decisions of the state tribunals in all cases to which they apply, " but "in the ordinary use of language it will hardly be contended that the decisions of Courts constitute laws. They are, at most, only evidence of what the laws are; and are not, of themselves, laws." In short, federal courts were only bound to follow state statutes, not the precedents of state courts. "The laws of a state are more usu-ally understood to mean the rules and enactments promulgated by the legislative authority thereof, or long established local customs having the force of laws."

If it appeared that Story had, with a wave of the hand, dismissed the entire Anglo-American common law concept of precedent, in which the state appeals courts' interpretations of statutes had the status of law—like a magician, what he had caused to disappear with one hand he recreated with the other. The Supreme Court's decisions, themselves no more or less than precedent than the state supreme courts, were binding on the state courts. "It becomes necessary for us, therefore, upon the present occasion to express our own opinion of the true result of the commercial law upon the question now before us . . . Undoubtedly, the decisions of the local tribunals upon such subjects are entitled to, and will receive, the most deliberate attention and respect of this Court; but they cannot furnish positive rules, or conclusive authority, by which our own judgments are to be bound up and governed." Note that under the *Swift* regime, two identical fact pattern cases might be resolved differently because one was adjudicated in state court and the other in federal court.[31]

Land was also transferred from generation to generation, and in the antebel-lum era sometimes by fraudulent means as obvious and odious as in the timber industry. The disputed estates in land often involved suitors from different states. Because parcels were held in trusts, these cases came to the federal courts under their equity jurisdiction. The trust was an old English device to hold together an estate when the rules for inheritance would have worked a hardship on one or more of the heirs. In "constructive trusts," the courts turned the administration of an estate into a trusteeship. Trustees were not to waste the estate or to use it for their own benefit. Sometimes these arrangements were so complicated that the federal circuit courts had to appoint "special masters," in effect auxiliaries of the court who took depositions, examined documents, and then reported to the court. Masters uncovered frauds that clever trustees hid and performed other invaluable tasks.

One especially convoluted case of massive fraud coming to circuit court as an equity suit involved the founding of the city of Toledo on the banks of the Maumee River border of the state of Ohio and the Michigan Territory. Insofar as it required the federal court to determine the boundaries of states, it is the perfect example of how judicial federalism might work to prevent interstate conflict. At the same time, it is a disquieting example of the misconduct of private and public fiduciaries typical of the "big barbeque" era of American politics. Founded in 1833 as part of Monroe County, Michigan, after the "Toledo War," the city was reestablished in Lucas County, Ohio. In 1835, a boundary dispute led both sides to arm militias who then spent a year issuing threats and baiting one another to start a fight. President Andrew Jackson and Congress intervened in 1836, giving the strip of land to Ohio and in return rushing Michigan statehood and adding to the state the Upper Peninsula.[32]

For twenty years before the controversy was settled and a decade after, a tale of failed land speculation and almost successful peculation played out. In *Oliver v. Piatt* (1845), an appeal to the U.S. Supreme Court from the Ohio federal circuit court (the record was over 400 pages long), beginning in 1817 with two land-development companies trading stock shares and titles among the company owners. The details of the case were typical of antebellum western land speculation. After the War of 1812, the British withdrew their troops from the American side of the Great Lakes, leaving behind the opportunity for speculation in land. At the end of the decade, two Maumee companies merged into one company and authorized one of the directors, one Martin Baum, to sell portions of the land around what would become Toledo as a township. Over the next decade the plots of land and then pieces of paper representing title to the land changed hands a number of times, in effect operating as a kind of investment capital/commercial paper. The problem began when the purchasers of the land wanted out, and found they could not pass legal title to their buyers. In the meantime, the Panic of 1819 had ruined the land development company. As Baum wrote to one correspondent, in 1824:

> The land speculation has truly been an unfortunate business, and no one can be more tired of it than I am; for it's me who has to stand the brunt of the company—suits, judgments, executions, with all its attendant vexations. First, our agents were crazy in making purchases at such high rates—then the madness of Congress in reducing the price of the public lands—change of times—scarcity of money—the impossibility of managing that species of property where so many are concerned; the change of sentiments of persons in holding real estate; in fact all and everything has operated against such speculations.

Baum dumped the entire matter on one William Oliver, who was in effect a trustee for the purchasers, but had his own plans—to wit, get as much out of the parcels of land as he could. (John H. Piatt was one of the original purchasers—hence the caption of the case). In the meantime, some of the land was donated to Michigan to begin a university, a genuine deed of trust. Under established trusteeship principles, Oliver was not to use these grants for other than their stated purposes, but he did, selling them off through agents who might or might not have known about the underlying misfeasance. With the buying and selling of the original lots going on apace, the paper trail grew massive and bewildering. The federal circuit court named a master in equity whose job it was to make sense of the various claims and counterclaims and report to the court, which did not please Oliver. In 1842, ordered to pay back what he owed, he appealed the circuit court decision to the Supreme Court. He lost.[33]

Federal courts' equitable jurisdiction also involved the judges in domestic disputes, for example enforcing trusts for family members and spouses who resided in different states. While these cases may not share the scope or consequence of an *Oliver v. Piatt*, they demonstrate how diversity jurisdiction promoted judicial federalism. A particularly illustrative case of this type was *Lewis v Baird* (1842). In it, an Ohio federal court had to referee a suit whose origin lay in land grants nearly a half-century old. Kentuckian John Lawson, a veteran of the Revolutionary War, had received for his service nearly 5,000 acres in the Ohio Territory. But Lawson was not a happy man. "A great number of witnesses have testified as to the habits of Gen. Lawson. It seems he was intemperate before he left Virginia, and that this habit became much worse in Kentucky. Indeed some of the witnesses say that his indulgences in this way were so excessive, as to render him unfit to transact any kind of business." Not surprisingly, Lawson was having marital difficulties. As a peace offering, he arranged a trust for his wife and those to whom she assigned title after he died, "and the said Lawson covenanted with the trustees that he would at no future time, 'offer any personal violence or injury to his wife, and that he would abstain from the intemperate use of every kind of spirituous liquors, and that if he should any time thereafter again offer any personal violence or injury to his wife, the trustees were authorised to dispossess him of the hundred and fifty acres of land.'" The reconciliation did not last, and she returned to her Virginia home, leaving him, the trust, and the various parcels behind. When she died, in 1809, she had not assigned the parcels. Lawson fell further into the slough of despondence. "After the last separation from his wife, he seemed to lose all respect for himself, his family and society. That he became utterly degraded, the associate of slaves; and was seen in the streets of Lexington imploring money from every person he met with to purchase spirits."

But a facet of Lawson's character was far more self-possessed. "When sober, which was sometimes the case, he was capable of transacting business. He was a lawyer by profession, and occasionally, as well after his removal to Kentucky as before it, was engaged in the practice of law." With his wife gone, he began selling off 3,000 acres of the land in the trust to various and sundry buyers, who then repatented (i.e., re-registered it in the deed book) it in their own names. The fraud was eventually discovered by her heirs, and they sought an injunction to bar the purchasers from repatenting the land. The battle joined in 1807 lasted until 1842, as the pieces of land changed hands almost faster than the heirs could follow. A myriad of depositions documented their efforts to regain what they argued the trust had conveyed. In the meantime, the county court in Kentucky had lost the original deed of trust. Judge Humphrey Leavitt of the Southern District of Ohio, hearing the suit, valiantly tried to sort out the conflicting claims and finally concluded that the claimants in equity had waited too long to file—laches barred the suit.[34]

Parenthetically, equity suits like *Oliver v. Piatt* and *Lewis v. Baird* particularly taxed the courts' clerks. For example, in the Circuit Court for the District of Missouri clerk Benjamin Hickman had to copy in the record book documents filed with the appeal from the district court. One account for debt ran to fifty-one pages, each beautifully handwritten folio page containing about 1,000 words. Typically, the suit was continued for years. *Barnes and Park v. Victor S. Jourdan*, ending in a consent decree for "one cent, balance of account," gave Hickman less trouble. Even more expeditious entries chronicled Charles Goodrich's many suits for patent infringement, some forty, on October 5, 1859, and April 25, 1860—all ending with the defendants agreeing not to reproduce Goodrich's patented vulcanized India rubber. The cases were all handled in the district court.[35]

Legitimate ventures like Goodrich's were built on credit. Canal companies and railroads, the leading speculative sectors of the antebellum economy after land speculation, all relied on the floating of stocks and bonds. By purchasing these or trading them, speculators were entering a network of credit and debt. Antebellum banks printed their own scrip (minting coin was the exclusive privilege of the federal government). Such bank notes freely circulated, but they too had little behind them but the confidence the drawer of the notes had on the bank. The morality of the business classes required strict attention to credit and debt. A man who did not pay what he owed was not considered creditworthy. But fire, flood, crop failure, and personal illness, added to the boom-and-bust cycles of the economy, called all of these moral injunctions into question, and the questions ended up in the courts.

Judges found that many of the speculative schemes of the period were shaky, and some were outright scams. Local and state bonds to raise capital for these ventures were traded like money, giving the unscrupulous and the greedy a chance to get rich quick. Private companies printed bonds for the most outlandish purposes. Two notorious cases presented these issues in stark form. In 1855,

Central American filibusterer William Walker printed bonds for his Nicaraguan adventure redeemable at 6 percent interest. They featured a picture of five volcanoes—hardly a visual inducement to investors. Still, the Bank of Louisiana handled the transaction. Stocks and bonds like Walker's were sold to or given to politicians in a position to further the interests of the promoters. Like moths to the flame, politicians seemed drawn to filibusterers like Walker. In 1854, former Mississippi Governor John A. Quitman found himself in federal circuit court in Louisiana when he tried to unload securities from a failed Cuban filibustering expedition in violation of the neutrality laws. A lawyer himself, Quitman should have known better than to invest. When called before a federal grand jury, he refused to offer any information about the scheme, citing his Fifth Amendment rights, though he did tell the jurors that the neutrality laws did not apply to him. Justice John Archibald Campbell, presiding in the circuit court, answered Quitman: "I have explained, in the charge addressed to the grand jury, my sense of the importance of the [neutrality] act of congress involved in this discussion, and my opinion of the policy in which it is founded. The honor of our country, [and] the fair repute of its citizens, in my opinion, require an exact observance of that act. It is a law binding upon our whole people, and the principles, which justify its violation, menace the order and repose of the whole confederacy." Quitman went to trial, but he was able to convince a jury not to convict him.[36]

Federal courts had to balance the needs of commerce as practiced, with easy credit and common indebtedness, against strict fiscal moralism. In some of these cases, like *Bank of Augusta v. Earle* (1839), they once again played the role of moderating what could have been serious interstate quarrels. In this particular case, a defaulter on a bond tried to escape creditors by arguing in federal court that the creditors had done business in the forum state illegally. In 1838, Joseph Earle, a Mobile, Alabama, businessman, faced payment of two bills of exchange he endorsed that were subsequently bought by firms in Georgia and Louisiana. The federal Circuit Court for the Southern District of Alabama found for Earle because Alabama had not chartered the foreign (out of state) firms to do business in Alabama.[37]

The U.S. Supreme Court reversed the circuit court decision. At its bar respected and expensive counsel argued the case, including Daniel Webster representing the interests of the Bank of the United States, for the case's general implications for banking and financial-paper law were far-reaching. In effect, Chief Justice Roger Taney's opinion for the Court announced the doctrine that corporations were citizens of the states in which they were chartered. He began by quoting the decision: "a bank incorporated by the laws of Georgia, with a power among other things to purchase bills of exchange, could not lawfully exercise that power in the State of Alabama, and that the contract for this bill was therefore void and did not bind the parties to the payment of the money" for such unauthorized operation in another state was "inconsistent with the rights and sovereignty of the states in which [such financial arrangements] are made." Georgia might give to its banks the power to collect on foreign commercial paper, but Georgia could not confer on its banks the power to use the courts of another state or the federal courts sitting in another state to collect on debts without the consent of the other state.

At the same time, Taney wanted to enable national commerce as well (he would sign on to Story's opinion in *Swift*) and, absent Alabama's explicit statutory bar on foreign banks' operation in the state, economic progress and the Full Faith and Credit Clause of Article IV, Section 1 ("Full Faith and Credit shall be given in each State to the public Acts, Records, and judicial Proceedings of every other State") promoted corporations' nationwide operation. So Taney concluded that Earle must pay what he owed to the Bank of Augusta. Surely Alabama would want this outcome: "It is but justice to all the parties concerned to suppose that these contracts were made in good faith and that no suspicion was entertained by either of them that these engagements could not be enforced."[38]

Taney's closing remarks implied that morality had some part in financial dealings. For much of the nineteenth-century judges routinely coupled law and morality. As New York judge and future U.S. Supreme Court Justice Samuel Nelson opined in one domestic relations case, the best decisions in court combined "sound law and sound morality."[39]

Slavery in the Antebellum Federal Courts

While Justice Story may have hoped that slavery would die out on its own accord, and the Marshall Court had decided slavery cases on the narrowest factual grounds, that ground grew into a chasm in the ensuing twenty-five years. Between 1836 and 1860 slavery suits would present the worst case scenario of the politicization of the courts, dragging them to the center of the struggle between free soil and slavery advocates.

When South Carolina Senator James Henry Hammond boasted in 1858 that "cotton is king," he was not far from the truth. The spread of cotton cultivation and its growing importance in the national economy was little short of astounding. From 7 percent of the value of the nation's exports in 1800, it had become nearly 60 percent of the value of all exports by 1860. In 1790, only 4,000 bales were produced. By 1860, more than 3.8 million bales were picked, packed, and shipped. Slaves were not necessary to plant or harvest cotton. In fact nearly 50 percent of cotton farmers had no slaves. But slavery and cotton did go together because profits depended upon the amount of cotton grown, and slave labor could increase the yield in direct proportion to the number of slaves employed. Slaves in the South thus multiplied from a little less than 700,000 men and women in 1790 to nearly four million in 1860, most working on gangs of more than ten slaves on plantations with the "black belt" soils conducive to cotton growing. High cotton prices convinced the children of the older inhabitants of the South to relocate west, with their slaves. The internal immigration also spurred the domestic slave market, making it profitable for planters in Virginia and South Carolina to sell slaves they did not need "down the river" to the Mississippi Delta. In the period to 1850, Louisiana (1812), Mississippi (1817), Alabama (1819), Missouri (1821), Arkansas (1836), Florida (1845), and Texas (1845) joined the Union as slave states.[40]

As slavery spread throughout the Southwest in the 1830s, an era of intense moral self-examination was sweeping the North. A "ferment" of reformism changed the way many Americans thought about themselves, and communal experiences as widely divergent as revival meetings and labor union meetings shared the notion that the human spirit could be perfected and society as a whole could be improved. Over time, the reform ideal moved from persuading the individual to repent to fostering reform associations and utopian religious sanctuaries, to seeking the aid of governments in imposing reform measures, to the most imposing and divisive of all the reforms—abolition of slavery.[41]

Slave cases did not make up a numerically significant portion of the antebellum federal courts' dockets. For the years 1789 to 1860, there were less than 100 of these cases recorded, the majority concerning the slave trade, fugitive slaves, or diversity cases in which a slave was part of an estate. In only thirty-three of the cases was slavery a central issue. It is possible that this figure, based on local reporters, underrepresents the importance of slavery in the courts and the law. The published records included cases heard. Cases settled "in the shadow of the courthouse" would not have been included.

Of the thirty-three cases reported in the district and circuit courts centrally involving slavery during the 1840s and 1850s, the plurality concerned the overseas slave trade. The second-largest group entailed the pursuit and arrest of suspected runaway slaves. Despite the laws against American shippers' participation in the overseas slave trade, southern ports were still visited by slavers who sold their illegal cargoes to American buyers. Typical of prosecutions for these violations was the 1845 indictment of a ship master and two seamen in the Circuit Court for the District of Maryland. The year before they were indicted, they had conspired with the captain of the ship *Montevideo* to keep slaves on board, when the slaves were not "inhabitants of the United States." When a repeat case of this type appeared on the docket of the Circuit Court for the Southern District of Georgia, an irate Justice James M. Wayne informed the grand jury: "A circumstance has recently occurred in this city which impresses the larger portion of its people, I may say all, with few exceptions, that the same vessel has been positively taken from this port to be engaged again in the same unlawful trade."[42]

Some northern federal judges found ways to enable suits for slaves' freedom. In *Polydore v. Prince* (1837), for example, next friends sued for West Indian slave Polydore's freedom based on his ill treatment aboard the ship *Prince*. Edward Fox, himself named to the Maine district court bench in 1866, was counsel for Polydore, and he argued before his predecessor Maine District Judge Ashur Ware that Polydore was a seaman aboard the ship, and seamen were entitled to the court's protection under admiralty law. Ware allowed the slave standing to bring the suit without putting up the statutory bond for court costs: "The libellant in this case is a servant, a slave in his own country, with no other friend or acquaintance here, than a minor, whom he attends in the quality of a servant. To require of him to enter into a stipulation for costs with sureties, would be the same thing in effect as saying that he had no right to ask redress in this court."

Could Polydore next sustain his suit for freedom? Ware quoted Joseph Story's influential treatise on *Conflict of Laws* (1834) to the effect that Polydore's status was determined by the slave laws of his domicile but qualified Story's reasoning, "If a Turkish or Hindoo husband were travelling in this country with his wife, or temporarily resident here, we should, without hesitation, acknowledge the relation of husband and wife between them; but the legal pre-eminence of the husband as to acts done here, would be admitted only to the extent that the marital rights are recognized by our laws, and not as they are recognized by the law of his domicile." Indeed, as state courts had determined when freeing bondmen brought by their masters or mistresses to free soil, "[i]t follows of course that when a slave passes into a country, by whose laws slavery is not recognized, his civil condition is changed from a state of servitude, to that of freedom, and he becomes invested with those civil capacities which the law of the place imparts to all who stand in the same category." But Ware hedged his bets—it was Polydore's mistreatment by the ship captain, rather than his status as slave on Maine's free soil, that led to his freedom. Fox would serve on the federal bench with distinction from 1866 until his death in 1881.[43]

John Kintzing Kane, district judge for the Eastern District of Pennsylvania from 1846 to his death in 1858, distinguished between his official enforcement of slave law and his personal views condoning abolitionism. Kane's son, Thomas, was his court clerk and a well-known abolitionist. He and his wife lived in the judge's Philadelphia home, a stop on the Underground Railroad for runaway slaves. The judge followed an ask-no-questions policy when it came to the African-American men and women who suddenly appeared and just as suddenly departed the house, but on the bench in 1855 he found abolitionist Passmore Williamson in violation of the Fugitive Slave Act of 1850 for aiding and abetting the Vigilance Committee of Philadelphia's underground railway efforts.

Williamson countered in the city's Court of Common Pleas with a suit for false arrest. Kane found Williamson in contempt for filing the suit, but the judge died before the issue could be resolved.[44]

Nothing in the laws criminalizing the external slave trade or in admiralty law regarding bound seamen hindered the internal slave trade. It was a major source of revenue for its operators. But the carrying of slaves from place to place, particularly in the border states' slave trades, provided opportunities for slaves to "steal themselves," in the words of runaway and abolitionist Frederick Douglass. Afraid of this, southern members of Congress demanded stronger federal measures to recapture runaways. The Fugitive Slave Act of 1850 brought the federal government directly into the business of slave catching. The law empowered federal judges to name commissioners to hear and decide fugitive slave cases in summary hearings, without any process other than arrest by a federal marshal. The federal judges and the commissioners were not to require indictments, hold trials, or empanel juries, nor allow the alleged fugitive to confront witnesses or have counsel. In short, the detainee could not assert any of the procedural guarantees under the Bill of Rights. Thus, even as northern states ended slavery, free persons of color in the North did not possess the same rights as persons of European extraction in the antebellum federal courts. The very paradox at the heart of federal law on slavery underlay this distinction. As Chief Justice Taney explained in 1859, "It is true that a slave is the property of the master, and his right of property is recognized and secured by the constitution and laws of the United States; and it is equally true that he is not a citizen, and would not be embraced in a law operating only upon that class of persons. Yet, he is a person, and is always spoken of and described as such in the state papers and public acts of the United States."[45]

The increasingly acerbic language with which members of Congress assailed one another over slavery should have urged Taney to continue Marshall's wiser or more prudent minimalist approach to slave questions. But Taney had other ideas and in the waning years of his long tenure from 1836 to 1864, his dicta on slavery came to define his contribution to American jurisprudence.

Like Marshall, Taney was a man of many faces. A scion of the planter elite, he practiced law in the city of Baltimore. Taney was a practicing Roman Catholic in a nation that barely tolerated Catholicism. In his youth, he freed most of his own slaves (taking care of the needs of his older bondsmen as well), and showed some signs of dislike of the institution itself, but later in life he would become a defender of slavery. His career in public office included important posts in the federal government, where he balanced states' rights constitutionalism with nationalism. When the southern states seceded and Maryland remained in the Union, Taney stayed at his post.[46]

For a man who owed his high office to politics, Taney had a positive gift for misreading political currents. As attorney general (1831–1833) and secretary of the treasury (1833), he so infuriated members of the Senate that they refused to confirm his permanent appointment to the Treasury and denied him a post on the Supreme Court the first time that Jackson submitted his name. In 1836 the Senate finally confirmed him as chief justice. In duties overlooked by his critics, Taney was a reliable and diligent circuit court judge, rarely missing sessions in Virginia, Maryland, and Delaware. On the bench, he authored decisions promoting enterprise and contributed to a nuanced refining of judicial federalism. In an atmosphere so filled with vilification by the slavery question, perhaps no federal judge could have avoided calumny from one side or the other. But Taney's overreaching unnecessarily wounded himself and the Court.[47]

With the annexation of Texas and the war with Mexico, antislavery opinion in Congress saw a plot to expand "the empire of slavery," and proslavery members began to speak of secession openly. The debate over the admission of California as a free state, in 1850, the adoption of the Fugitive Slave Act, a concession to the slave South, and the passage of northern state "personal liberty laws" overtly flouting the Fugitive Slave Act, all proved that the division over slavery had worsened. The advent of "Bleeding Kansas," with its escalating violence between pro- and antislave migrants, truly poisoned the sessions of Congress. Members began to carry weapons to the chambers, and one proslavery congressman, South Carolina's Preston S. Brooks, caned abolitionist Senator Charles Sumner into insensibility as he sat at his Senate desk. Northern newspapers were inflamed by the episode; southerners sent Brooks canes to replace the one he broke over Sumner's head.[48]

It was in this increasingly vitriolic climate of opinion that the antebellum federal courts heard a series of slave cases, *U.S. v. Libellants and Claimants of the Schooner Amistad* (1841), *Prigg v. Pennsylvania* (1842), *Jones v. Van Zandt* (1847), *Strader v. Graham* (1851), the disputed rendition of runaway slave Anthony Burns, and *Dred Scott v. Sanford* (1857). During the years between its inception and its resolution, the *Amistad* case was a subject of great public interest only surpassed in later years by *Dred Scott*. In June 1839, a Cuban schooner carrying fifty-three slaves sailed from Havana to another port on the island. Along the way, the slaves rose up; killed the captain, cook, and crew members; and ordered the two planter-owners aboard to sail for Africa. Instead, they managed to bring the ship into United States territorial waters, where it was boarded by American sailors and brought to the port of New London, Connecticut.[49]

The *Amistad* presented familiar issues both of salvage (that is, who could legally benefit from the saved ship and cargo) and the legality of the slave trade under international treaties. As a salvage case, the question was whether the cargo of the ship—the Africans—belonged to the men who came aboard (two naval officers) and brought the ship into the American port, the Cuban owners, or the two Spanish men who had purchased the majority of the slaves and who, after the uprising, were to have sailed the ship to Africa under the orders of the slaves. There were also questions of crimes at sea (the slaves had killed at least two crew members) and the jurisdiction of the federal court over the case. The district court over which Judge Andrew Judson presided referred the question of criminal jurisdiction to the circuit court. Sitting in the circuit court, Justice Smith Thompson ruled that the case was properly before the district court—it had jurisdiction—over the case in admiralty but not over the alleged crimes (as serious crimes they belonged to the circuit court). The question then became who owned the ship and whether the Africans were slaves or free. The queen of Spain intervened in support of the Cuban owners, Spanish subjects, resting the case upon a maritime treaty between Spain and the United States ratified in 1821. As a question of salvage, the case was of little importance, and could have ended in the district court with a decree that the ship be returned to its Cuban owners.[50]

The alleged slaves also petitioned for their freedom, arguing that they were free when the alleged slave traders kidnapped them and carried them from their homeland to Cuba (violating Spanish law) before their transshipment on the *Amistad*. Justice Thompson found that the district court could also hear arguments on the detention of the slaves. For this reason, as a freedom suit, the case became a highly publicized and politicized one, closely watched by southern slave interests and northern abolitionists. At the circuit court preliminary hearing on habeas corpus writs for the incarcerated slaves, Justice Thompson had made clear his abhorrence of slavery but continued that he was bound by existing slave law. Did that law apply to the high seas? Van Buren's secretary of state, John Forsyth, a virulently proslavery Georgian, tried every trick to return the slaves to their owners by executive decree. But helped by abolitionists and ultimately represented by former secretary of state, president, and current member of Congress John Quincy Adams (who had coauthored the treaty with Spain in 1819), the slaves' suit raised vital questions about the slave trade's legality, the morality of bondage, and the right to rebel. At the time, Adams was waging what seemed a one-man war in the House of Representatives to lift the "gag order" that the Congress had placed on antislavery petitions.[51]

Judge Judson, once again hearing the case, noted that Spain had outlawed the slave trade in 1817. He decreed that the alleged slaves were in fact free and should be given to the president of the United States to be returned to their homes in Africa. The circuit court concurred (Thompson joining Judson). But the owners wanted the slaves, and the queen, with the support of Secretary of State Forsyth asked the U.S. attorney for the district to appeal the circuit court's affirmance of the district court's decree to the Supreme Court.

The Supreme Court had before it evidence that the human cargo were not Cuban slaves by birth and not simply en route from one Cuban port to another, but were newly taken from Africa. What was more, the documents the ship's master carried were a fraud to get around Spain's agreement with Great Britain not to trade in African slaves. Co-counsel for the slaves Roger Baldwin urged, "The American people have never imposed it as a duty on the government of the United States, to become actors in an attempt to reduce to slavery, men found in a state of freedom, by giving extra-territorial force to a foreign slave law. Such a duty would not only be repugnant to the feelings of a large portion of the citizens of the United States, but it would be wholly inconsistent with the fundamental principles of our government." Story was sympathetic but wary.[52]

Story's nationalism and his fear that the debate over slavery could destroy the Union (a fear far greater in 1841 than in the early 1820s) cautioned him against an eloquent denunciation of slavery. His caution was seconded by Taney, who signed on to the opinion. Instead of fulminating on the evils of slavery, Story wrote a technically clear but limited opinion based on his wide-ranging knowledge of conflict of laws. When one jurisdiction (the United States) was bound to render judgment under the laws of another jurisdiction (Spain), the Spanish law should govern. Story read Spanish law and the treaty of 1819 to bar transatlantic trading in slaves.[53]

> It is plain beyond controversy, if we examine the evidence, that these negroes never were the lawful slaves of Ruiz or Montez, or of any other Spanish subjects. They are natives of Africa, and were kidnapped there, and were unlawfully transported to Cuba, in violation of the laws and treaties of Spain, and the most solemn edicts and declarations of that government. By those laws, and treaties, and edicts, the African slave trade is utterly abolished; the dealing in that trade is deemed a heinous crime; and the negroes thereby introduced into the dominions of Spain, are declared to be free.

He agreed with counsel for the Africans that the evidence proved they had been taken in Africa and transported to Cuba in violation of the treaty. He affirmed the lower courts' rulings save for one item: the Africans were not to be delivered to President Van Buren (and thus to the mercy of the Spanish) but were free to go immediately.

Prigg presented a far more vexing political question to the Court the following term. An 1826 Pennsylvania law required that anyone seeking to recapture a runaway slave obtain a certificate from the state that the person sought was in fact a runaway slave. Margaret Morgan and her children were either runaway slaves or free persons of color (the census listed her as free) from Maryland living in

Pennsylvania. Edward Prigg, a neighbor of the Maryland owner, found Margaret and her children and returned them to Maryland in the middle of the night, without getting a certificate from Pennsylvania. For violating its laws he was indicted, and Pennsylvania sought his extradition from Maryland to stand trial. The two states agreed that he would be tried, and his conviction was appealed to the Pennsylvania Supreme Court, which upheld the lower court trial verdict. The two states now directly appealed to the Supreme Court, which had original jurisdiction when one state sued another.[54]

Article IV, Section 2 of the Constitution mandated rendition of fugitive bondsmen and women to their owners, and the federal Fugitive Slave Act of 1793 based on this clause permitted slave catchers to bring alleged runaway slaves before any free state magistrate prior to taking them from the state back to their supposed legal owners. In theory, the Pennsylvania anti-kidnapping law did not apply to such fugitives. It merely protected free persons of color domiciled in the state from being carried off illegally.

Story knew that the case had immense political consequences; that it reached deeply into state-federal relations; and that he must treat it with utmost care. He wrote, "Few questions which have ever come before this Court involve more delicate and important considerations; and few upon which the public at large may be presumed to feel a more profound and pervading interest." He knew that the Rendition Clause was of utmost importance to South Carolina and Georgia in the drafting and ratification of the federal Constitution and that the slave South regarded the return of its wayward property as essential to its welfare and wealth. The Fugitive Slave Act of 1793 and the Constitution's Rendition Clause could not be sidestepped. In his opinion, the duty to return runaways was absolute and the rights of southern property holders must be secure. Applying this to the Pennsylvania law, he found it in violation of the federal Constitution. Prigg's conviction was reversed and the anti-kidnapping law voided. At the same time, *Prigg* was an agonizing case for Story. As "a judge from the constitution" he wrote to a friend a year later, he could not have decided the case otherwise.[55]

Other members of the Court, notably Taney and Justice Peter V. Daniel of Virginia, signed on to Story's view of the Rendition Clause but resisted his view that states could not be compelled to assist in the rendition of runaways. They thought that every state had the duty to assist slave catchers. The purpose of the Pennsylvania law was evidentiary—to ensure that the slave catcher had evidence. The problem with this for Pennsylvania's case in *Prigg* was that Prigg did have evidence from the Maryland owner, but the Pennsylvania authorities refused to issue the certificate anyhow. (On the other hand, one of Morgan's children was born in Pennsylvania, making that child free by the state law. Maryland law, under principles of comity, should have regarded that child as free, but she was enslaved along with her mother and siblings.) Using *Prigg* as its authority, antislavery majorities in northern state legislatures barred state magistrates from assisting in the recapture of alleged runaways. Even Story's son, William Wetmore Story, tried to spin the decision as a "victory for freedom," allowing the free states to escape the burden of enforcing a policy that they abhorred.[56]

Justice John McLean, who joined the Court in 1829, dissented. He was something of a throwback to men with backgrounds like Samuel Chase and William Paterson, indeed to President Jackson himself. The justice grew up in a farming family that moved from New Jersey to Virginia, then Kentucky, and finally Ohio, seeking to better its opportunities. Much of his view of the world came from the egalitarian strains in Methodism, reinforcing his own salt-of-the-earth background. He abhorred slavery:

> No one has held in greater abhorrence than myself the principles of slavery. With me this has not been a mere matter of theory. Some eight or ten colored persons are now free who were made so by my money, when I owed more debts that the value of my property. . . . I might ask how many of those have done more than I have to liberate individuals from bondage.[57]

In one case, he ruled that "wherever the master seeks a profit, by the labor of this slave in this state, he forfeits all right to the possession and services of such slave." But as a judge in a federal system that incorporated the domestic (i.e., state) law of slavery in the Constitution, McLean felt an obligation to uphold the rights of slaveholders when those rights were established by an act of Congress. He would run for the presidency as, first, a Free Soil Democrat (Free Soilers opposed the expansion of slavery into the western territories), and later, under the new Republican Party banner (the new Republicans formed in 1854 to oppose the spread of slavery). He wrote 247 opinions for the Court and two notable dissents—in *Prigg* and in *Dred Scott*—and died while serving, in 1861.[58]

In *Van Zandt* the Court ruled that an Ohio man aiding and abetting the escape of runaway slaves had violated the provisions of the Fugitive Slave Act of 1793. He had to pay a fine. Writing for the Court, Justice Levi Woodbury of New Hampshire did not find the case novel or especially difficult to decide. It was simply a matter of protecting the right of private property. Indeed, the case was made a cause célèbre not by its facts or law, but because counsel for Van Zandt, including Ohio's Salmo n P. Chase and New York's William Henry Seward, both Whigs with higher political ambitions and superb legal skills, had argued that Congress lacked the power to enact the Fugitive Slave law. Seward already was and Chase would soon become a United States Senator, and in less than a decade they would help found the Republican Party. In 1864, Chase would become chief justice of the Supreme Court.[59]

Figure 4.3 Cartoon published in 1850 titled "Effects of Fugitive Slave Law." In the antebellum South, the law was praised and its enforcement urged. In the free North it was mocked and decried and its enforcement resisted. Credit: Library of Congress.

A unanimous Court in *Strader* (1851) ruled that the abolitionists who helped a group of slave musicians to escape from their Kentucky owner were liable for damages under Kentucky law. The owner argued and won in a Kentucky court that the three slaves were boarded on a steamer in Louisville and transported without his knowledge to Cincinnati, where they were aided and abetted in their journey to Canada. The defendants' counsel argued that the men were not slaves at all, for they had been sent to perform in Cincinnati Ohio, and the Northwest Ordinance of 1787 banned slavery in states formed from the territory. The Supreme Court decided that it had no jurisdiction in the case (hence could not hear the appeal)–it was a Kentucky case under Kentucky law. Chief Justice Taney: "Every State has an undoubted right to determine the status, or domestic and social condition, of the persons domiciled within its territory; except in so far as the powers of the States in this respect are restrained, or duties and obligations imposed upon them, by the Constitution of the United States. There is nothing in the Constitution of the United States that can in any degree control the law of Kentucky upon this subject." Taney had limned the essential states' rights view of federalism, but did not stop there. He opined "The argument assumes that the six articles which that Ordinance declares to be perpetual are still in force in the States since formed within the Territory, and admitted into the Union. If this proposition could be maintained, it would not alter the question. For the regulation of Congress, under the old Confederation or the present Constitution, for the government of a particular territory, could have no force beyond its limits." Taney did not find that the Northwest Ordinance had been unconstitutional, perhaps because the Ordinance was now moot. Still, the growing expansiveness of his opinions, in particular through the use of dicta, was ominous.[60]

Figure 4.4 Chief Justice Roger Taney of Maryland, 1859, whose tenure was almost as long as Chief Justice John Marshall's and far more controversial. Credit: Library of Congress.

Prigg, *Strader*, and *Van Zandt* did not turn federal courts into agents of the "slaveocracy," whatever outraged abolitionists might claim. Federal officers did not act as de facto slave patrollers scouring the brush for runaways. But federal marshals and commissioners aided and abetted the slave catchers and that compromised federal justice in the eyes of antislavery forces. For example, when Anthony Burns, a nineteen-year-old runaway from Richmond, Virginia, was discovered and detained in Boston, federal marshals and a federal commissioner came under attack from abolitionists. Most cases of runaways were expeditiously dispatched under the Fugitive Slave Act of 1850—the accused did not have a right to counsel and could not compel the attendance of witnesses on his behalf or the production of evidence of his freedom. On this occasion, Richard Henry Dana Jr., one of Boston's leading attorneys, agreed to represent Burns in a hearing before federal commissioner Edward Greeley Loring. No great friend to slavery, Loring thought that he "had no discretion" under the Act but to order the detention of Burns, and Burns did not resist. A mob gathered outside the courthouse jail where he was held and determined to free him by force. In the melee, James Batchelder, deputized by the federal marshal to guard the prisoner, was fatally shot. When city police could not quiet the angry streets, President Franklin Pierce, a proslavery Democrat from New Hampshire, dispatched federal troops to keep order. Predictably, after the rendition hearing, Burns was transported back to his owners and resold. Later ransomed from his current owner, he became a minister in Canada. Loring's reputation suffered irredeemable harm. The newspapers made a feast of the events, southerners concluding that northerners could not be trusted to return runaways. As law, the case had little significance, changing nothing. As news, it was a bombshell, one more proof of the intimate tie between law and politics.[61]

Thus far, slave cases had raised all the political, judicial federalism, and separation-of-powers specters that Madison and the framers had feared when they created a federal courts system. But the courts had skirted the political question by deciding the cases on narrow statutory grounds, sailed safely between conflicting free-state and slave-state laws, and more or less conformed to the dictates of Congress and the presidency. But nothing the courts had done, or could have done, lessened the potential for disorder and disunity that each new slave case posed. The nation was moving west. Would slavery move with it? Could Congress bar slavery from a territory? Taney's obiter dictum in *Strader* had suggested that Congress had the power to bar slavery from a territory before the Constitution was passed, and the Constitution explicitly incorporated the acts of the Confederation, but after the compromises the Constitution had made with slavery, could any territory strip slaveholders of their human chattel when it became a state?

When the terms of California's admission as a free state, the Fugitive Slave Act of 1850, and statehood for Kansas became political issues in the 1850s, the political system could not contain sectional discord. Political parties fractured, old compromises failed, and newly-elected President James Buchanan of Pennsylvania in 1857 faced the prospect of imminent disunion. Some historians agree with William Seward, the Republican senator from New York, who in 1858 called the conflict between slavery and freedom "irrepressible," and Abraham Lincoln of Illinois, who warned in the same year that "a house divided against itself cannot stand."[62]

"The Self-Inflicted Wound": *Dred Scott v. Sanford* (1857)

The slavery jurisprudence of the antebellum federal courts came to a climax with *Dred Scott v. Sandford*. Dred Scott was the slave of U.S. Army doctor John Emerson and traveled with him to army posts in the free state of Illinois and free territory of Minnesota, where he and the doctor were domiciled. At Fort Snelling in the Minnesota Territory, Scott married a slave named Harriett and had children, a marriage to which Emerson consented and which was recorded. In 1843 Emerson returned to a family home in Missouri, a slave state, and Scott went with him. Emerson died in 1846, and Scott sued for freedom for he and his family. After two trials and four years had passed, the Missouri trial court ruled in his favor. The Missouri Supreme Court reversed that decision in 1852. In the midst of the crisis over slavery in the territories, a majority of that court abandoned its own precedents that if a slave was freed in the North, the individual's return to Missouri did not reimpose bondage. Northern personal liberty laws, the response to the Fugitive Slave Act of 1850, angered Missouri slaveholding interests, and the majority opinion of the state's Supreme Court in *Dred Scott* reflected that anger. The court found Scott, his wife, and their two daughters to be slaves.[63]

But Scott's cause had also gained new friends—free soil and abolitionist interests that saw his case raising crucial issues. Because Dr. Emerson's estate had a New York executor, John Sanford, Scott's counsel Roswell Field brought a suit for freedom in federal circuit court under federal diversity jurisdiction. This litigation could only go forward if Scott were deemed a citizen in the federal court. Sitting in St. Louis, District Judge Robert Wells, a native Virginian who moved to Missouri after it gained statehood, allowed counsel to argue the jurisdictional issues. Wells found that "the law is for the plaintiff [Scott]" and permitted the case to go to trial. The jury found Scott a slave in Missouri and therefore diversity did not exist. A slave did not have standing to bring a suit on the basis of diversity of citizenship.[64]

With the circuit court decision a dead end for Scott, his new counsel, Montgomery Blair, one of the founders of the new Republican Party (not to be confused with the party of Jefferson), filed a writ of error from the circuit court to the U.S. Supreme Court. Sanford's defense was conducted by former and future U.S. Senator Reverdy Johnson, a proslavery Democrat from Maryland. The political clout of the opposing counsel signaled the growing importance of the case. Dred Scott's counsel had based the case for his freedom in part on the Northwest Ordinance, and the Constitution had explicitly incorporated the territorial ordinances of the Confederation. The Court could have declined the invitation by citing the political question doctrine (political questions would be left to elected government bodies) established in *Luther v. Borden* (1849), but the case was now so widely discussed and had become so important to the debate over slavery in both North and South, that justices on the Supreme Court felt obliged to take it on. Oral argument in 1856 took four days, and the Court's final ruling was delayed another year, after the presidential election of 1856. It was reported at the time that President-elect Buchanan approached Taney for a "brief chat" before Buchanan took his oath of office. They may have discussed the case, and Buchanan may have urged Taney to settle the matter once and for all.[65]

There was no doubt that newly elected Democratic President Buchanan wanted Bleeding Kansas and the popular sovereignty question resolved. His predecessor, Franklin Pierce, had tried to settle the problem by executive decree, and failed. Congress had not only stumbled over the issue, it had brought the legislative branch to its knees. Buchanan, himself a lawyer, hoped that the federal courts could do what the other two branches had not—settle the question once and for all. *Dred Scott* was thus a test of separation of powers, the relationship of federal and state courts, and the role of courts in the most vexing political issue of the age.[66]

There were three sources of law the Court might draw upon to accommodate Buchanan's desire. The first was the Comity Clause of the Constitution. If northern states could be made to give "full faith and credit" to the "public acts, records, and judicial proceedings" of southern courts as specified in Article IV Section 1 of the federal Constitution, and follow the provisions of Section 2 of that article, requiring the return of persons "held to service or labor" in southern states, perhaps the South would be satisfied. If, in turn, the southern states (as they had before the 1850s), allowed slaves freed in the North to return to the South as free persons, the dispute might be mitigated. Unfortunately, the Comity Clause of the Constitution did not look like a promising place to find a solution against the background of northern states' personal freedom laws—not while "fire-eaters" in the South were opening mail from the North to be certain that it did not contain abolitionist literature.

The next source of law within the traditional jurisprudential role of courts was the interpretation of congressional legislation. Under Section 3 of Article IV, Congress had "the power to dispose of and make all needful rules and regulations respecting the territory or other property belonging to the United States." This power was expressed in the Missouri Compromise in 1820 and the Kansas-Nebraska Act of 1854. The former barred slavery in lands acquired in the Louisiana Purchase north of the 36°30' latitude line. This would have included Kansas. The Kansas-Nebraska Act repealed the Missouri Compromise and gave the settlers of the territory the privilege of deciding whether it would join the Union as a free or slave state. The Court might simply have interpreted these statutes, in effect deferring to Congress, but by 1857, it had become clear that Congress could not compromise the passions the pro-slavery and antislavery forces engendered.

Finally, the Court might find legal grounds to settle the slavery controversy in its own precedents. But in the past the Court had prudently steered away from the sort of sweeping ruling that Buchanan wanted. Still, by basing a ruling solely on these precedents, including the dictum in *Strader*, the Court could have resolved *Dred Scott* without churning slavery law.

While the Court might still have saved its store of public confidence, or at least not exposed itself to the virulent politics of the day, by issuing a narrow ruling, perhaps along the lines that the circuit court trial envisioned, division over slavery on the Court had come to mirror divisions in the nation. Facing the prospect of a wide-ranging antislavery opinion by Justice McLean, Chief Justice Taney expanded his own opinion. As Justice Charles Evans Hughes later wrote, Taney's opinion in the case was a "self-inflicted wound." Its contents were not binding precedent, for only Justice Daniel signed on to it, but by not deferring to the elective branches and seeking to settle the slavery issue once and for all, Taney put the Court in the center of the most divisive issue in national politics.[67]

Joined by six of the other justices, Taney ruled that the Missouri supreme court and the lower federal court were correct—under Missouri law Scott had no case and Missouri law disposed of the suit. Nor should the case have come to the federal courts, for Scott was not a citizen. The law behind this decision was clear, and it was enough to resolve the case. But Taney was not done. He added two dicta, readings of history and law that were not necessary to resolve the case (and were not subscribed to by the other six justices), but would, if followed, have imposed on all African Americans a species of civil servitude.

Taney wrote that no person of African descent brought to America to labor could ever be a citizen of the United States. They might be citizens of particular states, but this did not confer national citizenship on them, for "they were not intended to be included, under the word 'citizens' in the Constitution, and can therefore claim none of the rights and privileges which that instrument provides for and secures to citizens on the United States." Adding gratuitous insult to injury, Taney continued, blacks "had for more than a century before [the drafting of the federal Constitution] been regarded as beings of an lower order, and altogether unfit to associate with the white race, either in social or political relations; and so far lower that they had no rights which the white man was bound to respect."[68]

Taney had not finished. In a second dictum he opined that the Fifth Amendment to the Constitution, guaranteeing that no man's property might be taken without due process of law, barred Congress from denying slavery expansion into the territories. Although Article IV, Section 3 of the Constitution had explicitly given to Congress full and untrammeled authority to set laws and regulations for the territories, it could not rule out slavery because the Fifth Amendment was added to the Constitution after ratification, and it must be read to modify Congress's powers over the territories. In effect, Taney retroactively declared the Missouri Compromise of 1820 unconstitutional.

What might Taney have written? Justice John Catron, whose circuit duties included Missouri, was not present at the circuit court when it heard the case. (By the 1850s the justices were slacking off on their circuit duties.). From his opinion in a Supreme Court case, one can see how he would have reasoned had he been present at the circuit court. "The defendant [Sanford] pleaded to the jurisdiction of the Circuit Court, that the plaintiff was a negro of African blood; the descendant of Africans, who had been imported and sold in this country as slaves, and thus had no capacity as a citizen of Missouri to maintain a suit in the Circuit Court. The court sustained a demurrer to this plea, and a trial was had upon the pleas, of the general issue [that is, the facts], and also that the plaintiff and his family were slaves, belonging to the defendant. In this trial, a verdict was given for the defendant." For Catron, the only question the federal circuit court, a trial court, had to determine was whether Dred Scott was a slave in Missouri, under Missouri law. The trial found it so. "The judgment of the Circuit Court upon the plea in abatement is not open, in my opinion, to examination in this court [i.e., the U.S. Supreme Court] upon the plaintiff's writ." He sensed, rightly, that Taney's revised opinion, which he had read before filing his own and to which he did not wholly subscribe, was a time bomb with a short fuse.[69]

Catron's more cautious opinion might have saved the Court from controversy, for without the majority of the Court on board, Taney's dicta were not constitutional law, and he had put his court and all the federal courts in the position of defending slavery. More so than the acts of Congress, the decree of the highest court in the federal system dictated outcomes in the lower courts. This is called the rule of recognition, and Taney's Court had removed all wiggle room that federal judges might have in protecting those who helped runaway slaves or protecting free persons of color accused of being runaway slaves or protecting state personal liberty laws.

The Penumbras of *Dred Scott*

Had it not poked a stick into a nest of snakes, Taney's opinion should have quieted the contest between free states' courts and federal courts over slavery, itself a threat to judicial federalism. Instead, as *Ableman v. Booth* (1859) proved, nothing was resolved by Taney's attempt at judicial statesmanship. Inadvertently he had opened the door to the very state-federal conflict that he wanted to keep out of the courts. Wisconsin had become a state in 1848 and, after 1856, was a bastion of the new Republican Party. Even its Democratic Party, though split into factions, had by 1856 agreed that slavery had no place in the state. Wisconsin enacted some of the strongest personal liberty laws in the country. At the same time, the new federal district judge in Wisconsin, Andrew Miller, was a Polk Democrat and not a Free Soiler. As events would prove, the relation between the federal courts and the state courts was a microcosm of the nation's dilemma: slavery the worm in the bud of federalism.[70]

The test of that relationship began in 1854 when abolitionist editor Sherman Booth was arrested for violating the Fugitive Slave Act of 1850. He had abetted the rescue of a runaway Missouri slave, Joshua Glover, from U.S. Marshal Stephen Ableman. Booth led an antislavery mob that broke into the Milwaukee jail where Ableman had confined Glover, and Booth freed him. Booth then sought a writ of habeas corpus from a Wisconsin state judge to remove the case from Miller's federal court to the state court. The Wisconsin judge granted the writ, ordering Booth released from federal custody, ruling in effect that state law was supreme in the matter, though a federal law had been allegedly violated. Ableman appealed to the state supreme court, which affirmed Booth's release.[71]

The Wisconsin Supreme Court refused to recognize the authority of a federal judge. Thought by the governor who appointed him to be "a good states' rights man," Vermont-born Chief Justice Luther Dixon, however, had by this time become a Republican. He opined: "The only question that is or can be made on the entering and conforming to these mandates is: Does the constitution of the United States confer on congress the power to provide by law for an appeal from the courts of the several states to the supreme court of the United States, and to authorize that court in the exercise of its appellate jurisdiction, to review and reverse the judgments of the state courts in the cases specified in the 25th section of the judiciary act approved the 24th of September, 1789?" Dixon understood that the case was an important one and the underlying question required careful analysis. "I have been over it again and again, and that to the utmost of my ability, and with a solicitude becoming the position I occupy, and which I never before experienced, I have studied and considered every argument, for and against, within my reach." At the same time as he pronounced judgment on himself, Dixon knew that he was flying in the face of a federal law and grounded his view on the Constitution and the Judiciary Act of 1789. In these, he found "that the framers of the constitution contemplated that cases within the cognizance of the courts of the United States, would arise in the state courts in the course of their ordinary jurisdiction; and that the state courts would and must incidentally take cognizance of and decide cases arising under the constitution, laws and treaties of the United States." Within this body of cases, "that there would be a very large class of cases under the first and most important clause of the section which could never be reached by the federal courts, either by virtue of their original or appellate jurisdiction." *Ableman* was such a case for him.[72]

The marshal then appealed to the U.S. Supreme Court, which held, in a unanimous opinion by Taney, that the Wisconsin Supreme Court had wrongly asserted the supremacy of state courts over federal courts. In cases arising under the Constitution and laws of the United States, Taney wrote, "the State Court . . . claimed and exercised jurisdiction over the proceedings and judgment of a District Court of the United States . . . has set aside and annulled its judgment, and discharged a prisoner who had been tried and found guilty of an offence against the laws of the United States . . . And it further appears that the State court have not only claimed and exercised this jurisdiction, but have also determined that their decision is final and conclusive upon all the courts of the United States." Taney was not a states' rights advocate along the lines of a John C. Calhoun, at least not on this occasion. "Although the State of Wisconsin is sovereign within its territorial limits to a certain extent, yet that sovereignty is limited and restricted by the Constitution of the United States . . . And the sphere of action appropriated to the United States is as far beyond the reach of the judicial process issued by a State judge or a State court, as if the line of division was traced by landmarks and monuments visible to the eye."[73]

In the same year as *Ableman* asserted federal courts' supremacy over state courts when Congress had imposed criminal penalties for some act, the trial of John Brown for treason against the state of Virginia showed that state courts could take cases properly belonging to federal courts without a whimper of protest by federal authorities. On October 18, 1859, Brown and his small band of radical abolitionists attacked a federal arsenal at Harpers Ferry. After a short siege, a wounded Brown and four of his followers were captured by a federal force under the command of Colonel Robert E. Lee. Brown's actions were as clear a violation of the federal Crimes Act of 1790 as one could imagine— occurring in a federal facility and involving the destruction of federal property. Even if the charge of treason did not apply (Brown was not waging war against the United States nor aiding its enemies in time of war), the Assimilative Crimes Act of 1825 provided that federal courts could apply state criminal law when no federal law applied to criminal acts committed on federal property. Though the Western District of Virginia federal court was sitting a mere twenty-five miles away, the U.S. attorney for the western district of Virginia did not ask District Judge John White Brockenbrough to issue an order to remove Brown from state custody, which Lee and his (federal) troops had consigned Brown, nor did the judge send his marshal to arrest Brown for trial in a federal court.[74]

At the state trial, the charge was not the federal offense, but treason against Virginia, inciting slaves to rebellion, and murder. A grand jury found true bills on all three counts. The trial began on October 25 and continued for a little over a week. Brown pled not guilty to the treason charge. The state's counsel explained why the outcome of the trial was so important to Virginia (and by proxy, the slave South). Brown had "come into the bosom of the Commonwealth with the deadly purpose of applying the torch to our buildings and shedding the blood of our citizens . . . manumit our slaves, confiscate the property of slaveholders, and . . . make it another Haiti. Such an idea is too abhorrent to pursue." The prosecution's case rested entirely on the state's law.

Could Virginia prosecute for treason against the state or had the Constitution and the Federal Crimes Act of 1790 preempted state action on this offense? According to William Rawle's *A View of the Constitution* (1825), "The United States therefore justly reserved to itself the right to punish this offense [of treason]," and the states have "abstained from intermeddling with prosecutions of it." But Rawle was long dead, and with him were interred the lessons of the Whiskey Rebellion. Virginia hanged Brown.[75]

The *Dred Scott* case and the John Brown raid and trial polarized the national debate over slavery, and sectional discord bent federal jurisdiction back and forth like a loblolly pine in a high wind. To save the courts from the storm, Congress might have taken away from the lower federal courts (and the Supreme Court's appellate jurisdiction) all matters concerning slavery. One could argue that Article III provided a basis for this step. Congress had entire control over what is today called "stripping" of jurisdiction. Congress might, for example, strip diversity jurisdiction from the federal courts or even deny to the Supreme Court the authority to hear appeals from the state courts.

In fact, when Lincoln debated Stephen Douglas during the 1858 U.S. Senate campaign in Illinois, he hinted that the Supreme Court's *Dred Scott* decision should not be the last word on slavery's expansion into formerly free territories or states. Later, in the midst of mild and conciliatory gestures to the secessionists during his first inaugural address, he warned:

> I do not forget the position assumed by some that constitutional questions are to be decided by the Supreme Court, nor do I deny that such decisions must be binding in any case upon the parties to a suit as to the object of that suit, while they are also entitled to very high respect

and consideration in all parallel cases by all other departments of the Government. And while it is obviously possible that such decision may be erroneous in any given case . . . At the same time, the candid citizen must confess that if the policy of the Government upon vital questions affecting the whole people is to be irrevocably fixed by decisions of the Supreme Court, the instant they are made in ordinary litigation between parties in personal actions the people will have ceased to be their own rulers, having to that extent practically resigned their Government into the hands of that eminent tribunal.[76]

When Lincoln won election to the presidency in 1860, the South Carolina legislature called for a special convention to decide whether the state would depart the federal Union. The delegates agreed that the victorious Republicans in Washington, D.C. posed a grave threat to the future of slavery. By excluding slavery from the western territories, limiting the internal slave trade, and otherwise hindering the legal rights of slave owners, Republican majorities in Congress and a Republican president might undermine the very foundations of the state's wealth and its social system. The unanimous decision of that convention to secede, followed in rapid succession by secession conventions in Georgia, Alabama, Mississippi, Louisiana, and Florida, and Texas, posed a devastating threat to the Union's survival and, with it, the entire federal courts system. By the end of April, 1861, Tennessee, Virginia, North Carolina, and Arkansas had joined what Confederate lawyers called the Confederate States of America.[77]

PART II

COURTS AND THE FOUNDING OF MODERN AMERICA, 1861–1929

The survival test of the Confederacy was the Civil War, and the Union prevailed. Although federal military efforts were not at first directed to ending slavery, early on in the war Union Army commanders regarded slaves as contraband of war and refused to return them to their masters. This doctrine, somewhat altered, became the basis for Lincoln's Emancipation Proclamation of January 1, 1863, freeing all slaves in Confederate-held lands. Three amendments to the Constitution followed the defeat of the Confederacy, ending slavery, defining citizenship as national rather than based on residency in a state, requiring states to provide equal protection and due process for all American citizens, and finally denying to any state the authority to restrict the franchise on the basis of race. Reconstruction was a great experiment in legal reformation of a nation torn apart by slavery, but the war had not destroyed racism in the North or in the South, and Reconstruction would not achieve its legal aims until nearly another century had passed.[1]

Once again the federal courts stood at the center of the maelstrom. Civil rights acts and enforcement acts made federal courts the front line of Reconstruction reform in the South. That initiative would largely fail, but so important were the federal courts to the revival of commerce and land speculation, that even as the Reconstruction experiment in civil rights adjudication stumbled, the business of the federal courts in the South and the North reached new heights.

Whatever its flaws, internal contradictions, and partisanships, Reconstruction constitutionalism projected a vision of equality before the law. With the violent end of that experiment on the dark and bloody ground of "redemption," federal judges were in one sense liberated from the burden of imposing equality on a society not ready for it. But judging is never performed in a vacuum, and judges bring to court their own experience, a mix of past presumption and present perception. What then if the past world of the life-tenured judge is so out of tune with the present world in which he finds himself, that all the rules that govern the world seem to him up for grabs? If that happens, a yawning gulf opens between the unelected, life-tenured bench and an elected Congress and presidency, leaving judges at the not-so-tender mercies of public outcry and dismay. Poised at times at its brink in the period from 1861 to 1929, the federal judiciary did not tumble into this chasm. Not always, and not perfectly, it changed with the times. That is the story we tell in Part II.[2]

The great challenge for the federal judiciary in this period was to keep pace with a nation and a world that was changing faster and more profoundly than anyone expected. The United States concluded the Indian Wars that had defined the nation's existence since its founding and triumphed in the Spanish-American War and the first of two world wars. It went from an overwhelmingly rural emerging nation to a largely urban superpower. Towering smokestacks of steel factories and mountains of coal slag appeared in the midst of a landscape of farms and shops. New technologies knitted a loosely affiliated federation of regions into a national economy centered on production and consumption. The shift to an automobile-centered way of life was in full swing as the first of the great suburban sprawls reached from Boston to Washington, D.C. in the East, in a great spider web from Chicago to the surrounding plains, and from San Diego to San Francisco in the West. The economics of scale had become the byword of the economy, replacing domestic self-sufficiency. In oak-paneled and electrically lit boardrooms, boards of directors of corporations wielded enormous power on a scale and scope undreamed of before the Civil War.[3]

The technologies that made these changes possible carried with them unforeseen consequences. The massive, irreversible demographic shift from rural and small town to city and suburb fashioned an increasingly impersonal, modernist way of life, along with both anxiety and innovation in social and cultural forms. The slower horse-and-buggy days of the telegraph, the country store, and a self-satisfied faith in individualism and opportunity much romanticized in the mythology of yeoman republicanism were fast disappearing. The family grew smaller and more child-centered. A new realism in art, literature, and architecture, followed by the rise of modernist abstract art, challenged classical themes and values. Feminism fostered the image of the "new woman": educated, career seeking, and liberated from constraining courting rituals.[4]

Aiding in the transformation of judicial thought to keep pace with these changes in culture and society was a new way of thinking about the law. In the first decades of the twentieth century, at Harvard, Yale, Columbia, and Penn, law school teaching was shifting from "classical formalism" to "legal realism." Formalism assumed that law was a "closed" logical system in which judges could deduce the right answers and apply them to cases. The new jurisprudence tutored the next generation of judges to the study of law as practiced, to gathering and analyzing social science data, and, for some, to reform. The American Law Institute, founded by a group of law professors, lawyers, and judges ostensibly to bring order and uniformity to rapidly evolving law, churned out model codes and *Restatements* of the laws of agency, contracts, torts, and conflict of laws. These, under the prodding of Penn's Law School dean William Draper Lewis, gently but firmly urged change on courts and legislatures.[5]

The structure of the federal courts system was profoundly altered in this period. A layer of dedicated courts of appeal was added between the district trial courts and the Supreme Court, and Supreme Court justices' circuit riding ended. The creation of a conference of senior (chief judges in modern parlance) circuit judges promoted uniformity and efficiency in the courts. That effort continued throughout the century, in later years giving the federal courts a standard set of rules for civil and criminal procedure.

None of the efforts to modernize the federal courts could shield them from the winds of partisanship. Indeed, because the courts handled the hot-button public issues of the day—taxation, corporate finance, segregation, First Amendment claims, and labor relations, to name a few—it would have been impossible to avoid political scrutiny. What was more,

presidents and their parties continued to examine the political credentials of nominees to ensure that they were not antagonistic to party aims.
Insofar as the judiciary was part of the government, public scrutiny was
not in itself a bad idea, but it raised untoward and unwanted questions
from both left- and right-wing partisans about the impartiality of federal
courts.

5

The Courts in Crisis Times, 1861–1876

In the period 1861–1876, the years of Civil War and Reconstruction, the Madisonian Compromise faced its greatest peril. Not the first line of defense of the Union, the courts nevertheless had to determine the lawfulness of wartime congressional acts and presidential decrees. At stake was the separation-of-powers system the framers had embedded in the Constitution. The threat to the relation of federal to state courts in federalism was even more obvious, as the states of the Confederacy replaced the federal courts with Confederate tribunals. Insofar as secession was a political and a legal stand, no worse example of the impact of political conflict on the federal courts can be found. After the war, charged with enforcement of new kinds of statutory regulations arising from a new concept of federalism and with the interpretation of three amendments to the Constitution, the courts faced a new set of challenges to the Madisonian Compromise.

Abraham Lincoln, an experienced and able lawyer, understood the crisis's legal ramifications. His first inaugural address explained: "I take the official oath to-day with no mental reservations and with no purpose to construe the Constitution or laws by any hypercritical rules; and while I do not choose now to specify particular acts of Congress as proper to be enforced, I do suggest that it will be much safer for all, both in official and private stations, to conform to and abide by all those acts." Secession he held to be a violation of the "perpetual" Union the Constitution fashioned, to which the southern states had agreed by ratification or by petition for admission to the Union. "In your hands, my dissatisfied fellow-countrymen, and not in mine, is the momentous issue of civil war. The Government will not assail you. You can have no conflict without being yourselves the aggressors. You have no oath registered in heaven to destroy the Government, while I shall have the most solemn one to 'preserve, protect, and defend it.'" An assault on federal lands, arsenals, and the mails, however, were federal crimes, and Lincoln warned anyone who undertook them that the federal courts were still open.[1]

Even after hostilities erupted, Lincoln sought a swift resumption of peacetime legalities. Central to this project was the continuous operation of federal courts in the seceding territory. When the Confederacy was formed, federal courts only functioned in a handful of coastal enclaves occupied by Union troops, and all but two of the southern district judges resigned their commissions. As a matter of jurisprudence, however, the federal courts in the South never closed. They simply did not hold sessions during the conflict. When the Confederacy collapsed in 1865, all the decisions of its courts came into question. In a series of cases, the federal courts accepted the private law determinations of Confederate courts but not the public law or the legislation of the Confederacy or the Confederate states. In effect, when the federal courts resumed operation in the defeated Confederacy, they acted as if the Confederates had never left the Union.[2]

Like their handling of Confederate private lawsuits after the war, throughout the crisis federal courts upheld the ideal and the practice of rule of law. Rebel prize captains and blockade runners were tried not in special or military courts but in regular circuit courts. The defendants had able legal counsel. So, too, confiscations of rebel property were not summarily processed but at hearings held in the U.S. Court of Claims. Indeed, the entire confiscation effort was marked by "an agonized, intractable, ideological impasse," in which "relatively little property was actually confiscated." The Treason Act of 1862, which literally applied would have led to the trial and conviction of the entire rebel officer corps, was not enforced, a lenience almost unparalleled in history. Facing the violence of an unreconstructed white South, federal courts still heard and enforced the Civil Rights and Enforcement Acts.[3]

In the closing years of the war and for the next decade, the majority in Congress led an experiment in equal protection of the law for the former slaves. Three amendments to the Constitution and a series of Civil Rights and Enforcement Acts defined this commitment. This experiment, called Reconstruction, involved the federal courts in a myriad of ways because at the heart of Reconstruction lay the ideal that civil rights and civil liberties that belonged to all Americans would be enforced in federal courts.

The Courts and Civil War

The first, and as events were to prove, the most controversial tests of wartime federal law came as the war was just beginning. By the end of May 1861, federal judges in commission for Alabama (William G. Jones); Arkansas (Daniel Ringo); Florida (McQueen McIntosh); Georgia (John C. Nicoll); Louisiana (Theodore McCaleb and Henry Boyce); Mississippi (Samuel J. Gholson); North Carolina (Asa Biggs); South Carolina (Andrew McGrath); and Virginia (James

Halyburton and John Brockenbrough) resigned. Anticipating Kentucky's seces-sion (despite the Unionist sentiment of many of its political leaders) and expect-ing that Confederate military operations would carve the state from the Union, Thomas Monroe stepped down from the federal bench there. The exception was John Watrous of Texas, who had held the post from 1847 but could not hold court during the war. [4]

Brockenbrough's case was typical. Born in Hanover County, he practiced law in Lexington in the Shenandoah Valley of Virginia. A lifelong Democrat, he resigned his federal post in May 1861 to serve as the judge of the Confederate dis-trict court and represent the district in the Confederate Congress. Unpunished for his adherence to rebellion against the United States, Brockenbrough went on to found the law school at Washington and Lee University. He died in 1877, honored by his students and the legal community of western Virginia. [5]

The motives behind the actions of federal judges like Brockenbrough are not hard to find. John A. Campbell of Alabama resigned his Supreme Court seat with some reluctance and hoped for "peace, peace, peace" between the "two confederacies." South Carolina Judge Andrew G. McGrath was less conciliatory. The day after Lincoln's election, McGrath announced in open court:

> Feeling an assurance of what will be the action of the State, I consider it my duty, without delay, to prepare to obey its wishes. That prepara-tion is made by the resignation of the office I have held. For the last time I have, as a Judge of the United States, administered the laws of the United States, within the limits of the State of South Carolina. While thus acting in obedience to a sense of duty, I cannot be indifferent to the emotions it must produce. That department of Government which, I believe, has best maintained its integrity and preserved its purity, has been suspended

He was the secretary of the South Carolina secession convention, served briefly as a Confederate district court judge, and succeeded Francis Pickens as South Carolina governor during the last year of the Confederacy. [6]

North Carolina Judge Asa Biggs explained why he resigned after North Carolina joined the Confederacy. He had served his country in Congress and in its courts, but his attachment to his state outweighed oath, office, and nation.

> Whenever any State in her Sovereign capacity (and I mean by that, the people of a State duly and legally assembled in a convention by the proper authority, with the same formalities and regularity as con-ventions were held to ratify and adopt the Constitution of the United States originally) shall solemnly so decide she has the right for sufficient

cause (of which she must be the judge, as upon her alone rests the heavy responsibility for such a fearful act) to voluntarily and peaceably secede from the Union, which she voluntarily entered: and thereupon, a citizen of such State is absolved from his allegiance to the United States.[7]

It was an awesome question, and Biggs hoped, in the closing days of peace, that no judge would have to render an opinion on it, but secession and war came. Biggs wrote to President Lincoln, "Sir:—I hereby resign my office of District Judge of the United States for the District of North Carolina, being unwilling longer to hold a commission in a Government which has degenerated into a military despotism. I subscribe myself yet a friend of constitutional liberty." Like Brockenbrough, Biggs would accept an appointment as a Confederate district court judge, and after the fall of the Confederacy continued in private practice until his death in 1878.[8]

Figure 5.1 Judge Asa Biggs of North Carolina. Former U.S. Representative and senator, he resigned his commission as federal judge with the coming of secession. Credit: Library of Congress.

Northern federal judges took a different view of secession. As Judge David A. Smalley told a Vermont grand jury on January 14, 1861: "persons owing allegiance to the United States have confederated together, and with arms, by force and intimidation" had violated the 1790 law against treason. Such "outrageous acts" could not be justified under state law, even were the state still in the Union. In the unlikely event that any of the Confederates should appear in the vicinity of Vermont, they were to be apprehended and indicted.[9]

The closer to the scenes of war, the more disruptive to the federal courts the fighting was. In the District Court for the Eastern District of Missouri, for example, Judge Samuel Treat, a Democrat and Pierce nominee, "stood solidly with the Union" despite the threats posed by local Confederate militias. Treat was a Harvard College and Harvard Law School graduate and owed his place more to his birthright (Pierce's own New Hampshire) than to any "Doughface" sentiments he might have harbored. A strong believer in due process when the federal courts were open, Treat bristled when the army would not release a suspected Confederate sympathizer after Treat had issued habeas corpus for the prisoner, but his loyalty to the Union was never suspect. Treat published his views in an 1863 St. Louis newspaper editorial: "the pernicious heresies of nullification and secession, which have at length ripened into treason and rebellion, have always found in me an unyielding opponent." In the circuit court that met in St. Louis, in July 1861, Treat heard Supreme Court Justice John Catron instruct the grand jury that "giving aid to the confederate cause constituted a treasonable offense." For his own part, though a states' rights Democrat and a well-regarded Nashville resident, Catron remained loyal to the Union. Though threatened with death by Confederate vigilantes, he continued to ride circuit in Kentucky and Missouri during the war.[10]

Federal courts in the Eastern District of Missouri—a cockpit of guerilla warfare, recruiting for the Confederate Army, and spying—were virtually shuttered in 1861, recording but one civil case and no criminal cases, by the next year 204 civil cases were begun or continued, a total (averaging the two years) that was roughly comparable to the yearly dockets for the rest of the war. Although military provost marshals arrested suspects and only answered to the district military commanders rather than the federal judges, regular criminal proceedings resumed against those suspected of conspiring against the federal government as well as those who did not pay taxes, hijacked postage stamps, and committed other less mundane offenses. In 1862 there were thirty prosecutions, in 1863, fifty-eight prosecutions, in 1864, seventy-five prosecutions and 1865, thirty-six prosecutions. These were based on grand jury indictments, though not all went to trial as the defendants disappeared into "the bush."[11]

While Vermont seemed free of the virus of treason and Missouri grand juries indicted rebel conspirators, Maryland remained a hotbed of Confederate sympathizers. The most serious test of the rule of law in that state's federal courts began with a military arrest, continued with a war of words between Chief Justice Taney and newly elected President Lincoln, and ended quietly in a federal circuit court. Lincoln moved swiftly against supporters of secession in areas under federal control. On April 27, 1861, he gave to military officers the authority to arrest individuals supporting secession by word or deed, in effect suspending the right of habeas corpus. In Maryland, pro-Confederate mobs had rioted and pro-South political leaders were drilling antigovernment militias. One ringleader was Maryland assemblyman John Merryman, a terrorist who had helped destroy bridges to prevent the movement of federal troops south. He was arrested by military order and held without bail for a military tribunal. Merryman's counsel sped to Washington seeking a habeas corpus writ from the member of the Court who rode circuit in Maryland—none other than Chief Justice Taney. The irony of a Confederate conspirator asking for federal relief was apparently lost on Merryman's important friends, including Taney, who traveled to Baltimore to secure his release. The ordinary procedure would have been to order the federal marshal to serve the writ on Merryman's custodians, presumably General George Cadwalader, commander of the federal troops in the city. Eventually the marshal of the circuit court did serve the writ, to no avail. For Lincoln had already suspended the operation of the writ in Maryland, as District Judge William Giles had learned on May 2 when a father sought that relief to undo his son's enlistment. This set the stage for the first of a series of confrontations between the Democratic incumbents on the federal bench and the new Republican president and his congressional majority.[12]

Though frail and often absent from the Court because of illness, Taney had lost none of his intellectual ability. While he traveled to Baltimore as the chief justice, once there he could only speak as a circuit court judge. Thus his opinion on the matter did not have the weight of a U.S. Supreme Court decision. Nevertheless, he wrote as if it were: "The application in this case for a writ of habeas corpus is made to me under the 14th section of the judiciary act of 1789 which renders effectual for the citizen the constitutional privilege of the writ of habeas corpus. That act gives to the courts of the United States, as well as to each justice of the supreme court, and to every district judge, power to grant writs of habeas corpus for the purpose of an inquiry into the cause of commitment." This question was settled as early as Ex Parte Bollman (1807), the precursor to Aaron Burr's trial for treason. Taney continued, "The petition was presented to me, at Washington, under the impression that I would order the prisoner to be brought before me there, but as he was confined in Fort McHenry, in the city of Baltimore, which is in my circuit, I resolved to hear it in the latter city."[13]

On the spot (the written opinion appeared three days later, on June 1) he declared that the president had no power to suspend the writ or authorize others to ignore it; the military had no authority to supplant the normal course of justice or to disobey the courts in an area not in active rebellion; and Union officers could not arrest anyone except army personnel. The Constitution provided that the writ might be suspended in time of "rebellion or invasion," when "the public safety might require it," Taney allowed, but this provision appeared in Article I, under the powers of Congress, not in Article II enumerating the powers of the president. Taney issued the writ.[14]

Maryland teetered on rebellion. Martial law kept the Confederate sympathizers in check. Would release on habeas corpus allow other Merrymans to agitate against the very civil power that protected their legal rights? Would acceptance of the writ become precedent on other circuits? The latter possibility was not only part of Taney's thinking (one reason why he signed his opinion as the chief justice rather as the circuit justice), and his action would influence at least two other federal judges in similar cases. In any case, his opinion in *Merryman* became the occasion for southern defenders to claim that Lincoln was a tyrant who flouted the Constitution and the federal courts.[15]

Taney defended the rule of law and the powers of the federal courts, but he understood, if he did not sympathize with, Lincoln's plight. Taney had taken an oath to preserve and defend the Constitution, but to him and to Lincoln that oath had different implications. Even had they not come from opposite sides of the political world, a justice of the Supreme Court and the commander in chief of federal forces had different duties. Perhaps Taney was reminded of Justice Henry Brockholst Livingston's opinion in another treason case, *U.S. v. Hoxie* (1808): "As judges, we are not sent here merely to preside at trials, to preserve order, and to regulate the form of proceeding. We have a much higher and more important trust committed to us: it is our right and our duty to expound the law." Faced with conspiracy in the border states and active rebellion in the Confederate states, Lincoln could not rely on civil process. He did not ask the Maryland U.S. attorney to seek an indictment of Merryman for treason. In prior cases the Whiskey rebels and John Fries were convicted of treason by federal circuit court juries for doing pretty much what Merryman had done. The practical problem in prosecuting Merryman for treason was that a Baltimore grand jury might not indict or a trial jury convict, particularly when the trial was conducted by the Supreme Court justice riding that circuit—again Taney. By contrast, the trials of the Whiskey rebels in the 1790s were held in Philadelphia, far from the scene of their activities around Pittsburgh. Merryman's case never went to trial.[16]

Washington, D.C., though filled with federal troops, was not immune to suspicions of pro-Confederate sympathy—even among the judiciary. While upholding the rule of law in the face of stern executive admonishments was not necessarily pro-Confederate, it did lead to suspicion. In October 1861, Judge William Merrick issued a writ of habeas corpus to remove one prisoner from military custody, but the provost marshal arrested the lawyer carrying the writ. Merrick was a Franklin Pierce appointee, and not much loved by some of the Republicans, but his action was entirely proper. The circuit court found the provost marshal in contempt of court, but the court's marshal would not deliver the contempt citation to his military counterpart. The stalemate ended when the Republican majority in Congress abolished the circuit court and created a new Supreme Court for the district. The new court was both a local and a federal court, replicating the many faces of the district's "circuit, district, and criminal courts. None of the judges who had held the provost marshal in contempt were returned to the bench."[17]

Taney refused to resign, going about the capital city "bent by the weight of years, his thin, nervous, and deeply furrowed face . . . gave him a weird, wizard like expression." The oldest of the Court's members at eighty-seven, he was only a little more feeble than some of his fellow justices, but no one wanted to retire, least of all Taney. "For the last two or three years [he] on account of falling health, took very little part in public affairs; and he was by many suspected of leaning strongly in his sympathies toward the Southern side of the great issues which divide the nation." The day after he died, Maryland adopted a new constitution barring slavery. Lincoln and Secretary of State William Seward, long Taney's political adversaries, nevertheless visited with Taney's two daughters at the Taney residence. In a break with tradition, however, Congress at first refused to appropriate funds for a bust of the chief justice for the capitol. Senator Charles Sumner, one of the strongest opponents of slavery, opined that Taney's name and reputation would be "hooted down the page of history." Taney's longtime friend, Maryland Senator Reverdy Johnson, replied that Taney's reputation as a "learned jurist" would, in the fullness of time, exceed Sumner's.[18]

Congress Acts, the Courts Follow

Suspension of the writ of habeas corpus in time of war was not untoward—that is why the Constitution provided for it. Wartime exigencies in combat areas might require the detention of dangerous individuals. Taney cited Congress as the only branch of the federal government that could suspend the right to habeas corpus. That too was a correct reading of the Constitution. (Of course a court could refuse to issue the writ even when it remained on option.) Congress, devoid of the departing southern Democrats, was a largely Republican body when called into special session by Lincoln in the summer of 1861. Lincoln reported his controversy with Taney, leaving to Congress the matter. He suspended the writ by executive proclamation in September 1862 after the battle of Antietam. Congress belatedly authorized suspension of the writ the next year.[19]

Meanwhile, in a series of loyalty oath and confiscation enactments, the wartime Congress attempted to define the scope of and impose punishment for the rebellion, enforcement for which was divided between the provost marshals and the federal courts. The first of the oath acts was the July 2, 1862, so-called Test or Ironclad Oath: "every person elected or appointed to any office . . . under the Government of the United States . . . excepting the President of the United States" was to swear or affirm that they had never previously engaged in criminal or disloyal conduct. Those government employees who failed to take the 1862 Test Oath would not receive a salary; those who swore falsely would be prosecuted for perjury and forever denied federal employment.[20]

Congress passed two confiscation acts. The first in 1861 gave to federal authorities, in practical terms the armed forces, the right to seize the property of anyone in rebellion against the United States. It applied everywhere in the country, including territory claimed by the Confederacy. Steamboats carrying cotton on the South's waterways were fair game, even if it was not clear whether the consignment and the crew were part of the Confederate war effort. Slaves working on Confederate military installations were also fair game. Slaves who escaped and went to Union Army camps were not included in the law but were not returned to their masters under the international law of "contraband." The Act was signed into law by President Lincoln on August 6, 1861. Under Section 2, "such prizes and capture shall be condemned in the district or circuit court of the United States having jurisdiction of the amount, or in admiralty in any district in which the same may be seized, or into which they may be taken and proceedings first instituted."[21]

Figure 5.2 Cotton shipments from southern ports to New York continued during the Civil War, sometimes in violation of the Confiscation Acts. Sketch of cotton at the port of Savannah. W. T. Crane, *Frank Leslie's Illustrated Newspaper*, 1865.

A second Confiscation Act passed on July 17, 1862. It defined the crime of treason in no uncertain terms. "That every person who shall hereafter commit the crime of treason against the United States, and shall be adjudged guilty thereof, shall suffer death, and all his slaves, if any, shall be declared and made free; or, at the discretion of the court, he shall be imprisoned for not less than five years and fined not less than ten thousand dollars, and all his slaves, if any, shall be declared and made free." The alternative sentencing provision reflected the realities of secession—Lincoln's courts were not going to condemn every Confederate soldier to death.[22]

The new statutes added many cases to the criminal side of the district court dockets, but the increased caseload was not matched by an increase in judicial personnel. Instead, additional burdens were laid on members of the executive branch. The attorney general assumed the task of supervising the Confiscation Acts. The secretary of the treasury took charge of violations of the Non-Intercourse Act of July 13, 1861, banning trade with persons and companies in the seceding states, as amended and enlarged on May 20, 1862.[23]

Every departing ship from a northern port was watched if it was suspected that its cargo was intended for a Confederate port. When the George Darby was loading in the port of New York, for example, its cargo raised suspicion. "The government detectives, who sedulously supervised in secret the outfitting of the vessel in this port, and watched every step in her preparation, were obviously cautioned that she could not be interfered with whilst moored in the harbor, and waited until she cast off from her dock to arrest her in the act of violating the law 'in proceeding' from this port to Beaufort [S.C.]. The arrest of the vessel was virtually concomitant with her casting off from her moorings, as the seizing officers went immediately on board her." While army officials simply confiscated and sold at auction some of the property seized under the acts, owners and merchants could take their claims for restitution to the federal courts, and sometimes won.[24]

Section 5 of the July 1861 Act barred all commercial intercourse between inhabitants of the Confederate states and the rest of the Union. Goods and merchandise, together with the vessels or vehicles conveying such goods, coming from the Confederate states to the Union or going in the reverse direction were forfeited to the federal government. The effect of this statute meant that some diversity suits in federal courts involving commercial transactions, for example the delivery of goods, or the non-payment for the delivery of goods, by a party in one of the Confederate states against a party in the Union were effectively barred as well. The Acts seemed to expand the jurisdiction of the federal courts, giving them the task of determining what was and was not commerce with the enemy, hence what was and was not forfeit. Section 5, however, stripped them of diversity jurisdiction in normal suits at law, for example in life insurance cases where northern insurers refused to pay benefits to southern widows. After the war, the resumption or the commencement of these suits contributed to the swelling dockets of the federal courts.[25]

While federal agents' findings could be appealed to the federal courts, not every appeal succeeded. The facts in *U.S. v. 129 Packages* (1862) were typical of these cases. The claimant, desiring to ship goods to Memphis, Tennessee, applied to the surveyor of the port of St. Louis for a permit under federal regulations "pursuant to the act of July 13, 1861." The shipment, he averred, contained 100 barrels of cement. The permit was granted for the cement. The surveyor of the port, who had the duty of examining the cargos, found that they did not contain cement but whiskey "packed in cement." Obviously, the shipper wanted to avoid payment of the excise tax on alcoholic spirits. The entire shipment was seized, including 129 packages "that did not contain the contraband." Plaintiff lost in the district court.[26]

Draft-dodging cases also came to the district courts. The draft never provided more than a small portion of the Union forces. After the draft act of 1863 passed, federal courts heard cases of resistance to the draft. On some occasions, these cases entailed violent resistance. For example, in the Northern District of Ohio, Judge Hiram V. Willson presided over trials resulting from the "Battle of Fort Fizzle." Draft resisters in Holmes County mobbed federal officials trying to enroll draftees. The provost marshal detained four of the resisters, but a mob descended on the jail in Millersburg and freed the four men. The draft resisters then constructed a "fort" to protect themselves, which federal troops had to assault. In the end result, in May 1864, twelve of the protestors found themselves in the federal district court. One was convicted and sentenced to six months hard labor, but President Lincoln pardoned him before he served his full sentence.[27]

Lincoln had initially opposed the Confiscation and Non-intercourse Acts, believing that they would push the border states to side with the Confederacy because confiscation of Confederates' slaves would incite Unionist slave owners. He nonetheless signed them because they would aid the Union's wartime effort. He was not yet in favor of general emancipation, though in September 1862 he warned Confederate slaveholders that slaves in any portion of the country still in rebellion as of January 1, 1863, would be considered free under federal law. This preliminary Emancipation Proclamation was issued under his authority as commander in chief of federal forces.[28]

Although international law forbade the seizure of private property of noncombatants, the rule only applied to war between sovereign nations. The Confederacy was never recognized as such by Britain or France and certainly not by the federal government. Congress never declared war on the Confederate States of America. Lincoln believed that the rebellion was not universally supported in the Confederate states, and that Unionists might not be able to protect themselves from rebellious local or state governments until the war was over—hence the Act of March 12, 1863, "To provide for the collection of abandoned property and for the prevention of frauds in insurrectionary districts within the United States." The operative provision of this Act was that "[a]ny person claiming to have been the owner of any such abandoned or captured property may, at any time within two years after the suppression of the rebellion, prefer his claim to the proceeds thereof in the court of claims." In effect, anyone who elected to remain in the Confederacy had the chance, when hostilities in that area had ended, to prove their loyalty. Property taken by the Confederacy for its use or by federal troops for their use might then be compensated by the federal government, at some discount.[29]

Congress created the U.S. Court of Claims in 1855 to determine pension claims arising from the Mexican-American War. Determinations by this three-judge commission went to Congress, which then authorized the secretary of the treasury to disburse the funds. Under the 1863 law, the Court of Claims was enlarged to five judges and given the authority to order compensation to Unionists for property the Confederacy confiscated. Loyalty was the basis for such awards, though Lincoln and his successor, Andrew Johnson, wanted to extend the program to former insurrectionists who took the loyalty oath. Lincoln's Amnesty Proclamation of December 8, 1863, exempted Confederate officials and those who departed federal office (including judges) to serve the Confederacy, but otherwise offered "restoration of all rights of property, except as to slaves." The May 22, 1872, Amnesty Act would restore the right to vote to all former Confederates and the right to hold office to all but a few Confederate leaders—those who resigned from Congress and served in the Confederate government and those who held military commissions from the United States who served in the Confederate armed forces.[30]

During the war years, federal courts' dockets overflowed. In a single year, 1863, there were filed in Illinois's two districts 674 cases, in New York's 1,594, in Pennsylvania's, 217, and in California's, 90. The types of cases reflected the districts' disparate economies, legal histories, and present population mix. For example, California land grants from the Spanish government, the Mexican government, and the U.S. government were especially difficult to untangle, as Spanish and Mexican land law was derived from Roman code models rather than English common law. Under Mexican law, huge grants of land were at the discretion of the governor. In 1851 Congress passed "An Act to Ascertain and Settle Private Land Claims in the State of California" creating the California Land Commission and requiring all land grants under the Mexican government to establish their validity. Appeal of the Commission decisions resided with the federal district courts, burdening them with almost endlessly complex claims. Some historians sympathetic to the dispossessed Mexican owners have called

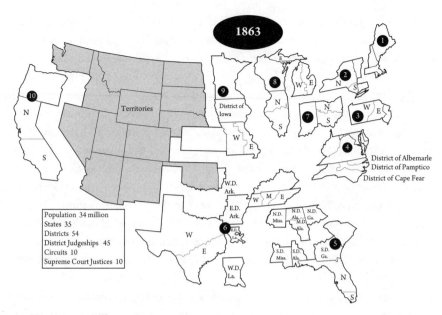

Figure 5.3 The federal circuits in 1863. Source: Wheeler and Harrison, *Creating the Federal Judicial System.* Courtesy of the Federal Judicial Center.

this a "land grab," while others find the original grants riven with corruption. Kentucky, Tennessee, and Louisiana, portions of which had been won back from the Confederacy, posted a handful of cases. More were handled by military courts' summary proceedings. In 1864, the Supreme Court had over 350 cases docketed, some waiting over two years for the Court's decision. In 1865, Chief Justice Salmon P. Chase wrote in his diary that he was wearied by "the painful monotony of hearing, reading, thinking, and writing on the same class of subjects and in the same way, all the time—morning, noon, evening, and night" in the circuit courts.[31]

Treason and Piracy in the Wartime Courts

The idea of amnesty was a carrot to draw rebels back into the fold. The stick was criminal prosecution for waging war against the United States. While captured Confederate officers and men were exchanged for captured Union soldiers until the middle of 1863, a practical concession of the belligerent status of the Confederacy, Confederates who participated in the naval war against the United States faced trial in federal courts for piracy or treason. The question then turned on whether the Confederacy was an independent nation and its naval agents operated under letters of marque, as permitted by international law, or the Confederate seamen were United States citizens, guilty of the crime of treason, or of piracy, which the Federal Crimes Act of 1790 expanded to cover the offense at sea or "any river, haven, basin, or bay, out of the jurisdiction of any particular State."

Two sets of trials, one for treason and the other for piracy on the high seas, convened in New York City and Philadelphia respectively, demonstrated the federal courts' and the Lincoln administration's commitment to both the stick and the carrot. In the first case, T. Harrison Baker was the captain of the CSS *Savannah* when it took a northern vessel for a prize on June 2, 1861. The *Savannah* and her crew were captured by a U.S. Navy vessel the next day and conveyed to New York City to await trial on charges of piracy. A month later, a U.S. naval vessel overwhelmed the crew that the Confederate raider *Jeff Davis* put aboard a captured northern merchant vessel, the *Enchantress*. William Smith and his fellow Confederate crewmen were taken to Philadelphia to face charges of treason.[32]

Four months passed before the two crews came to trial. By that time, both had gained the assistance of formidable legal teams. Although it was an unpopular step for him, prominent New York City attorney Daniel Lord offered to defend the *Savannah* crew. He had gone to Yale with the prize captain's father. Algernon Sullivan, founder of the prestigious law firm of Sullivan and Cromwell, was hired by the Confederate government to join the defense. In the circuit court they argued that the taking of the prize ship was not piracy because the sailors acted under the assumption that the Confederacy was a legal government and they had letters of marque from Confederate President Jefferson Davis. Lincoln's attorney general Edward Bates hired a special counsel, William M. Evarts, to prosecute. Justice Samuel Nelson presided over the trial in the circuit court, along with District Judge Samuel Betts.

In the meantime, counsel for the *Jeff Davis*'s prize crew had assembled in Philadelphia, and trial in the circuit court commenced. Leading defense counsel was George M. Wharton, a prominent local attorney who would become one of the great benefactors of the University of Pennsylvania. Justice Robert C. Grier, a Pennsylvanian almost unknown in political circles when President James K. Polk chose him, presided, along with District Judge John Cadwalader.

In both cases jury selection proved critical. Under questioning by the bench, jurors who indicated that they could not come to a fair verdict were dismissed. Jury selection took a few hours in both courtrooms, a not uncommon stretch of time for important trials in this era of American law. The composition of the jury panel was not actually a cross-section of those who were, in theory, eligible to serve. The most recent study of nineteenth-century American juries suggests that by the time the panel was seated its members reflected the "elite" of the community.[33]

The defense sought in cross-examination and summation to establish what they could not prove with documentary evidence—that the Confederacy was a nation and its sailors acted in conformity with the laws of war between belligerents. The second prong of their argument was that if the Confederacy was not a belligerent, then the imposition of a blockade of its ports and the seizing of its merchant shipping by the U.S. Navy was itself illegal. One could only impose a blockade, according to the law of nations, on an enemy nation, which would have made the Confederacy's privateering legal under the law of nations. What was more, an active exchange of prisoners, especially officers, was already in progress. If the Confederate officers were committing treason, how could they be repatriated? No matter the fine ironies of the defense—the jury convicted the Philadelphia privateers the same day that their defense closed. In New York City, Justice Nelson admitted into evidence documents that Grier had either excluded or qualified, for the charge of piracy of the *Savannah* crew offered a line of defense that the indictment for treason had not allowed the *Jeff Davis* crew. If the defense could convince the jury that the Confederacy was a sovereign nation, or at least that there was some genuine evidence to that effect, the defendants were not pirates. The jury in the New York case was divided: eight found the defendants guilty, four disagreed. A new trial was ordered. Before that trial began, President Davis sent word to Lincoln that for every member of either crew executed, a randomly selected Union prisoner of war would be executed. Lincoln relented and exchanged all but two crew members, the two unfortunates having died in prison. Two years later, in *The Prize Cases* (1863), the Supreme Court's majority deemed the seizure of Confederate vessels legal. In time of Civil War, the legitimate government could blockade the rebels' ports and seize their property at sea. Grier wrote the majority's opinion. Nelson dissented, along with Catron, Clifford, and, unsurprisingly, Taney.[34]

Lincoln's Judges

Like Thomas Jefferson and Andrew Jackson, Lincoln regarded judicial appointments as a source of patronage, though he never nominated someone who was unqualified. Party loyalty mattered, though he crossed party lines on occasion. Personal friendship did not hurt either. But above all, he wanted a strongly Unionist federal bench. He named thirty-six men between March 4, 1861, and his death in April 1865. Four, David Cartter of New York, George Fisher of Delaware, Abram Olin of Vermont, and Andrew Wylie of Pennsylvania, comprised the first bench of the newly refashioned District Court for the District of Columbia that Congress created in 1863. None of these men were southerners, and none had the taint of prosecession. Others, like Brigadier General

Richard Busteed of New York and Henry Clay Caldwell of Iowa, were serving in the Union Army when Lincoln tapped them. They were sent south—Busteed to Alabama and Caldwell to Arkansas, when the war was over. So, too, Edward Durell of New Hampshire, was sent to preside over the District Court in New Orleans soon after the city was retaken from the Confederacy. New York–born John Underwood, whose antislavery views were tolerated by his Virginia neighbors but whose Unionism during the secession crisis required that he briefly leave the state, was assigned to the Eastern District of Virginia. Some of the appointees were Unionists forced to leave the South after their states' secession, like John Jay Jackson Jr. of West Virginia, and Connally Trigg, returning to his native Tennessee. George Washington Lane abandoned his practice in

Figure 5.4 Judge Richard Busteed, Irish born Union Army officer, attorney, and Reconstruction Era federal judge in Alabama. Credit: Library of Congress.

Huntsville, Alabama, and accepted a judgeship for the Northern District of Alabama, but died in 1863, never having had the chance to serve in his nation's courts.

These and Lincoln's other nominees proved themselves loyal Republican defenders of Reconstruction after the war, though some of them, like Busteed, did not demonstrate a judicial temperament. He reopened court as soon as the state reentered the Union in 1865. The marshals, clerks, and U.S. attorneys reappeared. But all was not quiet. Busteed did not want military authorities telling him who he could admit to practice in his court. "It is plain," he complained in court, "that the civil power and the military control cannot coexist in the same sphere . . . the sword must yield to the statute or the statute to the sword." Busteed's enemies tried to have him impeached and failed. Only one Lincoln choice, Mark Delahay, of Kansas, was a disgrace, resigning in 1873 after impeachment in the House.[35]

A few federal judges had held court in what was nominally Confederate territory during the war. District Judge Underwood sat in Alexandria, Virginia, after the town was occupied by Union troops. Jackson held court in West Virginia when it joined the Union as a new state in 1863. After the federal judge of the Northern District of Florida, McQueen McIntosh, resigned his federal commission and took up one from Governor Madison Perry as a Confederate state judge, the southern district's federal judge William Marvin convened federal court in Key West. He sat until 1863, when Lincoln replaced him with Thomas Jefferson Boynton, formerly the U.S. attorney for the district.

Some of the transitions in personnel were especially dramatic. In Tennessee, West Humphreys had presided over the three federal districts after President Pierce appointed him in 1853. In 1862, after accepting a judicial appointment from the Confederacy, Humphreys was impeached and convicted (in absentia) of various crimes and misdemeanors and removed from his post by the Senate, more a symbolic gesture than anything else. Humphreys served the Confederacy until the end of the war and later began a private practice in Nashville. The only penalty for his crimes in office was disqualification from further federal office. Lincoln named and the Senate confirmed Trigg to replace Humphreys.

Through the first year of the war, six Democrats remained on the Supreme Court, but with the passing of Justice Daniel in 1860, the demise of Justice McLean the next year, and the resignation of Justice Campbell, Lincoln had the chance to add three Republicans to the bench. Ohio's Noah Swayne was the first, arriving on the Court at the beginning of 1862, shortly followed by Samuel F. Miller, an Iowan, in July of that year, and then David Davis of Illinois, in October. When Congress, in the Judiciary Act of 1863 created a tenth seat, Stephen J. Field, a strongly Unionist Democrat from California, became the last addition to the

Taney Court. These were relatively young men, free of the taint of proslavery and secessionist views, and they brought new energy to a court that had lost prestige.

Swayne, a Quaker from Pennsylvania, came by his dislike for slavery young: his parents were antislavery activists. Long service as the U.S. attorney for the federal district court in Ohio followed. By 1856, Swayne was a Republican stalwart, and in 1860, he backed Lincoln. A robust figure of a man, he would also support a robust version of freed slaves' civil rights and liberties after the Civil War. Swayne served until 1881.[36]

Born in Kentucky to a farm family that had come from North Carolina, Miller read law on his own and joined the Kentucky bar in 1847, at the age of thirty-one. He opposed slavery, but Kentucky did not, and he shifted his practice to Iowa, where he freed his slaves. An impressive physical figure in the courtroom, a wonderful storyteller, and a very sharp intellect, Miller became a leader in the antislavery movement and joined the Republican Party at its inception in 1854. He was a dominant figure on the Court, especially in constitutional cases, until his death in1890.[37]

Davis was a veritable giant of a man at nearly 300 pounds. Born and reared in Maryland, he went west to find his fortune, establishing a solid law practice in Bloomington, Illinois, followed by a judgeship. Davis was Lincoln's campaign manager in 1860, "the Achilles" of his campaign and close advisor during his presidency. He was the executor of Lincoln's estate. He remained a politico on the Court, thought about running for president himself, and resigned in 1877 to become a senator from Illinois. .[38]

As nimble and slight as Davis was solid, Field of California was perhaps the most brilliant addition to the Court since Justice Story. Field came from a remarkable Connecticut family: his brothers were David Dudley Field Jr., a leader of the New York City bar and a pioneer in legal procedural reform, and Cyrus Field, one of the most successful merchants in the country, supervised the laying of the first transatlantic telegraph cable. Field traveled to California during the gold rush of 1849, where he established a prosperous law practice, served as a judge on the new state's supreme court, and wrote the state's legal code (incorporating some of his brother's ideas about simplified pleading). Under the Judiciary Act of 1863, the new justice was tasked with handling a new circuit composed of California and Oregon—perfect for Field. He would sit until 1897, an avatar of laissez-faire economics and an opponent of state and federal regulation of the economy.[39]

Presiding over the Court was Chase, a deeply religious man and an avid abolitionist. A Dartmouth College graduate who studied law under leading practitioner William Wirt, he was not an especially forceful or creative legal thinker or effective leader on the bench. Chase's ambitions remained political, and even after he was confirmed he hungered for the Republican nomination for president.[40]

Figure 5.5 Chief Justice Salmon P. Chase and his Supreme Court brethren posed as a group for the first time in 1867. From the reader's left, the members are David Davis, Noah H. Swain, Robert C. Grier, James W. Wayne, Chief Justice Chase, Samuel Nelson, Nathan Clifford, Samuel F. Miller, and Stephen J. Field. Credit: Collection of the Supreme Court of the United States.

In late April 1865, with the war all but over and travel along the coast and cross-country becoming safer, Chief Justice Chase, never content with books of precedents and dry pleadings, and perhaps already planning his third run for the presidency in 1868, determined to tour the Fourth (his own) and Fifth Circuits. Promising to provide "observations" of the former Confederate states to President Lincoln's successor, Andrew Johnson of Tennessee, Chase and a small entourage of journalists boarded a steamer and left Washington, D.C.

On the night of May 10, 1865, in Hilton Head, South Carolina, harbor, Chase's vessel happened to drop anchor alongside the warship carrying the captured president of the Confederacy, Jefferson Davis. The two men knew one another from their overlapping service in the U.S. Senate and chatted amiably. But an executive order kept Davis in custody, and Chase left the matter in the hands of the executive branch. Davis would remain a military prisoner until 1867. For his part, Chase was concerned about the legal proprieties of custody and, more important, about the possibility of trial before a military tribunal. The conspirators in the Lincoln assassination had been tried by the military, even though the civil courts in the District of Columbia were open. The 1861 law provided serious penalties against "insurrection" and the 1790 Federal Crimes Act prescribed death on conviction of treason, both crimes fitting Davis's role in the Confederacy. Moreover, Davis showed no remorse about his wartime conduct. A Washington, D.C. grand jury issued such an indictment against Davis, but it came to naught. Later, a grand jury empanelled for the U.S. Circuit Court for the District of Virginia (Davis was then held in Fortress Monroe, Virginia) brought another indictment, and two others followed. With Chase opposing trial and general pardons flying all over the former Confederacy, the Davis case fell apart. Indeed, none of the political or military leaders of the confederacy would be convicted in civil courts for either of these offenses.[41]

Riding circuit on the other coast, in California, Field found himself sharing the bench uncomfortably with old adversaries from his gold rush days. Judge Ogden Hoffman Jr., for one, complained of living in "Field's shadow and finding him a personal nemesis." Hoffman was a New Yorker, well educated, erudite, and polished. So was Field. In one important way, the two men were opposites. Hoffman was a defender of the rights of the Chinese in the state and did not share Field's barely concealed racist attitudes toward them. Their mutual antipathy came to a head when Hoffman opened the January 1865 session of the circuit court and Field was nowhere to be found. Unwilling to proceed with cases, Hoffman simply logged them in the docket book along with the record of various newcomers seeking naturalization and lawyers wishing to litigate in the federal courts. When Field appeared in May, he took charge of the court, doing most of the questioning of counsel and almost blatantly ignoring Hoffman. While Field was not the only justice to find his circuit-riding duties burdensome or the only justice who did not get along with the members of the lower court bench in his circuit, Field's attempt to create "ninth circuit law" and to be the California judge ruffled feathers in both his native state and Washington, D.C.[42]

Reconstruction Begins

Hoffman and the other judges and justices on the circuit courts had new and enlarged duties when the Reconstruction of the Union began. Between 1864 and 1876, congressional legislation would provide for new causes of civil action, removal of cases from state courts, habeas corpus reform, and additional excise taxes, among other initiatives. In addition, suits based on three "Reconstruction amendments" and a surge in debt relief filings would keep federal courts busy during this period.

The cascade in the business of the courts was partly the result of Congress resetting the agenda of the federal courts. There was nothing new about Congress's latest initiatives. From 1789 on Congress had tinkered with the federal courts' shape and jurisdiction. More profound and lasting was the way that the legislative program of Reconstruction shifted the boundary of state and federal jurisdiction. Reconstruction legislative activity also thrust the federal courts into the maelstrom of postwar partisanship in a fashion similar to the courts in the late 1790s. Reconstruction efforts inextricably bound together the partisan and the legal. Republican Party advocates of Reconstruction needed all their political strength to push through legal reforms; Democratic critics of Reconstruction's legal reforms regarded them as a smokescreen for Republican Party ascendency.

Lincoln wanted a swift end to the war and had no desire to punish individual southerners for secession. His wife was southern, and she had lost three brothers in the Confederate Army. Lincoln also did not want a long bloody guerilla war to follow the formal surrender of the South. Thus, in his second inaugural address he promised a merciful restoration of the Union, "with malice toward none and charity for all." He had already promised a general amnesty for all but the leaders of the Confederacy. His one condition was that southerners accept the end of slavery.[43]

Many in the Republican majority in Congress, whom Lincoln had not consulted on his amnesty program, rejected his approach. Some, including Pennsylvania's Thaddeus Stevens in the House and Massachusetts's Charles Sumner in the Senate, wanted the conquered South to be treated as unorganized territory and pass through the steps to be admitted to the Union that territories followed. In 1864, Republican Congressman Henry Winter Davis of Maryland and Senator Benjamin Wade of Ohio drafted a bill that would have required a majority of former Confederates to swear loyalty, that only those who had not taken part in secession could be delegates to conventions to draft new state constitutions in the South, and that all officers above the rank of lieutenant and all civil officials were to be forever disenfranchised. Lincoln vetoed the bill. But Lincoln supported a Thirteenth Amendment, ending slavery, and when it passed by a two-thirds vote in both houses on January 31, 1865, there was cheering and tears in the gallery of the House. The republic would now experience the "new birth of freedom" Lincoln promised in his Gettysburg Address. The amendment stated that Congress would have the power to enforce the end of slavery by legislative means. Ratification of the amendment by former Confederate states was a prerequisite to return to the Union under Lincoln's plan.[44]

After the assassination of Lincoln, President Johnson, a staunchly Unionist Democrat chosen in 1864 to balance the ticket, continued Lincoln's program of "presidential reconstruction." Although he grew up poor and had no love of the planter aristocracy, he had equal contempt for people of color. He absolutely opposed giving black people the vote, believing them only one step removed from "barbarism." He preferred limited government to the vast expansion of federal power that the war brought and wanted Reconstruction left to the states when they were readmitted to the Union. With Congress in recess in the summer of 1865, there was no one to slow his pace readmitting the former Confederate states as swiftly as possible. According to one leading student of the period, "the result was a disaster." No sooner had the former Confederate states fulfilled the conditions he had set and restored their governments, they passed legislation (anecdotally called "black codes") effectually imposing bondage on the newly freed slaves.[45]

In the meantime, those federal courts that had ceased functioning in the former Confederate states reopened. Lincoln had selected Unionists to replace the judges who resigned. Most but not all were Republicans. In 1866, Johnson named four men to southern districts—John Erskine in Georgia, George Bryan in South Carolina, George Washington Brooks in North Carolina, and Robert Hill in Mississippi. None of these men held office under the Confederacy. In fact, the Senate confirmed all nine of Johnson's nominees for the district courts, a show of cooperation between the Republicans in the Senate and the executive branch in the otherwise troubled Johnson presidency. (The Senate did not act on Johnson's lone nominee for the Supreme Court, his attorney general Henry Stanbery.)[46]

No federal justice was available in South Carolina until 1866, when Bryan accepted Johnson's request to serve. Asa Biggs's North Carolina successor was G. W. Brooks, another Johnson appointment confirmed in 1866. Robert A. Hill held the Mississippi district court judgeship from 1866 until 1891. He was a native of North Carolina but had moved to Mississippi six years before the war began and during the war served on a local probate court. Erskine served in the Northern and then the Southern Districts of Georgia. He was in private practice during the Confederacy.

Outraged by the black codes and increasingly disenchanted with Johnson's lenient management of Reconstruction, the Republican majority in Congress asserted itself when the body reassembled at the end of 1865. Reminiscent of the initiative it exercised in the era of the first Judiciary Act and the Process Act, Congress added a new category of public litigation to the jurisdiction of the courts—civil rights. The first effort along this line was the Civil Rights Act of 1866, enacted over President Johnson's veto. It envisioned a major shift in the relationship of states to federal courts and the place of the federal courts in ordinary life. The Act defined citizenship and made it a federal offense to deny to any citizen the right to participate fully in civil activities, including (but not limited to) the right to make and enforce contracts; sue and be sued; give evidence in court; and inherit, purchase, lease, sell, hold, and convey real and personal property. It removed "the badge of servitude," in its sponsor Illinois Senator Lyman Trumbull's words, from the former slaves. Its "nondiscrimination" terminology anticipated but did not employ the equal protection and due process of law language of the Fourteenth Amendment adopted two years later. Some historians argue that the Fourteenth Amendment's purpose was to give retroactive constitutional sanction to the act.[47]

The struggle between the Republicans in Congress and Johnson continued with the reorganization of the judicial circuits. The Judiciary Act of 1866 was a partisan maneuver, in part intended to reduce southern influence on the federal courts and in part to deny to Democrats seats on the Supreme Court. It reduced the number of justices, "no vacancy in the office of associate justice of the supreme court shall be filled by appointment until the number of associate justices shall be reduced to six," effectually denying to Johnson the ability to name new members. It redrew the boundaries of the judicial circuits so that only two, the Fourth and the Fifth, were primarily southern. "Between 1837 and 1862, five of the nine circuits consisted exclusively of slave states. The tradition of appointing a justice from each circuit allowed Southerners to dominate the Supreme Court." No longer: "the districts Maryland, West Virginia, Virginia, North Carolina, and South Carolina shall constitute the fourth circuit; that the districts of Georgia, Florida, Alabama, Mississippi, Louisiana, and Texas shall constitute the fifth circuit."[48]

As the prewar Democratic justices left the Supreme Court bench and Johnson was replaced in the White House by Ulysses S. Grant, the Judiciary Act of 1869 returned the seven-member Supreme Court bench to nine members. The seats were filled with loyal Republicans. The first was Connecticut-born William Strong. A Yale College graduate and Law School attendee (the Law School did not begin to award degrees until 1843, twelve years after he left), he served as a U.S. Representative from Pennsylvania and later as a justice on the state supreme court. He was in private practice when tapped by Grant. Strong was about as far from a Radical Republican as one could get in the party, and he did not favor an active judicial role in civil rights.

Joseph P. Bradley of New Jersey filled the second vacancy. A graduate of Rutgers College, he was self-taught in the law and spent his career as a counsel for railroads and other business clients in Newark. A conservative Republican, he had an unshakeable belief that "[a] dull equalization of wealth would smother enterprise, produce listlessness, and induce a man, instead of aiming to support himself by his own exertions, to depend for his support upon the rest" of society. He too was not a strong supporter of civil rights (his hometown of Newark, New Jersey was a hotbed of racist feeling), and his views on the Civil Rights Acts' limitations on federal enforcement—that Congress could not pass a law that would supplant or render nugatory state and municipal regulations of local criminal conduct—would play a major role in the demise of Reconstruction. Eccentric but brilliant, Bradley wielded considerable influence on the Court during his tenure from 1870 to 1892.[49]

The third of the trio, Ward Hunt, was a successful New York state lawyer and judge and one of the pillars of the Republican Party in the years before the war. He strongly supported the Fifteenth Amendment. He was no friend to women's rights, however. His arbitrary conduct of the trial of Susan B. Anthony for voting in violation of the Enforcement Act of 1870—he dictated a verdict of guilty to the jury—was later explicitly rejected in *U.S. v. Taylor* (1882). A severe stroke would limit his role on the Court. Because Hunt did not meet the eligibility requirements for a judicial pension—serving ten years on the bench and reaching the age of seventy—Congress had to pass a special retirement bill to induce him to resign. Hunt's infirmity was not the first time that a justice was incapacitated, nor would it be the last.[50]

Grant nominated Morrison R. Waite to replace Chase as chief justice. Well known and respected in his adopted state of Ohio, Waite gave up a remunerative practice in Toledo (estimated at $25,000 a year) to move to Washington and accept the newly raised salary of $10,000 authorized for him by Congress. Waite opposed slavery but was not particularly friendly to the rights of the freedmen. An advocate of states' rights rather than strong central government, he believed in deference to elected bodies, a stance that protected state legislation on subjects as disparate as grain elevator prices and race crimes. He thought himself a steady, no-nonsense manager of his more opinionated and volatile brethren, and set an example with his diligence, modesty, and even temper.[51]

New Laws . . .

In part the Reconstruction legislation program relied on revitalized federal courts for its effectiveness. A series of congressional acts which may or may not have been aimed to assist the freedmen shaped public litigation. Even before Congress took Reconstruction into its own hands, the Separable Controversies Act of 1866 prevented southern litigants from using the existing diversity requirement (no two parties could come from the same state) to prevent non-southern litigants from removing their suits to southern federal courts. There was evidence that southern parties to suits added a fictitious party to defeat pure diversity (the rule that all parties to the suit had to be from different states) and that southern debtors used such devices to avoid paying lawful prewar debts to northern creditors. The Act allowed the out-of-state party to sever the part of the suit where pure diversity existed from the rest of the suit, and remove that part to the federal courts (a step reminiscent of the way that the Judiciary Act allowed British creditors to remove their suits from state to federal courts). So, too, the Prejudice and Local Influence Act of 1867 allowed removal when a party could establish, to the satisfaction of the federal judge, that "he has reason to and does believe that, from prejudice or local influence, he will not be able to obtain justice in such state court." Both Acts expanded the diversity jurisdiction (and the dockets) of federal courts.[52]

The Habeas Corpus Act of 1867 was another of the remedial statutes, this one shifting civil rights enforcement to federal courts. Congress had restored the writ in 1866, and the new Act amended the Judiciary Act of 1789 to give all federal courts the authority to issue writs of habeas corpus to state officials. The particular purpose may have been to aid freedmen and women detained and sold to prison farms in the South after a conviction for vagrancy, one of the many ways in which southern black codes reenslaved former slaves. The federal judge did not have to accept the local officials' account of the detention but could inquire about the facts on his own. This intrusion in state criminal proceedings was without precedent and shifted the boundaries of federal and state criminal jurisdiction in profound ways that persist to this day.[53]

The Fourteenth Amendment, proposed on June 13, 1866, and ratified by the required three-fourths of the states on July 9, 1868, posed complex questions for federal courts. The amendment's Section I reads:

> All persons born or naturalized in the United States, and subject to the jurisdiction thereof, are citizens of the United States and of the State wherein they reside. No State shall make or enforce any law which shall abridge the privileges or immunities of citizens of the United States; nor shall any State deprive any person of life, liberty, or property, without due process of law; nor deny to any person within its jurisdiction the equal protection of the laws.

Students of the period have argued that the ratification of this amendment so fundamentally changed the shape of national law and federalism that it created a second constitution. Certainly it is true that suits brought in federal court based on the Equal Protection and Due Process Clauses of the Fourteenth Amendment have substantially enlarged the powers of the federal government to intervene in ordinary life. The amendment is also the source of a huge body of judicial opinion and legal scholarship.[54]

With the election of Grant, congressional Reconstruction found a friend. Safe from the prospect of Johnson naming his favorites to the Supreme Court, Congress once again reordered its shape. The Judiciary Act of 1869 restored the Court to nine members and established nine separate judgeships for the U.S. circuit courts. It also allowed judges to retire without losing their salary. Lyman Trumbull of Illinois reported it out of the Senate Judiciary Committee on February 3, 1869, assuming that its way through Congress was paved with political and jurisprudential good intentions. The rebellion was over, and reform of the courts was long overdue. Popular among litigants and litigators, at the same time, the naming of new judges by a Republican president and a Republican majority in the Senate would reward loyalty to the party and the Union in the South.[55]

But the Act did not pass easily. Lyman and his allies in Congress had ignored the justices' wishes to be relieved of circuit riding. Motives for this continuing resistance to their pleas included the old fear that a distant Court would be indifferent to local attitudes. Some members of Congress may have deferred to the desire of local bar leaders to see the justices in person. Many legislators feared changing a system nearly 100 years old. There was no avoiding the question of how to replace the circuit courts should circuit riding be abolished, a question that would continue to divide congressmen well into the next decades. Still, the Act lessened the demands of circuit riding. Justices were required to attend each circuit court within their assigned circuit only once every two years, a recognition of their frequent prewar absences from their circuits. The new circuit judges exercised the same authority as the justices in the circuit sessions. A circuit court could be held by the circuit judge, the justice appointed to the circuit, the district judge, or by any combination of two of them, thus making easier the simultaneous meeting of different circuit courts within a given circuit. The more efficient distribution of judicial responsibilities and the retirement clause offered the promise of a more active federal judiciary, but by adhering to the system of dual trial courts and maintaining the circuit duty of Supreme Court justices, the Act fell short of the proposals to eliminate the circuit courts and create a middle tier of wholly appellate courts.[56]

Judges named to the circuit courts under the 1869 Act had very similar credentials to the district judges—in fact, many had been district judges. For example, the new Seventh Circuit judge was Thomas Drummond. He had practiced law in Galena, Illinois, briefly served in Congress, and was a close friend of Lincoln. He was confirmed as a federal district judge for the District of Illinois in 1850 and was an obvious choice for the new circuit post when it was created. Indiana's new circuit court appointee, Walter Gresham, was born and practiced law in the state. Like many in the Old Northwest, Gresham thought slavery wrong but was not an abolitionist. He joined the new Republican Party and when war came, raised a regiment of Indiana volunteers and fought alongside Grant at Shiloh Court House and the siege of Vicksburg. Grant would name him to the district court in 1869 and former Union General Chester A. Arthur, at the end of his term in the White House, would name Gresham to the circuit court in 1884, when Drummond retired.[57]

Congress mollified local legal authorities who might have been upset by the Judiciary Act of 1869 with the Conformity Act of June 1, 1872. It provided that the civil practice and procedure in federal district and circuit courts (other than in equity and admiralty matters) must conform to the practice and procedure used by the state courts for similar civil cases "as near as may be" at the time. The Process Acts had linked federal to state procedure as the latter stood in 1792, and in many states procedure had been revised since that time. The Act did not apply to rules of evidence that the federal courts had adopted or Congress had imposed on federal courts. The Federal Rules of Civil Procedure, which became effective in 1938, superseded the Conformity Act.[58]

The Conformity Act's passage should be seen in the context of Reconstruction. The Civil Rights Acts and the Enforcement Acts had made, perhaps inadvertently, the federal courts into the second line of defense of freedmen's legal rights. (The military commission courts were the first.) Senator Trumbull led the discussion of the bill, and the debate turned on whether it should include language making intimidating or tampering with grand and petty jurors in federal courts a contempt of court. Everyone in the Senate chamber knew what was at stake. William Stewart of Nevada, a Republican stalwart and author of a number of Reconstruction acts, wanted to add the provision to the bill. Trumbull offered that jurors in his state had not complained of undue outside influence. What was more, "it was important that the bill should pass" because it would ease the burden of courts "in civil matters"—in effect, arguing that relieving all the federal courts of inconveniences and inconsistencies in civil suits had a higher priority than strengthening the contempt powers of federal judges in the Reconstruction South. Steward reluctantly conceded the point and withdrew the amendment. The bill passed without the contempt provisions.[59]

With legislation like the Conformity Act, Congress clearly viewed the federal courts as important agents in knitting the nation together again. But not all of these acts were concessions to state practice. That is to say, the federalism of the Reconstruction Era was different from the federalism of 1787 and 1789. A striking illustration of the difference was the Jurisdiction and Removal Act of March 3, 1875: "An Act to determine the jurisdiction of circuit courts of the United States, and to regulate the removal of causes from State courts, and for other purposes." While it might seem on its face a part of the integration of the new circuit judiciary into the fold, that appearance was deceptive. It granted the U.S. circuit courts what Marshall in *Osborn* had foretold: the jurisdiction to hear all cases arising under the Constitution and the laws of the United States, as long as the matter in dispute was worth more than $500. The statute also made it possible for plaintiffs and defendants in cases before state courts to remove a case to a U.S. circuit court whenever the matter involved a question of federal law or if any members of the parties were from different states. The last of the Civil Rights Acts of the era, passed in 1875, afforded those individuals barred from public accommodations on the basis of their race to bring suit in federal courts. This Act, like its predecessors, was not some expression of empty idealism or ritual posing—it was the capstone of the plan to use the federal courts to ensure the gains of Reconstruction. By adopting an expansive interpretation of federal jurisdiction, in the long run the Act fundamentally changed the role of the federal courts in the federal system, the most sweeping extension of judicial power since the short-lived Judiciary Act of 1801.[60]

Since 1789, federal jurisdiction had been divided between the federal courts and state courts, with the latter hearing most cases involving federal law if both parties were residents of the state. In the first half of the nineteenth century, Congress occasionally expanded the right of removal to federal courts in order to protect specific areas of federal authority such as enforcement of customs regulations during the War of 1812 and the collection of revenue following South Carolina's attempt to nullify tariff laws in 1833. During and after the Civil War, Congress more frequently included removal provisions in acts designed to protect civil and political liberties in the former Confederate states, but the right of removal continued to be extended only in attempts to enforce specific policies. The uneasy, back and forth contest between state and federal courts entered a new stage in Reconstruction.

Perhaps the shift in the boundary between state and federal courts had become inevitable, for the federal courts were fast becoming far more elite than the state courts in recruitment, salary, and prestige. The Madisonian Compromise rested in part on the idea that justice in the federal courts would not be affected by local bias. Whether or not "parity" existed after 1875, and the implications of that claim today (for example, for federal habeas corpus protection for minority defendants in state criminal courts), the controversy goes back to the Reconstruction Era. As Congress opened the doors of the federal courts to civil litigants, it allowed liberal removal of suits to federal courts.[61]

... And Busy Courts

Peacetime brought a surfeit of business to the federal courts. Alleged Unionists came to the U.S. Court of Claims revealing what they had (allegedly) successfully hidden during the insurrection—that they really were loyal. A wide range of fact patterns marked these cases. Moses Adler, a Louisiana sugar and cotton planter on Bayou Teche, gave his goods to the Union forces for a chit, then took the oath of allegiance. Presenting the chit and reasserting his loyalty, he sought repayment for the goods. Although the Union quartermaster refused to reimburse Adler, the Court of Claims ordered him paid $13,000. By contrast, consider the case of Georgian Benjamin H. Zellner. His thirty bales of cotton were seized by a special treasury agent in 1865. Zellner brought his case to the Court of Claims, insisting that he did nothing to aid the Confederacy. The government could not prove him wrong, but neither could he offer any evidence of his loyalty. His claim was dismissed.[62]

While all the judges on the Court of Claims had experience in state and federal government, one, David Wilmot, had more of a hand in creating conflict than his brethren. Wilmot, who served from 1863 to 1868, was a lawyer from the northeastern corner of Pennsylvania, early a free soil advocate in the Democratic Party, and the author of the Wilmot Proviso of August 8, 1846, that no territory taken as a result of the Mexican-American War be open to slavery. This would have shut the door to the expansion of slavery into the Southwest and California. The resulting furor demonstrated how divided the political parties and the sections were. Wilmot would become one of the founders of the Republican Party and after a brief stint in the U.S. Senate, accepted his commission on the Court of Claims.[63]

Legal consequences of military actions also found their way into the postwar federal courts. Perhaps the most notorious cases concerned the federal occupation of New Orleans during the war. There, General Benjamin Butler established courts under martial law. He did this without authorization from Lincoln or Attorney General Edward Bates. Nonetheless, Butler proceeded to order that Confederate money still in circulation was not legal tender and then sat as the sole judge of his own court to ensure that all debts were paid in U.S. dollars. Shortly thereafter Lincoln appointed New Yorker Charles Peabody as a "provisional judge" for the city and its environs, an appointment under Lincoln's powers as commander in chief rather than any act of Congress. "And I do hereby authorize and empower the said judge to . . . appoint a prosecuting attorney, marshal, and clerk of the said court." The appointment was to "continue during the pleasure of the President, not extending beyond the military occupation of the city of New Orleans, or the restoration of the civil authority in that city and the State of Louisiana."[64]

When the war ended, the lending banks sued in Louisiana state court to recover the difference in value between the loan in Confederate and U.S. dollars. The argument was that Butler's military commission and Lincoln's provisional courts were unconstitutional—an ironic argument for formerly Confederate banks to proffer. Under the Act of 1869, the case came to the Supreme Court. In *Mechanics Bank v. Union Bank* (1874) it ruled that as the occupation of the city was constitutional so were the provisional courts. "That clause of the Constitution has no application to the abnormal condition of conquered territory in the occupancy of the conquering army. It refers only to courts of the United States, which military courts are not."[65]

Despite the fact that the resumption of federal court sessions represented the triumph of the Union over the Confederacy, southerners had no hesitation turning to federal courts for civil relief during Reconstruction. In fact, compared with the prewar district courts' dockets, postwar private litigation was booming. In the Northern District of Georgia, for example, after the resumption of federal authority, the March 1867 minutes recorded seventy-one civil cases and fourteen federal crimes, most of the latter were failure to pay fees under federal statutes. There was also one patent infringement case. A year later, the court spent three weeks hearing 151 civil suits and 121 federal criminal indictments for violation of the Revenue Act of 1867. Typical was the indictment of Thomas Harris for "distill[ing] without paying the special tax." Most of those indicted under the Revenue Act confessed and paid the fines. There were also three indictments of mail clerks who had defaulted on bonds that they were required to post.[66]

The Bankruptcy Act of 1867, the work of the same Radical Republican majority in Congress that imposed occupation of the former Confederate states, was welcomed in the South and brought many propertied white people to the federal courts seeking relief for debts incurred during secession. In 3,180 filings, all but 404 voluntarily filed by debtors from the Southern District of Mississippi, South Carolina, and the Eastern District of Tennessee, white southerners gained the aid of the federal courts. Southern sympathizers in the Eastern District of Missouri benefited from the Act—within the first year of its operation there were 581 filings. Bankruptcy petitions flooded the Northern District of Georgia's federal court. The Act's relatively high level of exemption of personal property from discharge to creditors stabilized a southern economic system made fragile by wartime expenditures, reattached the interest of southern lawyers to the federal courts, and reintegrated the southern economy into northern credit markets.[67]

Reconstruction congressional acts had a similar impact on northern courts' dockets. In the Circuit Court for the District of Massachusetts, for example, the caseload was 472 filings in 1857, 508 filings in 1858, 557 filings in 1859, and 627 filings in 1860. These represented the usual array of civil suits for debt, along with personal injury suits against the Boston and Maine, and the Boston and Worcester Railroad, and suits against the City of New Bedford, the capital of the whaling industry. The war years dampened the caseloads and reversed the growth of the docket, with 496 filings in 1861 and 489 filings in 1862. But the upward trend reappeared at the end of the war, the court hearing and determining 963 cases in 1865 and a whopping 1229 cases in 1866, many of them the same revenue cases as the Northern District of Alabama faced. The Bankruptcy Act brought another bumper crop of cases, 1,062 in 1867 and 1,145 in 1868 to the Massachusetts district court. Recourse to the federal courts was national, not sectional.[68]

The expanded business of the federal courts required the creation of the Department of Justice. The Supreme Court's justices lobbied Congress for more uniform supervision of federal law enforcement within the attorney general's office, particularly when departments of the federal government argued against one another in cases coming to the Court. On June 22, 1870, Congress responded. The most recent scholarly accounts of the new department find that it promoted "the separation of government lawyers from regular partisan politics, and the professionalization of the government lawyer" and improved "consistency and uniformity" in the legal opinions of the federal district attorneys. It was a nationalizing step at the time when the nation was reuniting itself and a professionalizing step when the professionalization of the legal fraternity was gaining momentum. To this new federal department, headed by the attorney general, was given much of the administrative business of the federal courts, including budgeting. The law also created the office of the solicitor general, whose job it was to represent the federal government in litigation before the Supreme Court.[69]

While removal and other provisions of congressional acts may have shifted the boundary of judicial federalism, new duties for the federal courts in the Reconstruction Era did not precipitate conflict with the state courts. State courts' dockets rose as fast as federal courts'. The boom years in California brought 196 cases to its highest court during the July and October terms of 1860, but in the same terms for the year 1875, the number of suits in the state's supreme court was 380. The war years had slowed litigation in Illinois—a mere 179 cases came to its supreme court between 1863 and 1866—but by 1871 the docket swelled to an average of over 275 cases per year. The Indiana Supreme Court heard over 900 cases in the year before the war, but by 1871, that number had grown to nearly 1,500 cases a year. Kansas's Supreme Court was only burdened with 101 cases in 1866, but by 1872 the load had risen to nearly 400 and four years later it was 481. Removal did not stop former Confederates from marching off to their own supreme courts. Before war came, at the June 1859 and January 1860 meetings of the Alabama Supreme Court, 238 cases were filed. The December 1876 session of the court heard 232 cases. Mississippi's Supreme Court heard and determined 128 cases; by 1876, with Reconstruction ended (through extralegal means to be sure), its supreme court heard 321 cases. The same pattern held in North Carolina, whose supreme court adjudicated 321 cases in 1859–1860 sittings, and over 600 in 1876.[70]

Checks and Balances

While the quarrel between Congress and President Johnson was the period's most visible example of a rugged separation of powers, Congress and the federal courts carried on their own running battle over jurisdiction, standing, and other procedural matters. Although largely Republican in membership, Congress and the federal courts continued to experience fractious moments. Could Congress take from the federal courts jurisdiction over certain kinds of cases and certain kinds of claimants—"jurisdiction stripping"? Could the federal courts resist such quasi-judicial actions by the legislative branch? In *Ex Parte McCardle* (1869) and *U.S. v. Klein* (1871) the tussle became obvious.

The two *Ex Parte McCardle* cases arose from a set of disputed elections. William H. McCardle of Vicksburg was the very model of the unreconstructed Confederate. Virulent in his newspaper editorials, he called for the end of military occupation, the permanent disenfranchisement of the freedmen, and a lily-white Mississippi government. Charged with impeding the implementation of the Congressional Reconstruction Act of March 2, 1867, he challenged the military tribunal that tried him. On his appeal for release on a writ of habeas corpus, the Supreme Court heard two days of oral argument from the finest legal minds in the country, Senator Trumbull for the United States and David Dudley Field for McCardle. Counsel for both sides had pled their cases extraordinarily well according to contemporaries, but the justices' minds were already made up.[71]

Oral argument closed on March 9, 1868, and eighteen days later Congress repealed the statute under which McCardle sought relief in the federal court. In effect, Congress was telling the Court that the entire matter was political and could be settled by the Act. McCardle's political activities in Mississippi played opposite to McCardle's legal strategy, however. If the matter was not one of jurisdiction but a political question, the Court should have declined to hear the case under its own precedent in *Luther v. Borden* (1849). Then, the Court chose not to intervene in Rhode Island's Dorr War because it was a political question left to the elected branches of government. Whether Congress could "strip" the courts of jurisdiction over cases like McCardle's by repealing the law under which he was indicted remains a controversial matter.[72]

Justices Grier, an old Democrat, and Field, a younger one, wanted to reach a decision (presumably favoring McCardle's appeal) before Congress passed the repeal act. But Chief Justice Chase delayed a final decision until after Johnson vetoed the repeal bill and Congress passed it over his veto. There was no wiggle room for the Court, but Chase, presiding over the impeachment trial of President Johnson in the Senate, once again postponed a decision on McCardle's appeal. When the Court spoke, after the election of 1868, Grant had won the White House and Congress was once again solidly Republican. Chase then wrote for the majority, "It is quite clear, therefore, that this court cannot proceed to pronounce judgment in this case, for it has no longer jurisdiction of the appeal; and judicial duty is not less fitly performed by declining ungranted jurisdiction than in exercising firmly that which the Constitution and the laws confer." What Congress had given by statute Congress could take away by statute. Chase could not forgo a closing comment, defending the Court from a too intrusive

Congress. He hinted that the case might properly come before the Court if McCardle brought a motion for a habeas corpus outside of the scope of the 1867 Act. A year later, in *Ex Parte Yerger* (1869), a unanimous Court restated its capacity to issue the writ for a petitioner held in a military prison.[73]

Klein raised similar separation of powers issues. In February 1864, Victor F. Wilson of Vicksburg, a wealthy cotton merchant, took advantage of President Lincoln's amnesty proclamation. When he died, the administrator of his estate, John Klein, sought compensation for over 500 bales of Wilson's cotton that the government had sold as abandoned property. The Abandoned and Captured Property Act of 1863, an inducement to southerners like Wilson to accept a pardon, promised compensation to claimants who had not aided the rebellion. Klein averred that Wilson's pardon meant that he should not be considered a rebel. In May 1869, the Court of Claims accepted this position. The U.S. Supreme Court, in a series of other cases, had found in favor of similar claims. In the meantime, furious at Johnson's liberal pardon policy, Congress repealed the Abandoned and Captured Property Act and enacted a law barring claims for confiscated property under the color of a presidential pardon. The legislation was clearly directed at decisions like *Klein* and a handful of other cases pending in the Court of Claims, though the language of the statute sounded merely jurisdictional.[74]

In passing the 1870 Act Congress directly interfered in ongoing litigation, an action far beyond mere jurisdiction stripping. The Supreme Court challenged Congress when *Klein* arrived on its docket. The Court told lawmakers not to dictate the outcome of a particular case nor infringe the right of pardon lodged in the executive branch. The old issue of separation of powers had reared its head and roared. Chief Justice Chase, joined by all but two of his brethren, opined that in the 1863 law "[t]he government recognized to the fullest extent the humane maxims of the modern law of nations, which exempt private property of non-combatant enemies from capture as booty of war. Even the law of confiscation was sparingly applied. The cases were few indeed in which the property of any not engaged in actual hostilities was subjected to seizure and sale." What was more, the president's power to pardon was not subject to legislation; it was the exclusive prerogative of the executive branch, whatever Congress might say. Those who acted under the color of a pardon become part of a "national obligation" vital to ending the war and ensuring the peace. Finally, the Court of Claims, though created by Congress, was not an agency of Congress. Article I courts were part of the judicial branch of government. Congress's action was, in the opinion of the justices, "not an exercise of the acknowledged power of Congress to make exceptions and prescribe regulations to the appellate power . . . We must think that Congress has inadvertently passed the limit which separates the legislative from the judicial power."[75]

The Court had spoken as if it had the final word in matters of its own jurisdiction, but Congress had other ideas. In 1874, facing its own backlog of cases, the Supreme Court in *Vannevar v. Bryant*, decided that diversity suits required all parties to be citizens of different states. Members of Congress objected to that restriction on diversity suits. Representative Luke Poland of Vermont introduced legislation to restore the right of removal in all civil cases in which one of the defendants was a citizen of a state other than that in which the suit was filed. Although the House rejected this modest extension of removal and passed a bill to make only minor revisions in the law, Senator Matthew Carpenter of Wisconsin proposed amendments to guarantee the right of removal in any civil case arising under federal law or in which there was diversity of citizenship, with the $500 threshold applying to both categories of cases. The House accepted that version of the bill, which President Grant signed in March 1875. Congress had told the Court that it had the final say over diversity jurisdiction.[76]

Representative Poland and Senator Carpenter had other motives than mere procedural fairness when they proposed their legislation. They wanted to ensure that federal courts would enforce the Civil Rights Acts in the South. Their proposals also reflected an important truth about diversity jurisdiction not connected to Reconstruction. As the nation expanded, the federal courts' diversity jurisdiction went with the courts. In a parallel fashion to the way that recapitulation of the district and circuit court system in the western portion of the country ensured the uniformity of the federal judiciary, so diversity jurisdiction tied the various sections' courts together. Through suits removed to federal courts through diversity, litigants and lawyers from different parts of the country were brought together in a single place—the federal courtroom. Diversity jurisdiction kept the federal courts truly national courts. [77]

A last important facet of Reconstruction era legal innovation from a federal courts' standpoint was the way it redefined private law and public law. In the antebellum period, slaves were private property. Although federal and state law protected that property, buying, selling, leasing, and inheriting slaves was regulated by private markets; and when disputes came to court, they were handled as matters of private law. In the Reconstruction years, the fate of the former slaves lay in the courts' enforcement of civil rights statutes, that is, as a matter of public law.[78]

Reconstruction Ends

The high watermark of Reconstruction came in the Enforcement Acts of 1870 and 1871. The former repeated key provisions of the 1866 Civil Rights Act, then went further, providing remedies for conspiracies by private individuals to deny anyone rights guaranteed by federal law. Perpetrators would be tried in federal courts as felons and if convicted, "disabled from holding, any office or place of honor, profit, or trust created by the Constitution or laws of the United States." The word "disguise" in the text referred to the hoods worn by members of the Ku Klux Klan when they violated the rights of the freedmen and women.[79]

The Enforcement Act of April 20, 1871, also known as the Ku Klux Klan Act, completed the definition of civil rights crimes: "if two or more persons within any State or Territory of the United States" conspired against the federal government, violently opposed its officers in the performance of their duties, or "by force, intimidation, or threat" interfered with the execution of federal laws, they were guilty of a federal offense. More controversial were the conspiracy provisions of the Act, penalizing those who "conspire together for the purpose of" the foregoing proscribed activities. While the final clause of the Fourteenth Amendment might arguably be the basis for the conspiracy provisions, the amendment referred to states, hence state officials, while the conspirators might be private citizens. It might also have rested on the General Welfare Clause in the Preamble and Article I.[80]

The Enforcement Acts provided a federal remedy for victims of civil rights offenses. The U.S. attorneys could bring suits against violators, as could private individuals. The Acts were in theory effective tools by which the courts could constrain extralegal bodies like the Klan. For example, in the winter and spring of 1871, a band of forty Klansman led by former Confederate major James Avery coursed over York Country, South Carolina, terrorizing the freed black population. A black man named Amzi Rainey resisted, and the Klansmen raped his elder daughter in his sight and then lynched him. U.S. attorneys, empaneling grand juries, brought the KKK members involved to trial, Circuit Judge Hugh Lennox Bond presiding. Bond shared the bench with District Judge George Bryan, an aged South Carolina plutocrat who had supported the Confederate government but was chosen in 1866 by President Johnson to sit in judgment of former Confederates and former slaves. Bryan was not sympathetic to the defendants' goals, but he knew them and understood their sense of disentitlement. Both judges also realized that the grand and petty jurors might face the fury of the defendants' family and associates. Fifteen of the grand jurors and eight of the trial jurors were black. The exclusion of those with Klan sympathy to some extent determined the racial composition of the panel, but the county was majority black and its juries reflected, for the first time, the actual demography of the jurisdiction. The juries found the terrorists guilty. For a time the trials so weakened the Klan that it could no longer operate openly in the state. The U.S. Supreme Court declined to hear the defendants' appeal.[81]

The constitutional question of whether the indictments could be founded on the Fourteenth Amendment was the centerpiece of the defense. The Klansmen were not state officials nor did they act as though under state government orders. Judge Bond skirted that issue in his opinion denying the motion to quash the indictments. "After the prolonged and very able argument of counsel upon this motion to quash, we feel embarrassed, gentlemen, that, upon so little deliberation, we are to pass judgment upon the grave questions raised here. But the fact that so many persons are now in confinement upon these charges and that so many witnesses are in attendance upon the court, at great personal expense, makes it necessary that we should not delay longer." Yet he did find that nine of the eleven counts were unsustainable, and Bond's silence on the constitutionality of the Enforcement Acts suggested that the prospects for equal treatment under law based on the Fourteenth Amendment were tenuous.[82]

Along the Mississippi, "Redeemers" were busy implementing the "Mississippi Plan" to regain control of the South from the Republicans and their African-American allies. Some were members of the Klan, others were not. The plan was simple—frighten or assassinate the black voters; persuade the white Republicans to switch allegiance; regain control of the southern state governments; and bluff the Republican administration in Washington out of military or legal responses. White "gun clubs" and "bulldozers" kept blacks from the polls.[83]

One case from Louisiana tested the federal courts' willingness to protect the new rights of freedmen against private violence. In the wake of a violently contested 1872 election year in the state, a white militia armed with rifles and a small cannon overpowered and killed a group of former slaves at the parish courthouse in Colfax, Louisiana. Most of the freedmen were assassinated after they surrendered, and nearly fifty more were killed later that night after being held as prisoners for several hours. The U.S. attorney for the district, J. R. Beckwith, ordered the arrest of the ringleaders of the massacre and brought them to trial under the Enforcement Act of 1870. Citing *Prigg*, Justice Bradley sitting in the circuit court opined, "It seems to be firmly established . . . that congress has power to enforce, by appropriate legislation, every right and privilege given or guaranteed by the constitution." But the Fourteenth Amendment could not give to Congress jurisdiction over crimes by individuals except crimes against the United States. Ordinary criminal jurisdiction over murder like that at Colfax belonged to the states. "When it is declared that no state shall deprive any person of life, liberty, or property without due process of law, this declaration is not intended as a guaranty against the commission of murder, false imprisonment, robbery, or any other crime committed by individual malefactors, so as to give congress the power to pass laws for the punishment of such crimes in the several states generally."[84]

The district judge, Edward Durell, did not concur with Bradley, thus the case went to the Supreme Court on a writ of error. In *Cruikshank v. U.S.* (1875), Chief Justice Waite, writing for all the justices but Ward Hunt, worried that the Enforcement Act prescribed federal punishment for individuals who were not agents or officers of the state of Louisiana. Congressional acts under the Fourteenth Amendment could only reach "state action." The court found every one of the sixteen counts against the defendants invalid. The opinion instructed victims of discriminatory criminal acts by private persons to turn to the state courts for relief. As Waite intoned, "We have in our political system a government of the United States and a government of each of the several States. Each one of these governments is distinct from the others, and each has citizens of its own who owe it allegiance, and whose rights, within its jurisdiction, it must protect." A robust concept of states' rights after the war had done what the secession movement could not do—protect the absolute authority of an armed white population to brutalize its black fellow citizens. Even though the blacks were also citizens of the United States, "[t]he duty of a [federal] government to afford protection is limited always by the power it possesses for that purpose."[85]

By the mid-1870s, Reconstruction was faltering. Waning northern support, a depression beginning in 1873 and not ending until 1881, and the success of the southern "Redeemers" after the general pardon of 1872 may have doomed the experiment in equal protection of the law, but a split in the Republican Party finished the job. By 1876, the Democrats had regained control of all but three of the former Confederate states. Newly-elected President Rutherford B. Hayes kept his election promise to remove the remaining Union troops from the South. The long agony of Jim Crow began.[86]

The return to power of the white Democratic power structure did not diminish the allure of civil law practice in the federal courts. Democratic litigators and litigants were not opposed to federal courts in principle. For example, southern corporate lawyering was built on the wide shoulders of the southern rail development and lawyering for the railroad companies in federal court "guaranteed income" and garnered "prestige." In this, leaders of the (white) southern bar were much like leaders of the northern bar. Led by cases involving railroads and railroad companies, in 1876, there were 14,397 civil suits pending in U.S. district and circuit courts. In 1877, the number had leapt to 20,570 and the next year to 22,005. A dangerous backlog was building. The Supreme Court, the only final appeals court in the federal system, was averaging over 1,200 cases each year on its docket but terminating on average only a little more than 400. This left a backlog of more than 800 pending cases each year adding to the existing backlog.[87]

The themes that had shaped the first federal courts—the close ties between politics and law, shifting and contested separation of power boundaries within the federal government, and the state courts' rivalry with the federal tribunals—had taken on new and complex shapes in the crisis times of the Civil War and Reconstruction. The dispute over diversity jurisdiction reopened another old controversy: which branch of the federal government was to decide such questions. Congress's powers under Article I and Article III directly challenged the Supreme Court's view of its own procedural rule-making authority. In the years after 1876, as the federalism question receded, contentions over rule making moved to the foreground. The Reconstruction Amendments and the postwar judicial acts had shifted some of the burden of adjudication from state to federal tribunals and, more important, had opened new avenues for litigants to press their claims on the federal courts. The politics of congressional expansion of the circuits and the placement of district courts remained but was not as important as it had been prior to the war. New players in the federal courts appeared— powerful corporations and the emerging industrial labor unions.

The growing backlog of cases called for innovative ideas and new forms of judicial organization. While increased awareness of European legal scholarship and law reform movements provided an impetus for reform and resulted in the dissemination of new ideas in jurisprudence, institutional reform of the courts came from within the legal fraternity and, initially at least, revolved around a reconceptualization of the courts and lawyering. The ideal was "scientific government" in which legislatures and courts did not clash but joined with professionally trained lawyers, trade commissions, boards of experts, and local authorities to "rationalize law" and thereby reduce the burden on the courts. It was a bold project, suited to the explosion of entrepreneurial and professional activity in what Mark Twain had slyly caricatured as the "Gilded Age."[88]

6

The Gilded Age Courts, 1877–1896

The "Gilded Age" was a time of striking transitions and highly visible contradictions when a largely rural nation became increasingly urbanized and a few accumulated great wealth and displayed it conspicuously while many labored in soot-covered cities and ill-lit factories. Metropolises like New York City and Chicago warehoused millions of immigrants from foreign lands (over thirteen million entered the country during the Gilded Age) and nearby rural areas seeking jobs. Cities hosted giant corporations whose headquarters filled new "skyscraper" office buildings. At the same time, unrest and violence in the city pit newcomer against native born, rich against poor, and labor against capital in a witch's brew of poverty, illness, crime, and corruption.[1]

Big was better, or so the giants of industry seemed to think. Labeled robber barons by some; celebrated as industrial statesmen by others, they brought the nation into the modern age of business organization. In 1860, the largest business enterprises employed thousands, were capitalized at one million dollars, and served a national market. In the Gilded Age, behemoths like Standard Oil employed tens of thousands, were capitalized in the tens of millions, and reached global markets. The new middle-management corporation, with layers of "general managers" between different divisions of the corporation, and squadrons of middle managers reporting to the general managers, abetted by investment bankers and aided by corporate lawyers, came to dominate the country's economic development. The value of manufactured exports rose from $205 million in 1895 to $485 million in 1900, increasing its share of total exports from 25.8 percent to 35.3 percent. By the end of the Gilded Age in the mid-1890s, American heavy industry stood alongside food production and staple crop enterprises as the leading sectors in the national economy, exceeding them in terms of capital investment and market value.[2]

Most of the new ventures were risky, but the rewards seemed worth the risk. Reducing the risks was the task of an emerging cadre of very able commercial lawyers. These men not only advised and represented venture capitalists, they fine-tuned doctrines that safeguarded capital from unscrupulous operators of "bucket shops" (betting parlors masquerading as stock exchanges) and unwary buyers of industrial futures. From curbing the excesses of risk in trading futures to securing the capital of insurers, lawyers made the heady entrepreneurship of the age a little sounder. Many of these lawyers practiced in the federal courts.[3]

The Busiest Courts in the Land

The transformation of the economy and demography of the nation meant that some judicial districts would be more heavily patronized by litigants than others. Given that the busiest districts would also be those in centers of commerce, industry, and invention, these districts would face and resolve the most novel and complex cases. So it was in the Southern District courts of New York in the Gilded Age. We start with this story because the performance of the court demonstrates with the greatest clarity the challenge to the federal courts to changing with the times.

In the Gilded Age it seemed that all roads—rail, canal, and newly paved— led to New York City. The shipping industry, the insurance industry, the rails, the fabricators of clothing and culture, the investment banks, and the New York Stock Exchange all called "The City" on Manhattan Island home. Manhattan (Kings County, Queens County, Bronx County, and Richmond County joined New York County as boroughs in 1898) was a landscape of contrasts: elegantly appointed Fifth Avenue mansions and Central Park West palatial apartments housed the families of the rich; Lower East Side tenement slums teemed with the families of the poor. President Rutherford B. Hayes joined "the frock coated trustees and their wives in silk dresses" at the opening of the Metropolitan Museum of Art while not far away entire immigrant families jammed into poorly lit sweatshops, living quarters doubling as miniature clothing factories.[4]

To the Southern District courts of New York came a microcosm of Gilded Age America. In its courtrooms disreputably garbed counterfeiters of liquor excise tax stamps stood at the same bar as elegantly attired scoundrels like New York stockbroker "Diamond" Jim Fisk and "robber barons" like Jay Gould. In its courtrooms practiced lawyers who got their degrees at night schools and lawyers with degrees from the top law schools. When the giant industrial combinations faced federal legal action for monopolizing supply and fixing prices, Sullivan and Cromwell lawyers James Brooks Dill and William Curtis stepped in with a solution: the mega corporation, by which an interlocking directorate of formerly competing companies could control prices and supplies. Fisk and Gould, two of the richest men in America, owed their fortunes to the courtroom skills of Thomas Shearman and John William Sterling, founders of one of the great corporate law firms. Wall Street lawyer S. C. Dodd helped fashion the

Standard Oil oligopoly, and attorney Elihu Root and his partners assisted in the creation of the Sugar Trust. This was lawyering New York City style.[5]

The corporations needed top-flight lawyers like Shearman and Sterling, for the city was a center of corporate finance. With its neighbor, the Eastern District (created in 1865) covering the city of Brooklyn and the rest of Long Island, the Southern District courts almost capsized in the flood of post-Reconstruction litigation from 1865 to 1891. The sheer numbers are staggering, all the more because of the comparison with other jurisdictions. By the end of the Civil War, nearly twice as many cases were pending in the Southern District of New York (4,132) as in the second-busiest circuit in the nation, Eastern Pennsylvania, with (2,226). By contrast, the Northern District of New York had but 535 cases pending, and the other states in the Second Circuit, Connecticut and Vermont, had a combined total of 116 awaiting resolution. The load of cases filed in the Southern District's courts grew after the Civil War, and the backlog of cases followed suit. By 1884, there were over 6,000 cases pending in its courts. It took an average of three years for these suits to be resolved, by which time the backlog had grown further. The Eastern District and the Northern District of New York's courts and the federal courts of Connecticut and Vermont did not keep pace with the 1,500 or so private (civil suits) filed each year in the Southern District, the other districts' courts combining with fewer than a 1,000 a year. It did not alleviate the Southern District courts' burden that almost all the customs cases for the port of New York went to them, along with complex patent and copyright cases. These were the type of cases that were not easily resolved and clogged dockets for years.[6]

Fortunately for (some of) the parties to these suits, one of the country's foremost experts on patent and admiralty law sat first on the district court in the Southern District, then on its circuit court, and finally as a member of the Supreme Court, with circuit-riding duties in the Second Circuit. Samuel Blatchford served the district court from 1867 to 1878, when he became a circuit court judge. Blatchford owed his appointment to the most powerful and admired figure in the state's electoral politics—lawyer and founder of the Republican Party William Henry Seward. Seward was a reformer, an abolitionist, a feminist, and a promoter of public education in upstate New York. Young Blatchford was his secretary. Unlike Seward, whose path led to the Senate, Lincoln's cabinet, and a place in history, Blatchford preferred law practice (he was one of the founders of the firm that would eventually become Cravath, Swaine & Moore) and then the bench. Along the way he became the reporter of the New York Court of Appeals (the state's highest tribunal). Chester A. Arthur appointed both Blatchford and Horace Gray, chief justice of the Massachusetts Supreme Court and an influential legal and historical scholar, to the Supreme Court in 1882. Their opinions were models of learning and good sense.

Blatchford was a believer in the vital role of courts in the growth of the economy. He told a Washington, D.C. audience in an address celebrating 100 years of American patent law, "In the administration of the patent laws by the courts of the United States, the proper rights of inventors have been firmly maintained, while the abuses which crept in, in consequence of improper reissues of patents, have been corrected."[7] As evidence, Blatchford cited Chief Justice Taney's opinion in the Samuel F. B. Morse patent case—finding that absent a practical, operating model of an invention, an idea for the invention could not be patented—but Blatchford might well have been thinking of a more recent case that his successor as circuit judge, William James Wallace, heard on the bench and for which Blatchford was the case reporter. Like Blatchford, Wallace had spent the eight years on the district court before his elevation as circuit court judge. (In 1891 he would become one of the new federal courts of appeal judges.)[8]

American Bell Telephone Company v. People's Telephone Company (1884) epitomized the southern district's complex patent litigation. Even more important, it demonstrated the vital role that the federal courts played in releasing the energy of capitalism. Without protection of inventions, and the investment in business based on invention, and the protection of invention by patent, the post–Civil War economy could never have achieved the remarkable growth it did.[9]

A master in equity appointed by the court had heard and recorded nearly 500 witnesses swear that either Alexander Graham Bell had invented the telephone, and thus his American Telephone Company deserved its patents, or that a rural Pennsylvania mechanic named Daniel Drawbaugh had perfected a telephonic device much earlier than Bell. To be sure, Bell's company had fought off other competitors over the course of the seventeen years of Bell's initial patents. His lawyers had filed over 600 infringement suits against Bell's imitators. But Drawbaugh's counsel presented neighbors who testified that they had seen and heard his machine work years before Bell's patent application was filed. None of them was an expert, and all of them were locals. Though in fact an equity suit, the patent case resembled the old English trial by compurgation (also known as "wager of law"). In these, each side marshaled crowds of witnesses who swore that their party's tale was truthful.[10]

Judge Wallace had to decide whether to issue the injunction against Drawbaugh's People's Telephone Company. Wallace summarized the core of the case. "The defendants contend that long before Bell had perfected his invention, and long before its mental conception by him, Drawbaugh had not only made the same invention, but had perfected improvements in organization and detail which Bell never reached." The transmitter of the Drawbaugh phone was "a porcelain tea cup" and the receiver a tin can. Other household items completed the design. Drawbaugh's wife, pregnant and bedridden, testified to hearing the phone ring in their house when he first transmitted over the teacup. Wallace weathered the testimony of the "cloud" of witnesses substantiating Drawbaugh's own testimony, yet one set of facts seemed to him to trump all their recollections. Drawbaugh had never tried to patent any of his alleged inventions. It was only when Bell succeeded that Drawbaugh duplicated the Bell design and started marketing rival telephones. Collateral evidence demonstrated that Drawbaugh's other attempts at inventing electrical mechanisms had ended in ludicrous failure. Nor was Drawbaugh able to recall the steps he had taken to create his telephone. Wallace reported Drawbaugh's words, " 'I had a number of crude apparatuses, but can't remember exactly the shape of any of them. I had membranes stretched over hoops,—over a hoop, I remember that; and I had electromagnets and the arrangement was varied. I don't remember exactly the arrangement.' " At the end of his thirty-page opinion, Wallace granted the injunction.[11]

The federal District Court of the District of Columbia was not as busy as the courts of the Southern District of New York, but among its suits were some of the most famous—or infamous—of the time. To be sure, it was unique in the federal system, both a municipal court for the District and a federal court, roles it performed as the successor to the circuit court for the district. One of these criminal prosecutions—the trial of Charles Guiteau for the assassination of President James A. Garfield—was arguably the most important federal criminal trial of the century. Guiteau's personal history was a tour through the byways of religious zealotry and radical reform in the Gilded Age, as well as law practice in his native Chicago, a brief career as a political speech writer, and finally disappointment seeking a federal job. On July 2, 1881, Guiteau ambushed Garfield at a train station in Washington, D.C. and shot the president twice. The second bullet, lodged in the spine, eventually caused Garfield's death from sepsis on September 19, 1881. On October 14 the assassin was indicted. A month later, after a voir dire (examination to determine jurors bias and competence) of 175 men, the panel was completed and the trial commenced. On January 25, 1882, the jury returned a verdict of guilty. Through all of this, Judge Walter S. Cox gave Guiteau every opportunity to speak for himself (though at one point throwing his arms up in dismay at Guiteau's rambling), appointed a series of able counsel for the defendant, and ran a fair trial, even by the modern standards of the Federal Rules of Criminal Procedure.[12]

Cox, a longtime resident of Georgetown who had graduated Harvard Law School and combined practice in D.C. with a teaching appointment at Columbian University (renamed the George Washington University in 1904), was appointed to the D.C. District Court in 1879 by Rutherford B. Hayes. Guiteau's primary counsel was his brother-in-law, George Scoville, whom he scolded throughout the trial. The prosecutor was George Corkhill, plainly not amused by the antics at the defense table. Nevertheless, the crowds at the courthouse each day turned the trial into a holiday outing. Though a "state trial" in the old English sense of

Figure 6.1 The trial of assassin Charles Guiteau, pictured on the witness stand in 1881, created a media sensation. Credit: *Harper's Weekly*.

the word, it was not rigged for the prosecution. As one observer who sat through the entirety of the proceedings noted, "On Judge Cox's management of the trial almost unqualified commendation can be bestowed."[13]

The record of the trial itself was published in two volumes and became a best seller. Guiteau's ultimate plea of not guilty by reason of insanity was unpersuasive at the time, though later observers have suggested that he might have had some form of schizophrenia. Nevertheless, he knew right from wrong and was in possession of all his faculties when he pulled the trigger. On these issues, Judge Cox's charge to the jury is a model of its kind, and at twenty-eight printed pages almost as long as Wallace's opinion in *American Telephone*. Uppermost in Cox's mind was that the trial not only be fair but also that it be perceived as fair. "With what difficulty and trial of patience this law has been administered in the present case, you have been daily witnesses. After all, however, it is our consolation that not one of these sacred guaranties has been violated in the person of the accused." While this solemn opening to the charge was something of scripted boilerplate, Cox's patience with the antics of the defense—matching Wallace's with Drawbaugh's claims—demonstrated a genuine commitment to a fair trial. To the insanity plea, Cox reminded the jury that "it is equally true that a defendant is presumed to be sane and have been so at the time when the crime charged against him was committed; that is to say, the government is not bound, as a part of its proofs, to show, affirmatively, that the defendant was sane." Nothing convinced Cox that Guiteau was deranged, possessed, infirm of mind, or delusional when he planned or executed the crime. The judge conceded that the insanity defense had become so popular, and so nebulous, as to lead to abuses, but that was not true of this case. A note to the published version of the charge by Francis Wharton turned a simple murder trial into a treatise on the insanity plea. The trial of Guiteau can rightly be called "the trial of the century," at least for the federal courts.[14]

Courthouses, Courts, and Judges in the Gilded Age

The huge Second Empire–style courthouse for the Southern District in Foley Square, completed in 1880, was an imposing example of the growth of the federal government as a whole during the postwar period. After the war, the Treasury Department embarked on the nation's first centrally directed program of court building. In 1866, with the appointment of Alfred B. Mullett as the superintending architect in the Treasury Department, an "entrepreneur and a bureaucrat" molded by the war years, the building program took off. Although he only served until 1875, by that time major construction projects were begun in New York, Boston, Washington, D.C., and elsewhere. Under the guidance of Mullett's successor, William Appleton Potter, Gilded Age courthouses joined with railroad stations and opera houses as monuments to an enthusiastic urban boosterism. Far more than functional, these Second Empire and neo-Romanesque structures dominated the business districts of New York City, Chicago, and Philadelphia. They courthouses featured all the modern conveniences, including plumbing. But getting a new courthouse was not easy—not only did Congress have to appropriate the funds, but the courts also had to wait as other claimants on a new building's space lobbied local politicians and congressional representatives over location and other matters. Students of Gilded Age corruption would not be surprised to learn that the building of courthouses in that era entailed patronage and pork barreling.[15]

Far from the bustle of a Chicago, New York City, or Philadelphia, federal judges had to do without such basic creature comforts as flush toilets. The territorial judges did not have life tenure, but they carried the federal law with them to the far corners of the nation. Consider the travels and travails of Samuel Chipman Parks, a Republican stalwart appointed to be the first territorial federal judge in the Idaho Territory (1863–1867) and subsequently a federal judge in the New Mexico Territory (1878–1882) and the Wyoming Territory (1882–1886). Moving west with the frontier, Parks was born in Vermont, educated in Indiana, and practiced in Illinois, where he was one of the first Republicans to back

Figure 6.2 The Southern District courthouse, completed in lower Manhattan in 1880, was a monument to the new building program for federal courts. It housed the district and circuit courts and, after 1891, the courts of appeal. Supplanted by the modern Foley Square Courthouse in 1936, the 1880 structure was razed three years later. Credit: General Services Administration.

Lincoln for the presidency. He lived to the age of ninety-seven, witnessing the Mexican-American War, the Civil War, the Spanish-American War, and the onset of World War I, not to mention the Indian Wars. He carried his law books with him, "a wandering frontier lawyer" holding court in wayside inns, opera houses, and town halls—a man whose rugged individualism and commitment to the rule of law was an ornament to the bench and bar. Shortly before his death, he even published an imaginary account of President William McKinley's trial for killing thousands of Filipinos. A reincarnated George Washington, foreman of the trial jury, pronounced the verdict: "guilty as charged."[16]

Appointees to the federal district and circuit courts in these years were men whose outlook and experience were shaped by the hard times and self-sacrifice of the Civil War era and its aftermath. Out of the destruction of war came a desire for healing and a demand for justice. War's memory taught duty, courage, and fatalism. Memory also stirred romantic images of martial ardor and sacrifice. Survival made them realists.[17]

Of the 124 appointments to Article III courts between January 1, 1877, and December 31, 1896, a near majority had served in the opposing forces during the war. Allegiance had been largely dictated by where the future judges were practicing, for example Kentucky lawyers joining the U.S. Army and Tennessee attorneys the C.S.A. Army. John Marshall Harlan of Kentucky's service in the Union Army made him an ideal candidate for being appointed to one of the southern seats on the Supreme Court. Bearing arms for the Confederacy was, however, no bar to later elevation to the federal bench. For example, District Judge Thomas Settle was selected by President Grant, though Settle had been a captain in the Confederate Army. Emory Speer, during the war a private in a Georgia infantry regiment, was in 1885 named by President Arthur to the District Court for the Northern District of Georgia after service as the U.S. attorney there, though both Grant and Arthur were Union generals as well as Republican presidents. Former Confederate soldiers even found seats on the Supreme Court: for example, Edward D. White of Louisiana and Lucius Q.C. Lamar of Mississippi sat on the high bench alongside former Union soldiers. To be sure, after the hostilities had ended, the future judges had to take the oath of allegiance necessary to practice in federal courts.

The Gilded Age appointees had similar career paths as those named to the federal bench prior to the hostilities, save for their military service during the war. Many of them had held local and state offices during or immediately after the conflict and apprenticed with a practicing attorney (i.e., "read law") rather than attending law school. They were to "combine the qualities of able lawyers with those of perfectly pure, single-minded and upright citizens," according to a letter from Governor Jacob Cox of Ohio, he a former Union Army general, to Senator George Frisbie Hoar of Massachusetts. The bulk of them came to the bench from private practice during or after the war years. Almost all of the midwestern appointees had left East Coast birthplaces to practice law in Ohio, Michigan, Missouri, and other Midwest states. Some, like Augustus Seymour of New York and North Carolina, and John Williams had gone South to begin practices after the Civil War. New Yorker John Underwood, a judge in the Eastern

District of Virginia, chaired the Virginia constitutional convention mandated by the Reconstruction Acts. Although dismissed as unscrupulous and self-dealing "carpetbaggers" by "Redeemers," men like Seymour, Williams, and Underwood brought legal acumen and honesty to a region of the country that needed a rebirth of law and order.[18]

Only one of the new federal judges, Charles Swayne of the Northern District of Florida, endured the ignominy of impeachment. Confirmed in 1890, he was impeached in 1904. Although the House of Representatives divided on the charges, the majority concluded that his offenses included neglect of his official duties; improper appointments of bankruptcy commissioners; partiality to certain lawyers practicing in his court and "oppression and tyranny" to other counsel; mal-administration of bankruptcy cases; and peculation. Swayne, testifying before the Senate, first denied everything, and then, arguing "in the alternative" (a style of pleading that had replaced single-issue writ pleading) insisted that even if the facts alleged were true, everything he did was in proper keeping with his duties. Whatever fell in between was "inadvertent" error and did not amount to a "high crime or misdemeanor." On February 25, 1905, after nearly two months of mulling over the accusations and his response, the Senate met and acquitted him. Perhaps some of the animosity against Swayne in the accusations derived from the fact that he too was a carpetbagger.[19]

The appointment of circuit judges did not relieve the burden on Chief Justice Morrison R. Waite. Instead, his steady work habits were sorely tested as the Court's caseload expanded. When a nervous breakdown took him away from his duties for a time, fellow Justice Samuel F. Miller remarked, "I always knew that [Waite] did a great deal more work than I," referring not only to the administrative labors of the chief justice but also to Waite's habits of reading every word in the briefs and handling every piece of correspondence. Still, the Court was fighting a losing battle. Each year the number of cases awaiting decision rose. By the end of Waite's tenure in 1888 it was higher than 1,550. The Court was churning out many hundreds of opinions a year, up from the double digits of the prewar period, but still falling behind. With appeal to the Supreme Court relatively easy, most of these cases were similar in content to those the district courts heard: contracts, torts, insurance, and negligence. Comparatively few involved civil rights or any of the newer causes of action. The backlog in all the federal courts increased 86 percent, from 29,000 to 54,000 cases. Federal question jurisdiction and diversity jurisdiction were in part responsible, but the simple fact was that more and more businesses were turning to the federal courts, particularly after the 1873 downturn, to pursue debtors who crossed state lines.[20]

In addition, during this period the number of Supreme Court justices willing and able to write opinions declined. Justice Nathan Clifford, a Democratic holdover from the prewar court, refused to resign until a Democrat was elected president, but he was infirm much of his tenure and did not do his share of the work. Ward Hunt's stroke in 1878 rendered him speechless and prevented him from holding a pen. Some of the justices, notably Clifford, insisted on writing long opinions, which delayed their arrival and added to the burden on the other justices. On top of this, until 1911 the justices were still supposed to ride circuit, though few of them actually carried out this chore.[21]

Some help for Waite and the Court was on the way. In the 1869 Judiciary Act, Congress provided pensions for retiring justices, and between 1869 and 1877 Justices Robert C. Grier, Samuel Nelson, and David Davis retired. In the next few years, Justices Hunt, Strong, and Noah Swayne stepped down. A new cadre of postwar judges took their places. The first addition to the Waite Court, John Marshall Harlan, would become one of the most noteworthy members of the federal judiciary. Born into a well-to-do Kentucky family, owner of slaves, and for a time vocal member of the anti-immigration American (Know-Nothing) Party, there was little in his early career to distinguish him from others in the border state elite. During the war he joined the Republican Party, led Union troops in battle, and was later elected attorney general of Kentucky. In 1876, he represented the state at the Republican Presidential Convention and carried his delegation for the eventual victor, Rutherford B. Hayes. Hayes never forgot a friend and when Justice Davis's seat fell vacant, Hayes put him up for it. Although some Republicans suspected Harlan's late conversion to the cause (he had opposed the Thirteenth Amendment for a time), the nomination sailed through the Senate on a voice vote in early 1877. He came to hate slavery, but his views of the freedman can best be called paternalistic. He never abandoned the belief that whites were superior.[22]

Harlan was a maverick on the Court, often so powerfully in dissent that others claimed he had "dissent-ery." His dissents in the *Civil Rights Cases* (1883) and *Plessy v. Ferguson* (1896), his defense of Congress's imposition of an income tax and antitrust laws, and his belief that the Fourteenth Amendment incorporated the Bill of Rights in *Hurtado v. California* (1884) endeared him to later generations of constitutional jurists even as they set him at odds with his brethren at the time.[23]

As the appointment of Harlan demonstrated, party affiliation and personal loyalty were vital considerations of presidents and senators when selecting members of the federal judiciary. Like their prewar predecessors, almost all the members added after 1865 had political experience and well-known party affiliations. The justices were fully aware of the politics of the day and how it affected their appointments. One striking example of the impact of party affiliation came during the tumultuous campaign of 1876. In the presidential election, Democrat Samuel J. Tilden led Republican Rutherford B. Hayes in popular votes, and 184–165 in the Electoral College, but disputed electoral votes in a number of states left 20 electoral votes in doubt. Congress created a fifteen-member electoral commission of ten members of Congress and five Supreme Court justices, divided by party affiliation. The commission gave Hayes all 20 votes. The three Republican justices on the commission voted for every Hayes elector, the two Democratic justices for every Tilden elector. After which, both sides complained about the partisanship of the other.[24]

Separate and Unequal

Not so hidden behind the election of 1876 dispute was the great political issue of the antebellum period: sectionalism. Both candidates were northerners and both had supported the Union, but the role that their respective parties had played late in the insurrection were revisited in the course of the campaign. The Civil Rights and Enforcement Acts and the Reconstruction Amendments may have been the Republicans' attempt to end sectional legal differences once and for all, but the legislation was largely abhorrent to the Democrats. They preferred to defer to state governments. Applied to the project of Reconstruction, that meant concessions to redemption of the South by its prewar leadership. The South's domestic law, once the great shield of chattel slavery, had by 1877 became the sword of segregation. In this context, Hayes's willingness to undo the Reconstruction Act of 1867 was less a compromise of principle than an admission that it had failed.[25]

With the demise of Reconstruction, Jim Crow laws multiplied. Jim Crow was an antebellum caricature of an illiterate, sexually promiscuous black man; a singing and dancing character in minstrel road shows always played by a white man in blackface. By the Gilded Age, the term had gained a second more insidious meaning:state-mandated (though often privately enforced) segregation of the races in public arenas, education, railroad stations, and restaurants. Public facilities for people of color were invariably worse than those whites.[26]

Reconstructionist federal courts had a mandate to protect the civil rights of the freedmen, but the ruling in *U.S. v. Cruikshank* (1875) had sent a chilling message to Republican radicals and civil rights advocates who opposed Jim Crow. The Enforcement Acts were passed under the Fourteenth Amendment's provision: "The Congress shall have power to enforce, by appropriate legislation, the provisions of this article." But the Gilded Age federal courts were not willing to give the Fourteenth Amendment or the Enforcement Acts an expansive reading. Perhaps this owed to the long-standing reluctance to give Congress a blank check regarding the courts' involvement in local criminal affairs. It may also be that, with the demise of Reconstruction, federal courts in the South perceived that imposing such an expansive role for the federal courts over a reluctant, even hostile, former Confederacy would result in widespread resistance to court orders. The upshot was that the *Cruikshank* doctrine skewered the freedmen on the horns of a tragic dilemma. On the one hand, if a state acted to protect the freedmen, it was intruding into the exclusive realm of congressional powers. If a state did not act to protect the freedmen from private agents' discriminatory conduct (including violence), Congress could not provide a remedy. The application of the state action doctrine of *Cruikshank* was relentless.

The federal courts explained why Congress could not protect the rights of the freedmen when they were violated by private persons in the *Civil Rights Cases* (1883). The cases were a collection of five suits arising in Kansas, California, Missouri, New York, and Tennessee, four of which involved federal prosecution of individuals operating public commercial enterprises who refused admission or service to people of color. Prosecution rested on the provisions of the Civil Rights Act of 1875 or, in *Robinson and Wife v. Memphis and Charleston Railroad*, a civil suit to "recover the penalty of $500 given by the second section of the act; and the gravamen was the refusal by the conductor of the railroad company to allow the wife to ride in the ladies' car, for the reason, as stated in one of the counts, that she was a person of African descent." Circuit Court Judge John Baxter presided, a jury found for the defendant railroad, and Robinson appealed when he lost. The other cases came to the Court because the circuit court bench certified a division of opinion.

With only Justice Harlan dissenting, the Supreme Court found that the Civil Rights Act of 1875's public accommodations section exceeded the power given to Congress under the Thirteenth and Fourteenth Amendments. Justice Bradley wrote for the majority that public conveyances, inns, parks, theaters and other facilities run by private individuals could not be brought under the umbrella of federal law. The Thirteenth Amendment did not extend to gaining service at an inn or amusement park and the Fourteenth Amendment only applied to state actions and actors. Justice Bradley: "It is State action of a particular character that is prohibited. Individual invasion of individual rights is not the subject-matter of the amendment."[27]

Harlan's dissent came to a different conclusion. "The opinion in these cases proceeds, it seems to me, upon grounds entirely too narrow and artificial. I cannot resist the conclusion that the substance and spirit of the recent amendments of the Constitution have been sacrificed by a subtle and ingenious verbal criticism." Harlan saw the tragic irony in the Court's stance. In the years before the Civil War, the federal government had acted directly and forcefully to protect the master's property in his slave. The Fugitive Slave laws trumped all state legislation. "With all respect for the opinion of others, I insist that the national legislature may, without transcending the limits of the Constitution, do for human liberty and the fundamental rights of American citizenship, what it did, with the

sanction of this court, for the protection of slavery and the rights of the masters of fugitive slaves." Harlan knew firsthand that southern Democratic leaders
never intended to treat the freedmen as full citizens, much less equals, instead
reinstituting "burdens and disabilities which constitute badges of slavery and
servitude," against which Congress could and had legislated.[28]

On the other hand, the Court majority was unwilling to interfere when the
state imposed segregation on its population. Lower federal courts had a mixed
record on enforcement of the Civil Rights Acts after the end of Reconstruction.
Provisions for removal under the first Civil Rights Act fared better than criminal
prosecutions under the Enforcement Acts. But on the whole, the federal courts,
during the Reconstruction Era the bulwark of protection for the freedmen, were
increasingly in line with the retreat after 1877. The federal courts' stance on civil
rights litigation brought them into closer alignment with the state courts and
with post-Reconstruction congresses and the presidency, an ironic triumph for
the Madisonian Compromise.[29]

In *Plessy v. Ferguson* (1896) the Court, with Harlan again in dissent, explained
why the state could mandate the separation of the races while Congress could
not mandate equal treatment of the races. No one on the Court denied that there
were races and that the white race was the superior one. Even Harlan conceded
this. "The white race deems itself to be the dominant race in this country. And
so it is, in prestige, in achievements, in education, in wealth and in power. So,
I doubt not, it will continue to be for all time, if it remains true to its great heritage and holds fast to the principles of constitutional liberty." Although Harlan
did not expand on this dictum, it reflected the notion that the "ruling race" was
Anglo-Saxon or Teutonic or Nordic, and the superiority of one people over all
others was literally in the blood. A more extreme version of the ruling-race or
"herrenvolk" ideology concluded that that the darker races of Africa and the
"yellow" races of Asia should bow to the imperialism of the age. Segregationists
like Tennessee Senator John Tyler Morgan read the Reconstruction Amendments
as proof that people of color needed special nurturing. Writing in 1890, he
opined that some legal protection was needed "to save the negroes from the
natural decay of their new-born liberties, which would result, necessarily, from
their natural inability to preserve their freedom."[30]

In 1892, plaintiff Homer Plessy and counselor Albion Tourgeé tested
Louisiana's version of this racialist ideology. Two years earlier, the state passed
a railroad car segregation law. Plessy was selected by a committee of his fellow Afro-Creoles because he could "pass" for white, and they arranged for the
conductor and a detective to detain and then arrest Plessy after he bought his
first-class ticket and refused to switch to the black car. It was a "test case." The
committee lost its case in the Louisiana courts (where John Ferguson was a trial

court judge) but appealed to the Supreme Court on Thirteenth Amendment and Fourteenth Amendment grounds.[31]

Tourgeé, a civil rights advocate and former Reconstruction agent in North Carolina, former U.S. Solicitor General Samuel F. Phillips (who had represented the government in the *Civil Rights Cases* ten years earlier), and local counsel James Walker argued that the Louisiana Separate Car Act violated the Reconstruction Amendments and the common law of common carriers. The Court was not impressed. Justice Henry Billings Brown wrote for the majority, dismissing both constitutional and common law grounds for the suit, then continued to explain the need for segregation. There was no need for this passage in the opinion; it was not the basis for denying the appeal as a matter of law. As such, it was just as much dicta as Chief Justice Taney's remarks about black citizenship in *Dred Scott*. But Brown thought it needed to be in the opinion to refute Harlan's expected dissent. "The object of the amendment was undoubtedly to enforce the absolute equality of the two races before the law, but in the nature of things it could not have been intended to abolish distinctions based upon color, or to enforce social, as distinguished from political equality, or a commingling of the two races upon terms unsatisfactory to either." A law that limited where a person of one color could sit on a train and did not so restrain a person of another color did not disparage, harm, or make any assertion about the first person. "If this be so, it is not by reason of anything found in the act, but solely because the colored race chooses to put that construction upon it . . . We think the enforced separation of the races, as applied to the internal commerce of the State, neither abridges the privileges or immunities of the colored man, deprives him of his property without due process of law, nor denies him the equal protection of the laws, within the meaning of the Fourteenth Amendment."[32]

The long-established usages of discrimination presumed that segregation was part of a natural order. Brown continued, "If the two races are to meet upon terms of social equality, it must be the result of natural affinities, a mutual appreciation of each other's merits and a voluntary consent of individuals." The alternative, that "social prejudices may be overcome by legislation, and that equal rights" could be "secured to the negro . . . by an enforced commingling of the two races" was a social impossibility more than a legal one. "Legislation is powerless to eradicate racial instincts or to abolish distinctions based upon physical differences, and the attempt to do so can only result in accentuating the difficulties of the present situation . . . If one race be lower to the other socially, the Constitution of the United States cannot put them upon the same plane." Equal but separate, Brown found, did not violate the Thirteenth or the Fourteenth Amendments.[33]

Harlan's dissent in *Plessy* echoed his dissent in the *Civil Rights Cases*.

In respect of civil rights, common to all citizens, the Constitution of the United States does not, I think, permit any public authority to know the race of those entitled to be protected in the enjoyment of such rights. . . . I deny that any legislative body or judicial tribunal may have regard to the race of citizens when the civil rights of those citizens are involved. Indeed, such legislation, as that here in question, is inconsistent not only with that equality of rights which pertains to citizenship, National and State, but with the personal liberty enjoyed by every one within the United States . . . [The federal laws,] if enforced according to their true intent and meaning, will protect all the civil rights that pertain to freedom and citizenship . . . These notable additions to the fundamental law were welcomed by the friends of liberty throughout the world. They removed the race line from our governmental systems.

Harlan concluded: "Our Constitution is color-blind, and neither knows nor tolerates classes among citizens. In respect of civil rights, all citizens are equal before the law." Ironically, it was Harlan's dissent that introduced the term "separate but equal," regarding it as a perverse reading of the intent of the framers and a distortion of the reality of discrimination.[34]

Caseloads and Court Reform

Overworked, Waite died of pneumonia on March 23, 1888. It could be said with some truth that the burden of cases killed Waite. In 1880, there were 1,212 cases sitting on the docket of the Supreme Court. In the same year, 369 were decided. In 1888, the number pending had grown to 1,571 cases; the Court decided 423. The vast majority of these were appeals from the district and circuit courts in common law matters or suits begun by the U.S. attorneys.[35]

The members of the Supreme Court were fully aware that the Reconstruction statutes and constitutional amendments had made federal courts more attractive to litigants. At the same time, they knew that former Confederates now seated in Congress were arguing against the expansion of the federal courts. Most important, they knew that the only substantial relief the federal judiciary, in particular the Supreme Court, could expect would come from Congress. Thus they caged their plea for reform of the judicial system in neutral terms. From the comments of those within the judicial branch, one would assume that the increase in caseload had no political context—that it simply happened and needed to be remedied. As Associate Justice William Strong wrote in 1881, the ideal of reform was that "[t]here would no longer be any complaint of a denial of justice. Every question respecting the force and effect of Congressional statutes, or respecting private rights declared or protected by Federal power, would be met and answered in due time; the embarrassments now so often felt in governmental operations would be removed, and certainty would be given to the relations of the citizen to the Government."[36]

Waite's premature death had little immediate effect on court reform plans in Congress. Southern Democrats, fully recovered from their electoral losses after the war, pressed in the opposite direction, seeking to roll back the jurisdiction and autonomy of federal courts to the era before the Judiciary Acts of the Reconstruction period. They hammered away at diversity jurisdiction, winning House approval of bills that would have crippled diversity in the federal courts. The Senate, with its Republican majority, refused to accede. In 1882 the Senate passed a reform bill, the work of former Supreme Court Justice Davis, now a senator from Illinois. It would have combined the existing district and circuit courts' jurisdiction, created a new tier of appeals courts in each of the circuits, and ended the circuit riding of the Supreme Court members. The new intermediate courts of appeal were to be staffed by district and circuit court judges and Supreme Court justices. A modification of earlier reform proposals by Senators Trumbull and Ira Harris of New York, like their efforts, Davis's unwieldy compromise died in the House. For their own part, although they cast the issue as one of clean government and the opposition as speaking for corrupt railroad and land speculation interests, the best the southern Democrats could get was the Judiciary Act of 1887, "increasing the amount in controversy necessary to enter federal courts from $500 to $2,000 and eliminating the ability of plaintiffs to remove a case they had brought in state court."[37]

In the spring of 1890, the House of Representatives took another look at the overburdened federal judiciary. The debate over what would in the end be called the "Evarts Act" reflected all three themes that first appeared in the framing of Article III and the Judiciary Act of 1789: the overlapping of law and politics, the competition of national and state interests inherent in federalism, and the separation of powers tug-of-war between the federal courts and Congress. The debate was one of the fullest and most revealing expositions of sectional views of federal courts since the end of Reconstruction and as significant for the shape and operation of the federal courts as the debate over the original Judiciary Act. What the judges said to be a simple matter of numbers, members of Congress regarded as a test of the very purpose of a national judiciary.[38]

On September 20, 1890, with the Republicans at least temporarily in the majority in both houses, Illinois Republican Joseph Cannon, speaking for the Judiciary Committee and the Committee on the Rules, introduced a measure that would form the basis of the debate. It would have created intermediate courts of appeal. In 1801, the Federalist Judiciary Act included a variant of this structure, though the jurisdictions of the two sets of courts would have been quite different (the Cannon proposal courts were purely appellate; the Federalists courts were largely trial courts). In any case, the 1801 Act fell to the Jeffersonians' broad assault on the Federalist judiciary. By 1890, the nation was larger, national government was more comprehensive, and the federal courts' jurisdiction, and consequently its workload, had grown.[39]

Leading the opposition to the plan were southern Democrats. Almost all had strong connections to the fallen Confederacy. All opposed expansion of the federal government. They were lawyers but local rather than national in their experience and ties. It was politics—but not just Democratic versus Republican politics—that motivated them. Their cause was sectional on a scale reminiscent of the years before the war when Congress was hamstrung by sectionalism. To be fair, the argument against centralized federal courts went all the way back to 1789, but then it was not sectional. Now it was.[40]

William C. Oates of Alabama led the charge. Oates, a lawyer, went to war in 1861 and served until he lost an arm in the defense of Petersburg. He then returned to his law practice and won a seat in the Alabama State Assembly, and then in the U.S. House of Representatives. Oates asserted that the bill's altera-tion of the function of the circuit courts reduced the power of the district courts, making the process of appellate judicial determination, at least in terms of actual location, less local and more hierarchical. Oates plainly yearned for a time in the past before the elaboration of the federal government's administrative system in the war years, and feared a future in which judicial federalism would give way to a centralized system. He wanted judicial power to reside with the familiar, the accessible, and the nearby. That this method of allocating responsibility for litigation should lend itself to the Democratic domination of the South should come as no surprise. The two fit together seamlessly.[41]

When Republicans replied that the courts were merely rule-bound adminis-trative agencies with little discretion, nonpartisan, and no danger to local institu-tions, Democrat Clifton Breckinridge of Arkansas, another Confederate veteran, voiced his fear that a federal Department of Justice working hand in hand with a Republican-dominated judiciary might try to reverse the work of the redemp-tion of the South. Breckinridge fulminated, "Is [the proposal] not a very great, if not a radical, modification of our present judicial system?" Cannon fired back that the measure was the consensus of every bar throughout the land. The law-yers wanted it. The judges wanted it. Surely it was a nonpartisan project. It was a technical adjustment to correct a technical problem. He won a respite—the bill was not killed. But it was not passed. The Democrats all knew that President Benjamin Harrison, a Republican, would be making the appointments to any new judicial posts. Even if Reconstruction was a dead letter and the civil service reform Pendleton Act of 1883 had reduced the number of offices in the presi-dent's appointing power, judgeships were still patronage posts worth contesting.

Even if, as seemed likely, the Democrats returned as majorities to both houses after the election of 1890 (which turned out to be the case), Harrison would remain in the White House until March 1893.[42]

John Henry Rogers, another Arkansas Democrat and Confederate war veteran, supported the bill: make the existing circuit courts into dedicated appeals courts and add two judges to each circuit court. Eliminate the Supreme Court justices' circuit riding. Better a limited revision of the system rather than a more thoroughgoing reform. He reported that he and the other members of the Judiciary Committee had labored mightily to produce the draft. He lamented that nothing could be done about corporate forum shopping, but he denied that eliminating the evils of circuit riding through permanent circuit courts of appeal would produce disharmony in the law. "[T]hat great central power, the Supreme Court of the United States," would rectify any differences between the circuits. With Rogers's comments ending debate, the House voted the bill up, 131 to 13, with 183 not voting. The bill then journeyed to the Senate. In 1896, Democratic President Grover Cleveland named Rogers to the District Court for the Western District of Arkansas, the former Confederate infantryman faithfully serving on his old enemy's courts until he died in 1911.[43]

In the upper house, Evarts took the lead in the debate on court reform. Born in 1818, to a Boston lawyer turned Congregationalist preacher, Evarts could trace his lineage back to the founding of the colony. Though his father's death in 1830 left his family in strained circumstances (and taught Evarts the importance of personal finances), he attended the prestigious Boston Latin school, Yale College, and Harvard Law School. With these strong academic credentials and the social capital he earned from his schooling, Evarts began a long, distinguished, and well-compensated practice in New York City, at the peak of his career earning well over $75,000 a year. He did not neglect public service. After a stint as an assistant district attorney in New York, from 1849 to 1853, in 1855 he became an organizer in the newly founded Republican Party. The fulsome compensation he received for his legal services for the federal government during the Civil War helped convince opponents of the proposed Department of Justice that its cost to the federal treasury was far more manageable than outsourcing the government's legal representation to men like Evarts. He served as one of Johnson's defense attorneys in the president's impeachment trial before the Senate, and Johnson rewarded him with an appointment as U.S. attorney general. Evarts advocated enfranchisement for the freedmen but supported readmission of un-Reconstructed, former Confederate states.[44]

Indeed, firmly opposed to the so-called rule by bayonet approach to the South, Evarts assisted the legal team that brought about Rutherford B. Hayes's ascension to the presidency in 1877. Evarts believed in freedom of enterprise, the paramount rights of private property, the due process of law limitation

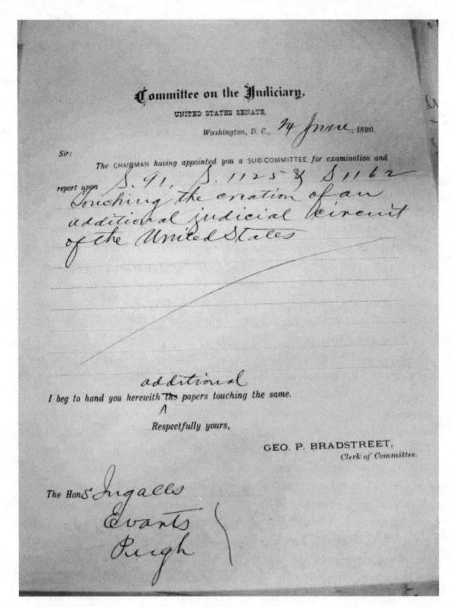

Figure 6.3 The House Judiciary Committee signed a bill in 1890 to replace the circuit trial courts with dedicated courts of appeal in each circuit. A revised version would later be called the Evarts Act of 1891, creating the circuit courts of appeal. Credit: House Judiciary Committee.

on government regulation of the economy, and in the moral rectitude of the American businessman. Consistent with these principles, he performed his duties as Hayes's secretary of state, and as president and one of the founding members of the New York State Bar Association and the American Bar Association.

Elected to the U.S. Senate in 1885, Evarts became a solid partisan for Republican policies. When the circuit courts of appeal bill came to the Senate, this thin, aged veteran of every aspect of federal governance saw it as a boon to lawyers and a capstone project of federal court reform dating back to 1800. Evarts offered his own bill to the Senate with the Rogers bill apparently stalled in the lower house, then lent his support to the Rogers bill when it arrived in the Senate.[45]

On September 19, 1890, Evarts spoke on the House bill. His contribution was more the momentum his career and reputation added to the movement for reform than major substantive addition to the debate. Indeed, his own proposal was only marginally different from Rogers's. Evarts did propose that the Supreme Court justices would only have to hear appeals in diversity cases they chose, on writs of certiorari (literally "to be examined"). As well, appeals based on constitutional questions would bypass the circuit courts of appeal and go directly to the Supreme Court. After the Senate was treated to a series of amendments that covered everything from the geographical shape of the circuits to the treatment of appeals from the Indian territories, Evarts portrayed the circuit courts of appeal as a neutral reform that relieved the Supreme Court of its overwhelming caseload. The terms he used were as instructive as the general content of his arguments. Four times he referred to the "administration of justice" and three times to the "judicial establishment." A conscious advocate of a more substantial national state, he frankly portrayed the courts as the best administrators for a nation that required more and more administrative expertise.[46]

One again, a chorus of opposition arose from southern senators. None were carpetbaggers. All had served the Confederacy. George Vest, for one, was not persuaded that another level of federal courts was necessary or proper. He practiced law before and after the Civil War in Missouri, during which he represented Missouri in the Confederacy's House of Representatives, then in its Senate. He returned to national political life in the 1870s, serving in the U.S. Senate from 1879 to 1903. His arguments repeated House southern Democrats' rejection of professional, unelected, central power. He compared the workload of federal judges unfavorably to that of state judges and denounced justices working in "the shadow of the [national] Capitol . . . They were unresponsive to any constituency, and life tenure isolated them from the will of the people." Vest's solution to the Supreme Court's heavy workload was to subdivide the bench. With a smaller number of justices deliberating and multiple panels at work, they could supposedly dispose of the burgeoning caseload three to four times more quickly. There would be no need to create more unelected judges.[47]

Vest continued. Would not this intermediate level of appellate scrutiny merely serve corporations seeking to delay litigation until it died? Pushed by the questioning of northern Republicans, Vest made his last stand. Paraphrasing some unnamed English judge, he asserted that "all justice should be administered in a manner acceptable to suitors; in other words, that the courts of the country should be popularized as far as possible . . . It is a country based upon the will of the people. It is a country that appeals in all its laws and in all the administration of its laws to the consent and confidence and affection of the people."[48]

Like punch-drunk fighters throwing wayward roundhouse blows in the fifteenth round, the two sides in the Senate missed the point of one another's arguments and staggered toward the end of the debate. One by one the amendments to the Evarts bill went down to defeat. On September 24 the Senators at long last voted, 41 to 6 in favor of passage with 31 absent. After a conference committee ironed out minor differences and more debate, in both houses the measure was adopted. [49]

The Act as amended provided for an additional Article III judge in each circuit and entirely new dedicated circuit courts of appeal. Judges named to the new courts of appeal would also be confirmed as members of the circuit courts' benches. The new courts would hear appeals from the district courts. Unlike the old circuit courts, the new courts of appeal were not trial courts. These new courts would fashion their own administrative rules, appoint clerks and marshals (as the existing district and circuit trial courts already did), collect fees (according to the Supreme Court schedule), and have the power to establish their own guidelines for the conduct of business. The law set a principal city where the court of appeals would sit: Boston for the first circuit, New York City for the second circuit, Philadelphia for the third circuit, Richmond for the fourth circuit, New Orleans for the fifth circuit, Cincinnati for the sixth circuit, Chicago for the seventh circuit, St. Louis for the eighth circuit, and San Francisco for the ninth circuit, and "in such other places in each of the above circuits as said court may from time to time designate." None of the initially designated seats for the courts was in a rural area and none was in the geographical center of the circuit. The choice of fixed seats in urban areas recognized the growing importance of cities in America and was a convenience for corporation lawyers who had offices in those cities. Note that all of them were railroad hubs—a major source of litigation in the federal courts and a major source of business for the federal bar. The designation of principal cities also fit the building program of the federal architects.[50]

After the Evarts Act passage, the old circuit trial courts' dockets showed a steady decline in caseload. In the Eastern District of Pennsylvania, for example, the October session for 1891 had 364 new filings and a year later, the filings were down to ninety. In 1893, they had fallen to forty-two. Yearly totals for the April and the October sessions fell from about 140 filings per year during the rest of the nineteenth century, to about 120 per year until 1911. Even these caseloads are misleading because some of these suits involved multiple visits to the court in the same session or over a series of sessions of cases first brought before the

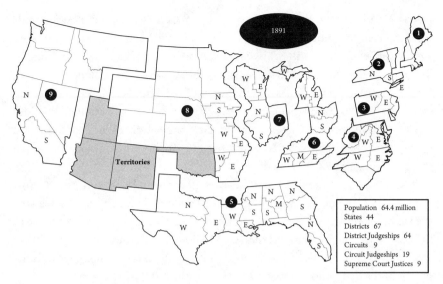

Figure 6.4 Federal judicial circuits in 1891. Source: Wheeler and Harrison, *Creating the Federal Judicial System,* courtesy of the Federal Judicial Center.

Evarts Act passed. Almost all of these were diversity suits, and many involved complex banking, railroad, and other commercial issues.[51]

Cases in the old circuit courts involving more than one session were as complex as they were interminable. Take, for example, *U.S. v. Five Parcels* (1893–1896), better known as the Gettysburg Battlefield Memorial cases. In them, the Gettysburg Battlefield Memorial Association created by Congress to protect "battlelines" and state "monuments" at Gettysburg sought the aid of the circuit court to remove offending private trolley lines like those of the Gettysburg Electric Company. The defendant companies replied that the fund set aside by Congress for the purchase of the land by eminent domain (the power of the government to take private property with compensation) was almost exhausted by earlier purchases, rendering the taking a virtual condemnation. Court of Appeals Judge George Mifflin Dallas, a Philadelphia attorney and scion of the illustrious Dallas dynasty, sitting on the circuit court, agreed. Nowhere in the Constitution did he find grounds for taking private property for the purpose of preserving a battlefield. He scolded U.S. Attorney Ellery Ingham's case for the government, depending as it did on a single clause of the Constitution—the Taxation Clause in Article 1, Section 8. Dallas found that clause "wholly irrelevant" to the case at hand. The opinion read like one of Dallas's lectures at the University of Pennsylvania law school; succinct and brooking little dissent. District Judge William Butler was not convinced. "I do not propose to enter an argument to sustain my views," he promised, then wrote an opinion three times as long and equally learned as Dallas's. Butler concluded that "the land described in the petition is adjacent to the Gettysburg National Cemetery." If no other grounds were asserted for eminent domain, this would have been sufficient—for there were veterans of that battle who would still be interred in those holy grounds. The case ended up as *U.S. v. Gettysburg Electric Railway Company* (1896), Butler's view trumping Dallas's. In his peroration, Justice Rufus Peckham waxed eloquent: "Such action [that Congress took to preserve the battlefield pristine] touches the heart, and comes home to the imagination of every citizen, and greatly tends to enhance his love and respect for those institutions for which these heroic sacrifices were made."[52]

The caseloads of the district courts were unchanged by the Evarts Act. Now the primary trial court venue for the federal system, district court caseloads in the years between the creation of the circuit courts of appeal and the demise of the old circuit courts in 1911 averaged 11,500 new cases filed each year. There was no trend up or down. The lowest year, with the nation emerging from the depths of the depression of 1893, was 1899, with 10,035. The year with the most new filings was 1907, at the end of another dip in the economy, with 15, 801.[53]

But new congressional enactments, added to the shift of more traditional serious federal crimes from the circuit courts, kept the district courts' grand juries busy. For the final nine years of the nineteenth century and the first decade of the twentieth, the Eastern District of Pennsylvania District Court averaged over seventy cases of these new statutory types per year. Philadelphia, where the court met, was a busy industrial, commercial, and overseas trade center, and as one would expect, the court disposed of immigration, customs, and fraud suits the government brought. In addition to the familiar prosecutions for mail fraud, theft from the mails, evasion of taxes on distilled alcohol, forgery, counterfeiting, and "secreting" an article of value in the mail without paying proper postage, however, the Eastern District sessions saw new offenses like violation of the Oliomargarine Act of 1886 (protecting the butter industry), sneaking Chinese laborers into the country in violation of the 1883 ban on Chinese immigration, making false entries on bank accounts contrary to the National Banking Act of 1863, and "depositing in the U.S. mail certain circulars declared unfit for mail." The clerk variously depicted these dangerously immoral packets as "cards with bad language," "obscene letters," and "inflammatory letter in mail," but more often than not the postmasters had discovered birth control devices banned from the mails by the 1873 "Comstock Act." In 1873, Anthony Comstock persuaded Congress to bar obscene materials—including birth control instructions— from the U.S. mail. It criminalized manufacturing or sending through the mails "an obscene book, pamphlet, paper, writing, advertisement, circular, print, picture, drawing or other representation, figure, or image on or of paper or other material, or any cast instrument, or other article of an immoral nature, or any drug or medicine, or any article whatever, for the prevention of conception."

Nothing matched the Southern District of New York's Comstockery cases— over fifty "obscene books" in a single year were ordered destroyed. In these cases, grand juries routinely brought indictments (more than 90 percent of the time), and defendants almost always pled guilty and paid the fines. In short, the Gilded Age district courts had become managers of an increasingly diverse and intrusive body of federal criminal law affecting a far larger portion of the population's daily lives than before the war. What was more, although federal criminal prosecutions in the district courts were few relative to prosecutions in state trial courts, the enlarged criminal jurisdiction of the district courts following the spurt of economic regulatory enactments in the 1880s and 1890s was a burden unanticipated by the proponents of the Evarts Act.[54]

Time and place still mattered in federal courts' business of course. To the Eastern District of Pennsylvania, for example, headquarters for many of the nation's railroads, came a slew of cases involving railroad receiverships. Railroads expanded their track and their commerce immensely after the recovery from the 1873 crash. Success brought its own problems, as companies competing for the same routes, particularly in the Middle Atlantic states, overbuilt and oversubsidized the expansion. One answer was the acquisition of rival firms and their right of ways. No rail firm was more aggressive in this than the Pennsylvania Railroad, the largest in the country. But too much expansion squeezed the capital reserves of larger lines like the Pennsy and its great rival the Reading Railroad. Curbs on railroad price-fixing and gouging that state governments and the federal Interstate Commerce Commission imposed after 1887 made a precarious situation even more perilous for the rail lines. When the crash of 1893 cost the companies freight revenues, they faced bankruptcy. At the request of a creditor, the federal court could come to the rescue, using its equitable powers to fashion a receivership, keeping the railroad line going while it reorganized its operations and paid off a portion of its debts. In the meantime, a mix of counsel for shareholders, creditors, financiers, and the railroad's lawyers appeared in court to argue over divvying up the remaining assets.[55]

Brought in equity, the railroad cases often took years to come to a final decree. For example, in *Van Siclen v. Bartol* (1899), a bondholder was upset because the reorganization plan left him empty-handed. He found that the court would not hold the reorganization committee liable for not informing him of its revision of the plan. The railroad had gone into receivership in 1891, but the first plan to repay the bondholders a portion of their principal failed in 1895. The second reorganization plan was filed with the district court in 1895, and Van Siclen was notified but he did not request his share until a week after the assets had been divided—too late, the court found—for him to collect leaving him without grounds to sue the reorganization committee. The most he could collect was $181 (with interest dating to 1895), his share of the expenses owed to the reorganization committee. In other cases a receiver was not held responsible for leases to rolling stock that the line, to which they were lent, temporarily used; nor could a creditor, even with judgment in his favor, sell property in the hands of a receiver. Three hundred and eighteen of these kinds of cases came to United States courts in the single decade of 1890–1899.[56]

At the other end of the nation, over the course of the same decade, grand juries sitting in San Antonio for the Western District of Texas heard 377 indictments for "military expedition," "conspiracy," and "exporting arms to Mexico" during the "Garza War" (1891–1893). Catarino Garza was born in Mexico and migrated to Brownsville, Texas, as a teenager. There he published a newspaper and became a leader in the Mexican-American border community. Urged on by friends from Mexico and expatriates in Texas, he joined the struggle against Mexican dictator Porfirio Diaz. Crossing the border to engage in armed raids against Diaz strongholds was a violation of American neutrality laws. These forbade aiding and abetting a revolution against a "friendly power" unless the United States had recognized the rebels as a belligerent power. Federal attorneys asked the military to capture and bring to trial the "Garzistas." For three years the rebels fought Diaz's forces and their U.S. allies; the rebellion finally ended with the capture and trial of its ringleaders. Given that many of the suspects were apprehended in Mexico by U.S. troops, the cases presented complex legal questions. Thomas Sheldon Maxey presided over the trials, allowing Garza to delay his own trial because he had become ill. Maxey, a Virginia lawyer who had served in the Confederate Army, may have had special insight into what would make men rebel against a government. In the end, juries convicted almost all the defendants including Garza, but the punishment was limited by the statute (although some of the defendants were extradited to Mexico at the conclusion of their jail time). The court remained embroiled in later border conflicts. For example, in 1913 a grand jury indicted one Emiliano Zapata (of later insurrectionary fame) for violation of the Neutrality Act.[57]

After their creation in 1891, the new courts of appeal soon grew busy. Unlike the district and circuit courts' dockets, the courts of appeal caseloads showed a clear upward trend, from a low in 1893 of 704, to 1,245 in 1911. The rise was even more dramatic in the busiest courts of appeal. In the Second Circuit Court of Appeals, for example, with its burden of regulatory cases, trademark and patent suits, and labor versus capital struggles, the number of appeals went from seventy-six in 1891 to 196 in 1900 and 323 in 1910. The same upward trend was true in the Third Circuit Court of Appeals, from twenty-six in 1892 to 133 in 1904 and 156 by 1915. The Fourth Circuit Court of Appeals docket grew as well, albeit more slowly and with lower totals from thirty-seven in 1892 to fifty-eight in 1895 and about the same each year thereafter until the eve of World War I. The Seventh Circuit Court of Appeals opened in 1891 with twenty-seven cases. The next year saw sixty-eight new cases docketed. By 1897 this number had risen to ninety-seven new cases. By the new century, the court had more than 100 new filings on average a year.[58]

Short on judges from their inception, the courts of appeal were slow in clearing their growing backlog. Delays led to the carryover of cases from session to session. In the Fourth Circuit Court of Appeals, by the late 1890s, the docket books averaged over 150 cases a year, and the new century brought a further increase to over 230 cases on average each year. The clerk's docket report for 1909, for example, recorded cases from three years earlier still being adjudicated in the court, and a total of 317 cases newly filed and pending. The same pattern held true through the eve of World War I, with totals in the low three hundreds. The D.C. Court of Appeals, created by statute in 1893, was immediately busy, with 281 cases docketed in 1893. The number dropped to 134 in 1894 and averaged a little over 100 a year until 1913, with temporary rises to 135 in 1905 and 158 in 1910. Thereafter, the average remained steady at 135. Nearly swamped, already feeling the pinch of too few judges covering too many cases, the courts of appeal were struggling to dispose of as many cases each year as were filed in that year, but new cases kept arriving at an increasing rate, further clogging the dockets.[59]

The Evarts Act was the end result of the twenty-year debate on the expansion of the federal court system, and it has a place in the history of the federal courts nearly equaling that of the Judiciary Act of 1789. But proposed and defended to reduce the backlog in the Supreme Court, the Act contrariwise spurred litigation rates in the federal courts. Just as highway planners have discovered that building additional lanes on a highway does not relieve traffic, but instead attracts more traffic, in creating courts of appeal Congress added to the federal court loads. In a further irony, passed as a compromise measure to allay state court suspicion of rival federal courts, the Evarts Act enabled the national government's judiciary to play a greater role in American self-government. And if the Judiciary Act of 1891's purpose was to reduce the load on the Supreme Court and speed its handling of cases, its success was mixed. At first, the burden on the Supreme Court was reduced from an average of the mid-500s in the 1880s, peaking at 636 in 1890, down to 383 in 1891, 290 in 1892, but then beginning to creep upward to 341 in 1894, 386 in 1895, then into the mid-500s new cases each year in the first decades of the new century. The courts of appeal cases were being appealed to the Supreme Court. One benefit to the justices' personal lives and health was undeniable however—they no longer had to ride circuit as often.[60]

Gilded Age Federal Judges

Presidents Benjamin Harrison and Grover Cleveland named ten men to fill the new courts of appeal slots. All were confirmed in the Senate. They included Dallas; William Ball Gilbert, a Republican state legislator and practicing lawyer in Portland, Oregon, who served from 1892 until his death in 1931; Nathan Goff, a West Virginian whose service in the Union Army and whose Republican credentials brought him the post of U.S. attorney for the district, a nineteen-year stint on the Fourth Circuit Court of Appeals, followed by another term representing the state in the U.S. Senate; Andrew P. McCormick, a former Confederate officer who became a Republican after the war, thereafter a state judge, a federal attorney for the Eastern District of Texas, a district judge, and finally an inaugural member of the Fifth Circuit Court of Appeals; and Joseph McKenna, a California Republican and former attorney general of the United States who would leave the Ninth Circuit Court of Appeals to join the justices on the Supreme Court in 1898. William L. Putnam, a Democrat from Maine who opposed secession, was named to the First Circuit Court of Appeals; Walter Henry Sanborn, a St. Paul railroad lawyer, to the Eighth Circuit Court of Appeals, and Nathaniel Shipman, whose service on the federal district court in Connecticut preceded his appointment as Second Circuit Court of Appeals judge. William Howard Taft accepted appointment to the Sixth Circuit Court of Appeals, a stint followed by his service as governor general of the American-occupied Philippines, secretary of war, the presidency, and finally the center chair on the Supreme Court. William A. Woods, an Indiana lawyer and federal district judge, became a Seventh Circuit Court of Appeals judge. Harrison and Cleveland avoided the mistake of John Adams's "midnight judges" appointed in 1801; the appointees to the new courts of appeal came from both parties.[61]

What can be said—or rather cannot be said—of this judge list as a whole is tremendously important to understanding recruitment and service on the federal bench in the Gilded Age. Elite lawyering in that era was different from top-drawer lawyering in the antebellum period. Some of these lawyers exemplified the "organizational synthesis" pioneered by the leaders of the major corporations. They formed partnerships and centralized their operations. Led by the example of men like David Dudley Field of New York, educated at top law schools like Harvard, Yale, Columbia, and Penn instead of reading law in a practitioner's office, they brought sophistication and learning to practice in the federal courts. They also earned more in retainers and hourly billing than their predecessors, joining the upper level management of the corporations they served as a new professional elite. The founding of the American Bar Association by Simeon Baldwin in 1878, bringing together "the best men of the bar" from all over the country, signaled the arrival of this elite bar.[62]

But most of the judges named to the federal courts in these years were not members of the new elite. They were almost all small city or town lawyers whose public service and important political connections attracted the attention of the president, the attorney general, or their senators and at the same time made judicial office attractive. They came to the attention of the president because he knew them, or his attorney general knew them, or because a member of Congress from their state and their party supported their cause. Many had worked for the railroads—it was the most lucrative retainer a lawyer could have—but with a few exceptions (Associate Justices Stanley Mathews and Samuel Blatchford) they were not the elite members of the railroad bar.[63]

The new bench reflected the recruitment patterns of an older period, featuring letters of support to the attorney general or the president from local bar associations. That pattern had served the federal courts, and the nation, well. The eastern and midwestern backgrounds of the Gilded Age western federal judges, like the spread of the district and circuit court system across that nation itself, united a judiciary that now stretched from ocean to ocean. For example, Moses Hallett, the sole district judge for the District of Colorado, was born and raised in Illinois and practiced law in Chicago before the war. James H. Beatty, who sat on the bench in the District of Idaho during this period, was reared in Ohio, served in the Union Army, taught school in Mississippi, and practiced law in Missouri before his appointment. Hiram Knowles, the district judge in the District of Montana, was born in Maine and practiced in Nevada before his was elevated to the bench. Ohioan George Sabin was succeeded by Indiana's Thomas Hawley on the Nevada bench, and Cornelius Hanford, who occupied the bench in Washington, came from Iowa. He alone among the district judges had early removed himself to the far West. Though the decentralized system of trial courts still reflected its compromise federalism origins, the common background of the judges and the new appeal provisions furthered the creation of a uniform national law.

The perhaps unfortunate side effect of the persistence of older recruitment patterns was a bench that did not fully comprehend how profoundly different America was from the pre–Civil War years when the judges and justices entered the bar. Their notions of law, of the economy, and in particular the relationship of government, capital, and labor were rooted in a society and culture passing from the scene. The Supreme Court presented the most obvious examples of this cultural lag. For example, Waite's replacement, Melville W. Fuller, gained his place because Democratic President Grover Cleveland hoped to secure Illinois support for his reelection in 1888. A younger Fuller had gone west to seek his fortune when prospects in his native Maine paled, much like Justices Miller and Field. During the Civil War, he had flirted with Illinois Copperhead Democrats, and with the war's end, he built a very lucrative legal practice representing business interests in Chicago. He combined prewar states' rights philosophy with an even stronger laissez-faire stance and a fierce antagonism to unions (perhaps a result of his corporate law practice in Chicago during the Haymarket riots). Fuller gets high marks for his administrative skills, hostility to class legislation, solicitude for individual property rights, and for restoring the "traditional" balance between federal and state regulation of the economy. He earns a somewhat lower grade for "a slender stock of judicial ideas," his defense of wealth against public regulation, and presiding over a Court that "turned a blind eye to racial segregation."[64]

To a greater extent than the members of any prior Courts save John Marshall's, the justices on Fuller's Court shared a common outlook: a fervent belief in laissez-faire capitalism. First to join Fuller was David J. Brewer, a Yale graduate, who had studied at Albany Law School and then apprenticed in his uncle David Dudley Field's office. There he learned firsthand how the greatest of all the corporate lawyers of this time plied his trade. Brewer then went west to Leavenworth, Kansas, where he served at every level as a state judge. He ruled in favor of the Kansas system of segregation in the schools—the system overturned in *Brown v. Board of Education of Topeka, Kansas* (1954). He cited the overriding importance of local control of the schools as "dear to his heart," which in practice amounted to white control of blacks' lives and fortunes. Serving from 1890 to 1910, Brewer had little use for "the paternal theory of government" and generally opposed government regulation of rates, wages, working conditions, and prices. "I believe the time is not distant when the evils resulting from this assumption of a power on the part of government to determine the compensation a man may receive for the use of his property, or the performance of his personal services, will become so apparent that the courts will hasten" to overturn all such legislation. But he was not opposed to all government intervention—he believed that the courts should and could intervene to protect private property. For example, he strongly supported the "labor injunction" by which courts could, on the petition of owners of businesses, enjoin workers from striking and criminally punish any worker who violated the injunction.[65]

President Harrison next appointed Henry Billings Brown, whose opinion in *Plessy* would repeat the racist clichés of the age. He joined the Court in 1891 after serving for fourteen years as district judge for eastern Michigan. A year later Harrison selected George Shiras Jr., a Pennsylvania Republican, who appreciated the value of railroads and big business. Shiras served for ten terms and Brown for fifteen. Harrison had a chance to name a fourth justice, Howell E. Jackson, whose long service as counsel to the railroads and his personal friendship with both

Cleveland and Harrison gained him a place on the Sixth Circuit federal bench and then appointment to the Supreme Court. In ill health when appointed in 1893, he died two years later at home in Nashville, Tennessee, from tuberculosis.

President Cleveland added two justices to the Fuller Court. Edward D. White, selected in 1894, entered Louisiana politics as a Democratic "Redeemer" when the state's government returned to its prewar lily-white shape. He believed in states' rights and defended the sugar monopoly of his clients—a lawyer who served his wealthy masters with fierce loyalty. He was serving as a U.S. senator from Louisiana when appointed to the Court.[66] The following year Cleveland appointed his close friend Rufus W. Peckham, a New Yorker from a family of lawyers. On the state court Peckham generally opposed regulatory legislation and was stridently antiunion and probusiness. To him, as for his brethren on the Fuller Court, private property was sacred.[67]

The Federal Courts and the Trusts: Separation of Powers Revisited

With the Congress ending its experiment with civil rights legislation, the Compromise of 1877 leading to the withdrawal of federal troops from the former Confederate states, and the courts pronouncing Reconstruction done, there seemed little likelihood of confrontation between the federal courts and the other branches of the federal government. That calm ended with the passage of the Sherman Antitrust Act of 1890. For the next forty years the federal bench's views of the sanctity of private property came up against the will of Congress in a series of antitrust cases.

In the years after 1877 a veritable revolution occurred in the institutional and financial structure of the largest corporations. Industrialists like steel magnate Andrew Carnegie achieved a near monopoly of formerly competing firms, creating a conglomerate that controlled much of the supply of steel products, though he insisted that competition was the lifeblood of industry and invention. Other industrial leaders sought to concentrate the supply of raw materials in their own hands in what has been called "vertical monopoly." John D. Rockefeller's Standard Oil Company led the way in this business innovation. On the financial side, the commercial or business trust was pioneered by lawyers William Nelson Cromwell and John B. Dill to integrate the management of these giant business concerns by moving (fictive) assets to trusts. The trust protected firms like Rockefeller's Standard Oil Company from state regulations against restraint of trade. Against such "combinations" that restrained free trade, Congress passed the Sherman Antitrust Act of 1890.[68]

Aimed at the great combinations of corporations that effectually monopolized an industry in restraint of free trade, the Sherman Antitrust Act of 1890 statute reflected a very old idea—the inherent value of free market competition—in a time when markets were increasingly controlled by corporate producers. While these may or may not have been more efficient than a marketplace of many smaller businesses, the Act had a strong moral component. Competition was good; unfair or conspiratorial efforts to restrict competition were bad. A movement to repeal the law the year after it went into effect failed, not because of insufficient lobbying efforts (the trusts spared no expense to buy the vote), but because the old ideology was so deeply entrenched in American voters' minds.[69]

The Sherman Act gave a powerful weapon to the federal government to combat the trusts. The key provision, Section Four, enabled U.S. attorneys to bring suit in federal court both to "prevent and restrain such violations of this act." These suits came before a district judge and could be appealed after 1891 to the courts of appeal. Acting in the public interest, the federal government became the prosecutor of monopolists, though under the Act individuals and companies could bring their own suits. The discretion given the district attorneys was immense. That discretion was exercised with great caution. Over the course of Sherman Act antitrust jurisprudence (1890–1914), relatively few cases came to trial. Of the twenty-one suits brought between 1890 and 1900, half resulted in court-ordered injunctions against the defendants. The law's mechanisms did not act as a deterrent, however, as manufacturers, railway owners, and mine owners continued to form monopolies.

The government won the first two of these suits, U.S. v. Jellico Mountain Coke (1891) and U.S. v. Trans-Missouri Freight Association (1892). Thereafter, the result was mixed, as U.S. v. E.C. Knight had a chilling influence on intrastate manufacturing monopolies. The first labor case, U.S. v. Workingman's Amalgamated Council of New Orleans (1893) laid the groundwork for the antilabor injunction, about which more in the next chapter. In the period 1900–1914, the cases slowed to a trickle, though the government almost invariably won, notably against the Swift and Armour meat-packing companies, and the Northern Securities and Standard Oil Trusts.[70]

One reason for the relative paucity of suits was the outcome of the first of the great antitrust cases. The federal government prosecuted the E.C. Knight sugar-refining company and other refining operations, all part of the same sugar trust, for violation of the Act. The Act stated that "every contract, combination in the form of trust, or otherwise, or conspiracy in restraint of trade and commerce among the several States is illegal, and that persons who shall monopolize or shall attempt to monopolize, or combine or conspire with any other persons to monopolize any part of the trade and commerce among the several States, shall be guilty of a misdemeanor." The American Sugar Refining company was buying up its competitors, including E.C. Knight, in an attempt to control all refining in the country and following that, control, supply, and pricing. The case came to the Circuit Court for the Eastern District of Pennsylvania in 1894, and U.S. Attorney Ellery Ingham once more stood before District Judge Butler (as he had in the Gettysburg eminent domain case), once more arguing that a company violated an act of Congress. Once again Ingham lost. Butler found the company had nothing to do with interstate trade, and so could not come under the rubric of the statute. After a failed appeal to the Third Circuit Court of Appeals, the government appealed to the Supreme Court. Chief Justice Fuller agreed with the lower court ruling. To him it seemed as simple as ABC. A: "[T]he monopoly and restraint denounced by the act are the monopoly and restraint of interstate and international trade or commerce, while the conclusion to be assumed on this record is that the result of the transaction complained of was the creation of a monopoly in the manufacture" of sugar. B: "The fundamental question is, whether conceding that the existence of a monopoly in manufacture is established by the evidence, that monopoly can be directly suppressed under the act of Congress in the mode attempted by this bill." Congress had the power to regulate interstate commerce, but, C: "that which belongs to commerce is within the jurisdiction of the United States, but that which does not belong to commerce is within the jurisdiction of the police power of the State." The refineries were manufacturing plants wholly within the states of Delaware, Pennsylvania, and New Jersey.[71]

One might view the case as proof that the checks and balances system worked, or alternatively that the will of the people had been frustrated by a judiciary out of touch with the realities of modern industrial financial practices. Indeed, between 1897 and 1904, 4,227 firms merged again and again until "they had consolidated to form 257 corporations." By 1904, 318 companies controlled about 40 percent of the nation's manufacturing output. In seventy-eight industries, a single firm produced over half that industry's output. At the top of these pyramids of industry were the trusts that enabled the tobacco, sugar, oil, steel, and other industries to reduce competition and control the labor market. However one viewed *E.C. Knight*, it heralded a renewed test of the Madisonian Compromise, a test that would soon become far more arduous as a new reform movement took shape.[72]

In their resistance to state and federal regulatory regimes at the end of the Gilded Age, the federal courts had embraced the ideas of laissez-faire free market. But the business conditions which, before the Civil War, had given rise to this ideology no longer held sway. Among academics, journalists, and reformers, the ideology itself was under attack. "The popularity of laissez-faire was ebbing" by the middle 1890s as new theories of how the economy actually worked were adopted by a new generation of academically trained social scientists. Views of the "iron laws" of economics might have come into flower on the Court, but in the country they were fading.[73]

A gap was opening between the mental landscape of the federal bench and the actual landscape of industrial concentrations. The consequence of this disparity between judicial ideology and economic reality ill fitted many members of the federal bench to make concessions to popular distrust of giant business combinations. A jurisprudence that made sense in an older era seemed out of place, making the federal courts targets of those whose actual enemy was the large corporation. This critique of the federal courts was gaining traction in the states, with the result that state regulation of the economy was increasingly common. Railroads, banks, and industries then challenged these state regulations in federal courts, creating the potential for an escalating cycle of cases, criticism and crisis in judicial federalism. Scholars might concede that "[t]o engage in conflicts with the political branches is the Court's prerogative," but such contests only prove that the courts were inescapably political institutions, and if they were out of sync with popular political opinion, the reputation of the courts would suffer.[74]

Federal Courts in the Progressive Era, 1897–1919

While the creation of the courts of appeal was the most far-reaching institutional alteration of the federal court system since the Judiciary Act of 1789, the impact of the Evarts Act was eclipsed in the public mind by the spectacle of federal courts, state legislatures, and Congress at odds over what appeared to be "judicial solicitude" toward the large corporations and the railroads. That controversy is the proper beginning of this chapter.[1]

Decisions like *E.C. Knight* drew the courts to the center of the political arena, dismaying "a broad cross section of public opinion." The Court's decisions brought attacks on all levels of the federal judiciary, amplified because federal judges were not subject to election and had life tenure. One Populist-Democratic governor, Claude Matthews of Indiana, sounded the alarm of a judicial federalism skewed toward the central government: "The federal courts have in recent years been reaching out and gathering to themselves jurisdiction in matters that are within the province of the states alone. I think this tendency should be resisted." Nebraska lawyer and Populist leader William Jennings Bryan, who captured the Democratic Party nomination in 1896, aimed his barbs directly at the Court. "They criticize us for our criticism of the Supreme Court of the United States. My friends, we have made no criticism. We have simply called attention to what you know. If you want criticisms, read the dissenting opinions of the Court. That will give you criticisms."[2]

Bryan was defeated decisively in the 1896 presidential election, and the Populist movement he led never quite recovered its electoral strength, but a new reform movement, called by its members "Progressivism" was gaining prominence, and it would take up the hue and cry against the federal courts. Leading Progressives were educated, urban professionals and business people. They shared a moralizing absolutism and the ideal of clean, efficient government by professionals like themselves. In order to bypass city and state political machines, Progressives pushed for and won the secret ballot, a constitutional amendment for the direct election of senators, and changes to several state constitutions providing referenda, ballot initiatives, and the recall of state officials. Progressives also sought and achieved a constitutional amendment allowing the collection of national income taxes. Not so admirable was the almost unthinking snobbery and indifferent racism that lurked at the edges of the Progressive reform, expressing itself in anti-immigration legislation, the refusal to return to the Reconstruction agenda of equal rights, and an imperialism that assumed the "little brown brother" (Governor General William Howard Taft's patronizing term) of the Philippines and other newly acquired territorial possessions supposedly required the paternal ministrations of the white race.[3]

The Populists' antagonism to the federal courts had been, in part, parochial, a suspicion of the federal government that recalls some themes found in the opposition to the Evarts Act. The Progressive campaign against the federal courts was more sophisticated, driven by opposition to federal injunctive powers, substantive due process review of state regulation of the workplace, and the federal courts' apparent resistance to legislative reform initiatives. To be sure, the Progressive movement was not monolithic. Some Progressives were far more conservative than others. But all agreed that some reform of the federal courts was desirable. "In the years following 1900, Progressives turned the populist attack on the federal judiciary into a staple of political debate."[4]

The Assault on the Federal Injunctive Power

Because federal tribunals were courts of equity, federal judges could issue injunctions. Until 1908, a single district judge could command the parties before the court (or even a party not present in court) to do or not do some act in all kinds of suits. Most common in nuisance suits and cases of trusteeship, the federal injunction had a wide range of uses, including antitrust injunctions. They could even be leveled ex parte at individuals or groups who were not in court. Although governed by clear and strict rules, the issuance of injunctions by individual judges remained discretionary.[5]

Throughout the period covered in this chapter, Progressive critics of the federal courts focused on their wide-ranging injunctive power. For example, Progressive Governor George Sheldon of Nebraska blasted its district court for enjoining a state rate schedule for rail haulage of farmers' grain, "I believe the federal courts have abused the privilege of injunction." He wanted a constitutional amendment to curb judicial use of that power. While the Progressives were not particularly sympathetic to the industrial labor movement, the antilabor injunction's spread aroused the suspicions of liberal politicians, respected jurists, and teachers of law. Such injunctions were sought by manufacturers and businesses to curb or prevent labor union work stoppages. While temporary injunctions of this sort were often issued against organizations, for example an entire union, they were enforceable against individual officials of the union. Failure to obey led to contempt citations and jail, even when the labor leaders had no notice of the injunction and were not represented in court when the injunction was issued. Theodore Roosevelt admonished the courts on this score. "In this matter of injunctions there is lodged in the hands of the judiciary a necessary power which is nevertheless subject to the possibility of grave abuse. It is a power that should be exercised with extreme care and should be subject to the jealous scrutiny of all men."[6]

The labor injunction, more properly termed an antilabor injunction, had long been a hot-button issue for labor reformers. *In Re Debs*, a suit arising from an injunction against the American Railway Workers Union for closing the rail yards in 1894, had moved the antilabor injunction to the top of the reformers' agenda. Although the basis for the injunction was not the Sherman Antitrust Act, *Debs* could be read to prove that the Sherman Antitrust Act allowed injunctive relief for a business facing organized labor activities. In the years after *Debs*, the great preponderance of injunctions came from state courts, but federal courts found grounds for enjoining labor activity in some 100 of the 118 applications between 1877 and 1930. As Judge Taft of the Sixth Circuit Court of Appeals wrote, ruling in a Railroad Engineers Union strike, "neither law nor morals can give a man a right . . . to withhold his labor" in violation of a contract or in support of another local of a national union. After the injunction, predictably, the strike failed.[7]

More forceful denunciations of this judicial curb on otherwise legal labor organizing and strike tactics bewailed the injunction as unwonted misuse of judicial power—"government by injunction"—and argued that the federal judiciary had willfully usurped the role of Congress. As Thomas Carl Spelling, a New York City lawyer and author of a treatise on injunctive remedies (as well as books on bossism, trusts, monopolies, and other abuses of public power), told the House Judiciary Committee in 1908, "The courts, supposedly the representatives of the Government and handmaids of public justice, are thus guaranteeing to a certain class immunity against the ordinary vicissitudes and hazards of business. And they are doing this in a country of supposed equals, and in order to do it are robbing thousands and millions of men of their liberties."[8]

In 1903, 1906, and 1910, Congress provided some respite from the outcry against the federal injunction by requiring a three-judge panel for injunctive relief, respectively, to hear antitrust cases, cases when an order of the Interstate Commerce Commission was challenged, and most controversially, when a petitioner sought to bar a state from enforcing its own laws. The immediate cause of the third iteration of the three-judge court was widespread reaction against *Ex Parte Young* (1908). In that case the Supreme Court refused to issue habeas corpus to free the attorney general of Minnesota. The previous year Attorney General Edward Young, a lawyer and schoolteacher from Chippewa County and former member of the state legislature, had ignored a circuit court's temporary injunction barring Minnesota from applying its railroad rate regulations. Judge Walter Sanborn had not only enjoined the state from enforcing its own rate laws, when Young ignored the order, Sanborn ordered him jailed for contempt of court. The state was a hotbed of reformism and the successful petitioners were stockholders of the railroad whose rates the reformers had targeted.

The Supreme Court upheld the district court order. Progressive leaders were furious. North Carolina Senator Lee Slater Overman, a Progressive Democrat, told his colleagues that they should "not allow a federal court to enjoin the enforcement of a state statute." The least the legislators could do was prevent a single federal judge from stopping a state from enforcing its own laws. Old-fashioned federalism and Gilded Age born reformism combined to demand the enlarged panel in such cases. Like its predecessors, the Three-judge Act of 1910 did not make the three-judge panel mandatory. Instead, it gave the lower courts some discretion in determining whether a three-judge panel was appropriate, and it did not apply to the antilabor temporary restraining orders. As with many patchwork enactments, critics soon found that the panels consumed time and judicial resources while litigants could never be certain whether they would get a three-judge panel.[9]

In Congress, reformers continued to campaign against the antilabor injunction. Henry DeLamar Clayton Jr. of Alabama led the way. Though his 1912 anti-injunction bill failed of passage, he was able to get its core inserted in the Clayton Anti-Trust Act two years later. Shortly thereafter, President Woodrow Wilson chose Clayton for the Northern District of Alabama bench. The Clayton Act barred federal courts from indiscriminant antitrust injunctions against labor unions. As Section 6 of the Act explained, "The labor of a human being is not a commodity or article of commerce. Nothing contained in the antitrust laws shall be construed to forbid the existence and operation of labor, agricultural, or horticultural organizations. . . . from lawfully carrying out the legitimate objects thereof; nor shall such organizations, or the members thereof, be held or construed to be illegal combinations or conspiracies in restraint of trade, under the antitrust laws." Section 20 of the Act went even further, explicitly barring injunctive relief to employers unless "necessary to prevent irreparable injury to property, or to a property right." So long as strikers used "peaceful means" to make their case to the public or to other workers, no contempt charges for violating an injunction could be filed against the organization or any member of it. This did not stop federal courts from interpreting the statute to allow the very conduct it seemed, on its face, to denounce.[10]

The Progressives, *Lochner v. New York*, and the Recall Movement

At the national level, the most prominent Progressive was President Theodore Roosevelt. The leader of the liberal wing of the movement, Roosevelt actively sponsored most of the reform legislation passed during his administration. Although his handpicked successor, William Howard Taft, actually "busted" more trusts than he did, Roosevelt's trust-busting gained greater publicity. Roosevelt recalled the time early in his tenure as president when he was "waked to a dim and partial understanding that the courts were not necessarily the best judges of what should be done to better social and industrial conditions." It was not that the judges were bad men on these occasions, but their decisions were wrong. "They knew legalism, but not life."[11]

The prime occasion for Roosevelt's frustration with the federal courts was one case from his state of New York. In *Lochner v. New York* (1905) the Supreme Court refused to defer to the state legislature's findings—findings based on the kind of factual evidence that Progressives admired. *Lochner* involved a challenge to the New York Bakeshop Act of 1895. On health grounds, it limited the hours a baker could be made to work to ten per day or sixty per week. Joseph Lochner, whose bakery in Utica did not quite fit the horrible conditions of the tenement bakeries the Act's progressive promoters had portrayed, refused to obey and, held liable, refused to pay his fines. His counsel argued that the Act violated Lochner's and his workers' freedom to enter contracts, freedom arguably protected from a state's interference by the Due Process Clause of the Fourteenth Amendment. Although the state legislature twice passed the Act unanimously, and the state's courts declined to honor his claims, the Supreme Court agreed to hear the case.[12]

In by far the majority of state regulatory regimes, the federal courts allowed the states' laws to stand. States could pass laws protecting the health and welfare of their inhabitants. In these cases, however, one does not see deference to the states or to federalism so much as the federal courts imposing their own doctrinal test. Thus, the same line of cases can be read as empowering the Supreme Court, as the guardian of the Due Process Clause, to review state legislation that unconstitutionally interfered with private property rights. In *Lochner*, Justice Rufus Peckham wrote for the majority: "The [Bakeshop Act] necessarily interferes with the right of contract between the employer and employees . . . The

Figure 7.1 Joseph Lochner photographed in his bakery in Utica, New York, 1904.
Credit: Photograph by Dante Tranquille, courtesy of Mrs. Joanne Brady.

general right to make a contract in relation to his business is part of the liberty of the individual protected by the Fourteenth Amendment of the Federal
Constitution." State regulations of economic activities or individual rights were
not unconstitutional per se, but "there is a limit to the valid exercise of the police
power by the State . . . Otherwise the Fourteenth Amendment would have no
efficacy and the legislatures of the States would have unbounded power."[13]

Harlan dissented. He cited prior cases in which the Court had deferred to legislatures and social science evidence. "The right to contract in relation to persons
and property or to do business, within a State, may be 'regulated and sometimes
prohibited, when the contracts or business conflict with the policy of the State
as contained in its statutes.' " When could and should a court override the state?
Rarely and with great trepidation: "Upon this point there is no room for dispute;
for, the rule is universal that a legislative enactment, Federal or state, is never

to be disregarded or held invalid unless it be, beyond question, plainly and pal-pably in excess of legislative power." Harlan then presented a mini-brief, drawn from a variety of social science and government reports, to show that the bakery industry was indeed dangerous to its employees. Justices Edward D. White and William Rufus Day agreed.[14]

Roosevelt's first nominee to the Supreme Court, Oliver Wendell Holmes Jr., had no love lost for laboring men's rights, but he too dissented. He did not see why Peckham's economic ideology should be constitutionalized, any more than any judge's personal views of liberty should trump a legislature's. Here he wrote, "This case is decided upon an economic theory which a large part of the country does not entertain . . . I strongly believe that my agreement or disagreement has nothing to do with the right of a majority [in a legislature] to embody their opinions in law . . . The Fourteenth Amendment does not enact Mr. Herbert Spencer's *Social Statics*."[15]

After *Lochner*, the Progressive assault on the federal courts gained momen-tum. To contemporary critics the Supreme Court seemed to have forgotten the compromise inherent in the Judiciary Act of 1789's Section 25. (A little

Figure 7.2 Oliver Wendell Holmes Jr. 1914, when he was already recognized as one of the finest penmen in the history of the Court. Photograph by Harris and Ewing. Credit: Library of Congress.

history lesson would have reminded critics that John Marshall's Court had taken a similar stand in *McCulloch*—and faced a similar chorus of objections.) The *New York Times*, a paper generally supportive of the federal courts, recognized that President Roosevelt and Congress "appear to distrust the federal courts." The critics' barbs stung members of the judiciary. As Judge William Wallace, the Second Circuit senior judge (in modern parlance the chief judge) told an evening gathering in New York, "I wish to depreciate and denounce the recent attempts that have been made to censure federal judges because some of them have seen fit closely to hew to the line of their judicial duty."[16]

In the meantime, the doctrinal rigidity that marked opinions like *Lochner* had found one brilliant critic from the heartland of the country. Roscoe Pound, the son of a Lincoln, Nebraska, lawyer, led a law school campaign to blast federal courts' formalistic style of judging. After service as dean of the new law school at Nebraska, Pound accepted positions at Northwestern, Chicago, and then Harvard Law School. In an influential 1908 law review article, Pound took the Supreme Court to task for its "mechanical jurisprudence." He insisted that modern, enlightened courts should bow to legislatures when the representative branches were accommodating public needs. That was the lesson of his "sociological jurisprudence," a combination of enlightened European jurisprudential trends and his own liberal Republican progressivism. He feared that courts' decisions were, or seemed to be, bent on protecting the wealthy classes against the working classes.[17]

The recall of judges movement was a second, even more direct assault on the independence of the federal judiciary. Debate over recall resuscitated much older arguments about separation of powers, checks and balances, and added newer arguments about democracy. The result was the bedding of odd fellows—the last of the Southern opponents of the federal courts making common cause with the younger advocates of progressive reform. Walter Clark of North Carolina straddled these alliances, a former Confederate soldier, a sitting state supreme court justice, and in his later years, a progressive Democrat, Clark wanted a truly democratic bench. He rooted his argument in what might today be called the doctrine of a living Constitution: "When the Constitution of the United States was adopted at Philadelphia . . . a representative democracy was an experiment, and there was a frankly expressed fear of committing power to the masses." The country had proved that a government resting on a broad base of suffrage could endure and prosper, a world of change from that the framers of the Constitution inhabited. "The unnatural thing is, not its adoption in 1787, but the retention, unchanged, of the non-elective features of the [1787] Constitution in 1904." The most unnatural of those provisions seemed to Clark to be an unelected judicial branch.[18]

In an address to his own state bar association in 1912, Oklahoma Senator Robert Owen made the strongest case for recall. Infuriated that President Taft had vetoed a bill for the admission of Arizona because its state constitution would have included recall of state judges, Owen thundered, "The Federal judiciary has, in my opinion, become the bulwark of privilege and ought to be made immediately subject to legislative recall by the representatives of the people for the safety of the people and for the stability of the property of the masses—of the producers of the Nation." In the lower house, Owen's call was echoed by Minnesota's James Manahan. Manahan had moved not only to the left as the Progressive movement gained steam, he had shifted his allegiance from the Democratic to the Republican Party. An ally of Progressive leader Robert La Follette of Wisconsin, Manahan's sponsorship carried the weight of the most liberal wing of the Progressive alliance. He too used the state bar association as his forum, and then arranged for his words to appear in the *Congressional Record*: "It is urged that the recall of judges would subject the judiciary to the clamor of the mob, that we must have a fearless judiciary. The man who believes the people are a mob does not believe in republican form of government . . . A fearless judge would never fear the people. A cowardly judge would fear the people less than he would the political boss and big business men who made him."[19]

Despite the fervid language of the Progressives, the recall of judges movement did not turn out to be a serious threat to the independence of the federal judiciary. Even Roosevelt would concede that the movement aimed to challenge the federal courts' interpretation of law rather than punish individual judges for exercising their official duties. He wrote in 1914:

> My contention is that we are not concerned with the question whether Mr. Taft and his followers are right or wrong in holding that the judge-made laws . . . are "the best laws we have." We are greatly concerned, however, with the question as to whether we have or have not the right to decide these questions for ourselves instead of having them decided for us by men whose decisions we regard as unjust . . . This is all that is meant by the somewhat misleading term "recall of judicial decisions." What we aim to accomplish would be better expressed by the phrase "the right of the people to review judge-made law."[20]

A third Progressive project to curb the unwonted independence of federal judges would involve Congress imposing term limitations or other than impeachment and trial provisions to remove federal judges. The problem with this most sweeping of all changes in the system of federal courts was that it would have seriously diminished the appeal of service on the federal bench. As it was, some of the judges had given up far more lucrative legal practices to accept elevation to the federal bench. Without the protection of good conduct tenure, recruitment would have been far more difficult. As it was, one *New York Times* editorial joked, "no sane man would give up a practice of which the income was $30,000 a year for a salary of $3,000." Senator (and shortly to be Justice) George Sutherland explained in 1913:

> Judges are selected for their learning, ability, and impartiality, but if they are to be made subject to reversal by the vote of a majority, such men will inevitably disappear from the bench and politicians will take their places who will very naturally endeavor to ascertain the drift of popular sentiment before deciding, and decisions instead of reflecting the intelligent and independent judgment of the judge will voice the speculations of the politician as to what the opinion of the majority is likely to be.[21]

Although in the end the reform program came to no more than incremental adjustments of procedure like the Three-judge Act, the disrespect of the federal judiciary in all of these reform campaigns seemed very real to federal court defenders. In the words of Ezra Thayer, dean of Harvard Law School, the reform proposals were a club to brandish over the head of the federal courts wielded by their political foes, notably Roosevelt, in a "popular demonstration" of opposition to the courts' refusal to give fullest rein to congressional legislative intent. Inadvertently, for this was not their intent, Sutherland and Thayer had demonstrated the truth of what Roosevelt had averred—that the Court was an institution in a political system subject to partisan attack. "Judicial usurpation" of the more properly exercised functions of elected state and federal bodies continued to be a theme of Progressives.[22]

A more telling setback to the Progressives' program came in 1918 and involved a centerpiece of progressive reform—child labor. The invention of fast camera film at Eastman Kodak and the development of motion pictures at Eastman and at Thomas Alva Edison's labs enabled reformers to document and present to the nation the face of child labor. Reformers like New York City's Lewis Hine traveled throughout the country's mines and mills, sweatshops and street corners, capturing the faces of children old before their time. In stark contrast to the emerging child-centered family culture of the middle classes, the images of children denied a childhood appeared in newspapers, movie theaters, and mass circulation magazines. The National Child Labor Committee lobbied in statehouses and the Capitol to end the practice, and in the 1916 Keating-Owen Child Labor Act seemed to have won the fight.[23]

The constitutionality of the Keating-Owen Act was contested in *Hammer v. Dagenhart* (1918). Despite widespread support in the country for some limitation on child labor, powerful industrial interests, particularly southern textile mills and mines, did not want such limitation. These companies, closed to black workers by the racism of both owners and white employees, needed child labor to operate profitably. Poor southern white families, strapped for cash, reluctantly sent out sons and daughters, including preteens, to work around dangerous machines and in mines with few safety controls. Because these were manufacturing enterprises, rather than commercial ones, *E.C. Knight* prevented Congress from forbidding child labor in them directly. Congress moved instead to criminalize the interstate shipment of products that came from child labor.[24]

During hearings on the bill the National Association of Manufacturers and the textile mills' spokesmen laid the groundwork for the court challenge: Using the Commerce Clause was just a screen for Congress to intrude on the province of state government. If North Carolina did not want to protect its children, then Congress could not—even if those children were also citizens of the United States and had the privileges and immunities of all U.S. citizens. The Act of 1916 nevertheless passed both houses, and President Woodrow signed it into law. A challenge was almost immediately forthcoming in the District Court for the Western District of North Carolina, where a three-judge panel found the legislation unconstitutional and entered a decree enjoining its imposition.[25]

When the case was appealed to the Supreme Court, Justice William Rufus Day opined for a five-judge majority: "By means of a prohibition against the movement in interstate commerce of ordinary commercial commodities," Congress seeks, "to regulate the hours of labor of children in factories and mines within the States, a purely state authority. Thus the act in a twofold sense is repugnant to the Constitution. It not only transcends the authority delegated to Congress over commerce but also exerts a power as to a purely local matter to which the federal authority does not extend."[26]

Justice Holmes dissented. "The act does not meddle with anything belonging to the States. They may regulate their internal affairs and their domestic commerce as they like. But when they seek to send their products across the state line they are no longer within their rights." Congress had the authority to regulate any commerce which left the state—witness the Pure Food and Drug Act and the White Slave (Mann) Act. Holmes allowed himself a brief contrary-to-fact analysis of the majority's logic. "If there were no Constitution and no Congress [the products' ability] to cross [another state's] line would depend upon their neighbors. Under the Constitution such commerce belongs not to the States but to Congress to regulate." The Court would strike down child labor laws repeatedly thereafter, and child labor was not prohibited by federal law until 1938, by which time two more generations of young people had lost their childhoods in the mills and mines, while many had died or been crippled. Ironically, had North Carolina acted to bar child labor, the plaintiff, a father who wanted his two underage sons to work in a North Carolina mill, could have brought suit in federal court against the state. *Lochner* was a precedent on point. His counsel would have argued that the law violated the children's liberty of contract. (In contract law minors lacked the power to enter or enforce contracts, but the parents might have brought the suit as a violation of their right to their children's earnings.)[27]

The Federal Bench in the Progressive Era

Just as the Progressive reform campaign affected the output of the federal courts far less than it did the other branches of the federal government, so the Progressives "success at the polls did not much change the ideological composition of the federal bench as a whole. As Presidents Roosevelt, Taft, and Woodrow Wilson were to a greater or lesser degree Progressives, one would expect that men with Progressive backgrounds and opinions would be their nominees for judicial office. To some extent this was true, particularly when the president saw the courts as policy-making agencies, but only Taft, a former court of appeals judge, paid particular attention to almost all of the nominees' political views, and of the three chief executives he was the least attached to Progressive reform and the most attentive to the professionalism, as he saw it, of the nominees. Indeed, overall, and for the first years of all three presidents' administrations, patronage was a more important concern than professional attainments or ideological fit.[28]

Roosevelt nominated and the Senate confirmed seventy-two judges for the district and circuit courts, and circuit courts of appeal (court of appeals judges also served on the circuit courts until these courts' demise in 1911) and three justices for the Supreme Court between 1901 and 1908. Two nominees for district court posts, Oscar Hundley, for the District of Northern Alabama and Milton Purdy, for the District of Minnesota, were rejected by the Senate. Roosevelt stated his criteria in private correspondence: "My first consideration has in every case been to get a man of the high character, the good sense, the trained legal ability, and the necessary broad-mindedness of spirit all of which are essential to a good judge. . . . Political considerations have been in every instance not merely subordinated, but completely and entirely subordinated to the considerations above, and in a large number of cases they have been completely eliminated." Reading this disclaimer of partisanship more critically than, perhaps, Roosevelt intended it be read, one can see that political considerations did have a place in his thinking. But that thinking was not entirely along ideological lines. Instead, at first it was the input of Republicans in the Senate that introduced the political element. Only in the last two years of his tenure did Roosevelt begin to look for "more liberal" nominees.[29]

Two of the judges named to the lower courts would later go on to sit on the Supreme Court—Edward T. Sanford of Tennessee and Willis Van Devanter of Wyoming. Neither was particularly progressive there, Sanford a moderate conservative and Van Devanter an opponent of government intervention in the marketplace. Roosevelt paid closer attention to the three judges he chose for the Supreme Court, Oliver Wendell Holmes Jr. of Massachusetts, William Rufus Day of Ohio, and William Moody of Massachusetts. But only the last of the three conformed to his reformist expectations.[30]

Holmes had seen combat in the Civil War and returned to Cambridge, Massachusetts, far less idealistic than when he had left. For a brief time a professor at Harvard Law School, where he had earned his degree, and then a judge on the state's Supreme Judicial Court (at the end of his service its chief justice), Holmes had a reputation as a scholar and a jurist when Roosevelt appointed him, in 1901. But Holmes was no starry-eyed reformer. He believed in deference to the elected branches of federal and state government, which would pit him against more conservative members of the Fuller Court, but in matters of labor unions and civil rights, he had no sympathy for minorities or the working man. His terse and telling turn of phrase and his brilliance, particularly in dissent, brought him praise from contemporary legal academics; but his indifference to the plight of the underdog made him less than a hero to the Progressives. Judging was pragmatic work that did not change the world, nor should it, in his opinion.[31]

Day was serving on the Sixth Circuit Court of Appeals (having been appointed by President William McKinley, his childhood friend) when, in 1903, Roosevelt tapped him for the Supreme Court. His antipathy to the trusts endeared him to the president, but he was hardly a reformer on the bench, his important states' rights opinion striking down the Keating-Owen Child Labor Act notwithstanding. Moody was an associate of Roosevelt's, serving as his attorney general. His views of trusts matched the president's own, and Roosevelt chose him for the Supreme Court in 1906. But Moody's health broke down, and Taft persuaded him to retire in 1910. Day retired in 1923.[32]

In terms of other federal court appointments, one could say that on the whole their educational attainments were greater than their predecessors', but their judicial temperament was little different. Typical of the educational background of many of them, Elmer Adams, who sat on the District Court for the Eastern District of Missouri from 1895 and was elevated to the Court of Appeals for the Eighth Circuit in 1905, was a graduate of Yale College and Harvard Law School. But he was not a Progressive. Adams had a strong reputation and was a Republican and briefly a carpetbagger; that was enough. The same was true of Van Devanter, also a Republican and a conservative. He had served as a U.S. attorney in the District of Wyoming along with other posts of trust, including a short stint as chief justice of the Wyoming Supreme Court, when Roosevelt named him for the Court of Appeals for the Eighth Circuit. For Albert Anderson, service on the District of Indiana district court would lead, after twenty-three years, to a stint on the Court of Appeals for the Seventh Circuit. These were career judges, men of reliable probity who were willing to set aside private practice or political ambition and spend their mature years in robes. The list had one noteworthy novelty: German-born Jacob Trieber, commissioned to sit on the Eastern District of Arkansas in 1901, was the first Jewish federal court judge. Students of his jurisprudence noted, "In cases involving civil rights, he was generations ahead of his time." Fifty-eight of the seventy-two inferior court judges died during their service, suggesting that they preferred to stay on the bench rather than retire. The one constant was that overall fewer of Roosevelt's appointees had prior judicial experience than one might expect if professionalism were his primary concern. In the final years of his second term, only 50 percent of the nominees had sat on state or federal court benches. These were also the years when his ideological commitment to Progressivism showed itself most strongly.[33]

While the character of the vast majority of the new appointments was above reproach, a handful carried with them to their new office the same disabling greed that had brought disrepute to the railroad and mining moguls in the Gilded Age. Indeed, the lure of Klondike gold was too much for Arthur H. Noyes. A minor Dakota and Minnesota lawyer and politician appointed in 1900 territorial judge in Alaska, when he appeared in Nome to take office he regarded the bench as an opportunity to get rich. Noyes owed his appointment to the Republican boss of bosses in the Northwest, Dakota's Alexander McKenzie. McKenzie had a hand in fashioning the Alaskan mining code and then formed his own mining company to take advantage of the code. He needed an ally on the bench, and Noyes played that role. Although Noyes would later deny any collusion, he appointed McKenzie receiver in a series of cases of disputed mining claims (one side of the dispute being McKenzie's own interests), and McKenzie began to mine the claims himself. When the defendant miners successfully appealed their case to the Ninth Circuit, the judge refused to obey its order to remove McKenzie and have him surrender all the gold dust he had taken from the claims—a practical impossibility as very little that the boss had grasped could be pried from his hands. The matter was soon an embarrassment to the Republican Party, and Elihu Root, U.S. attorney general, recommended Noyes removal. Roosevelt complied on February 24, 1902. Noyes's short and less than storied career in the gold fields ended soon after it had begun.[34]

Another of those who did not finish his term was Robert W. Archbald. He too was a McKinley choice, in 1901, for the District Court for the Middle District of Pennsylvania. Taft nominated him for the Third Circuit Court of Appeals, to which post the Senate confirmed him in January1911. The Act establishing the U.S. Commerce Court "to enforce all orders of the Interstate Commerce Commission and to hear all challenges to the commission's rulings" empowered the president to name five judges as its bench. Archbald was one of these. The latter post appealed to Archibald's unsavory appetite for bribery. Impeachment proceedings against him began on April 23, 1912 and ran through nearly an entire month of testimony before the judiciary committee. The facts of Archbald's greed were boldfaced. For example, he purchased a coal dump in his native western Pennsylvania, then arranged in his own court for "gifts" from lawyers and parties in suits involving the sale of a part of his purchase to the Erie Railroad. Stock manipulations, special treatment, solicited "favors," and other misdeeds followed. The judiciary committee of the lower house presented the body with thirteen articles, and it voted 223 to 1 for all thirteen articles, principally for self-dealing, bribery, and extortion. President Taft cooperated in the investigation. There was also a general article of bringing the federal court into "disrepute." The Senate convicted him on five of the thirteen articles on January 13, 1913.[35]

Co-incident with Archbald's fall, Congress abolished the Commerce Court. Part of the same Mann-Elkins Act that extended the three-judge court to injunctions against states enforcing state law, the court lacked organizational focus. Not fully a part of the federal system, not really a super-regulatory agency, its decisions were appealable to the Supreme Court, and more than half of those that were appealed were reversed. Pleasing neither the Progressives (who thought it in bed with the railroad companies) nor the conservatives (who resented its jurisdiction over rail rates), it was a target of criticism from its inception. Even the ICC, which had favored the creation of the court, by the end of 1911 opposed it. With its authority so often curtailed, it could hardly have succeeded in its mission even without the Archbald scandal. Taft fought hard to save it, vetoing the two bills abolishing it, but after the election of 1912, Taft was gone and the Democratic majority reenacted the abolition bill. President Wilson signed it.[36]

The demise of the Commerce Court cannot be attributed to the weakness of its bench. Archbald to one side, the other members had unimpeachable credentials. Martin Knapp of the Second Circuit and later the Fourth Circuit had been appointed to the Interstate Commerce Commission by President Harrison, a Republican, reappointed by President Cleveland, a Democrat, and then named head of the Commission by President Roosevelt. He was serving as the head of the Commission in 1910 when he was elevated to the bench. He was also a respected mediator in the often acrimonious negotiations between railways and railway workers' unions. John Emmet Carland had served as a district judge in the District of South Dakota for fourteen years before he joined the Eighth Circuit Court of Appeals and the Commerce Court in 1910. William Henry Hunt was serving as the governor general of Puerto Rico when President Roosevelt tabbed him for district judgeship in the district of Montana. Prior to his service in Puerto Rico, Hunt had served in just about every capacity in Montana's state government. He was the last of the "at large" circuit court judges in 1910, and after the abolition of the Commerce Court was assigned to the Ninth Circuit Court of Appeals. Chicago's Julian Mack had a distinguished career on the appeals courts' bench, serving in the Seventh Circuit Court of Appeals, the Sixth Circuit Court of Appeals, and the Second Circuit Court of Appeals. Before his illustrious tenure on the federal bench, Mack, as one of the first Chicago juvenile court judges, was a pioneer in treating juvenile offenders with special concern, focusing on their youth and family background.[37]

Other Roosevelt appointees, like Kennesaw Mountain Landis, gained increased fame after they left their judicial posts. Landis was born in Ohio, reared in Indiana, and read law before practicing in Chicago. He then decided to attend YMCA school of law in Louisville. Roosevelt named him to the District Court for the Northern District of Illinois in 1905, on which tribunal he served until 1922. On the bench he was famous for jumping in to question witnesses and allowing no nonsense from counsel. Landis presided over the Standard Oil antitrust suit, and he fined John D. Rockefeller's corporation nearly $30 million, a record, for violations of the Sherman Act. A fiercely patriotic man (named after the Civil War battle in which his father fought), during World War I Landis heard a draft-resisting case involving over 110 defendants. His instructions to the jury led to an almost 100 percent conviction rate. The only acquittals were defendants who attended court in their newly issued military uniforms. At the time, left-leaning journalist John Reed described Landis's appearance: "Small on the huge bench sits a wasted man with untidy white hair, an emaciated face in which two burning eyes are set like jewels, parchment-like skin split by a crack for a mouth; the face of Andrew Jackson three years dead." In 1920 Landis accepted another position—commissioner of baseball. The national pastime had been tarnished by the "Black Sox" scandal, gambler Arnold Rothstein's successful attempt to buy the World Series in 1919. Landis refused to allow the White Sox players involved in the scandal, including Shoeless Joe Jackson, to return to the major leagues, and set a standard of rigid probity when it came to gambling and the game.[38]

President Taft appointed fifty-six men for service on Article III courts. The recess appointments of John Moses Cheney to the Southern District of Florida, Richard E. Sloan to the District of Arizona, and Clinton W. Howard to the Western District of Washington in 1912 were not acted on by the Senate. Oscar Richard Hundley, twice turned down by the Senate after Roosevelt recess appointments, failed to gain confirmation after Taft tried again in 1909.

Despite these setbacks, Taft's primary consideration seemed to be professionalism, but to him that not only meant prior service on the bench, it also meant men of sober and conservative instincts. He was wont to correspond with leading members of the local bar, far more so that Roosevelt. Taft was also influenced by political considerations, but he was not as beholden to members of the Senate as Wilson would be. Some of the nominees, like Taft himself (professor and dean at the University of Cincinnati Law School), had been law school teachers. These included Alexis Angell (University of Michigan); Julian Mack (Northwestern, University of Chicago); John McPherson (Penn); William Schofield (Harvard); Willis Van Devanter (George Washington); John Warrington (Cincinnati); and Charles A. Willard (Minnesota). Willard and James Francis Smith both sat on the Philippine Supreme Court when Taft was governor general there. Like Willard and Smith, almost all of Taft's choices had served in state or federal judicial office and had experience in private practice. Almost none had been general counsel to large corporations. Indeed, if one had to draw up a composite picture of them, they would have resembled Taft himself—steady men, men of experience, and men who could be trusted to read the law as a given and not bend to the winds of current opinion. [39]

There were a few who did not quite fit this composite. Perhaps the most notable of them was Learned Hand. New York's Hand had strong Republican progressive credentials, but failure to win elective office had turned him in the direction of a judicial post. On the Southern District of New York bench, Hand was a consummate penman, a strong believer in judicial restraint (judges should not act or think as legislators), deference to the elected branches, and First Amendment rights. Indeed, he was a pioneer in the latter, as his opinion in the *Masses* case (1917) would demonstrate. On the Court of Appeals for the Second Circuit, and as its chief judge, he led what many believed was the most learned bench in the land.[40]

One can see in his choices for the Supreme Court something of Taft's personal agenda. Taft had hungered for the post of chief justice himself, or so he told confidants, but with Fuller's passing, Taft reached into the Court itself and selected Justice Edward D. White of Louisiana for the chief justiceship. Taft, a former federal appeals court judge, liked what he saw in the heavy-set, courtly White, but, more important, Taft wanted the job himself as the capstone to his career. The ailing and elderly White did not step down when Taft lost his bid for reelection, however, and Taft's gambit, if such it was, did not work.[41]

As the new chief, White promoted camaraderie on the bench, courtesy among the justices, and even limited his cigar smoking to accommodate the nonsmokers on the Court. White was comfortable in the Court's setting—the old Senate chamber, still close and clubby in its atmosphere. It was too dark for some of the justices to see beyond the first row of counsels' desks, but that did not bother White, whose severe cataracts limited his vision all the time. A floor below, their library and conference room, formerly their first chamber in the Capitol, was

Figure 7.3 Judge Learned Hand, photographed in 1924. His clear thinking and longevity on the federal bench would elevate him to the pantheon of great judges. Credit: George Grantham Bain Collection, Library of Congress.

so dank and foul smelling that Justice Holmes was known to mutter obscenities when White, courteous to a fault, refused to curb the long-windedness of some of their brethren.[42]

White and the associate justices worked at home because they had no offices in the Capitol. Congress allowed them a $2,000 home office subsidy to supplement their $14,500 salaries (the chief made $500 more), and provided another $2,000 for them to hire stenographic clerks or secretaries. White Court clerks were a mix of law students enrolled in evening classes and law school graduates. Most were hired because they had experience working as stenographers in various government agencies or in local D.C. law firms. Some served multiple terms. For example, one of White's clerks, William H. Pope, was with him for eighteen years.[43]

In 1919 Congress appropriated funding for "law clerks" in addition to the funds allotted the justices to hire legal secretaries. A year later Congress specified a salary of $3,600 for one law clerk and a salary of $2,000 for one stenographic secretary. The choice of the former had some precedent in the 1880s, when Justice Horace Gray hired Harvard Law School honor graduates as clerks, initially paying them himself. Justice Holmes and later Justice Louis Brandeis resumed Gray's practice, establishing the modern clerkship model of recruiting students from elite law schools and mentoring them on to brilliant careers after a term or two of service.[44]

It was not until 1930 that Congress provided funds for each circuit court of appeals judge to hire a law clerk. In 1936 Congress authorized district court judges to appoint law clerks, but only in thirty-five districts and only if they could demonstrate "need." Nine years later, all district judges were allowed a clerk if they could show a certificate of need—a requirement that was not dropped until 1959. As federal judicial caseloads have risen, the number of law clerks retained by judges has too. Supreme Court justices now employ four clerks who rotate annually, but some lower court judges now prefer clerks who will serve a minimum of four years.[45]

Taft crossed party lines to appoint three Democrats to the Court. Two were southerners, and many saw their selections as a final gesture of bringing the South into the Union. Horace H. Lurton (1910–1914) of Tennessee was a former Confederate soldier, whom Taft had served with on the Sixth Circuit Court of Appeals and was impressed by his ability. Joseph R. Lamar (1911–1916) came from the social and professional elite of Georgia, and Taft had come to know him not through politics but through personal contact—a chance encounter at a spa followed by socializing and golf. Though still recovering its infrastructure and its fiscal stability (Lamar was a railroad lawyer and the beneficiary of the rise of the New South's business interests), the South was once again a dominant force in Congress (southern members voting as a bloc) and on the Court.[46] The third Democrat was Mahlon Pitney, who had been serving on the state supreme court of New Jersey and then as chancellor of the New Jersey court system. His appointment in 1912 was more controversial than the southern Democrats': liberal senators opposed his antilabor, anti-Progressive record, and he was narrowly confirmed.

Taft elevated Wyoming's Van Devanter from the Court of Appeals for the Eighth Circuit to the Supreme Court in 1911. An able craftsman as both lawyer and federal judge, he lobbied for the seat (though not the first or the last person to do so) and occupied it for twenty-six years. He was no particular friend to railroads and bowed to Congress when it limited its regulations to interstate commerce and would become a part of a conservative bloc on the Court. A man of great personal charm, he contributed much to the deliberations of the Court in conference, but he suffered from writer's block, or "pen paralysis" as he called it, during his tenure from 1911 to 1937.[47]

Taft did choose one genuine Progressive for the Supreme Court, Republican governor of New York Charles Evans Hughes. In New York, Hughes had begun to engineer the same kind of liberal reform regime as had Robert LaFollette in

Wisconsin. Formerly a professor of law at Cornell, an advocate of investigating and uncovering wrongdoing in service industries like insurance and utilities, and a believer in the rightful role of government in the economy, Hughes could have been a major player on the bench had he not interrupted his service in 1916 to run for the presidency. He returned to the Court in 1930 as President Herbert Hoover's choice for chief justice. Taft had political reasons for selecting Hughes. Not only was he a Republican, he also was the leader of the liberal wing of the party, and Taft saw Hughes as a potential rival in the forthcoming 1912 presidential poll. Moving him to the Court removed him from the electoral lists. To sweeten the deal, Taft even hinted that Hughes might be his choice for the center seat, should that become vacant. For his part, Hughes was profoundly tired of campaigning and did not intend to stay on as governor. As he later wrote, the qualifications for a justice of the Court were "learning, ability, integrity, and independence" of mind, qualities essential for a Court deciding constitutional questions of the greatest significance. He recognized that there would be political fallout from these decisions, for their subject matter had already divided the country and the national parties. He did not need to add that he thought himself well suited to stand above those party considerations when he accepted Taft's offer. The appointment suited both men, and Congress approved "promptly and painlessly" a week after its submission.[48]

More than Taft and Roosevelt, Woodrow Wilson was attentive to placing Progressives on the bench. He understood the importance of a judiciary compliant with Progressives in Congress and his presidency. Although he was comfortable with Jim Crow, thinking forced separation best for both races, his "new freedom" credo included reforms in banking, labor law, and other Progressive agenda items that would have to pass muster in the courts. During his stay in office, from 1913 to 1921, he nominated and the Senate confirmed sixty-nine men to the district and circuit courts of appeal. Of these, Chicago's Samuel Alschuler (1915, to the Seventh Circuit Court of Appeals), a trusted friend of the labor unions; Learned Hand's cousin Augustus Hand (in 1914 to Southern District of New York; and by Coolidge, in 1927, to the Second Circuit Court of Appeals), a noteworthy exponent of freedom of speech; and Henry Clayton, of the Middle District of Alabama and antitrust fame, who had impeccable Progressive credentials. Another Progressive, John H. Clarke, would ascend from the Northern District of Ohio to the Supreme Court in 1916. A few were embarrassments: Martin Manton of the Second Circuit Court of Appeals, for example, would disgrace the federal courts by taking bribes, and after his resignation, by conviction in federal court for bribery and extortion. All of Wilson's appointees were Democrats, a partisan tradition going back to Jefferson and Jackson but not true of Lincoln, Cleveland, and Taft.[49]

Wilson's vision of Progressivism might be limited by his belief in the superiority of the white race, but it would have been difficult for Wilson to find many white candidates for the federal bench who did not share that view. For example Clayton was a Progressive, but he was "committed to white supremacy." Similarly, Wilson's first pick for the Supreme Court did not see any reason for civil rights reform. Former Tennessee Democratic politician (he ran once, unsuccessfully, for public office) James C. McReynolds was Wilson's attorney general from 1913 to 1914. McReynolds was outstanding as a trust buster, but by the time of the appointment to the Court, there was no love lost between Wilson and this narrow-minded, often blunt, eccentric. Gossip at the time claimed that Wilson proposed his name to the Senate to rid the cabinet of him. His irascibility and incivility to Jews and liberals on the Court, and his reactionary views on many subjects, limited his effectiveness during his tenure from 1914 to 1941.[50]

Wilson's second appointment, Louis Brandeis, was a "fearful shock" (Taft's words) to McReynolds and other advocates of conservative jurisprudence. Not surprising, for as one student of the Court depicted Brandeis, he was "of an entirely different cast of that of the colleagues he joined, in outlook and experience." From a very successful Boston practice, Brandeis had emerged as "the people's advocate," a defender of social justice who used the courts for liberal ends. In speaking for consumer groups and labor unions in legislative hearings and court cases, Brandeis make plain his views, for example, on labor unionism: "The disclosures incident to the labor policies of the strong trusts and particularly the hours of labor, wages, and conditions . . . are making many Americans recognize that unions and collective bargaining are essential to industrial liberty and social justice."[51]

Wilson held Brandeis dear and adopted many of his ideas. "The new freedom" ideology that carried Wilson to victory in 1912 was largely Brandeis's creation. Wilson's formulation of a renewed spirit of "absolutely free opportunity"—free from the control of big business, a return to an older, simpler, purer America—had an almost religious quality. Brandeis explained it in more practical terms: "no economic problem in America is as important today as that presented by the Money Trust—the control which a few financiers exercise over the capital of America . . . the greatest economic menace of today is . . . these few able financiers who are gradually acquiring control over our quick capital." But so odious did many find Brandeis's relentless advocacy (and his Judaism) that Wilson did not dare bring the Boston lawyer into his cabinet.[52]

Instead, in 1916, Wilson proposed that Brandeis replace Justice Lamar. The confirmation battle was incredibly bitter, as both Taft and McReynolds lobbied against the appointment. For four months, witnesses for and against Brandeis trooped up Capitol Hill. In particular, railroad interests stung by Brandeis's testimony in favor of ICC rate setting, corporate leaders furious at Brandeis's role in framing the Clayton Antitrust Act, and banking spokesmen determined to pay Brandeis back for his articles on "Breaking the Money Trust," saw the confirmation as the occasion to vent their spleen.[53]

The argument made against him was that he was no lawyer and unfit to be a judge because, according to one newspaper, "Mr. Brandeis is a radical, a theorist, impractical, with strong socialistic tendencies. That he is given to extravagance in utterance, inspired by prejudice and intolerance. That he is a self-advertiser, reckless in his methods of seeking personal exploitation." A petition of fifty-five Boston lawyers, most of whom had crossed swords with Brandeis and lost, pronounced that Brandeis did not have "their confidence." Brandeis was also the first Jewish person nominated for a seat on the Supreme Court at a time when anti-Semitism was rife in the country. Some of the opposition to his confirmation came from that source. But Wilson stood by his man and wrote to the committee, "I perceived from the first that the charges were intrinsically incredible by anyone who had really known Mr. Brandeis. I have known him . . . He is a friend to all just men and a lover of the right, and he knows more than how to talk about the right—he knows how to set it forward in the face of his enemies." Wilson lined up his allies in the Senate and the nomination was confirmed on June 5, 1916, 47 to 22.[54]

On the Court Brandeis would prove a man of exquisite personal probity, recusing himself whenever a case touched any of his earlier interests or his financial holdings, treating his colleagues with respect and courtesy, and taking great pains with every case that came the Court's way. His opinions were predictably liberal, and often he found himself in dissent, particularly in matters of racial justice, civil liberties, free speech, and labor unions. He almost always favored deference to legislative acts and judicial restraint. Holmes and Brandeis developed a warm relationship from the start, and Brandeis was able to persuade Holmes to soften some of his hard-edged realism.[55]

Postcards from the South

In the first decades of the twentieth century, mail from the South included a new and popular product—postcards gruesomely depicting lynching. Southerners kept the grainy images of "poisoned fruit" as treasured souvenirs of the most effective way to enforce white supremacy. In a private conversation with the producer of D. W. Griffith's openly racist movie, *Birth of A Nation*, Chief Justice White admitted that he had been a member of the Ku Klux Klan and had, in the violent closing days of Reconstruction in New Orleans, "walked my sentinel's beat through the ugliest streets of New Orleans with my rifle on my shoulder." The Klan, despite congressional legislation banning hooded vigilantism, made a strong comeback during the Wilson presidency. Even before the Klan's resurgence, a wave of lynching and race riots gave rise to an alliance of white and black reformers in the National Association for the Advancement of Colored People. In 1910, the NAACP began to bring cases to the federal courts seeking relief from state law and state courts.[56]

In *Franklin v. State of South Carolina* (1910), the first of the NAACP cases, the Supreme Court deferred to local juries and state courts. Pink Franklin was a sharecropper who refused to plow a field until later in the day. A constable, acting under a South Carolina law that made such refusals criminal, burst without warning or warrant into Franklin's home, and Franklin killed the constable. The all-white trial jury found Franklin guilty of murder, even though key pieces of evidence were withheld from Franklin's defense counsel. The Supreme Court was not about to oversee every criminal trial in which a claim of racial discrimination was made. "The States have the right to administer their own laws for the prosecution of crime, and the jurisdiction of this court extends only to the reversal of such state proceedings where fundamental rights secured by the Federal law have been denied by the proceedings in the state courts" Justice Day concluded. Franklin was executed.[57]

Were federal courts to return to the Reconstruction Enforcement Acts' regime, they would be inundated with challenges to racialist state court decisions. There was no constitutional reason for federal courts to defer to state courts in criminal cases, however. Day's narrow view of "fundamental rights" implied that for him and the majority of the justices, the Fourteenth Amendment's Due Process and Equal Protection Clauses did not "incorporate" (that is, impose on the states) the guarantees of the Fourth, Fifth, and Sixth Amendments. Where Congress had acted, however, there were grounds for the federal courts to intervene in state criminal prosecutions. The Habeas Corpus Act of 1867 tilted the federal-state judicial relationship in this direction, allowing for removal of an individual in the custody of the state to the federal court issuing the "great writ." The Act was a product of the Reconstruction Congress at its high tide, based on the assumption that southern state courts would use the vagrancy statutes of the first "black codes" to effectually re-enslave the freedmen.[58]

But that was before Jim Crow replaced cotton as king in the South and federal courts took down much of the Reconstruction Era safety net for the freedmen. In 1915 the Supreme Court revisited the Habeas Corpus Act. New Yorker Leo Frank was jailed in Atlanta, facing execution for allegedly murdering Mary Phagan, a worker in the pencil factory he managed there. The trial in the state court was patently unfair, filled with anti-Semitic vituperation against the defendant. The prosecution was allowed license to promote these views among the jury pool; judge Leonard Roan made clear to the jury his view that Frank was guilty; the coverage in the newspapers made a mockery of the ideal of impartial trial; and the riotous conduct of crowds outside the courthouse cowed everyone inside it. Prosecutor Hugh Dorsey would use the public outcry to vault himself into the governorship.[59]

The Georgia Supreme Court did not find any reason to order a new trial. The federal district court found no grounds to issue the writ, and on the Supreme Court Mahlon Pitney, agreed. "As to the 'due process of law' that is required by the 14th Amendment, it is perfectly well settled that a criminal prosecution in the courts of a state, based upon a law not in itself repugnant to the Federal Constitution, and conducted according to the settled course of judicial proceedings as established by the law of the state, so long as it includes notice and a hearing, or an opportunity to be heard, before a court of competent jurisdiction, according to established modes of procedure, is 'due process' in the constitutional sense." Pitney, who would not defer to states in social legislation questions, thought this kind of case different. "The rule stands upon a much higher plane, for it arises out of the very nature and ground of the inquiry into the proceedings of the state tribunals, and touches closely upon the relations between the state

Figure 7.4 The first day of the Leo Frank trial, Atlanta, Georgia, 1915. Credit: Library of Congress.

and the Federal governments." A robust federalism (of the pre-Reconstruction sort) dictated deference to the state's court.[60]

Justice Holmes and Justice Hughes dissented. Holmes wrote, "The petitioner alleges that the trial was dominated by a hostile mob and was nothing but an empty form," a fact (if not an interpretation of fact), that no one in any of the courts that heard the case could doubt. "Whatever disagreement there may be as to the scope of the phrase 'due process of law,' there can be no doubt that it embraces the fundamental conception of a fair trial, with opportunity to be heard. Mob law does not become due process of law by securing the assent of a terrorized jury." When the outgoing governor, John Slaton, commuted the death sentence, a mob broke Frank out of prison and hanged him. The mob included a former governor of the state, a sitting state superior court judge, and the mayor of the city of Marietta, where the lynching took place. Many years later, a witness admitted that he had perjured himself at the trial and revealed the actual murderer. Frank was posthumously pardoned in 1986.[61]

Frank was but one instance of the perversion of Southern Populism into a frenzy against outsiders, immigrants, Jews, Catholics, and people of color. Nine men sitting in a courtroom in Washington, D.C. could not curb all of these excesses even had they wished it. But flickering points of light for civil rights reformers were rulings like *Bailey v. Alabama* (1911), the first of the "peonage cases." In it, the Court refused to admit the extent or nature of state-sponsored or state-allowed oppression of minorities. Instead, the majority found technical grounds to invalidate discriminatory laws, albeit without exploring the racial nature of the discrimination.[62]

The "peonage cases" demonstrated that federal courts could still impose fair play on Jim Crow state courts. At the beginning of the 1900s, to ensure that its white planters had a ready supply of cheap black labor, Alabama made it criminal to receive an advance for labor under a contract and either fail to perform the labor or fail to continue to labor for the period of time stated in the contract. Failure to complete the contract subjected the laborer to a term of forced labor. Conviction turned a free labor relationship into peonage—a form of labor barred by the Federal Peonage Act of 1867. In fact, the sponsors of the Act in Congress foresaw the re-enslavement of black agricultural workers through statutes like Alabama's. The Alabama law also included an instruction judges were to give to the jury that nonperformance of the agreed upon labor was presumptive evidence of the intention to defraud, in effect making the defendant guilty until proven innocent: "the refusal of any personal who enters into such contract to perform such act or service, or refund such money, or pay for such property, without just cause, shall be prima facie evidence of the intent to . . . defraud . . . his employer." This 1907 addition to the 1903 criminal statute closed any avenue the laborer had to escape conviction. Because many of these so-called contracts were verbal and the only witnesses were the (black) laborer and the (white) boss, the evidentiary burden the new law placed on the laborer was almost insurmountable. Not surprisingly, all-white juries routinely found the accused guilty. Alabama had found its way back to the black codes the state legislature passed in 1865.[63]

Not every Alabama judge, lawyer, or lawmaker subscribed to these ideas. Alabama had its fair-minded conservatives, like federal Judge Giles Jones, who presided over violations of the federal antipeonage laws. Jones, a former governor, was hardly a civil rights advocate (having supported the disenfranchisement of the state's African Americans), but Booker T. Washington among others lobbied Theodore Roosevelt to appoint Jones to the district court bench. Jones thought the Alabama law corrupted the legal system itself. It induced and rewarded the perjury of the employer. At the trials in the federal courts, Jones "methodically explained to grand and petit jurors why peonage was illegal. He did not stop there. He added that peonage robbed a man—any man—of the most precious of all rights, the right to benefit from his own labor." The point made, Jones meted out very modest punishments to violators of the federal law.[64]

Alonzo Bailey was a black farm laborer caught in the web of debt and dependence that the Alabama law wove. He sought a writ of habeas corpus in federal court to free him from his incarceration under the state statute. The state's attorney general explained in oral argument before the Supreme Court why Bailey should not be granted the get-out-of-jail card. "The statute was to punish fraudulent practices and not mere failure to pay a debt . . . if a rule of evidence which excludes the defendant from testifying as to his motives has the effect of making the rule of evidence prescribed by the statute a conclusive rule, it is due to the particular facts and not to the statute itself." He added that Alabama did not violate federal law against peonage, because the Alabama law did not mention peonage.[65]

Hughes's opinion for the majority turned on the Alabama trial court's instructions. Ordinarily, it was the burden of the state to produce such evidence. Alabama simply took the word of the employer, the person who would directly benefit from the conviction. Hughes also noted the penalty for conviction was forced labor for a term far longer than would repay the advance. The labor was due to a private individual—the employer—even though the offense was against the state (as in all criminal cases). So the state, in effect, had reduced a free laborer to a peon working for a private employer. "It is not permitted to accomplish the same result" by changing the criminal law to make the defendant in such cases guilty until proven innocent, then exclude all evidence of his innocence.[66]

The Federal Courts Go to War

The world went to war in 1914. The United States attempted a policy of neutrality, but it clearly favored the Allies—giving nearly $2.3 billion in loans to Britain and France and only $27 million to the Central Powers. So long as Germany refrained from sinking passenger ships with its submarines, however, President Wilson hoped for peace. He won reelection in part with the slogan "he kept us out of war." When Germany's submarine campaign struck at all vessels heading for Allied ports, including American ships, in early 1917, Wilson finally asked Congress for a declaration of war.[67]

As war approached, Department of Justice lawyers had begged Congress to pass an act to punish "political agitation" that undermined, or might undermine (with discretion left to federal prosecutors to decide what actions fit that category) the "safety of the state." The safety of the state translated into support for the Wilson administration's war policies. The Act was to be used against those who spread "disloyal propaganda." Some members of Congress, particularly Progressive Senator William Borah, objected that too broad a statute would stifle all political speech. The author of the Act, constitutional scholar and Harvard Law School professor Charles Warren, reassured him it would not. His draft originally included a censorship provision, but members of Congress rejected this, in part because the president was to be the censor.[68]

The Espionage Act of 1917 and the Sedition Act of 1918 were wartime measures. They could not have been passed by Congress without the war, but they remained on the books after the war. In addition to spelling out the varieties of espionage, the first Act had an omnibus Section 3, part of which punished anyone who, in wartime, "shall wilfully make or convey false reports or false statements with intent to interfere with the operation or success of the military or naval forces of the United States," a categorization of what constituted antiwar speech and publications giving great discretion to federal prosecutors, "or shall wilfully obstruct the recruiting or enlistment service of the United States." There was in addition a penalty for conspiracy to violate the Act so broadly defined that it could cover anyone who met with or agreed with someone who acted in furtherance of antiwar activities. The Sedition Act of 1918 added punishment for "any disloyal, profane, scurrilous, or abusive language about the form of government of the United States . . . or the flag of the United States, or the uniform of the Army or Navy."[69]

In the war years, the checks and balances in separation of powers were replaced by a federal troika—all three branches pulling together to support the war effort. The U.S. attorneys and federal judiciary played their part, trying and convicting those indicted under the wartime acts. There were three exceptions to this common effort, however, exceptions that proved the rule that federal law stands on constitutional and statutory foundations, and the Constitution could be read as a statement of the highest aspirations of the framers. The three federal judges who enunciated these values in their opinions would all be overturned or wrote in dissent, but together their efforts represented the highest calling of judging, speaking justice to power.

Learned Hand in the Southern District of New York heard the first case under the sedition law. The radical cadre around the Greenwich Village magazine, *The Masses*, overlapped Hand's circle of friends in the New York Progressive movement. The magazine openly opposed the war and accused the great corporations of fostering it to make profit from the carnage. The "merchants of death" theme was hardly un-American, and the writers for the magazine, including leading literary talents like Sherwood Anderson, were not unpatriotic, but the message was all the more threatening to the Wilson administration for its persuasive elegance. Postmaster Thomas Patten, following orders from Washington, D.C., barred sending the magazine to its subscribers, and the editors sought an injunction in federal court—Hand's court––prohibiting Patten from acting.[70]

Hand found that the government did not make its case because it misread the statute. Nothing he saw in the magazine would "cause" Americans to refuse to fight, unless the statute intended to make all criticism of the government a crime. This surely was not what Congress had in mind, Hand concluded. Such an interpretation "is so contrary to the use and wont of our people that only the clearest expression of such a power justifies the conclusion that it was intended." Words so remote from action, and protest meetings so peaceful in their conduct, surely did not violate the law. Hand did not rely upon the First Amendment, but his reasoning provided a test for what might and might not "incite" mischief under the Espionage Act. If Congress had the power, which he conceded, to suppress seditious speech in wartime,

> I would like to know to-day, how many men and women there are in America who admire the self-reliance and sacrifice of those who are resisting the conscription law on the ground that they believe it violates the sacred rights and liberties of man .. I recall the Essays of Emerson, the Poems of Walt Whitman, which sounded a call never heard before in the world's literature, for erect and insuppressible individuality, the courage of solitary faith and heroic assertion of self. It was America's contribution to the ideals of man ... It was a revolt of the aspiring mind against that instinctive running with custom and the support of numbers, which is an hereditary frailty of our nerves.[71]

The federal courts did not follow Hand's cue. The full bench of the Court of Appeals reversed him, and the Supreme Court adopted its own standard quite distinct from his. The latter's cases were *Schenck v. U.S.* (1919), *Debs v. U.S.* (1919), *Frohwerk v. U.S.* (1919) and *Abrams v. U.S.* (1919). They all resulted in short decisions, for the applicable law seemed easy. Holmes wrote for a unanimous Court in the first three. Then he dissented in the fourth.

Holmes's dissent in *Abrams* has become part of the pantheon of statements of American ideals, alongside the Declaration of Independence, Lincoln's Gettysburg Address, and Wilson's Fourteen Points. In *Schenck,* Holmes had led the Court to adopt an "evil tendency" test. The time and place of the speech determined whether it had an evil tendency. Holmes conceded that "in many places and in ordinary times the defendants in saying all that was said . . . would have been within their constitutional rights . . . [but] the character of every act depends upon the circumstances in which it is done. The most stringent protection of free speech would not protect a man in falsely shouting fire in a theater and causing a panic."[72]

But the war was over when the Abrams case arrived in the Southern District of New York. A "Red Scare," an antiradical sweep inaugurated by Wilson's Attorney General A. Mitchell Palmer after the war ended, troubled Holmes. Holmes's young protégeé, Harvard Law School professor Felix Frankfurter, joined with Harvard Law School Dean Roscoe Pound to document the evils of the Red Scare. Leading intellectuals who were not socialists, men like John Dewey, were making the case for a broad reading of First Amendment liberties, and Holmes respected these men. Learned Hand was corresponding with Holmes, and Brandeis, a friend and ally on the Court, would join in the dissent.[73]

The five defendants in *Abrams v. U.S.*, all young anarchists born in Russia, dropped leaflets in English and Yiddish from a Lower East Side Manhattan window criticizing President Wilson for sending troops to suppress the Bolshevik takeover in Russia. They were indicted under the provisions of the 1918 Sedition Act, a more restrictive statute than the 1917 Espionage Act, under which Judge Hand heard *The Masses.* Observers of the trial in the federal district court, with Judge Clayton of Alabama on temporary assignment, were treated to Clayton's Alabama court ways. For example, he told the jury to rely on "their good, common, out-of-doors sense . . . that men used before law books were written" to decide if the defendants had the requisite intent to violate the law. But his conduct of the trial was tainted by his open animus to the defendants. Clayton's Progressivism had no place for foreign-born radicalism. Charging the jury before they deliberated, he even apologized after a fashion for any "reference, or comment, or expression of opinion which the court [i.e. Judge Clayton] may have made" during the trial. Then Clayton prefaced his sentencing of the defendants

to the maximum penalty with a two-hour tongue lashing on the "devilish ingenuity" of enemies of the war effort, and why anarchists like the defendants would
never understand what it was to be an American.[74]

Counsel for the defendants sought bail, and Judge Augustus Hand granted
a series of delays to allow the accumulation of funds. With the defendants free
for the time being, the Supreme Court expedited their appeal. Clayton's conduct of the trial was not the basis for the appeal to the Supreme Court, however.
Instead, it was based on a First Amendment claim. The majority of the justices,
with Justice John H. Clarke's opinion citing the three Holmes opinions, found
that the defendants' leaflets violated the Espionage Acts. Clarke concluded that
"the purpose of this [leaflet] obviously was to persuade the persons to whom it
was addressed to turn a deaf ear to patriotic appeals in behalf of the government
of the United States" and that was tantamount to a conspiracy to defeat the war
effort.[75]

In dissent, Holmes found that the leaflets "in no way attack the form of government of the United States" nor that the authors intended any such act. A strict
reading of the Espionage Acts must find real intent, he opined. What was more,
"The principle of the right to free speech is always the same. It is only the present
danger of immediate evil or an intent to bring it about that warrants Congress
setting a limit to the expression of opinion." The four defendants' leaflets were
"silly" publications, and in any case, political speech was privileged. "Congress
certainly cannot forbid all effort to change the mind of the country." History—
the history of a great democracy—offered a different lesson.

> When men have realized that time has upset many fighting faiths, they
> may come to believe even more than they believe the very foundations
> of their own conduct that the ultimate good desired is better reached by
> free trade in ideas–that the best test of truth is the power of the thought
> to get itself accepted in the competition of the market, and that truth is
> the only ground upon which their wishes safely can be carried out. That
> at any rate is the theory of our Constitution.[76]

Nothing in the Constitution included such free markets of ideas (any more
than the Constitution incorporated laissez-faire doctrines on commerce),
but Holmes added this potent idea to the store of constitutional truths. The
Constitution "is an experiment, as all life is an experiment. Every year if not every
day we have to wager our salvation upon some prophecy based upon imperfect
knowledge." This was a living constitution, one that grew and embraced larger
truths and freedoms. It was a tolerant constitution that had room for many contradictory opinions. Brandeis concurred.[77]

The third case was *Colyer v. Skeffington* (1920), a suit heard in a District of Massachusetts court, where the defendants sought to enjoin the government from deporting suspected enemy aliens. The case concerned a third wartime statute, the Anarchist Exclusion Act of 1918. It provided that "aliens who are members of or affiliated with any organization that entertains a belief in, teaches, or advocates the overthrow by force or violence of the Government of the United States or of all forms of law" were subject to deportation. Lumping together socialists, communists, and anarchists, and raising the emotional level of his warnings to fever pitch, Attorney General Palmer asked Congress to increase his budget tenfold to counter a massive conspiracy against the federal government. [78]

The Palmer raids particularly targeted Russian immigrant workers, whether or not they were members of a radical group, and included more than a handful of U.S. citizens. Aided by Department of Justice lawyers and a new agency called the General Intelligence Division led by lawyer J. Edgar Hoover, federal officers and state and local police interrogated men and women who might, but generally did not, understand English. Even though the impetus and much of the manpower for the roundups came from the Department of Justice, the authority for these proceedings was the secretary of labor. By law, only he could issue warrants for the arrest of alien violators of the Immigration Acts, and deportation required a hearing by an immigration inspector. By the end of winter of 1920, the Anarchist Exclusion Act sent hundreds of deportees to federal courts seeking relief.

The first objections to the wholesale arrests had been raised in liberal journals of opinion like *The Nation* and *The New Republic*. For their opposition, their editors were branded as fellow travelers of the "Reds." Francis Fisher Kane, the U.S. attorney for the Eastern District of Pennsylvania, resigned in protest. In his letter of resignation to President Wilson and Attorney General Palmer, he wrote: "It seems to me that the policy of raids against large numbers of individuals is generally unwise and very apt to result in injustice. People not really guilty are likely to be arrested and railroaded through their hearings . . . We appear to be attempting to repress a political party . . . By such methods we drive underground and make dangerous what was not dangerous before." The new secretary of labor, William Wilson, was not a great friend of the roundups, and his first assistant, and later acting secretary, Louis Freeland Post canceled more than 2,000 warrants. Of the more than 10,000 arrested, 556 resident aliens were eventually deported.[79]

In the meantime, the legal academy began to protest the government's apparent indifference to the First Amendment rights of the detainees. On May 28, 1920, a hastily assembled National Popular Government League, published

To the American People: A Report of the Illegal Practices of the United States Department of Justice blasting the Department of Justice's handling of the detentions. Harvard Law School's Frankfurter, Pound, and Zechariah Chafee led the way, but Kane also signed the report. It documented cruel and unusual treatment of the detainees, punishment before any proof of violation of law, illegal arrests and seizures, and "provocative" interrogation, a euphemism for the third degree. The authors concluded, "It has always been the proud boast of America that this is a government of laws and not of men . . . There is no danger of revolution so great as that created by suppression, by ruthlessness, and by deliberate violation of the simple rules of American law and American decency."[80]

On June 23, 1920, First Circuit Court of Appeals Judge George Weston Anderson rendered his ruling on the habeas corpus proceedings for 112 detainees held on Deer Island in Boston Harbor. A Wilson nominee and an avidly liberal Progressive, Anderson had been on the bench for two years. He had previously served as U.S. attorney for the District of Massachusetts. His opinion was a melding of fact and statutory interpretation commonly found in Progressive writing. He was conscious of the challenge in this case: the evidence comprised over 1,600 typed pages. "Under such circumstances, it seemed the plain duty of this court to afford the fullest opportunity both to the petitioners and to the government to present all facts arguably pertinent." He saw the issue as extending far beyond the petitions presented to the court, for "at the opening of the hearing the cases were said by counsel on both sides to be, in many important aspects, test cases of the legality of an undertaking of the government to deport several thousand aliens."[81]

Anderson's opinion was more than a determination on the issuance of the writ—it was an exemplar of the coming of age of Progressive jurisprudence, of the melding of judicial examination of legislative intent and extensive factual findings. Anderson was plainly offended that throughout their interrogation, the detainees had no access to counsel. Now they did. Anderson appreciated the voluntary efforts of Frankfurter and others. "I desire to express my appreciation of their unselfish and highly professional endeavors to assist in the proper determination of a cause involving, directly, the fundamental rights of a large number of aliens but poorly equipped with means or knowledge to protect their rights."[82]

Anderson then explained to the other branches of the federal government the essential role that courts played in America. His version of separation of powers echoed John Marshall's, as did the style of argument in Anderson's opinion. He would concede the limitations of his court, then with a simple twist or a single phrase, arrive at the opposite conclusion—the vital role of courts in the checks and balances system. "It has been repeatedly held that the right to exclude or to expel all aliens, or any class of aliens, absolutely or upon certain conditions, in war or in peace," is "an inherent and inalienable right of every sovereign and

Figure 7.5 George Weston Anderson, 1916, U.S. attorney for the District of
Massachusetts, two years before he became a federal judge. Credit: Library of Congress.

independent nation, essential to its safety, its independence, and its welfare."
Anderson seemed to agree, then he spun about and added that the court was
"required by the paramount law of the Constitution, to intervene."[83]

He conceded the limitation of courts when the intent of Congress was clear.
He did not want the case to be read as part of the long controversy between the
two branches of the federal government. "Otherwise stated, there is no constitutional limit to the power of Congress to exclude or expel aliens. An invitation once extended to the alien to come within our borders may be withdrawn.
He has no vested right to remain." Congress, not the courts, determined immigration law. Similarly, he insisted that he wished no quarrel with the executive
branch, the other long-standing rival to the authority of the federal courts within
the federal system. "It is also familiar and perfectly well-settled law that the
courts have no jurisdiction, on habeas corpus proceedings, to interfere with the
proceedings in the Department of Labor concerning the exclusion or the expul-
sion of aliens, unless and until there is some error of law in that department."
The "unless" was the exception: "unless the proceedings in that department are

unfair, thus lacking some of the essential elements of due process of law." The "unless" in Anderson's view was the essence of his court's duty. "In these habeas corpus cases, therefore, it may be said that the primary function of the court is to try, not the right of the alien to enter or to remain in the United States, but to try the trial of the alien in the Department of Labor."

Then he wrote a sentence that should stand with Marshall's "it is a Constitution we are expounding" in the annals of American jurisprudence: "It may, however, fitly be observed that a mob is a mob, whether made up of government officials acting under instructions from the Department of Justice, or of criminals, loafers, and the vicious classes."[84]

The litany of abuses the government perpetrated against the detainees made up the bulk of the opinion. "Necessarily a raid of this kind, carried out with such disregard of law and of properly verified facts, had many unexpected and some unintended results." Men and women were gathered up in the night and held in cells without access to counsel, much less to the basic necessities of life. "It was under such terrorizing conditions as these that these aliens were subjected to questionnaires, subsequently used as, and generally constituting an important part of, the evidence adduced against them before the immigration inspectors." What could have excused the inhuman, not to mention illegal, process in so many cases? "Pains were taken to give spectacular publicity to the raid, and to make it appear that there was great and imminent public danger, against which these activities of the Department of Justice were directed." The propaganda effort did not persuade Anderson, not after he weighed the facts. "The arrested aliens, in most instances perfectly quiet and harmless working people, many of them not long ago Russian peasants" were not dangerous aliens. The entire episode was designed to humiliate and frighten the detainees, as if they were already proven criminals. The comparison to the chain gangs of former slaves, paraded out of the work farms at the beginning of the day, runs through the account like an ominous shadow. The suspected anarchists "were handcuffed in pairs, and then, for the purposes of transfer on trains and through the streets of Boston, chained together . . . the handcuffed and chained aliens were exposed to newspaper photographers and again thus exposed at the wharf where they took the boat for Deer Island" in Boston harbor. On the island, sanitary facilities were inadequate; heat and light were absent; food was rotten; and the detainees were herded together like cattle. "In the early days at Deer Island one alien committed suicide by throwing himself from the fifth floor and dashing his brains out in the corridor below in the presence of other horrified aliens. One was committed as insane; others were driven nearly, if not quite, to the verge of insanity." Anderson allowed return of all the writs—if the men and women were to be deported, it would be after fair trial. For opponents of the Red Scare, Anderson's opinion shone like a lighthouse beacon over a stormy sea—until it was partially reversed by the First Circuit Court of Appeals. Indeed, most of the lower federal courts fell in line with the repression of dissent and deportation of its utterers.[85]

Good judges follow the law, enforcing it fairly. Great judges have the vision to see beyond and above the particular case at hand to the great foundations of law in social life. In *The Masses, Abrams,* and *Colyer,* Hand, Holmes, and Anderson rose to the latter category.

Hand's opinion in *The Masses,* Holmes's dissent in *Abrams,* and Anderson's findings in *Colyer* elevated the federal courts above the bitterness of partisan politics and the rush to judgment common in time war. But it was Taft, not Hand, Holmes, or Anderson who would leave the deepest impress on the federal courts in the decade of the 1920s. By the end of the previous decade, White's faltering powers and refusal to step down irritated the man who had elevated him to the chief justiceship. Taft still hungered for the post. White obliged Taft in May 1921, dying from complications of a bladder operation. With fellow Ohio Republican President Warren Harding's full support, Taft was nominated and confirmed as chief justice within a month.

Taft would deny in public but readily admit in private that the previous years had thrust the federal courts into the maelstrom of politics. Reformers' complaints about conservative benches during the Progressive Era made clear that the judicial system was fully part of the political realm. The recall movement so successful against state judges not only brought the courts into the public eye, it also pit state government against federal government. So, too, did courts' overturning of state regulatory regimes. The cries of "government by injunction" heard in Congress and the courts' refusal to follow congressional intent to interpret federal acts in antitrust and price-control cases rejuvenated the old contest over checks and balances in the federal government. The courts during the Great War seemed more than willing to follow Congress and the president in wartime suppression of dissent, but the inadvertent consequence of that cooperation would be even closer ties between federal jurisprudence and politics. Sedition cases, as in the late 1790s, freed judges to embed their personal political ideology in their legal opinions. If there were "nobler, and more lasting" constitutional "legacies," they would not bear fruit for decades.[86]

Federal Courts in the Age of Anxiety, 1921–1929

During his presidential election campaign of 1920, Senator Warren G. Harding of Ohio told a Boston audience, "America's present need is not heroics, but healing; not nostrums, but normalcy; not revolution, but restoration; not agitation, but adjustment; not surgery, but serenity; not the dramatic, but the dispassionate; not experiment, but equipoise; not submergence in internationality, but sustainment in triumphant nationality." Harding's gift for platitude, honed by his years of writing newspaper editorials, had not deserted him. Still, the war years had seen tumult at home and devastation and loss abroad. The influenza epidemic of 1918–1920 brought more agony and death. While his appeal for serenity helped Harding win the Oval Office, it did not capture Americans' experience in the 1920s. Instead, the twenties were an age of anxiety.[1]

Harding was right in one respect. The war had scarred the American psyche. The easy confidence in the economic growth and modernization of the nation state that preceded the war had become its casualty. The Klan reappeared, as did an uncompromising religious fundamentalism, the two sometimes linked in their antagonism to Catholics and Jews. As one Klansman gave witness, "I found Christ through the Klan." By contrast, some intellectuals embraced "modernism" in art, literature, and music, with its cynical edginess and its brutal acceptance of reality. Modernist writers proposed that men did not go to war in heroic self-sacrifice; they were sent like cattle to slaughter. Many of these artists and writers, like young Ernest Hemingway, departed the states for Paris and other foreign parts. Another, Gertrude Stein, called the self-exiles a "lost generation."[2]

The Harding and the later Coolidge administrations had a similar antipathy toward the concerns of organized labor. In workers' attempts to organize, business and political leaders alike saw the specter of "Bolshevism"—the routine moniker for any kind of social welfare agitation. After all, the newly-formed American Civil Liberties Union under Roger Baldwin advocated for the free speech rights of dissenters whether they were union organizers, pacifists, or anarchists. What could be more suspicious than that? Business leaders went even further, inventing company-controlled labor organizations, company-provided social clubs and recreation centers, and industrywide blacklists, company police forces, and other security measures to combat would-be organizers. Although the economy provided work, the wages for that work stagnated along with labor's struggle to organize over the course of the 1920s.[3]

A fierce consumerism characterized many Americans' response to the deprivations of wartime. Sinclair Lewis began his novel, *Main Street*, "The story would be the same in Ohio or Montana, in Kansas or Kentucky or Illinois, and not very differently would it be told up York State or in the Carolina hills. Main Street is the climax of civilization. That this Ford car might stand in front of the Bon Ton Store" was the ultimate goal of every American, or so it seemed to the jaded eye of the author. New consumer durables like washing machines and refrigerators were de rigueur purchases for those who could qualify for credit and make the down payment. New electronic technologies brought the sounds of radio into the home, and the number of stations jumped from thirty to 600 during the decade. Radio personalities like Will Rogers, the cowboy humorist, became household names. But the more the house or apartment filled with such items, the more were needed to satisfy the addiction of "conspicuous consumption."[4]

How the federal courts would ride out the tides of radicalism and conservative reaction was a matter of concern to Chief Justice Taft. He wrote to his friend

Figure 8.1 "Return to Normalcy" was the winning electoral slogan of Warren G. Harding, here shown at his inauguration in 1921. Credit: Library of Congress.

George Sutherland in 1922, after the former Utah senator's confirmation to the Supreme Court, "I write to congratulate you from the bottom of my heart on your appointment to the [Supreme Court] bench . . . a supreme judge needs to keep abreast of the actual situation of the country so as to understand all the phases of important issues which arise . . . I should judge that the court is about to enter upon another period of agitation against its powers. . . [as] when Thad Stevens and the radical Republicans defied the Court, and when William Jennings Bryan and the income tax decision were made a part of the 1896 campaign."[5]

Chief Justice Taft's Courts

President Harding preferred to name less controversial judges than Hand and Anderson. The one man he knew from their common Ohio roots who fit this bill exactly was Taft. Perhaps no man was better suited by experience or personal inclination to be chief justice than Taft. With amiability, firmness, and honesty he served his country. He found time before he went to the Philippines as governor general to act as dean of the Cincinnati School of Law, and after he left the White House he taught at Yale Law School. Above all, he loved being a judge and yearned to be the chief justice. As he confessed, after Calvin Coolidge was elected president in 1924, "I would rather have been chief justice than president." Physically imposing (he could have held his own with Justice David Davis), an able manager and efficient executive, he expected and returned loyalty.[6]

On the Court, Taft was far more than first among equals. He found a tribunal overwhelmed with unfinished business and a system of districts and circuits largely without central direction. Taft set about changing both of these situations. He had the personal and professional clout to press Congress for reforms in the structure and operation of the lower courts, to seek greater control by the Court over its own docket, to influence the recruitment of judges, and to set the tone for the operation of the Court. To begin, he arranged with Harding's attorney general, Ohio politician Harry Daugherty, to have a say in every federal judicial appointment, then lobbied for the men he wanted on the Supreme Court. Most often, he got his way. He urged his colleagues to work as a team, show courtesy to one another, and not dissent. As a result, Taft dissented in only 1.2 percent of the cases the Court heard.[7]

Taft pressed Congress for greater bureaucratic autonomy for the courts, emending the existing system. While the Department of Justice continued to administer the judicial branch (a function that passed to the Administrative Office of United States Courts when it was created in 1939), the 1922 statute creating the Conference of Senior Circuit Judges enabled the chief justice to work more closely with the senior judges in managing the entire system of courts. In 1925, Congress, again at Taft's urging, amended the Judiciary Act of 1789 to allow the Supreme Court to largely select those cases it wanted to hear. While his plan for reform of pleading in federal courts failed, his desire for a Supreme Court building, with chambers for each justice, a conference room and separate library, and a courtroom whose dignity would match the Court's own, would come to fruition after his death. Congress acceded to his wishes, and he threw himself into planning the new "marble palace." He did not live to see its completion in 1935, but it was a monument to his vision for the Court. Given his influence as chief justice in the process of staffing the Supreme Court (he had a hand in naming five associate justices) and his success in reorganizing the administration of the lower federal courts, one could say of Taft with truth that he was the head of the federal court system.[8]

Taft's impact on his own Court's membership was immediately evident. In September 1922 Harding asked Congress to confirm Sutherland to the Supreme Court, and the Senate obliged by a voice vote the next day, an honor usually reserved for a sitting senator (Sutherland had served from 1905 to 1917). The English-born, Utah politician had been Harding's close advisor

Figure 8.2 Chief Justice William H. Taft (*third from left*) and the associate justices admire architect Cass Gilbert's model for a new Supreme Court building in 1929. Taft not only persuaded Congress to fund the building, but he also supervised its planning and initial construction. Credit: Collection of the Supreme Court of the United States.

during the campaign, a conservative whose views matched Harding's and Taft's. Sutherland had no love for legislative solutions to economic or social woes, or to the supremacy of the federal government over the states. His reading of the Fourteenth Amendment's protection for private enterprise barred federal and state social and labor legislation. At the same time, he found room in the Constitution to protect the right to a fair trial and to oppose prior censorship. He retired in January 1938, as the Court and the country swung away from his economic views.[9]

Pierce Butler joined the Court in December 1922, after William Rufus Day retired. He was a local politician and railroad lawyer in Minnesota when Taft prodded Harding to name him. Butler was a Democrat and a Roman Catholic, so Taft had to work hard to ensure Republican Party support. Butler's conservative views mollified the conservative Republicans in the Senate, and Taft pulled strings to bring doubters into line. His nomination ran into some trouble in the Senate from Progressives, especially Wisconsin's Robert La Follette. He remarked that the Butler confirmation was an example of the powerful few lording it over the many. In response, the chief justice wrote to Harding that the opposition to Butler in the Senate "is part of the program they are deliberately setting out . . . to attack you, the court, and the constitution. The more blatant they make it the better I think it will be to unite the conservative elements to resist their plotting against the present social order." Butler was confirmed and Taft was right about his man—Butler voted with Taft 90 percent of the time. He was a stalwart of the Court's conservative bloc until his death in 1939.[10]

The last of the Taft Court nominees was Harlan Fiske Stone, named in 1925. Stone, the U.S. attorney general, was a New Hampshire man, granite-like in his probity, intellectually inquisitive (he was a professor and then dean of Columbia Law School), and capable of great warmth and friendship (Coolidge had been his classmate at Amherst). On the Court he demonstrated time and again that he could hold his own with any of his brethren, sometimes driving Taft to distraction. Expected to be as conservative as his predecessor, Joseph McKenna, Stone would instead join with Brandeis and Holmes to form a liberal minority on the Court. His opinions would become the bedrock of a new kind of substantive due process, based not on property but democratic empowerment.[11]

Policing the Nation's Morals

Taft's demand for reform of the courts' structure coincided with a sudden surge in their business, the last remnant of the moral crusade of Populism. The Eighteenth Amendment was ratified on January 16, 1919 and acting Secretary of State Frank L. Polk certified the ratification on January 29. Connecticut and

Rhode Island rejected the amendment, and New Jersey ratified it two years after it went into effect. The amendment read in part: "After one year from the ratification of this article the manufacture, sale, or transportation of intoxicating liquors within, the importation thereof into, or the exportation thereof from the United States and all territory subject to the jurisdiction thereof for beverage purposes is hereby prohibited." Ratification came more promptly than any previous amendment.[12]

On October 28, 1919, Congress passed the Volstead Act, providing the means for enforcement of the amendment. Wilson vetoed the bill, but Congress overrode his veto on the same day. Members were eager for Prohibition to commence. The burden on the executive branch was immediately felt, as the Act provided for "the Commissioner of Internal Revenue, his assistants, agents, and inspectors [to] investigate and report violations of the . . . Act to the United States attorney for the district in which committed, who shall be charged with the duty of prosecuting" offenders. The Act had some unintended but ironic similarities to the Fugitive Slave Act of 1850--the Volstead Act expanded the federal government's prosecutorial apparatus through the appointment of commissioners but was accompanied by widespread violations. Taft himself thought the Act unenforceable, and predicted, correctly, that it would heavily overburden the federal courts' docket, although he supported its enforcement. Whether anyone recognized these historical markers of likely resistance to the Act at the time of its passage, Taft, believed that the federal courts would stagger under the weight of the new revenue cases. Although he did not stress the point, he and his brethren were well aware that the whole project of enforcing the Volstead Act put federal revenue agents into every community in the country, increased the federal government's oversight of ordinary social activities (e.g., making and drinking alcoholic beverages), and added more to the administrative burdens of the executive and judicial branches than any congressional initiative since the (temporary) supervision of the draft during World War I. Others on the Court opposed Prohibition for precisely these reasons: that it impermissibly violated traditional norms of federalism.[13]

The results of the new law were immediately apparent. In 1917, there were 19,628 federal criminal cases commenced in the district courts. In 1920, this figure stood at 55,587, of which 5,095 were Volstead Act prosecutions. Throughout the 1920s, the totals of federal crimes prosecutions commenced varied from 54,487 in 1921 to 86,348 in 1929. The number of Volstead cases rose through the decade, from 21,297 in 1921 to 71,298 in 1929. In 1929, 83 percent of federal criminal proceedings involved Volstead Act violations. Federal judges all over the country recognized the problem of overloaded dockets and the report of the Conference of Senior Circuit Judges warned: "The business, civil and criminal, in the Federal Courts continues to increase in volume." Once again the busiest of the districts were those in and around New York City. "Some twelve Judges have been assigned from other circuits to sit in the Eastern, Southern and Western Districts of New York from time to time since July 1st, 1924, and some reduction has been made in the arrears. But it is perfectly evident that no real remedy will be afforded except by increasing the number of District Judges in that Circuit."[14]

Even with an increase in the apparatus of enforcement, violators' counsel could find cracks in the system. The "booze lawyers" fought hard to delay convictions. The percentage of acquittals and dismissed cases rose from 15 percent in 1920 to 26 percent in 1929. In San Francisco the docket with Prohibition cases was so backed up that newly appointed district Judge John Slater Partridge told the *Examiner* that "the situation here is unprecedented and one of the worst in the country." In his March 1929 inaugural address, President Herbert Hoover sounded the alarm: "We are fortunate in the ability and integrity of our Federal judges and attorneys. But the system which these officers are called upon to administer is in many respects ill adapted to present-day conditions. Its intricate and involved rules of procedure have become the refuge of both big and little criminals. There is a belief abroad that by invoking technicalities, subterfuge, and delay, the ends of justice may be thwarted by those who can pay the cost." [15]

One of the most notorious of the Volstead Act violators was Chicago "outfit" mastermind Alphonse Capone. By using violence to conceal his operations, to drive off or kill off rivals, and by bribing officials, Capone was never successfully prosecuted under the Volstead Act, though he brought in from Canada and sold huge quantities of outlawed spirits. The federal government charged him with income tax evasion. He could not truthfully report his ill-gotten gains, and when a plea bargain fell through, he was tried and convicted. One episode from the trial has become almost legendary. Informed that Capone's agents had tampered with his trial jury pool, the presiding judge, James H. Wilkerson, in an extraordinary step, simply replaced the pool with another jury pool waiting for a trial next door. Wilkerson was a Chicago attorney, U.S. attorney for the district. He was neither cowed nor impressed with Capone, despite knowing all about the gangster's violent ways. With a bravura only matched by his misconduct as a crime lord, Capone's attorneys appealed the conviction, citing *Cruikshank*. They argued that the indictment was faulty for not specifying what Capone had worked so hard to conceal—the criminal operations that generated the income. Seventh Circuit Court of Appeals Judge William M. Sparks, a veteran prosecutor from Indiana, wrote for the panel denying the appeal. Capone went to prison and there his health deteriorated. Others took control of his criminal operation, however. The rewards of crime created by the Volstead Act were a far greater motivation than the fear of prosecution.[16]

It took nearly a decade to bring Capone to justice. Part of the problem, as Chief Justice Taft understood, was the relative paucity of trial court judges.

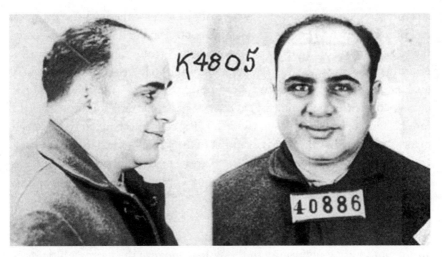

Figure 8.3 Al Capone mug shot. Courtesy: FBI, United States Bureau of Prisons.

Although the number of cases had risen more than 325 percent, on average, only slightly over 120 district judgeships heard these cases. That figure did not rise very much, certainly not in proportion to the rise in criminal prosecutions, going to 128 judgeships in 1929 and 136 the next year. Nor were these evenly distributed over the districts. Some judges, particularly in New York City, Detroit, Chicago, and Cleveland, bore a disproportionate share of the load. One solution was to provide for relief from less burdened circuits. Another was to end Prohibition. The Judiciary Act of 1922 assayed the first step. Repeal of the Eighteenth Amendment did not come as easily.[17]

The Creation of the Conference of Senior Circuit Judges and the "Judges' Bill"

Taft cited the impact of the Volstead Act in his plea for reform of the federal courts' administrative apparatus, in particular the ability to deploy judges temporarily to districts where caseloads had spiked. He knew this part of his plan for a more efficient distribution of the judicial workforce would, in the context of the Volstead Act, spur some opposition. He told the American Bar Association in 1922, when the first of his proposals was making its way through Congress, that it "ends the absurd condition, which has heretofore prevailed, under which each district judge has had to paddle his own canoe and done as much business as he thought proper."[18]

But Taft's vision for the courts reform went beyond the immediate crisis. His program for reform of the lower courts had long been in his thinking, and it was a clear example of the Gilded Age's "organizational synthesis," by which local and regional variation gives way to central control and uniformity. At its center, the establishment of the Conference of Senior Circuit Judges (the equivalent of today's chief judges), a part of the reform of the judicial code, represented the fruition of a long process of reform. In the past, the various districts had developed their own administrative practices and the variation promoted the forum shopping begun after the Civil War. The centrifugal pull of so many sets of local rules, sped by the rapid expansion of the judicial system itself in the new century's first two decades, threatened to create serious disharmonies. In 1921 incoming attorney general Harry Daugherty created a committee to consider reforms of the federal judicial system, which Taft joined when he became chief justice. Daugherty's committee had already discussed the idea of a conference of senior (chief) circuit judges. The final version of the Conference proposal was an attempt to bring uniformity to the system and give the judges a little more control over information presented to Congress on the functioning of the courts and, according to some students of the courts, more subtly "elude or erode state judicial power."[19]

The unwieldy title, "An Act for the appointment of an additional circuit judge for the Fourth Judicial Circuit, for the appointment of additional district judges for certain districts, providing for an annual conference of certain judges, and for other purposes" suggested its multiple purposes, a kind of omnibus reform composed of diverse pieces. The first was a substantial expansion of the judicial system to handle the rapidly increasing caseload, a total of twenty-four new district judgeships and one additional circuit judgeship (so that all the circuit courts of appeal had three judges). Most of these new slots reflected the growth (and growing legal business) of cities: Boston, New York City, Philadelphia, Pittsburgh, Dallas, Miami, Detroit, Cleveland, Nashville, Chicago, Minneapolis, St. Louis, Kansas City (Missouri), San Francisco, Los Angeles, Albuquerque, Tulsa, and Phoenix. The changing shape of the judiciary reflected a nation becoming more urban. The tide of immigration had slowed—the Immigration Quota Acts of 1920 and 1924 had seen to that—but the internal tide of immigration from countryside to city had increased greatly after the war. By 1926, as a result of the Act, the number of district judgeships jumped to 121, nearly an 18 percent increase.[20]

The administrative role of the chief justice expanded as well. Perhaps unfairly, opponents of the plan in Congress regarded and resented this as a coup. Taft had advocated the creation of the Conference and critics railed at what they saw as Taft's stance as "commander in chief" of the judiciary. Typical of these complainants, John Shields of Tennessee, a Democrat and former chief of his state supreme court, fulminated, "The Chief Justice has no more to do with the judges of the district courts of the United States, and with the trial of cases, and procedure in those courts, or the congestion of business in them, than does King George. His interference is purely voluntary and officious."[21]

Taft denied any such ambitions, but not only did the new statute refashion the old distribution of authority between center and periphery in the judicial system, it also gave to the chief justice an official forum for promoting his agenda. Taft wanted further change to come from the top of the system. The statute complied with his wishes. Before the Act, each circuit acted as if it were "a feudal barony, isolated from the others and accountable to no one." The Act changed all that: "It shall be the duty of the Chief Justice of the United States . . . to summon to a conference . . . the senior circuit judge, i.e. the chief judge, of each judicial circuit." The chief justice (or his substitute in case of disability) could summon—a command—chief judges in the circuits to attend, an authority nowhere contemplated in the Constitution or the Judiciary Act of 1789. If a senior circuit judge was unable to attend, the chief justice (or his substitute) could summon a different circuit or district judge to attend. The authority to substitute a particular judge similarly was new (because the Conference was new). Finally, "It shall be the duty of every judge thus summoned to attend said conference, and to remain throughout its proceedings, unless excused by the Chief Justice." Nothing like this existed previously (federal judges only having to hold court at the stated times and places). No wonder some members of Congress and some of the judges bridled at the new rules.[22]

The statute directed each senior district judge, in advance of the Conference, to provide the senior circuit judge a report on the condition of the district's docket with recommendations, if any, "as to the need of additional judicial assistance" in the coming year—data and recommendations that each Conference participant was to present to the full conference. Although the Conference only met for a day or two in September (unless it was called to a special session or its business required additional meeting time), journeying to Washington, D.C. from the West Coast or the High Plains was time-consuming. Train travel was the only reliable means, and it could take two days and a number of rail line switches to make the journey. Once in the District, the judges assembled in the conference room adjacent to the Supreme Court chamber in the Capitol, where "[t]he Chief Justice, or, in his absence, the senior associate justice, shall be the presiding officer of the conference." The attorney general was to report to the Conference subjects "as may seem in the interest of uniformity and expedition of business," particularly on "causes or proceedings in which the United States may be a party." (Recall that the administrative organ of the federal courts was the Department of Justice, which the attorney general led.)

The Act imposed duties on the senior circuit judges, to wit: "Whenever any district judge by reason of any disability or necessary absence from his district or the accumulation or urgency of business is unable to perform speedily the work

Figure 8.4 Chief Justice Taft (*third from right*) and senior circuit judges from the Conference of Senior Circuit Judges call on President Calvin Coolidge at the White House, 1924. Credit: Library of Congress.

of his district" the senior circuit judge could "designate and assign any district judge of any district court within the same judicial circuit to act as district judge in such district." If no judge within the circuit could be found, the chief justice could reach out to another circuit and with the consent of its senior circuit judge designate someone from that district temporarily reassigned. In short, the new code provisions gave to the chief justice and the senior circuit judges a species of appointment power to reassign judges to other circuits from those to which they had been appointed by the president and Congress. Taft regarded this authority not as a shift in separation of powers but as an aid to the overburdened district judges. Whether viewed as a consolidation of power at the top of the judicial system or a long overdue reform, the new system was as important as any the Progressives had proposed, though it leaned away from their desire to lodge judicial accountability with nonjudicial bodies in favor of judicial self-policing.

The Act systematized and centralized what had been a much older practice with regard to the disability of a district judge. Beginning in 1850, a justice on circuit (and after 1869, a circuit judge) could reassign a district judge within a circuit in case of the disability of another district judge. If the circuit judge was unavailable or the designated district judge did not fulfill his duties, the chief justice could reassign a district judge to a district court in a contiguous circuit. In 1907, Congress empowered the chief justice to reassign a district judge from any circuit in case of disability, but only after a certificate of disability was issued by the circuit judge of the receiving circuit. In response to the extraordinary caseloads in the Southern District of New York, Congress in 1913 passed a law allowing the chief justice to reassign a district judge from any circuit—with the judge's consent and the approval of the senior circuit judge of the circuit—to hold district court in the Second Circuit.[23]

Long before Taft's success in creating the Conference, he planned to seek another concession from Congress: increasing the Court's control over its own docket. It had to hear certain types of appeals from the circuit courts of appeal, for example, and cases under its original jurisdiction. A series of congressional acts from 1903 to 1916 had exempted mandatory direct appeal of bankruptcy cases, trademark cases, and Federal Employers Liability Act cases. The further limitation of mandatory review was Taft's project, but his fellow justice and ally Van Devanter spoke vigorously in favor of the limitation of mandatory Court review in testimony before the House Judicial Affairs committee in 1922. Taft anticipated and rejected arguments that it gave the Supreme Court a "too wide discretionary power." But the proposal languished until 1924.[24]

As the Supreme Court's caseload leaped from 713 new appeals in 1923 to 854 in 1924, Taft direfully predicted a skyrocketing docket. A renewed effort by Van Devanter led to the resumption of hearings. He told the congressmen, "It is not too much to say that one-third of the business which now comes to the Supreme Court results in no advantage to the litigants or the public . . . Cases coming from a State court have already passed through two courts; and so of cases coming from a [federal] circuit court of appeals. In each instance the case has been through a court of original jurisdiction and an appellate court. Of course, most of them have been rightly decided. Our obligatory jurisdiction operates to give a review in a third court as of right, even though the decision is obviously correct." The ABA had opposed the bill until Taft intervened, and Taft had a powerful ally—Coolidge praised the bill in his successful campaign to retain the presidency. The bill passed the House in a voice vote on February 2, 1925, and the Senate, with one negative vote, the next week.[25]

Named the "Judges' Bill" because it came from the Court, Coolidge signed it into law on January 28, 1925. It cut back significantly on "mandatory" appellate review, limiting it to those cases "where is drawn in question the validity of a statute of any state, on the grounds of its being repugnant to the Constitution, treaties or laws of the United States, and the decision is against its validity." Further, mandatory review was restricted to the federal question presented in the pleadings and, again, only when review was sought be the party relying on state law.[26]

Only 754 new cases were docketed in 1925 and that number fell to 732 in 1926. Watching from on high (at Harvard Law School), Felix Frankfurter lauded the Act. He thought that the Supreme Court should only concern itself with issues of great national importance. But he predicted that the Court's docket would once again grow.[27]

The Judges' Bill did not bar appeals from other federal or state court decisions, merely moving them to a discretionary category and having them arrive at the Court through the request for a writ of certiorari from the appellants. After all, according to Justice Van Devanter's testimony before the Judiciary Committee, if at least four of the members voted certiorari, the Court would take a non-mandatory appeal. Taft had promised serious consideration of the granting of all such writs, a promise he may have meant to keep, but one that left the hearing of such appeals entirely to the discretion of four of the nine justices. The legislation largely relieved the Court of its role of appellate error-corrector and moved it toward its current primary role as an adjudicator of national issues. But the Act did not materially change the number of cases the Court disposed each year in the remainder of the 1920s—that figure remaining fairly constant in the mid-800s. What is more, as Frankfurter had predicted, in the next decade, the yearly average of cases disposed would creep up to the mid-900s. [28]

A final act of institutional importance in 1929 broke the Eighth Circuit into two parts, primarily to divide its court of appeals. "The six Circuit judges in the Circuit . . . make up two Supreme Courts . . . in the 8th circuit. And this prevents the uniformity of decision that is very necessary in one Circuit having theoretically only one Circuit Court of Appeals." Despite some opposition from judges in the circuit concerned about traveling arrangements should the old circuit be divided, the chief justice favored the division. When the actual lines of division were proposed in Congress, however, the opposition grew stronger. The hearings revealed controversy over where courts of appeals would sit, but these cavils were overcome. The Eighth, as revised, included the Dakotas, Nebraska, Iowa, Minnesota, Missouri, and Arkansas, retaining the interregional character of the old circuit. A new circuit, the Tenth, not to be confused with the short-lived circuit from 1863 to 1866, now included Wyoming, Kansas, New Mexico, Colorado, Oklahoma, and Utah—a plains region.[29]

One bridge Taft wanted to cross was too far for Congress to follow. The Supreme Court issued the rules of procedure for the entire federal system in matters of admiralty and equity, a power going all the way back to the Judiciary Act of 1789 and made explicit in 1842. In the revised judicial code of 1911, Congress allowed the Court to reframe the relationship between suits in equity and law cases, making it easier to move from one docket to the other. But attempts to unify the two dockets had stalled. A year later, the ABA's president Thomas Shelton proposed that the Supreme Court have the task of rewriting all federal procedural rules. That would have opened the door for the Court to unify the law and equity dockets. Fully aware of the assault from the left on the courts, Shelton saw procedural reform as an

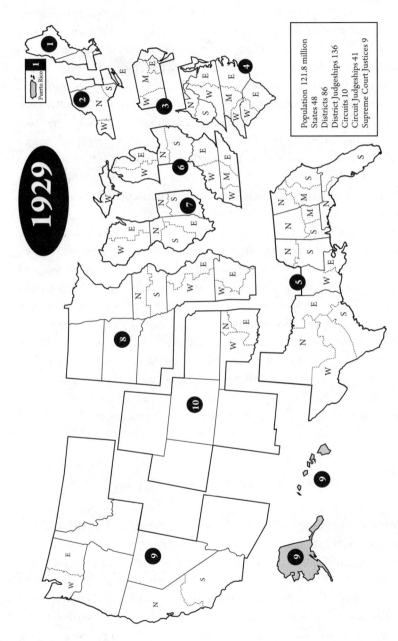

Figure 8.5 Judicial circuits, 1929. Source: Wheeler and Harrison, *Creating the Federal Judicial System*, courtesy of the Federal Judicial Center.

Population 121.8 million
States 48
Districts 86
District Judgeships 136
Circuits 10
Circuit Judgeships 41
Supreme Court Justices 9

1929

antidote to political criticism. If one wanted to divorce "the courts from politics and political influences and require them and the Bar to clean their own house . . . [and] if lawyers and judges are to be held solely responsible, as in right they should, then they must be given the power to correct the evil by putting into practice all necessary reforms in the courts." Henry Clayton, while working on his own Anti-trust Act of 1914, laid Shelton's proposal before Congress at the end of the year. Clayton saw the unification of the docket as a boon to the ordinary man who sought justice in federal courts. Clayton's proposal lay on the table until 1914, opposition from, among others, Progressives like Thomas J. Walsh of Montana, barring its way forward. The Law and Equity Act of 1915 in Michigan showed that states were moving in the direction of New York's Field Code, but the federal government lagged behind. The Federal Law and Equity Act of 1915 permitted litigants to adjudicate the equity claims first, and then have the legal issue settled by a jury, but the two dockets remained separate. Clayton still pressed for a uniform meta-procedure. By 1917 a sitting federal district judge, he lamented that no lawyer or judge could predict which state's procedural law (under the Conformity Act) would be applicable in any particular case. Worse, there was no procedural uniformity among the states, some adopting unification of law and equity, others not. "It is believed by nearly all of those who have studied the subject that the remedy for the highly unsatisfactory condition in federal procedure ought not to be attempted through the medium of a rigid legislative code, and unamendable, except by the slow process of legislative regulations." Instead, the answer was in some version of the Shelton Plan—letting the Supreme Court determine the uniform rules for all civil litigation in federal courts. Walsh remained adamant. "Mr. Shelton and his associates among the members of the American Bar Association who try cases in many States, but the humble lawyer whose practice is confined to the State in which he resides may be pardoned for looking at the matter in quite a different light." The plan languished.[30]

The Taft Court's New Nationalism

A perhaps unintended byproduct of Taft's attempt to restrict the jurisprudence of the Supreme Court to matters of national importance was the increased visibility and impact of the Court's decisions in First Amendment cases. There was relatively little litigation of freedom of speech questions until the World War I era. All that changed with the Taft Court. Taft was a nationalist. His entire legal and political career was in service to the nation. What was more, he oversaw the courts in an era of national expansion—the acquisition of an overseas empire, the rise of nationwide corporate and industrial entities, and the growing role that federal law played in everyday life—and wanted the federal courts to promote that nationalism.

In deciding appeals from state statutes that impinged on First Amendment claims, the Taft Court was revisiting federalism. While it was true that the boundary between state courts and federal courts, as well as between state statutes and the federal Constitution, was always shifting, the Taft Court continued what Reconstruction federal jurisprudence had begun. In the "incorporation" of the Bill of Rights, the Taft Court redrew the boundaries of federalism. Incorporation meant the imposition of the eight amendments on the states through the Due Process or Equal Protection Clauses of the Fourteenth Amendment. Taft did not see the Court as the great defender of the powerless and the oppressed, but his administrative reforms—in particular turning the face of the Court to issues of constitutional importance—started the Court on this road. Incorporation meant an increasing portion of the Supreme Court's attention to appeals from state court would be explicitly based on these amendments. And if plaintiffs in civil suits and defendants in criminal cases could appeal state court decisions to the federal courts based on freedom of speech, freedom of the press, criminal procedure, and the other guarantees of the Bill of Rights, no state court decision on any of these issues would ever be final. Incorporation was the nuclear option in the contest between the two judicial systems begun in 1789.[31]

Examination of incorporation of the First Amendment in the Taft Court arrived from an unlikely source: Justice McReynolds. McReynolds applied the Fourteenth Amendment to what amounted to state suppression of free speech in *Meyer v. Nebraska* (1923) and to freedom of worship in *Society of Sisters v. Pierce* (1925). In *Meyer*, the state forbade the teaching of German in elementary schools. A German-language teacher sued. McReynolds saw the right of the teacher to ply his trade as a property right guaranteed by the Due Process Clause, similar in one sense to *Lochner*. "Mere knowledge of the German language cannot reasonably be regarded as harmful. Heretofore it has been commonly looked upon as helpful and desirable. Plaintiff in error [i.e., Meyer] taught this language in school as part of his occupation. His right thus to teach and the right of parents to engage him so to instruct their children, we think, are within the liberty of the amendment." So far, nothing new, but McReynolds continued that the Due Process Clause "without doubt . . . denotes not merely freedom from bodily restraint but also the right of the individual to contract, to engage in any of the common occupations of life, to acquire useful knowledge, to marry, establish a home and bring up children, to worship God according to the dictates of his own conscience."[32]

Incorporation applied in *Pierce* as well. The state's public school law as amended in 1922 required that "every parent, guardian or other person having control of a child between the ages of eight and sixteen years to send him to the public school in the district where he resides." No child might be sent to a parochial school, in effect outlawing Catholic schools. Behind the new law was a Klan attack on the Catholic Church to which the legislature had capitulated. The Society of Sisters, a Roman Catholic orphanage and school, sued. While the legislature argued that the new law would lower crime rates and dissipate any religious animosity among children, McReynolds judged that "[u]nder the doctrine of *Meyer v. Nebraska* . . . we think it entirely plain that the Act of 1922 unreasonably interferes with the liberty of parents and guardians to direct the upbringing and education of children under their control. As often heretofore pointed out, rights guaranteed by the Constitution may not be abridged by [state] legislation which has no reasonable relation to some purpose within the competency of the State." Again the hidden issue was whether the Free Exercise Clause of the First Amendment applied to the states. As counsel for the Society of Sisters argued, "The statute in suit trespasses, not only upon the liberty of the parents individually, but upon their liberty collectively as well. It forbids them, as a body, to support private and parochial schools and thus give to their children such education and religious training as the parents may see fit." McReynolds's formulation brought the Court a step closer to full incorporation of the First Amendment. Equally important, the entire Court subscribed to his opinion.[33]

McReynolds did not apply the doctrine to radical political speech, but in *Gitlow v. New York* (1925) the issue was squarely before the Court. New York State passed a "criminal anarchy" law "punishing those who advocate, advise or teach the duty, necessity or propriety of overthrowing or overturning organized government by force." Benjamin Gitlow and others in the "Left Wing Section" of the Socialist Party distributed a pamphlet that the state prosecutors decided violated the law. Gitlow's counsel argued that the statements were meant to be factual rather than hortatory, or in the alternative, mere advocacy of one system over another. The Court upheld his conviction in a 7 to 2 vote, but Justice Edward T. Sanford went on to state, "For present purposes we may and do assume that freedom of speech and of the press—which are protected by the First Amendment from abridgment by Congress—are among the fundamental personal rights and 'liberties' protected by the due process clause of the Fourteenth Amendment from impairment by the States."[34]

An American Dilemma Continues

Despite the incorporation doctrine's appearance, the federal courts in the 1920s were not a bastion for minority rights. They did not overturn Jim Crow legislation nor interfere when it was enforced by state courts. Most federal judges in the South were southerners, and they shared many of the same racial attitudes as the legislators and governors in the states where they sat. Jim Crow law was imbedded in federal court precedents like the *Civil Rights Cases, Plessy v. Ferguson*, and a flotilla of similar decisions.

When southern states flouted federal law openly, as in the Alabama peonage cases, federal courts would step in, but that step was taken with great caution. Take, for example, *Nixon v. Herndon* (1927), in which the NAACP hired Fred Knollenberg, an El Paso white lawyer who had often represented black clients, to speak for Dr. Lawrence Nixon's right to vote in the all-white Democratic Party primary. The suit was based on the Civil Rights Act of 1870 and sought damages against the two election judges (as it happened, both friends of Nixon's) who told him that they could not give him a ballot. Texas law forbade his casting a vote. In 1924, Judge DuVal West, presiding in the district court for the Western District of Texas dismissed the suit with costs to Nixon. West had a storied career before President Wilson selected him for the federal bench in 1916. Growing up in Austin, Texas, he recalled hunting trips with members of his family who knew, firsthand, stories of the Mexican-American War. West himself had been a railroad surveyor, cattle driver, insurance salesman, federal marshal, a commander of Texas volunteers in the Spanish American War, and had represented Wilson and American interests in Mexico, interviewing and reporting back his impressions of the various contenders for power, during the Mexican Revolution. His opinion in *Nixon* was not recorded.[35]

Dr. Nixon appealed to the Supreme Court. In oral argument the state replied in its own defense, "Because the Democratic party holds a nominating primary, can it be contended that outsiders can be forced upon the party over its expressed dissent?" The outsiders, presumably, were black voters in Texas. Counsel for the state asked for deference to its laws, customs, and the tradition of judicial federalism. Justice Holmes, who ordinarily favored deference to the elected branches of government, wrote for the majority a two-page opinion. "We find it unnecessary to consider the Fifteenth Amendment, because it seems to us hard to imagine a more direct and obvious infringement of the Fourteenth Amendment, which, while it applies to all, was passed, as we know, with a special intent to protect the blacks from discrimination against them." Holmes, always a believer in legislative intent, was right on target about the intent of the drafters of the Civil Rights Acts and the Fourteenth Amendment. [36]

In *Gong Lum v. Rice* (1927) racial discrimination was as obvious and invidious as it was in *Nixon*. Mississippi law segregated schools on the basis of white and nonwhite, a posture which a Chinese family disputed. The petitioners did not dispute the racialist doctrine underlying the segregation of elementary schools in the state. Taft wrote for a unanimous Court: "We must assume, then, that there are school districts for colored children in Bolivar County." So long as some education was offered colored students (Taft did not inquire whether the rubric of separate but equal was fulfilled), there was no basis in the Fourteenth

Amendment to challenge the segregated school system. Brandeis, though he privately supported the NAACP and was no racist, did not dissent. Perhaps he had concluded that the Court had no way to force Mississippi to obey. Holmes and Stone signed on as well.[37]

When the New York Stock Market crashed on Black Tuesday, October 29, 1929, a wave of bank failures, business failures, and a loss of confidence in the economy followed. The Roaring Twenties ended with despair as makeshift shelters—termed Hoovervilles by their inhabitants as satirical tribute to the inability of President Hoover to reverse the downward spiral—spread across the urban landscape. The federal courts' jurisprudence, so attuned to the needs of business, was soon challenged by what was already being called the "Great Depression."[38]

Taft feared that a "radicalism" loosed by the Depression would shortly overturn the government and run riot through the streets. Both the leader and the symbol of the federal courts in the 1920s, he rightly worried about his legacy in such troubled times. Though dying from cardiovascular disease, he tried to arrange for his replacement with the same bluff assurance that he had used to gain approval for the Conference and the Judges' Bill and the same heavy-handed lobbying that had brought Sutherland and Butler to the Court. Taft had sworn in Hoover and sat through the new president's inaugural address on a cold March morning, a duty hardly conducive to his failing health, but Taft privately worried that "Hoover is a Progressive" and the work that Taft and his Court majority had done would be undone by Hoover nominees.[39]

Taft was right—Hoover's appointees did not share the outgoing chief's views. He named former Associate Justice Charles Evans Hughes, then secretary of state, to the center chair. Hughes's nomination sparked acrimonious debate in the Senate. On February 24, 1930, eleven days after he was confirmed, liberal senators like William Borah, George Norris, Robert La Follette, and Burton Wheeler denounced Hughes for representing oil companies and other major corporations. None of these critics doubted Hughes's integrity or ability, but all worried that another conservative chief justice would only continue in Taft's path. By contrast, conservative southern senators were concerned that Hughes might be too liberal. Hughes proved all the doubters wrong. His patrician bearing and personal dignity, along with a sense of his own historical importance, added gravity to the Court. Brandeis in particular appreciated the new chief's evenhandedness. Hughes moved the conferences of the justices along expeditiously, cutting off tangential comments, something that Taft, for all his business-like manner, had not managed. Hughes did not hold private meetings at home with a few select members, a practice that Taft had adopted. During oral argument Hughes was at his best, keeping counsel on their toes and turning the occasion into a genuinely informative event.[40]

Hoover's nomination of Fourth Circuit Judge John J. Parker to replace the departing Justice Sanford narrowly failed: Parker's suspect antiunion, anti–civil rights views telling against him (though in reality his jurisprudence was more moderate). Hoover was successful with Pennsylvania attorney Owen J. Roberts. Roberts had never before sat on the bench, and though much liked on the Court, his shifting stances on key constitutional issues often puzzled Court watchers.[41]

A third Hoover appointee was, unlike Roberts, well known to students of the law. In 1932, replacing Holmes, New York jurist Benjamin Cardozo joined the Court. A "giant had replaced a giant," the newspapers wrote. The choice of a Progressive Democrat (Cardozo) by a moderate Republican (Hoover) was not without precedent (think of Field and Lincoln, or Taft and Hughes), nor would it be the last time (think of Justice William J. Brennan and President Dwight Eisenhower). What was more, Cardozo had powerful supporters in Attorney General William Mitchell and Chief Justice Hughes.[42]

Cardozo is perhaps the most enigmatic figure ever to serve on the Court, possibly the most brilliant, and certainly one of the most creative. Elected to the New York supreme court through reform politics in 1913 at the age of forty-three, he refused to acknowledge any partisan obligations. He served eighteen years on the state's highest court and can be said to be the father of modern mass tort and products liability law, but he claimed no pride of place in any of this. His Storrs Lectures at Yale University on the nature of the judicial process were a remarkable contribution to legal thinking. He concluded that change was the rule of law and "many of these changes have been wrought by judges." But the lectures were devoid of personal insights. On the Court, he was courteous but aloof. His opinions were often elegant, and he did not shy away from moralizing. Most of all, he weighed a "larger sense of judicial responsibility" above more traditional craft canons.[43]

Taft was right—with the Hoover appointees seated, the Court had shifted a little to the left. Nevertheless, if the seeds of a new era of the federal judiciary were planted, the old dilemmas of state vsersus federal courts, checks and balances, and, most notably, the political impact of judicial decisions were about to gain renewed life in this time of national crisis.[44]

PART III

NO LONGER THE WEAKEST BRANCH, THE COURTS FROM 1929 TO 1986

The Depression decade of 1930–1940 ushered in a profound alteration of the role of the federal courts in American life. Working with other branches of the federal government, the courts came to the aid of a nation teetering on the brink of economic collapse. Cooperation among legal academics, federal judges, and lawyers birthed new rules for civil and criminal practice in the federal courts, in particular the transformative Federal Rules of Civil Procedure of 1938. Along with the Rules Enabling Act of 1934, Congress's creation of an Administrative Office of the United States Courts in 1939 gave the federal courts a greater degree of administrative autonomy within the federal government. As in the period of the Civil War and Reconstruction, the resulting shifts in constitutional doctrine and legal practice would become permanent parts of federal jurisprudence.[1]

Between 1941 and 1945 a world war tested the nation's will to sacrifice its people for the goal of world peace, and out of that war came a growing commitment to equal justice. The close of the Second World War left the United States as the foremost economic, political, and military power in the world and placed the United States at the center of what is today called "globalism." Even Congress, traditionally reluctant to surrender any portion of American economic sovereignty, went along with the new program. As *Time* magazine dubbed it, the "American Century" in world affairs was well under way.[2]

At home, the federal government sired a welfare state, with programs like the Social Security Administration, creating a "safety net" of economic resources for ordinary people. In the process of averting the siren call of state socialism and countering domestic communism, the government bound itself to help the needy, the elderly, and the infirm. It showed a willingness to work with labor unions, an eagerness to sponsor higher education, and a growing commitment to civil rights and liberties.[3]

But all was not well with the victors. An emerging contest with the Soviet Union and its expanding list of allies erupted into the Cold War— a conflict both superpowers waged through proxies, espionage, and nuclear threat. African Americans returned from their meritorious service in the war against racist Nazi Germany and Imperial Japan to find Jim Crow alive and well in their native land. Their fight for civil rights began before the war but gained new impetus after it. The Civil Rights Movement that unfolded over the next three decades inspired other disempowered groups—women, Native Americans, Hispanics, and the gay, lesbian, bisexual, and transgendered—to seek their own liberation from unjust laws. These efforts did not produce uniform results and sometimes suffered setbacks. [4]

It was a moral lag in American society that had ill consequences everywhere. The "well mortised wall" of segregated schools, public places, and employment was beginning to show cracks, however, and over time they would bring down the wall itself. Federal courts inched toward a vision of law that transformed and protected the civil rights of minorities. More and more often, and with greater and greater effect, judges brought social and economic considerations—the mores of the times—into their decisions. What was more, "it was discovered that, at least sometimes, courts could affect vast policy change without provoking vast political opposition." The way ahead was not so much an upward progress toward a more just law reflecting a more just society, as a halting progression in which federal courts sometimes led, and sometimes followed, public opinion.[5]

Court watchers and insiders debated whether there was a "litigation explosion." Seen from the inside the legal system, whether an "explosion" existed depended on how one compiled and read statistical measures of court records, including cases filed, cases adjudicated, and cases pending. The length, complexity, and expense of litigation also required careful definition. Complex technological cases, for example disputes over patents for software, were profoundly different from prisoners' petitions for habeas corpus relief. Should cases as distinct as these be bundled together or split into separate categories? Seen from outside the system, scholars wondered if widespread social alienation led people to seek relief in the courts for ills that had, in previous years, been borne in painful silence. A "rights revolution" had transformed many people's understanding of the public obligations of private actors, an unfortunate event for some students of the courts, but a blessing in others' minds.[6]

A simple calculation of the *rate* of suits filed in federal district courts by dividing the total decadal figures for those filings by the adult population for that decade (add the census figure for over age twenty at the start of the decade to the census figure for the next decade and divide by two) shows that there were 3.97 cases on average filed in the 1960s per 10,000 adults; for the 1970s there were 6.14 cases filed per 10,000 adults; in the 1980s there were 8.29 cases filed per 10,000 adults; in the 1990s there were 8.75 cases filed per 10,000 adults; and in the first decade of the twenty-first century there were 9.77 cases filed per 10,000 adults. Litigation had increased—whether the term "explosion" was apt depended on the perspective of the observer.[7]

Whether the federal courts' steadily increasing caseload represented litigants' shift away from state courts was another matter of controversy over the second half of the twentieth century and into the twenty-first. In 1956, Chief Judge John Parker of the Court of Appeals for the Fourth Circuit expressed his pleasure that nineteenth-century forum shopping was no longer the norm. The output of the model codes and Restatements of Law by American Law Institute, along with what Parker regarded as the salutary effects of the Federal Rules of Civil Procedure of 1938 and improvements in communication, had led to a growing uniformity of substantive law and procedural practice in federal courts. The federal bench finally seemed committed to the "idea of an integrated national judicial system" in which federal courts led the way. Parker did not denigrate the role of the state courts or mention that they had always carried a far greater burden of the nation's litigation than the federal courts, but the implication of his piece was that Chief Justice Marshall's version of the Madisonian Compromise was the correct one. Thirty years later, Parker's celebration of the supremacy of the federal courts seemed premature to Judge Ellen Peters of the Connecticut State Supreme Court. She noted that state courts carried 95 percent of the "nation's judicial workload," were a major source of interpretation of federal law and the Constitution, and in light of the "new federalism" decisions coming from the U.S. Supreme Court, the role of the states was far closer to Madison's ideal of federalism than Marshall's.[8]

The managerial role of federal judges in the age of the Federal Rules of Civil Procedure of 1938 was also controversial, not because it raised the issue of judicial federalism, but because it raised the specter of greater discretion. As Judge William Campbell of the Northern District of Illinois told new judges, "no other job, no member in the Supreme Court, including the chief justice, has the power that you do" in managing litigation, but with that power came the obligation to be fair to all parties in the court. This was particularly important in managing public law disputes. While few judges could dispute that they were playing a far more important role in pretrial cut and thrust than they had before the promulgation of the Rules, managing discovery in particular, not everyone in the legal world was happy with that consequence. The gains in efficiency—increasing the number of cases resolved without trial—weighed in the scales against complaints that judges were no longer neutral arbiters.[9]

The educational and demographic composition of the federal judiciary changed in the period. Almost all the new appointees had college and law degrees rather than "reading law" in the office of a member of the bar. More striking still was the incrementally increasing diversity on the bench, as African American, Hispanic, Asian, female, and other demographic and cultural groups took their seats. While overall the numbers of minority group judges remained comparatively small, and the increase in percentages may seem significant because the starting point was so low, but if present trends are any indication, a still more diverse bench is the judicial system's future.[10]

The political affiliation of court personnel shifted with the political tides, but this was nothing new. From the 1950s through the 1980s, the benches were largely composed of the appointees of Democratic Presidents Roosevelt, Truman, Kennedy, and Johnson. These judges were "moderately liberal" in civil rights and social justice matters, generally willing to expand the jurisdiction of the federal courts. With the election of Richard Nixon, and continuing into the tenures of Ronald Reagan and George H. W. Bush, the bench moved in a "slightly more conservative direction." The ideological range of decisions by appointees of Democratic and Republican presidents was much narrower than one might gather from the popular press or from interest groups on the left and right, however, and when the decisions are even more carefully parsed by content, the labels liberal and conservative begin to lose some of their meaning (although as categories for political science and other studies, they are commonly accepted). Looking at the district judges appointed in this period, one sees relatively little variation (by political affiliation of the nominating president) in liberality in criminal cases. The judges chosen by President Lyndon Johnson rendered liberal decisions in 38 percent of the criminal cases they heard, versus President Reagan appointee's liberal decisions in 25 percent of the cases—but one must factor in the changing nature of criminal law in this period (on which see chapter 13). Liberal decisions in civil rights and civil liberties cases were similarly statistically close—President Johnson's district court appointees rendered liberal decisions in 56 percent of their cases, while President Reagan's appointees were liberal in 33 percent of the cases they heard. All the other presidential appointees fell within the Johnson-Reagan range. If differences in political party views were fully deployed in federal court rooms, one would expect far greater statistical divergence between Democratic and Republican administration's judicial appointees.[11]

Unlike ideological convergence on the bench discussed above, contentious confirmation hearings in the Senate became much more common in the 1990s and after than they had been in the 1970s and 1980s. Politically motivated conduct in the Senate confirmation process was not new, but it was extending to more and more nominees for every Article III judgeship.[12]

The three themes that framed the federal judiciary at its inception— factional politics, federalism, and separation of powers (and its handmaiden, checks and balances)—remained a part of the federal courts' history in more modern times. That much had not changed. But the increasingly important administrative apparatus of the federal courts gave them the support they needed to perform increasingly complex tasks.

9

The Courts in the Great Depression, 1929–1940

The Great Depression of 1929–1940 profoundly affected Americans' lives. While a series of stock market crashes at the end of 1929 and the beginning of 1930 were the most visible inciters of the general downturn in the economy, deeper causes were long at work. Growing debt, a mark of the expanding gap between the few ultra-wealthy and the many who lived at or near the poverty level, contributed to the downward spiral. With little extra to spend on durable goods, middle-class Americans could not sustain the consumer economy. The malign effects of embezzlement and stock fraud, which in boom times were rife, were now easily and painfully uncovered. Lagging foreign demand for American exports contributed to the woes of American industrial workers and farmers. European customers, facing their own depression, could not pay for their purchases. Industrial production in the United States was halved.[1]

Like a row of dominos falling, market losses by businessmen led to business failures, unemployment, and bank defaults. At its peak, unemployment in the U.S. would reach a quarter of the work force. One woman's diary lamented, "There are no jobs. Most of us have had no breakfast. Hunger makes a human being lapse into a state of lethargy, especially city hunger." In the countryside, dairymen who could not find buyers poured their milk out on the road in protest. Such terrible ironies marked a nation on the brink of panic.[2]

For a generation of future federal judges, the years of the Great Depression had a lasting impact. Abner Mikva, who would become a federal judge in 1979, recalled that growing up poor in Chicago left him with a strong sense of social justice. "We had all our clothing from relief. Everyone knew that if you wore a black wool cap and these big black shoes that they were relief shoes and a relief cap." Constance Baker Motley, who joined the Southern District of New York bench in 1966, recalled similar experiences in New Haven, her family's dark skin adding to their economic woes. (Samuel) Hugh Dillin, who joined the Southern District of Indiana in 1961, recalled a Depression Era youth spent on an Indiana farm. "When it came to a given community, all of the men in the community would band together and clean out a field and go on to the next one. It was a communal operation." Without the help of neighbors, no one's farm would survive. Warren Urbom, looking back from a career on the bench that began in Nebraska in 1970, recalled a visit to a relative in rural Nebraska during the "Dustbowl" years: "First, I was embarrassed that my sole pair of shoes had holes in the heels. Second [my hosts] had ginger ale in their icebox every day, and I thought if I ever grew up and could afford it, I would have ginger ale in my icebox all the time."[3]

In the slough of the Great Depression, it appeared that the old tensions between Congress and the federal courts and competition between the federal courts and the state courts had largely vanished. The Republican ascendency of the 1920s in all but the solidly Democratic South, was reflected in the recruitment and output of the judiciary, and ensured greater harmony with Congress, the presidency, and the state courts than at any time since Reconstruction. As days passed and government at every level seemed inadequate to the task of helping Americans, however, that harmony would prove illusory. Novel legislative and executive reforms after 1933 would confront a federal judiciary at first unwilling to surrender older ideas of its constitutional role. In the latter years of the decade, the harmony of federal courts and the other branches of the federal government was restored, only to reawaken the dragon of federal-state judicial confrontation.

The election of Franklin Delano Roosevelt in 1932 brought a shift in energy and character of federal involvement in the economy and with it the seeds of a confrontation with the federal courts unlike any in its virulence since Lincoln castigated the Taney Court. Roosevelt was not a radical in political or economic views, but many of his advisors, carried to Washington, D.C. from his New York governorship, did not buy into the nineteenth-century doctrines of laissez faire. Roosevelt certainly understood the need for action and characterized it, accepting the nomination in 1932 by pledging "a new deal for the American people." In the first hundred days of his administration, he laid the ground work for what would be later called the safety net: "a forty-hour workweek, a minimum wage, worker's compensation, unemployment compensation, a federal law banning child labor, direct federal aid for unemployment relief, Social Security, and a revitalized public employment service and health insurance." But at first Roosevelt and his "Brains Trust" engaged in a frenzy of experimental pragmatism. "Dr. New Deal" went to work.[4]

With the Depression largely unaffected by the early efforts of the New Dealers, and after the Democrats' gains in the election of 1934, the Roosevelt administration considered more basic egalitarian reforms. Among these were programs to provide jobs (the Works Progress Administration), the Social Security Act, the Rural Electrification Administration, and the National Labor

Relations (Wagner) Act of 1935. The last of these finished the work of the Clayton Act and the Norris-LaGuardia Labor Act of 1932, finally ending the antilabor injunction.[5]

The Business and Personnel of the Early 1930s Courts

The onset of the Great Depression loaded debt and bankruptcy cases on a federal judiciary already reeling from Volstead Act prosecutions. Judges looked to the National Commission on Law Observance and Enforcement (the so-called Wickersham Commission), created on May 20, 1929, by President Herbert Hoover, for signs that relief was on the way. Two years of commission data-gathering led by former attorney general George Wickersham revealed widespread corruption in local police forces and the use of unacceptable tactics to coerce confessions and gain convictions, but the blue ribbon panel stopped short of recommending the repeal of the Eighteenth Amendment. Dissenters on the panel warned that failure to repeal the amendment would only prolong the logjam in the courts.[6]

The dissenters, like the federal judges, understood the impact of prosecutions on federal courts' dockets. By 1929, the district court dockets stood at 86,348 new filings and would top out at over 92,174 in 1932. (After repeal of the amendment, the 1934 docket had 34,152 new cases.) In 1932 and 1933, the Conference of Senior Circuit Judges and the attorney general called for the creation of additional federal court judgeships, but Congress did not act, nor did a similar appeal the next year bring relief.[7]

Prohibition ended with the ratification of the Twenty-First Amendment on December 5, 1933, easing the logjam in the federal courts. In September 1933, Attorney General Homer Cummings reported to the Conference of Senior Circuit Judges: "The number of cases terminated exceeded the number filed during 1933, and there was a general decrease in all classes except private suits, as compared with the previous year." Congestion was reduced greatly in the criminal calendar as Volstead Act prosecutions wound down. The need for additional judgeships was still clear—particularly in New York and California. Congress was sympathetic but, the economy being what it was, would not bear the expense of greatly expanding the judiciary—the same stance that Congress adopted in the early nineteenth century when faced with the expansion of the nation to the West.[8]

An increase in the size of the judiciary nevertheless eased the burden individual federal courts bore. The Judicial Conference continued to seek more judgeships, and from November 1, 1929, to the end of 1939, 161 judges were confirmed for the lower Article III courts. This was slightly more than the 141 lower court judges confirmed from November 1, 1919, to October 31, 1929. In terms of authorized judgeships, the judiciary grew by 76 percent between 1920 (140 lower court, life-tenured judgeships) and 1940 (250 judgeships), including thirty-five new judgeships added between 1935 and 1940. The increase actually ran a little ahead of the increase in population, but one should figure into this fact that immigration laws in 1921 and 1924 sharply reduced the number of immigrants from eastern and southern Europe, a major source of population increase. Also, during the Depression, domestic birth rates fell. Nevertheless, the judiciary grew as the rest of the federal government increased in size.[9]

The problem of caseloads presented by the early Depression years was not simply an artifact of temporary conditions. Looming behind the stockpiling of cases on the dockets was the delay in resolving cases. In 1931, as the Conference and the Congress sought ways to deal with the backlog, legal academics did not stand on the sidelines in the crisis. Yale Law School Dean Charles E. Clark convinced the director of the American Law Institute, William Draper Lewis, to commission a new study of the *Business of the Federal Courts* with Clark as its reporter (chief draftsman). Clark was a man of immense energy and vision and assayed a scientific answer to the crisis of swollen dockets and delayed justice. His contribution to the "legal realist" program was a study of auto accidents and divorce in Connecticut that had already paved the way to "no fault" laws. For the new project he hired research assistants and persuaded colleagues to gather and tabulate data. Legal realists might be academics teaching in law schools, but they believed in bringing the real world into the classroom. Social science–informed empirical studies became part of the realist curriculum at Yale, Harvard, Columbia, and Penn, among other elite law schools. At Yale, professors William O. Douglas and Thurman Arnold helped Clark make sense of the data.[10]

Clark emerged confident that he had found the key to reform in the numbers. That federal courts had become the chief engine for the adjudication of "federal question" cases could not be denied. So, too, the docket was crowded by suits brought by the federal government itself–together over 80 percent of the docket. Although the burden of the criminal cases had eased by 1934 when the report was published, somewhat reducing its impact, Clark still offered conclusions about the federal dockets that fit a larger argument: delay in terminating cases did not result from the combat of parties so much as procedural clutter. Over and over, his collection of "trust worthy facts" in the form of tabulated data, presented as an objective and neutral form of analysis, to him revealed the truth of his "general hypothesis": reform procedure and delay in justice for all parties would vanish. Arnold told Clark that the data did not support some of Clark's proposals and reported to Frankfurter that "Charlie does not feel any too cheerful about" the apparent discrepancies. In particular, Arnold thought that the data did not prove the necessity of thoroughgoing procedural reform. Nevertheless, Clark denied that he had any other agenda than to "cast light" on future policies. A "quick and efficient disposition" of cases was the ideal, and a solution must be found. [11]

While Clark and his collaborators debated the causes of delay, debtors and creditors were seeking the aid of the federal courts in record numbers. Delay in resolving these cases meant real hardship for the parties. Under the terms of the 1898 federal Bankruptcy Act, debtors, including companies, could file for protection against their creditors without the creditors' consent. Referees appointed by the district judges handled these cases. The burden on these officials had grown to nearly intolerable levels. A veritable explosion of petitions: from a little more than 14,000 in 1919 and a little over 53,000 in 1928, the number grew to an average of 65,000 in the 1930s, each involving detailed accounts of who owed how much to whom. The referees held hearings and presented findings. But these could be challenged in the district courts. The numbers were cumulative—that is, bankrupts in prior years were still deeply in debt in coming years. It never went below 60,000 until 1937. In 1938, the Act was amended, easing filing procedures. Laboring under the burden, the courts averaged a remarkable 60,000 petitions discharged or concluded each year. But there were inevitable delays, made worse by the disdain that many lawyers had for bankruptcy cases.[12]

The impact of the bankruptcy and debt cases on the courts was visible to all—the old courthouses were bursting at the seams with litigants, clerks, and officials. New construction in 1932, 1933, and 1934 led to imposing federal courthouses and post offices in Montgomery, Alabama; Little Rock, Arkansas; Sacramento, California; Hartford, Connecticut; Ft. Myers and Miami, Florida; Columbus, Georgia; South Bend, Indiana; Dubuque and Sioux City, Iowa; Topeka, Kansas; Alexandria and Baton Rouge, Louisiana; Baltimore, Maryland; Springfield and Worcester, Massachusetts; Bay City, Michigan; Jackson and Meridian, Mississippi; Jefferson City, Missouri; Harve, Montana; Omaha, Nebraska; Las Vegas, Nevada; Camden, Trenton and Newark, New Jersey; Greensboro, North Carolina; Toledo and Youngstown, Ohio; Okmulgee and Ponca City, Oklahoma; Portland, Oregon; Lewisburg, Pennsylvania; Chattanooga and Knoxville, Tennessee; Beaumont, Ft. Worth, Lubbock, and Wichita Falls, Texas; Rutland, Vermont; Danville, Lynchburg, and Norfolk, Virginia; and Cheyenne, Wyoming. But nothing matched the skyscraping grandeur of the new Foley Square federal District and Court of Appeals building in New York City, completed in 1936. The architect, Cass Gilbert, had simultaneously worked on the U.S. Supreme Court building. Indeed, the base of the Foley Square courthouse resembled the entirety of the Supreme Court building, but atop the six-story base of the former was another thirty stories of functional office space capped by an Egyptian pyramid decorated with terra cotta and gold leaf. Together, these massive neoclassical office buildings covering entire blocks, reminded the observer of the potency of the federal government. A further note about these buildings—the Foley Square and D.C. structures were solely courthouses and associated offices, instead of combined post offices, customs houses, and court structures. With them, the federal judiciary expressed an identity separate from and superior to purely administrative federal offices. Recognizing the importance of the building program, local party leaders presided over the festivities when the new courthouses opened their doors. Altogether the federal building program, including the courthouses, told everyone who saw them that the Depression had not dispirited the national government despite hard times.[13]

The courthouses were administrative centers and the courts were, as they had been since their founding, quasi-administrative agencies. Not only did the clerks continue to see to their courts' affairs, they also recorded hundreds of thousands of petitions for naturalization. Working under the district judges, federal bankruptcy referees handled thousands of petitions for debt relief. The 1938 Chandler Act allowed bankruptcy referees to act in the stead of the judges for the purposes of administering oaths and taking evidence, and adjudicating the petitions, but the judges' burden was delayed, not lifted, by the new measure. Each bankruptcy was a tale of woe, of human suffering, closed businesses, and lost jobs–heart-wrenching reminders for the courts' personnel of the broken promise of a culture that celebrated enterprise and achievement.[14]

As the courthouse building boom suggested, the old cities of the East Coast were not the only sites of distress. In the Southern District of Texas, for example, Depression Era foreclosure cases constituted one-fourth of the docket, matched only by illegal immigration prosecutions. While big city Houston banks withstood the Depression by merging and reorganizing, local and rural banks needed the assistance of the federal courts to survive. In a show of cooperation between state and federal judicial authorities exhibiting the best of the Madisonian Compromise, federal courts adjudicated assaults on state regulations and state courts heard and resolved claims against federal regulations. The federal courts proved adept at balancing tests—for example, weighing state regulation of highways against the desire of cotton producers to haul huge loads of their crops by truck. The district court also worked in tandem with the state legislature to ensure that smaller businesses were treated fairly. Large-scale Texas oil and cotton interests, while not always happy with judicial determinations in these cases (no-juries—the relief sought was injunctive), were the long-run beneficiaries of this cooperative federalism.[15]

The district courts of the West and the Plains were open to the claims of family farmers too. Cultivators in western Missouri were just as hard hit by the Depression as those in southern Texas. Added to the horrors of the crop failures of the Dustbowl years, mortgage foreclosures had become an everyday nightmare. Though fiercely independent and local in their outlook, the farmers welcomed the Public Works Administration and the farm aid bills. Western District of Missouri Judge Merrill Otis upheld these measures despite opposition from private banks and utilities. Though he was a Coolidge Republican and generally unsympathetic to the New Deal, he understood that the farmers' plight was not of their own making. Some form of relief from Washington, D.C. was necessary and constitutionally permissible. But when Ozark farmers showed little patience for the course of the law and mobbed a federal marshal attempting to carry out foreclosure orders, Judge Otis read the farmers the riot act. The rule of law trumped the farmers' grievances, he told a grand jury specially convened to hear the case.[16]

While the circuits' courts of appeal did not face the same load as the district courts, appeals grew in number from about 2,200 in 1928 to average a little over 3,500 by the second half of the next decade and ran slightly behind the growth of population in the country. The averages concealed an important fact. As in the nineteenth-century courts, one could find regional variations in the output of the various circuits. The variation in the output of courts of appeal was not just a function of the varying caseload. It reflected the recruitment, experience, temperament, and traditions of the different circuits. As the second circuit's Judge

Figure 9.1 Foreclosures on family farms during the Depression were a source of great misfortune that spread across the country. The farms were then sold by banks.
Credit: Franklin Delano Roosevelt Library, courtesy of the National Archives and Records Administration.

Irving Kaufman wrote in 1977, the members of the different circuit courts of appeal were well aware and proud of these differences. Indeed, as Justice Byron White noted, somewhat wryly, "It has been said for a long time that there is not just one Supreme Court in this country, there are 12 regional supreme courts." Some of these circuit courts of appeal had developed their own "view" of certain areas of law according to Judge Henry J. Friendly of the Second Circuit. Litigators were also aware of this fact. When the federal government's lawyers wanted a liberal panel to hear their case, they shunned the Fourth Circuit, considered too conservative, and turned to the Second Circuit, reliably liberal—in the lawyers' minds at least. Such forum shopping could be a good thing, allowing complex issues to "percolate" through various circuits. It could also wreak havoc with the idea of a uniform law for all.[17]

The courts of the Southern District of New York were especially busy ones because of their location. Despite the New York Stock Exchange crash, the city of New York had continued as the financial center of the country. Its banks and other financial institutions were weakened, and many failed, but others survived the Depression. The banks continued to hold more than one-fourth of the nation's deposits. The many large law firms in the city serviced the banks' suits against their debtors and creditors. Many of these suits were handled in the state's courts, but diversity suits and suits raising federal questions under the U.S. Banking Acts of 1933 and 1935 came to the Southern District and then to the Second Circuit Court of Appeals. Watching the downward spiral of businesses from the Southern District Chief Judge John Knox wondered: "Where would all this stop? Bankruptcies had increased to unbelievable numbers." Charles Evans Hughes, who had been a prominent New York lawyer before his 1930 reappointment to the Supreme Court as chief justice, related to a 1939 gathering of the bar in New York City, "there is no more heavily burdened court" than the one sitting in Foley Square. Complex commercial questions were not the only ones the court faced. New York City was the center of the publishing industry, and suits over a wide variety of First Amendment, copyright, and antitrust issues came to the Court of Appeals.[18]

The Second Circuit included Vermont, Connecticut, and New York. On its Court of Appeals sat Harrie Chase, a Vermont man through and through, granite solid, conservative, "restrained and taciturn," and wary of innovation. Chase's colleague, Thomas Swan, a product of Yale and Harvard Law School, came to the court from the deanship of Yale Law School and brought with him a consummate professionalism and plenty of experience dealing with sharp-edged colleagues at Yale.[19]

Cousins Learned and Augustus Hand added a liberal feistiness to Chase's staidness and Swan's conservatism. Learned Hand, elevated in 1924, took senior status in 1951 but continued to serve until his death in 1961, his reputation growing throughout the period. Often promoted for a seat on the Supreme Court, he was blocked by Taft (ironic in light of the fact that Taft had appointed Hand to the federal bench in 1909), and then by the availability of other New Yorkers like Hughes and Benjamin Cardozo. Roosevelt was ready to appoint Hand in 1942, but advanced age (by then he was seventy) caused Roosevelt to reconsider.[20]

Like Learned, Augustus Hand was trained at Harvard College and Harvard Law School and sat on the District Court for the Southern District of New York until his own elevation to the circuit bench in 1928. Unlike Learned, Augustus was a Democrat, and a little more of his liberal instincts found their way into his jurisprudence than Learned allowed in his. Augustus's contributions to First Amendment law were as significant as Learned's, however. In *United States v. One Package* (1936), for example, he ruled that information on contraception was not per se pornography, giving the death blow to Comstockery; and in *United States v. One Book Entitled Ulysses by James Joyce* (1934), he found that the classic Joyce novel should be taken as a whole, and as a whole was not obscene. While his 800 legal opinions did not match Learned's over 4,000, and his reputation was overshadowed by Learned's, contemporaries valued his acute legal mind and his forward thinking. He died in 1954, a year after taking senior status.[21]

Compared to the testy and elegant intellectuality of the Second Circuit, hearings in the Eighth Circuit's Court of Appeals' panels exhibited plain-spoken good sense. People in the Eighth Circuit were familiar with economic distress long before the Wall Street crash. Faced with the crisis, the Court of Appeals members retained the same hardscrabble, conservative sensibility as the farmers whose foreclosure cases came to them on appeal. Unlike the members of the Second Circuit, the judges of the Eighth Circuit were homogeneous in their thinking and their backgrounds. The bench featured great continuity, with Minnesota's John B. Sanborn, a former tax commissioner, state court judge, and federal district judge; and Missouri's Kimbrough Stone, also a state court judge, serving from 1916 until he took senior status in 1947. Waiting for them on the bench was Coolidge's appointee Archibald Gardner of Iowa, formerly counsel for the Chicago and Northwestern Railway. Together on almost all matters before them, they turned out a harmonious brand of generally brief and unpretentious decisions, a court demonstrating a "team or family character" of collective thinking, as Sanborn law clerk Harry Blackmun recalled. Even the appointment of Joseph Woodrough, in 1933, a more liberal thinker who dissented on occasion, did not upset the bland collegial atmosphere of the Court of Appeals for the Eighth Circuit.[22]

A third proof of the truism that the circuits' courts of appeals reflected the values of the region and the collective judgment of the bench comes when one contrasts the decisions of the Eighth Circuit with those of the Ninth Circuit. The Ninth Circuit was hit by the Depression as profoundly as the Plains courts.

It included the Los Angeles region, a burgeoning center of oil wealth in the 1920s that faced both the agricultural depression and the loss of jobs in the Depression, and the Northern District whose center was San Francisco. While bank failures were not as drastic as in New York City, the region suffered and the court dockets rose. When a New Dealer, William Denman was added in 1935, sparks began to fly on the bench. A California native educated at the University of California at Berkeley, Denman earned his LL.B at Harvard Law School in 1897, practiced, and taught law at Hastings College of the Law and Boalt Hall (the University of California at Berkeley School of Law) in California. A "tireless reformer," Denman's adherence to the principles of the New Deal gained him Frankfurter's support, then Senator Hiram Johnson's, then Attorney General Homer Cummings's, and finally President Franklin D. Roosevelt's. On the bench already was Roosevelt's first nominee, Francis Garrecht. A Washington state lawyer, Garrecht was not as forceful in person as Denman but did share the newcomer's commitment to the New Deal. In 1936 Denman and Garrecht were joined by another Roosevelt appointee, Bert Haney, a Portland practitioner formerly chairman of the Oregon Democratic Committee, whose "combativeness" and commitment to the New Deal matched Denman's. With Garrecht, Denman, and Haney in the lead, arguably the Ninth became the most liberal court of appeals in the land. The idea of judges as advocates of economic reform remained something of a novelty however.[23]

Florence Allen, who joined the Sixth Circuit Court of Appeals in 1934, represented another New Deal Era novelty. As women entered the legal profession, it was perhaps inevitable that some among their number would seek judicial office. Allen had been the first female member of the Ohio State Supreme Court, a post she held from 1922 to 1934, and became the first female to sit on an Article III court when President Franklin D. Roosevelt named her. She would become its chief judge in 1958, take senior status the next year, and die in 1966, at the age of eighty-two, a pioneering jurist, and advocate of women's rights and world peace. Presidents Harry S. Truman named a second woman, Burnita Matthews, to the bench (U.S. District Court for the District of Columbia) as a recess appointment in 1949, and she was confirmed by the Senate in 1950. Dwight D. Eisenhower named a third, Mary Donlon, to the U.S. Customs Court, in 1955. Women were not added to the federal bench in significant numbers until the administration of President Jimmy Carter.[24]

President Taft had selected a number of men who were part-time instructors in law schools, but some notable New Deal additions were full professors or deans. In 1939 alone, eighteen new judges joined the district and nine the circuit courts of appeal, including, among the latter, law professors Armistead Dobie, Charles E. Clark, Calvert Magruder, and Wiley Rutledge. Rutledge, like Clark, was a law school dean, and Magruder was a professor at Harvard Law School. None

Figure 9.2 Florence Allen, after she was elected in 1920 to the State Supreme Court of Ohio. In 1934 she became the first woman to serve as an Article III judge. Credit: *Columbus Dispatch*.

of these men had been judges before their appointment to the circuit courts of appeal. Their selection may have reflected the fact that law school instructors and recent graduates played key roles in the expansion of the regulatory regime. (Rutledge and Clark had also supported the short-lived Court-packing plan.) Law school faculties were becoming nurseries of the federal judiciary.

The New Deal in the Court

The New Deal Era Supreme Court docket had swelled along with the lower courts'. In 1933, the Court agreed to hear more than a thousand cases. Over the next decade, the yearly figure never dropped below 900 new cases. Perhaps most important, the Court sat in final judgment on New Deal legislation and accompanying state legislation and state court decisions dealing with the continuing economic crisis. This role raised the visibility of the Court in the public eye. This story is well known among those who have studied the history of the 1930s or constitutional law, and here appears because it illustrates the place of the Supreme Court in the checks and balances system. A review of these New Deal cases also demonstrates how highly charged partisan issues and federal court decisions interacted. With the executive and the legislative branches pushing the limitations on "takings" (taking private property for public use) in the Constitution, the task of determining whether New Deal legislation and administrative mechanisms fell to the federal courts. Whether they deferred to Congress and the president, or resisted, political and legal consequences were inevitable.

A second set of cases coming before the federal courts tested the boundaries of judicial federalism. The federal courts in the 1920s had incorporated certain parts of the Bill of Rights, and the New Deal Era courts were called upon by defendants in criminal cases to extend this process. If the Court accepted this call, it would be further retreating from the deference to state criminal process it had shown in *Pink Franklin*. These New Deal Era cases further shifted the boundaries of judicial federalism and thus belong in this book.[25]

From 1932 through 1937 the Court found itself near the center of the vortex of New Deal politics. The four conservatives on the Court voted against federal programs, both structural and immediate, associated with the New Deal. Called in the press the "Four Horsemen of the Apocalypse," Justices Butler, McReynolds, Sutherland, and Van Devanter rarely broke ranks. If their views were conservative, they were no more conservative than one would expect from judges who had come to intellectual maturity in the last years of the nineteenth century. In the end, it was a common jurisprudence that brought them together, valuing a fixed rather than a changing law. They believed that in periods of great tribulation, like the Depression, the law must be even more stable or the Constitution itself would become an empty vessel.[26]

When the Court began to hear suits against far-reaching congressional acts involving the newly created National Recovery Administration (NRA) and Agricultural Adjustment Administration (AAA), McReynolds and his three cohorts found allies to overturn the legislation. In 1934, federal officials obeying orders from Hugh Johnson, boss of the NRA, to enforce provisions of the National Industrial Recovery Act were enjoined by the federal district court. Judge Randolph Bryant, sitting in the Eastern District of Texas, understood the importance of his decision. A Hoover appointee, he had served the district as its U.S. attorney for ten years. He opined: "This is another of those cases which have so frequently engaged the attention of the national courts involving as it essentially does a contest between state and federal authority and more particularly the extent to which the federal government may go in its exercise of authority in regulation of matters ordinarily committed to the regulation of the states." Here Congress had exceeded that authority by delegating to the NRA control over production, as opposed to interstate commerce. What was more, the Act evaded constitutional limitations on the authority of Congress and the president to intrude on the use of private property. Bryant cited *Hammer v. Dagenhart* as his authority.[27]

The Court agreed. Chief Justice Hughes, writing for the majority in *Panama Refining v. Ryan* (1935), found that the provision in the congressional Act "establishes no criterion to govern the President's course. It does not require any finding by the President as a condition of his action . . . so far as this section is concerned, it gives to the President an unlimited authority to determine the policy and to lay down the prohibition, or not to lay it down, as he may see fit." In short, it was an open-ended grant of absolute power from Congress to the president. This gave to the president the functions of a legislature, an unconstitutional delegation of authority from the legislative to the executive branch. In this case, the Court was tutoring the other two branches of the federal government in the doctrine of separation of powers.[28]

The stage was now set for an even more direct confrontation over separation of powers. A unanimous Court confirmed *Panama* in *Schechter Poultry v. United States* (1935). The Brooklyn, New York, orthodox Jewish slaughterhouse had violated the live poultry code of the NRA. The code was supposed to promote fair practices and competition among firms, protecting them and the consumer. The code included minimum wages and maximum hours. Had it been a state code, it would likely have passed muster. But a federal code for intrastate trade was problematic, for under *Adkins v. Children's Hospital* (1923) the minimum wage provisions were unconstitutional and, as in *Panama*, the legislation did not define the standards the NRA was to enforce. The NRA itself decided what was kosher and what not, and that made *Schechter* almost a straight replay of *Panama*. Hughes wrote for his entire Court. The code makers used the Depression crisis as an opportunity to impose administratively what the Fuller, White, and Taft Courts knocked down: minimum wage, maximum hours, no child labor, no yellow-dog contracts, and guaranteed collective bargaining.Hughes may have agreed with all of these provisions, but he found that the code violated the separation of powers in the Constitution. "The Congress is not permitted to abdicate or to transfer to others the essential legislative functions with which it is thus vested."[29]

A series of similar decisions followed, none unanimous, but all voiding key legislative enactments of the first New Deal. In *United States v. Butler* (1936) the Court struck down the Agricultural Adjustment Act as a violation of the Tenth Amendment. In *Carter v. Carter Coal Company* (1936) the Court invalidated the Bituminous Coal Conservation Act. Sutherland judged that coal production was not interstate commerce and so could not be regulated by Congress. In *Ashton v. Cameron County Water Improvement District* (1936) the majority overturned the Municipal Bankruptcy Act. McReynolds wrote for himself, Roberts, Sutherland, Van Devanter, and Butler. "The difficulties arising out of our dual form of government and the opportunities for differing opinions concerning the relative rights of State and National Governments are many; but for a very long time this court has steadfastly adhered to the doctrine that the taxing power of Congress does not extend to the States or their political subdivisions." The state-federal divide issue here joined the separation-of-powers issue and both aroused a storm of protest.[30]

Democratic newspapers reporting on the Court's 1935 and 1936 decisions made dire predictions that constitutional republicanism was at risk. After Roosevelt's smashing victory in 1936, he proposed to alter judicial branch membership. Most notably, he requested adding up to five new members of the Supreme Court for those over the age of seventy whom he somewhat uncharitably accused of being too old to keep up with the docket. The plan was part of an omnibus judiciary act, but the other provisions could not conceal the proposal's prime objective: adding new justices to the Court. Called "packing" the Court by its opponents, in fact public opinion varied widely. Some letters to the editor thanked Roosevelt: "the modernization and rejuvenation of our judicial system will be greeted by liberals, by workers and by all who have suffered from the law's delays and injustices and from ancient autocrats sitting on judges' benches," while others called for "Congress [to] resist this attack on our liberties and may our aroused people scotch the threat of dictatorship."[31]

All the justices viewed the packing plan askance. Justice Brandeis, whose friendship with Harvard Law School Professor Frankfurter and whose early defense of what would become many New Deal policies endeared him to the New Deal's lawyers, was particularly offended. On behalf of himself and his brethren, Chief Justice Hughes wrote to the Senate Judiciary Committee:

> An increase in the number of justices of the Supreme Court, apart from any question of policy, which I do not discuss, would not promote the efficiency of the court. It is believed that it would impair that efficiency so long as the court acts as a unit. There would be more judges to hear, more judges to confer, more judges to discuss, more judges to be convinced and to deride [sic]. The present number of justices is thought to be large enough so far as the prompt, adequate, and efficient conduct of the work of the court is concerned.[32]

Roosevelt's Judicial Procedures Reform bill would also have had a major impact on the lower courts. It would have created a flotilla of district judges available for temporary assignment to a district overloaded with cases. It would also have created a new quasi-judicial office called the "proctor" by which the justices could supervise the operations of the lower court. While something akin to these steps was already present in the Act of 1922, nothing of their scope existed in 1937. The proposals for the floating squadron had been around for a long time, and the notion of proctors came from the Ninth Circuit's Judge

Denman among others. These ideas were not directly related to the overturning of the first New Deal programs, but to the inundation of the federal courts with cases. Federal judges had been sending similar suggestions to Attorney General Homer Cummings for years prior to the 1936 election.[33]

The Reform bill never gained political traction, and the Senate quashed the initiative in 1937. By then, however, one member of the Court had shifted his views enough to let key measures of the second New Deal pass muster. The switch came first in *West Coast Hotel Co v. Parrish* (1937). Washington State had passed a minimum wage law in 1913, not an emergency measure, but an old Progressive Era act, much like the statutory limitation on hours challenged in *Muller v. Oregon* (1908). A commission determined the amount necessary for women to maintain their health and welfare. Elsie Parrish, a hotel chambermaid, filed suit for back wages: the difference between her pay packet and the commission's set minimum. The state supreme court found for Parrish. So did the new majority on the Supreme Court. By 5-4 votes the majority now upheld federal and state reform statutes.

The Justices went on to uphold the National Labor Relations Act and the Social Security Act. In *NLRB v. Jones and Laughlin Steel* (1937), the majority dumped the direct/indirect distinction in interstate commerce and allowed Congress to act on anything "in the stream of interstate commerce." *Steward Machine Company v. Davis* (1937) reversed a string of cases holding that Congress's power to levy taxes in the general welfare did not extend beyond the four corners—the enumerated powers—of the Constitution. *Helvering v. Davis* (1937) extended that reasoning to the social security tax that employers had to pay, along with employees, to fund social security benefits.[34]

Sometimes easily swayed by pressure from his brethren, genial Justice Roberts was the swing vote. At first unsure of his own abilities, when stung by collegial and public criticism of his opinions he shifted them. Some speculated that Roberts's changing views were influenced by the size of Roosevelt's reelection victory in 1936 or by his plan to enlarge the Courts. In fact, however, Roberts already had changed his mind about the key second New Deal cases and voted on them in conference before the election was even held. In other areas of law, Roberts was comfortable and consistent, for example in his support for civil rights and his belief that the Fourteenth Amendment incorporated the Free Exercise Clause of the First Amendment and the right to an attorney. He retired in 1945, returning to the University of Pennsylvania Law School as its dean.[35]

A second set of Supreme Court cases in this period came to the Court on appeal from the states. They were civil rights cases. In them, the Court examined the relation between state court decisions and state constitutions, on the one hand, and the federal Constitution on the other. In the process, the Court once more revised the federalism of the Madisonian Compromise.

The Great Depression hit the poor blacks of the South the hardest of all Americans. At the bottom of the socioeconomic ladder already, young black men took to the roads and rails to find employment. Two related cases stemming from this internal migration became a landmark on the path to true legal equality and signaled as profound a shift in the boundary between federal and state judicial power in criminal cases as *Pierce v. Society of Sisters* did in First Amendment cases. In 1931, in a Scottsboro, Alabama, courtroom, nine young black men were tried and convicted of raping two white women on a train. Their prosecution, based on perjured testimony of two vagrant women, exhibited all the malice, haste, indifference, and racial prejudice of many trials of blacks in Jim Crow southern courts. They patently did not have access to effective counsel in their capital cases, and counsel that the court ordered to represent them did not consult with them or take the time and effort to ascertain the truth. Though all they did was engage in a fight with white boys on the train, eight of them were condemned to death. "Black Americans were angry and indignant, but they were not surprised. They had expected the verdict . . . It was an old story."[36]

In *Powell v. Alabama* (1932), the Court heard their appeal. Counsel for the state made a similar argument to that in *Franklin v. South Carolina* and the Alabama peonage cases. "The question of due process is determined by the law of the jurisdiction where the offense was committed and the trial was had . . . Here the trials were in accordance with the constitution and statutes of Alabama." Justice Sutherland, who wrote for the majority, found, "There is a . . . recital to the effect that upon the arraignment they were represented by counsel. But no counsel had been employed . . . No one answered for the defendants or appeared to represent or defend them." Moreover, "Each of the three trials was completed within a single day." That was effective denial of the Sixth Amendment right to counsel, which the Fourteenth Amendment imposed on the state. Sutherland sarcastically continued: "That it would not have been an idle ceremony to have given the defendants reasonable opportunity to communicate with their families and endeavor to obtain counsel is demonstrated by the fact that, very soon after conviction, able counsel appeared in their behalf."[37]

The travail of the nine "Scottsboro Boys" was not over, however. Retried, they were again convicted. Counsel this time came from the New York City offices of the Labor Defense Fund, but the deck was again stacked. No black person was allowed to sit on the jury. At trial and then on appeal to the Alabama Supreme Court, the absence of black jurors from the panel was raised, overruled, and the conviction was upheld. Once more the Supreme Court heard the appeal, and in *Norris v. Alabama* (1935) found merit in it. Hughes wrote for the majority. "At the outset, a motion was made on [Norris's] behalf to quash the indictment upon the ground of the exclusion of negroes from juries . . . In relation to each county, the charge was of long-continued, systematic and arbitrary exclusion of qualified negro citizens from service on juries, solely because of their race and color, in violation of the Constitution of the United States."[38]

The Supreme Court long before, in *Strauder v. West Virginia* (1880), had announced that systematic exclusion of African Americans from jury duty by the action of the legislature or the state courts was a violation of the federal Constitution, but the Alabama law on jury eligibility—"all male citizens of the county who are generally reputed to be honest and intelligent men, and are esteemed in the community for their integrity, good character and sound judgment"—left wiggle room for the jury commission to exclude black men. And black men were always, with no exceptions, excluded. "It appeared that no negro had served on any grand or petit jury in that county within the memory of witnesses who had lived there all their lives."[39]

The Supreme Court of the United States is an appellate court and does not often engage in fact finding of its own. Here, with the State of Alabama patently lying about its jury selection policies, the Court wondered what was going on during Alabama jury selection. Was there bad faith in the production of evidence of the jury rolls when counsel for the defendants objected?[40]

> The question arose whether names of Negroes were in fact on the jury roll. The books containing the jury roll for Jackson County for the year 1930–31 were produced. They were produced from the custody of a member of the jury commission which, in 1931, had succeeded the commission which had made up the jury roll from which the grand jury in question [in the retrial] had been drawn. On the pages of this roll appeared the names of six negroes. They were entered, respectively, at the end of the precinct lists which were alphabetically arranged.

Apparently, to avoid the charge of excluding blacks without cause, the commissioners had altered the jury roll records after the appeal to conceal the violation.

Chief Justice Hughes had heard enough. "We think that the evidence that for a generation or longer no negro had been called for service on any jury in Jackson County, that there were negroes qualified for jury service . . . established the discrimination which the Constitution forbids." The Fifth Amendment guaranty of an impartial jury applied to Alabama. Sutherland, Van Devanter, and Butler joined in Hughes's opinion. McReynolds absented himself.

The other important civil rights pronouncement in this era was more subtle. Hidden in *United States v. Carolene Products* (1938), a case that had nothing to do with civil rights, was a footnote to the majority opinion that hinted at the Court's heightened awareness of civil rights issues. Justice Stone wrote the opinion, upholding Congress's authority to ban unsafe products from interstate commerce. Footnote number four in his opinion stated: "There may be narrower

scope for operation of the presumption of constitutionality when ... prejudice against discrete and insular minorities may be a special condition, which
tends seriously to curtail the operation of those political processes ordinarily to
be relied upon to protect minorities, and which may call for a correspondingly
more searching judicial inquiry." The note, the work of Stone's clerk Louis Lusky,
announced that henceforth a "more searching" scrutiny of racial or sexual discrimination resulting from a statute would trigger review of its constitutionality.
Artfully phrased in the negative—"nor need we enquire"—into such discrimination in the case before the Court, the note nevertheless gained a life of its own
very soon after it was prepared.[41]

Changing the Rules of the Game

The relationship between Congress and the courts was strained by Court review
of congressional regulatory acts. But as Congress's ultimate unwillingness to
pack the courts demonstrated, the members were willing to let the judges take
the lead on managing the judicial branch. Two major structural reforms gave
evidence of this commitment to separation of powers: the Rules Enabling Act
of 1934 and the creation of the Administrative Office of United States Courts
in 1939.

The Rules Enabling Act did not give the judiciary a blank check to reform
pleading in the federal courts, but it allowed the judges to take the initiative in
reform subject to the approval and ongoing oversight of Congress. The rebalanc-
ing of checks and balances one sees in this story was a series of compromises
worthy of Madison himself.

The pathway ahead had already been pioneered by David Dudley Field's
code of pleading in New York (1848) and parallel state reform efforts. The core
notion was simple: unite the law docket, where jury trial sorted out precise
issues presented in the pleadings, with the equity docket, in which pretrial depositions were allowed as evidence, and judges ordered remedies, like injunctions,
without the aid of jury verdicts (though judges might appoint special masters
to sort through the depositions parties presented to the court). The two kinds
of pleading had origins in England and were recognized in the Judiciary Act of
1789 as fundamentally different. The Field code not only did away with the separate dockets, it made it easy for joinder (combination) of parties of plaintiffs and
defendants with common interests, paved the way for class actions, and facilitated settlement short of the courtroom. In 1912, a revision of the federal rules
for pleading had taken a small step in this direction, allowing a suit brought in
the law side of the docket to include certain kinds of equitable practice. The Law
and Equity Act of 1915 allowed for the resolution of equity issues first, but the

1928 judicial code made clear that this provision only applied when such practices were prescribed by the laws of the state in which the courts were held rather than in all districts.[42]

In the revised Code of 1912, Congress had replaced writ pleading with fact pleading. Plaintiffs and defendants, instead of pleading and answering within the narrow confines of a predetermined set of issues, simply stated facts and asked for relief and replied in similar fashion. But fact pleading under the revised Code of 1912 still required parties to state the ultimate facts, placing on them responsibility for deciding what facts were justiciable and what facts were irrelevant. Intended to simplify pleading, fact pleading made the litigants' task more complex.[43]

From the time that he was president of the ABA, in 1914, then Yale Law Professor William Howard Taft pleaded for unified dockets. In the Supreme Court's center seat, Taft again argued for a blue ribbon commission selected by the Supreme Court to end the two dockets. As the chief told the ABA in 1922, three years before Charles Clark, then a professor at Yale Law School, ventured the first of his own modest proposals. "What I would suggest is that Congress provide for a commission . . . [to] recommend to Congress amendments to the present statutes of practice . . . authorizing a unit administration of law and equity in one form of civil action." The chief justice had in mind the power that the Supreme Court had thus far largely held in abeyance to frame the rules for pleading in federal courts. Hence the act "should provide for a permanent commission . . . with power to prepare a system of rules of procedure for adoption by the Supreme Court."[44]

Powerful opponents in the Senate, led by Thomas Walsh of Montana, an aging but still feisty Populist Democrat, feared that Congress would cede its control over the lower courts to a puppet commission of the Supreme Court. Walsh was a supporter of women's rights, democratic reform, and Woodrow Wilson, and no doubt harbored suspicion of rules that the conservative Taft Court would impose on Montana litigants. Taft was furious. Would "yahoos of the West" like Walsh stonewall needed reforms? In 1924, the Senate held hearings on a variety of versions of a reform bill, and sitting justices McReynolds and Sutherland testified that some reform would be welcome. The problem indicated by the sponsor of the bill, Senator Albert B. Cummins, an Iowa Progressive Republican, was that states feared substantive rights under state law would be trumped by Supreme Court procedural dictates. Lurking behind what seemed to be a straightforward matter of technical pleading was the old adversary–partisan politics. Cummins, like Walsh, knew that the Taft Court was a conservative one, and justices like Sutherland, Van Devanter, and McReynolds were bulwarks of that conservatism. Would Progressive state regulation of corporations and other business entities fall prey to the Supreme Court's antiregulation stance?[45]

Even before he had completed the study of the business of the courts, Clark had concluded that a thorough revision in federal civil procedure would begin with the unification of law and equity. Watching Congress dither, Clark, on the lookout for allies in academe, found one in Michigan Law School Professor Edson Sunderland and Sunderland's research fellow George Ragland, whose 1932 book in favor of expanded "discovery" rules Clark had favorably reviewed. As they understood unification, most of the work would be shifted from trial in court to lawyers taking evidence from both parties. This kind of discovery enabled both parties to see where they stood, instead of engaging in the ambush of one party by another at trial. The American Law Institute (ALI) model of panels with law professors, like Clark, as reporters and with leading practitioners and judges acting as advisors, was the perfect vehicle to fashion such a unified code, but to be effective the proposal must have more muscle than the ALI's Restatements of the Law and "model" codes. Clark had a solution even more thoroughgoing in mind. Persuade the Supreme Court to appoint him and his chosen aides to perform the task and then have the Supreme Court propose the new rules.[46]

Reenter Connecticut's Homer Cummings, the newly-appointed attorney general. Walsh had passed away, and with him much of the old Populist suspicion of a league of eastern plutocrats. Cummings was a Progressive Democrat, imbued with that movement's faith in efficiency and reform. He was vigorous in his role, and with Cummings's sponsorship the revival of the old Taft/ABA plan was sudden and effective. Clark later recalled: "So effective was this new leadership, that the bill became a law with surprising rapidity and unanimity of action." Chief Justice Hughes was on board as well, according to Clark: "The Conference, at the suggestion of the Chief Justice, considered appropriate methods for assisting the Supreme Court in the discharge of this highly important and difficult task, through the cooperation of the members of the Bench and Bar throughout the country, to the end that the views of the federal judges and of the Bar may find adequate and helpful expression."[47]

The Rules Enabling Act of 1934 did not solve the problems of pleading, but it passed the job from Congress to the Supreme Court, and from the Court to its chosen solons: "Be it enacted . . . That the Supreme Court of the United States shall have the power to prescribe, by general rules, for the district courts of the United States and for the courts of the District of Columbia, the forms of process, writs, pleadings, and motions, and the practice and procedure in civil actions at law." A concession to the critics of change followed. "Said rules shall neither abridge, enlarge, nor modify the substantive rights of any litigant." But Congress had approved, at least in principal, the core change Clark wanted. "The court may at any time unite the general rules prescribed by it for cases in equity with those in actions at law so as to secure one form of civil action and procedure for both: Provided, however, That in such union of rules the right of trial by jury as at common law and declared by the seventh amendment to the Constitution shall be preserved to the parties inviolate."

Congress retained ultimate control over the imposition of new rules. "Such united rules shall not take effect until they shall have been reported to Congress by the Attorney General at the beginning of a regular session thereof and until after the close of such session." These few lines sought to preserve the primacy of Congress in the separation of powers system, a remainder of the Madisonian Compromise. Discarded along the way was another part of that compromise— the Process Act principle that all civil actions in federal courts must conform their procedure to the states in which the court sat. This had never been true in equity, and insofar as the new rules were dominated by equitable procedure, that result was predictable. If, as promised, the new rules would not take any substantive right or grant any substantive right away from litigants, the revision nevertheless visibly shifted the relationship between Congress and the federal judiciary. When so much depended on procedure, the proposal for revision of the rules went far beyond mere technicalities.[48]

The Act raised also federalism questions. The use of local rules in federal courts had given an advantage to those members of the bar well versed in local practice. That voice had risen every time Congress contemplated new rules, especially when they would be framed by a federal commission. Insofar as the old rules originated in state practice, the manner of framing of the new rules and their uniformity across the land seemed to tip the old federal-state procedural equilibrium in favor of the central government. While states per se did not object, the local bar's jealous guardianship of its mastery of local rules might prove an obstacle to the new rules. But Clark had anticipated this source of objections, and the program of drafting new rules called for informational meetings all over the country. At least the local bar would have its say.

Following the passage of the Rules Enabling Act, Clark's machinations came to fruition. Chief Justice Hughes created an advisory committee to report to it a new procedural code. On June 3, 1935, the Supreme Court named the committee. Former Coolidge solicitor general and Hoover attorney general William Mitchell chaired it. At first, it was not clear that Clark would be the reporter, but he lobbied Mitchell hard and won that post. In the process Clark outmaneuvered Sunderland, his rival for the reporter's job, although throughout the committee's deliberations he treated Sunderland with utmost and sincere courtesy.[49]

The committee met through the fall and winter of 1935–1936 in Chicago and then Washington, D.C. Attendance at the meetings was excellent. The committee represented the elite national bar and the foremost law schools. It included, in addition to Clark, Mitchell, and Sunderland, George Wickersham; Armistead Dobie of the University of Virginia; Edmund Morgan of Harvard Law School;

Wilbur Cherry of the University of Minnesota; Edgar Tolman, secretary of the ABA; and Scott Loftin, president of the ABA who would serve the next year as a Senator from Florida; Joseph Gamble of Des Moines; Monte Lemann of New Orleans; Robert Dodge, a Boston attorney; and George Donworth, a Seattle lawyer and formerly a federal district judge.

Throughout the long sessions, the members exhibited all of the learning, meticulousness, and, on occasion, one-upmanship one would expect from such a group. One session was typical. At two o'clock on Sunday afternoon, November 17, 1935, the committee took up the last sentence of Rule 39, on representation of infants in federal litigation. Clark "took . . . from the equity rule" his position on the issue; Mitchell wondered how a guardian could be appointed before the court had jurisdiction over the case; Dobie said that some states provided for a guardian during the litigation; Dodge added that he knew of it; Clark whimsically asked if Dodge found the Supreme Court's views of the matter a little off; and Dodge joked, "I noticed they had made that mistake." Laughter followed. Cherry and Mitchell cited Minnesota and New York state rules for guardianship that might guide amendment of the draft rule, but Clark worried, "I suppose it could be argued that we are getting into substantive law." Clark knew that critics had already argued that the new rules impinged on states' substantive law. Wickersham reassured the group that they could leave it to the Court to decide the question, but it lingered: "I think there is a great danger in expecting to modify these rules after they are accepted." The Court would surely interpret the rules, but let Congress begin to tinker, and the entire project would be undermined. Clark warned that "uncertainty" posed greater dangers, but Mitchell countered that leaving the rule alone was better than opening the door to legislative amendment that the Rules Enabling Act seemed to have closed.[50]

Of the members, only Clark was a legal realist, but the entire project fulfilled a core realist premise: the law should reflect actual practice rather than rigid formality. Time after time, in the discussions, the notes that Clark prepared, and the end result, one finds terms familiar in equity pleading like "discretion" and "fairness." The rules promoted flexibility and easy amendment of pleadings in the name of justice to the parties. The committee left to judicial discretion the management of this flexibility, rather than Congress, further proof that the balance between the two branches of the federal government was changing.[51]

No sitting judge took part in the deliberations, but in 1936, a preliminary version was approved by the Supreme Court, and copies were circulated among various district judges. Three more revisions were submitted to these judges and local bar scrutiny in 1937. Their comments, particularly on the administration of pretrial discovery, proved particularly important to the committee in its deliberations. As Chairman Mitchell reminded the members, discovery was a centerpiece of the new rules, and there would be widespread "outrage" among bench and bar if nothing were done to constrain lawyers' "fishing expeditions" in opposing parties' records. He was right, and the committee responded by adding time, place, and other limitations. [52]

The Supreme Court approved the revisions on December 20, 1937. Hearings before the House of Representatives in March 1938 went well for the committee, ABA Secretary Tolman leading the congressmen through the Rules one by one, explaining how they would conform to or alter existing rules. In the Senate, however, Senator William King of Utah offered a resolution delaying the implementation of the Rules until Congress met again. According to the Rules Enabling Act, if Congress did not block the Rules, they would automatically go into effect. Tolman, Cummings, and Mitchell marshaled their troops for the hearings on King's resolution on April 18, 1938.

Cummings spoke first: "the work was not haphazard. It was scientifically planned . . . distinguished lawyers took time from their own activities . . . it is a monument . . . to the profession and to the Supreme Court." King demurred; the Senate had not time to go over the Rules, and it looked as though the rights of individuals established by state law would be overridden. Cummings rejoined, it was "hardly a mark of confidence in the work of the Supreme Court to make that suggestion." Mitchell testified next: "this was not a star chamber process." It took three and half years, and "thousands of copies were printed, everybody in the country had an opportunity to examine them." Though this was a bit of hyperbole, Mitchell continued in high dudgeon, "every class of lawyers," local, state, and national, "every federal judge," and "every bar association" had a chance to chime in, and many did. King persisted: rule making was the job of Congress. Mitchell shot back that Congress had given that job to the Court with the Rules Enabling Act. Senator Warren Austin of Vermont noted that Justice Brandeis was on record opposing the Rules. This interjection went nowhere, as Brandeis (unlike Cummings, a former senator, and Mitchell, a former attorney general) had little clout among the senators.

Mitchell then asked Arthur Vanderbilt, president of the ABA, to join the conversation, and Vanderbilt added that bar associations all over the country "spent days" in hearings with Tolman, Clark, Mitchell, and others members of the advisory committee. Herschel Whitefield Arant, dean of the Ohio State University College of Law, spoke for the American Association of Law Schools. (Like so many of the defenders of the new rules, including Clark and Dobie, Arant would become a judge, a member of the Court of Appeals for the Sixth Circuit in 1939.) He told the committee that the Rules "were one of the most forward-looking things that have been done in American jurisprudence in a long time." King was not moved: the Rules overturned over a century of laws, in particular the Rules of Decision in the Judiciary Act and the later Conformity Act that had protected individual rights. Arant replied that the Rules were procedural, not substantive, and would not take rights away from any litigant. Austin once more interjected this time with his concern about labor unions' rights. Tolman replied that labor unions testifying in the House had favored the new Rules. Tolman continued that the committee had received over 5,000 letters from lawyers and judges, including the strong support of the Utah State Bar Association (to which King belonged). The hearings were adjourned until the next month.[53]

A month later, on May 19, the subcommittee resumed hearings. By this time, King and other senators had time to go over the Rules and, more importantly, the notes to the Rules that Clark had prepared as the Rules' reporter. The parade of witnesses continued, this time however they were Senator King's. Drawn from the D.C. area on short notice, they were not quite as distinguished as those supporting the Ruless. P. H. Marshall, a D.C. lawyer, admitted, "I am a mediocre lawyer, of no distinction whatsoever," an appeal of sorts to his authority as the voice of the common lawyer. He and others in the D.C. bar had serious criticisms of the Rules. Some of those criticisms were answered by revisions, but others remained, particularly involving court orders to those not originally parties to the litigation.

Law Professor Charles Keigwin presented several difficulties that had revealed themselves to him as he lectured on the Rules at Georgetown Law School. "My predisposition is against any change. I think that most practicing lawyers feel that way." He had never heard a practitioner complain about the old rules. (Litigants' views were not mentioned in his testimony.) He added that the new rules were "unconstitutional." Senator Austin asked where in the Constitution did it forbid the joinder of law and equity? Keigwin conceded the point— nowhere. King rushed in to help his witness: were there not states that opposed the Rules because they seemed to impair certain rights conferred by state law? Keigwin did not pick up the cue, or he simply refused to follow it, conceding instead that most code-pleading states would have no problem with the Rules. King would not let the matter drop, "[D]o you think these rules, if they were enforced, would result in confusion and lawsuits?" Keigwin finally got the message: "I think there would be a good deal of that." Briefly caught off guard, Tolman weighed in with a memorandum, and a letter he solicited from another member of the D.C. Bar supporting the Rules.[54]

King had his day on the battlefield, but the Rules committee won the war. The Senate did not block them, instead adjourning without taking action, and the new Federal Rules of Civil Procedure went into effect on September 16, 1938. When the effort was done, Clark tried to write its history himself. Over and over, he cast his role as a simple one—a technocrat fixing a broken machine. As he wrote in an *American Bar Association Journal* 1937 issue on the work of the committee:

It has been shown that a vast adventure in cooperative intellectual endeavor by the bar of the entire country can be brought to the point of producing a coherent and clear-cut system of procedure, for approval or disapproval, as the event may disclose. It has been possible for the lawyers to organize and press through to statutory enactment authorization for an important law reform; for a committee from the profession of diverse experience and background to reach unanimity of belief as to the best practice code to be offered to the profession; for the lawyers all over the United States to spend time, which in total value, computed at professional rates, must reach a staggering amount, in judicious and meticulous scrutiny and criticism of the product; and finally, as now seems indicated, for the bar and bench as a whole to accept the result in a fine spirit of desire to make it a truly effective instrument for the administration of justice.

In fact his efforts were not transparent or merely technical. Concealed in his correspondence with Attorney General Cummings, academics like Sunderland, and members of the Court and Congress, along with the stenographic records of the meetings of the advisory committee, was a subtle mastery of compromise, manipulation, and a singular determination.[55]

Clark never conceded what in retrospect the historian of the courts can see plainly: the entire process, from the passage of the Enabling Act through the (silent) approval of the Rules, represented a challenge to the Madisonian Compromise of 1787–1789. Under Article III, Congress had the power to create lower federal courts and determine their jurisdiction. From the Process Acts of 1789 and 1792, through the Conformity Act of 1872, Congress had imposed on the lower federal courts hearing civil suits the obligation to use procedures of the state supreme court in which the federal court sat. Senator King had a point—by creating a general (later called a "trans-substantive") set of procedural rules, the Supreme Court was not only abrogating the Conformity Act, it was also taking unto itself the rule-making role Congress had exercised. Perhaps appeased by the shift in the Supreme Court's stance on New Deal legislation, Congress accepted the new Rules, for the Rules, like the Rules Enabling Act of 1934, provided that Congress was to have the final say on rules.

Congress restated its primacy with the Rules Enabling Act of 1940 (permitting the creation of federal rules of criminal procedure); the Rules Enabling Act of 1948 (permitting the federal courts to set the rules for its own business); the Rules Enabling Acts of 1949 and 1950 (giving to the Court rather than the attorney general the authority to report rules changes to Congress and prescribing the manner of such reports); the Rules Enabling Act of 1958 (a short-lived provision for the Conference rather than the Court to frame rules changes); the

Rules Enabling Act of 1964 (giving to the Court the power to prescribe rules for bankruptcy courts); the Rules Enabling Act of 1966 (adding courts of appeals to district courts in the scope of the rule-making power); and the Enabling Act of 1975 (adding rules of evidence to the list), all of which led back, in the end, to Congress. What the legislative branch had given with one hand it could always grasp with the other. The subsequent amendments, for example in 1982 requiring all the districts to publish their rules (currently revised to provide for website posting), showed that Congress had not stepped away from its older role. Indeed, additional amendments of particular portions of the judicial code (title 28 of the U.S. Code), resembled the kind of tinkering that Congress favored in the nineteenth century. The essence of the Madisonian Compromise in Article III and the Judiciary Act apportioning management of procedure to both Congress and the courts, though somewhat readjusted, remained in place because both Congress and the courts wanted it to remain in place.[56]

Although Clark, Tolman, and the other framers of the Rules defended them in the language of Progressive reform as a simple administrative step forward, they represented a major shift in pleading. "In large perspective, the Federal Rules [of Civil Procedure] made three basic changes. The first was simplified pleading. Pleaders are allowed to assert legal grievances, and legal defenses as well, in general terms. The second basic change was redesign of the rules governing joinder of parties and claims. Under the Federal Rules, joinder of parties and claims is based on the contours of the out-of-court transaction, not the legal categories in which the parties' conduct can be conceptualized. The third change was, of course, in discovery." Rule 1 united the two dockets in one form of action, but throughout the entire document it was equity pleading that dominated the Rules. Especially in the provisions for simply stating the harm and the type of relief requested (Rule 8), the easy introduction of counter-claims and cross-claims and the joinder of additional parties to all sides in the litigation, as well as permissive joinder and substitution of parties, creating complex litigation scenarios (Rules 13, 14, 19, 20, 24, and 25), pretrial conferences (Rule 16), class-action suits (Rule 23), and broad provisions for discovery by deposition and by production of the other's parties' records (Rules 26–33). Equity practice became the rule for all suits. Provisions for jury trial were preserved, but in suits for equitable remedies like injunction, there was no guarantee of jury trial. This was the sort of procedural shift that critics of the Rules called a violation of the Constitution.[57]

Although the reform of pleading had already taken place in many of the states (and others would follow after 1938), the new Rules had far-reaching consequences for lawyering and litigating. Law firms of dozens became law firms of hundreds and later thousands of associates, most of whose new duties consisted of taking depositions and searching through other parties' records. Complaints about delay centered on the pretrial process instead of the trial itself and on the perceived intrusiveness of judges (later and somewhat uncharitably called "managerial judging") in encouraging settlement of suits, and more troubling, about the use of procedural means to limit access to federal courts. Extensive discovery cost money and well-financed parties used it to exhaust the resources of less well-financed opponents. "As we sit in contemplation of the enormously powerful work of the drafters of the Federal Rules of Civil Procedure, we must be careful and thoughtful in our examination of the decisions made . . . years ago. We must understand that conversations about procedure are often used as vehicles for many other conversations that are difficult to have in a straightforward manner."[58]

As some of the academic critics of the Rules hinted, while the new rules may have made for greater justice in the outcome of cases, they did not shift the balance between the better funded party and the economically weaker party. In this sense they were not part of the liberalization of government and the equalization of benefits from government that the New Deal promised. Nor should one have expected such a redistribution-of-wealth outcome from a drafting committee drawn from elite bars and law schools. Indeed, the Rules gave an even greater advantage to better (and bigger) law firms than the older, less liberal rules of fact pleading.[59]

The next chapter in that story was written by the Court itself, in a case that otherwise was not very important. In *Erie v. Tompkins* (1938), a fact pattern eerily familiar to students of railroad negligence cases from the previous century, the Court heard an appeal from the Second Circuit. Mr. Tompkins was walking along a footpath next to an Erie Railroad track in western Pennsylvania. That part of the world is steeply mountainous with narrow valleys, and often the only flat portion of the land was taken up by the Erie, the Pennsylvania, and other railroads' rights of ways. It was a custom to walk alongside the tracks. This night, an Erie train's projecting door hit Tompkins and injured him. He brought suit in New York, where the railroad had its corporate headquarters, and the suit came to the federal district court there under its diversity jurisdiction (he wanted a $30,000 damage award, a sum sufficient to sue in diversity). The trial court heard the case, and its jury agreed that Erie was liable under common law rules for railroad liability, a doctrine of overarching federal law set in *Swift v. Tyson*. Pennsylvania law, by contrast, viewed Tompkins as a trespasser, and the rail line had no duty to pay for injuries it caused to trespassers. The Second Circuit affirmed the trial court. Both courts dismissed Erie's claim that the Rules of Decision provisions of the Judiciary Acts mandated that the case be decided according to state substantive law. The Supreme Court agreed with Erie and sent the case back to the district court to instruct the jury on the relevant state law. Justice Brandeis wrote for the Court.[60]

The question he faced was complex. Did the Rules of Decision provision apply to judge-made law (judicial opinions) and state statutes? In 1842, Story's opinion in *Swift* said no. Charles Warren, a Harvard Law professor, wrote an article in 1923 that said the original drafters of the provision had intended it to include judicial precedent and legislative enactment. Brandeis agreed with Warren. What is more, in an echo of King's witnesses' testimony on the likelihood of expense and confusion from federal rules of civil procedure, Brandeis invoked "[e]xperience in applying the doctrine of *Swift v. Tyson*, had revealed its defects, political and social; and the benefits expected to flow from the rule did not accrue. Persistence of state courts in their own opinions on questions of common law prevented uniformity; and the impossibility of discovering a satisfactory line of demarcation between the province of general law and that of local law developed a new well of uncertainties." The "injustice and confusion" resulting from the misuse of diversity suits to gain the aid of federal common law against local people was another of the many mischiefs of the *Swift* doctrine. For reasons of policy and justice, then, as well as for a correct reading of the Rules of Decision provisions, Brandeis determined: "Except in matters governed by the Federal Constitution or by Acts of Congress, the law to be applied in any case is the law of the State. And whether the law of the State shall be declared by its Legislature in a statute or by its highest court in a decision is not a matter of federal concern. There is no federal general common law." Congress could not change this, Brandeis supposed, for "Congress has no power to declare substantive rules of common law applicable in a State whether they be local in their nature or 'general,' be they commercial law or a part of the law of torts"—though in fact Congress could change it by simply repealing the Rules of Decision provisions. The Constitution gave Congress the authority to determine whether there would be a federal common law for its civil courts. The fact that Congress had not done this explicitly in the Rules Enabling Act, stating instead that no substantive right would be abridged by new procedural rules, was a matter to which Congress could attend whenever it so chose.[61]

The problem that *Erie* raised for the Federal Rules was the very same problem that Walsh, King and other critics of the Rules had raised. Where could or should a judge draw the line between a procedural (hence uniform federal) and a substantive (presumably state) matter? In *Erie*, the line was rather easily drawn—railroad liability was an old issue, once hotly contested, and the progenitor of doctrines as widely divergent as the "fellow servant rule" (employer not liable for injury to employee when fault was due to another employee's conduct), the balance of equity test (adjusting tort liability when benefit to community greater than harm to plaintiffs), the scope of workers compensation (state-imposed fixed-rate liability replacing lawsuits for injury to workers), and foreseeability of harm (another tort doctrine limiting liability when the harm was not foreseeable) but by the 1930s fairly well settled. What about patient-doctor confidentiality? Was that procedural or substantive? Or husband and wife confidentiality? Rule 23, governing class actions (multiparty litigation) was infuriatingly vague. What constituted "common" legal questions binding parties together? These issues, derived from the sometimes infuriating vagueness of the Rules, would generate thousands of law review pieces and volumes of contradictory judicial rulings. They were subject to hundreds of alterations and continue to roil academic and juridical authorities.[62]

Greater autonomy for the judiciary did not end with Congress's acceptance of the Federal Rules. It came a year later, in 1939, with Congress's creation of the Administrative Office of the United States Courts (AO). Notably, the Act ended the executive wardship of the courts' finances. The Office was to be supervised by the Judicial Conference. This made sense, as the immediate impetus for the AO came from Chief Justice Hughes, who asked the Conference to work with the ABA and the Department of Justice to fashion the new administrative agency. The agency was tasked with gathering and disseminating information, and was authorized to develop and submit (under the Conference's supervision) annual appropriations requests to the Budget Bureau for inclusion—without change—in the president's annual government-wide appropriations submission to Congress. The Act also provided for conferences of the judges and lawyers within each circuit. The director of the Administrative Office was to report to the Conference rather than the Supreme Court, evidence of the increasing importance of the Conference as an administrative body as well as a policymaking body (and, according to some sources, of the justices' reluctance to add this task to their adjudicative duties). The Administrative Office thus marked a further step toward making the federal courts an integrated system instead of a confederation of quasi-independent fiefdoms.[63]

The Conference arranged for a special session, in January 1940, "to consider questions arising in relation to the work of the Director of the Administrative Office of the United States courts." There was funding to manage, clerkships to approve, and "salary raises to recommend to Congress." The law gave the justices of the Supreme Court the task of appointing the director. Hughes's choice was Henry Chandler, a partner in Edgar Tolman's Chicago law firm, and Chandler held the post from 1939 to his retirement in 1956, neatly connecting the dots that Taft, Clark, Tolman, Cummings, and Mitchell had made in their outline for modernizing the court system.[64]

That is what changing the Federal Rules of Civil Procedure and the creation of the Administrative Office meant—uniformity of practice, closer administration of hitherto greatly independent circuits, and the appointment of full-time managerial professionals. Greater day-to-day independence of the judiciary from Congress and the executive branch did not, however, change the basic formula of separation of powers nor diminish the effectiveness of checks and balances. Congress still had the final say in procedural matters, an authority going back to the Judiciary and Process Acts of 1789 and in budgeting for the judicial branch. There was change, but it was change within the system, a dynamic giving the constitutional regime of separation of powers its flexibility and strength.[65]

Roosevelt's Very Own Courts

A temporary resolution of the separation-of-powers conflict between the Court and President Roosevelt came as it had during the Civil War, when Lincoln was able to select a compatible judiciary, and the Senate readily confirmed his nominees. Well before the Court-packing proposal was launched, Roosevelt had picked men for district and appellate posts who favored the New Deal's initiatives. Roosevelt, like President Taft, took a personal interest in the selection process. Political affiliation and policy orientation were his lodestars in choosing nominees. Often, Roosevelt suggested the nominee himself. When a Democratic senator suggested someone, they were careful to add that the individual favored the New Deal and was a loyal Democrat. Some of these nominees, like Denman and Woodrough, were openly in favor of the New Deal from its inception. Denman even wrote to Roosevelt that "the New Deal needs more federal judges." Others were not as well known to Roosevelt, for example Matthew Abruzzo of Brooklyn, New York, who came from the liberal Roman Catholic wing of the Democratic Party, one of a total of thirty-two Roman Catholics picked during Roosevelt's terms (a number eight times larger than Roosevelt's three predecessors, though Roosevelt served a good deal longer than any of his predecessors). Abruzzo was recommended by Democratic Party leaders in New York knowing that Roosevelt was grateful to urban Catholics who supported his administration. Roosevelt also appointed more Jews to the federal bench, for example Samuel Mandelbaum to the Southern District of New York. Mandelbaum's prior political experience included service as a Democratic state senator in New York.[66]

Roosevelt was not able to name anyone to the Supreme Court during his first term, but after the election of 1936, open slots appeared. First, and perhaps his most controversial choice for the Supreme Court, was Hugo L. Black, an Alabama senator and staunch friend of the New Deal. Indeed, the former rural storekeeper's son sometimes embarrassed the New York plutocrat in the White House with his attacks on privilege, corporate arrogance, and special deals. In this sense, Black was a Populist. He even supported the unions, a dangerous position to take in the Deep South, particularly when his wealthy Birmingham friends were fighting so hard to prevent unionization of the mines and mills.[67]

Although at first there were no objections to the nomination, Hiram Johnson, a liberal Republican senator from California raised the hue and cry, and the floodgates opened. Conservatives railed about Black's liberal voting record. The *Washington Post* outdid the senatorial critics: "If Senator Black has given any study or thought to any aspect of constitutional law in a way which would entitle him to this preferment, his labors in that direction have been skillfully concealed." Meanwhile, southern senators hated Black's pro-union stance and bewailed the appointment.[68]

The most damaging attack arose because of the revelation that Black was a former member of the Klan. As an ambitious young man, Black had found an ally during his rise in the Senate in the Klan, which he joined in 1923. He left officially two years later but did not renounce his Klan membership until a decade afterward. After all, at least some part of the Klan's message resembled the anti-privilege, antielite message of the Populists. In the end, senatorial courtesy saw him through, 63-16, but for the next few years critics demanded he step down. He served from 1937 until his death in 1971.[69]

In January 1939, Frankfurter filled the seat Cardozo's passing left vacant. Frankfurter was an immigrant, his family having fled to the Lower East Side of New York in 1894 to escape anti-Semitism in eastern Europe. Frankfurter starred as a student at Harvard Law School, returning in 1914 to the school from a brief stint in private practice and government service. As a professor, he introduced a seminar in administrative law. In it he mentored able and eager young men ready to enter and reform government. He was greatly loyal to Roosevelt and patriotic to a fault, lest anyone hold his Jewish background or his foreign birth against him.[70]

In oral argument, Frankfurter reverted to his professorial manner, posing sharp questions to counsel. In conference, however, he could go on speaking far too long, treating the other justices as though they were his students. His opinions and comments on other justices' drafts were miniature law school lectures. In his opinions, many of them concurrences, Frankfurter advocated judicial restraint, husbanding the political capital of the Court by deferring to the other branches of the federal government. He looked for ways to avoid deciding questions on constitutional grounds, including denying that a plaintiff had standing to sue, or finding that suits were moot or unripe for decision. Frankfurter sat from 1939 to 1962, beloved by his clerks but increasingly at odds with his liberal brethren, when a major stroke crippled him and he retired.[71]

The next-to-last Roosevelt nominee to the Hughes Court was another former law professor, William O. Douglas. Growing up in Yakima, Washington, after the death of his father, Douglas endured family poverty. He countered it with hard work and a vigorous outdoor life. He went on to a storied career as a law professor at Yale and Columbia and then to head the Securities Exchange

Commission. He was elevated to the Court in 1939, replacing Brandeis. At forty, next to the youngest man to serve (that was Joseph Story), Douglas would sit until 1975, setting the record for longevity on the Court (thirty-six years and seven months).[72]

Douglas was ambitious for the highest elective political office, much like McLean, Chase, Field, and Hughes. At the same time, he was a brilliant writer, giving speeches and publishing essays, in addition to dashing off stunning opinions "of creativity, novelty, and importance." From the first, his consistent support of the New Deal clearly put him in the liberal camp. With Black, he developed a warm if somewhat awkward friendship, but his early attachment to Frankfurter turned to vitriol. Frankfurter continued to treat Douglas like a student, and when Frankfurter pontificated, Douglas poked fun. "We all know what a great burden your long discourses are," he wrote to Frankfurter after one contentious conference session.[73]

The last addition to the Hughes Court was a Detroit Democratic politician, Frank Murphy, in 1940. Murphy was not a Washington, D.C. insider. Quite the contrary, this reforming Catholic mayor, and later governor, had an almost saintly disdain for favoritism. In Michigan, he proved that local and state government could be responsive to both unions and great corporations, provide relief to the poor in times of trouble, and promote social justice.[74]

Murphy was often a showman and sometimes a showoff. He never shunned publicity, and never tired of wearing the robes of righteousness and personal virtue. He emerged unscathed from the Senate hearings on his appointment as attorney general in 1939, after he lost his campaign for reelection in Michigan, by demonstrating how he alone ended the labor wars in his state. As U.S. attorney general, he fought against corruption in government and for civil rights in a highly visible manner. He was a member of the boards of the NAACP and the American Civil Liberties Union, groups that led the fight to end Jim Crow and protect the First Amendment. On the Court, he was an outspoken advocate of social justice. He died in his sleep in 1949.[75]

In 1940, war clouds loomed on every horizon. Europe was at war, a conflict that reached to Africa, the Middle East, and Asia. On the Atlantic shores of the United States, German submarines sank British ships. The Japanese invasion of China edged the Empire of the Sun and the United States toward a state of undeclared war. Attorney General Robert H. Jackson told the Conference on September 18, 1940, that the judiciary would soon be involved in the war, even though the country was still, nominally, a noncombatant. "He foresaw a greatly increased burden on the courts arising from the enforcement of the Selective Service Act, the Alien Registration Act, and the Espionage Act, and from condemnation cases, applications for naturalization, and deportation problems."[76]

Perhaps that call for unity would bring a cessation, if not an end, to political pressures on the courts and competition between state and federal tribunals. Surely it portended a new era of cooperation among the executive, legislative, and judicial branches of the federal government. The last of these hopes came true, but the wartime federal courts could not escape political controversy, nor did they allow state judicial and legislative activity to go unreviewed.

10

Federal Courts and the "Good War," 1941–1945

By the time that Chief Justice Hughes retired in April 1941, and Justice Stone was elevated to the center chair, the judges and justices of the federal courts confronted a far more implacable and wily enemy than the Depression. On December 7, 1941, the nation went to war. World War II was a monumental event, absorbing nearly ten million Americans into the army, four million into the navy, and 600,000 in the marines. The conflict entailed the most extensive conversion from peacetime to wartime production and finance (over $304 billion was spent on the war effort itself) in American history. The Office of Price Administration and the War Production Board were led by New Deal lawyers and leading corporate businessmen—opponents but a few years previously. "Dr. New Deal" had become "Dr. Win the War," turning the nation into an "arsenal of democracy."[1]

In popular memory, World War II is "the good war," and those who waged it on the Allied side are the "greatest generation." While the war effort was a remarkable achievement, it came at a cost. Rationing of gasoline and other consumer products reminded all Americans that the war imposed scarcity on the homefront. Children on the two coasts were especially affected, some running to and from school in fear that enemy bombs would rain down on the streets. The production of war materials afforded women an unparalleled opportunity to work outside the home, but the gains would prove temporary. Wartime personnel demands eased Jim Crow, though segregation in the armed forces remained the rule. John Reynolds, later a judge in the Eastern District of Wisconsin, recalled of his first day of training in the South, "Then I went to Mississippi . . . and we got off the train at Shelby and that very night a black kid was lynched. Right there. He was hung from a trestle, railroad trestle . . . And that was my introduction to what I considered the most foreign place . . . that I have ever been."[2]

Reynolds was properly horrified by the absence of law in Shelby. Had he begun his training on the other side of the country, at Bainbridge Island in Puget

Sound, he might have seen an equally haunting sight—thousands of Japanese Americans, clinging to a few personal belongings, assembled for dispersal to distant internment camps. In time of war, the judicial branch faces its greatest tests. The purpose of checks and balances in a system of separation of powers is to safeguard liberty against government tyranny. By apportioning the various functions of government among the three branches and giving to each checks on the others the framers hoped to erect barriers against oppression of individuals. As James Madison wrote in Federalist No. 48, the framers knew "that power is of an encroaching nature, and that it ought to be effectually restrained." When the courts act as handmaidens of the other branches, either rubber-stamping or effectuating oppressive policies, the system risks failure. When the courts bow willynilly to popular pressure, the rights of minorities go unprotected. For short periods of national emergency, or when war threatens, the urge to cooperate fully with the executive and legislative branches is almost irresistible. Courts that hold out against emergency measures put themselves in danger of censure, and judges who resist the call to arms can become targets of popular opprobrium. As jurist and scholar Geoffrey Stone has wisely written, "The central question, of course, is not how to protect constitutional rights [in time of war], but how to protect those rights while still allowing the government to respond effectively to a crisis." The U.S. attorney generals immediately preceding and during the Second World War—Frank Murphy, Robert H. Jackson, and Francis Biddle—were all determined not to follow the example of Attorney General Palmer's Red Scare. There would be no wholesale repression of dissent or deportation of dangerous aliens. But when national security seemed threatened, toleration narrowed and prosecutions followed. The first target of scrutiny was as in World War I: critics of the war effort and persons labeled as dangerous radicals. The second target was Americans of Japanese descent and Japanese immigrants, thousands of whom were forcibly interned in camps far from their homes. It was an ill-conceived and discriminatory policy in which the Congress, the executive branch, and the federal courts were all complicit.[3]

The Wartime Judges

One should not judge an institution on its worst day. Although the trials of dissidents and the relocation and internment of the Japanese Americans did not show the federal judiciary in its best light, those stories were hardly representative of the bulk of the judges' activities. Instead, the coming of war brought a wide range of new responsibilities, continuing trends already apparent and introducing new assignments for the judicial branch.

Attorney General Biddle reminded the Judicial Conference of the added burdens of wartime. In September 1942, he asked for the senior circuit judges' help in filling judicial vacancies promptly. He urged the judges to carry back the message to their circuits to expedite "hearings and appeals in cases where prompt decision is of immediate concern to the conduct of the war." Biddle wanted the judges to weigh the needs of wartime during litigation: "certain types of cases whose preparation and presentation would absorb too much time of army, navy, or civilian personnel essential in war work, or might disclose valuable information to the enemy. . . . It seems to me, however, that the Federal Courts, by weighing the hardships caused by the delay against the detriment to the war effort resulting from the absence of essential personnel, should be able to arrive at a practicable and fair solution of this problem." Finally, although Biddle did not give specifics, it is likely that another area of suits he wanted the judges to manage involved employer-labor relations, which were a vital part of the war effort that a strike or a work slowdown could harm. Biddle did not tell the judges how to decide cases, trusting their experience to manage their own caseload, but he told the judges to aid the war effort. [4]

The wartime bench was prepared for the managerial task. From the beginning of 1941 to the beginning of 1946, fifty-three men were commissioned to sit on district court benches. A comparison of their backgrounds with those of prior cohorts of judicial appointments reveals that more of the wartime appointees had served in managerial roles before they went on the bench than had any previous cohort of appointees. For example, in 1942, Stephen Brennan was in private practice in Albany when he agreed to serve the Northern District of New York. But in between, he was counsel to the state's tax department. John Bright closed his Middletown, New York, office to join the members of the Southern District of New York court, leaving behind his service as corporate counsel to the town. Robert L. Brown's private practice was in Butte, Montana. He served as assistant U.S attorney for the district, and then from 1945 until his death three years later he sat on the district court bench. Aloysius Connor was a member of the New Hampshire supreme court bench when he was appointed, in 1944, to its federal district court. All of these men, and the majority of their peers, had some form of managerial post before they were commissioned.

There were a few appointees, usually older men, who learned the law in a lawyer's office rather than going to law school, but they too had government experience before elevation to the federal bench. For example, Chase Clark, born in 1883, read law before practicing in Idaho and was its governor from 1941 to 1943 He served on the District Court for the District of Idaho from 1943 until his death in 1966. Thomas Davis, of Braselton, Georgia, was born in 1892, read law, and was the U.S. attorney for the Middle District there when in 1945 he moved to the bench. He died in office in 1969. Richard M. Duncan, of St. Joseph,

Missouri, was born in 1889 and read law before he went into private practice there. He was a U.S. congressman from Missouri when he accepted a judgeship in 1943. He died in office in 1974.

At a period in American history when life expectancy for white men was a little over sixty years, the longevity of many of the wartime federal judges was striking when compared with earlier cohorts of federal judges and to most Americans. Many not only lived into their seventies but also continued to serve, taking senior status, to the end of their lives. The longest lived of them in this period, Allen Hannay, served the Southern District of Texas from 1942 until his death, at age ninety-one, in 1983. Longevity could be a problem. Judge John Biggs, when named to the Third Circuit Court of Appeals in 1937, noted that the average age of the other members was seventy-seven. Most of them were "old and ill." The senior circuit judge was blind and senile. For such long-serving judges, trials were truly a trial, as Boston, Massachusetts's Charles Wyzanski, who served as a law clerk to both Learned Hand and Augustus Hand and went on to service in the New Deal Department of Justice, reported when in his seventies.[5]

From January 1, 1941, to December 31, 1945, sixteen men were named to the circuit courts of appeal. Like the district court nominees of the period, almost all had managerial experience, most often in public positions, or served the government in some other capacity. Noteworthy among these, Thurman Arnold had served in various New Deal agencies. He replaced Wiley Rutledge on the D.C. Circuit Court of Appeals in 1943. Arnold stepped down two years later to found one of D.C.'s foremost corporate law firms, and explained, "I think it was my preference for partisan argument, rather than for impartial judgment, that made me dissatisfied with a career on the appellate court ... to sum up, a person who is temperamentally an advocate, as I am, is not apt to make a good judge."[6]

Such honesty surely became Arnold as a man and a legal realist, but there were those on the bench who saw it as a bully pulpit. One of these was Jerome Frank on the Second Circuit Court of Appeals. A friend and ally of Arnold, Frank was a brilliant critic of classical jurisprudence in his academic writings. He was serving as the chairman of the Securities Exchange Commission when he was nominated and confirmed in 1941. He did not see judging as impartial at all. As he wrote in *Law and the Modern Mind,* "All judges exercise discretion, individualize abstract rules, make law ... efforts to eliminate the personality of the judge are doomed to failure. The correct course is to recognize the necessary existence of this personal element and act accordingly." Among his many contributions to American law from the bench was the concept of the "private attorney general," allowing suit when one does not have standing to bring the suit because of personal grounds, but because one is seeking to vindicate a wrong against the public, or by a public official, greatly expanding the concept of standing to sue and democratizing access to the courts.[7]

Additions to the Supreme Court also fit this description—men of experience in various branches of government in various places. The first was Attorney General Robert H. Jackson. Another of the Court's success stories, Jackson grew up on a farm in upstate New York. After completing high school, he took classes at Albany Law School and observed New York Court of Appeals arguments. In 1913, at the age of twenty one, he gained admission to the bar. He was immensely successful in private practice but took time to represent the poor and downtrodden as well as the well-to-do.[8]

Jackson's reputation as a lawyer and his steadfast Democrat politics brought him to FDR's attention as a friend and advisor, then in 1938 as solicitor general, and in 1940 as attorney general when Murphy went on the Court. A year later, Jackson followed. Expected, like Murphy, to follow a liberal activist line, instead he feuded with Black and was close to Frankfurter. Reliably deferential to government, he explained in his *The Struggle for Judicial Supremacy: A Study of a Crisis in American Power Politics* (1941), how a pre-1937 activist Court was "substituting its judgment for that of Congress and the way in which judicial review governed our society." On the bench he believed that liberty must make some concessions to order, and the rights that every citizen had did not include the right to undermine elected officials or the Constitution. The Bill of Rights was not "a suicide pact." Jackson's most famous aphorism was uttered in 1953: "reversal by a higher court is not proof that justice is thereby better done. There is no doubt that if there were a super-Supreme Court, a substantial proportion of our reversals of state courts would also be reversed. We are not final because we are infallible, but we are infallible only because we are final."[9]

Joining Jackson on the bench, though confirmed a month earlier, James F. Byrnes replaced McReynolds. Byrnes had even less formal education than Jackson but made up for it with drive, energy, and support for Roosevelt. In 1903, after reading law in Judge Benjamin H. Rutledge's chambers, he gained admission to the bar and began his practice at the age of twenty-one. He rose through the legal and political ranks, becoming a prosecutor in 1908 and earning a seat in the U.S. House of Representatives from 1911 to 1925. When he won a Senate seat, he carried his liberal (save for civil rights) politics into FDR's New Deal. He left the Court one year later for the White House to run the domestic war effort for the president. Byrnes ended his national government service as Truman's secretary of state, where he helped construct the beginning of the administration's approach to the Soviet Union.[10]

Roosevelt named Wiley B. Rutledge to replace Byrnes and gave Black, Douglas, and Murphy a solid fourth vote. Rutledge was one of the Court's great might-have-beens. Felled in 1949 by a massive stroke, he served only six years on the bench but earned the respect of friend and foe alike for his openness and forthright defense of civil liberties. Born in Kentucky in 1894, his father a

Baptist minister, Rutledge attended the University of Wisconsin at Madison and majored in ancient languages, fell gravely ill with tuberculosis, and sought a climate better for his health first in New Mexico then Colorado. He earned his law degree at the University of Colorado Law School in 1922, and two years later he became a professor there, moving to Washington University Law School in St. Louis, Missouri. In 1930 he became dean and five years later became dean of the University of Iowa College of Law. Like Stone, throughout his academic career Rutledge earned a reputation as a generous and personable teacher with strong liberal commitments. He came to Roosevelt's attention as one of the few law school deans who supported the Court-packing plan. Roosevelt picked him to serve on the D.C. Court of Appeals. There and on the Supreme Court, Rutledge grew into his new role as an outspoken liberal jurist.[11]

The Smith Act and the Federal Courts

As in World War I, the wartime federal courts were the not the front line of defense of national security. But the Smith Act (The Alien Registration Act) of June 29, 1940 early on brought the federal courts into the project of national defense. Insofar as the Act was defended and attacked in the political arena, and some of its targets were fringe political figures, Smith Act cases were politically charged. The Act criminalized certain kinds of expression that advocated the overthrow of the U.S. government. It also required all noncitizen adult residents to register with the government. Unlike the Espionage Act of 1917, the Smith Act was not limited to expression that hindered a legal government activity like the draft. Nor was it a wartime expediency, like the Sedition Act of 1918. Instead, it had been long in gestation during the years when communist and fascist organizations were gaining adherents in the country, against which Congress responded with the Foreign Agents Registration Act of 1938 and the Hatch Act of 1939, the latter requiring registration of members of the Communist Party.[12]

The Act that Howard Smith, a Virginia Democrat, drafted grew from these roots, but its prohibition of speech as well as antigovernment conspiracies was a step beyond all of its progenitors. Nevertheless, as the war approached and fears of dangerous radicalism once more emerged, it was a very popular measure. The House of Representatives voted it up 382 to 4, with 45 not voting, on June 22, 1940. In the Senate, a division was not called, in effect passing the House version without a vote. Roosevelt signed it on June 28, 1940.[13]

The key provision of the Act appeared in its first title. It penalized those who "with intent to cause the overthrow" of the government printed, published, edited, issued, circulated, distributed, sold, or publically displayed anything that advocated, advised, or taught the violent overthrow of the government; helped anyone else engage in such activity; or organized or helped organize "any society, group, or assembly of persons who teach, advocate, or encourage the overthrow or destruction of any such government by force or violence." Membership in such an organization was enough to bring an individual under the umbrella language of the Act. Unlike the World War I Acts, the individual did not have to write, speak, or take part in any of the proscribed activities.[14]

Title II of the Smith Act provided for deportation of aliens if they had ever been a member of a suspect organization, whether or not that membership was active. The third title required registration and fingerprinting of all aliens in the country within thirty days. Registration required the alien to provide, on oath, the organizations to which he or she belonged or had belonged. In effect, the Act introduced into federal law the old English "oath ex officio" that the Puritans had so hated. The alien who had at one time belonged to a proscribed group was trapped. If one did not take the oath, one would be deported. If one took it and lied, one would be deported. If one took it and admitted membership, one would be deported. U.S. Post Offices became registration centers. All aliens had to report any changes of residence within three months.[15]

Challenges to the Smith Act deportations, like those to the 1919–1920 Red Scare deportations, came to the federal courts. The most notable case was that of Harry Bridges, an Australian-born former communist union organizer on the San Francisco docks. The Smith Act allowed for deportation because of membership at any time. His case was then brought before a commissioner. A hearing resulting in an order for deportation was reversed by the Board of Immigration Appeals (BIA). In May 1942, Attorney General Biddle overruled the BIA and ordered Bridges deported. Bridges sought federal judicial review by filing a writ of habeas corpus with the Northern District of California federal court. Immigration and naturalization service district director I. F. Wixon explained to the court that the deportation order was Biddle's and his discretion was unreviewable. The court nevertheless heard the petition. Judge Martin Ignatius Welsh, formerly a Sacramento prosecutor confirmed in a new seat in 1939 (and who could not have been unfamiliar with Bridges's reputation for self-promotion), concluded the Act applied to Biddle because of his former membership. The deportation order was reinstated.[16]

Bridges contended that the sole purpose of the Act was his deportation, and Welsh did not ignore that claim. Bridges could not be deported under the Alien Agents Registration Act and that failure played into the passage of the Smith Act. But for Judge Welsh, the motives of members of Congress when passing an act of general application could not be questioned. Welsh quoted the Supreme Court opinion in *Soon Hing v. Crowley* (1885), a case in which the Supreme Court heard and affirmed a California court judgment that curfews on laundries, though obviously aimed at the Chinese community, could not be challenged

Figure 10.1 Union leader Harry Bridges, whose nearly decade-long travails involved federal courts at every level. Credit: Photo by Harris and Ewing, Library of Congress.

on the basis of the presumed bias of the legislature: "The motives of the legislators, considered as to the purposes they had in view, will always be presumed to be to accomplish that which follows as the natural and reasonable effect of their enactments ... The diverse character of such motives, and the impossibility of penetrating into the hearts of men and ascertaining the truth, precludes all such inquiries as impracticable and futile." Bridges's habeas corpus petition was denied. A sharply divided Ninth Circuit upheld the lower court. The majority found, "The point to be determined by us is whether the appellant had a fair hearing, and, if it appears from the record that he had, we are not at liberty to disturb the decision of the lower court." A vigorous dissent from Judge William Healy, joined by Judge Francis Garrecht, followed: "For those who cherish traditions of American justice it is permissible to believe that the alien should not be deprived of his freedom to remain here unless the truth of the accusation be fairly established. That it was not so proven must be patent, I think, to any candid person who takes the trouble to examine the record."[17]

Bridges was not done. The Supreme Court agreed to hear his appeal. There, in *Bridges v. Wixon* (1945), the Supreme Court found that the term "affiliation" with an organization in the statute must be read to mean taking part in its activities. Douglas wrote for the majority: "[H]e who cooperates with such an organization only in its wholly lawful activities cannot by that fact be said as a matter of law to be 'affiliated' with it." It was a stretch as far as statutory interpretation goes, but at the time, the United States was actively soliciting the assistance of the Soviet Union in the reduction of the Japanese enemy and the Cold War had yet to begin. Justice Murphy, whose long and supportive connection to the union movement made him particularly sympathetic to Bridges, was even more emphatic in his judgment: "Seldom if ever in the history of this nation has there been such a concentrated and relentless crusade to deport an individual because he dared to exercise the freedom that belongs to him as a human being and that is guaranteed to him by the Constitution."[18]

Why does the Harry Bridges case matter in a history of the federal courts? His victory did not vindicate some glowing principle of justice, whatever the rhetoric of his supporters might claim. Had organized labor not taken up his cause, one doubts whether he would have had the wherewithal to continue his appeals. His case came to the Supreme Court on certiorari—that is, because four of the justices wanted to hear it. The odds of that happening were slim, given the small percentage of writs of certiorari pleaded that the Court agreed to hear. What makes his case notable is that it demonstrates that the courts in war did not close their doors; they gave the deportation order of an alien, radical longshoreman much attention. That fairness ultimately overcame administrative expediency. Bridges was no saint, not even a victim in the sense that the Scottsboro Boys were, but he had the opportunity to make his case before the highest court in the land, and thus the case shows the checks and balances mechanism at work. Through the Smith Act, the entire weight of the Congress fell on Bridges, and the Department of Justice doubled down on that weight; the Court was not the handmaiden of Congress and the executive branch: Bridges was not deported.

Minneapolis Socialist Workers Party (SWP) members were not as fortunate. Like the socialists in the first year of World War I, the SWP's opposition to the government appeared to be a violation of the Smith Act. There was as well a residue of antiunion sentiment in the arrest of the Minneapolis and St. Paul leaders of Local 544 of the Teamsters, the local union controlled by the SWP.

Twenty-nine of the union officers and members of the party were indicted for the offense of plotting to overthrow the U.S. government, largely, but not wholly, based on the Smith Act. Attorney General Biddle, in urging the prosecution, took the view that the Smith Act had replaced the "clear and present danger" test of *Schenck* and the other First Amendment World War I sedition cases. The jury was not instructed in the test, despite defense counsels' motion for it, and found eighteen of the defendants guilty.[19]

The Eighth Circuit Court of Appeals upheld the convictions. The judges believed that Biddle's interpretation of the Act, overriding the clear-and-present-danger doctrine, was correct. Citing *Gitlow v. New York* (1925), Judge Kimbrough Stone, a Wilson appointee who served through the First World War period, explained, "While the doctrine of the Schenck case [per *Bridges*] has afforded practical guidance in a great variety of cases in which the scope of constitutional protections of freedom of expression was in issue, yet it is by no means of universal application. *Gitlow* . . . definitely determines that the Schenck case doctrine is not applicable in situations where the legislative body has, by statute, determined that 'utterances of a certain kind involve such danger of substantive evil that they may be punished.' " All of the SWP members convicted served at least a part of their sentences and the last of them left jail in February 1945.[20]

The Smith Act was also used to bring pro-Nazi activists to heel. The first of the cases was the prosecution of George W. Christians, head of the Crusader White Shirts. A federal court convicted him on June 8, 1942. The next of the trials brought together a collection of right-wing dissidents and Nazi sympathizers. Two years after the indictments, a trial commenced in Washington, D.C. The unwieldy thirty-three defendants pool, the ineptitude of some of the counsel, and the effective delaying tactics of others representing the defendants (twenty-four lawyers made over 500 motions, some against one another's clients' interests), led Judge Bolitha Laws to declare a mistrial on November 29, 1944. The next year, Judge Laws went on the Court of Appeals for the District of Columbia, no doubt relieved to leave behind the circus that had hastened the death of his predecessor at the trial, Judge Edward Eicher. Lampooned in the press as "the great sedition trial," the cases hung fire until the government dropped the prosecutions two years later.[21]

While the Nazi trials continued in the District of Columbia courts, the Federal Bureau of Investigation, under the leadership of its director, J. Edgar Hoover, turned its attention to another type of subversive group. The target was Manhood United, a utopian religious sect whose organization and theology anticipated Scientology. Self-appointed prophet and tax dodger Arthur Bell was the founder of Manhood United, and he challenged the constitutional validity of the FBI's raid on his headquarters and his arrest by bringing a civil suit in federal court against Hoover's agents. Bell's complaint averred that "in the early morning of December 18th, 1942, [the defendants did] search the homes of the individual plaintiffs herein without any warrants of search or seizures, and unlawfully to seize the papers, documents and effects of said plaintiffs and of 'Mankind United', and falsely to imprison the individual plaintiffs by unlawfully arresting some of the individual plaintiffs."[22]

Judge Ralph E. Jenney in the Southern District of California heard the case. Rather than dismissing it on the grounds that the federal agents acted within the scope of their authority as officers of the United States and that the searches and seizures were incidental to lawful arrests and were therefore valid, he explored a different rationale. He dismissed the suit for want of jurisdiction. "This action was not one that 'arises under the Constitution or laws of the United States.'" His ruling was upheld by the Ninth Circuit: "It will be noticed that Congress has enacted no law under the authority of the constitutional provision relied upon by plaintiffs as the jurisdictional basis giving United States Courts jurisdiction over torts in general." Three and a half years after the raid, on April 1, 1946, the U.S. Supreme Court handed down its decision in *Bell v. Hood*. The Court did not address whether Bell's Fourth and Fifth Amendment rights had been violated, but it did establish Bell's right to raise these issues in a civil suit in federal court. On remand, the district court again found no grounds for suit against the agents—if they acted within their official capacity, they were immune, and if they acted outside their authorized duties, there were no grounds for a federal suit against them.[23]

War Powers and the Relocation Cases

The trials of Harry Bridges and George Christians, along with Arthur Bell's suit against the government demonstrated how slowly the wheels of justice could grind. The great sedition trial began with justifiable grounds but ended in farce. So, too, Christians's and Bell's cases ended with a whimper. The suits stemming from the "relocation" of Japanese Americans began with a palpable injustice and ended decades later in belated reparations. In 1942, according to an act of Congress and a presidential order, more than 100,000 Japanese American citizens were forcibly removed from their West Coast homes and relocated to detention camps in the deserts and mountains of the West and Southwest. The evacuees' sole offense was their Japanese identity. There was no proof and little effort to find proof that individually or collectively they posed a danger to national security or the war effort. By comparison, the efficiency of the War Relocation Authority and the Western Civilian Control Administration in establishing and running the internment camps surpassed that of any of the New Deal administrative agencies.[24]

Figure 10.2 Residents of Japanese descent registering for evacuation and internment. Wartime Civil Control Administration, San Francisco, April 1942. Credit: Farm Security Administration, Library of Congress.

The sorry story of the forced relocation of Japanese Americans does not begin with the shock, panic, and embarrassment of the Japanese attack on Pearl Harbor. From the time of the Japanese Exclusion policies during the Progressive Era, western states' governments subjected Japanese immigrants and their children to denigrating treatment. Federal courts refused to intervene. The coming of the war in the Pacific brought these covertly sanctioned harassments to a head. After a string of successive defeats in the Pacific, at the urging of several military and civilian officials, on February 19, 1942, Roosevelt issued Executive Order 9066 that allowed the secretary of war and military officials to designate areas of the country from which people could be "excluded, expelled, restricted, or otherwise subjected to regulations the appropriate military authorities might impose at their discretion." Acting under this policy, Western Defense Command's Lieutenant General John L. DeWitt issued curfews for all those of Japanese ancestry residing within forty miles of the West Coast. His memorandum justifying the policy was so racist that Roosevelt administration officials rewrote it and hid the original. On March 18, 1942, Roosevelt issued Executive Order 9102 establishing the War Relocation Authority that gave DeWitt the wherewithal to forcibly remove

Japanese Americans to "relocation centers" in Colorado, Arizona, and other western states. On March 21, Congress passed legislation codifying this executive order. Within days DeWitt's military police forcibly detained and removed 112,000 Japanese Americans to the War Relocation Centers. About 70,000 were U.S.-born citizens. The hardships the curfew and later relocation forced on these individuals were devastating. Psychological trauma, economic devastation from the sale of their businesses and homes, and the separation from their communities wreaked a terrible toll on this population.[25]

The first legal tests of these policies came from Gordon Kiyoshi Hirabayashi and Minoru Yasui. Hirabayashi only reluctantly challenged the curfew after initially obeying. Yasui was an activist for the Japanese American Citizens League and mounted his case with the express intent of overturning the policy. By contrast, Fred Toyosaburo Korematsu had not tried to challenge the policy, but instead he hid in plain sight rather than obey the order. After hearings, Hirabayashi and Yasui were held for transportation to the camps. Judge Adolphus St. Sure, of the Northern District of California, was plainly troubled by the imposition of a martial rule when the civil courts were open and operating. St. Sure was a Progressive Republican appointed to the court in 1925. He heard the Korematsu case without a jury because the government and the defendant agreed to a bench trial. In ruling on Korematsu's case, St. Sure found that the exclusion order, resting on an act of Congress and a presidential order in time of war, left little room for Korematsu's resistance. He continued that Korematsu was entitled to bail while he appealed. A military policeman, following DeWitt's orders and violating the judge's, took Korematsu into custody. His counsel's offer to arrange for payment of a larger bail was ignored by the military policeman, and Korematsu was taken from the court and held at the military jail in the Presidio.[26]

When Korematsu's appeal was heard by a panel of the Ninth Circuit Court of Appeals, the judges did not agree on the grounds for continued detention. Judge Curtis Wilbur, a Hoover appointee who had come to the circuit court from the chief justiceship of the Supreme Court of California, found the case an easy one. Wilbur was the judge who wrote the majority opinion in *Bridges v. Wixon*. The U.S. Supreme Court had already spoken on the matter of Yasui's petition and "held the curfew restrictions valid. The Court did not expressly pass upon the validity of the evacuation order which is involved in the case at bar. However, the justices held that under the Constitution the government of the United States, in prosecuting a war, has power to do all that is necessary to the successful prosecution of a war although the exercise of those powers temporarily infringe some of the inherent rights and liberties of individual citizens which are recognized and guaranteed by the Constitution."[27]

Judge Denman did not agree with the grounds that his colleague had cited for denying the appeal. "It is with regret that I find myself in profound disagreement with a majority of my colleagues in their treatment of the claims of unconsti-tutionality and other illegalities . . . of General DeWitt's order to Korematsu. Korematsu is a fellow citizen, who [happens] . . . to have a common ancestry with the people under the dominion of the Japanese Government." His dissent was grounded on policy, the facts, and the law. As to policy, "Americans are to face a peace table at which our prestige and power will rest upon the belief of a world questioning Caucasian sincerity, a world which includes a billion Asiatics. There no one will shut his eyes to the [relocation camps]." The facts were just as plain to him—Korematsu posed no threat; indeed he was a model citizen. "In the course of the hearing, the Government admitted that not one of these 70,000 Japanese descended citizen deportees had filed against him in any federal court of this circuit an indictment or information charging espionage, sabotage or any treasonable act." The Constitution as well stood in the way of mass internments. The Circuit Court of Appeals had ignored Korematsu's claims that his case was based on racial discrimination. Denman wanted them included. "It is unjust to the appellant to omit from the summary of the contentions on which he relied."[28]

In opinions that Chief Justice Stone crafted, a unanimous Court rejected the challenges to the curfew in *Hirabayashi v. U.S.* (1943) and *Yasui v. United States* (1943). Stone considered three issues: whether Congress and the president had the authority to apply such a curfew; whether Congress and the president met the constitutional burden in doing so; and whether Congress could properly del-egate such an authority to the War Relocation Authority. His answer to all three questions was in the affirmative. He deferred to the decisions of the military, the executive, and the legislative branches considering the overall context of the imminent and immense danger of wartime. The "war power" in the Constitution meant that the political branches must be given the leeway they needed to meet present emergencies. "Where, as they did here, the conditions call for the exer-cise of judgment and discretion and for the choice of means by those branches of the Government on which the Constitution has placed the responsibility of warmaking, it is not for any court to sit in review of the wisdom of their action or substitute its judgment for theirs." Based on a low level "reasonableness" stan-dard of review, in effect the "rational relation" test applied not to the states in a due process suit but to Congress, Stone relinquished the judiciary's supervision of the matter.[29]

Although Douglas concurred, he tried to narrow the precedent. He empha-sized the immediacy, the threatened danger, and the difficulties of attempting to enact a more nuanced approach. Murphy's concurring opinion read more like a dissent. Though he too granted the good faith and intentions of the mili-tary authorities, he made it clear he found the blanket classification of a group because of race or nationality as liable to punishment without trial abhorrent. "Distinctions based on color and ancestry are utterly inconsistent with our traditions and ideals. They are at variance with the principles for which we are now waging war."[30]

Black delivered the opinion of the Court in *Korematsu v. U.S.* (1944) upholding forced relocation. Although he, unlike Stone, weighed the congressional enactment under the strict-scrutiny standard he helped formulate, the result was the same. "Like curfew, exclusion of those of Japanese origin was deemed necessary because of the presence of an unascertained number of disloyal members of the group, most of whom we have no doubt were loyal to this country. It was because we could not reject the finding of the military authorities that it was impossible to bring about an immediate segregation of the disloyal from the loyal that we sustained the validity of the curfew order as applying to the whole group." Like Stone, Black found the military acted within the authority Congress and the president had lawfully executed. "But exclusion from a threatened area, no less than curfew, has a definite and close relationship to the prevention of espionage and sabotage . . . when under conditions of modern warfare our shores are threatened by hostile forces, the power to protect must be commensurate with the threatened danger." He denied any racial aspect in the situation. "Korematsu was not excluded from the Military Area because of hostility to him or his race." Frankfurter, concurring, found that it was the "business of the . . . Congress and the executive . . . not ours."[31]

Justice Owen J. Roberts dissented. "I think the indisputable facts exhibit a clear violation of Constitutional rights." He found relocation on the basis of ancestry, as opposed to the curfew, to be a clear violation of the Constitution. "It is the case of convicting a citizen as a punishment for not submitting to imprisonment in a concentration camp, based on his ancestry, and solely because of his ancestry, without evidence or inquiry concerning his loyalty and good disposition towards the United States." Murphy, now dissenting, agreed with Roberts. "Such exclusion goes over 'the very brink of constitutional power' and falls into the ugly abyss of racism." Jackson dissented as well.

> Korematsu was born on our soil, of parents born in Japan. The Constitution makes him a citizen of the United States by nativity and a citizen of California by residence. No claim is made that he is not loyal to this country. There is no suggestion that apart from the matter involved here he is not law-abiding and well disposed. Korematsu, however, has been convicted of an act not commonly a crime. It consists merely of being present in the state whereof he is a citizen, near the place where he was born, and where all his life he has lived.[32]

After the 1944 election, in which Roosevelt had returned to the White House for a fourth term, and the war against Japan now raged over its home islands, the military exigencies claimed for relocation vanished like a mist at morning. Injustice alone was visible. Justice Douglas, explaining the Court's stance on *Ex Parte Mitsuye Endo,* neatly skirted the question of how the Court could uphold detention of Korematsu while invalidating the detention of Endo by ingeniously distinguishing the two cases. Korematsu had challenged the legitimacy of the initial detention order. Endo was challenging its continuation in her particular circumstances. Douglas concluded that she should have been granted leave from the detention center, whereas Korematsu was legally detained. Endo, like Korematsu, was "a loyal and law-abiding citizen." The WRA did not detain her for cause.[33]

Even when the Court provided relief, however, it did not do so on well-ordered legal grounds much less constitutional grounds. "We are of the view that Mitsuye Endo should be given her liberty. In reaching that conclusion we do not come to the underlying constitutional issues which have been argued." Why not spell out, as Roberts and his brethren had in dissent, the constitutional grounds for Endo's freedom? Because, as Douglas immediately continued, her case was not the same as the other Japanese relocation cases. Instead, "We must assume that the Chief Executive and members of Congress, as well as the courts, are sensitive to and respectful of the liberties of the citizen. In interpreting a wartime measure we must assume that their purpose was to allow for the greatest possible accommodation between those liberties and the exigencies of war."[34]

Justice Douglas's "must assume," like Frankfurter and Black's deference to the other branches of the federal government, was linked to wartime exigency. The tenor of their opinions strongly hinted that the checks and balances system the framers erected explicitly to limit the power of the executive was subject to a balancing test. When the war's outcome was still in doubt, the courts would show more deference to the branches of government actually waging the war. With the war coming to a close, the courts would begin to reassert their constitutionally mandated independence from the other branches. One may call the relocation cases an example of prudential jurisprudence, a realistic assessment of the political climate during the war. Had the Supreme Court in 1943 concluded that relocation violated the Constitution, the clash with the other branches would have resembled the clash over the relocation of the Cherokee in the 1830s and would probably have had the same result.

The concurring opinions in *Endo* took issue with Douglas's exculpation of the executive and the military. But there was no sense of regret, no concession of wrongheadedness in them—these very same jurists had not dissented in 1943 when dissent would have mattered more than concurrence in 1945. Murphy repeated his objections to the entire relocation program as he had made them two years earlier. "For the Government to suggest under these circumstances that the presence of Japanese blood in a loyal American citizen might be enough to warrant her exclusion from a place where she would otherwise have a right to go is a position I cannot sanction." Roberts disagreed with Douglas's skirting of the constitutional issues, as Roberts had dissented in *Hirabayashi*. "An admittedly loyal citizen has been deprived of her liberty for a period of years. Under the Constitution she should be free to come and go as she pleases." [35]

Though not the "self-inflicted wound" of *Dred Scott*, these decisions were not the Court's finest hour. Deference to Congress and the president in time of war notwithstanding, the Supreme Court, and the federal judiciary whose hierarchy it sat atop, could have spoken justice to power. Surely by 1943, when *Hirabayashi* came to the Court, it was evident to all the only danger to the Pacific Coast came from the looting of absent Japanese citizens' property by their white neighbors.

The shadow of the four cases reached into the 1970s and beyond. For his part, Justice Black told an interviewer in 1971: "I would do precisely the same thing today . . . people were rightly fearful of the Japanese" because "they all look alike to a person not a Jap." Justice Stanley F. Reed, formerly Roosevelt's solicitor general, recalled "maybe it was hysteria . . . but the record shows there were authenticated cases of such treasonable actions." Justice Douglas confessed, in 1974, "I have always regretted that I bowed to my elders and withdrew my opinion" condemning the camps. In a series of suits in federal court beginning in 1983, Peter Irons and other lawyers gained for Korematsu, Yasui, and Hirabayashi the ruling that their convictions under the relocation laws and orders were illegal. On November 10, 1983, Judge Marilyn Hall Patel of the Northern District of California vacated Korematsu's conviction, an act Judges St. Sure and Denman would have approved. Three years later, Judge Donald S. Voorhees of the Western District of Washington vacated Hirabayashi's conviction. The next year, Judge Mary M. Schroeder, writing for a three-judge panel on the Ninth Circuit, upheld Voorhees's ruling. In 1988 Congress appropriated $20,000 for each survivor of the camps, payment for three years of lost lives and suffering. No assessment was made or repayment offered for lost businesses and careers. In 1998, President Bill Clinton awarded Korematsu the Medal of Freedom. In 2012, President Barack Obama presented the same medal to Hirabayashi, posthumously.[36]

Civil Rights

Jim Crow laws might be seen to raise the same issues as the Japanese relocation cases, but the federal courts regarded challenges to all-white grand juries and all-white primaries in a different light. Perhaps the Scottsboro Boys cases cast their penumbras over these decisions. The Stone Court held discrimination on the basis of race in jury selection to be a violation of the Equal Protection Clause of the Fourteenth Amendment in *Hill v. Texas* (1942). Again the Supreme Court looked at facts, not just the fact that Texas made no attempt to refute the petitioner's claim that the grand jury, which indicted him for rape, did not have, nor ever had, any black grand jurors, although over 8,000 black inhabitants of the vicinage paid taxes to the county. Hill brought to the Texas Supreme Court hearing on his appeal two members of the grand jury commission. Both conceded that they chose grand jurors who they knew personally and thought would make good members. Chief Justice Stone's opinion continued the story: "An assistant district attorney for the county, who had lived in Dallas County for twenty-seven or twenty-eight years and had served for sixteen years as a judge of the criminal court in which petitioner was tried and convicted, testified that he never knew of a negro being called to serve on a grand jury in the county. The district clerk of the county, whose duty it is to certify the grand jury list to the sheriff... knew of no citations issued for negroes to serve upon the grand jury."[37]

The all-white primary was a patent attempt by Jim Crow Democratic Party leaders to deny to black voters any part in the election of federal officials. Louisiana had a long history of indifference to the provisions of the Fifteenth Amendment, but when the federal government brought suit against the registrars of voters in the primary, Judge Adrian Caillouet of the Eastern District found no grounds for the suit. Citing Justice McReynolds' opinion in a 1921 voting case, Caillouet concluded "the 'elections' therein referred to [in federal election law] are 'general' elections and not 'primary' elections, which are not final and of themselves do not 'elect' anyone to serve either in the Senate or House of Representatives; [the courts had] no power to control party primary elections, such as the Democratic primary election of September 10th, 1940." What was more, no primary "was ever intended at the time that the Constitution was adopted; 'primary' elections for the nominating of candidates for the offices of either Senator or member of the House of Representatives were not even within the orbit of the Convention's deliberations on the subject of representation in the National Congress, as 'primaries' were then unknown." Caillouet, a Louisiana native and Roosevelt appointee, had just taken his seat when this hot potato was handed him. He had not attended law school, following the older path of reading law and then taking the bar exam. His experience was limited to private practice. The Supreme Court reversed, determining, "Unless the constitutional protection of the integrity of 'elections' extends to primary elections, Congress is left powerless to effect the constitutional purpose, and the popular choice of representatives is stripped of its constitutional protection."[38]

Southern states persisted in using the all-white primary to exclude black voters in one-party Democratic states. The Legal Defense Fund of the NAACP, with Thurgood Marshall in the lead, and the American Civil Liberties Union, represented by Arthur Garfield Hays, brought suit in the name of Lonnie Smith against the Texas all-white primary. Judge Thomas Kennerly of the Southern

District of Texas found no grounds to order the end of the all-white primary. The primary was not an election; it was a mere party procedure, hence not covered by constitutional provisions or congressional action. He cited the Supreme Court opinion in *Grovey v. Townshend* (1935). Kennerly, like Caillouet, read law in his native Texas and then engaged in private practice until he was named to the court by Herbert Hoover in 1931. The Fifth Circuit, in a per curiam opinion, affirmed the lower court. In *Smith v. Allwright* (1944), Thurgood Marshall led the legal team for the appellant, this time successfully. Justice Reed, who was from Kentucky but had vigorously defended the constitutionality of the New Deal as FDR's solicitor general, delivered the opinion of the Court, concluding, "The [political] party takes its character as a state agency from the duties imposed upon it by state statutes; the duties do not become matters of private law because they are performed by a political party." The all-white primary was gone.[39]

A majority of the Stone Court also believed that state and local officials must obey federal law. In *Screws v. United States* (1945), a federal trial resulted in a jury verdict against a Georgia sheriff and his deputies who beat Robert Hall, an African American, to death after arresting him for stealing a tire. The defendants demurred in an appeal to the Fifth Circuit, but two of its three members affirmed the trial court's view that federal criminal law applied. Court of Appeals Judge Samuel H. Sibley dissented. After obtaining a law degree from the University of Georgia, he had practiced in Union Point, Georgia, from 1893 until he was elected to the Greene County court in 1905. Greene County had been one of the most heavily populated by slaves before the Civil War; its cotton plantations made it one of the richest counties in the state, but after the war it became one of the poorest counties. Race relations there had not changed much from the redemption era to the World War II years.[40]

Sibley's dissent read like that of a man whose upbringing and attitudes were rooted in local experience and "Redeemer" values. "Horror at what happened in this case has, I think, interfered with a calm consideration of the law involved. Certainly, if the evidence for the prosecution is credited, the appellants ought to be in the penitentiary. The question is, ought [it] to be in the penitentiary of the United States?" He preferred the rule in *Cruikshank* that the case belonged in a state court. The prisoner was handcuffed at the time he was beaten to death, but he was heard to utter curses at the sheriff and his men. Sibley related that "[i]t is also a custom in Georgia to strike one who calls you to your face a 'son of a bitch', but as the District Judge charged the jury in this case the privilege of resenting such words does not extend to an arresting officer." Presumably Hall's verbal offense to the officers contributed to his fate and mitigated the sheriff's offense.[41]

When the case came before them, the Supreme Court justices divided on whether that the United States could prosecute the local officials under the

Civil Rights Act of 1866. Roberts, Jackson, and Frankfurter argued that the case belonged in the Georgia courts on the grounds that federal prosecution subjected the defendants to far weaker punishment than Georgia law would impose. (Whether the three justices realized that no white Georgia jury would have convicted the three defendants remains a matter of conjecture.) Justice Douglas, writing for Chief Justice Stone, and Justices Black, Reed, and Rutledge, found that there was federal grounds for prosecution but sent the case back to the federal trial court because its judge had not instructed the jury that the sheriff and his deputies' acts must be "willful." Justice Rutledge wrote a concurrence in the course of which he took a swipe at Sibley's personal aside. "Generally state officials know something of the individual's basic legal rights. If they do not, they should, for they assume that duty when they assume their office. Ignorance of the law is no excuse for men in general. It is less an excuse for men whose special duty is to apply it, and therefore to know and observe it. If their knowledge is not comprehensive, state officials know or should know when they pass the limits of their authority, so far at any rate that their action exceeds honest error of judgment and amounts to abuse of their office and its function." Justice Murphy dissented. "Common sense" told him it was not necessary for the jury to be instructed in the willfulness of beating a handcuffed man to death.[42]

More important to the larger narrative of the federal courts, these cases all shifted the federalism balance, making the federal courts supervisors of state law in ways that the regulatory decisions of the New Deal years did not. Instead of deferring to state law, the wartime courts were applying the sort of strict-scrutiny standards that the Hughes Court had largely abandoned. Federalism was alive and well, but the exact boundary of state-federal juridical relations was shifting, and federal judges knew in which direction the shift was occurring.

The Federal Rules of Criminal Procedure and the Administrative Procedures Act

Matters of criminal procedure in the federal courts were also under review in the war years. The effort to make these uniform across the districts did not face the same problems as the Federal Rules of Civil Procedure because criminal procedure in federal courts was not tied to state procedure in the same way as the various Procedure Acts bound the federal courts to state civil processes. Except for adopting the state's rules for arrests, bail, and preliminary hearings, criminal procedure in federal cases was left to the federal courts from their inception. Nevertheless, the various districts had developed their own rules for issuing and returning criminal summons, subpoenas, and other writs, for time limits and for other materials of process. The Sumners Courts Act of 1940 directed the Supreme Court to prepare uniform rules: "to prescribe, from time to time, rules of pleading, practice, and procedure with respect to any or all proceedings prior to and including verdict." These were deployed in two parts: in December 1944 a comprehensive set of rules for process up to the verdict, and a year and a half later, a similarly comprehensive set of rules for post conviction, including appeals. The combined rules took effect on March 21, 1946.[43]

Former Attorney General Cummings saw the new rules of Criminal Procedure as companions to the Federal Rules of Civil Procedure that he had sponsored. In 1945, he wrote that the process by which Congress asked for the rules and the subsequent advisory committee draft, approved by the Supreme Court, represented the very best tradition of democratic lawmaking. It involved the two branches of the federal government in a cooperative effort. Unlike the debates over the Federal Rules of Civil Procedure, there was little acrimony in the acceptance of the draft. "Every worthy suggestion" was weighed. No "thoughtful proposal failed of a hearing." The advisory committee (attacked in the hearings on the rules for civil pleading for being out of touch with local feeling) was here, supposedly, merely a conduit (though it was staffed with the very highest caliber of judges, lawyers, and professors). The result was a code imposed on the bench and bar by neither branch of the government, but one arising, Cummings concluded, from the people themselves.[44]

Cummings's encomium to the democratic process was not entirely candid. He conceded that the American Law Institute (ALI) had a hand in the call for the new Rules. The ALI's annual meeting reported its desire for the new Rules to Hatton Sumners, the chair of the House Judiciary Committee, a presentation that could not be ignored given the elite membership of the ALI and its growing influence on American law. Then U.S. Attorney General Jackson had added his voice to the chorus. This was a command from the top down, not from the bottom up. Cummings continued that "the bench and bar" had come to agree that the advisory committee was a better way to fashion rules than incremental congressional action, another endorsement of expertise (and a retroactive defense of Clark's Federal Rules of Civil Procedure committee). This time the advisory committee was led by Alexander Holtzoff, at the time a special counsel in the attorney general's office, who in 1945 was named to the D.C. District Court, and Arthur T. Vanderbilt, New York University Law School's dean, noted reformer, and future chief justice of the New Jersey Supreme Court. Cummings conceded that the rules would need polishing and would be amended accordingly, as events would prove a prudent close to his piece.[45]

If the successful prosecution of the war had proved anything to leaders in Allied governments, it was the value of bureaucracies. Housed primarily in Washington, D.C., bureaus and agencies handled the details of rationing, war materials production, war information for the home front (including censorship), production of civilian goods, hospitals for the wounded, housing, and a myriad of other functions (including the relocation of Japanese Americans). In many cases, the hearings and decision making of these agencies took place behind closed doors. The Office of Price Administration (OPA), for example, had the power to set rent controls and other prices equal in scope to the activities of the constitutionally impermissible National Recovery Administration. Bureaus like the Office of Emergency Management spawned miniature bureaus, a complex hierarchy of the "fourth branch of government" impenetrable from the outside and largely autonomous. Of course the OPA and other discretionary agencies had critics, particularly vociferous ones, as the "administrative frenzy" diminished with the war's end.[46]

While Congress had in 1943 retroactively approved the first wartime agencies, a more thoroughgoing review of the entire process of agency operation awaited the end of the war. Judicial review of agency findings was nothing new—it had become fairly commonplace in federal courts in the last years of the New Deal. But in those years, the federal courts deferred to the expertise of the agencies more often than not. At the same time, one of the concerns of the federal courts had been the untrammeled rule making of the agencies, rooted in the claim of expertise and defended by academics and New Deal administrators.[47]

Congress, recognizing the necessity of administrative agency adjudication and the danger that the agencies posed to the public interest if they were not subject to more consistent review, passed the Administrative Procedure Act of 1946. The Act governed the agencies' hearings and required review of their findings in federal district courts. In theory, the new Act made uniform the various agencies' operations. In fact, there were gaps and slippages.[48]

Like the Federal Rules of Civil Procedure, the Act had been in the works for nearly a decade. Hearings on it had been contentious, some regarding them as a backdoor way of criticizing the New Deal, others claiming that the measure was simply a refinement of earlier enactments. Certainly, the drive toward administrative bodies established a fourth branch of the federal government, and under the terms of the creation of the first three branches, the administrative agencies should not have been free of checks and balances. In the Act, agency activity was divided into rule-making functions (how the hearings were to be publicized, who could come, and the like) and adjudicative functions (who won and who lost). The Act required the agencies to give notice of all rule changes and provide explanatory notes for each change. The body of the Act was a "statement of principles" rather than a detailed guide. That was left, along with a heavy load of administrative law cases, to the district judges.[49]

In the first place, it was not all that clear whether the Act changed the way in which the agencies were to function. Certainly, the long shadow of the district courts falling on the agency's operations must have had some impact on the outcome of hearings, given the open door for appeal in Section 10 of the Act. What was more, the court hearing a challenge to any outcome could, in theory, decide that the enabling legislation was unconstitutional. In this situation, the Act would have given the courts a power over congressional legislation that they did not have previously. Surely Congress did not want judicial review of administrative agency hearings to have such a draconian impact on separation of powers within the federal government—although the discussion of Section 10 in the Senate and House debates on the bill were murky at best and contradictory at worst. If the courts were to defer to the agency when substantial evidence supported the agency finding, did the agency or the court decide what and how much evidence met the "substantial" evidence standard? Attorney General Tom Clark told the Senate Judiciary Committee that, in the opinion of his committee on Administrative Procedure and the Bar, it did not confer on the courts any nonjudicial, that is, administrative, functions. These remained the province of the agencies themselves. The problem with this forthright limitation on the courts was that the courts, not the attorney general's office, would have to interpret the meaning of the statute.[50]

With the war concluded, the federal courts might have been given time to collectively catch their breath. But the peace imposed new and unprecedented burdens. The Cold War with our former ally the Soviet Union spurred a second Red Scare. New commitments emerged from the war, including taking a major role in the establishment of the United Nations and the institution of war crimes trials in Japan and Germany, calling on members of the federal judiciary to exercise not only wisdom but also prescience. The war had conferred on the presidency unprecedented powers to which the courts and Congress had acceded, but which peacetime politics would test. At home, the Stone Court continued the program of incorporation of the first eight amendments in the Bill of Rights. How would it readjust the relationship between federal and state courts, particularly in criminal cases? One of the foremost students of civil liberties, Paul Murphy, asserted, "The Court's favorable civil liberties record was in some ways one of the most remarkable aspects of the war period, particularly when one compares it with the bleak picture of World War I." Would that commitment to greater personal liberty continue? Attorney General Tom Clark hinted that it might not, calling the Conference's attention to the U.S. Code provisions "providing for the mandatory deportation of aliens convicted of certain types of crimes, unless the trial judge, at the time of passing sentence or within thirty days thereafter, recommends against deportation." Given the influx of refugees from Nazi Germany who had radical political backgrounds, this reminder could not have been a reassuring gesture to newcomers.[51]

Stone did not live long into this new era of the courts' labors. The chief collapsed on April 22, 1946, at his seat in the center of the bench, while announcing an opinion. He died that evening. At his funeral, the music included the old hymn "The Strife Is Over." In fact, for the nation and its courts, that strife was about to enter a new and bitter phase.[52]

11

The Courts and the Cold War, 1946–1954

Even if the end of World War II war seemed a triumph of liberty and human dignity over tyranny, a good war for a good cause, the ideals of the Atlantic Charter of 1941—freedom from fear and want—for which Americans fought abroad remained elusive on the home front. The challenge lay ahead to keep the nation safe from its foreign enemies while guaranteeing equal protection of law and civil liberty for all its people. In the face of a second Red Scare and the persistence of Jim Crow regimes, post–World War II federal courtrooms became legal battlegrounds.[1]

Truman's Judges

Recruitment of federal judges during the war stressed administrative experience. President Harry S. Truman adopted another model for many of his nominees. He turned to trusted friends and personal attachments, whose recommendations perhaps had disproportionate weight in his choices for the bench. Like Roosevelt's, about 26 percent of Truman's nominees lacked college degrees. But unlike every president who followed him, fully 20 percent of Truman's nominees had held elective political office. Sometimes, his "extravagant notions of loyalty ... prompted him to make many a crony appointment" to the bench from among these fellow politicians.[2]

For example, when a spot opened on the Eighth Circuit Court of Appeals in 1947, Truman picked District Judge John Caskie Collet, a friend and political ally. Collet had practiced law in Missouri until Roosevelt named him to the lower court at the urging of then Senator Truman. Collet and Truman vacationed together at Key West in 1946. Collet repaid the favor of elevation to the court of appeals, acting as an unofficial White House consultant during Truman's remaining years in office. When Collet left the district court bench, Truman turned to another Missouri political ally, "Roy" Winfield Harper. Harper was born in Gibson, Missouri, in 1905, he received A.B. and LL.B. degrees from the University of Missouri, worked for a time for Shell Oil, in St. Louis, and then in private practice in Steele. In 1934 he became Democratic County chairman of Pemiscot County, and resumed private practice from 1934 to 1947 in Caruthersville. In 1940 he served as chair of the campaign to reelect Truman to the Senate. After the war he became chair of the Missouri State Democratic Committee. Truman twice named Harper to the eastern district of Missouri by recess appointment to replace Judge Collet, and twice the Republican majority in the Senate refused to confirm him, only giving in to Truman on January 31, 1949, after Truman had been reelected. Harper assumed senior status on January 5, 1971, and served in that capacity until his death in 1994.[3]

Truman was not above naming someone as a favor to an ally. Herbert Lehman, elected to the Senate in 1950, interceded with the president to appoint Edward Weinfeld to the federal bench. Weinfeld had lobbied for the post for the past year, unsuccessfully, but Lehman's recommendation ("[Weinfeld's] appointment would be very pleasing to me") carried the day. Weinfeld's service on the Southern District's bench from 1950 to 1988 was a credit to Lehman's sponsorship and to the bench.[4]

Hubert Humphrey, elected to the U.S. Senate from Minnesota in 1948, had helped Truman win reelection. Humphrey wanted Truman to aid Minnesota Governor Luther Youngdahl, a liberal Republican. Truman knew Youngdahl, the only Republican to write Truman commending him for firing General Douglas McArthur. Truman complied by naming Youngdahl for a seat on the U.S. District Court for the District of Columbia for which he received a commission in 1951. Youngdahl later joked that Humphrey was happy to have helped and was also relieved that Youngdahl would not run against him for the Senate seat in 1954. Youngdahl would later distinguish himself as one of the federal judges unmoved by the rush to judgment in the second Red Scare.[5]

Overall (political favors notwithstanding), the single most distinguishing characteristic of Truman's nominees was their strong personal connections to the district in which they were to sit. These connections reinforced strong attachments to local values. For example, Edward Kampf, named to the Northern District of New York, had graduated from Albany Law School; and Roy Shelborune had a law degree from Cumberland Law School in Tennessee and returned to Kentucky to practice in Bardwell and Paducah for many years before he was chosen for the Western District of Kentucky. Francis Scarlett, of Brunswick, Georgia, received his law degree from the University of Georgia in 1913, and practiced in his hometown until 1946, when he was selected for the Southern District of Georgia. Samuel Driver, who practiced in eastern

Washington state after earning a law degree at the University of Washington, was picked for the district court seat in Spokane and served until his death in 1958.[6]

The pattern of parochialism in judicial appointments in the postwar period had an impact on the judiciary different from prewar parochialism. Before World War II, one could say that the country was a collectivity of distinct localities. After the war, the culture of the nation was becoming more homogenous and less local. By the early 1950s, over 50 percent of American households had at least one television set. Television was knitting the nation together in a way that local newspapers and radio stations did not. Television was national. In this sense, the continuing localism of the newly named lower federal judiciary was a throwback to an earlier time. Perhaps that was not wholly accidental. Truman wrote to one judge that "the appointment of federal judges is the most important thing that I do," and Truman's own career was a throwback to an earlier time of small town politics. One got ahead through personal service and reciprocal favors.[7]

In the main, then, the bulk of the Truman judges were like Truman, men of ordinary means and local attachments who had, as he had, risen from modest circumstances and proven their mettle in government service. Typical of these was Theodore Levin. Levin was born in Chicago, Illinois, in 1897, one of eight children of eastern European immigrants. Joseph and Ida Levin moved briefly to Canada and then brought their eight children back to Detroit, Michigan. Levin received a LL.B. from University of Detroit School of Law in 1920, and an LL.M. from the same institution in 1924. He was in private practice with his brother Saul in Detroit from 1920 to 1946. In the 1930s, Levin was part of a group of immigration lawyers who opposed the Michigan Alien Registration and Fingerprinting Act. He was a member of the executive board of the National Refugees Service Administration and an officer of the Michigan Commission on Displaced Persons. In 1933, Levin was appointed special assistant attorney general in an investigation into the Michigan Bank Holiday, and from 1944 to 1946 he served as a member of the Selective Service Appeal Board. On July 3, 1946, Truman selected Levin for the District Court for the Eastern District of Michigan. He was chief judge of the court from 1959 to 1967, and thereafter served in a senior capacity until his death. During his tenure as a federal judge, Levin joined with other judges in his district in an informal sentencing council to review presentencing reports and promote uniformity.[8]

David Bazelon had grown up in modest circumstances in Chicago. He earned a degree from Northwestern University in 1931. After a stint in private practice he was named assistant U.S. attorney for the Northern District of Illinois in 1935 by Roosevelt's attorney general, Homer Cummings. He then worked as the assistant U.S. attorney general for the U.S. Lands Division from 1946 to 1949. On October 21, 1949, when he was forty years old, Bazelon received a recess appointment from Truman to a new seat on the United States Court of Appeals for the District of Columbia Circuit and was nominated and confirmed the next year, the youngest judge ever appointed to that court. From 1962 to 1978 he served as chief judge; he took senior status in 1979 and served until his death in 1993. Bazelon was elected a Fellow of the American Academy of Arts and Sciences in 1970 in part because he was a pioneer on the bench in recognizing that mental disease was a plausible defense in a criminal prosecution. Beloved by his clerks, he was a forceful advocate of causes in which he believed and more than once was called a dangerous liberal.[9]

Truman's "Fair Deal" program included a genuine effort to advance the cause of civil rights, one reason why he saw merit in Levin and Bazelon perhaps, and he took executive steps in that direction, including the beginning of the desegregation of the armed services. Among other steps was the recess appointment on October 14, 1949, of William H. Hastie to the Court of Appeals for the Third Circuit, the first nonwhite judge named to a life tenured federal judgeship. To be sure, there was a partisan backstory. Hastie had helped swing black votes for Truman during the 1948 campaign. With the Senate back in session, Truman nominated him in January 1950 and had to press hard for confirmation. Hastie's distinguished career helped. An Amherst College and Harvard Law School graduate, Hastie had left private practice in D.C. to serve as an assistant solicitor in the U.S. Department of the Interior (1933–1937), a territorial judge in the Virgin Islands (1937–1939), and as governor of the Virgin Islands (1946–1949). He had also served as dean of Howard University's school of law from 1939–1946. Although a single judgeship hardly signaled the end of racial discrimination, it was a first step that civil rights advocates noticed and applauded.[10]

Truman looked to his former Senate comrades to fill vacancies on the Supreme Court. His first was Harold Burton, in 1945, then serving as Republican senator from Ohio, and his last was former Senator Sherman Minton, a Democrat from Indiana, in 1949. Minton, unlike Burton, had judicial experience, confirmed to a seat on the Seventh Circuit Court of Appeals in 1941 after losing his seat in the Senate. Truman knew, liked, and had worked with both men when Truman represented Missouri in the Senate. Truman's most important appointment to the Supreme Court was not a member of the Senate, however, but was a man for whom Truman had personal affection and respect. Truman selected his secretary of the treasury Fred M. Vinson to fill the center seat when Chief Justice Harlan Stone suddenly died.[11]

Vinson's life and character was similar to Truman's. Born in 1890 in the small town of Louisa, Kentucky, Vinson overcame many obstacles to reach the pinnacle of American judicial office. He demonstrated academic excellence, athletic prowess, and personality wherever he went. He returned to Louisa to practice law in 1911 until the United States entered World War I. Like Truman, he served in the armed forces. Thereafter, Vinson was a quintessential local politician, easy to know and work with, earning election as commonwealth attorney in 1921 and successive terms in Congress from 1924 to 1938, with the exception of one election in 1928 when the national Democratic Party's stand on Prohibition briefly cost him his seat. Roosevelt appointed him to the D.C. Circuit Court of Appeals. On the Court of Appeals he sided with the government and deferred to the legislative branch. After service as an administrator during the war, President Truman appointed him secretary of treasury, and on June 6, 1946 tapped him for the chief justiceship. Confirmation followed easily. But Vinson would prove unable to apply his administrative experience to managing what had become a bitterly divided bench.[12]

With the passing of Justices Murphy and Rutledge, additional Truman appointees would give Vinson, for a short time, a solid five-vote majority (with Justices Burton and Reed) on all issues except segregation. What was more, the new justices shared something of his background and approach to law, drawn as they were from government service. The first of these was Truman's attorney general, Tom C. Clark, named to succeed Murphy. Clark possessed a fine legal mind, a distinguished record in the Justice Department, and fulfilled Vinson's request for a friend on the Court on whom he could count.[13]

Born in Dallas, Texas, in 1899, Clark attended the Virginia Military Institute until financial reasons forced him home. Like Vinson, he volunteered for service in World War I but did not see combat. He earned his bachelor's and L.L.B. from the University of Texas and joined his father and brother in the family law firm before becoming a successful assistant district attorney. Local politics led to federal office. In 1937, after another stint in private practice, he went to Washington to serve in the Department of War, and after the United States entered World War II, he was the special assistant in the War Risk Insurance Office, the first of a series of agency positions, including civilian coordinator for Japanese internment. Much later in life, he admitted that was "the biggest mistake of my life." Truman made Clark attorney general where he continued his antitrust work, and, unlike Vinson, vigorously aided the civil rights movement, filing friends-of-the-court briefs in NAACP lawsuits, urging the FBI to investigate racial violence, and supporting an antilynching bill in Congress. Clark also undertook a thorough campaign against communism through Smith Act prosecutions of American Communist Party leaders. But by 1948, he soured on red-baiting, now a cause championed by Republican-dominated organs like the House Un-American Activities Committee (HUAC). From this platform of friendship and service to Truman, Clark ascended to the Court.[14]

A few months after the Clark appointment, Truman put another friend, Sherman "Shay" Minton, forward to replace Rutledge. Liberal groups favored the former senator from Indiana whose 1934 Senate campaign featured the slogan, "You can't eat the Constitution." A stint on the Seventh Circuit Court of

Appeals, from 1941, had shown Minton an advocate of restraint, deference, and practicality. The committee and the full Senate approved his appointment in October 1949. Minton remained committed to judicial restraint on the Supreme Court bench, consistently voting to uphold government actions. He believed the elective branches were the ones to secure the people's liberty and his role was to respect precedent and stay out of their way, a left-leaning stance in the context of the New Deal, but a far more conservative position in the postwar era of civil rights and civil liberties litigation. His gregarious, folksy manner made him many friends on the bench but accorded him little respect among court watchers. In 1956 he resigned from the bench due to ill health.[15]

The Vinson Court was outshined by the intellectual luminosity of the Court of Appeals for the Second Circuit (the 1948 revision of the judicial code changed the courts of appeal's terminology). Chief Judge Learned Hand's performance remained sterling despite his age. The appointments of Connecticut's Charles Clark in 1939 and New York's Jerome Frank in 1941 to a bench already graced by Learned and Augustus Hand had made the court, by the postwar period, "the strongest tribunal in the English speaking world" in the words of one practitioner. Encomia for judges are common among members of the legal profession, but rarely do they come while the judges are active. Retirement and death open the floodgates (although one suspects that bromides like "he was a real gentleman" is more palliative than praise). But those who practiced before "Learned Hand's court" agreed with academics and judges on other benches—the Second Circuit was a splendid collection of legal thinkers.[16]

Charles Clark had pioneered a realistic view of the operation of courts and had navigated the new Federal Rules of Civil Procedure past the shoals of the ABA and through the rough waters of Congress, major reform achievements. If Hand never quite warmed to the prickly New Englander (he privately referred to Clark as the GLAPP—"greatest living authority on practice and procedure"), he treated Clark with courtesy and respect. With Jerome Frank, whose views of judging and whose liberalism was even more radical than Clark's, Hand developed a genuinely warm and ultimately affectionate relationship. Frank's *Law and the Modern Mind* (1930) proposed that much judging was rooted in the personality of the judge. His role in pressing the New Deal agenda made him anathema to many lawyers representing corporate interests. But his contribution to the Second Circuit, notably his notion of the ordinary citizen acting as a private attorney general suing to fulfill government aims, was and remains noteworthy. When Clark and Frank went out of their way to tussle, sometimes over trivial matters, their competition only burnished the reputation of the court.[17]

One cannot leave an account of the Second Circuit Court of Appeals without some notice of Henry J. Friendly, named to it in 1959. Friendly had long been in corporate practice in New York City when Judge Medina vacated his slot.

Friendly lobbied for it, with Frankfurter among others supporting him. Friendly was a master of detail and a student of judging. He wrote well, showed great creativity when faced with immensely complex commercial litigation, and had little patience with poor lawyering, lazy judges, or incompetent arguments. Friendly's speeches and occasional writings, including essays on judging and on the business of the courts, are classics of their kind. His treatise on administrative law and regulation is still a textbook for students of the field. Like Frankfurter, his sharp intellect during oral arguments could cut counsel to shreds. Yet this retiring, shy man was also capable of great courtesy to younger lawyers.[18]

By the end of the 1950s, the Second Circuit Court of Appeals had an intellectual rival—the Court of Appeals for the District of Columbia. This was particularly true in the area of administrative law. Because of their jurisdiction, the District's courts heard many regulatory cases, in particular those challenging Federal Communications Commission and Federal Power Commission rulings. The judges on its bench developed a forceful and well thought out conception of "public interest" in these cases. But as Judge Bazelon explained, the court did not see itself as a referee among competing interests, simply awarding the victory to the side that scored "the most points," but as the guardian of the general public interest. When Warren Burger joined the Court of Appeals bench in 1956, Bazelon's New Deal liberalism faced a conservative counterpoise of considerable energy. Along with other President Eisenhower appointments to the District of Columbia's courts, Burger was conservative on the issues that mattered most to Bazelon, administrative law and criminal law (especially their differing view of the insanity defense). Leading two quite distinct factions on the courts, the two judges carried on an intellectual contest fully the equal of Clark's and Frank's on the Court of Appeals for the Second Circuit. Over the course of years, the Court of Appeals for the District would become a classroom for students of federal jurisprudence, sending a number of its judges to the Supreme Court bench.[19]

Cold War Justice

The Truman administration confronted what would be called the "Cold War"— a contest of information, economic aid, and armed force waged against the spread of worldwide communism and the threat of a hostile Soviet Union. At the end of the World War, the Allies had committed to the ideal of "collective security" embodied in the United Nations charter and a series of multilateral alliances. Despite American efforts at cooperation with the Soviet Union, tensions between "the superpowers" soon escalated and confrontation became a fact of postwar diplomatic and military life.[20]

With the threat to national security in mind, Truman signed Executive Order 9835. It launched the Federal Employee Loyalty Program. The order presumed that "the presence within the Government service of any disloyal or subversive person constitutes a threat to our democratic processes." Truman's program continued with the establishment of a "Loyalty Review Board" to prevent subversives from gaining federal posts and to weed out anyone already serving in a federal government job.[21]

Truman's initiative had unforeseen consequences. Stoked by the House Un-American Activities Committee's hearings, government pursuit of alleged agents and admirers of the Soviet Union reached a fever pitch. Most state governments and professional organizations followed the federal government's lead, ferreting out and firing current and former members of the Communist Party of the United States of America (CPUSA). On February 9, 1950, before the Republican Women's Club in Wheeling, West Virginia, junior Senator Joseph McCarthy of Wisconsin claimed to have a list of 205 communists then working in the State Department. Though the number often changed and McCarthy could produce no evidence in support of any of his numbers, his name became synonymous with the anticommunist campaign. "McCarthyism" ranged across the political landscape largely unchallenged for the next four years. Industries assembled black lists of proscribed persons. Hollywood, academia, and the professions followed suit. Even the ABA urged state and local associations to require loyalty oaths of their members. (The Association of the Bar of the City of New York refused, but the vote was close.) McCarthy's Senate subcommittee on investigations of the committee on government operations pursued alleged communists inside and outside government. Even those merely suspected of sympathizing with communism—"fellow travelers"—found their lives ruined.[22]

Congress supplanted these executive initiatives with the Internal Security or Subversive Activities Control Act of 1950. Colloquially known as the McCarran Act, after Nevada Senator Pat McCarran's role in its passage, the Act required communist organizations and their members to register with the Department of Justice, and members of the party then faced loss of citizenship, including the right to vote. The Act also made picketing federal courthouses a felony. President Truman had vetoed the Act, but with McCarthyism riding high, Congress overrode his veto. The executive branch never did seek full deployment of the Act against picketers or protestors, and while the federal courts initially did not question the curbs on the First Amendment the Act imposed, a series of cases later limited its application and Congress itself modified the Act in 1971.[23]

The pursuit of suspected communist activity was concentrated in the Northeast. Two federal trials of suspected Soviet agents in the Southern District of New York especially captured the public imagination and provided grist for the Red Scare mill. The two cases were criminal trials, one for perjury and the other for conspiracy to commit espionage. Both ended in guilty verdicts and both gained great notoriety. The first concerned a former government lawyer, Alger Hiss. The second ended with the execution of scientists Julius and Ethel Rosenberg for espionage, specifically for engaging in a conspiracy to relay secret information to agents of the Soviet Union.[24]

Harvard Law School graduate Hiss had served in the Department of Justice and the Department of Agriculture, and many thought him a trusted and trust-worthy public servant. His stint in the State Department during the final term of the Roosevelt presidency and the administration of Harry Truman seemed to confirm this assessment, until a former communist spy named Whittaker Chambers told the HUAC that he had known Hiss in the 1930s and Hiss was also a spy. Hiss sued Chambers for defamation, a mistake for Hiss as events proved, for in the ensuing legal battles, a federal grand jury indicted Hiss for perjury.[25]

On May 31, 1949, Hiss's first trial for perjury drew reporters from all over the nation to the Foley Square federal courthouse in lower Manhattan. Judge Samuel Kaufman, named the previous year by Truman after a career in private practice, presided over a swift jury selection, and the prosecutor, assistant U.S. Attorney Thomas Murphy, promised the jury that the case would be simple. It was not. Although much of the evidence presented by the prosecution's key wit-ness, Chambers, and the results of the FBI investigation seemed to prove that Hiss had been a member of the Communist Party, Hiss could not be indicted or tried for espionage because the statute of limitations had expired. Instead, the prosecution had to establish the fact of espionage to prove that Hiss had lied to federal prosecutors. Chambers was not tried, having turned state's evi-dence before a congressional committee, but that grant of immunity made his testimony suspect. Chambers's own admission of perjury on prior occasions did not help.

The trial was a media circus. Hiss's character witnesses included Illinois Governor Adlai Stevenson, Supreme Court Justices Frankfurter and Reed, and 1924 presidential candidate John W. Davis, the dean of the New York City bar. The jury divided, eight voting guilty and four voting not guilty. The Department of Justice ordered Hiss tried once again. In December 1949, with Judge Henry Goddard presiding, Hiss was convicted. Goddard was a veteran on the bench, serving since 1923. He admitted evidence favorable to the prosecution that Kaufman had excluded, and when the jury convicted Hiss, Goddard sentenced the former advisor to presidents to five years in a federal penitentiary. Goddard also denied Hiss's motion for a retrial based on new evidence, ruling that the evidence, even if admitted, would not have changed the jury verdict.[26]

The trial of the Rosenbergs, part of a larger investigation of the commu-nist connections among scientists involved in the U.S. Army's World War II

Manhattan Project to develop an atomic bomb, was even more spectacular. Both were Communist Party members and were part of a largely ineffectual spy ring with relatives and coworkers. Whether or not Ethel had much to do with the spying or the information they passed to their KGB handlers was particularly useful (they did not have access to a lot of secrets about the atomic bomb, and the Soviets already had better sources in the Manhattan Project), they were indicted for conspiracy to commit espionage under the 1917 Act. The FBI gathered many witnesses and a great deal of physical evidence. Defenders of the couple argued then and later that the documents had been fabricated and the witness testimony was unreliable or coerced, but the U.S. attorney, Irving Saypol, deemed it sufficient for the prosecution to succeed.[27]

The trial began on March 6, 1951, before Judge Irving R. Kaufman (no relation to Samuel Kaufman). Kaufman was a Truman appointee who had been on the bench for a year and a half before which he had served as a special prosecutor in the Justice Department. Kaufman moved the trial along swiftly. He conducted the voir dire (examination of potential jurors) himself, and seating a panel only took a day and a half. Throughout the trial, Saypol seemed to think that he could convince either Ethel or Julius to confess. Perhaps with that in mind, he engaged in a series of private conversations with Judge Kaufman, a violation of judicial ethics for Kaufman and a violation of prosecutorial ethics for Saypool. The conspiracy charge under the 1917 Espionage Act could result in a death sentence, another tool the government used to persuade Julius to confess. Kaufman made clear to all in the courtroom his belief that the defendants were guilty, although his rulings on evidence and his instructions to the jury were technically correct.[28]

Students of the case have speculated that Kaufman viewed himself, quite rightly, as a young star (he was only forty years old) destined for higher judicial office. His sentencing of the couple to death row, however, came as something of a surprise. While public opinion favored it, he went beyond the pale by lobbying against efforts to appeal the sentence and later attempted to quash public criticism of his handling of the trial. One veteran New York lawyer with personal knowledge of the matter concluded that his handling of the sentencing "indelibly stained Kaufman's reputation." It certainly followed him to the grave, becoming the headline of his obituary in the *New York Times*. He did not get the seat he wanted on the Court of Appeals for the Second Circuit until 1961.[29]

On June 17, 1953, Justice Douglas stayed the execution, but a special session of the Supreme Court ordered by Vinson while Douglas was away on vacation vacated the stay, Justices Douglas, Black, and Frankfurter dissenting. The Rosenbergs were executed on June 19, in the electric chair. They swore they were innocent to the end.[30]

In what was a continuation of the World War II era of good feelings between the executive branch and the federal courts, the courts backed up the president in the loyalty oath cases. The Truman administration had introduced widespread use of loyalty oaths to enact a cheap, public, and efficient way of finding out whether federal employees had connections to communist or communist-affiliated organizations. Certainly, some of these employees had far left-of-center histories. J. Robert Oppenheimer, who headed the Manhattan Project, was a leftist, a stance common among intellectual and reform circles before the Second World War. Young people who flirted with communism—before the horrors of Soviet-style collectivism became public knowledge—were now at risk for their past conduct. If they did not take the oath, they could be fired from their jobs. If they did and admitted knowingly belonging to an organization dedicated to the overthrow of the U.S. government, they faced the same penalty. In *Gerende v. Board of Supervisors* (1951), for example, the Supreme Court upheld Maryland's loyalty oath law for political candidates; and in *Garner v. Board of Public Works* (1951), it upheld a Los Angeles ordinance of loyalty oaths for city workers.[31]

In addition to the cooperation of Congress, the Department of Justice, and the federal courts in the prosecution of suspected communists, loyalty cases exhibited reciprocity among state and federal courts. In the Madisonian Compromise, the framers assumed a healthy rivalry would exist between the two systems and sought ways to ameliorate it. In the heyday of McCarthyism, the two systems cooperated. Deference to the states' courts in loyalty cases reached its apogee in *Adler v. Board of Education* (1952). In it, the Court upheld New York's Feinberg law. Going further than the Smith Act in its definition of the offending conduct, the Feinberg law stipulated that belonging to any organization on a previously published list of proscribed organizations constituted a prima facie case for dismissal or disqualification as a public schoolteacher. Proscribed conduct included saying or writing anything that "willfully and deliberately advocates, advises or teaches the doctrine that the government of the United States or of any state or of any political subdivision thereof should be overthrown or overturned by force"; printing, publishing, editing, or selling any book, newspaper, or other writing promoting the proscribed doctrines; and, even more broadly and vaguely, the law included whoever joined an organization that advocated such stances. If one failed any of these tests, he or she could not teach in the state. The determination of which organizations and publications violated the law was left to the Board of Regents of the state, making it the prosecutor, judge, and jury in the case. In order to avoid penalties, someone who was no longer a member had to admit, in public, that he or she had been a member and had ended the relationship. Otherwise, simply belonging to an organization, or quoting or saying anything in private conversation fitting, in the opinion of the state, any of these categories, was grounds for dismissal from a public school teaching position, whether the opinions were published or spoken in the course of one's employment or in the classroom. The New York Court of Appeals, the state's highest tribunal, found that the law was enacted in good faith "[t]o meet conditions thus found to exist and as a preventive measure against the dissemination of subversive propaganda among children in the public schools."[32]

The majority of the U.S. Supreme Court found the Feinberg law acceptable. Justice Minton wrote for Vinson, Burton, Jackson, Reed, and Clark: "A teacher works in a sensitive area in a schoolroom. There he shapes the attitude of young minds towards the society in which they live. In this, the state has a vital concern . . . That the school authorities have the right and the duty to screen the officials, teachers, and employees as to their fitness to maintain the integrity of the schools as a part of ordered society."[33]

The dissenters in *Adler* worried that in the passions of the moment, the Court exaggerated the threat to students in metal shop from a mechanical arts teacher who might have belonged to a radical fringe organization. Justices Black, Frankfurter, and Douglas agreed that the law went too far. Black saw fundamental principles of intellectual inquiry and freedom at stake: "This is another of those rapidly multiplying legislative enactments which make it dangerous—this time for school teachers—to think or say anything except what a transient majority happen to approve at the moment." Frankfurter had done some research into the matter and in a closely reasoned and much longer dissent, struck at the incongruity between the actual danger and the breadth of the Feinberg law and its predecessors: "During the thirty-two years and ten years, respectively, that these laws have stood on the books, no proceedings, so far as appears, have been taken under them." Douglas's dissent featured his usual dash and style: "I cannot for example find in our constitutional scheme the power of a state to place its employees in the category of second-class citizens by denying them freedom of thought and expression."[34]

When the Congress spoke clearly, so did the Vinson Court in *American Communications Association v. Douds* (1950) and, more notably, in *Dennis v. United States* (1951). The legislation at issue in *Douds* was section 9(h) of the Taft-Hartley Act of 1948. A Republican-sponsored act intended to reduce suspected communist influence on organized labor among other objectives, the legislation required union leaders to file affidavits with the National Labor Relations Board swearing they were not members of the Communist Party or believed in the violent overthrow of the U.S. government. The penalty for evasion was loss of union recognition by the Board. Vinson wrote for the majority that Congress could impose the regulation on the union leaders under its authority to regulate interstate commerce. He found the threat of communist-controlled labor unions ordering politically motivated strikes to be of sufficient concern to warrant the measure. Frankfurter and Jackson concurred in part, but both wrote independently that the Court should have found the parts of 9(h) that restricted the right to have a political opinion, or to reject one, to be invalid.[35]

The following year Vinson directly confronted the free speech issue in *Dennis*. The case arose out of Attorney General Tom Clark's orders to prosecute the leaders of the CPUSA for violating the 1940 Smith Act, which forbade advocacy of or conspiracy to advocate the violent overthrow of the government. The case was another of what were becoming popularly known as the "Foley Square [Communist] Trials" in the Southern District of New York. Eugene Dennis was the secretary general of the CPUSA. In 1948, he and ten other party leaders were indicted under the Smith Act for advocating the violent overthrow of the federal government. Judge Harold Medina presided over their trial (*U.S. v. Foster*) in the Southern District of New York. The trial lasted from jury selection on January 17 through October 14 when Medina pronounced sentence. The crux of the indictment and of the prosecution's case was that communist doctrine, which the eleven men openly espoused, called for the overthrow of capitalist regimes, including that of the United States. It was not alleged that the eleven men conspired to accomplish this goal or that they had such a plan or that they acted in furtherance of this general goal, but that they taught the doctrine. The case thus fell on the outside edge of the First Amendment. The danger of communist teachings seemed so great, no matter how remote the likelihood that these men would actively try to lead a revolution, that the eleven men were convicted by a jury.[36]

For Judge Medina, a former Columbia Law School professor, the case became an ordeal, as defense counsel raised objections, made motions, and generally harassed the bench. Noisy pickets outside the courtroom further inflamed the scene within. Because of intellect and achievement, Medina was a perfect choice for the assignment—the son of immigrants, a star student at Princeton and Columbia University Law School, a practitioner of note in New York City between the wars—an avatar of all that elevated the practice of law in the city and on the bench. His most noteworthy case as a trial attorney was the successful defense of Anthony Cramer on the charge of treason before the same federal court on which he would sit. Medina was confirmed unanimously in 1947 to the Southern District's court. But the conduct of the defense lawyers showed that even the most principled and fair-minded of judges has his limits. The defendants' attorneys used the courtroom as a platform to attack the prosecution rather than simply defend their clients. His response was to fine counsel for contempt and order various defendants incarcerated during portions of their trial.[37]

On appeal, Judge Learned Hand once again had to find a formula to weigh the danger of radical speech against the protections of the First Amendment. Hand's thinking went all the way back to his 1917 opinion in *The Masses* case, and he repeated his views when the court of appeals upheld the verdict in *Dennis*. Here, Hand applied a tort (civil harm or wrong) standard: if the harm was so great, in this instance the danger of communist subversion, even if unlikely to occur (for the communists were few and powerless), then that harm outweighed the communists' free speech rights. The test did not address the constitutionality of the statute itself.[38]

Chief Justice Vinson, writing for a majority of the Court, adopted Hand's formula: "In each case, they must ask whether the gravity of the 'evil,' discounted by its improbability, justifies such invasion of free speech as is necessary to avoid the danger." Vinson warned that government did not have to wait to act as the Communist Party organized, infiltrated, and gathered strength. The Smith Act was clear and constitutional—and the Communist Party to which Dennis and the others belonged had as its policy the violent overthrow of our government. Frankfurter's concurrence was long and tortured, including a history of free speech doctrine and its various rationales, but in the end, he deferred to Congress's judgment (in the Smith Act) and the fact that his friend judge Learned Hand sustained the conviction. Jackson's concurrence concluded, "This prosecution is the latest of never-ending, because never successful, quests for some legal formula that will secure an existing order against revolutionary radicalism . . . The judicial process simply is not adequate to a trial of such far-flung issues. The answers given would reflect our own political predilections and nothing more." Although his opinion sounds as if he was leaning toward dissent, in the end he bowed to the judgment of the government.[39]

Black's dissent asserted that "Congress shall make no law . . . abridging the freedom of speech" in the text of the First Amendment meant exactly what it said—"no law." Douglas's dissent conceded some power to the government. "If this were a case where those who claimed protection under the First Amendment were teaching the techniques of sabotage, the assassination of the President, the filching of documents from public files, the planting of bombs, the art of street warfare, and the like, I would have no doubts." But, he said, that was not what the government proved, for all its thousands of pages of testimony and its truckloads of evidence. "So far as the present record is concerned, what petitioners did was to organize people to teach and themselves teach the Marxist-Leninist doctrine contained chiefly in four books."[40]

Habeas Corpus Cases

A quiet habeas corpus revolution spanned this same period. At the same time as Congress was seeking out loyalty risks, it provided a further expansion of habeas corpus relief to state prisoners. Perhaps meant as a belated remedy for the relocation cases (it came at the same time as the Japanese American Evacuation Claims Act), the 1948 Habeas Corpus Act codified provisions for federal district judges to issue habeas corpus relief to those convicted and sentenced for offenses against the state, wherein the petitioner alleged that the state had violated his or her federal constitutional rights. The issuance of the writ was discretionary and if issued, it then led to a hearing in a federal court on the underlying constitutional questions. There has been, in the years since the end of World War II, an "ebb and flow" in the tide of these petitions, governed in part by more or less expansive readings of the grounds for federal intervention. Federal courts wrestled, for example, with conflicting interpretations of the requirement that petitioners had "exhausted" state remedies. Did that term limit or simply channel the flow of petitions? What if a petitioner had inadvertently omitted a step in the state's appeals process?[41]

In later years, the number of petitions for habeas relief would become a subject of much controversy, particularly when coupled with federal court criminal procedure decisions on interrogation and search and seizure. But the roots of these issues did not spring from the 1948 Act any more than from suspected "leniency" toward criminals on the part of judges like Bazelon. Instead, the story of the evolution of federal criminal procedure began fifty years earlier, with the fuller exploration of Bill of Rights jurisprudence. That development, rather than ahistorical complaints about a permissive society or courts "soft on crime," is the appropriate context for discussion of habeas corpus relief after World War II.[42]

Civil Rights: From Separate and Unequal to Desegregation

Truman declined to run for reelection in 1952, and newly-installed President Dwight D. Eisenhower had limited interest in the civil rights initiatives that Truman inaugurated. Eisenhower had grown to manhood in an army that was as segregated as any Jim Crow state, but as president, he believed that inequalities based on race "in areas of federal responsibility," such as federal contracts on military bases in the South, must yield. As he wrote to Governor James F. Byrnes, of South Carolina, where such executive action might "run counter to customs in some states" the federal government's writ must run unobstructed. Nothing in this program intruded on those areas of policy, for example education, traditionally assigned to the states; however, Eisenhower had opened the letter to Byrnes by mentioning desegregation in the schools. Byrnes's reply, unanswered, was that the "Court has no right to legislate." Byrnes insisted that the "right of the state to exercise its police powers to make distinctions among people" was well established, and that Eisenhower himself had agreed that such matters were "local," not federal.[43]

Eisenhower presided over the next stage of civil rights litigation, but took little role in it. He said in his first State of the Union address:

> We know that discrimination against minorities persists despite our allegiance to this ideal. Such discrimination—confined to no one section of the Nation—is but the outward testimony to the persistence of distrust and of fear in the hearts of men . . . This fact makes all the more vital the fighting of these wrongs by each individual, in every station of life, in his every deed . . . Much of the answer lies in the power of fact, fully publicized; of persuasion, honestly pressed; and of conscience, justly aroused. These are methods familiar to our way of life, tested and proven wise.[44]

Missing from that invocation of the value of individual tolerance was a commitment to any executive or legislative civil rights program (other than in the military and the District of Columbia). Eisenhower did understand, however, that foreign eyes were closely watching how Jim Crow divided the nation in two. The leaders of the communist bloc recognized that Jim Crow was a powerful tool in their contest for the minds and hearts of people of color in the Third World. In appealing to African and Asian peoples, Soviet propagandists could point to state-mandated segregation of the races in a large portion of the United States.[45]

Members of Congress opposed to segregation were hamstrung by the tenaciousness of its southern delegations. Lily-white southern state governments were in the grasp of segregationist politicians. Reform must come from the source least theoretically disposed to legislate—the federal courts. But courts could not initiate cases, even were the judges disposed to use such cases to further legal equality among the races. For this reason the Legal Defense Fund (LDF) of the NAACP had to play a leading role in desegregation.[46]

Throughout the 1930s, the NAACP had focused its energies on ensuring that allegedly separate but equal facilities were actually equal. Charles Hamilton Houston, from his post as the dean of Howard University Law School, recruited young lawyers for the cause and looked for suitable plaintiffs. Future federal judges such as William H. Hastie, Thurgood Marshall, and Spottswood Robinson III were among the first LDF litigators. Facing the well-entrenched forces of Jim Crow, the civil rights lawyers had to adopt what one of their younger members Jack Greenberg called a "tactically cautious yet strategically bold technique." It might seem piecemeal, but its target was the entire Jim Crow system. The lawyers knew that a black man or woman who sued Jim Crow was likely to face retaliation from white neighbors. It was never easy to find willing and courageous plaintiffs—but the LDF did.[47]

As his health declined, Houston passed the baton to his able student, Thurgood Marshall. Marshall's legal team, with the financial support of ordinary African Americans and white liberal groups committed to their cause, sought to engineer a legal revolution—step by step.[48]

The LDF suits targeted four areas of segregation: transportation, housing, unions, and higher education. In all of these areas of ordinary life blacks faced discrimination.The way ahead was hard. For example, as in the voting rights cases, a lower federal court upheld the separate but equal provisions in railway dining cars. The railroad company simply put a wooden partition between the tables for whites and blacks, so whites did not have to sit next to blacks. In *Henderson v. Interstate Commerce Commission* (1948) a three-judge district court in Maryland (petitioners sought injunctive relief) heard the suit, and Judge William T. Coleman wrote for the panel: "We are satisfied, without further quoting from or analyzing the report of the [Interstate Commerce] Commission, that the inequality which we found to exist in the Railway Company's earlier dining car regulations, as respects the facilities afforded white and Negro passengers, has been removed by the Railway's amended regulations." On direct appeal (under federal rules provisions for three-judge panels appeal went directly to the Supreme Court), the Court reversed the Maryland decision. *Henderson* joined an array of cases ending Jim Crow in public transportation, in housing, and union membership.[49]

The most visible LDF target at the end of the 1940s was education. Here the potential defendants were public institutions, thus the central obstacle was not the *Civil Rights Cases* (1883) but *Plessy v. Ferguson* (1896) and its "separate-but-equal" reading of the Fourteenth Amendment's Equal Protection Clause. The LDF began with graduate and professional education suits. As in the other areas of discrimination, in the education cases trial courts found for the defendants, sustaining the denial of equal access to public education. The first two cases came from Oklahoma. In *Sipuel v. Board of Regents* (1947) the state Supreme Court held, "We conclude that petitioner is fully entitled to education in law with facilities equal to those for white students, but that the separate education policy of Oklahoma is lawful and is not intended to be discriminatory in fact, and is not discriminatory against plaintiff in law for the reasons above shown." Ada Sipuel could go out of state for her education with a tuition grant from the state that was not available to whites, so eager was Oklahoma not to provide equal opportunities for her in the state. "Or if she preferred, she might attend a separate law school for negroes in Oklahoma." There was no such school. Four days after the oral argument, the Vinson Court issued a per curiam opinion in *Sipuel v. Board of Regents of the University of Oklahoma* (1948) ordering the state to provide Sipuel a legal education "in conformity with the equal protection clause of the Fourteenth Amendment and provide it as soon as it does for the applicants of any other group."[50]

Oklahoma sought to preserve segregation by hastily opening up a law school for "coloreds"—hiring three attorneys and setting aside three rooms in the state capitol and access to the capitol law library, hardly equal though obviously separate. Arguing against the state, Marshall did not challenge *Plessy* directly, but Justice Rutledge did: "the equality required was equality in fact, not in legal fiction." Oklahoma successfully evaded integration of its premier law school, but the maneuver only lasted one year. Although the Supreme Court had not ordered the state to admit her, in 1949, state authorities conceded, the makeshift law school was closed, and Sipuel entered the real one. She graduated in 1951.[51]

In the meantime, the justices faced an even more egregious case of discrimination, again from Oklahoma. George McLaurin gained admission to a doctoral program under *Sipuel*, but the university, effectuating a state law passed to deal with his admission, "required [him] to sit apart at a designated desk in an anteroom adjoining the classroom; to sit at a designated desk on the mezzanine floor of the library, but not to use the desks in the regular reading room; and to sit at a designated table and to eat at a different time from the other students in the school cafeteria." A unanimous Supreme Court ruled that these special arrangements failed all constitutional tests. In *McLaurin v. Oklahoma State Board of Regents* (1950) one can hear the same tone of sharp rebuke as in the Court's second Alabama peonage case. "The Fourteenth Amendment precludes differences in treatment by the state based upon race." But again the Court limited its holding to the circumstances of the case.[52]

On the same day, the justices dealt with the University of Texas Law School's whites-only policy in *Sweatt v. Painter* (1950). In many ways the facts presented a much more difficult situation than the obvious deficiencies in facilities and treatment of black students in *Sipuel* and *McLaurin*. The State of Texas proposed to open a second law school at the Austin campus reserved for African Americans, the Texas State University for Negroes. Once more a unanimous Court, speaking through Vinson, found the proposed accommodation unacceptable. Vinson compared the state's premier school with the blacks-only institution, not only in terms of accreditation, number of faculty, library, and facilities, but he also considered the job opportunities available after attending the law school. Vinson declared "petitioner may claim his full constitutional right: legal education equivalent to that offered by the State to students of other races. Such education is not available to him in a separate law school as offered by the State." No mention was made of *Plessy*.

A second set of cases concerned the education of the young and impressionable. They came from federal district courts in which the LDF directly attacked "separate but equal." In these, lower federal courts in South Carolina, Virginia, and Kansas, upheld state-mandated separation of the races. The judges in these courts averred that they were bound by earlier Supreme Court decisions. They had no discretion to rule otherwise. Only the Supreme Court could overrule its own precedents. Of course, a trial court may interpret the application of a Supreme Court ruling according to the each judge's reading of the decision. Also, a trial court judge is free to choose among diverse competing precedents when all are on point.[53]

In the Kansas case, *Brown v. Board of Education*, the state permitted school districts to segregate or integrate. Topeka segregated its elementary schools. The three-judge federal court that heard *Brown* would not override the state law and would not order white schools to admit black students. As Tenth Circuit Judge Walter Huxman, a former Democratic governor of the state, wrote for his brethren on the *Brown* district panel, "As a subordinate court in the federal judicial system, we seek the answer to this constitutional question in the decision of the Supreme Court when it has spoken on the subject and do not substitute our own views for the declared law by the Supreme Court." In a later interview, Judge Huxman revealed that "there was no way around" *Plessy*, but he hoped that the Supreme Court would find a way. Petitioners appealed his decision to the Supreme Court. *Brown* was the lead case, joined by the Court with three other cases, from South Carolina, Virginia, Delaware, and another from the District of Columbia decided at the same time.[54]

The three-judge district court that heard and decided *Briggs v. Elliott*, with an opinion by Circuit Judge Parker, found that the facilities in South Carolina's rural Clarendon County schools were not equal, but the reason was not discrimination so much as the economic deficiencies of the Clarendon County region. "The defendants contend, however, that the district is one of the rural school districts which has not kept pace with urban districts in providing educational facilities for the children of either race, and that the inequalities have resulted from limited resources." Governor Byrnes and the state legislature had promised in the future to make up the difference, although no positive steps had been taken. Nevertheless, as equity presumed good faith on the part of the defendant state (petitioners sought injunctive relief), Parker continued, "[h]ow this shall be done is a matter for the school authorities and not for the court, so long as it is done in good faith and equality of facilities is afforded." Petitioners had asked the federal courts to provide appropriate relief. Parker replied, "One of the great virtues of our constitutional system is that, while the federal government protects the fundamental rights of the individual, it leaves to the several states the solution of local problems . . . local self government in local matters is essential to the peace and happiness of the people in the several communities." The "peace and happiness" Parker cited referred to the potential for white violence against blacks if the court should order the end of segregation, an argument that would be repeated by southern officials for the next twenty years.[55]

Parker was a distinguished jurist, had served on the Fourth Circuit Court of Appeals from 1925 to 1958, the last ten years of which he was its chief judge, and had been nominated for a seat on the Supreme Court in 1930. A born and bred North Carolinian, he did not hide his sympathy for the defeated South, telling one gathering of Georgia lawyers, "When I think of the lawyers of Georgia . . . whom I know and love and respect, . . . I think also of the great figures who have added glory to this bar in the past . . . Judge [T. R. R.] Cobb . . . and Alexander H. Stephens . . . I feel that their spirits still linger here and that their presence add to the dignity of all your deliberations." Parker knew that Cobb was a staunch defender of slavery who wrote the Confederate Constitution and died in its army. Stephens was vice president of the Confederate States of America and spent a brief time in a federal prison. Parker had also given a speech in which he defended the "grandfather clauses" exemptions from literacy tests for voting if an individual's ancestor had voted, effectually subjecting would-be black voters (whose ancestors were slaves) to franchise restrictions white voters did not face. He added that he thought it unlikely that the mass of African American voters could ever fulfill the obligations of republican citizenship.[56]

Parker's opinion was lauded by the state's white leaders. Governor Byrnes called it unanswerable, but that did not persuade the dissenter on the panel. District Judge J. Waties Waring was educated in Charleston, the descendant of Confederate leaders, and a son of the South deeply wedded to its traditions. He practiced law in Charleston for nearly forty years before Franklin D. Roosevelt named him to the Eastern District court in 1942. He was nevertheless frustrated by the injustice of separate and invariably unequal laws. After listening to Thurgood Marshall argue the case for the petitioners, Waring grew impatient with Judge Parker's temporizing, and his dissent hinted what everyone in the courtroom and on the bench knew or should have known—South Carolina had no more intention of equalizing its educational facilities than it did of abolishing segregation itself. "If this method of judicial evasion be adopted, these very infant plaintiffs now pupils in Clarendon County will probably be bringing suits for their children and grandchildren decades or rather generations hence in an effort to get for their descendants what are today denied to them." In effect, he was accusing his brethren of conspiring with the state government to deny the petitioners their long overdue rights. For his courage, Waring was ostracized by polite society and threatened by racist terrorists. To students of civil rights, however, his name will always be honored. In the meantime, plaintiffs appealed to the Supreme Court.[57]

Prince Edward County in Virginia bore some of the same characteristics as Clarendon County. Fifty miles west of Richmond, today the county is still largely rural. Race relations there were not as hostile as in Clarendon, but in 1951 black students refused to attend schools admittedly unequal if measured by building conditions, curricula, and transportation. In *Dorothy E. Davis, et al. v. County School Board of Prince Edward County* (1952), the district court ordered the defendants forthwith to provide substantially equal curricula and transportation but would not order the end of the discriminatory system itself. Petitioner's attorney Spottswood Robinson III (later a judge on both the District and Circuit Courts for the District of Columbia) argued that "Virginia's separation of the Negro youth from his white contemporary stigmatizes the former as an unwanted, that the impress is alike on the minds of the colored and the white, the parents as well as the children, and indeed of the public generally, and that the stamp is deeper and the more indelible because imposed by law." Judge Albert Bryan did not find that Robinson's argument compelled a desegregation order. To his thinking, and that of the other members of the three-judge court, there was sufficient evidence from "distinguished and qualified educationists and leaders in the other fields" that separate and truly equal would not stigmatize black students. Custom trumped any disparity in expert evidence. "Separation of white and colored 'children' in the public schools of Virginia has for generations been a part of the mores of her people. To have separate schools has been their use and wont." Bryan, a Truman nominee in 1947, knew whereof he spoke. He was born, bred, and educated in eastern Virginia. President Kennedy would name him in 1961 to the Fourth Circuit, where he sat until his death in 1984.[58]

Among the cases joined in *Brown*, there was one ray of light. In Delaware, Chancellor Collins Seitz (confirmed to the Court of Appeals for the Third Circuit in 1966), whose powers included the provision of equitable remedies, took a step that the federal judges in South Carolina and Virginia refused to take. In *Gebhart v. Belton*, parents of black students living in New Castle County brought a suit in the Delaware Court of Chancery. They sought to enjoin enforcement of provisions in the state constitution and statutory code that required the segregation of Negroes and whites in public schools. The Chancellor gave judgment for the plaintiffs and ordered their immediate admission to schools previously attended only by white children. The Delaware Supreme Court affirmed his decision. The defendants and the school board appealed to the Supreme Court to prevent desegregation.[59]

After the first oral argument, in 1952, the Court ordered further briefs on the questions of what the framers of the Fourteenth Amendment intended for public schools and what remedies were possible considering the numbers of students, jurisdictions, and local conditions involved. Before reargument took place, Vinson died on September 9, 1953. Eisenhower's nominee to replace him in the center chair would have the challenge and the opportunity to resolve the matter, and new chief justice Earl Warren would play a decisive role in that resolution. Warren was born in Los Angeles in 1891, grew up in Bakerfield, and earned his college and law degrees at the University of California, Berkeley. He served in the army during the First World War and plunged into Republican politics in Oakland after the war. His rise from county district attorney to attorney general to three-time governor of the state was meteoric. He was a vigorous advocate of Japanese relocation during the war, a stance he later "deeply regretted" and apologized for. After throwing his support to Eisenhower at the 1952 presidential convention, he was promised the next seat on the Supreme Court. That turned out to be the center chair, and for his leadership of the Court from 1953 to 1969 he has been called "Super Chief."[60]

In many ways, the first decision of note in the Warren Court, *Brown v. Board of Education* (1954), showed both the promise and the limitations of the judiciary in American life. A court can declare the law and decide a case, but social engineering on a broad scale may be beyond the ability of even the most determined tribunal. Warren understood this, and he deserves much of the credit for fashioning the approach to *Brown* and its many progeny, as well as some criticism for how the Court handled one of the most controversial cases in its history.[61]

As Justice Oliver Wendell Holmes Jr. noted, hard cases make bad law. No case could have been harder than undoing at a stroke what nearly one hundred years of segregation had done in public education. The system of separate schools was rooted in the fiscal, social, and psychological life of much of the South (and some parts of the North). Justice Frankfurter's fear that courts were inadequate to deal with these kinds of problems had much truth. Courts would play a vital role in the end of segregation, but there were obstacles that the best intentioned of courts could not, by themselves, overcome.[62]

At first, Black, Douglas, Burton, and Minton favored destroying *Plessy* outright; Vinson and Reed were reluctant to dismiss such an important precedent. Frankfurter and Jackson pleaded for special arrangements so the Court could properly address what was a deeply divisive local matter. Consistent with their concern about the local passions invested in segregation, the justices (led by Frankfurter) consolidated the cases but made the lead case the Kansas suit. Thus they took the southern edge off the question.[63]

After more than a little one-on-one lobbying of his brethren by Warren, the opinion of the Court was unanimous, and Warren wrote it. From its emphasis on the importance of public schooling to American life, to the plain language that took its reasoning from one point to the next, to the forward-thinking rejection of segregation as a moral wrong, the California progressive shone through. It was a short opinion—barely ten pages—that Warren read from the bench. He reported that the historical foray into the Reconstruction congressional records could not guide the Court because that record was inconclusive. History did show that "[i]n the first cases in this Court construing the Fourteenth Amendment, decided shortly after its adoption, the Court interpreted it as proscribing all state-imposed discriminations against the Negro race." "Separate but equal" was a later retreat from the goals of Reconstruction in general and the Fourteenth Amendment in particular.[64]

Warren and his Court read the Fourteenth Amendment simply. "What is this but declaring that the law in the States shall be the same for the black as for the white; that all persons, whether colored or white, shall stand equal before the laws of the States, and, in regard to the colored race, for whose protection the amendment was primarily designed, that no discrimination shall be made against them by law because of their color?" While this reading might be viewed

Figure 11.1 Desegregation plaintiffs' attorneys shaking hands on the steps of the Supreme Court after the *Brown* decision came down. Left to right: George E. C. Haynes, Thurgood Marshall, and James M. Nabrit, Jr. Credit: Library of Congress.

as the continuation of the higher education line of cases, Warren went far beyond those precedents. He read the Fourteenth Amendment in light of the Thirteenth Amendment, following the steps that the Reconstruction Congress itself had taken to find "[t]he right to exemption from unfriendly legislation against them distinctively as colored—exemption from legal discriminations, implying inferiority in civil society, lessening the security of their enjoyment of the rights which others enjoy, and discriminations which are steps towards reducing them to the condition of a subject race."[65]

Warren opined that education was the key to success in American society:

> It is doubtful that any child may reasonably be expected to succeed in life if he is denied the opportunity of an education. Such an opportunity, where the state has undertaken to provide it, is a right which must be made available to all on equal terms.

He then asked:

> [D]oes segregation of children in public schools solely on the basis of race, even though the physical facilities and other "tangible" factors may be equal, deprive the children of the minority group of equal educational opportunities? We believe that it does . . . To separate them from others of similar age and qualifications solely because of their race generates a feeling of inferiority as to their status in the community that may affect their hearts and minds in a way unlikely ever to be undone.[66]

Segregated education indelibly stigmatized black school children. In 1954, common sense revealed what in 1896 prejudice had denied: the negative impact on the education of black students, particularly in the lower grades, seemed obvious to Warren. Warren and the Court concluded that "in the field of public education the doctrine of 'separate but equal' has no place. Separate educational facilities are inherently unequal. Therefore, we hold that the plaintiffs and others similarly situated for whom the actions have been brought are, by reason of the segregation complained of, deprived of the equal protection of the laws guaranteed by the Fourteenth Amendment."[67]

The fifth case did not come from the states. It came from the District of Columbia. In *Bolling v. Sharpe* the Fourteenth Amendment would not apply (the District is not a state), but the Due Process Clause of the Fifth Amendment might afford black petitioners a basis for ending segregation in the district. The District Court for the District of Columbia had dismissed the petition. *Bolling* was decided the same day as *Brown* in a separate decision but with the same reasoning. John Marshall Harlan's voice in the *Civil Rights Cases* and *Plessy* had not been lost after all, despite the cacophony of racism that drowned him out at the time.[68]

In what would become something of a millstone around the otherwise simple and powerful language of *Brown*, at Warren's request, his clerk Earl Pollock added a footnote (number 11) to the written opinion. The footnote cited studies of the psychological impact of segregation on young people. The LDF had either commissioned the studies or introduced them in the arguments, so the note was one-sided. The studies cited included "K. B. Clark, Effect of Prejudice and Discrimination on Personality Development (Midcentury White House Conference on Children and Youth, 1950)," the famous white and black dolls study showing that black children thought white dolls were "good dolls" and black dolls were not. Later critics of the Court's supposed reliance on "sociological jurisprudence" and of the methodology of the doll study (no controls, no repetition) have misunderstood or exaggerated the importance of the evidence and note 11. The note and the studies were not crucial to Warren's thinking. He did not need to know what black children thought about dolls to know that forced separation was a stigma in itself.[69]

Warren's opinion did not explicitly overrule *Plessy*, a fact that had great significance. He said that the rule in *Plessy* did not apply to public education. *Plessy* was not concerned with education, though it would become the precedent on which segregation of schools was based. Instead, it concerned transportation. To overrule *Plessy* would have been tantamount to saying that all state segregation was unconstitutional. The Court would follow this path in the years to come, but at the time, it was more cautious.[70]

The justices worried about enforcement of their decision from the first moment that lawyers argued the five cases under Chief Justice Vinson and again when Warren replaced him. Frankfurter worried that Minton and Reed might not be enthusiastic about the Court sweeping aside what southern legislatures and local school boards had fashioned over so many years. Warren was in favor of ending segregation, had no hesitation about the Court so ordering, but like Frankfurter and Jackson understood that enforcement was the real problem for consensus on the Court. Justice Reed, who was born and raised in Kentucky and had practiced law there before joining the New Deal, was hesitant as well. According to one of Reed's law clerks at the time, Warren persuaded Reed to sign on by appealing to his patriotism and warning that he would be isolated from the rest of the Court if he dissented.[71]

Warren had his unanimous Court, but he needed to pay a substantial price for that consensus: the opinion would only rule on segregation in education and, more important, a separate implementation decision, *Brown* II, would wait upon testimony from the attorney generals of the states. Hopefully, this would give the southern legislatures time to accommodate to the new order. Because

Figure 11.2 The Supreme Court, 1954. Left to right. Seated: Felix Frankfurter, Hugo Black, Earl Warren, Stanley Reed, William O. Douglas. Standing: Tom Clark, Robert H. Jackson, Harold Burton, and Sherman Minton. Credit: Collection of the Supreme Court of the United States.

of the "considerable complexity" involved in desegregating tens of thousands of schoolchildren in thousands of school buildings in multiple jurisdictions specifically arranged to segregate, Warren's opinion invited reargument on implementation not only to the parties to the class action but also to the U.S. attorney general and to the attorneys general of the states involved. Intended to avert the risks of disobeying the ruling and disrespecting the Supreme Court, the delay would do the exact opposite. But no judge has a crystal ball underneath his or her robes.[72]

In times of uncertainty and unrest, the judgments of contemporaries are rarely the same as the judgments that history later imposes. This is certainly true of the federal courts in this period. The federal courts have a store of public confidence, something akin to deposits in a bank account, to which they deposit and on which they can draw. Contemporaries, with some notable exceptions, regarded the civil rights decisions as risky withdrawals from that store of goodwill. Perhaps such matters better belonged to the elected branches of the federal government or to the states. In finding that a large portion of the country's long habits of discrimination violated the federal Constitution, and in the process overturning sixty years of precedents, the Supreme Court withdrew a sizable sum from that bank account. For this act, history has judged the Court's stance a proper readjustment of both federalism and checks and balances. At the same time, the federal courts' involvement in the second Red Scare, generally approved at the time, was later seen as an unnecessary deference to a panicky public and a super-patriotic Congress.

From both perspectives, the work of the federal courts seemed incomplete. How would the civil rights initiative fare in the hands of the lower federal courts after *Brown* II? Would a robust attachment to the First Amendment mark the next round of free speech cases? Would caseloads, swelled by these developments, as well as appeals of administrative agency rulings, severely test the capacity of the federal courts?

12

Federal Courts in the Civil Rights Era, 1955–1969

In the years from 1955 to 1969, a flood of civil rights cases washed up on the steps of federal courthouses. The relief promised in *Brown* II required the good faith efforts of public school boards and local and state officials. Federal judges had an array of equitable powers to ensure compliance. The transition to a unitary school system could have gone relatively smoothly. The goal was clear. But the spirit of many localities, led by prosegregation politicians, was unwilling. Long years of litigation lay ahead for desegregation forces.[1]

Civil rights suits were a relatively small portion of the federal courts' business in these years. The number of civil rights suits increased significantly after the passage of the Civil Rights Act of 1964, from 709 filings in that year to 1,123 cases in 1965. Even as the civil rights docket grew, civil rights related cases as a percentage of the caseload remained small. It was not the number of cases, then, that made civil rights adjudication so important in the history of the federal courts, but the way in which these cases raised basic questions of politics, separation of powers, and federalism.[2]

Civil Rights and Remedies

Not since the slavery controversy had a constitutional question so thrust the federal courts into the maelstrom of national politics as *Brown v. Board of Education*. No imposition on the time, energy, prudence, and activity of the federal judiciary matched the long effort to implement *Brown*. Civil rights' remedies elevated the federal courts to a central place in American domestic policymaking, exposing the judges to considerable backlash from parties before the courts and from those in the polity who not only opposed a judicial solution to segregation but also the end of desegregation itself.[3]

The immediate response to *Brown*, however, seemed acceptance of the new order. Governors in Alabama and Arkansas promised compliance. Jim Folsom of Alabama conceded, "when the Supreme Court speaks, that's the law." In some of the border states of the South, notably Kentucky and Maryland, desegregation faced protests but moved apace. In other states like Delaware, however, protests closed the schools, and local and state officials began a campaign of foot dragging. The argument of the foot-draggers was that white parents were not ready to have their children sit next to black youngsters, and that if such an event were mandated, violence would ensue. It was the heckler's veto argument, and in the months after *Brown*, it gained momentum. "Citizens councils" organized to prevent desegregation, and politicians in the former Confederate states, calculating where the votes were, began to backpedal as well.[4]

Fervent opponents of desegregation warned of a race war. The Jackson, Mississippi, *Daily News* ominously predicted: "Human blood may stain Southern soil in many places because of this decision . . . white and negro children in the same schools will lead to miscegenation . . . and mongrelization of the human race." Southern congressmen and politicians joined in a "Declaration of Constitutional Principles" on March, 12, 1956, that announced a well-organized, state-government-sponsored massive resistance to the decision. The Declaration accused the Court of a "clear abuse of judicial power" that would undo the "habits, customs, traditions and way of life" of southerners "founded on elemental humanity and commonsense." It would create chaos and confusion, "destroying the amicable relations between the white and Negro people of both races." Desegregation would plant "hatred and suspicion where there has been heretofore friendship and understanding." Nearly every former Confederate state's member of Congress except for the delegations from Tennessee and Texas believed that massive resistance would force the Court to back down or change course. Only Senators Estes Kefauver and Albert Gore of Tennessee and Lyndon Johnson of Texas refused to sign, along with twenty-eight members of the Tennessee and Texas House delegations, including Speaker of the House Sam Rayburn of Texas.[5]

While on the one hand President Eisenhower never came out in favor of *Brown*, his attorney general, Herbert Brownell, openly favored the end of segregation. He sent Simon Sobeloff, the solicitor general of the United States, to present this position to the Court. Sobeloff put the weight of the executive branch of the federal government behind desegregation. On the other hand, Eisenhower's opponent in the 1956 presidential campaign, Adlai E. Stevenson, urged gradualism. He needed and hoped for Democratic votes in the South and could not afford to offend its segregationists. Most northern liberals agreed that southern blacks must exercise patience, advice that slowed the legal battle for equal protection.[6]

Brown II (1955), the implementation decision, with its call for individual suits and "all due deliberate speed," was not what the LDF team wanted. Warren opined in *Brown* that "[b]ecause these cases arose under different local conditions and their disposition will involve a variety of local problems, we requested further argument on the question of relief." After hearing from the attorneys general of the southern states, the Warren Court determined that "[f]ull implementation of these constitutional principles may require solution of varied local school problems." The simple fact was that local compliance rested on local school officials. They were best placed for "elucidating, assessing, and solving these problems." In this planned remedy, courts became a last resort for the parties rather than the formulator of the plans. "Courts will have to consider whether the action of school authorities constitutes good faith implementation of the governing constitutional principles." While this structure of settlement was the traditional role for courts sitting in equity, in these cases it left the lower court judges playing deep safety in a prevent defense. In his *Memoirs*, Warren would write that "the federal courts made meaningful many spin offs from [*Brown*] and with minor exceptions those courts met every test in following the Supreme Court" in the desegregation cases—a very generous view.[7]

The jurisprudence of equity requires good faith by the parties. That might be presumed but was hardly true of most of the local school boards, much less of the state governments in the South. District judges in the South were white southerners who had grown up with segregation. Some would press hard for the end of segregation. Others dragged their feet. School board members and state officials who did not obey desegregation orders could be held in contempt of court, but what federal judge was going to send an entire school board to jail? Knowing this, and determined not to follow the Supreme Court's lead, local and state school boards delayed, denied, and disobeyed *Brown* II with ill-concealed dodges like pupil placement and step-by-step (school year by school year) plans, all of which would take more time for the local board to study.

The story is not one of a centrally directed monolithic judiciary. In the implementation of *Brown* one finds little evidence of the organizational synthesis of earlier iterations of institutional reform. Instead, the very language of *Brown* II reinvigorated and empowered regional variation. The failure to nationalize desegregation was proof that this fiercely local aspect of federalism was still potent.

In a number of cases, federal judges approved local plans featuring delays in their implementation. Sometimes the delays camouflaged the local board's intention to resist desegregation. In 1957, the Dade County (Miami) School Board had no desire to desegregate its schools. According to Judge Joseph Patrick Lieb, "It is deemed by the Board that the best interest of the pupils and the orderly and efficient administration of the school system can best be preserved if the registration and attendance of pupils entering school commencing the current school term remains unchanged . . . until further notice the free public school system of Dade County will continue to be operated, maintained and conducted on a nonintegrated basis." Black parents brought a suit. The judge found no grounds in the suit for his court to order the school board to act. The Court of Appeals for the Fifth Circuit reversed and remanded. The state came up with a complicated pupil-placement plan that required individual parents to petition the board for placement of their student in a particular school. Individual school boards then delayed ruling on the petitions. The parents again turned to the district court, and Judge Lieb found the pupil-placement plans were an adequate remedy. "The Court finds that the Florida Pupil Assignment Law enacted by the Legislature of Florida since the filing of this suit meets the requirements of such a plan and the demands of the plaintiffs . . . No reference whatever is made in the Act to consideration of race or color of the pupils." Again the Fifth Circuit reversed and remanded.[8]

Judge Lieb was born in Minnesota, served for many years as an FBI agent, and moved to southern Florida and a private practice in Tampa. Eisenhower chose him for the district court in 1955. Lieb's reasoning in denying petitioners' pleas in both Dade County cases was rooted in the narrowest of readings of the command "all deliberate speed" in Brown II as well as deference to state laws clearly intended to delay or deny desegregation. He was not deterred when the Fifth Circuit overturned his decisions in increasingly stentorian language. In 1962, he was redeployed to the newly created Middle District of Florida, and there, with the Kennedy administration Department of Justice and the Court of Appeals watching over his shoulder, he ordered integration of the schools notwithstanding the Florida pupil-placement laws.[9]

The step-by-step plans many Deep South school boards adopted to delay actual desegregation passed muster in more than Lieb's court. In one Georgia case, Judge Frank A. Hooper not only allowed the Atlanta school board an additional two years to put a twelve-year plan in place, he told the LDF attorney for the petitioners, Constance Baker Motley, that he put as much stress on the "deliberate" as on the "speed" in Brown II. In the Southern District of the state, Judge Francis Muir Scarlet determined that a pupil-placement plan that used intelligence tests to resegregate schools did not violate Brown, as its purpose was not to separate students by race. The school board was then allowed additional time to collect the data to implement its plan.[10]

The Louisiana Parish school boards were also recalcitrant, and efforts by the Fifth Circuit to mandate effective desegregation ran into opposition not only from the local officials but also from one of the district judges. In Hall v. West (1964), Fifth Circuit Court of Appeals Judge John Minor Wisdom admonished the lower court judge, Elmer Gordon West, for the "startling, if not shocking, lack of appreciation of the clear pronouncements of the Supreme Court and this Court during the past year which make it perfectly plain that time has run out for a district court to temporize for the purpose of making accommodations." Judge West, a Louisiana State University–educated lawyer and Baton Rouge practitioner selected by Kennedy in 1961, thought it a matter of personal honor to respond. "However, in this most unusual case, since the opinion rendered by the Court of Appeals is so injudiciously couched in personal terms, and is so written as to directly, and by clear implication accuse me, personally, of refusing to accept my responsibilities as a Judge of this Court, of wasting precious judicial time, of acting in an 'unusual' and 'shocking' manner, and even intimating that I have, in some way, acted unethically in the handling of this case, I would be a poor judge indeed, and less than a man, if I were to let such an obvious attack on my personal integrity go unnoticed." Judge West's response sounded much like the antebellum southern honor code, in which a gentleman publically insulted was required to challenge his opponent to a duel, unless an apology was forthcoming. None was in this case. Judge West, however, finally ordered the school board to bring in a plan.[11]

By contrast, some district judges in the Fifth Circuit interpreted *Brown* II in the fullest sense of *Brown* I, and pressed school boards for desegregation forthwith. Among these, J. Skelly Wright of the Eastern District of Louisiana, including the City of New Orleans, led the way. New Orleans, with its diverse population of African Americans, Creoles, Italians, Irish, and other ethnically proud groups, was always different from the rest of the Deep South. Wright grew up in the city and attended both Loyola College and Loyola University College of Law. The natural rights philosophy of the Jesuits made its mark on him, as did teaching American history in high school. And when he was named to the district court bench, in 1949, he already had a strong moral sense that segregation was wrong. In 1951, he ordered desegregation at LSU, and after *Brown* he pushed for the end of segregated schools in New Orleans. The city, disregarding *Brown*, put up all manner of objections to the suit. Wright knocked them down one after another: "In their first preliminary defense, the defendants say that this action is in effect a suit against the State of Louisiana, which has not consented to be sued, and therefore, this court is without jurisdiction. But a suit against officers or agents of a state acting illegally is not a suit against the state." The city's counsel found an error in the pleading. Wright refused to dismiss on that ground. "The objection . . . even if well taken, would not result in a dismissal of the action, but only in the giving to the plaintiffs time to amend." A third, equally feeble objection followed: "Defendants also move to dismiss on the ground that no justiciable controversy is presented by the pleadings. This motion is without merit . . . The defendants admit that they are maintaining segregation in the public schools . . . If this issue does not present a justiciable controversy, it is

Figure 12.1 Fifth Circuit Court of Appeals Judge John Minor Wisdom, a civil rights stalwart, 1977. Credit: Photo by H. J. Patterson. Courtesy of the New Orleans *Times-Picayune*/Landov Media.

difficult to conceive of one." Last but not least, the city argued that the black parents had not exhausted their administrative remedies. Wright had heard that one already: "As a practical matter, plaintiffs here have exhausted their administrative remedies. They have petitioned the Board on three separate occasions asking that their children be assigned to nonsegregated schools. The Board not only has refused to desegregate the schools, but has passed a resolution noting the existence of the present suit." He would brook no nonsense, and his opinion was devoid of arcane nuance. Do it, he ordered. His efforts brought him and his family social ostracism and death threats. In 1962, President Kennedy named Wright to the D.C. Court of Appeals bench, removing him from the front lines in Louisiana. Wright died in 1988, honored by his peers and his many clerks.[12]

Judge Frank Johnson Jr. of the Middle District of Alabama may have owed his appointment to patrons in the Republican Department of Justice and friends in the old line Democratic organization, but from the moment of his appointment in 1955, he showed a streak of pragmatic activism, coupled with a sure sense of social justice, in fashioning his desegregation decrees. Early in life he developed a sense of the casual injustice with which the white establishment treated black citizens. In law school in Tuscaloosa, his lodestar was Justice Harlan's dissent in *Plessy*. In case after case coming from Birmingham and Montgomery city schools, Johnson developed a style of creative and expeditious injunctive relief that would mark much of the later district court management of desegregation. He would retain hands-on supervision, making it easier for all parties, even those who dragged their feet, to know what they had to do. He faced the same harassment and threats of violence as other southern judges who confronted segregation, and with every threat, every disingenuous plea for more time, his conviction that the time had come for an end to the injustice grew stronger.[13]

Whether chiding or aiding the district courts' judges, the Fifth Circuit Court of Appeals bore the brunt of the civil rights legal campaign, its judges were crying out, when, oh when, shall the task be done? A leader emerged among them— "General" Elbert Tuttle. Alongside Judge Wisdom and Judge Richard Taylor Rives (the only Democrat among the three), Tuttle demanded compliance, but it was not merely a respect for the rule of recognition that motivated him. Born in California, educated in Hawa'i and New York, Tuttle was a newspaper reporter, a World War II combat veteran (at the age of forty-eight reaching the rank of brigadier general), and one of Attorney General Brownell's liberal Republican cadre of lawyers when President Eisenhower tapped him for the Fifth Circuit in 1954. Tuttle made no bones about his opposition to segregation when *Brown* was decided. Indeed, he optimistically assumed that the decision's opponents would "fall in line." He had hoped for a "forthwith" order from the Supreme Court in 1954 and was disappointed that the Court allowed delay in compliance. Tuttle's distinguished service on the Fifth and then the new Eleventh Circuit continued until his death in 1996, a mere ninety-nine years old.[14]

If one case best depicted Tuttle's approach to the law, it would be his response to the challenge segregationists made to the Civil Rights Act of 1964. Some of the provisions of the Act concerning public accommodations appeared to resemble the same provisions of the Civil Rights Act of 1875 struck down by the Supreme Court in the *Civil Rights Cases* (1883). Here, the challenger was the Heart of Atlanta Motel. When the motel owner's counsel sought injunctive relief against the imposition of the statute, Tuttle wrote for the three-judge district court: "Title II declares the right of every person to full and equal enjoyment of the goods, services and facilities of any hotel or motel which provides lodging to transient guests if it contains more than five rooms for rent or hire." The motel was one of the largest in the state capital, often hosted out-of-state guests, and so was fully in the stream of interstate commerce. The commerce clause of Article I thus applied, allowing Congress to require the motel to house all guests in a nondiscriminatory manner. Tuttle concluded: "Heart of Atlanta Motel, Inc . . .

together with all persons in active concert or participation with them, are hereby enjoined from . . . Refusing to accept Negroes as guests in the motel by reason of their race or color." The general had spoken—an order in plain terms and easily understood.[15]

Throughout the 1960s the federal courts chipped away at the massive resistance of the segregationist Deep South. But its lower federal court judges did not always press for good faith compliance with *Brown* II. Open defiance to the court of appeals in their circuit or the Supreme Court is rare for district judges, but it did happen. The vast majority of district judges came from the region in which they sat, shared its values, and valued its customs. It was genuinely hard for them to knock down the well-mortised wall of segregation. If they did, they faced ostracism from their social set and threats of violence from segregationist vigilantes.[16]

For all of these reasons, the effort to end Jim Crow through court action was hard going. Mississippi, for example, presented the federal courts with twenty-nine individual cases at the end of 1968, in each of them local and state officials respectfully asking for more time. The same problems occurred in the Fourth Circuit, where Virginian massive resistance delayed compliance. In a few school districts, for example Richmond, compliance came early. There school board chair Lewis F. Powell Jr. insisted that the public schools stay open and desegregation begin. The result was "token" integration based on residential segregation because dropping legal barriers to desegregation left residentially segregated school districts in place. Still, in vain Powell tried to convince U.S. Senator Harry Byrd to shift his vehement opposition to all desegregation. Powell's stand may have influenced Governor James Lindsay Almond's decision to reopen the public schools in the rest of the state and assay gradual accommodation to the Court's orders, however. Almond told Senator Byrd that as governor he could not and would not defy federal law. Almond did not advocate wholesale desegregation, however. When the Supreme Court finally dropped the "all deliberate speed" formula in *Green v. County School Board of New Kent County, Virginia* (1968), courts of appeal told district judges that all deliberate speed was no longer acceptable. One grade at a time was no longer acceptable. Genuine integration began.[17]

The end of "all deliberate speed" accelerated desegregationists' turn to the courts. By 1970, the Court of Appeals for the Fifth Circuit, stretching from Miami to El Paso, had become the busiest in the nation, with civil rights and voting rights cases leading the way. Appeals had increased twelvefold from 1960 to 1964 and doubled again by 1970. According to the Administrative Office director's annual report, the Fifth Circuit had 2,014 filings, leading the next circuit, the Second, by nearly 700 filings. The Fifth had fifteen appeals court judgeships, leading the Ninth Circuit, the next highest, by two judges. After Congress increased its judgeships to twenty-six in 1978, the difficulty of operating an appellate court that size led its judges to petition Congress to split the circuit in two, thus creating a new Eleventh Circuit, consisting of Alabama, Georgia, and Florida, with a new court of appeals. Congress complied in 1980. The New Fifth Circuit comprised the districts of Mississippi, Louisiana, and Texas.[18]

The Fourth and Fifth Circuits were not the only ones to with nationally noticed desegregation cases. The city of Little Rock, Arkansas, sat at the southern end of the Eighth Circuit. Following *Brown* II, Fayetteville, the seat of University of Arkansas's central campus, desegregated its schools. It seemed that Arkansas was ready to desegregate quietly. Judge John Miller approved a plan for the city of Little Rock that featured phased desegregation from the high school down to the first year of elementary school. The Eighth Circuit Court of Appeals heard the plan and agreed. But the state courts intervened, barring the plan, and local resistance, spurred by Governor Orval Faubus, led to violence. The Eastern District of Arkansas was short of judges, and the chief judge of the circuit, Archibald K. Gardner, following the course laid out in the Judiciary Act of 1922, designated Ronald Davies, of the District of North Dakota, to temporary service in the district. "I didn't even know what case I would get when I was ordered to go down there," he recalled in 1987. The desegregation case fell to him. He decreed that the state courts had no jurisdiction in the matter and ordered the school board to implement its plan forthwith. Violence outside the high school and inside its classrooms did not deter nine black students from entering the school, in part because President Eisenhower sent soldiers of the 101st Airborne Division to patrol inside and outside Central High School. The Court of Appeals backed Davies.[19]

With Davies returning to North Dakota, the school board, citing the violence, then petitioned District Judge Harry J. Lemley, the next federal judge to preside over implementation of the plan, to delay implementation for three years, and he acceded to their request. Lemley had "roots in the south" according to the local newspaper, and after holding hearings in the summer of 1958, determined that "the pattern of Southern life" embedded in separation of the races needed more time to change. The Court of Appeals refused to back down. Newly seated Court of Appeals Judge Marion Matthes wrote for a divided panel: "a plan of integration, once in operation . . . suspended because of popular opposition thereto, as manifested in overt acts of violence . . . the fires, destruction of private and public property, physical abuse, bomb threats, intimidation of school officials, open defiance of the police department of the City of Little Rock by mobs," was a perfect example of the heckler's veto, and it could not defeat a legal commitment to genuine desegregation. Chief Judge Gardner dissented. He had been sitting on the Court of Appeals since 1929 and was familiar with state- and local-mandated segregation of schools. "Having in mind that the school officials and the teaching

Figure 12.2 Federal troops escorting four black students to Little Rock Central High School to protect them from protesters, 1957. Credit: Library of Congress.

staff acted in good faith and that the school officials presented their petition for an extension of time in good faith" a delay should be granted. A "cooling off" period would allow the school board to implement the plan in good order, he judged. He did not address the possibility that if violence could derail a plan in 1958, a resumption of violence could derail it at any time thereafter.[20]

A unanimous Supreme Court upheld Matthes's ruling in *Cooper v. Aaron* (1958). When the board decided to close the school, Judge Miller, once more managing the case, heard petitioners seeking an injunction to keep the schools open, and he found the law closing the schools unconstitutional. He ordered them reopened. Other Arkansas cities reluctantly, even grudgingly, opened their public school doors to all their children.[21]

While school boards and federal judges were jousting, civil rights advocates were making advances on other fronts, though none came easily. On December 1, 1955, Rosa Parks refused to leave the "whites only" section of a city bus in Montgomery, Alabama. Her arrest for violating the city ordinance became the starting point for a remarkable movement in American history. The NAACP had been looking for another test case to challenge state-required segregation, and the respectable secretary fit the bill. Soon, local civil rights activists organized a bus boycott with the support of neighborhood black churches including one led by Dr. Martin Luther King Jr. The eloquent, spiritual Atlanta-bred King modeled the movement he was soon to lead on that of Mohandas K. Gandhi, whose nonviolent resistance policies helped gain India independence from Britain.

Founded in 1957, King's Southern Christian Leadership Conference (SCLC) joined the Congress for Racial Equality (CORE) and the NAACP in organizing against the white supremacist South.[22]

The end of the bus boycott came when a federal court ruled that segregation on the buses violated the equal protection clause of the federal Constitution. In *Browder v. Gayle* (1956), a case that tested *Plessy* directly, Court of Appeals Judge Richard T. Rives, writing for himself and Judge Frank Johnson on the three-judge court, found that all the plaintiffs had standing to bring the suit and that they satisfied the Federal Rules criteria for a class action. Bus drivers for the city had ordered them to the back of buses. The city had claimed it merely followed Alabama law. That law conferred on the bus drivers the authority to segregate the seating. The court brushed away the argument that state court remedies should be sought and only when denied should the case be heard in federal tribunal. If the grounds for the suit lay in federal law or the U.S. Constitution, there was no need for plaintiffs to exhaust state remedies. Segregation in public facilities may have had the sanction of custom, but "there is, however, a difference, a constitutional difference, between voluntary adherence to custom and the perpetuation and enforcement of that custom by law." Judge Rives had struck at the heart of Justice Brown's justification for separate but equal seating assignments in Louisiana's Separate Car Act. Citing an array of cases from the 1940s and 1950s, the court found that *Plessy* no longer applied. "We cannot in good conscience perform our duty as judges by blindly following the precedent of *Plessy*" when "under the later decisions, there is now no rational basis upon which the separate but equal doctrine can be validly applied to public carrier transportation within the City of Montgomery and its police jurisdiction."[23]

Rives was born and would die in Montgomery. He read law and practiced law there up to his confirmation to a seat on the Fifth Circuit Court of Appeals in 1951. Courtly, respected, he "never lost sight of his roots" in rural Alabama. He knew what customs prevailed there, but his duty as a judge and his sense of fairness dictated that separate but equal had no place in public accommodations.[24]

District Judge Seybourn Harris Lynne dissented. He had joined the Northern District bench in 1946 after service on county and state circuit courts. Like Rives, his attachment to soil and the customs of Alabama ran deep. His grandfather had served in the army of the Confederate States of America, then started a law firm, in which Lynne's father and he practiced. Having taken part in the state courts' refusal to provide the kinds of remedies that plaintiffs sought in *Browder*, he offered a segregationist reading of *Brown*: "It seems to me that the Supreme Court therein recognized that there still remains an area within our constitutional scheme of state and federal governments wherein that doctrine [of separate but equal] may be applied even though its applications are always constitutionally suspect." Given his reading of Chief Justice Warren's recent refusal to overturn

Plessy outright, Lynne worried that "a comparatively new principle of pernicious implications has found its way into our jurisprudence. Lower courts may
feel free to disregard the precise precedent of a Supreme Court opinion if they
perceive a 'pronounced new doctrinal trend' in its later decisions." A significant
passage of time, not recent jurisprudential fashions, should convince trial court
judges to abandon long-held opinions about the law and race relations. "I would
dismiss the action on the authority of *Plessy v. Ferguson.*" Seven years later, Lynne
ordered Alabama Governor George C. Wallace to admit the African-American
students that he refused to allow entrance to the state university. "I love the people of Alabama," he said, but he insisted that the law of the land came first. "I
know many of both races are troubled and like Jonah of old, are 'angry even unto
death,'" he wrote. "My prayer is that all of our people, in keeping with our finest
tradition, will join in the resolution that law and order will be maintained."[25]

In the meantime, King's inspirational message spread to college campuses.
In Greensboro, North Carolina, on February 1, 1960, four freshmen from the
North Carolina Agricultural and Technical State University initiated a sit-in at
a Woolworth's lunch counter reserved for whites. In subsequent days they were
joined by others including students from a local women's college. White suprem-
acists brandishing Confederate flags attacked them, drawing international media
attention to the protest. As the practice spread to other cities throughout the
South, so did the confrontations and the boycott of those establishments that
refused to serve African Americans. In April of that year, African-American
students from across the South meeting in Raleigh, North Carolina, followed
the advice of experienced civil rights activist Ella Baker and formed their own
organization independent of SCLC, CORE, and the NAACP—the Student
Non-violent Coordinating Committee (SNCC). Although some lunch counters
continued to segregate well into 1965, despite the Civil Rights Act of 1964, the
Greensboro Woolworth lunch counter relented on July 25, 1960.[26]

Unwilling for the slow process of litigation in federal courts to work its way
through segregationists' intransigence, or, more likely, to gain national attention
for the Civil Rights Movement, in the spring of 1961, SNCC members participated in a CORE-planned challenge to the still-segregated interstate buses.
Called the freedom rides, the two buses' riders met violent attacks by Ku Klux
Klan members and their sympathizers in local law enforcement. At first, federal
judges in Mississippi, on the Fifth Circuit, and the Supreme Court were reluctant to provide habeas corpus relief to the freedom riders, jailed by local police,
until the petitioners had exhausted their appeals to the state courts (according to
the rule applied to convicts in state prisons). Judge Sidney Mize of the Southern
District of Mississippi decided instead to order a moratorium on freedom rides,
although the constitutionality of such an order restricting interstate commerce
was arguable. Judge Mize was born in Mississippi, educated in Mississippi, and

practiced in Gulfport, Mississippi, before President Roosevelt appointed him to the Southern District of Mississippi bench. A per curiam decision from the U.S. Supreme Court and an order from the attorney general integrated the buses officially, but the violent confrontation over integration in the South would continue throughout the 1960s.[27]

Shortly thereafter, Judge Mize denied James Meredith's request for an order admitting him to the University of Mississippi. Meredith was fully qualified, but Mize ruled that "[t]he management and control of the University of Mississippi and all other state institutions of higher learning in the State of Mississippi is vested in the Board [of Regents]." Apparently federal law stopped at the Mississippi state line. The admissions officer who refused to allow Meredith to register testified that, in his opinion, Meredith was not a citizen of the state. Mize agreed:

> The overwhelming weight of the testimony is that the plaintiff was not denied admission because of his color or race. The Registrar swore emphatically and unequivocably [sic] that the race of plaintiff or his color had nothing in the world to do with the action of the Registrar in denying his application. An examination of the entire testimony of the Registrar shows conclusively that he gave no consideration whatsoever to the race or the color of the plaintiff when he denied the application for admission and the Registrar is corroborated by other circumstances and witnesses in the case to this effect.[28]

The Fifth Circuit overturned Mize with the somewhat exasperated comment that the judge should know what everyone else knew. "A full review of the record leads the Court inescapably to the conclusion that from the moment the defendants discovered Meredith was a Negro they engaged in a carefully calculated campaign of delay, harassment, and masterly inactivity."[29]

Diversifying the Bench

One parallel to the resistance to desegregation of schools and public facilities was the agonizingly slow desegregation of the federal bench. President Eisenhower made no African-American nominations for the federal bench. In fact, at least one of his nominees to the Fifth Circuit Court of Appeals, in 1955, Benjamin F. Cameron of Mississippi, was an avowed segregationist, and another, G. Harrold Carswell, tapped in 1958 for the Northern District of Florida, had made inflammatory racist remarks during a campaign for a congressional seat from Georgia ten years earlier. Other potential nominees, like Solicitor General

Sobeloff, whose role in promoting desegregation was well known, were blocked for a time by southern senators. Sobeloff would earn a place on the Court of Appeals for the Fourth Circuit in 1956, his credentials among the Maryland members of the bar (he was chief judge of Maryland's highest court, the Court of Appeals, from 1952 to 1954) and his service as U.S. solicitor general (from 1954 to 1956) outweighing any animus among southern senators for his support for civil rights. On the Court of Appeals for the Fourth Circuit he played a vital and positive role in assuring the root and branch dismantling of school segregation, reversing the course that Chief Judge Parker had piloted for the circuit. But the bottom line was that none of these nominees was African American.[30]

Unlike his predecessors, save Truman, President John F. Kennedy named African Americans to highly visible judicial posts. His appointees, James Parsons, Wade McCree Jr., and Thurgood Marshall, were all well-known in civil rights circles, although political payback played a major role along with the aim of diversifying the bench. The president was aware of the importance of the African American vote in northern cities, and his choices can be seen in that light.[31]

All three African American choices were highly qualified. Parsons was an assistant U.S. attorney for the Northern District of Illinois when President Kennedy toured Chicago with him. Kennedy kept a promise to the Chicago Democratic machine and Parsons was nominated to the Northern District of Illinois and confirmed in the first year of the new administration. When Parsons joined the bench, its judges had courtesy memberships in the Union League Club, an elite cultural and social organization. When the board of the club denied Parsons membership, all his colleagues resigned theirs and with him joined the rival Standard Club.[32]

With Chicagoland gaining a federal judge of color, political pressure from Detroit grew for McCree. He was serving as a judge in a Michigan circuit court, in Detroit, when Kennedy selected him for the District Court for the Eastern District of Michigan. In 1966, he was named to the Court of Appeals for the Sixth Circuit by President Johnson. He resigned that seat in 1977 to serve as President Jimmy Carter's solicitor general, and when Carter's term ended, McCree accepted a professorship at the University of Michigan Law School.[33]

Thurgood Marshall was lead counsel for the LDF when Kennedy asked him to serve on the Court of Appeals for the Second Circuit. The nomination took some courage on Kennedy's part, for southern Democratic congressmen had little love for this tough-minded grandson of a former slave. Marshall grew up in Jim Crow Baltimore, to a father who worked as a dining car waiter and a mother who taught in a segregated elementary school. Marshall worked as a bellhop to put himself through college at Lincoln University in Pennsylvania and Howard University Law School, both black schools, because Maryland denied blacks admission to its premier undergraduate and graduate institutions.

At Howard, Marshall found two mentors: Dean Charles Hamilton Houston and William Hastie. Under Houston's direction, Marshall joined the NAACP's litigation team, the Legal Defense Fund. "Mr. Civil Rights," as he was known well before he and his LDF teammates won the cases joined in *Brown*, knew that the Court's enforcement decision to proceed "with all deliberate speed" in *Brown* II made the desegregation of schools much harder. The appointment to the Second Circuit doubled his income but removed him from the advocacy of the cause he valued so highly. Despite a nearly year-long confirmation fight, bespattered with the vitriol of southern Democrats, he gained Senate approval. When Johnson made him solicitor general, he solidified his reputation as one of the nation's ablest civil rights advocates, winning fourteen of nineteen cases. Many of those cases protected the landmark civil and voting rights legislation of the Johnson presidency. In 1967 Johnson chose Marshall for the Supreme Court. Confirmation followed a month and half later.[34]

Next, Johnson selected A. Leon Higginbotham for the Eastern District of Pennsylvania in 1964. His nomination was confirmed within a month. Although that space of time was not unusual for candidates, the fact that confirmation was not prolonged by southern senators' delaying tactics, as were Hastie's and Marshall's, was a novelty. Higginbotham was in private practice in Philadelphia at the time but had served in various state official capacities. President Jimmy Carter's choice of Higginbotham for the Court of Appeals for the Third Circuit went just as swiftly through the Senate. Higginbotham was an articulate student of slavery and the law, of racism in American history, and of the long road ahead to genuine racial equality. He would retire in 1993 and join the faculty at Harvard Law School. [35]

Another Johnson choice was Constance Baker Motley, the first female African American to sit on the federal bench. Senator James O. Eastland of Mississippi, chair of the Judiciary Committee, held up her confirmation hearings for months. She recalled that President Johnson refused to send any names for judgeships to the Senate until he relented. Joining her was Spottswood Robinson III, a veteran of the LDF and the Prince Edward County segregation case. Robinson would serve in the District Court (1964) and later the Court of Appeals (1966) for the District of Columbia. The desegregation of the federal judiciary was picking up speed.[36]

Earl Warren's Supreme Court

From 1954 to 1969 Court watchers routinely called the Supreme Court "Warren's Court." Certainly the unanimity of the Supreme Court on desegregation issues had a good deal to do with Warren's personal influence on his brethren. That influence did not arise from his technical sophistication, the elegance of his prose, or the depth of his thinking. Accused of results-oriented judging, it was true that he sometimes abandoned well-established precedents in favor of a progressive result. Unlike Chief Justice Taft, Warren did not have much influence on who would join him on the bench. Although he and President Eisenhower were both Republicans, the two men were not particularly close. With President Kennedy, Warren's relations were genuinely cordial and even deferential, but Warren was not a confidant, and Kennedy had his own agenda when it came to Supreme Court appointments. Lyndon Johnson had "only a passing acquaintance" with Warren and did not consult him about appointments to his Court. In the final analysis, the term "Warren Court" reflected the chief's larger than life presence, his charisma, rather than his political clout. It was a quality that made his the popular face of the Court and at the same time his visibility brought him more than his share of abuse from those who opposed the liberal direction of his jurisprudence.[37]

Following the sudden death of Robert H. Jackson from heart failure, Eisenhower looked to John Marshall Harlan II, the grandson of the great dissenter, to fill the seat. Eisenhower had appointed him to the Court of Appeals of the Second Circuit only thirteen months earlier. Some southern senators, notably Eastland of Mississippi, objected to the nomination to express their displeasure with the ruling in *Brown*. Other senators objected on the grounds that Harlan's undergraduate degree from Princeton and graduate study at Balliol College, Oxford, as a Rhodes Scholar made him a part of the one-world conspiracy of the United Nations and its supporters. Nevertheless, he was confirmed by the Senate in March 1955.[38]

Justice Harlan proved to be a lawyer's lawyer with a conscience, a believer in hard and careful work, and the value of detail. He gained a reputation as one of the Court's ablest and most prolific writers. He was Frankfurter's natural ally. They respected one another and agreed on 80 percent of the cases. One wag went so far as to declare that Harlan, a courtly gentleman on and off the bench, was Frankfurter "without the mustard." When Frankfurter retired, Harlan became the standard bearer of judicial restraint, federalism, and deference to legislatures, but he shared with his grandfather a concern for civil rights, especially those of African Americans, and free speech. Much respected by his brethren, he exercised great influence in the Conference. He retired in September 1971.[39]

When Sherman Minton stepped down, in late 1956, Eisenhower had another chance to shape the supreme tribunal. Largely in order to demonstrate his bipartisanship in an election year, he decided to nominate a Democrat. Attorney General Brownell had come to like and admire New Jersey Supreme Court Justice William J. Brennan Jr. Eisenhower went along with his attorney general's recommendation, with a recess appointment in October and then confirmation in January when the new Congress convened. Brennan had been hesitant, but Brownell told him, "you can't say no to the president of the United States." Brennan would exercise an immense influence over American law for the next thirty-four years, his almost cherubic optimism, his immense delight in the politics of coalition building, and his sense of right and wrong coming through every decision in which he took part.[40]

Commitment to liberal reform came naturally to Brennan. Born in 1906, in Newark, New Jersey, to Irish immigrants, Brennan grew up amidst the boom times of the industrial Northeast. His father became a staunch supporter of organized labor, a foe of dirty dealing, and a crusading politician. Brennan attended Harvard Law School, joined the army at the outset of World War II, and with the peace he reentered private practice. But public service beckoned again, and Brennan helped overhaul the state's antiquated, complex, malfunctioning judicial system. In recognition for his effort, he gained appointment to the superior court in 1949, the appellate division of the superior court in 1950, and the New Jersey Supreme Court in 1952.

While he did not always write elegant opinions, his grasp of the nub of legal issues, his vision of a living constitution, and his ability to bring together majorities around the extension and protection of civil liberties and civil rights made him an especially effective justice. As he wrote in 1961, the Constitution's "genius . . . rests not in any static meaning it might have had in a world that is dead and gone, but in the adaptability of its great principles to cope with current problems and current needs.". He served until 1990.[41]

As the 1960s opened, Warren and his colleagues, including additional Eisenhower nominees Charles Whittaker and Potter Stewart, found their values and experience put to the test. Whittaker, who long had trouble writing opinions and suffered from depression, would step down after five terms. Stewart's twenty-two-term tenure was a different story. Yale College and Yale Law School educated, Stewart had served on the Court of Appeals for the Sixth Circuit when he replaced Harold Burton. On the Court from 1959 to 1981, Stewart wrote opinions expressing a sound, common-sense approach to the most complicated legal and doctrinal issues. Modest, hardworking, and fair-minded, he was a centrist on the Court.[42]

Kennedy's first appointment to the Court, a 1962 replacement for Whittaker, was Byron R. White. In many ways he resembled the short-lived president. White was tough-minded and realistic in his thinking and pragmatic in his view of law. A magna cum laude graduate of the University of Colorado, White was a star athlete, who played professional football for Detroit and Pittsburgh. During the 1940 and 1941 football seasons he simultaneously attended Yale Law School. After Pearl Harbor, White became an intelligence officer in the Pacific theater, writing the report on the sinking of

Jack Kennedy's PT 109. He returned to Yale to complete his degree, earning first-in-his-class distinction. In 1946 he clerked for Chief Justice Fred Vinson and then returned to Colorado to practice law. His general practice for mostly corporate and wealthy clients earned him a comfortable living. A man blessed with these athletic and intellectual gifts might have sought a political career, but his almost virulent distaste for those seeking to publicize his life (in part a reaction to the assault by the press during his college and professional football playing days), restricted him to organizing for the Democratic Party in Colorado. At Robert Kennedy's request, he helped lead a national campaign for his brother's presidential bid.[43]

White's judicial philosophy was honed when he served as a deputy attorney general under Robert Kennedy. He favored vigorous enforcement of the law to deal with the increasing turmoil over civil rights for African Americans but deferred to political bodies in other matters. On the Court, White believed in neutral principles, a philosophy of judging in which only fair procedures and a commitment to the legal process should govern the outcome of a case. Straightforward to the point of brutal honesty, incisive in his opinions, he would serve until 1993.[44]

Kennedy's other appointee, Arthur J. Goldberg, rose from modest circumstances to great political influence and legal office, like the man he succeeded, Justice Frankfurter. As a child on Chicago's West Side, he held several jobs to help keep his Russian immigrant family afloat. His intellectual gifts and hard work enabled him to graduate high school at fifteen. While he worked during the days, he attended Crane Junior College, then De Paul University at night. At Northwestern University School of Law, he graduated first in his class, the next year adding a graduate degree in law. He began a distinguished law career working at Pritzker and Pritzker in Chicago and after a time started his own practice, focusing on labor law. After the war, he became general counsel for the United Steelworkers of America in 1948 and represented the Congress of Industrial Organizations. Goldberg played an integral part in its 1955 merger with its rival, the American Federation of Labor. He served as the new organization's special counsel until 1961 when Kennedy tapped him to become the secretary of labor. When Frankfurter announced his intention to retire after failing to recover fully from a stroke, Kennedy had little difficulty putting Goldberg in the so-called Jewish seat. Although he would only occupy it for three terms, from 1962 to 1965, Goldberg's votes were a part of the Warren Court's civil rights revolution. He wrote the majority opinion in Escobedo v. Illinois (1964), requiring police to inform suspects of their right to remain silent, and his concurrence in Griswold v. Connecticut (1965) placed the right to privacy in the Ninth Amendment. During his short tenure on the Supreme Court, he brought an activist attitude to social and economic issues.[45]

President Johnson pressed Goldberg to trade his seat on the Court for the ambassadorship to the United Nations, ostensibly to help negotiate an end to the Vietnam War. In fact, Johnson wanted to place his personal attorney and confidant, Abe Fortas, in the Jewish seat. Though he would have a rewarding career as a diplomat and D.C. lawyer, Goldberg always regretted his short stay at the marble palace. Fortas's appointment did not tilt the ideological balance of the bench, however. He was as liberal and activist as Goldberg.[46]

Like some Shakespearian tragic hero, Fortas possessed the makings of a great justice, perhaps a great chief justice, but that did not happen. The child of two orthodox Jewish immigrants, Fortas grew up in Memphis, Tennessee, and attended Yale Law School after graduating first in his class at Southwestern College in Memphis. Fortas's mentor at Yale was Professor William O. Douglas, who encouraged him to apply social conscience to public service, even if he elected to remain in private practice. Although Fortas accepted an appointment to his law school's faculty, he soon followed in his mentor's footsteps to Roosevelt's New Deal agencies, eventually rising to the highest positions at the Interior Department.[47]

Fortas was highly effective in his administrative posts, but in 1946, he quit government work to form the highly successful D.C. law firm of Arnold, Fortas & Porter. There he did not abandon public service even though the firm's bread and butter were large corporate clients. In 1962, he won his most notable Supreme Court victory. An indigent Florida defendant named Clarence Earl Gideon appealed his felony conviction on the ground that he could not afford legal representation. Fortas took on Gideon's cause without pay (pro bono publico). In *Gideon v. Wainwright* (1963), the Court mandated that the state provide attorneys for indigent defendants in felony cases. Justice Douglas recalled that Fortas's presentation of Gideon's appeal was the best he had ever heard in all his tenure on the Court.[48]

Through his connection with president Johnson, Fortas became the ultimate inside-the-beltway operator. Without his permission, Johnson publically mentioned him as his nominee in July 1965. Fortas was reluctant to join the Court, for it would have meant a prodigious loss of income. But he acquiesced, and Johnson formally named him at the end of the month. On the bench he proved to be an able judicial craftsman. He wrote the majority opinion for *In re Gault* (1967), which extended self-incrimination and right to counsel rights to juveniles, and *Tinker v. Des Moines* (1969), which recognized the symbolic speech rights of grade school and high school students. The first was longish, the second relatively terse, but both demonstrated the exceptional commitment to detail of a veteran, top-flight litigator.[49]

The last of Johnson's appointments to the Supreme Court was Thurgood Marshall. His contributions to the Warren Court helped advance the causes of the weak, underprivileged, and vulnerable. He wrote for the Court in *Stanley v. Georgia* (1969), protecting the privacy rights of individuals with regards to obscene material, and *Benton v. Maryland* (1969), applying the double jeopardy protection of the Bill of Rights to the states. As the only justice who faced invidious racism every day of his life, including once being mistaken for the elevator operator in the marble palace, Marshall wrote with real authority on injustice. A man of good humor who enjoyed the bully pulpit his seat on the Court provided, he stepped down in 1991 because of accumulating health problems.[50]

Political Questions Revisited

Civil rights cases were not the only ones in which the federal courts of this period faced the old dilemma of state-federal relations. The most basic of all rights a citizen of a republic can claim is the right to vote. In two streams of voting rights cases coming to the federal courts—the denial of the rights of minorities to cast votes and the malapportionment of state legislatures and congressional districts—the Court elected to revisit the "political question" doctrine. Although the Supreme Court had avoided the latter in *Colegrove v. Green* (1946), it had already intervened to prevent the Fifteenth Amendment from evisceration by state political parties and one-party state legislatures in *Smith v. Allwright* (1944), ending the Texas all-white primary and in *Terry v. Adams* (1953), finding unconstitutional the Texas Democratic Party's attempt to evade *Smith* by holding a private primary closed to black voters.[51]

In *Baker v. Carr* (1962), Brennan wrote for a 6-2 majority declaring that the Equal Protection Clause of the Fourteenth Amendment allowed the federal bench to hear cases involving state legislative districting. The Court had once again entered a "political thicket," this time where the politics of state districting had hitherto been too overgrown for federal courts to intervene. The Court, as in desegregation, was once again ahead of Congress and the federal executive. Over the strenuous objections of Justices Frankfurter and Harlan, who berated the majority for their disregard of their proper—limited—role within a democratic system, Brennan reasoned that the Court was ensuring democracy.[52]

Once the door was open to judicial scrutiny of apportionment, additional cases arrived at the Court. Douglas's majority opinion in *Gray v. Sanders* (1963) included a formulation so simple and resonant, "one person, one vote," that ordinary Americans could understand what the Court was doing. The Georgia "unit" districts at issue in *Gray*, designed to make the black vote for members of Congress disappear, soon gave way to other challenges, leading to a revolution in reapportionment of both state legislatures and congressional districts that rivaled the Civil Rights Movement. "One person, one vote" was the formula used by the court to shift power to urban populations earlier deprived of their proportional share.[53]

Lawyers brought suits in Alabama and Colorado to see if state legislatures would act without waiting for the Supreme Court to intervene. Both went to the Court on appeal, and in *Reynolds v. Sims* (1964) and *Lucas v. Forty-Fourth General Assembly of Colorado* (1964), a majority put the Court's seal of approval on the reapportionment drive. As the District Court for the Middle District of Alabama explained in *Sims v. Frink* (1962), despite the clear message of *Baker*, states were finding ways to retain malapportioned legislatures. The veil of rationality donned by the state officials was as translucent to the courts as the veil of pupil-placement plans in desegregation cases. In a per curiam opinion, Court of Appeals for the Fifth Circuit Court Judge Rives and District Judges Johnson and Daniel H. Thomas determined that petitioners' "rights concerning the apportionment of representatives and senators among the counties of the State of Alabama" required that the court look beyond the historical and customary rules for districting. These were, "when considered as a whole, so obviously discriminatory, arbitrary and irrational" that a court-imposed reapportionment was the only guarantee of constitutional fairness. All three men were born and bred Alabamians, and all three knew what everyone else in the state knew, that the plans and the contingency plans and all other plans proposed by a segregationist legislature and governor's office were designed to dilute black voting power.[54]

Not every case involved denial of a racial minority's right to have its full weight counted. As in *Baker*, municipal voters brought suits to gain a fair count of their numbers in state elections. But the grounds for ordering relief were the same in both types of suits. Countering two different defenses from state officials on appeal to the Supreme Court, one a majoritarian argument, the other a regionalist one, Chief Justice Warren declared in *Lucas v. Forty-fourth General Assembly*, (1964), "The weight of a citizen's vote cannot be made to depend on where he lives," and "that certain rights exist which a citizen cannot trade, barter, or even give away." The chief justice's most direct statement of the basis for court-imposed reapportionment came in *Reynolds v. Sims* (1964): "Citizens, not history or economic interests, cast votes. People, not land or trees or pastures, vote." The formula of one man, one vote was not a mathematical one, for states had some leeway in reforming districts and gerrymandering was still possible. The formula was a constitutional one, a mandate that states not dilute the voting power of any of the population groups within the state. Although it sounded akin to the individualistic idealism of the nineteenth century, it protected those insular and isolated minorities described in footnote 4 to *Carolene Products*.[55]

The last, often unnoticed, case in the reapportionment line immediately after *Reynolds* was *Germano v. Kerner* (1964, 1965) in which a federal district court in the Northern District of Illinois refused to delay hearing a reapportionment case while the same case was before the state court. Illinois, like many of the states in these suits, had drawn its state districts to favor less populous rural areas rather than the more densely populated region around Chicago. Judge William J. Campbell told Illinois, the respondent, "The right of a [federal] court to declare a particular election system violative of the Equal Protection Clause of the Fourteenth Amendment to the Constitution can no longer be questioned." The federal court had already entered a final injunction in the case. "Not only would our turning of this case over to the Illinois Supreme Court (assuming it would want the case) fail to hasten its final disposition (ignoring that a final disposition has already been reached) but ... would most probably occasion delays sought to be precluded by the very statute upon which defendants rely." The Supreme Court, in a per curiam opinion in *Scott v. Germano* (1965), vacated the federal court injunction. The district court was instead ordered to step back to supervise the case, fixing a time limit for the state to reapportion the voting districts. Whether prudence, the perceived impact of criticism of its reapportionment decisions, or a concern to maintain a more traditional balance between state and federal courts had motivated the Supreme Court to adopt this stance, the result was to empower state legislatures and courts in the reapportionment process. [56]

That Solomonic decision had the opposite of its intended effect. Instead of providing guidance to the lower state or federal courts, it fostered litigation. The Supreme Court had given Illinois until the election of 1966 to create fairer districts, but who was to determine if the new districts comported with the reapportionment cases? If Illinois had this task, then it was a judge in its own cause. If the job belonged to the federal district court, then, as Judge Campbell had predicted, the stay of its proceedings was simply a delay, not a settlement.

According to the federal courts' reapportionment jurisprudence, successful challenges rested on the Fourteenth Amendment's Equal Protection Clause. They were not political in any sense of the word. But the judges surely knew that state legislative reapportionment was partisan from beginning to end . The majority party in the legislature would try to maximize advantage by designing voting districts that diluted the other party's voting strength. That was the reason that the dominant party in state governments fought so hard to retain absolute control over apportionment.

In entering these cases, the court also revisited the Madisonian Compromise on federalism. Decisions like *Reynolds* and *Germano* did not tell the states how to reapportion, but they did tell the states when the drawing of district lines violated constitutional protections. State courts and federal courts found themselves fencing not only over the district lines the legislatures drew, but over the respective roles of state and federal courts in supervising the line-drawing process.

Insofar as the decisions directly or indirectly (state legislatures drew boundaries of congressional districts) affected the composition of Congress, reapportionment also raised federal checks and balances questions. When Congress passed the Voting Rights Act of 1965, it tacitly conceded that the relationship among the branches of government had been altered by the Court and that Congress needed to regain the initiative.[57]

A second stream of voting rights cases came to the federal courts via the 1965 Act. The legislation complemented President Johnson's civil rights initiative. It explicitly aimed at those states, counties, and cities whose laws or ordinances had wholly or in part discriminated against minority voters in the past. Section 5 prohibited those instrumentalities of government with a history of discriminatory voting practices from altering voting regulations without first obtaining "preclearance" from the U.S. attorney general or a three-judge panel in the District Court for the District of Columbia. In *South Carolina v. Katzenbach*, (1966), the Court found the Voting Rights Act as a whole to be constitutional, and in *Allen v. State Board of Elections* (1969), the Court allowed a suit by a private citizen under Section 5. In both cases, the Court found no inconsistency between the Voting Rights Act's provisions and the Court's reapportionment cases.[58]

Congress Steps Up

Alongside congressional activity directly affecting the courts' caseload were reforms in the delivery of legal services to the poor, the management of the docket, and the training of newly-appointed members of the bench. The 1964 Criminal Justice Act provided for modest compensation and reimbursement of expenses for attorneys appointed to represent indigent federal defendants. As amended in 1970 the Act authorized the creation of public defender offices in each district as counterparts to the U.S. attorneys. Congress also dealt with pretrial incarceration in the 1966 Bail Reform Act. Its "partiality for pre-trial release," wrote future District of Columbia Circuit Judge Patricia Wald, "is designed to reverse the old system's pattern of pretrial detention."[59]

The 1968 Federal Magistrates Act replaced the old fee-based United States Commissioner system with U.S. magistrates (now magistrate judges, discussed in the next chapter). In the same year, Congress created the Judicial Panel on Multi-district Litigation to assign cases filed in many districts about a common event (an airline disaster, for example) to a single judge for pretrial proceedings. The Panel replaced a 1962 Coordinating Committee for such litigation that Chief Justice Warren had created within the Judicial Conference in response to a wave of multidistrict electrical equipment antitrust suits.[60]

The creation of the Federal Judicial Center in 1967 demonstrated how the judiciary, the legislative branches, and the executive could work hand-in-hand to improve to delivery of justice. In the 1950s and 1960s, the Judicial Conference had instigated a "patchwork of research and continuing education programs" in response to changes in the nature and quantity of federal caseloads. They included studies of the management of protracted cases, and seminars for district judges, bankruptcy referees, and federal probation officers. Congress provided funds for a few of the seminars, but other projects were funded by squeezing money out of other accounts, or, as one judge complained, "having 'to go . . . hat in hand, begging foundations.'" Chief Justice Warren found these arrangements unacceptable and, working with Californian Warren Olney, whom he had placed as director of the Administrative Office, wished for an independent agency in the judicial branch, separately funded, to plan and execute a coordinated program of analysis and education. Warren believed that challenges facing the federal courts could not be remedied by "a continuous tinkering in order to rectify every little outcropping of inefficiency . . . Our strength must come mainly from improved methods of adjusting caseloads, dispatching litigation . . . resolving complicated issues, eliminating non-essential ones, increasing courtroom efficiency, and through dispatch in decision making and appeal." Warren appointed a Special Committee on Continuing Education, Research, Training, and Administration, chaired by retired Justice Stanley F. Reed, to prepare draft legislation for approval from the Conference and then submit it to Congress. In early 1967, while the Committee was still in the drafting stage, Warren pressed for completion of the bill. Olney reported to the Committee that the Chief Justice "personally . . . made . . . overtures to the White House with the result that the proposal for a judicial center had been incorporated in the President's [crime] message." In late 1967, Congress sent the Judicial Center bill to President Johnson, who signed it en route to South Vietnam to meet with U.S. troops.[61]

When the Hurly Burly's Done; When the Battle's Lost and Won

As the decade of the 1960s came to a close, it appeared that the federal courts had weathered the storm of protest that civil rights and voting rights cases had raised. Congress had stepped up with helpful legislation. But two episodes at the close of the era revived the hurly burly that had surrounded the courts for the past two decades. Both were battles that no one really won. The first was outgoing President Johnson's attempt to name Justice Fortas as Chief Justice Warren's successor. The second was the trial of a group of antiwar protestors at the Democratic National Convention in Chicago.

When in 1968 Warren wrote to Johnson to inform him that he would retire as soon as a successor was confirmed, the president picked Fortas as Warren's replacement. Though initially the appointment had the support of a majority of the Senate, at his hearing, Fortas faced sharp attacks on his character (for advising Johnson on a regular basis while on the Court), his morality (for extending constitutional free speech protections to what others considered lurid films), and, most devastating, his ethical judgment (for accepting $15,000 for teaching a law course paid for by clients at his former law firm). While none of these activities could have been prosecuted (or were), they exposed Fortas to fierce criticism in Congress. A battered, besmirched, and weary Fortas withdrew himself from consideration for the center chair. This did not end his travails, for *Life* magazine broke a story on Fortas's acceptance, later rescinded, of an annual $20,000 from a charitable foundation established by a shady former client named Louis Wolfson. Assailed for this lapse in judgment, with threats of impeachment emanating from Congress, Fortas resigned from the Court in May 1969.[62]

The story of the "Chicago Eight" (later reduced to seven when one of the defendants was removed from the courtroom) began a year earlier. The Tet Offensive in Vietnam during the first days of the new year convinced vital segments of the American public that the war was unwinable. Protests against continued involvement in the war turned ugly. D.C. court judges could smell in their chambers the smoke rising from riot sites in the capital.[63]

With the nation sharply divided by the war and the antiwar protests, the Democratic Party determined to hold its presidential convention in one of the most predictably Democratic cities in the country, Mayor Richard Daley's Chicago. What the Democratic National Committee's organizers did not appreciate was that another group of organizers, led by Students for a Democratic Society's (SDS) Tom Hayden and others, planned a counter-convention. Piggybacking on the SDS, counterculture icons Jerry Rubin and Abbie Hoffman arrived to stage their own version of a be-in, a public demonstration of their contempt for authority. The city's police department, unsympathetic to the counterculture and plagued with a history of violent treatment of radical organizers going back to the Haymarket riots of 1886, were to play their own role in the events. When the Daley administration refused to give the groups parade permits, the confrontation with the city, televised because of the coverage of the convention, became national news. On three days in the last week of August, demonstrators and police clashed in the parks around the convention site, a real-life television drama of broken bones and bleeding heads. Inside the convention hall that night, Senator Abraham Ribicoff of Connecticut condemned the "Gestapo tactics on the streets of Chicago," while Mayor Daley, in full view of television cameras, "shouted obscenities and anti-Semitic slurs at the senator." A later investigation called the police response "a police riot."[64]

The battleground cleared, Chief Judge William J. Campbell of the Northern District of Illinois, a Roosevelt appointee, convened a grand jury to determine whether any federal laws had been broken. On March 6, 1969, it returned indictments against eight of the protestors for the crime of conspiracy. Allegedly, they had crossed state lines with the intent to commit a riot. Trial before Judge Julius Hoffman began on September 24 and continued until February 18, 1970.

Media coverage of the events of the preceding August, along with incoming President Richard M. Nixon administration's determination to deal sternly with street protests and radical politics, ensured that the trial would be widely and closely covered. It was an important event for the federal courts as well, for few trials brought federal criminal trial procedure into such sharp focus as the Chicago Eight (later seven) trial would. On top of all this, the Northern District of Illinois was the third largest in the nation, its bench only bowing to the Southern District of New York and the Central District of California in numbers of judgeships. Even without the Democratic National Convention and the demonstrations, all eyes would be on the Chicago courtroom.

Judge Hoffman was an Eisenhower appointee, and at seventy-three years of age was impatient with the theatrical displays of the defendants and the repeated disrespect defense counsel William Kunstler and others showed the bench, an antipathy which in turn bred the judge's prejudicial conduct of the trial. Judge Hoffman truly loved Chicago, where he was born and raised. His undergraduate degree was from Northwestern, just north of the city in Evanston, and his law degree was from Northwestern Law School, in the near North Side of the city. He practiced in the city and then became a Cook County trial judge. His sense of personal affront at seeing the parks of the city filled with demonstrators added injury to the insult of having his courtroom turned into a circus. (One defendant, Bobby Seale, was bound and gagged during much of the trial after he engaged in a shouting match with the judge.) But Hoffman waited until the jury was deliberating its verdict to issue 159 contempt citations to the defendants and their counsel. A year before he died, he remained feisty and unapologetic. "I did nothing in the trial that I'm not proud of . . . I presided with dignity. When I felt I had to be firm, I was firm." He was proud that "we let certain kinds of lawyers know there are certain kinds of things you don't do when you're trying a lawsuit in the highest trial court in the land."[65]

Unfortunately, the proceedings lent itself to the defense's attempt to portray the indictments as partisan because Hoffman refused the defense's request to ask potential jury members about their views of the war or whether they had followed the riots in the media. After its deliberations, the jury found all not guilty of conspiracy, but five guilty of traveling across state lines with intent to riot, a violation of the Civil Rights Act of 1968.[66]

Figure 12.3 More than 1,000 demonstrators gathered in front of the federal courthouse in Seattle, Washington, in 1970, to protest contempt-of-court sentences against seven defendants at the Chicago conspiracy trial. Credit: AP Photo/Barry Sweet.

While the district court bench, led by Judge Campbell, publically stood behind Hoffman, calling his conduct of the trial "excellent," all three of the judges on a panel of the Court of Appeals for the Seventh Circuit voted to overturn the verdicts and most of the contempt citations. Judge Thomas Fairchild explained that the prosecutor "went at least up to, and probably beyond, the outermost boundary of permissible inferences from the evidence in his characterizations of defendants." Hoffman (though not named in the opinion) had erred in not asking jurors about their knowledge of the events: "Despite the district court's earlier assurance that the voir dire would cover pretrial publicity, the only explicit reference to publicity was to that which might occur during the trial." Hoffman had "lulled" defense counsel into not submitting these questions to prospective jurors. The judge had arbitrarily excluded written evidence on the defendants' purpose in coming to the convention. The tone of the Court of Appeals was especially striking when it came to prosecutorial and judicial conduct:

> There are high standards for the conduct of judges and prosecutors, and impropriety by persons before the court does not give license to depart from those standards . . . The district judge's deprecatory and often antagonistic attitude toward the defense is evident in the record from the very beginning. It appears in remarks and actions both in

the presence and absence of the jury . . . These comments were often touched with sarcasm, implying rather than saying outright that defense counsel was inept, bumptious, or untrustworthy, or that his case lacked merit . . . these remarks were not justified thereby and fell below the standards applicable to a representative of the United States.[67]

Watching from her post on the D.C. Superior Court, so-to-be District Judge Joyce Hens Green recalled that Hoffman was "unable to cope with intended disruption, behaved poorly and became the scorn of the nation, the embarrassment of the judiciary." Not so of the retrial begun in October 1973, conducted with learning and patience by Judge Edward T. Gignoux, of the U.S. District Court for Maine. Gignoux, assigned by Chief Justice Warren Burger, found David Dellinger, Abbie Hoffman, Jerry Rubin, and Kunstler guilty of contempt but concluded that no punishment other than his finding was necessary. "From the foregoing, it is apparent that the contumacious conduct of the defendants and their lawyers cannot be considered apart from the conduct of the trial judge and prosecutors. Each reacted to provocation by the other, and the tensions generated during four and a half months of so acrimonious a trial cannot be ignored."[68]

Chief Justice Warren, himself a veteran politician of no mean distinction, recognized the problem that a lack of public confidence in the federal judiciary posed, but he had no solution to it other than to offer that the courts must be free of partisanship. He had "left politics" when he donned judicial robes and was not about to reenter politics in his retirement, though his memoirs show that every criticism of him and his Court stung.[69]

Despite criticism of the Warren Court, ranging from disgruntled elements of the public to jurists and politicians concerned that the Court had moved too far too fast to the left, at the end of the 1960s, the federal courts had emerged as the first place to look for relief in cases of segregation, denial of civil liberties, criminal procedural rights violations, and other often unpopular cases. Indeed, not since the Judiciary Act of 1789, not even in the flush of Reconstruction experimentation with the Civil Rights and Enforcement Acts, had Congress so entrusted the courts with the fulfillment of a national agenda as it did with the Civil Rights Act of 1964 and the Voting Rights Act of 1965. Both enactments directed private litigants to seek redress in the federal courts. The courts were thus bidden by Congress to execute the other, often overlooked portion of the Madisonian Compromise—to be a place of redress for individuals when state and local governments were hostile or indifferent to individual rights.

Reform and Reaction, the Federal Courts, 1969–1986

In the closing years of the 1960s, American self-government appeared to many to stand at a crossroads. Reaction, sometimes violent, to the assassinations of Martin Luther King Jr. and Robert F. Kennedy, race riots, and demonstrations against the Vietnam War seemed to engulf the nation. In his 1969 inaugural address, President Richard Nixon called on citizens to take consolation in "this orderly transfer of power" and to "celebrate the unity that keeps us free." Yet Justice William O. Douglas worried that "the stresses and the strains in our system have become so great and the dissents so violent and continuous that a great sense of insecurity has possessed much of the country." Indeed, a "law and order" backlash was building in response to this sense of insecurity, and it reflected, in part, opposition to the civil liberties and procedural protections associated with the Warren Court. Although the long night of Jim Crow appeared to be ending—the courts having successfully presided over a transformation of ordinary life unlike any since the end of slavery—the nation's confidence in the government and law seemed perilously low.[1]

Observers outside and inside the federal judicial system warned that the need for reform was "boiling over." Yale Law professor Grant Gilmore, delivering the 1974 Storrs Lectures, pronounced the federal courts "crisis-ridden." Two years after he was installed as Chief Justice, Warren E. Burger told the American Bar Association in 1971, "Essentially the problems of the federal courts, in common with state courts and indeed much of the entire fabric of our national life, are suffering from an accumulated neglect. This disrepair became an acute problem as the load increased, and we cannot ignore it any longer." Chief Justice Burger, whose tenure spanned the period covered in this chapter, had watched with alarm from his post on the Court of Appeals for the District of Columbia during the 1960s as public criticism of the Warren Court built to a crescendo. Once confirmed in his new post as head of the judiciary, his plans for reform included speeding up adjudication and trials, making procedure more uniform, ending diversity jurisdiction, and promoting alternatives to litigation.[2]

Nixon's Judges

Burger was not alone in his urgent call for major reforms. He viewed the problems in institutional terms. President Nixon, himself a lawyer, saw the problems in terms of personnel on the bench. Nixon won the election in part because of

Figure 13.1 Chief Justice Warren Burger addressing a meeting of the American Bar Association, with the annual report on the *State of the Judiciary*, New Orleans, Louisiana, 1983. Credit: Bettman/Corbis/AP Images.

public reaction against the Warren Court's jurisprudence on crime. Nixon promised a new era of law and order, and in the fall of 1968 "the federal courts became a campaign issue." Part of the fulfillment of his campaign pledge lay in a revamping of the federal judiciary. The largest part of that effort was directed to filling judicial posts with individuals whose views matched the president's agenda.[3]

Nixon did not take a personal interest in most of the lower court appointments, at least not until the last months of his presidency. Instead, a variety of his advisors, including Attorney General John Mitchell, assistant to the president John Ehrlichman, and members of the Department of Justice handled the details of vetting potential nominees. There was no single set of ideological stances that qualified a potential nominee, although candidates were supposed to be "strict constructionists" of the Constitution. While some advocates of that stance admitted later that it did not mean very much, it did eliminate certain candidates who were "soft on crime." Nixon also had to deal with a Senate dominated by the opposing party. Scholars evaluating his selection process concluded that connections to members of Nixon's administration and support for his campaign meant more than conformity to any fixed jurisprudential philosophy.[4]

Over his six and half year tenure, Nixon had the opportunity to name 216 district and circuit court judges, considerably more than Kennedy (123) or Johnson (165). Thirteen of the judges were Democrats. One appointee, Cornelia G. Kennedy, for the Eastern District of Michigan, was female. Judge Kennedy was later named to the Court of Appeals for the Sixth Circuit by President Jimmy Carter. President Nixon chose six African Americans for these courts.

Nixon asked Judge Warren Burger of the D.C. Court of Appeals to lead the Supreme Court. Burger attended the University of Minnesota and after graduation he worked as an accountant for an insurance company by day while he took classes at the University of Minnesota, then at St. Paul College of Law (now William Mitchell). In 1931, the twenty-four-year-old Minnesotan received his LL.B. magna cum laude and an appointment to teach a contracts course, an appointment he held until 1948. He also joined a law firm, where he specialized in probate, corporate, and real estate law. Burger helped elect Republican Harold Stassen governor of Minnesota, and when Stassen came up short in his try for the Republican nomination for president in 1952, Burger enabled Eisenhower to gain Minnesota's delegates. President Eisenhower took notice and appointed him an assistant attorney general for the civil division in 1953. There, he made a name for himself by mastering admiralty law and prosecuting the loyalty oath cases. His performance led to a place on the D.C. Circuit Court of Appeals.[5]

Burger's passion was an efficient legal system, making him the inheritor of William Howard Taft's legacy. His confirmation as chief justice in late spring of 1969 gave him the platform he needed to call for reform. He aimed at speeding cases through the system and reducing overcrowded dockets. At the National

Conference of the Judiciary, held in Williamsburg, Virginia, in 1971, Burger called for the creation of a central resource for the state courts—a "national center for state courts." He also played a major role in creating an Institute for Court Management to improve the training of court managers. He strongly supported state-federal judicial councils that would meet periodically and reduce tensions when state and federal courts had scheduled cases involving the same attorneys for the same time slots. He encouraged state chief justices to introduce a National Center for State Courts to perform similar functions to the Federal Judicial Center—providing research and analysis of court operations and case management. He oversaw improvements to the Court's grounds, equipment, and procedures; limited oral argument to one hour instead of two; and by example urged his colleagues to eliminate reading of entire opinions from the bench unless there were exceptional circumstances. He even changed the shape of the bench from straight to three sides of a hexagon to maximize the justices' visibility of other justices.[6]

Central to Burger's plan was enhancing the administrative framework within the circuits and the creation of new subject matter tribunals. He successfully lobbied Congress for the creation of the Office of Circuit Executives and abetted an earlier proposal for the creation of the Court of Appeals for the Federal Circuit (a court with a national subject matter jurisdiction to hear appeals from district court patent cases and from the Court of International Trade and several administrative agencies). He was also a leader in the expansion of the role of magistrate judges, which is discussed at the end of this chapter. On occasion his reach exceeded his grasp, as in his advocacy for an intermediate court of appeals to deal with the conflicting decisions of different circuits. Some of his reform schemes encountered opposition, but there is no doubt that he had a vision for a smoothly operating system of justice at the federal and state levels.[7]

Burger's take-charge management style produced some ill-will among the brethren. His occasional refusal to follow conventions in assigning opinions, his inability to frame issues clearly when he was writing for the Court, and his pettiness when crossed brought unfavorable comparisons to his predecessor. However, his capacity for friendship, his work ethic, and his commitment to the job gained him a high rating among Court watchers. In 1986, after seventeen years of often exhausting service, Burger retired to become head of the nation's commission to commemorate the bicentennial of the Constitution.[8]

President Nixon's next nomination to the Supreme Court, for the seat Fortas had vacated, was an attempt to repay immediate political debts. The Republican Party's successful "Southern Strategy" helped him win the 1968 election. When Fortas left the Court, Nixon recalled, "I asked [attorney general] John Mitchell to direct the search for a Supreme Court justice." They selected Clement F. Haynsworth Jr. of South Carolina, who then was chief judge of the Court of

Appeals for the Fourth Circuit. He seemed assured of confirmation until questions arose over his handling of a case in which he had a personal stake. Nixon claimed that "the pack mentality" of the critics swayed the Senate. Haynsworth was denied the seat, in a 55 to 45 vote.[9]

Nixon's second choice, G. Harrold Carswell, fared even less well. Though he had been a district judge in Florida and was serving on the Court of Appeals for the Fifth Circuit at the time of his nomination, the American Bar Association expressed concern about his lack of experience and overall lack of distinction. This prompted Republican Senator Roman Hruska of Nebraska to defend the nomination: "Even if he is mediocre, there are a lot of mediocre judges and people and lawyers, and they are entitled to a little representation, aren't they? We can't have all Brandeises and Cardozos and Frankfurters and stuff like that." But it was Carswell's own words that came back to haunt him. In a speech he made while on the hustings for a seat in the Georgia legislature before he gained a federal judgeship, he said: "I yield to no man as a fellow candidate or as a fellow citizen in the firm, vigorous belief in the principles of White Supremacy, and I shall always be so governed." The Senate rejected him 51 to 45.

Nixon and Mitchell pushed the nominations all the way through to final vote. Nixon, by his own admission, relished a fight to the finish. Part of his motivation was his loyalty to those who had carried his presidential campaign to victory. Mitchell's successor, Richard Kleindienst, was not so partisan, and in the course of the confirmation hearings of Democrat Prentice Marshall to the Northern District of Illinois, was reported to have remarked that the "the Constitution calls for the advice and consent of the Senate, not the advice and consent of the Republican Caucus."[10]

After losing bruising battles over Haynsworth and Carswell, Nixon and the Senate embraced a relatively uncontroversial conservative from Minnesota, Harry A. Blackmun. Though a boyhood friend and long-time colleague of Burger—both were from the Minneapolis-St. Paul region, and both seemed to share philosophies of law—Blackmun's career differed in key ways from Burger's. Blackmun attended Harvard College and Harvard Law School. He clerked for Judge John B. Sanborn of the U.S. Court of Appeals for the Eighth Circuit and in the course of private practice became resident counsel for the famous Mayo Clinic as well as teaching courses at the University of Minnesota Law School. In 1959 Eisenhower picked him for the Court of Appeals for the Eighth Circuit. Blackmun gained a reputation there as a conservative of conscience, sympathetic to immigrants, laboring poor, and women.

In the spotlight that membership on the Supreme Court throws on its members, he did not, at first, seem very impressive, particularly to liberal Court watchers, but that view was premature. He did not put his head in the law books and keep it there, but listened to public opinion, his family, and his friends. When new justices appeared, he was the first to greet them. Slow to write when he was assigned a case early in his tenure, and capable of some stubbornness when a case he had written was ignored or narrowed, he retired in 1994.[11]

When Hugo Black's poor health led him to retire, Nixon named another southerner, the gentlemanly Richmond attorney Lewis F. Powell Jr. Although Nixon had followed Eisenhower's example (with Brennan) of selecting someone from the opposite party, Powell's views were closer to Nixon's than Brennan's were to Eisenhower's. In civil rights, Powell was a pragmatist. The NAACP rated him an acceptable candidate, and he was confirmed by the Senate at the end of 1971, with only Fred Harris, an Oklahoma populist Democrat, dissenting. On the Court, Justice Powell advocated judicial restraint and deference. He believed that the Constitution and the Civil Rights Act of 1964 protected minority rights and became a key swing vote on an often deeply divided Court. He retired relatively young in 1987.[12]

Nixon's appointee to replace Justice Harlan, William H. Rehnquist, joined Powell on the Court on the same day in January 1972. Rehnquist attended Stanford on the GI Bill. With bachelor's and master's degrees in political science in hand, he went on to get another master's, in government, then a Stanford Law degree in 1952. First in his class at Stanford, he made a reputation for himself as a brilliant conservative. As a clerk for Justice Robert H. Jackson, he continued to impress contemporaries with both his intellectual abilities and his well-articulated opposition to the Court's civil rights jurisprudence.[13]

After his clerkship, Rehnquist combined private practice with political activism for political causes in his adopted city of Phoenix, Arizona. These brought him to the attention of another Republican in Arizona, Richard Kleindienst, who recommended Rehnquist to be Nixon's assistant attorney general in charge of the Office of Legal Counsel. In this position, Rehnquist helped vet potential nominees to the federal bench and worked to undo the Warren Court's liberal criminal justice rulings. In his first years on the Court, he often found himself in dissent, but by the end of the 1980s, having moved to the center chair and been joined by new bench-mates, he more often led a majority.[14]

Watergate

On September 15, 1972, a federal grand jury indicted seven men for their June 17, 1972, break in at the Democratic National Committee Headquarters in the Watergate office and residential complex. A "cover-up" orchestrated at the highest levels of the administration, including presidential advisors John Ehrlichman and H. R. Haldeman, soon entangled the president himself. He had not ordered the break-in, indeed, he did not know about it but did take part in the subsequent attempt to obstruct justice. In effect, he would be the eighth man standing on the dock of public opinion.[15]

D.C. District Court Chief Judge John Sirica presided over the trials of the burglars and the subsequent evidentiary hearings. Sirica was no stranger to Washington D.C. or to its political partisanship. Born of immigrant working-class parents in Connecticut, he was schooled in the District of Columbia and went to Georgetown Law School there. He was in private practice from 1926 until 1930, when he joined President Hoover's Department of Justice. He returned to private practice in 1934. Sirica was a registered Republican, actively campaigned for Eisenhower in 1952 and 1956, and was rewarded with a seat on the D.C. District Court in 1957. Never widely known before the trials, facing as much media attention as Judge Hoffman in the Chicago Seven trial, Sirica rose to the occasion. Captured in the media coverage of the Watergate trials was his fierce commitment to get at the truth in the face of admitted perjury and obstruction of justice. As Court of Appeals for the District of Columbia Judge Harold Leventhal described Sirica, in an opinion upholding one of the convictions, "Judge Sirica's palpable search for truth in such a trial was not only permissible, it was in the highest tradition of his office as a federal judge." Though critics would later decry his tough tactics, at the time Americans needed to see the face of justice, and his weathered countenance represented the nation's indignation. Though not born to greatness, greatness found him.[16]

On March 23, 1973, Judge Sirica read aloud in court a letter from James McCord, one of the burglars, reporting his own perjury and the fact that the defendants had been pressured to remain silent. Trying to staunch the loss of confidence in his administration, Nixon replaced Attorney General Richard Kleindienst, who was not involved in the cover up, with Elliot Richardson, whose probity in public and private life was above reproach. Richardson hired former Solicitor General Archibald Cox, a Harvard Law School professor, as a special prosecutor. When a Senate special committee investigating the affair heard that there was a voice-activated recording system in Nixon's office, Cox sought the tapes. Nixon refused to turn them over, and he asked Richardson to fire Cox. When Richardson refused, Nixon turned to Deputy Attorney General William Ruckelshaus. Both resigned rather than comply. Acting Attorney General Robert Bork fired Cox.[17]

Arguing against turning over the tapes, Nixon's personal counsel James St. Clair told Judge Sirica that the tapes were protected under the doctrine of executive privilege. The case thus became a test of checks and balances at the highest level of government. Faced with the president's refusal to turn over the tapes when served with the subpoena he issued, Sirica opined that no one was above the law in the American system of government. It was as succinct and complete a statement of the rule of checks as balances as any of the framers might have

Figure 13.2 Judge Sirica and the defendants and counsel listen to the Nixon tapes during the Watergate hearings in 1974. Credit: Sketch by Betty Wells. Courtesy of Stanley Kaplan.

written. "What distinctive quality of the Presidency permits its incumbent to withhold evidence? To argue that the need for Presidential privacy justifies it, is not persuasive. On the occasions when such need justifies suppression, the courts will sustain a privilege." John Marshall, presiding over the treason trial of Aaron Burr, in 1807, had written in similar fashion to President Jefferson when Aaron Burr sought documents in Jefferson's possession for his defense against the charge of treason, and with some petulance Jefferson complied. The vastly increased power of the presidency in the federal system over the years from 1807 to 1973 did not sway Sirica. Marshall's view of the law was Sirica's. "To argue that it is the constitutional separation of powers that bars compulsory court process from the White House, is also unpersuasive. Such a contention overlooks history." Was the federal judiciary still the weakest branch? Perhaps, but a proposition "that the Court has not the physical power to enforce its order to the President is immaterial to a resolution of the issues. Regardless of its physical power to enforce them, the Court has a duty to issue appropriate orders. The Court cannot say that the Executive's persistence in withholding the tape recordings would 'tarnish its reputation,' but must admit that it would tarnish the Court's reputation to fail to do what it could in pursuit of justice." The U.S. Supreme Court upheld Sirica's order. With impeachment looming, the president resigned the office.[18]

Ford, Carter, and Reagan Appointments to the Federal Bench

President Gerald Ford made only one addition to the Supreme Court. When Justice Douglas's disability from strokes led him to retire, Ford picked a fellow midwesterner, John Paul Stevens. The second-oldest and the third-longest serving justice when he retired in 2010, Stevens's thorough craftsmanship and wide reading habits showed through all his opinions. A child of wealth from Hyde Park, a neighborhood on the South Side of Chicago, he served in the navy during World War II and inspired in part by his clerkship with Justice Rutledge, came to see the law as an evolving reflection of a democratic people's values. An antitrust litigator in Chicago and a moderate Republican, he was a Nixon choice for the Court of Appeals for the Seventh Circuit in 1970. On the Supreme Court, he moved from a moderate conservative position to a fairly consistently liberal one, a course similar to Blackmun's (though Stevens would insist that he had not changed his views—the Court had merely moved to the right).[19]

President Jimmy Carter never had the opportunity to fill a vacancy on the Supreme Court, but he made major contributions to the history of the federal courts' recruitment. Carter bade his attorney general and close friend, former federal appeals court Judge Griffin Bell, to create and head a merit panel on appointment to the courts of appeals. The merit panel in turn created panels for each of the judicial circuits. Carter encouraged members of the Senate to form their own vetting groups for the districts, though not all members of the upper house took advantage of this opportunity. Carter also asked Bell to run the potential nominees by him and according to documentary evidence in the Carter library, Bell commented extensively on the potential choices. Carter was not a lawyer and depended on Bell as much as on the merit panels, but his was a hands-on presidency, and it should come as no surprise that he wanted a hand in selecting the finalists.[20]

With the opportunity to fill 117 new district and 35 new circuit judgeships created by the Federal District and Circuit Judges Act of 1978, the merit panels were an innovation of great potential significance. Although Senators in twenty-nine states agreed in principal to establish merit vetting for district judgeships, that promise was never realized, and indeed the ideal of selection based solely on merit never quite fulfilled Carter's campaign promises of nonpartisanship.

Over 95 percent of the choices were Democrats (hardly likely if party affiliation were not part of the selection process). Frank Johnson was a Republican and sailed through the merit committee hearing on his appointment to the Fifth Circuit; Democratic Senator Howell Heflin from Alabama joining and Bell and Carter in support of the nomination. Not every potential appointee was as well known as Johnson. For example, Arthur Alarcón recalled being interviewed by the merit committee for a post on the Court of Appeals for the Ninth Circuit. At the time he was a middle level California appeals court judge. The circuit merit panel met with him in a federal courthouse in San Francisco. It was only the second time he had been there, but he so impressed his interrogators that he was nominated and confirmed without much further ado. Alarcón was a Republican, as it happened, a fact that the Carter White House knew. So, too, was Carolyn Dineen King, who was nominated and confirmed for the Court of Appeals for the Fifth Circuit. She was in private practice in Houston when the circuit panel suggested her. In an ABA oral history she recalled her childhood, her parents the only Republicans in a 100 percent Irish neighborhood in Syracuse. Good grades and pluck enabled her to gain honors at Smith College and Yale Law School. She recalled how being a woman made finding a job in the public sector difficult. A job interview with the U.S. attorney in Houston, the city where her husband found his legal job, made a big impression on her. There were no Republicans in the U.S. attorney's Texas, or at least working in his office, he reported. He had "'hired him' an African American and he had 'hired him' a Mexican" but he wasn't ready to "hire him" a woman. Eventually he did hire a woman, and when King became a judge, she and the U.S. attorney became fast friends. [21]

As governor of Georgia Carter "appointed more women and minorities to his own staff, to major state policy board and agencies, and to the judiciary than all of his predecessors combined." As president, he was committed to making the judiciary more representative of the American people, not quite an affirmative action initiative, but something very close to it. His appointments to the District of Columbia courts signaled his intent. To the district court he named African-Americans John Garrett Penn and Norma Holloway Johnson, and women— Johnson and Joyce Hens Green. His appointments to the District's Court of Appeals included Patricia M. Wald, his assistant attorney general for legislative affairs and a well-known civil liberties lawyer. Abner Mikva was the second of his choices. Mikva was a former Democratic congressman. Harry T. Edwards was the second African American to serve on the District's Court of Appeals after Spottswood Robinson III. Prior to his appointment he had been a law professor at Michigan and Harvard and was recognized as an expert on labor law. Finally, Carter appointed Ruth Bader Ginsburg, a law professor at Columbia and head of the women's rights project at the ACLU, to the Court of Appeals for the District. The District's Court of Appeals is second only to the bench of the Supreme Court in visibility, and Carter's appointments were symbolic of his commitment to a diverse bench. The nine men and women he selected exceeded the demographic pattern of his picks for the other federal judgeships—as two were African-American males, one was an African-American woman, and three were white women.[22]

President Ronald Reagan wanted the federal judiciary to reflect his administration's priorities. While the president did not continue the circuit-level panel, Attorney General William French Smith urged members of the Senate to continue to use committees to examine the credential of potential nominees. But like his immediate predecessors, Reagan had made judicial appointments an important talking point in his campaign, and his administration would pay considerable attention to the backgrounds of nominees. One of Reagan's most specific promises was to appoint a woman to the Supreme Court. He soon got his opportunity.[23]

When Justice Potter Stewart retired in the summer of 1981, Reagan nominated Sandra Day O'Connor. The Senate quickly confirmed her nomination, unanimously, making her the first woman to serve on the Court. O'Connor had spent her early childhood on her parents' ranch in southeastern Arizona, a sprawling 155,000 acre enterprise. Isolated from other children, she read voraciously and eclectically. She earned both her undergraduate degree and her law degree at Stanford. Despite a splendid academic record and service as an editor of the law journal, as a woman her only offer of employment in the legal world was as a legal secretary at a large firm in Los Angeles. Instead she turned to politics. By 1965 O'Connor had established a reputation as a sharp, able, and conservative Republican in Arizona politics, serving as an assistant state attorney general, in the state Senate where, in 1973, she became the first female majority leader, and on the bench of the Maricopa County Superior Court. In 1979, due at least in part to her refusal to run against him for governor, Democrat Bruce Babbitt appointed O'Connor to the Arizona Court of Appeals.[24]

On the Supreme Court O'Connor proved to be a flexible and pragmatic judge, and she would often be a swing vote when the other members divided evenly. Indeed, because she sensed the politics of the Court and the political mood of the nation, she was almost always in the majority. O'Connor carved out influential opinions on subjects such as religious freedom and affirmative action before retiring in 2006 after twenty-five years on the Court.[25]

Filling openings on the lower courts was left in the hands of trusted Reagan subordinates, in particular Attorney General William French Smith and his successor, Edwin Meese. Their plans did not include merit panels. Instead, "the highest levels of the White House staff . . . played an ongoing, active role in the selection of judges." The process ensured a greater uniformity of views among the new nominees than one found in Carter's recruitment process. According to one judge added to a Court of Appeals in this round of appointments, Smith and Meese were looking for young, conservative, intellectually active jurists and found them in the law school teaching the ranks. Meese developed a screening process that indirectly included political affiliation and directly sought candidates' views on subjects that were important to the Reagan administration. Potential nominees later recalled that they were asked about their judicial philosophy, their personal views, and their background. These interviews were conducted with uniformity and precision, and observers concluded that they had an impact on the ideological composition of the nominees sent to the Senate, although the members of the Department of Justice who conducted the interviews denied that they focused on any one set of issues or sought any one set of responses.[26]

Various liberal political action groups mounted vigorous campaigns against some of the nominations. The nomination of Jefferson Sessions III, U.S. attorney for the Southern District of Alabama, for the district court was denied a majority on the Senate Judiciary Committee in 1986 after his insensitive comments about African Americans were revealed. Sessions was later elected to the Senate. Only Reagan's personal intervention and a good deal of horse trading got Daniel Manion's confirmation for the Court of Appeals for the Seventh Circuit through the Senate with a tie vote. These issues came to a head in the prolonged and highly visible Senate hearings on the confirmation of Robert Bork to the Supreme Court. Bork was a University of Chicago and University of Chicago Law School product and Yale Law School professor for many years and a somewhat more orthodox, even doctrinaire, advocate of law and economics. Reputed to be capable of "great charm" in private, in public Bork appeared cold and harsh. He believed in private choice theory, free markets, and a light hand for the government in the private sector—including doubts about the legitimacy of the reasoning in *Brown v. Board of Education*.[27]

Bork was certainly qualified for the bench by virtue of his service in the solicitor general's office, his education, and his intellect. His jurisprudence, rather than any close ties to Meese or Reagan, gained him a nod for an open slot on the D.C. Court of Appeals, and Bork was confirmed in February 1982. When he was asked to serve on the Court of Appeals, he later recalled that he was hesitant. He had just left Yale Law School and returned to his old law firm. Visits from a succession of increasingly higher ranking Department of Justice officials finally swayed him. He took a serious cut in salary and found himself in "a life sentence to the Law Review." He was unhappy because, he recalled, "it's an isolated job . . . everybody's busy and you don't drop in on a judge to kick around a legal question because the judging has become too much of an assembly line process—get the stuff out." The bulk of the cases were "not very interesting as law because what you're doing is second-guessing a prudential decision by some regulator." As the Reagan appointees on the Court became the majority, relations among the judges became "a little less jolly." Bork did not always agree with his most recent colleagues. After six years, light appeared at the end of the tunnel: President Reagan asked him to join the Supreme Court.[28]

Bork's confirmation hearings for the D.C. Court of Appeals had been easy, he recalled: one hour; no vetting beforehand; no visiting with various senators. Five and a half years later, Bork's experience in the Senate was diametrically opposite from what he faced in 1982. In the 1986 election year, the Senate changed hands, going from a Republican to a Democratic majority. This did not bode well for confirmation. Since the Harding administration, when a president and a Senate majority were of opposite political parties, the Senate rejected or forced withdrawal of Supreme Court nominees in four of fifteen, or over one-quarter, of the cases; while only four of thirty-nine nominations for the Supreme Court, a little over one-tenth, were rejected or withdrawn when the Senate majority and the president were of the same party. In a series of what Bork defenders regarded as excruciatingly partisan and Bork opponents viewed as "extremely high quality" hearings, expert witnesses, including a number of law professors, testified for and against his candidacy. Was he simply a consistent advocate of the jurisprudence of originalism or heartlessly indifferent to an evolving notion of rights? Did his unwillingness to find the right to privacy in the Constitution reflect principled reasoning or stubborn resistance to changing national values? The widely televised hearings gave the viewing public a look at the confirmation process at its most contentious. The Senate rejected his nomination, 58 against, 42 in favor, with six Republicans and two Democrats crossing party lines. Bork reportedly told friends that he had faced "the first all-out political campaign with respect to a judicial nominee in the country's history," a campaign that had "reached record lows for mendacity, brutality, and intellectual vulgarity." While some commentators concluded that the Bork nomination changed the process of appointment profoundly, anyone familiar with the Louis Brandeis and John Parker confirmation hearings might disagree.[29]

In 1981, Professor Richard Posner took a seat on the Court of Appeals for the Seventh Circuit. Born in New York City and a graduate of Yale College, Posner attended Harvard Law School, clerked for Justice Brennan, and became a noted advocate of the "law and economics" theory of judicial reasoning at the University of Chicago Law School. Though he worked in Lyndon Johnson's Department of Justice and was a nominal Democrat, he was one of Reagan's first nominees in 1981. Though a young man when confirmed at forty-two years of age, Posner was already a true public intellectual. Since his confirmation, his productivity on the bench and as a scholar has been simply remarkable. He has written books about the decline of the public intellectual, the process of judging, plagiarism, *Bush v. Gore*, the impeachment of President Clinton, the reputation of Justice Cardozo, pragmatism, capitalism, sex and the law, terrorism, and a series of hornbooks and casebooks on the economic interpretation of law, among other subjects. Posner's law and economics jurisprudence led to a liberal stance on such matters as the decriminalization of drug use, the legality of partial birth abortion, and prisoners' rights.[30]

A third noteworthy Reagan choice, J. Harvie Wilkinson III, was as sharp-minded as Bork and Posner, without the combativeness of the former or the doctrinal commitments of the latter. Although he had served on the bench, he was young (forty) when appointed, educated at Yale College and University of Virginia Law School, with experience in the Reagan administration (briefly a deputy assistant attorney general), articulate (four books and counting), and a former Supreme Court clerk (to Justice Powell). His opposition to affirmative action programs and his concern about the role of the courts in reproductive rights cases also fit the views of the president. In environmental, freedom of speech, and gun control cases, Wilkinson proved that he was far more independent-minded than his initial backers would have anticipated, however. His 2012 essay on *Cosmic Constitutional Theory* explained why the courts should restrain themselves from trying to change the world: First, it was not their job. Second, judging was not an intellectual endeavor that lent itself to theorizing. Finally, cases in which judges exceeded the bounds of prudence often had untoward consequences. Better to leave policymaking for the elected bodies of government. Short-listed on more than one occasion for a seat on the Supreme Court, Wilkinson's reflective views on the limitations of judging, not to mention his moderate views on a number of issues, may actually have harmed his chances. [31]

Judge Antonin Scalia, a fourth Reagan and Meese selection, was like Bork, Posner, and Wilkinson, an intellectual student of law, a skilled craftsman of opinions, and a powerful voice for judicial restraint. Born in Trenton, New Jersey, Scalia was the only child of a schoolteacher and a professor. He grew to adulthood in Queens, New York, went to Georgetown University as an undergraduate, and then Harvard Law School. Always a superior student, he found a job immediately at a Cleveland law firm, and in 1967, became a law professor at the University of Virginia. In 1971, he entered the Nixon administration and stayed on in President Gerald Ford's Department of Justice. He taught at the Georgetown University Law Center, then at the University of Chicago Law School. In 1982, President Ronald Reagan appointed Scalia to the U.S. Court of Appeals for the District of Columbia Circuit.[32]

On the Court of Appeals Scalia's specialty was the powers (and limitation of the powers) of federal agencies. He affirmed agency decisions nearly 60 percent of the time, though one should note that in many cases the agencies' decisions restrained the federal government's role in the economy. His only support for expansion of federal governmental powers lay in the criminal justice area. He had little occasion to write about civil rights, privacy, or other socially controversial matters. Most often his views represented the conclusions of the majority of the panel on which he was serving. The highest level of agreement was with Judges Robert Bork, James Buckley, Laurence Silberman, and Kenneth Starr, others who had served in Republican administrations or had been a Republican member of Congress.[33]

Scalia's reputation as a conservative jurisprudent made him a natural choice to join the Reagan Court. Indeed, few justices could point to as consistent a philosophy of judging and reading of the Constitution as Scalia's. He advocated a plain sense, plain-meaning rule for interpreting the Constitution, a variation of the doctrine of originalism, and disparaged surveys of legislative intent in interpreting statutory language. Perhaps it helped his cause that in 1986 the Republicans held a majority of seats in the Senate. In any case, his confirmation was unanimous.[34]

By contrast, Reagan's appointment of Justice Rehnquist to replace Burger in the center seat roiled controversy in the Senate. All the old charges, with some new additions, made against Rehnquist when he was appointed to the Court reappeared. The Senate nevertheless voted 65-33 to confirm Rehnquist as chief justice, and on September 26, 1986, he moved over two seats. While Rehnquist had often dissented alone on the Burger Court, after he became chief justice he found himself more often in the majority as he was joined by other conservative justices. His colleagues greatly appreciated his administrative efficiency and his sense of humor. He was a realist and wisely concluded the final edition of his widely read history of the Supreme Court: "Placed in the context of U.S. political history [the Court] has had a great deal to say about whether the political solutions to major national problems devised by the legislative and executive branches would be allowed to proceed."[35]

The last of Reagan's appointees to the Court was Anthony Kennedy, a sitting Court of Appeals for the Ninth Circuit judge, whom Reagan selected after Bork's nomination was defeated and D.C. Circuit Judge Douglas Ginsburg withdrew his name from consideration. A Stanford undergraduate and Harvard Law School product, Kennedy was a sound choice. On the Court of Appeals and later the Supreme Court, Kennedy was a moderate conservative without a doctrinaire view of law, often a swing vote joining O'Connor. After she retired, wags called his tenure the "Kennedy Court."[36]

While much in the Nixon, Carter, and Reagan appointments process will seem familiar to readers of earlier chapters, one less familiar theme deserves some attention. Special interest groups always had a hand in suggesting nominees and wrangling over confirmations. In the wake of the rise of the Moral Majority and New Feminism movements, among others, the characteristics of groups seeking a voice on the federal courts broadened in the final years of the Reagan administration. United by issue orientation rather than regional or ethnic ties, these groups often had specific criteria in mind to measure the fitness of candidates. Insofar as the groups' importance to the bases of the major political parties mattered, these criteria became very visible parts of the nomination and confirmation process.[37]

Managerial Remedies

One area in which the federal courts and advocacy groups came in regular contact was in the courts' management of controversial matters like desegregation, prison administration, products liability, and reapportionment. By the late 1960s, "managerial judging" on these and other subjects was a fact of life in the district courts. Even the term had established itself as the rubric for a wide variety of judicial techniques. The Federal Rules of Civil Procedure provisions for discovery and class action opened this door, and civil rights cases and mass tort suits drew federal judges through it.[38]

The novelty of federal managerial judges in the late 1960s and after was that judges were engaged not only in managing the pretrial and trial portions of suits, they were managing remedies as well. In the early stages of desegregation litigation under *Brown* II, judges facilitated the process of remediation in tradition ways. They maintained, in varying degrees, a neutrality—not an indifference to desegregation, but a distance from the nuts and bolts of desegregation plans. They conducted evidentiary hearings, ruled on motions, and reacted to the parties. The Court dropped the "all deliberate speed" formula in 1968 and mandated speedy compliance; however, the judges became managers of the remedy. For example, in the mid-1960s, "virtually all blacks in Charlotte [North Carolina] were still attending all-black schools." District Judge James B. McMillan was not satisfied with the school board's compliance or with his predecessor's view that the board had done enough. Although a North Carolinian born and bred, and new on the federal bench, the litigation "educated" him about the realities of white southern resistance to *Brown*. With the help of John Finger, an expert on the subject, McMillan ordered a comprehensive busing plan. "This is political dynamite and will cause a real commotion. But let's go ahead," he told Finger. In *Swann v. Charlotte-Mecklenburg* (1970), they did. Indeed, in a remarkable turnabout in later years, the school board "aggressively" pursued the goal of desegregation. In the Southern District of Texas, Judge Woodrow B. Seals began to take an active role in the desegregation of Corpus Christi schools. He consulted directly with lawyers and witnesses, gathered information on the district, found busing a suitable remedy to end de facto segregation, and "announced an ambitious" busing scheme for Corpus Christi and stayed involved in the process to ensure compliance with his orders.[39]

Judges managing the posttrial stage of the litigation in order to gain compliance confronted a variety of obstacles in the path to integration that tested their patience and their managerial skills. Massive white flight from city school systems to suburbs undid the fairest-minded desegregation plans. In Detroit, for example, where long-time residential segregation had led to de facto school segregation in the city, black families sought integration of the city's schools. White flight, however, had taken many wealthier white families outside the city limits. In *Bradley v. Milliken* (1971) (on appeal *Milliken v. Bradley*), federal judge Stephen Roth, a Kennedy appointee who had been a refugee from communist Hungary, presided over a forty-one day bench trial. The suit pitted the city, in the person of student Ronald Bradley, against Governor William Milliken. In the meantime, a plan for busing children across districts was approved in Pontiac, Michigan, and the *Swann* opinion came down.

Roth found that the state had failed to provide equal educational opportunities to the inner city children, in effect using districting to recreate de jure segregation. "The City of Detroit is a community generally divided by racial lines. Residential segregation within the city and throughout the larger metropolitan area is substantial, pervasive and of long standing. Black citizens are located in separate and distinct areas within the city and are not generally to be found in the suburbs. While the racially unrestricted choice of black persons and economic factors may have played some part in the development of this pattern of residential segregation, it is, in the main, the result of past and present practices and customs of racial discrimination, both public and private." After consultation with the parties, he fashioned a comprehensive regional busing plan. What was more, he continued over the course of three more years to refine and enforce the remedy. In the name of the white families who had left the city to avoid sending their children to Detroit schools, the state of Michigan fought back. It stood behind the concept of neighborhood schools and regarded the city limits as the proper limit of any busing plan involving the city's children. On appeal, it won its case.[40]

In Nashville, Tennessee, the effort to desegregate the public school system began in 1956 and finally resulted in a comprehensive busing plan for the Davidson County school district. It was fashioned by district judges William E. Miller and his successor L. Clure Morton. Miller, a native Tennessean and 1955 Eisenhower appointee, had managed the litigation in the traditional fashion, hearing and determining motions after his original order to the district to desegregate. He struck down a statewide parent preference plan that did not compel integration but allowed a "grade-a-year" plan that in effect maintained a dual system of schools through the 1960s. At the end of that decade, Judge

Miller ordered the district to prepare a busing program. Judge Morton was not happy with the plan, however, and called on experts from the U.S. Department of Health, Education, and Welfare to assist him in achieving racial balance in the metropolitan public schools.

Morton was a Nixon appointee, a longtime Republican, and a close friend of Republican Senator Howard Baker. He was determined to see that the schools desegregated. The new plan featured ratios and zones to ensure that no school had a majority of minority students. The result was fury coming close to violence by antibusing parents. Two scholars who studied these events found that "[a]ll this activity was directed at one man, Judge L. Clure Morton." Federal marshals became de facto bodyguards as the judge worked to ensure the plan's success. White flight took the form of parents sending their children to private schools, effectually resegregating public education. Black parents responded by condemning busing and calling for increased funding for schools, once again in almost entirely black neighborhoods.[41]

Other judges faced even more vexing difficulties as they tried to manage the desegregation remedies they had ordered. Judge W. Arthur Garrity in the District of Massachusetts wrestled with a hostile Boston City Council, a candidate for mayor who was running on a platform of civil disobedience, and an enraged Irish community in South Boston that refused to integrate its schools by busing their children. The Boston city schools imbroglio became national news. Unable or unwilling to move to the suburbs as the white parents of Detroit had, South Boston white residents mobilized massive resistance to the Garrity plan. Garrity might have had divided loyalties, as he was the handpicked choice of the Boston-Kennedy clan that derived much of its political clout from Boston's Irish population, but he was a man of strict moral conscience and fidelity to the rule of law. When it fell to him to manage desegregation of the Boston schools, he appointed masters in equity to aid him, including a former attorney general of the state, a former justice of the state supreme court, and a former U.S. commissioner of education. In *Morgan v. Hennigan* (1974), his seventy-four page densely detailed opinion, combined tables and statistical findings with a narrative that resembled a social science monograph. Unlike Roth in *Milliken*, Garrity did not extend the ruling to the surrounding communities: "The court denied a motion of the city defendants to join numerous cities and towns around Boston as defendants, partly on the ground that the proposed defendant cities and towns had not been charged by the plaintiffs with contributing to the violation of their constitutional rights." But he found that open enrollment and controlled transfer plans earlier inaugurated by the city school board were inadequate remedies for the pervasive fact of continuing segregation. Busing was the answer. "Southie won't go" was the response of antibusing activists, along with anonymous promises to murder the judge. Ostracized by former friends, reviled by his fellow city citizens, Garrity nevertheless arranged for the plan to cover the entire city and prepared to supervise its implementation.[42]

The burden of managing remedies sometimes had a profound impact on the judges. Not only did it absorb much of their time, it altered the way they looked at desegregation. Judge McMillan's background in rural North Carolina had not made him sympathetic to the plight of black city school children but reviewing the facts did. Judge Roth was initially skeptical of the arguments that the Legal Defense Fund of the NAACP made, but as the evidence he acquired began to mount, his views changed. He became far more responsive to the plight of the inner city school children and to the efforts of the city school board to provide the parents with truly integrated schools. Judge Garrity would have preferred some other remedy than citywide busing, but the facts he gathered left him little choice.[43]

After watching with frustration nearly twenty years of Little Rock school district's attempts to avoid integration, Judge Henry Woods, a Little Rock Arkansas native appointed to the district bench by President Carter, recused himself from further involvement in the case. His last decree had ordered a unitary or consolidated school district, but it was overturned by the Eighth Circuit's judgment that consolidation was not constitutionally warranted. His regret and dismay were palpable in his final opinion:

Figure 13.3 Boston police escort school buses carrying black students to and from high school to protect them from protests of court-ordered busing in 1974. Credit: Bettman/Corbis/AP Images.

In my years as district judge in this difficult case involving the three
school districts in Pulaski County, I have attempted to oversee the
implementation of positive desegregation plans which would benefit
all children in the public schools. To that end, I have sought the help of
the most progressive and able persons in this country . . . Whatever the
plan finally mandated by the Court of Appeals, those who take as their
part delay and obstruction will have won. For those people, delay is victory, regardless of the cost to the school children or to a community
economically stagnant because of the "school mess."[44]

Complex class-action suits involving products liability and mass torts also
called for managerial judging of remedies. Although these were class actions
suits, they differed from civil rights litigation. The civil rights class action resulted
in injunctions affecting all concerned, but did not directly transfer funds into
the hands of the successful party (though school district funding formulas were
directly effected). By contrast, the plaintiffs in products liability and mass tort
cases wanted monetary awards to repair the damage that the defendant's products had caused. A distinction between the two kinds of class-action suits was
foreseen in 1966, but attempts at a simple distinction spawned a new generation
of Federal Rules of Civil Procedure, in this case Rules 14, 22, and 23, governing
certain kinds of multiparty litigation.

The older class action included permissive joinder (of defendants and plaintiffs to the suit), impleading (allowing defendants to bring another party into the
suit or plaintiffs to add another defendant), and interpleader (a plaintiff can ask
the court to have third parties litigate a dispute over the plaintiff's property—
to avoid multiple claims on it). Inclusion of the class action in the earliest versions of the Federal Rules was designed to improve the efficiency of the courts
without sacrificing fairness to parties. But the overarching concept had problems
when applied to specific cases: When did the rights or fact situation of one or
more of the parties not conform to the others? When did the remedy sought for
the class not fit the harm to one party or others? How were parties to be notified? How were parties able to "opt out" of the class and bring their own suit?
Successive Rules revision committees tried to iron out these wrinkles, an effort
that never seemed finished.[45]

These technical questions aside, the broadening of the category facilitated the
filing of class action civil rights cases—indeed, some commentators have concluded that the purpose of the amended rule was to facilitate civil rights litigation by avoiding the need to file suits in more than one district. But broadening
the rules did not come to grips with the class-action suits that sought monetary
relief.[46]

So courts suggested, the advisory committee made proposed amendments, and Congress approved four categorical requirements for certifying class-action suits. The first was "numerosity"—the size of the potential class. Federal courts would be deluged if thousands of claims were filed when a single class action could adequately and fairly accommodate all the claimants. Commonality of claims, including common facts and legal theories under which the litigation was begun, had to be established. The claims or defenses of any one member of the class named in the action had to be typical of the others in the class that the named litigant supposedly represented. The same was true of the named defendant. Finally, the class members had to have adequate legal representation. All of these bore on the certification of a class, apart from the remedy segment of the litigation. [47]

Judicial management became a regular part of the class action when the underlying claim was product liability. A note to the revision of Rule 23 suggested that a mass accident was not a proper subject for class action, as matters of liability and causation might be significantly different for individual members of the plaintiff class. Defective products suits, however, were certified for "dispersed" members of the class. Typical of these was the class action against the Dalkon Shield intrauterine device. The case was certified in 1981 and decertified in 1982, and finally certified, tried, and settled in *In Re A.H. Robins Co* (1989).[48]

Robins, a major pharmaceutical firm, bought the license to market the birth control device from Dalkonand, at first marketed it widely and successfully. By 1980, however, the complaints by women whose use of the shield had led to a wide range of harms, from pelvic infections to infertility, had reached a level that Robins began to send letters to doctors warning that infections were a common side effect if the shield was in place for more than a limited period of time, the idea being that it was the user's misuse of the product, not a defect in the product itself, that caused the harm. This was the basis of the company's defense against the mounting number of lawsuits. By 1981, plaintiffs were winning suits against Robins, and the punitive damage awards (based on Robins concealing internal evidence of defects) were mounting steeply.[49]

Robins stopped marketing the product the next year but did not issue a recall until 1980, when litigants offered irrefutable evidence that the device caused widespread infertility problems and heightened the risk of pelvic infection. Individual claimants were winning damages as early as 1975, but the number of diversity cases was cascading, and some judges were taking steps to join the plaintiffs to manage the cases and fund the monetary rewards. A district court in California was the first to certify the class action. The Ninth Circuit reversed the certification under the theory that each plaintiff had to prove that the device had caused her injury, a proximate causation doctrine common in tort law. The defendant pharmaceutical company losing suit after suit and paying out large monetary rewards then asked for class-action certification in a Virginia district court, but the reasoning of the Ninth Circuit continued to bar certification. In the course of a series of federal suits against Robins in Minnesota, plaintiffs lawyers discovered evidence that the company had not only known about the dangers, it had also destroyed internal documents that warned of the dangers. In 1984, ten years after the first suit was filed in a Wichita, Kansas, federal court, with the punitive awards mounting still higher and plaintiffs winning all their cases, the company withdrew the product from the market. At the same time, Robins again sought the consolidation of the cases in one federal jurisdiction, as it happened, in the Eastern District of Virginia. In 1984, Judge Robert Merhige, who had nearly two decades earlier managed the desegregation of the Richmond schools, found himself managing the Dalkon Shield litigation. His decision in the former case, busing students across school district lines, was highly controversial (and ultimately reversed), but it was matched in boldness by his handling of the Dalkon Shield cases. He sympathized with defendant's request for certification of all the cases as a class action but denied the request for res judicata (the issue had already been settled). Still, he worked with the parties to reach a solution that did not deny plaintiffs adequate recompense while keeping the company afloat, perhaps by denying punitive damages. In 1985, he arranged a meeting of judges handling the cases, but soon afterward Robins's petition for bankruptcy ended his plan to manage the entirety of the litigation from his courtroom. In an exchange in his courtroom, in which one plaintiff's lawyer asked Judge Merhige if he had sought to have all the cases brought to his court, he replied, "I am a judge, not a huckster, I don't advertise for business."[50]

In 1985, the Dalkon Shield plaintiffs turned their guns on Robins's insurance company, Aetna. Aetna disputed their extent of liability in the matter. By this time, courts were managing how Robins might emerge from bankruptcy and the various suits against Aetna. The various issues were soon turning on whether the federal courts had or could manage the payouts of damages. The Agent Orange, asbestos, and other mass products tort cases' payouts were similarly at stake, a kind of fictive issue joinder of class actions the courts faced, as all eyes turned to *Robins*. Judge Merhige had certified the suits against Aetna as a class action. The Court of Appeals for the Fourth Circuit upheld the certification in an opinion by Judge Donald Russell, "In summary, we take it as the lessons to be gleaned from the authorities already cited and discussed to be . . . that the 'trend' is once again to give Rule 23 [the civil procedure rule governing the certification of class action suits] a liberal rather than a restrictive construction, adopting a standard of flexibility in application which will in the particular case 'best serve the ends of justice for the affected parties and . . . promote judicial efficiency.'"[51]

The pendulum swung against permissive certification in the next decade. With *Robins* as precedent, district courts were certifying class actions in mass torts. But appellate courts reversed, determining that defendants with stronger cases than *Robins* were caving in and settling rather than face certification of a class action. Central to these appellate decisions to decertify cases were tobacco-related suits and asbestos exposure suits. Some of the decisions involved the old tort law element of causation. Others involved payouts from a limited fund. None of the reversals slowed the more general advance of managerial judging however.

The Other Civil Rights Revolution

The Dalkon Shield plaintiffs were women, and the litigation overlapped what may be called the other civil rights revolution in the federal courts. Women's rights litigation in the 1970s centered on the debilities and inequalities suffered by women. Although feminism was already a well-established ideology when women obtained the vote and women began to serve in government, the Civil Rights Act of 1964 expanded the public law guarantees for women; Title VII included sex in the suspect categories of discrimination in education, occupation, and the public sphere. The creation of the Equal Employment Opportunity Commission furthered the goal of equal pay for equal work. Author and activist Betty Friedan's 1966 idea for a National Organization for Women (NOW) led to a drive for legal reform. The capstone of the movement was the call for an Equal Rights Amendment to the Constitution.[52]

Legal issues of special interest to women included the right to equal treatment in insurance and pension payouts, the right to be safe from harassment in the workforce, and the right to manage their own reproductive experience. Under the provisions of Title VII, women were beginning to bring suits to federal courts to establish these rights in practice. Some of these women's cases involved new causes of action, that is, new grounds for bringing suit within the jurisdiction of the federal courts based on acts of Congress.[53]

The success of the other civil rights revolution must in some degree be credited to law schools' admission of women in increasing numbers and the part these graduates played in litigating women's issues. For a time, the Ivy League law schools sandbagged levies against the rising flood. One example will suffice to make the case. In 1945, one law student recalled, Harvard Law Professor Roscoe Pound saw a woman at the back of his classroom and thundered, "I don't permit women in my classes. Get out!" Four years later, Dean Erwin Griswold reported to the Harvard faculty that "many able men are turned away from our classes each year," but, "a small number of unusually qualified women students" would be admitted the next year. The number of women practicing law increased from fewer than 7,000 in 1960 to over 13,000 in 1970, but various subtle obstacles and not so subtle quotas still limited women's enrollment to less than 5 percent of the total in these years. It is impossible to document how many women sought entry to law schools like Harvard intending to engage in public law, but the relative numbers of women law school graduates in the public sector, particularly in government service, is easily proven. When judicial clerkships were opened to women, they "enthusiastically" and successfully sought them. Even more important, from a handful of women joining men as teachers of law in the 1960s, the ratio of men to women in these positions is approaching one to one. One of these female professors, Ruth Bader Ginsburg, would play a crucial role in carrying the civil rights revolution into the realm of ending sex discrimination in the law. As Justice Elena Kagan told a meeting of the New York City Bar Association in 2014, "As a litigator and then as a judge [Ginsburg] changed the face of American antidiscrimination law."[54]

Ginsburg grew up in New York City, in a family of modest means. Both parents sacrificed the comforts of their later years for their only daughter's education, and Ginsburg made the most of the opportunity. She starred at Cornell University and then at Harvard Law School before finishing at Columbia Law School. Even the top women graduates of elite schools could not break into the major New York City firms, just as O'Connor discovered in California, nor gain judicial clerkships. As Ginsburg later wrote, "a woman, a Jew, and a mother to boot" was a triple handicap. She found a job teaching at Columbia Law School, then Rutgers–Newark, then back to Columbia.[55]

By the beginning of the 1970s, Ginsburg was fast becoming one of the most successful advocates of legal equality for women. In 1971, Ginsburg was co-counsel in *Reed v. Reed* (1971), in which the Court struck down a law that discriminated on the basis of sex—in this case gender distinctions in Idaho's estate law—based on the Equal Protection Clause of the Fourteenth Amendment. The next year, she co-founded the Women's Rights Project at the ACLU. In 1973, she argued *Frontiero v. Richardson* (1973), in which the Court found that provisions for benefits given to members of the armed services cannot discriminate on the basis of sex.[56]

The decisions were triumphs for Ginsburg and women's equal rights. The next year, in *Cleveland Board of Education v. LaFleur* (1974) she successfully advocated the end of discriminatory pregnancy leave policies, and in *Corning Glass Works v. Brennan* (1974) she played a key role in the effort to gain women the same pay as men for the same work under the Equal Pay Act. Her team reversed the discriminatory policies of the Social Security Administration in *Weinberger v. Wiesenfeld* (1975), convincing the Court that unequal pay for widows and widowers raising minors violated the Due Process Clause of the Fifth Amendment. In *Craig v. Boren* (1976) the majority of the Court elevated gender-specific legislation to intermediate level of scrutiny above the rational-relation test and below the strict-scrutiny test. The Oklahoma law in question allowed women to purchase low alcohol beer at age eighteen but restricted male purchasers to age twenty-one and over. Brennan's opinion struck down the statute, but the test he used was far more important than simply equalizing the age at which young people could buy near beer. To pass the new test for equal protection under the Fourteenth Amendment (though Brennan, writing for a 7 to 2 majority, insisted that he had not created anything new) a state law that discriminated against women "must serve important government objectives and must be substantially related to the achievement of those objectives."[57]

In the 1970s the right to a safe and legal abortion absorbed many of the other women's causes in the same fashion as the drive for abolition of slavery absorbed many northern reform movements in the 1850s. Two graduates of the University of Texas School of Law in Austin, Sarah Weddington and Linda Coffee, were largely responsible for the federalization of a woman's right to end a pregnancy in a case that would become known as *Roe v. Wade* (1973). Texas had a very old law that made the performance of an abortion a felony. The woman undergoing the procedure was not a party to the offense. There was no exception for rape, incest, or the health of the mother, save when her life was at stake. Georgia had recently altered its law, following guidelines from the American Bar Association, the American Medical Association, and the Model Penal Code, to allow an abortion if a panel of doctors agreed that continuing a pregnancy endangered the health of the patient. That process was challenged in *Doe v. Bolton* (1973). Because petitioners in both cases sought injunctive relief against states enforcing their own laws, three-judge district courts heard the cases.[58]

In the Northern Texas District, Circuit Judge Irving Goldberg, writing for his two colleagues, based his decision on the right to privacy elucidated in *Griswold v. Connecticut* (1965): "On the merits, plaintiffs argue as their principal contention that the Texas Abortion Laws must be declared unconstitutional because they deprive single women and married couples of their right, secured by the Ninth Amendment, to choose whether to have children. We agree."[59]

When the two cases came to the Supreme Court, Chief Justice Burger, who voted with the majority, assigned the opinion on both to Justice Blackmun. He rested the right to an abortion upon the Due Process Clause of the Fourteenth Amendment. Presumably that meant that any state regulation had to survive strict scrutiny. Blackmun began with the stark reminder that Texas and Georgia had made abortion into crimes, although the two statutes had a different cast, the latter reflecting "advancing medical knowledge, and . . . new thinking about an old issue." In the time between the passage of the former and the adoption of the latter, changing legal and social ideas on population growth, pollution, poverty, and race had intervened.[60]

The choice of ending a pregnancy in its early stages was now a fundamental right, protected by the Fourteenth Amendment's right to privacy. That right was not absolute, however. States had a right to protect incipient human life that grew as the pregnancy continued, so that "at some point in time [in the pregnancy]" the state could assert a compelling interest in protecting the potential human life the fetus represented. From having served for many years as legal counsel to the Mayo Clinic, Blackmun wanted as well to tie the opinion to medical science. He proposed the division of a pregnancy into trimesters. In the first of these, a woman only needed the consent of her doctor. In the second and third trimesters, the state's interest in the potential life allowed it to impose increasingly stiff regulations on abortions. Blackmun insisted that the Court could not enter a discussion of when human life began, for neither Blackmun nor the majority of the Court for whom he wrote "was not in a position to speculate" on that question, nor did he think that the Court or the states could turn religious or moral presumptions into medical facts.[61]

Justice White dissented. White saw the crucial cases as those in which women simply wanted to end a pregnancy that did not endanger them. They might be motivated by shame, convenience, economics, or "dislike of children." The Court had turned women's "whim, or caprice" into a constitutional principle, although there was nothing in the Constitution's language to sustain that judgment. To convenience a mother, and for little more, the Court had "disentitled" the legislatures of all fifty states from weighing the "relative importance of the continued existence and development of the fetus, on the one hand, against a spectrum of possible impacts on the mother, on the other hand." Justice Rehnquist's joined Justice White's opinion and wrote his own dissent. The plaintiff was not pregnant at the time of the decision, so the Court overreached itself in providing her with a relief she did not need and could not claim. There was no right of privacy involved, for the abortion was not a private act. If liberty was lost, it was lost through "due process of law." The state's regulation of abortion did not have to rest on a compelling interest, only a rational one, and the states' statutes surely had a rational relationship to the goal of saving the unborn child.[62]

The 7 to 2 decision invalidated most of the abortion laws in the country and nationalized what had been a very local, very personal issue. Roe would become the most contested and controversial of the Court's opinions since Dred Scott, to which some of its critics, including Justice Antonin Scalia, would later compare it. Women's rights advocates got a decision that recognized a right, but only barely, and with qualifications, on a constitutional theory ripe for attack. Opponents of the right to an abortion argued that the human life began at conception, and the state had a duty to protect the unborn child from that time forth. From the announcement of the decision, they would mobilize and wage war against what seemed to them to be Roe's desecration of religion, motherhood, and the family. In ensuing years, the position a nominee took on *Roe* would became a litmus test for judges selected to the federal bench and the Supreme Court itself. Congressional and presidential elections turned on the abortion rights question, as new and potent political action groups, in particular religious lobbies, entered the national arena for the first time to battle over *Roe*.[63]

Rising Judicial Caseloads and the War on Crime

Although never approaching the load that the states' courts carried, from the 1920s a growing percentage of the nation's overall criminal law business began in the federal courts. This was a result of congressional action and elective politics. The Volstead Act prosecutions resulted from an act of Congress. The criminalization of the sale of marijuana in the 1930s was part of an anti-Mexican immigration campaign, and anticrime initiatives in the Kennedy, Johnson, Nixon, and Reagan presidential campaigns, along with congressional activity following those campaigns, brought more cases to the federal courts. Civil rights initiatives in Congress and in the executive branch similarly led to federal litigation. Insofar as all of these developments increased federal courts' purview over private acts, they shifted the relative role of federal and state courts in litigation, with an attendant impact on federalism.[64]

In the Burger era, two of the most controversial of these initiatives were the Comprehensive Drug Abuse, Prevention and Control Act of 1970 and the creation and the growth of the Drug Enforcement Administration (DEA). Both had a visible impact on the federal courts' caseloads. Created by a Nixon executive order in July 1973 to put the war on drugs under one roof, the DEA included at the outset 1,470 special agents and a budget of less than $75 million. The perception in both the Nixon White House and Congress in these years was that drug use had expanded immensely and was responsible for both the rise in gang violence and the illegal activities of foreign drug cartels supplying the domestic market. With offices in foreign countries and a series of domestic "task forces," the DEA's consolidation of drug enforcement meant many more prosecutions. These were based on traditional police investigatory methods and the implementation of a wide variety of intelligence-gathering measures. At the same time, the passage of RICO (the Racketeer Influenced and Corrupt Organizations) in 1970 gave federal prosecutors more leverage than ever before against organized crime, allowing them to bring charges against mobsters as conspirators and as perpetrators.[65]

As the number of controlled substances included in the criminal drug abuse category increased, the criminalization of the sale and use of these substances, added to existing criminal prosecution of heroin and marijuana, nearly doubled the number of such cases coming to the courts. What is more, a larger percent of these involved trial and conviction than other types of federal criminal prosecutions (for example for white-collar crime). In 1970, a total of 38,182 criminal indictments came to the federal courts, of which 3,511, or 9 percent, involved narcotics. In 1976, the total of criminal cases on the federal courts' dockets was 39,147, of which 6,198 were drug crimes, or 16 percent. Given the demographic composition of the offender pool, the decision to pursue drug "pushers" at the street corner level meant that the defendants in these cases (and the convicted population) were overwhelmingly African American and Latino. Drug convictions soon tripled the federal jail population.[66]

Beyond Article III Judges

The civil rights era of the 1960s seemed to give way to an era of burgeoning litigation in the federal courts in the 1970s and beyond. The fewer than 59,000 civil case filings and 30,000 criminal filings in 1960 more than tripled by 1986. At the same time, the relative proportion of civil litigation in federal and state courts shifted dramatically. Though both dockets grew apace in this period, and states continued to bear a far greater burden of that increase, the "distribution" of the cases noticeably altered, with a larger proportion landing in the federal courts. In the same period, Congress increased the number of district judgeships from 368 to 517.[67]

Structural and political barriers precluded open-ended increases in the number of district judgeships, but the courts, sometimes with help from Congress, continued to seek other ways to handle the caseload. One way was by expanding the role of judges appointed to fixed terms by the courts. Another was greater use and numbers of court-employed attorneys—law clerks and staff attorneys—to assist with research, drafting, and case management. Neither development was free of controversy over the proper limits of delegation.

At the same time, no one could miss the fact that the federal courts were becoming a sizable administrative entity, of which the judges remained both the most important and the smallest part. In a fashion not unlike that of the executive branch, the number of federal court employees had risen in numbers in the postwar era such that by 1995 only 3.2 percent of court employees were judges with Article III's tenure and salary protections, down from 6.9 percent in 1970.[68]

The growth in the federal judicial workforce included attorneys to assist individual judges, dating back at least to late nineteenth-century Supreme Court justices who retained such attorneys as "secretaries." "Law clerks," in today's parlance, are typically recent law school graduates who work directly for individual judges to assist in legal research and drafting and related tasks. In 1930, Congress authorized circuit judges to hire law clerks, and in 1936 Congress authorized law clerks for a small number of district judges. In response to frequent requests from the judiciary, Congress slowly increased the numbers in later years.[69]

The role of law clerks became important enough that by 1979 the Judicial Conference pressed Congress for more control over resources for law clerks. After considerable negotiation with Congress, the Conference established the number of clerks to which different types of judges would be entitled, and Congress agreed to give the judges some discretion in how to fund these positions. As federal judicial caseloads and budgets increased during the last four decades of the twentieth century, the number of law clerks rose steadily. Today, Judicial Conference guidelines authorize circuit judges to select four law clerks, district judges two, and bankruptcy and magistrate judges one. Each judge is also authorized one clerical "judicial assistant," although many use this authorization to hire another law clerk instead. Today's law clerks typically perform quasi-judicial functions, such as preparing memoranda on legal issues and composing drafts of judicial opinions. Some judges have eschewed the practice of hiring short-term law clerks in favor of "career" clerks, who are hired with the expectation that they will serve for at least five years, something of a throwback to the clerks hired by the justices in the early twentieth century.

In addition to "elbow law clerks," who work directly for (sit at the elbow of) an individual judge, staff attorneys and clerks who work for the entire court have become more prevalent. In the 1970s, courts of appeal began to employ staff attorneys to screen appeals into different dispositional tracks (such as oral argument or not). As part of a 1975 pilot project, district courts began hiring "pro se law clerks" to help process petitions filed by prisoners without lawyers seeking review of their convictions and other relief. In 1981, the Conference authorized such hires for all courts receiving at least 300 petitions annually, and in 1998 approved appointment of death penalty law clerks to assist in cases brought by prisoners seeking relief in capital cases. All courts of appeal have small staffs of "preargument" or "conference" attorneys to help parties narrow the issues in specified types of civil appeals and perhaps reach a settlement. Today there are more than 400 staff attorneys in the appellate courts and more than 400 pro se and death penalty law clerks in the district courts.[70]

Congress, at the urging of the Judicial Conference, overhauled the courts' long-standing commissioner system with a 1968 statute creating the position of United States Magistrate, with a formal title change to Magistrate Judge in 1990. Presently, the Judicial Conference determines the number of magistrate judge positions, subject to Congress providing the funds to support them. Appointed by the district judges in each district to either renewable eight-year, full-time positions or four-year, part-time positions, their numbers grew from 83 full-time and 450 part-time positions in 1971, to 280 full-time and 177 part-time positions by 1986, and in 2014, 534 full-time and 36 part-time magistrate judges. By stat-ute, the selection process includes public notice of vacancies and the assistance of "merit selection panels" to identify and recommend candidates.[71]

The shift from a system dominated by part-time magistrate judges to one almost exclusively of full-time officers has been matched by an expansion of duties and concomitant debate about how much of the district judges' work should be assigned to what some termed "para-judges," not appointed through the process prescribed in the Constitution. The 1968 statute left discretion over magistrates' duties largely in the hands of district courts, subject to lim-its prescribed in the statute. The Judicial Conference in March 1975 pushed for greater use of magistrate judges by encouraging all districts to embrace a check-list of duties these judges performed in districts that used them robustly. These duties included conducting civil pretrial conferences, ruling on motions in civil cases, reviewing and filing reports to district judges for the disposition of litiga-tion filed by prisoners and appeals by Social Security claimants, and serving as special masters in civil cases. In criminal cases, magistrates conducted pretrial conferences, ruled on motions, and conducted arraignments. Practices varied widely from district to district. In 1979, Congress authorized magistrates to conduct civil trials if the parties consented to preside over misdemeanor trials if defendants waived their right to a trial before a district judge.[72]

On the one hand, credit for these statutes goes in part to Burger's activities, in part to the Conference, and in part to the lobbying of the magistrates them-selves. Whether Burger led or followed, there is no question that Burger praised Congress for the Magistrate Judges Act. In his yearly report to the ABA on the federal courts, he told the members, "Congress wisely created the new office to relieve judges of some of their duties," which allows them to conduct trials and perform tasks central to their function. Burger wanted the purview of the magis-trate judges expanded. In 1979 it was.[73]

On the other hand, concern about the growing number and jurisdiction of the magistrate judges echoed older cavils about the expense and independence of the federal judiciary. As one recent recitation of this complaint hints, concerns about "the increasing utilization of magistrate judges and staff law clerks" are likely to continue. What is more, while "the practice of delegating to magistrate judges varies enormously from district to district . . . non-Article III judges are handling major civil matters." From a historical perspective, some of these con-cerns may be assuaged. Looking back to the first years of the federal courts, one finds that clerks were performing many quasi-judicial functions with a discretion that would have astounded today's judges. Questions raised by magistrates' rou-tinized handling of matters submitted to Article III courts is not just a question of competence—judges supervise these processes closely—but the issue of del-egation itself. Nowhere in the first Judiciary Acts does such delegation appear, although from the inception of the lower courts, the vital importance and broad powers of court officers and commissioners was assumed proper. Congress underwrote these assumptions in the 1976, 1979, and 1990 Magistrates Acts. In any case, unless a great many more Article III judges are deployed, the staff handling of filings will remain accepted routine. "Suffice it to say for now that the question of undue delegation is a critical one underlying case management and one that involves tradeoffs between risks of increasing staff and the real dangers of enlarging the number of judges on appellate courts."[74]

Along with changes in the magistrate judgeship, Congress altered the status and function of bankruptcy judges. While district filings tripled in the period, bankruptcy filings more than quadrupled, from about 110,000 to almost 478,000 in 1986.[75] This increase helped prompt a major change in the federal bankruptcy system in 1978. An 1898 statute had established the position of referee as an administrator for bankruptcy cases in the district courts. Congress gradually assigned the referees many of the district judges' bankruptcy duties, and a 1973 rules change adopted the title of bankruptcy judge.[76]

The 1978 Bankruptcy Act created new bankruptcy courts with expanded jurisdiction to hear all cases "arising under" and "related" to bankruptcy proceedings. Congress's goal was a single tribunal for legal disputes related to bankruptcies and to end confusion over the responsibilities of bankruptcy judges, district courts, and state courts by vesting the new bankruptcy courts with all of the authorities of courts of law, equity, and admiralty, including conducting jury trials. The bankruptcy courts could enforce their orders, which could be appealed first to a panel of bankruptcy judges and then to a court of appeals. The president, with the Senate's consent, would appoint them to fourteen-year terms.

The powers of the new judges led to another episode of separation-of-powers contests, reminiscent of those after the Civil War. In 1982, the Supreme Court held unconstitutional the broad jurisdiction granted in the 1978 Bankruptcy Act and ruled that jurisdiction over state common law issues that were only marginally related to a bankruptcy could not be conferred on judges lacking the tenure and salary protections of Article III. Congress responded with the 1984 Bankruptcy Amendments and Federal Judgeship Act, which established the bankruptcy courts as a "unit" of the district courts, granted district courts "original and exclusive jurisdiction of all cases arising under" the bankruptcy laws, and original but not exclusive jurisdiction over "all civil proceedings arising under" or "arising in or related to cases under" the bankruptcy laws. The district courts could refer all of these matters to the bankruptcy judges, whom the respective courts of appeals would appoint to renewable fourteen-year terms, again through a statutorily mandated process involving recommendations from merit-selection panels. As of September 2014, there were 349 bankruptcy judgeships, including thirty-four temporary judgeships, authorized for the districts.[77]

The question of federal jurisdiction over cases related to a bankruptcy has become increasingly complex since the reorganization of the bankruptcy courts. Statutes and court decisions gradually expanded bankruptcy court jurisdiction over a range of actions deemed "related" to bankruptcy proceedings. In 2011, however, the Supreme Court ruled unconstitutional Congress's vesting bankruptcy courts with jurisdiction over certain state law counterclaims because their judges lacked Article III protections.[78]

During the 1970s and 1980s, debate emerged about whether the federal courts had become "bureaucratized" by the expanding numbers and roles of court-appointed judges and attorney assistants. What parts of a district judge's responsibilities were essential to the judicial function under Article III? What judicial duties could legitimately be devolved onto judges who lacked life tenure and other guarantees? How much influence did, and should, law clerks and staff attorneys exercise over the outcome of cases? The debate continues to this day, driven less by competing theories of court administration and more by the press of cases, making magistrate judges, bankruptcy judges, law clerks, and staff attorneys an integral part of the federal judicial machinery.[79]

If not quite the fulfillment of Chief Justice Burger's plans for the federal courts, the Burger years brought a more cooperative federalism and a more efficient and better defined separation of powers. What the Burger era of administrative reforms could not accomplish was the insulation of the courts from ideological special interest agitation outside the halls of government or from party politics within those halls. For those students of the courts who believe that they are part and parcel of the political process, this fact needs no explanation. For those who insist that the courts are relatively insulated from partisan currents by the canons of judging, by precedent, and by concern for the good opinion of their fellow judges and members of the bar, the Burger years' were hopeful ones.

Afterword

The Federal Courts, 1987–2015

*Written by John S. Cooke and Russell R. Wheeler, with Daniel S. Holt and Jake Kobrick of the Federal Judicial Center History Office.

Writing an afterword to this sweeping and rich history of the federal courts is no small challenge. Fortunately, the preface provides a fitting roadmap for describing the years from 1987 to 2015: the courts continued to function in a "world in motion," and as the introduction explains, their activities were still framed within the three concentric rings of separation of powers, federalism, and political currents.

The World in Motion

Following the Soviet Union's collapse and the Cold War's end, asymmetric warfare and terrorism became the predominant threats to international security. Global trade and migration mushroomed. The new millennium was accompanied by tremendous scientific and technological advances, including the exponential growth of computing capacity and the Internet. Economic boom was followed by bust and a stagnant recovery.

The United States became more diverse. By 2013, non-Hispanic whites in the total population had fallen to 62 percent, an all-time low. Women and members of racial and ethnic minorities became more prominent in American professional and political life, highlighted by Barack Obama's 2008 election as president.[1]

Political divisions widened as the country seemed to coalesce into "red state/ blue state" regions and communities. Compromise became more difficult on social issues like abortion, gay rights, and gun rights and on economic ones, such as taxes and health-care policy.[2]

These changes affected the issues confronting the federal courts and the courts' composition and operations. Like the society it served, the federal bench grew more diverse. Polarization seemed to feed the litigation boom and to feed

Table A.1 **Active status circuit and district judges: gender and race/ethnicity***

Date	Totals	Gender		Race/Ethnicity				
		Male	Female	White	African American	Hispanic	Asian American	Other**
1/1/85	640	586 92%	54 8%	562 88%	48 8%	24 4%	5 1%	1 <1%
1/1/95	759	634 84%	125 17%	648 85%	69 9%	35 5%	5 1%	2 <1%
1/1/05	817	620 76%	197 24%	664 81%	90 11%	57 7%	6 1%	0
1/1/15***	812	545 67%	267 33%	606 75%	107 13%	78 10%	26 3%	2 <1%

* Source: Federal Judicial Center Federal Judicial Biographical Directory. Percentages may not total 100 due to rounding; see also note ***.

** "Other" refers to American Indian for 1985 and 1995 and to both American Indian and Pacific Islander for 2015.

*** For 2015, the sum of the numbers in the race and ethnicity categories exceeds the total number of active judges because seven judges identified themselves by reference to multiple categories.

off its results. Judges adopted, or adapted, case management and administrative measures to meet the demands of a litigious society.

Appointments: Diversity, Division, Delay

Presidents and senators stepped up efforts of earlier decades and produced a more diverse federal judiciary. Between 1985 and 2015, the number of active status judges increased by about a quarter but the number of women on the bench increased almost fivefold, African Americans more than doubled, Hispanics tripled, and Asian-Americans increased over fivefold. Table A.1 summarizes the changes.

At the Supreme Court, Sandra Day O'Connor, appointed in 1981, was until 1993 the only woman to serve there. By 2015, three more women had been appointed: Ruth Bader Ginsburg, Sonia Sotomayor, and Elena Kagan. Thurgood Marshall was the only African-American justice in the Court's history upon his appointment in 1967. Clarence Thomas, who replaced him in 1991, became the second. Sotomayor became the first Hispanic justice in 2009.

In 2015, all the justices were Ivy League law school graduates, eight from Harvard or Yale, one from Columbia. In mid-1986, the justices came two each from Harvard and Stanford and one each from Howard, William Mitchell, Northwestern, Washington and Lee, and Yale. All the justices in 2015 came to the Court from a U.S. court of appeals except former Solicitor General Kagan. In 1986, four justices had come to the Court from federal appellate courts, two from state appellate courts, and three from private practice (two of the three had been serving short stints in the Justice Department). Observers also noted that since 2010 for the first time in its history, no Protestants served on the Court (six Roman Catholic, three Jewish).

Changes continued in the preappointment professional backgrounds of district and circuit judges. Perhaps most notable was the increase, from a minority in the 1950s to a majority by the 2000s, in the percentage of judges with substantial experience working in the public sector, including experience as state court judges, and federal magistrate and bankruptcy judges.[3]

Among the explanations for this shift was a lengthening nomination and confirmation process that could send a private practitioner into professional limbo for an extended period, with confirmation hardly assured. (Private practitioners must begin transferring clients to other lawyers in advance of possible confirmation to avoid disruption of representation; public attorneys and sitting judges do not face the same problem.) Table A.2 shows that median days from initial nomination to confirmation increased, from a little over a month for Reagan's circuit and district appointees, to over seven months for Bush's and Obama's circuit appointees, and for Obama's district nominees. And some, of course, waited much longer. Chief Justice Rehnquist and Chief Justice Roberts commented

Table A.2 **Confirmation rates and median days, nomination to confirmation**

	Courts of Appeals			District Courts		
	Noms./ Confs.	Rate	Med. Days	Noms./ Confs.	Rate	Med. Days
Reagan (1981–89)	94/83	88%	37	309/292	94%	37
H. W. Bush (1989–93)	53/42	79%	78	189/150	79%	92
Clinton (1993–2001)	90/66	73%	139	347/305	88%	99
G. W. Bush (2001–09)*	84/60	71%	219	284/261	92%	142
Obama (2009–9/1/15)	61/54	89%	229	289/254	89%	215

• G. W. Bush confirmations do not include Roger Gregory (Fourth Circuit), who received a recess appointment a month before Clinton left office and was renominated and confirmed early in the Bush administration, and Charles Pickering (Fifth circuit), a recess appointee whose subsequent nomination was not confirmed.

on the adverse impact of such delays in their *Year-End Reports on the Federal Judiciary* in 1997, 2001, 2002, and 2010.[4]

Confirmation rates for district nominees held relatively steady, save for the dip for George H. W. Bush. That downturn was a function mainly of Congress's creating a large number of judgeships in late 1990: although confirmations increased over previous numbers, they did not keep pace with the surge in nominations. Rates for courts of appeals nominees declined steadily from Reagan to George W. Bush, then increased for Obama, standing at 89 percent in September of his seventh year in office.[5]

Obama's relatively high confirmation rates were unlikely to hold through the end of his term. In November 2013, his district and circuit confirmation rates were only in the 70 percent range. Then, Senate Democrats reduced from 60 to 51 the number of votes necessary to invoke "cloture" (i.e., to end a "filibuster" and thus allow a vote) on a district or circuit nominee. Republicans had earlier threatened to do so in May 2005, at which point Bush's circuit confirmation rate was in the 60 percent range, but seven Democrats and seven Republicans agreed to oppose both a rules change and more filibusters (except in unspecified "exceptional circumstances").[6]

Following the 2013 rules change, the Senate became a judicial confirmation juggernaut, approving from November 2013 through 2014 more than a third of Obama's total six-plus years of district confirmations and a quarter of his total appellate confirmations. Yet the whirlwind of confirmations in 2014 was less the result of the rules change—relatively few of the confirmations faced enough nay votes to have sustained filibusters under the old rules—than Senate Democrats' decision to expend political capital to push through as many nominations as possible before the anticipated, and since realized, Republican takeover of the Senate and a sharp drop-off in confirmations. Despite this brief uptick, 1987–2015 saw long-standing Senate traditions of comity and cooperation yield to polarizing tactics that made the process of staffing the federal judiciary a victim of larger political battles.

The Litigation Era Continues: More Work for the Courts

The increase in cases from 1987 to 2015 was significant even if not as dramatic as in the 1970s and 1980s. Some litigants were drawn by a perceived willingness of the courts to provide relief. Others were directed to the courts by legislation or driven there by the other branches' inability to resolve controversial policy questions.

From 1987 to 2014 annual filings in the courts of appeals increased by over half to almost 55,000. Civil and criminal filings in the district courts went up by a quarter, to over 376,000. On the civil side, the biggest growth, almost two-thirds, to 61,000, were cases filed by prisoners, either protesting the conditions of their confinement or seeking review of their convictions through habeas corpus. Labor and employment-related cases grew by half, to over 32,000, due partly to expanded civil rights laws. On the criminal side, reflecting shifting legislative and executive branch law enforcement priorities, drug cases grew by almost half, to over 25,000 defendants, and immigration cases, principally the felony of illegal reentry, grew almost tenfold, to 22,000. Bankruptcy cases (which fluctuate with the economy) increased by 75 percent, to slightly under a million.[7]

The Judicial Conference periodically recommended large "omnibus" judgeship bills during the period to keep pace with the increased filings, but Congress enacted only one in 1990. Such bills faced the same polarization that vexed the confirmation process and concerns, even among some judges, about too large a judicial branch. Nevertheless as a result of the 1990 Omnibus Act and some piecemeal legislation in later years, life-tenured district judgeships increased by 18 percent to 673, and circuit judgeships saw a smaller increase, 7 percent, to 179. During the same period, bankruptcy judgeships grew by half, to 349 positions, and magistrate judges by 23 percent, to 573 (and a shift to many more full-time than part-time positions). For the first time in the federal courts' history, term-limited judicial positions outnumbered life-tenured positions.[8]

Compounding the rise in cases overall was the rise in "pro se" cases, that is, cases brought by persons without an attorney. Most, but hardly all, pro se litigants were prisoners. In 1987 such cases were too few to merit separate reporting, but by 2014 they had grown, for example, to more than 25 percent of the district court civil docket, 81,000 out of 295,000 cases. Pro se litigants rarely understand the litigation process, so their pleadings and presentations obliged judges and their staffs to devote special care to ensuring that their claims are fairly examined (including, as described in chapter 13, creating staff positions specifically for attorneys to work on these cases).

Litigation became more complex. The courts saw more multidistrict litigation—cases filed in separate districts based on the same event, such as an airplane disaster or an allegedly defective product. An increase in patent cases, from just 1,100 in 1987 to 5,600 in 2014, reflected in part the rapid growth in science and technology. Although still relatively few, most patent cases were complex because of highly technical subject matter and high monetary stakes, so they consumed more of the courts' time and attention than did most cases. Technology also complicated other cases. Vast amounts of electronically stored information, including e-mail and other data, made discovery—through which parties share (or resist sharing) information to prepare for trial—more time-consuming and expensive, as when the storage medium required sometimes obsolete and hard-to-acquire technology to reveal information.[9]

Expanding technology affected federal courts and public opinion about them in other ways. In 1978, Congress had delegated judicial review of government applications to undertake national security–related investigations, principally domestic electronic surveillance, to the Foreign Intelligence Surveillance Court (the FISC) (and a separate Court of Review). FISC members are district judges, designated by the chief justice to serve seven-year nonrenewable terms in addition to their regular duties. National security investigations ramped up after the September 2001 attacks. After a government contractor leaked vast stores of data about them in 2013, they became more controversial. So did the FISC. Some legislators, journalists, and government officials attacked its largely nonadversarial, nonpublic procedures; FISC defenders said more elaborate procedures were unnecessary given the nature of its work. Critics also said no single individual should be responsible for designating its members (pointing to overrepresentation of Republican appointees and former prosecutors among the fifty-eight judges who served on it since 1979), but some analysts questioned the significance of those background characteristics to FISC decision-making and said that alternative designation regimes risked more problems than the process in place. In June 2015, in response to some of these concerns, Congress made minor modifications to the FISC, including provision for the appointment of lawyers to make arguments in addition to the presentations of Justice Department attorneys.[10]

Committees, Caseloads, Congress

In the late 1980s, talk of "crisis" in the courts recurred as it did in earlier decades and in retrospect seems somewhat overblown. In 1988, Congress created a blue ribbon commission, the Federal Courts Study Committee. Its report's "Overview" referred to "the impending crisis of the federal courts" and anticipated a query in the 1995 report of the Judicial Conference's Long Range Planning Committee: "Has the Crisis Arrived?" The Conference's Long Range Plan contained ninety-three recommendations designed to "conserve the judicial branch's core values." Congress also established a Commission on Structural Alternatives for the Federal Courts of Appeals, primarily to consider whether the Ninth Circuit's court of appeals was too large in territory and judgeships to function effectively.[11]

Judges, not just their caseloads, received committee attention. In 1990, reacting to the impeachment and removal of three federal judges in the 1980s, each for serious crimes, Congress created the National Commission on Judicial Discipline and Removal, which among other things examined how chief circuit judges and judicial councils administered the Judicial Conduct and Disability Act, enacted in 1980. Fourteen years later, Chief Justice Rehnquist, reacting to congressional criticism, appointed a small committee chaired by Justice Breyer to examine the matter again.[12]

The studies and reports sometimes produced administrative adjustments within the judicial branch. The Breyer Committee, for example, which found that chief circuit judges and judicial councils were largely treating complaints as the 1980 Act intended, nevertheless made recommendations that led the Judicial Conference to strengthen oversight of the Act's administration. Committees' recommendations, though, rarely led to legislative consensus; any legislative fixes were incremental. In 1990, Congress, responding in part to a Brookings Institution report, *Justice for All* (instigated by then Senate Judiciary Chair Joseph Biden), enacted the Civil Justice Reform Act (known informally as the "Biden bill"), after deleting requirements for detailed case management practices. Many judges already used some of them but objected to legislative mandates imposing them uniformly. The Act required districts to develop cost- and delay-reduction plans. Perhaps more important, it required the Administrative Office to publish semiannual reports of backlogged civil cases by name of judge—a first—to spur judges to move old cases.[13]

Some judges and members of the legal academy turned their attention to narrowing federal jurisdiction, hardly a novel recommendation. In the mid-1990s, they worried about statutes that "federalized" criminal and civil law, as seen in the growing number of federal prosecutions of acts that had previously been prosecuted exclusively or primarily in state courts (including firearms, drugs, gambling, loan sharking, sexual abuse, and violence against minority groups). About 60 percent of civil cases were brought under statutes that grant a right of action in federal court, such as laws prohibiting discrimination in employment. These laws had the salutary effect of producing national standards and more uniform enforcement of civil rights, but they added to the federal courts' workload. By the early 1990s, the Judicial Conference and the Justice Department were repeating earlier calls for Congress to consider the "judicial impact" of legislation on caseloads and costs to the federal courts before passing new laws. As articulated in the Conference's *Long Range Plan*, the judiciary's official stance was that "Congress should be encouraged to exercise restraint in the enactment of new statutes that assign civil jurisdiction to the federal courts and should do so only to further clearly defined and justified federal interests." Critics saw this recommendation as a smokescreen to limit federal judicial protection of important rights.[14]

Congress did limit access to the federal courts in a few areas. The 1996 Antiterrorism and Effective Death Penalty Act narrowed the grounds and time limits for state prisoner habeas petitions, supporters arguing that federal courts were unnecessarily injecting themselves into the business and infringing on the integrity of state courts. The1996 Prisoner Litigation Reform Act sought to reduce the volume of prisoner civil rights claims, which initially fell by nearly one-third. However, likely as a result of the burgeoning prison population, prisoner cases grew again, albeit probably more slowly than they would have without the two statutes.[15]

The 1995 Private Securities Litigation Reform Act limited what supporters saw as frivolous securities fraud class action suits, and the 2005 Bankruptcy Abuse and Consumer Protection Act imposed stricter filing requirements on potential bankruptcy petitioners. Although other factors surely played a role, including larger economic trends, overall bankruptcy filings declined by about 40 percent.[16]

Other legislation, however, opened the federal courts to more litigation. The 2002 Multiparty, Multiforum Trial Jurisdiction Act allowed victims of mass accidents to file in federal court, their consolidated cases replacing a proliferation of individual state court cases. The 2005 Class Action Fairness Act relaxed diversity jurisdiction requirements for many class actions on the rationale that state courts were abusing class-action remedies and federal courts could more effectively ensure that unmeritorious cases did not advance. There followed a

72 percent increase in the number of federal diversity class action suits between 2001 and 2007.[17]

The legislation that had the most far-reaching effect on federal courts during 1987 to 2015 was the Sentencing Reform Act, part of the Comprehensive Crime Control Act of 1984. The Sentencing Reform Act was the product of years of debate over federal sentences. Liberals, such as Senator Edward Kennedy, were mainly concerned about federal judges' broad sentencing discretion and sentence disparities from one judge to the next, even for similar crimes by similar offenders. Conservatives such as Senator Strom Thurmond believed that federal sentences were too lenient in light of the offenses in question. Congress's solution, drawing on state experience, was to create a seven-member United States Sentencing Commission within the judicial branch to develop mandatory guidelines for imposing sentence. Its members—three federal judges and four non-judges with experience and expertise in federal sentencing —were to be appointed by the president and confirmed by the Senate. Separate from the guidelines, Congress enacted mandatory minimum sentences for many crimes, further restricting judicial discretion. [18]

The Commission issued its first set of guidelines on November 1, 1987. Thereafter, many judges criticized their rigidity, complaining about unfair results that they attributed to curtailed judicial discretion and to prosecutors' enhanced control over sentencing outcomes through their charging decisions and the leverage that the stiffer guidelines penalties enabled them to exercise in plea bargaining. On the other hand, some judges defended the guidelines.[19]

In *United States v. Booker* (2005), the Supreme Court held that the mandatory nature of the guidelines unconstitutionally infringed on the defendant's right to have a jury decide facts that determine the limits on potential punishment. *Booker* left the guidelines in place but only as advisory. Judges still generally followed them—the guidelines remained part of federal court furniture—but exercised greater discretion to sentence outside the prescribed range.[20]

Coupled with the federalization of many crimes, the guidelines contributed to the nearly tenfold increase in the federal prison population from 1980 to 2014. By 2015, members of both political parties were questioning the wisdom of incarcerating so many people at so much expense.[21]

Legislative-Judicial Confrontations

A 2003 statute (prior to *Booker*) further restricted judges' limited authority to "depart" from guideline sentences, and it enhanced legislative monitoring of departures. A few months later, in a rare step symptomatic of heightened legislative-judicial tensions dating from the mid-1990s, the Judicial Conference

voted "overwhelmingly" to urge repeal of those provisions because Congress
had failed to consult the judicial branch about them. Chief Justice Rehnquist
later said that although it was Congress's prerogative to consult whomever it
wishes, "it surely improves the legislative process at least to ask the Judiciary its
views on such a significant piece of legislation." The Conference vote was institutional, not partisan. Twenty of the twenty-five members who voted on repeal
of the House's Republican-sponsored statute were Republican appointees.[22]

At the Conference's next meeting, then-chair of the House Judiciary
Committee, F. James Sensenbrenner (R-Wis), defended the statute as
"a legislative response to long-standing Congressional concern that the
Sentencing Guidelines were increasingly being circumvented by some federal
judges through inappropriate downward departures" (that is, more lenient
sentences than guideline formulas prescribed). He also protested "sustained
criticism [of his Committee] for its constitutionally-mandated legislative and
oversight actions concerning the federal judiciary" and threatened to withdraw
the statutory authority by which chief circuit judges and judicial councils act
on complaints of judicial misconduct (which, as noted earlier, led Chief Justice

Figure 1.1 Judge Julia S. Gibbons, chair of the Conference's Budget Committee, speaks
with Sen. Chris Coons (D-Del.), left, and Sen. John Boozman (R-Ark.), respectively,
ranking minority member and chair of the Senate Appropriations Subcommittee
on Financial Services and General Government. James C. Duff, director of the
Administrative Office of the U.S. Courts, is at right. 2015. Credit: U.S. Courts.

Rehnquist to appoint the Breyer Committee, whose report in turn led the Judicial Conference to beef up oversight of the Act's administration).[23]

These incidents were but one scene in a drama of heightened judicial-legislative contentiousness reminiscent of similar periods in the nineteenth and twentieth centuries. The modern era saw bills to curtail federal jurisdiction in sensitive areas such as school prayer and same-sex marriage (none passed), investigations into judicial procedures, and a 2003 "House Working Group on Judicial Accountability," about which the then-House majority leader said "We ... are putting America's judges on alert. We are watching you."[24]

Despite these tensions, legislative-judiciary interaction necessary to maintain the judicial branch continued. The checks and balances system was meant to preserve republican government, not to pit one branch of the government against the others. Indeed, Congress treated the judiciary's funding requests somewhat better than those of most executive branch agencies. Court funding between 2003 and 2005 rose from $4.9 billion to $5.5 billion. And despite some furloughs and layoffs after the 2011 Budget Control Act, federal courts remained in general much more generously resourced than state courts. [25]

Adjustments in People and Processes

The number of judicial branch employees (excluding judges) grew from 18,000 in 1987 to 28,000 in 2013 (quadrupling the 1970 figure of 7,200), an increase that Congress supported with increased funding—three quarters of a billion dollars in 1970 (adjusted for inflation) compared to $6.5 billion in 2015. The increases in cases, money, and personnel, in effect, turned many federal courthouses from small businesses into midsize companies and necessitated a more decentralized management structure. Although federal courts historically prized their local autonomy in judicial matters, the Administrative Office of the U.S. Courts, upon its 1939 creation, administered its statutory authority in a highly centralized manner, purchasing all equipment, supplies, and services for federal courts across the country. The Judicial Conference, and the Administrative Office itself, realized this arrangement was unsustainable as the judicial branch expanded, and thus instigated a major program to delegate authority to the courts, along with national standards, training, and oversight to try to ensure that this delegated authority was used properly.[26]

The courts adopted technological tools both to help with the increased workload and encourage transparency. A Case Management/Electronic Case Filing System gradually weaned courts and lawyers from paper filings and records in most cases, and the PACER system (Public Access to Court Electronic Records) made most case files available on the Internet, although some protested PACER fees to access public records.

Judges refined other methods to move cases to resolution expeditiously. In 1995, the Judicial Conference officially endorsed "active case management," a concept that had existed for decades. While subject to various interpretations and applications, active case management typically consists of judges using pre-trial conferences and other procedural tools to work with the parties to move cases to a "just, speedy, and inexpensive determination." Alternative Dispute Resolution (ADR), which had also existed for some time, received new empha-sis, providing parties in-court programs of mediation and other techniques, either to avoid trial or to streamline it. The Conference endorsed ADR as well, and 1998 legislation required each district to offer but not require some alterna-tive forum to most civil litigants.[27]

Some would-be litigants, hoping for faster outcomes, turned to private mediation and arbitration services. This competition created an incentive for the courts to be both accessible and cost competitive, a challenge noted in the Judicial Conference's 2010 Strategic Plan for the Federal Judiciary. Although some judges worried that wealthy commercial litigants who could afford higher priced alternatives would eschew the courts, making the courts predominantly a forum for litigants of limited means, that seems to have been more of a con-cern for state courts. On another front, some legislators and others argued that the 1925 Federal Arbitration Act as interpreted by the Supreme Court forced individual consumers into mandatory arbitration, barring them from the federal courts in disputes with more powerful companies.[28]

The use of active case management and ADR contributed to a broader devel-opment in both federal and state courts: what some called the "vanishing trial." Most civil cases have long been resolved through settlement or on pretrial motions, but, starting in the 1980s, the portion (and actual number) of trials fell steadily. In 1986, 6 percent of federal civil cases reached trial. By 1991 it was 4 percent, and fell to a mere 1 percent (a little fewer than 3,000 trials) in 2014. Thirteen percent of criminal defendants—most of whom plead guilty—received a trial verdict in 1991 versus 3 percent in 2014.[29]

The decline in the rate and number of federal trials prompted debate among judges, lawyers, and academics. One prominent commentator argued that the federal judicial establishment's encouraging active case management, ADR, and procedural mechanisms like summary judgment (by which a judge decides a case without trial if the case turns solely on legal, not factual, disputes) dis-couraged "adjudication as a touchstone of thriving democracy." A district judge responded that "[l]aw professors and judges should stop bemoaning disappear-ing trials," which litigants increasingly disfavored "because of the unacceptable risk and expense."[30]

Caseload pressures had a major impact on the courts of appeals, where cases per judgeship greatly outpaced district court cases. From 1987 to 2014, filings per district judgeship increased on average by 7 percent, compared with a 46 percent increase for judgeships in the regional courts of appeal. Appellate filings rose from over 35,000 in 1987 to almost 55,000 in 2014 (down from a peak of 68,000 in 2005), but Congress added appellate judgeships only once. The 1990 omnibus bill lifted the total judgeships in the regional courts of appeals from 156 to 167. Partly due to caseload pressures, the classic appellate model of oral argument before a three-judge panel followed by a published opinion became an illusion in most cases. Staff attorney screening of cases for summary disposition without argument or published opinion began in the 1970s. By 1987, a little over half of cases disposed of on the merits (as opposed to procedural terminations—cases improperly filed, for example) received oral argument, falling to 32 percent in 2001, and to 19 percent by 2014. In merit terminations, published opinions fell from 31 percent in 1991 to 20 percent in 2001 to 12 percent in 2014—but with significant variation among courts, from 46 percent in one court of appeals to 6 percent in another.[31]

Appellate courts reduced published opinions and oral argument in part because the increased caseload included proportionately fewer cases that needed either. But judges and lawyers worried about a lack of uniformity with each court using its own mix of procedures to accommodate varied caseloads. Others asked whether the proliferation of unpublished opinions threatened the uniformity of federal law across the country.

This concern with uniformity became even more important as the Supreme Court decreased the number of cases to which it gave full plenary review each term—177 in 1975, the peak year, down to fewer than 80 cases per term in the decade ending in 2015.[32]

The Supreme Court

The Court, unlike other federal courts, has almost total discretion as to which cases it will grant review and formally decide. In 1987, the Court received 4,493 petitions for review, a number that peaked at 8,857 in the 2006–2007 term and has remained near that level. While the number of petitions per year nearly doubled, as noted above, the number of cases the Court granted for review fell by about half.[33]

Ideological divisions within the Court have long been a subject of interest. While 5-4 decisions and partial concurrences in high-profile cases garnered headlines, in the twenty years since 1995 they did not grow as a portion of total decisions, fluctuating from term to term, comprising between 15 and 30 percent of all decisions. The contentious 5-4 splits should not obscure the fact that the Court typically rendered a large portion of its decisions unanimously. The proportion of unanimous decisions has generally been between 40 and 50 percent in the three decades prior to 2015, peaking at 66 percent in the 2013–2014 term.[34]

As ever, and perhaps more than ever, due to divisions that crippled the other branches' ability to resolve difficult issues, the courts were called upon to decide contentious questions across a wide range of matters, and the most controversial of these inevitably reached the Supreme Court. One indication that the Court was increasingly expected to decide controversial social, economic, and political questions was the increase in the proportion of cases with briefs filed by "amicus curiae"—individuals and groups not party to the litigation but hoping nevertheless to influence its outcome. Such cases were in the 45 percent range in the 1940s and 1950s, rose to 85 percent in 1986, and were close to 100 percent in the 2014 term.[35]

In 2015, constitutional interpretations and legal doctrines were still evolving in many of these headline-grabbing topics. Only a brief description of the Court's major holdings is warranted here.

In the more than forty years since *Roe v. Wade* (1973) upheld the right to an abortion, the decision remained one of the Court's most debated rulings. Legislatures enacted various laws to overturn or narrow it. Notwithstanding changes in the Court's membership, *Roe* by 2015 withstood all direct challenges, while the Court further defined the contours of the right to an abortion, upholding some specific restrictions and striking down others.[36]

In *Obergefell v. Hodges* (2015), the Court held that same-sex couples have a constitutional right to marry, striking down state laws that prohibited or failed to recognize this right. *Obergefell* marked a striking turnaround from the Court's relatively recent 1986 decision in *Bowers v. Hardwick*, which upheld criminal penalties for intimate sexual conduct by same sex couples. The Court had overturned *Bowers* in *Lawrence v. Texas* (2003), holding that criminalizing such acts was a denial of due process, and after *Lawrence* several states, through legislation or judicial decisions, extended to gay and lesbian couples the right to marry. This trend received added impetus from the Supreme Court in *United States v. Windsor* (2013), which struck down a statute forbidding the federal government from recognizing such marriages for most purposes.[37]

After avoiding a Second Amendment question for over 200 years, in 2008 the Court held in *District of Columbia v. Heller* that the amendment accords to individuals a constitutional right to own firearms, but that the right may be subject to reasonable limitations. That made it likely that courts will be asked to review a variety of state and local regulations regarding gun ownership.[38]

Cases affecting elections have come to the Court for a long time. The Court's most direct foray into an election came in its 2000 decision in *Bush v. Gore*, which put an end to the disputed vote recount in the pivotal state of

Florida in the presidential election. The Court said that any further effort by the Florida courts to refine the recount process would deny equal protection to, and effectively disenfranchise, some voters. The decision generated heated debate but had the unequivocal result of ensuring George Bush's election to the presidency.[39]

Campaign finance, redistricting, and voting rights questions continued to reach the Court. Based on its precept that political spending equates to political speech, the Court disfavored campaign finance restrictions. *Citizens United v. Federal Election Commission* (2010) held that restrictions on corporations' independent "electioneering communications" violate the First Amendment. In *McCutcheon v. Federal Election Commission* (2014), the Court found that restricting aggregate campaign donations by a single donor violates the First Amendment. Based on principles of federalism and on the difficulty of separating nonjusticiable political questions from politically motivated gerrymandering, the Court largely, but not entirely, left redistricting decisions to state legislatures. And, again based on federalism, as well as the belief that racial attitudes and animus have changed, the Court made it easier for states to impose procedural requirements on the right to vote.[40]

Progress in race relations in America in the sixty years since *Brown v. Board of Education* itself gave rise to difficult cases. Efforts by public institutions to achieve or maintain racial and ethnic diversity even in the absence of direct discrimination against minority groups raised the question whether the Constitution is truly color-blind. When, for example, may race or ethnicity be considered when making college or graduate school admissions decisions? The Court visited this question several times. It had not as of 2015 completely barred considering race and ethnicity in such decisions, but it made it increasingly difficult for states to justify using them as criteria.[41]

The United States' response to the September 11, 2001, attacks on the World Trade Center and the Pentagon drew the courts, and ultimately the Supreme Court, into the debate about the balance between national security and individual rights, and about the president's powers to wage war against a shadowy collection of non-state actors. The president, with express authority from Congress, used military force against the perpetrators of the September 11 attacks, Al Qaeda, primarily in Afghanistan. The government also aggressively pursued suspected terrorists elsewhere, including within the United States.[42]

Domestically, this pursuit led to the prosecution of many suspected terrorists in federal courts, including Zacarias Moussaoui, the so-called twentieth 9/11 hijacker. Moussaoui and others were prosecuted using regular criminal laws and procedures; most were convicted, and several, like Moussaoui, received life sentences. These cases, while not routine, involved few novel legal issues, and none reached the Court.

Figure A.2 Chief Justice John G. Roberts, Jr., and the Judicial Conference, 2013. Seated left to right: Chief Judge Sandra L. Lynch (1st Cir.); Chief Judge Dennis Jacobs (2nd Cir.); Chief Judge Theodore A. McKee (3rd Cir.); Chief Judge William B. Traxler, Jr. (4th Cir.); Chief Justice John G. Roberts, Jr.; Chief Judge Edith Hollan Jones (5th Cir.); Chief Judge Alice M. Batchelder (6th Cir.); Chief Judge Frank H. Easterbrook (7th Cir.); Chief Judge William Jay Riley (8th Cir.). Standing, Second Row: (left to right) Chief Judge Mark L. Wolf (D. Mass.); Chief Judge Carol Bagley Amon (E.D. NY); Chief Judge Gary L. Lancaster (W.D. Pa.); Chief Judge David Bryan Sentelle (DC Cir.); Chief Judge Randall R. Rader (Fed. Cir.); Chief Judge Alex Kozinski (9th Cir.); Chief Judge Mary Beck Briscoe (10th Cir.); Chief Judge Joel F. Dubina (11th Cir.); Chief Judge Deborah K. Chasanow (D. Md.); and Chief Judge Sarah S. Vance (E.D. La.).

Standing, Third Row: (left to right) Judge Thomas A. Varlan (E.D. Tenn.); Chief Judge Richard L. Young (S.D. Ind.); Judge Robert S. Lasnik (W.D. Wash.); Judge Robin J. Cauthron (W.D. Okla.); Judge Rodney W. Sippel (E.D. Mo.); Judge W. Louis Sands (M.D. Ga.); Chief Judge Royce C. Lamberth (D. DC); Chief Judge Donald C. Pogue (Int'l Trade); and Judge Thomas F. Hogan, Dir, AOUSC. Credit: U.S. Courts.

More controversially, the government detained without trial persons whom it deemed "unlawful enemy combatants" and prosecuted some of them in military commissions (military tribunals similar to courts-martial). Most of those detained were non-U.S. citizens captured in Afghanistan or elsewhere abroad. One was a U.S. citizen captured in Afghanistan. The fate of several of these detainees did reach the Supreme Court.

In *United States v. Hamdi* (2004), the Court ruled that even a U.S. citizen who the government alleges was captured overseas while fighting against the United States is entitled to a habeas corpus hearing before a federal judge. In several other cases, the Court ruled that the jurisdiction of federal courts extended to the United States naval base at Guantanamo, Cuba, and that persons detained there were entitled to review of their detention. The Court also held that the Geneva Conventions applied to these detainees, and that although persons detained at Guantanamo could be tried by military commission, the procedures originally established by the president failed to comport with requirements of the Conventions. These decisions left the president with broad powers in the war on terrorism, but they also demonstrated the Court's willingness to enforce limits on that power under the Constitution and international law.[43]

The Patient Protection and Affordable Care Act of 2010 was so identified with President Obama that it came to be known as "Obamacare." Opponents took their fight against it to the courts, contending, among other things, that requiring individuals to purchase health insurance exceeded Congress's constitutional power to regulate commerce. The Act survived when Chief Justice Roberts, joined by four other justices, wrote the opinion of the Court upholding it, but he relied on Congress's power to levy taxes. In so doing, he set forth a restrictive view of the commerce clause that could limit Congress's exercise of such power in the future. Such a limitation would be consistent with the Court's renewed emphasis on federalism in some areas such as states' sovereign immunity. In 2015, the Act survived another challenge—this one statutory—when the Court ruled that, despite language that arguably allowed federally subsidized insurance only when States established insurance exchanges but not when the federal government did, Congress intended to permit subsidies in both instances.[44]

In its decisions on abortion, gay rights, guns, elections and campaign finance, diversity initiatives, national security, health-care policy—and other issues too

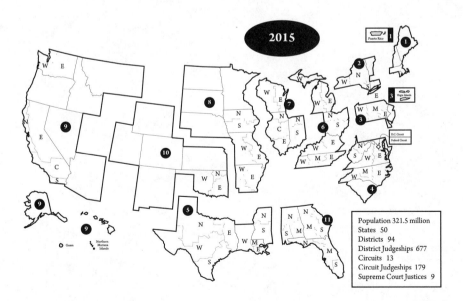

Figure A.3 Federal judicial circuits in 2015. Source: Wheeler and Harrison, *Creating the Federal Judicial System*, courtesy of the Federal Judicial Center.

numerous to discuss here—the Court had vocal supporters and vehement critics (including the dissenting justices in many of these cases). Fans of one set of decisions were often the biggest critics of others. Each of the justices was in the majority in some of these cases and in dissent in others. But what all of these cases had in common was a Court that sat comfortably at the center of the three rings where law, governmental structure, and politics converge and confidently decided the controversies presented to it.

In a history of all the federal courts, however, it should not be forgotten that these headline-grabbing cases constitute only the very tip of an iceberg. If the remaining 2,200 or so cases that the Supreme Court formally decided after 1987 represented the rest of the iceberg below the tip but above the waterline, then the millions of cases resolved by the federal courts during that period were the enormous mass below the surface. The vast majority of cases in federal courts, and even most of those reaching the Supreme Court, did not involve constitutional questions. Instead, they turned on interpretation and application of statutes, regulations, and precedents, as well as determination of the particular facts in the case. Most cases "matter," in a direct sense, only to the parties and their lawyers. But, as in the thirteen chapters that precede this afterword, in the aggregate the work of the federal courts has continued to reflect and affect the fabric and growth of the nation, socially, economically, and politically.

Conclusion

Whither the Federal Courts?

The conundrum that all historians of living institutions face at the end of their books is that the work must come to an end, but the institution's history does not. Our account of the federal courts now closes, but such closure cannot produce a certain prediction of things to come. The afterword gave some indications of current trends, but we cannot know the future. History may nevertheless help us understand how we got here.

In 1994, former Supreme Court Justice Lewis F. Powell, prefacing Gerald Gunther's magnificent biography of Judge Learned Hand, praised the author's evenhandedness and neutrality. It was a restraint that the mature Hand had extolled in his own jurisprudence. Gunther himself embraced it out of a respect for the role of federal judges "within the confines set by the executive and legislative bodies." Only through this self-imposed restraint could the judge avoid pouring "personal preferences" into his or her decisions.[1]

The authors of the present volume have attempted to follow this admirable advice, though in a scholarly recounting of past events and people it is not always possible, or even desirable, to avoid all judgment. Setting aside the epistemological question—can the historian every really know enough to be objective—the historian who does not add the value of studied judgments to the recital of past facts is a mere antiquarian. That value derives from looking at the present in long historical perspective; from comparisons over time and space; and finally from weighing those results in the context of changing political, social, and economic influences on the courts and the judges. In a conclusion to a work such as this one, judgments of this sort are not only inevitable, they are essential.[2]

Some of these judgments are obvious. The continuities we identified at the outset are still in place. First, for all the efforts of those within the judicial branch and in other branches of the federal government regarding the judiciary, the goal of greater uniformity of practice seems to remain just around a corner or shrouded in the mist ahead. As one federal appeals court judge recently commented, "The lack of uniformity among the lower federal courts about the best way to respond to the ballooning caseloads and, at least since the late 1980s [has spurred renewed consensus] that greater judicial management is essential." While the goal of dispatch and uniformity might benefit litigants and litigators, herding judges toward these ends is an endless and thankless task. One could also argue that variety is essential to the operation of courts over so vast a land and varied a people. Insofar as litigation in federal courts reflects very different aims and outlooks of region and ethnicity, and a variety of outcomes in the district courts gives the courts of appeal and the Supreme Court a chance to weigh alternatives, perhaps one should not expect or demand precise uniformity of outcomes.[3]

In a second example of continuity between past and present, today fears of a "fiscal cliff" have become a regular part of the planning for the federal judiciary. The salaries of the judges lag far behind the highest remuneration in private sector. This is nothing new. From the 1790s, when Rhode Island District Judge Marchant and South Carolina District Judge Bee both petitioned Congress for a pay raise, that complaint has cast its shadow over the relation between the judiciary and Congress. Overall, the judicial system has not been starved compared with the other nonmilitary institutions of the federal government, however. "In 1978, federal court outlays were one-tenth of one percent of all outlays; now they are two-tenths of one percent. They were 41% of what Congress spent on itself in 1978, a figure that's now 157%." Not all of that largesse has affected judicial salaries. In part because of the disparity between compensation in the public and the private sectors, it is harder and harder to recruit federal judges from the ranks of practitioners and professors. More recently, sequestration of funds has put up hurdles to the operation of the courts, and such "budgetary shortfalls" are expected to continue. As Chief Justice Roberts noted in his 2012 end of year report, "Even though the Judiciary consumes such a tiny portion of the federal budget, it must continue to do its part to search out cost savings in the face of the government's budget deficit," a message he repeated in his 2013 report.[4]

A third continuity hides within what seems to be a discontinuity. Since the terrorist attacks on the country on September 11, 2001, the war on terror, a war without end against numberless unseen enemies, has not only made war the natural state of public life in the United States, it also has thrust the federal courts into the maelstrom of war-related adjudication. On the one hand, American history has always been as much a history of war as of peace. The nation was conceived in the War for Independence, and subsequent territorial acquisition on the continent of North America, in the Caribbean, and in the Pacific was accompanied by war or the threat of war. A four-year Civil War redefined federalism and the role of the federal courts. The Indian Wars were a constant in American history until the twentieth century. On the other hand, the old adage that in war the laws are silent was never true of our courts. American law making and consequent judicial interpretation of those laws was never busier than during wartime. Twenty-first century counterterrorism efforts and full-scale conflicts in the Middle East simply continued this pattern.[5]

This last continuity derives at least in part from the geographic situation of the nation. From their inception the federal courts, like the nation they served, had one eye on the Atlantic world and one eye on continental expansion. The result was a melding of domestic and international concerns. Today's federal courts face a myriad of continental and international law questions, including the application of treaty provisions and the adoption of customary international law. This simply continues the role the federal courts played in the struggle among the great imperial powers of Britain, France, and Spain for control of the Western Hemisphere at the end of the eighteenth century. Then and now, the use of international law precepts and statutes has been shaped by the perceived needs of national interest and "traditional constitutional doctrine."[6]

With these continuities as context, we conclude our study where it began, with the three themes of federalism, checks and balances, and the influence of politics on the courts and the courts on politics. Although they do not pose the threats to the existence of the federal courts in the twenty-first century that they seemed to pose at the inception of the federal government, they still frame the federal courts' story.

Once upon a simpler time, advocates of the lower federal courts defended the imposition of a detailed system of federal courts on existing states and their judicial bodies as insurance against biased adjudication. Opponents warned that such courts would undo the compromises inherent in federalism. History proved both sides right. The progress of the courts went hand-in-hand (though never smoothly) with the elaboration of the nation-state's powers. But the state courts were not swallowed by the federal courts. Instead, a workable balance was achieved in caseload and jurisdiction.[7]

So, too, early signs of tension between the other branches of the federal government and its courts did not grow into entrenched rivalry. While control over certain matters continues to divide legislators and judges, Congress has ceded to the federal judiciary much of the initiative for the amending process and limiting or expanding substantive purview while keeping its hand in. Relations with the executive have not always been amicable, but judges remember who appointed them, and presidents obey, if sometimes reluctantly, the orders of the federal courts. If periodically the independence of the judiciary within the federal government seemed to be stalled at a "crossroads" in the checks-and-balances highway, separation of powers was never meant to facilitate high-speed decision making. It is what it is—a system to check and balance governmental powers in which the judiciary plays a vital role.[8]

Finally, history reveals that the federal courts continue to have one foot in the political process while not becoming adjuncts of the democratic process or partisan alignments. "Federal judges in the United States are by nature and necessity politicians." True, in certain cases, the federal courts may have appeared to jump with both feet into the political arena, but public opinion, the canons of judging, and the judges' self-discipline have prevented much of the politicization that the framers feared. The recent trend toward greater partisan distrust in the confirmation process is far more disturbing evidence of the part that politics plays in the history of the federal courts. Delay, filibuster, "nuclear options" to bypass filibusters, and other aspects of senatorial handling of presidential nominations have proven that the politics of appointment at all levels of the federal judiciary is still in place.[9]

Located within the three themes that run through this *Essential History*, the federal courts have not only survived, they emerged as one of the framers' most successful creations. They have adapted from a republican system of limited popular participation in limited federal government to a fully developed democracy with a powerful federal presence in everyday life. "They harmonize the Constitution with the demands of majoritarian politics." Federal judges are everywhere in the news. No longer the weakest branch, the federal courts are an essential part of the most successful and most copied constitutional regime in history and, even more important, an indispensable part of Americans' everyday lives.[10]

NOTES

Introduction

1. Richard H. Fallon Jr., John F. Manning, Daniel J. Meltzer, and David L. Shapiro, *Hart and Wechsler's The Federal Courts and the Federal System*, 6th ed. (New York: Foundation, 2009), 287; Richard A. Posner, *The Federal Courts: Challenge and Reform* (Cambridge, MA: Harvard University Press, 2009), 256.

2. Alexander Hamilton, Federalist No. 82, in Clinton Rossiter, ed., *The Federalist Papers* (New York: New American Library, 1961), 494.

3. Munn v. Illinois, 98 U.S. 113 (1877); Plessy v. Ferguson, 163 U.S. 537 (1896).

4. On the origin of the term "Madisonian Compromise," an academic coinage, see Michael G. Collins, "Article III Cases, State Court Duties, and the Madisonian Compromise," *Wisconsin Law Review* 1995, (1995), 42, citing Henry M. Hart Jr. and Herbert Wechsler's canonical *The Federal Courts and the Federal System* casebook of 1953. It reappeared in every edition thereafter, most recently in Fallon et al., *Federal Courts*, 7–9. Academics like Alison L. Lacroix, *The Ideological Origins of American Federalism* (Cambridge, MA: Harvard University Press, 2011), 180; and Charles Gardiner Geyh, *When Courts and Congress Collide: The Struggle for Control of America's Judicial System* (Ann Arbor: University of Michigan Press, 2009), 45 adopt it as though it was established usage. It is now common currency. See, e.g., Lumen N. Mulligan, "Did the Madisonian Compromise Survive Detension at Guantanamo," *New York University Law Review* 85 (2010), 539–540. We have used it to describe a range of compromises that actually took place, as well as the conceptual framework that the compromises created.

5. Politics here and hereafter is a bundle of related notions—political affiliation (party, movement), political ideas (policy preferences, ideology), and partisanships (attachment to persons or factions). This constellation of sometimes distinct and disparate notions would be untenably vague if it were not for the fact that Americans mix all of it together when they think about politics. Even "the act of defining something as political" imports a myriad of such notions. Eugene Lewis, *American Politics in a Bureaucratic Age: Citizens, Constituents, Clients, and Victims* (Washington, D.C.: University Press of America, 1977), 41.

6. Clinton Rossiter, *Parties and Politics in America* (Ithaca, NY: Cornell University Press, 1964), 39; Finley Peter Dunne, "The Supreme Court's Decisions," *Mr. Dooley's Opinions* (New York: Russell, 1901), 26; Lee Epstein, William M. Landes, and Richard A. Posner, *The Behavior of Federal Judges: A Theoretical and Empirical Study of Rational Choice* (Cambridge, MA: Harvard University Press, 2013) (ideology and partisan identification is important, though less so in the lower courts); Andres Sawicki, David Schkade, Cass R. Sunstein, and Lisa M. Ellman, *Are Judges Political?: An Empirical Analysis of the Federal Judiciary* (Washington, D.C.: Brookings Institution, 2006) (on controversial political issues federal appeals court judges tend to divide along partisan lines).

7. Lanell Yulee-Williams v. Florida Bar, no. 13–499, 575 U.S. ____ (2015), 1 (Roberts, C.J.); Alexander M. Bickel, *The Least Dangerous Branch: The Supreme Court at the Bar of Politics* (Indianapolis: Bobbs Merrill, 1962), 80.

8. Jeffrey Rosen, *The Most Democratic Branch: How the Courts Serve America* (New York: Oxford University Press, 2006), 69 and after; Oliver Wendell Holmes Jr., *Speeches by Oliver Wendell Holmes* (Boston: Little, Brown, 1900), 17.

9. Lee Epstein and Jeffrey A. Siegel, *Advice and Consent: The Politics of Judicial Appointments* (New York: Oxford University Press, 2005), 43–44, suggest that the spurts of expansion and confirmation come when the president and the majority of the Senate are of the same party.

10. Felix Frankfurter and James M. Landis, *The Business of the Supreme Court of the United States: A Study in the Federal Judicial System* (New York: Macmillan, 1928), 251; Henry J. Friendly, *Federal Jurisdiction: A General View* (New York: Columbia University Press, 1973), 3. Posner, *The Federal Courts*, 59, 274. Note that these books were not simply compendia of facts; all had public policy aims.

11. Frederick Jackson Turner, "The Significance of the Section in American History," (1925) in John Mack Faragher, ed., *Rereading Frederick Jackson Turner* (New Haven: Yale University Press, 1998), 201, 215–216.

12. "Report of the Commission on Revision of the Federal Court Appellate System, December 18, 1973," 3; "Commission on Structural Alternatives for the Federal Courts of Appeal, Final Report, December 18, 1998" (with special thanks to Russell Wheeler for suggesting a close reading of the Commission's reports); Irving R. Kaufman, "The Second Circuit: Reputation for Excellence," *American Bar Association Journal* 63 (1977), 201. In some sense the way in which judges in one circuit looked at decisions in other circuits (even though these were not compelling precedent) created a "system" of the courts.

13. See, e.g., David A. Skeel, *Debt's Dominion: A History of Bankruptcy Law in America* (Princeton: Princeton University Press, 2001), 2–3 and after (U.S. bankruptcy law unique and pervasive); Robert J. Gordon, ed., *The American Business Cycle: Continuity and Change* (Chicago: University of Chicago Press, 2007); Jonathan Levy, *Freaks of Fortune: The Emerging World of Capitalism and Risk in America* (Cambridge, MA: Harvard University Press, 2012), 2, 84–85.

14. Nathan James, "The Federal Prison Population Buildup: Overview, Policy Changes, Positions, and Options," Congressional Research Service, January 22, 2013, http://i2.cdn.turner.com/ cnn/2013/images/08/20/crs.federal.prisons.jan.2013.pdf.

15. Martin Luther King Jr., Speech at Western Michigan University, December 18, 1963; http:// www.wmich.edu/sites/default/files/attachments/MLK.pdf; James C. Cobb, *Away Down South: A History of Southern Identity* (New York: Oxford University Press, 2005), 214.

16. Abram Chayes, "The Role of the Judge in Public Law Litigation," *Harvard Law Review* 89 (1976), 1281–1316; Robert E. Keeton, *Judging* (St. Paul: West, 1990), 182–184, 207–208. Is "bench presence" an adequate measure of the role of judges? See William G. Young and Jordan M. Singer, "Bench Presence: Toward a More Accurate Model of Federal District Court Productivity," *Penn State Law Review* 118 (2013–2014), 55–80.

Part I

1. Robert Middlekauff, *The Glorious Cause: The American Revolution, 1763–1789* (New York: Oxford University Press, 1982), 585–596.

2. Benjamin Franklin, "Observations Concerning the Increase of Mankind" [1751] in Leonard W. Labaree et al., eds., *The Papers of Benjamin Franklin* (New Haven,CT: Yale University Press, 1959), 4:225; Charles Sellers, *The Market Revolution Jacksonian America, 1815–1846* (New York: Oxford University Press, 1992), 3–32 (land speculation and commerce).

3. Larry W. Yackel, *Reclaiming the Federal Courts* (Cambridge, MA: Harvard University Press, 1994), 38.

4. Slavery cannot exist without positive law sanction: "the relation of the owner and the slave is a creature of municipal law." Commonwealth v. Aves 35 Mass. 193, 217 (1836) (Shaw, C.J.). The *Aves* opinion represented a long line of reasoning going back before the Revolutionary War. The case was cited widely for Chief Justice Lemuel Shaw's terse and telling rule. In federal

courts it was adopted as well. "But this circumstance [of some states barring slavery] does not affect the domestic institution of slavery, as other States may choose to allow it among their people, nor impair their rights of property under it, when their slaves happen to escape to other States." Jones v. Van Zandt, 46 U.S. 215, 230 (1847) (Woodbury J.)

5. Dred Scott v. Sandford, 60 U.S. 393 (1857); Abelman v. Booth, 62 U.S. 506 (1859); Robert William Fogel and Stanley L. Engerman, *Time on the Cross: The Economics of American Slavery* (Boston: Little, Brown, 1974), 59–106 (profitability of slavery); Earl M. Maltz, *Slavery and the Supreme Court, 1825–1861* (Lawrence: University Press of Kansas, 2009), 300.

Chapter 1

1. Daniel J. Meltzer, "The Judiciary's Bicentennial," *University of Chicago Law Review* 56 (1989), 423–424. Julius W. Goebel, *Antecedents and Beginnings: Oliver Wendell Holmes Devise History of the Supreme Court*, Vol. 1 (New York: Macmillan, 1973), 1, argued that the federal system of courts began "when the first colonies were planted on the North American continent" implying that the beginnings of the U.S. Supreme Court were planted in the first days of colonization. By contrast, Frankfurter and Landis, *The Business of the Supreme Court*, 6, argued that the origins of the federal judicial system lay in the unique conditions of American "sectionalism," itself the root of both federalism and the politicization of law not present in England or the colonies.

2. Charles H. McIlwain, *The American Revolution: A Constitutional Interpretation* (New York: Macmillan, 1924), 8 and after (constitutional claims of the Revolutionaries vital part of the resistance to Parliament); John Phillip Reid, *Constitutional History of the American Revolution* (Madison: University of Wisconsin Press, 1995), 101 (Revolution's great achievement was change in constitutional ideas); Bernard Bailyn, *The Ideological Origins of the American Revolution* expanded ed. (Cambridge, MA: Harvard University Press, 1992), 160–229 (novelty of Revolutionary constitutionalism); but see William W. Crosskey, *Politics and the Constitution in the History of the United States* (Chicago: University of Chicago Press, 1953), 363 (common law was received as national law in the formative era of the nation).

3. Peter Charles Hoffer, *Law and People in Colonial America*, 2nd ed. (Baltimore: Johns Hopkins University Press, 1998), 146; Bernard Bailyn, *The Ordeal of Thomas Hutchinson* (Cambridge, MA: Harvard University Press, 1974), 14, 43.

4. The novel conception of "branches" of government appeared at the same time. For example, in the same passage that he discussed separation of the legislature and the magistracy, Montesquieu used the term "branches" of government. See *Spirit of the Laws*, trans. Thomas Nugent (New York: Colonial Press, 1900), 1:152. James Madison later dated the concept to the founding period in a letter to Edward Everett, in 1830, published in the *North American Review* in October of that year, and quoted by Joseph Story's *Commentaries on the Constitution of the United States* (Boston: Hilliard, 1833), 1:377.

5. Gordon S. Wood, *The Creation of the American Republic, 1776–1787* (Chapel Hill: University of North Carolina Press, 1969), 151–152; John Adams, "Thoughts on Government" in Robert J. Taylor, ed., *Papers of John Adams* (Cambridge: Harvard University Press, 1979), 4:86–93.

6. Adams, "Thoughts on Government," in Taylor, ed., *Papers*, 4:92. But see Edward Purcell, "The Ideal of Judicial Independence" *Tulsa Law Review* 47 (2011), 144 (arguing that Adams was not looking forward to a new regime of checks and balances with judicial independence at its center, but recycling older ideas about checking overreaching legislative and executive departments).

7. Wood, *The Creation of the American Republic*, 161; John Ferling, *John Adams: A Life* (New York: Oxford University Press, 2010), 155–156.

8. Adams, "Thoughts on Government," in Taylor, ed., *Papers*, 4:92; Alexander Hamilton, Federalist No. 78, in Rossiter, ed., *Federalist Papers*, 470; John Jay, charge to the grand jury, April 12, 1790, in Maeva Marcus et al., eds., *Documentary History of the Supreme Court of the United States, 1789–1800* (New York: Columbia University Press, 1985–2007) [hereafter *DHSC*] 2:26.

9. Massachusetts Constitution of 1780, in Benjamin Perley Poore, ed., *Colonial and State Constitutions* (Washington, D.C.: United States Government, 1877), 1:968–969; Pennsylvania Constitution of 1776, ibid., 2:1540.

10. The few exceptions involved attempted impeachment of state judges, notably Samuel Ashe in North Carolina and Thomas McKean in Pennsylvania. Both states' chief justices survived the effort. See Peter Charles Hoffer and N. E. H. Hull, *Impeachment in America, 1635–1805* (New Haven: Yale University Press, 1984), 87–95; Douglas Scott Gerber, *A Distinct Judicial Power: The Origins of an Independent Judiciary* (New York: Oxford University Press, 2011), 113.

11. Articles of Confederation [1778–1781], article 9; Henry J. Bourguignon, *The First Federal Court: The Federal Appellate Prize Court of the American Revolution, 1775–1787* (Philadelphia: American Philosophical Association, 1977), 77, 124–125.

12. Peter S. Onuf, *The Origins of the Federal Republic: Jurisdictional Controversies in the United States, 1775–1787* (Philadelphia: University of Pennsylvania Press, 1983), 11, 17, 18, and after.

13. Report of the Commissioners, Annapolis, Md., September 14, 1786, usconstitution.net/annapolis.html.

14. George Washington to Henry Lee, October 31, 1786, in John C. Fitzpatrick, ed., *Writings of George Washington* (Washington D.C.: U.S. GPO, 1931–1944), 29: 34.

15. Hamilton, Federalist No. 78, in Rossiter, ed., *Federalist Papers*, 464. Peter Charles Hoffer, *Rutgers v. Waddington: Alexander Hamilton, the End of the War for Independence, and the Origin of Judicial Review* (Lawrence: University Press of Kansas, 2016) discusses examples of these cases.

16. On the Virginia Plan's nationalizing impetus, see Max M. Edling, *A Revolution in Favor of Government: Origins of the U.S. Constitution and the Making of the American State* (New York: Oxford University Press, 2003), 73 and after, and Lance Banning, *The Sacred Fire of Liberty: James Madison and the Founding of the Federal Republic* (Ithaca, NY: Cornell University Press, 1995), 111–137.

17. Madison's Notes, May 29, 1787, in Max Farrand, ed., *Records of the Federal Constitution* (New Haven: Yale University Press, 1911), 1:21. Note that the Virginia impeachment, unlike impeachment in Parliament, was not a criminal proceeding, for there was no criminal penalty on conviction and only applied to misconduct in office, not to any other offense, as in the English model. Models and precedent for a national supreme court existed in almost all the states in 1787. Although the new state constitutions varied a good deal, all except Georgia had some form of supreme court. Much that would appear in the document the framers drafted that spring and summer of 1787 in Philadelphia came directly from the state constitutions. As Madison would write in Federalist No. 39, the guide the delegates used for the new federal Constitution was the states' constitutional provisions. For example, "the tenure of the ministerial offices [in the federal government] will be a subject of legal regulation, conformably to the reason of the case, and the example of the State Constitutions," in Rossiter, ed., *Federalist Papers*, 242. The term "corresponding powers" originates in Hoffer and Hull, *Impeachment in America*, 269–270.

18. New Jersey Plan, Farrand, ed., *Records*, 1:242–245.

19. Farrand, ed., *Records*, 1:120; 3:594.

20. Farrand, ed., *Records*, 1:124.

21. Farrand, ed., *Records*, 1:124. The problem with attributing more precise motives to the framers or giving more precise meaning to the language they adopted is that historians are largely dependent on the notes taken by James Madison. These were neither stenographic nor verbatim. Nor were they publically available until 1840, after Madison's death. No one who was at the Convention was alive when they were published, and thus no one could contradict, amend, or add to what Madison decided to write. One may simply assert that he tried to be as accurate as possible, but even then, he did not have time to hear and write everything that was said. Adding to the incompleteness of the record, he elected not to keep notes on the deliberations of the various committees of the Convention to which he was named, a severe gap in the record given that so much of what transpired in the Convention took place in committee meetings. This gap is especially glaring for the five days in September when the Committee of Style (on which he served) reduced the twenty-three articles framed by the Committee of Detail to seven and entirely recast the Preamble. See James H. Hutson, "The Creation of the Constitution: The Integrity of the Documentary Record," *Texas Law Review* 65 (1986), 1–40 (one cannot gain original intent of framers due to inaccuracy and imprecision of the original

sources), and Peter Charles Hoffer, *For Ourselves and Our Posterity: The Preamble to the Federal Constitution in American History* (New York: Oxford University Press, 2013), 65–82 (the work of the Committee of Style).

22. Farrand, ed., *Records*, 1:124.
23. Farrand, ed., *Records*, 1:290–292.
24. Farrand, ed., *Records*, 2:37–41.
25. Farrand, ed., *Records*, 1: 421.
26. Farrand, ed., *Records*, 2:42. Parties were evil, so the founders thought. Thomas W. Perry, *Public Opinion, Propaganda, and Politics in Eighteenth-Century England* (Cambridge, MA: Harvard University Press, 1962), 183; Bernard Bailyn, *To Begin the World Anew: The Genius and Ingenuity of the American Founders* (New York: Random House, 2004), 118.
27. Farrand, ed., *Records*, 2:42.
28. Farrand, ed., *Records*, 1:125, 2:45.
29. Farrand, ed., *Records*, 2:80, 183.
30. Farrand, ed., *Records*, 2:428. Gerhard Casper, *Separating Power: Essays on the Founding Period* (Cambridge, MA: Harvard University Press, 1997), 142, suggests that the conferral of equitable jurisprudence on the federal courts was "unwittingly created by the drafters of Article III." This is not so. Johnson's Connecticut practice would have included equity, as would the other members of the Committee of Style—King, Hamilton, and Morris. Unlike a lawsuit, a suit in equity began with a simple English-language complaint stating the grievance and the kind of relief desired rather than a law case opening with the filing of one of the formulary writs. The judge had jurisdiction over the parties before him rather than over the physical object of the suit. He could command the parties to do or not do acts and punish noncompliance with contempt citations. The two most common versions of this equitable power were the means of "discovery" (principally taking evidence by deposition rather than by testimony in court) and the issuance of injunctions. See Peter Charles Hoffer, *The Law's Conscience: Equitable Constitutionalism in America* (Chapel Hill: University of North Carolina Press, 1990), 7–29.
31. Farrand, ed., *Records*, 2:429.
32. James Madison to Thomas Jefferson, October 24, 1787, in William T. Hutchinson et al., eds., *Papers of James Madison* (Chicago: University of Chicago Press, 1977), 10:207.
33. On the role of Gouverneur Morris, see Hoffer, *For Ourselves and Our Posterity*, 69–79.
34. For example, under Article I, Congress created the territorial courts. The constitutionality of these was upheld in American Insurance Company v. Canter, 26 U.S. 511 (1828). Note that the term "inferior" used throughout the debates and in Article III did not have a pejorative connotation. It simply meant that such courts occupied a position in the system beneath the Supreme Court. Today, inferior has a different first meaning. For that reason, we have elected to call these courts the "lower" federal courts, a term closer to the original understanding.
35. The discussion in the Convention revolved around a proposed "council of revision" like that in New York and Pennsylvania. It first appeared in the Virginia Plan, and Madison supported it in the debates, but in the end, it went nowhere. The discussion is noteworthy however for, among others, George Mason's suggestion that federal judges may have "further use" than just sitting on the bench. Farrand, ed., *Records*, 2:78. See Russell Wheeler, "The Extrajudicial Activities of the Early Supreme Court," *Supreme Court Review* (1973), 123–130, and James T. Barry, "The Council of Revision and the Limits of Judicial Power," *University of Chicago Law Review* 56 (1989), 260–261. The term "judicial review" was not used at this time, indeed, it was not in common currency in the nineteenth century. See, e.g., Keith E. Whittington and Amanda Rinderle, "Making a Mountain Out of a Molehill? *Marbury* and the Construction of a Constitutional Canon," *Hastings Constitutional Law Quarterly* 39 (2012), 826.
36. Farrand, ed., *Records*, 1:97. Did Gerry mean to limit judicial review to matters in which the Court was policing its own turf? Yes: Robert Lowery Clinton, *Marbury v. Madison and Judicial Review* (Lawrence: University Press of Kansas, 1989), 74–78; no: Larry Kramer, *The People Themselves: Popular Constitutionalism and Judicial Review* (New York: Oxford University Press, 2004), 70. All three of these members of the convention must have known that state supreme courts in Connecticut, New York, and North Carolina had all claimed for themselves the duty and privilege of laying state legislation on the courts' functions against the text of the state constitution and finding the acts of the assemblies

unconstitutional. But this principle of judicial review of legislation related to the function of the courts, a narrow area of governance that immediately concerned the state supreme courts. Whether the state precedent was applicable to the U.S. Supreme Court would be determined, perhaps, by the latter court itself. "Eight times," Fallon et al., *The Federal Courts*, 12, n. 67.

37. James Madison, September 27, 1787, in the Confederation Congress, in Merrill Jensen, John P. Kaminski, and Gaspare J. Saladino, et al., eds., *Documentary History of the Ratification of the Constitution* (Madison: University of Wisconsin Press, 1976–) [hereafter *DHRC*] 1:339.

38. George Mason, "Objections to the Constitution," circulated October 1787, in Jon L. Wakelyn, ed., *The Birth of the Bill of Rights: Major Writings* (Westport, CT: Greenwood, 2004), 233; Brutus, "To the Citizens of the State of New York," *New York Journal*, October 18, 1787.

39. A Farmer, *Maryland Gazette* [1787] in Herbert J. Storing, ed., *The Complete Anti-Federalist*, vol. 5, *Maryland and Virginia and the South* (Chicago: University of Chicago Press, 1981), 38–39; Federal Farmer, "Letter 18," January 25, 1788, *DHRC*, 14:12–15 (authorship); Storing, ed., *Complete Anti-Federalist*, 2:240.

40. For the debates in Virginia, see *DHRC*, 10:1474–1556, Marshall at the ratifying convention, ibid., 1429, 1480; Editorial Note, "Virginia Ratifying Convention," in Herbert A. Johnson, et al., *The Papers of John Marshall* (Chapel Hill: University of North Carolina Press, 1974–2006), 1:252–255. The debate is tracked in Pauline Maier, *Ratification: The People Debate the Constitution, 1787–1788* (New York: Simon and Schuster, 2010), 286–291.

41. Madison, *Federalist No. 47*, in Rossiter, ed., *Federalist Papers*, 301; Madison, Federalist No. 51, in ibid., 322. At the time, Publius was widely read but the authors of its various essays were not identified until Douglass G. Adair's seminal article, "The Authorship of the Disputed Federalist Papers," *William and Mary Quarterly* 3rd ser. 1 (1944), 97–122, 235–264.

42. Hamilton, Federalist No. 22, in Rossiter, ed., *Federalist Papers*, 150. On Hamilton at the New York ratification convention, see Maier, *Ratification*, 352–353.

43. Hamilton, Federalist No. 83, in Rossiter, ed., *Federalist Papers*, 497; Hamilton, No. 78, ibid., 465–466.

44. Proposed New York Amendments: Linda Grant DePauw, Charlene Bangs Bickford, Kenneth R. Bowling, and Helen E. Veit, eds., *Documentary History of the First Federal Congress, Debates in the House of Representatives* (Baltimore: Johns Hopkins University Press, 1972—) [hereinafter *DHFFC*], 4:19.

45. David P. Currie, *The Constitution in Congress: The Federalist Period, 1789–1801* (Chicago: University of Chicago Press, 1997), ii, 5 and after (second constitutional convention), 119 (crucial role of Madison at first Congress).

46. "Amendments Proposed by the Virginia Convention, June 27, 1788," in Ralph Ketcham, ed., *Anti-federalist Papers* (New York: Penguin, 2003), 223–224; *DHFFC*, 4:17.

47. James Madison to Samuel Johnston, July 31, 1789, in *DHSC*, 4:491; Samuel Livermore, August 29, 1789, *DHFFC*, 11:1330–31; Christopher Gore to Rufus King, March 29, 1789, citing the thoughts of Massachusetts Supreme Judicial Court Justice Francis Dana, and James Sullivan to Elbridge Gerry, March 29, 1789, *DHSC*, 4:371, 372.

48. The Diary of William Maclay, June 29, 1789, *DHFFC*, 9:91. William Vans Murray to John Quincy Adams, 1800, quoted in Stanley Elkins and Eric McKitrick, *The Age of Federalism* (New York: Oxford University Press, 1993), 894, n.79. The primary and still cited source for the notion of compromise is Charles Warren, *The Supreme Court in United States History, 1787–1821* (Boston: Little, Brown, 1923), 1:8–11.

49. On the absence of the Virginia Resolves provisions for federal courts in Madison's proposed amendments, Compare *DHFFC* 4:17 (Virginia Resolves) with Madison proposal, June 8, 1789, and June 16, 1789, *DHFFC*, 11:803–804, 821–827; exchange of James Jackson and James Madison in the House, June 8, 1789, *DHFFC*, 11:807–809.

50. *DHFFC*, 5:192–193.

51. Diary of William Maclay, June 23, 1789, *DHFFC*, 9:87; Richard Henry Lee to Patrick Henry, September 14, 1789, Henry Family Papers, Library of Congress. The even division of members of the Senate committee computed is in Robert N. Clinton, "A Mandatory View of Federal Court Jurisdiction: Early Implementation of and Departures from the Constitutional Plan," *Columbia Law Review* 86 (1986), 1526.

52. James Madison, June 16, 1789, *Annals of the Congress*, 1st cong., 1st sess., 464. Note that of the two places in the Constitution giving Congress the authority to establish inferior federal courts, Article I and Article III, which was the basis for the Act? By one account, Article III is "vague," hence the need for legislative clarification, and Article I is clear, hence no need for clarification. Randa Issa, "Judiciary Act of 1789," in David Andrew Schultz, ed., *Encyclopedia of the United States Constitution* (New York: Infobase, 2009), 399. According to scholars, contemporaries seem to have assumed Article III was the foundation for the Act. See, e.g., Maeva Marcus and Natalie Wexler, "Judiciary Act of 1789," in Maeva Marcus, ed., *Origins of the Federal Judiciary* (New York: Oxford University Press, 1992), 13–14; Crowe, *Building the Federal Judiciary*, 30–31. But no evidence from the papers or debates definitively establishes that the Act was not based on Congress's powers in Article I.

53. Diary of William Maclay, June 22, 1789, *DHFFC* 9:85; Hamilton, Federalist No. 82, in Rossiter, ed., *Federalist Papers*, 469.

54. Here and after, Judiciary Act of 1789, 1 Stat. 73 et seq. Jurisdiction under the Judiciary Act of 1789 is explained in Fallon et al., *Federal Courts*, 22–26. Was this compromise a wise one, or like the three-fifths compromise, one in which everyone had to swallow hard to get it down? The answer, seen in context, seems clear: it was a brilliant, durable, and workable solution to the problem of judicial federalism. Of course, one may with hindsight disapprove the entire federalist endeavor. See Sanford Levinson, *Framed: America's Fifty-One Constitutions and the Crisis of Governance* (New York: Oxford University Press, 2012), 165 (system created too much diversity and uncertainty).

55. On federal question jurisdiction, Akhil Amar, *America's Constitution: A Biography* (New York: Random House, 2005), 227–229, finds an answer to the question in the "coiled tightly" text of Article III, whose first portion used the word "all" but whose second paragraph did not. In this "two-tier" arrangement, "all" meant federal questions. It is not clear whether this ingenious solution was in the minds of the framers, however, or just the scholar's.

56. See, e.g., Cary v. Curtis, 44 U.S. 236, 245 (1845) (Daniel, J.); accord: Sheldon v. Still, 49 U.S. 441 (1850).

57. Geoffrey C. Hazard, Jr. and Michele Taruffo, *American Civil Procedure: An Introduction* (New Haven: Yale University Press, 1993), 16–17; E. N. Griswold, "The Narrative Record in Federal Equity Appeals," *Harvard Law Review* 42 (1929), 486–488. The Judiciary Act and the Process Act made clear that the admiralty and equity rules had a foreign origin. They went back to English practices and beyond that to old Roman Law of Nations. As William Rawle concluded in his *View of the Constitution of the United States*, 2nd ed. (Philadelphia: Nicklin, 1829), 258, "the word equity [in the Rules of Decision Act] means equity as understood in England." The peculiar structure of the federal system of courts may have been an example of American exceptionalism, but the law in federal courts was not solely American in origin. See David L. Sloss, Michael D. Ramsey, and William S. Dodge, "The U.S. Supreme Court and International Law: Continuity and Change," in Sloss et al., eds., *International Law in the U.S. Supreme Court* (New York: Cambridge University Press, 2011), 2 ("from its earliest decisions in the 1790s, the Supreme Court has used international law to help resolve some of the major controversies on its docket").

58. Alexander Hamilton to William Rawle, January 20, 1794, William Rawle Papers, Historical Society of Pennsylvania. On the Federal Rules of Civil Proceedure' drafting and adoption, see chapter 9.

59. See, e.g., Robert L. Jones, "Finishing a Friendly Argument: The Jury and the Historical Origins of Diversity Jurisdiction," *New York University Law Review* 82 (2007), 997–1101. Posner, *The Federal Courts*, 210–212, hypothesizes what would happen if Congress, as it could, took diversity suits away from the federal courts.

60. See, e.g., Anthony J. Bellia Jr. and Bradford R. Clark, "The Law of Nations as Constitutional Law," *Virginia Law Review* 98 (2012), 729–838; and David M. Golove and Daniel Hulsebosch, "A Civilized Nation: The Early American Constitution, the Law of Nations, and the Pursuit of International Recognition," *New York University Law Review* 85 (2010), 932–1066. Golove and Hulsebosch argue that the federal Constitution "is best understood, in historical perspective, as an international document" whose purpose was to demonstrate that the new nation belonged in the community of nations (934).

61. Process Act, September 29, 1789, 1 Stats. 93; Fallon et al., *Federal Courts*, 537. In 1792, Congress conceded to the U.S. Supreme Court the authority to make rules for its own and the lower federal courts internal proceedings. This was confirmed by later statutes. Fallon et al., *Federal Courts*, 538–539.
62. Oliver Ellsworth to Richard Law, August 4, 1789, *DHSC*, 4:495.
63. *Pennsylvania Packet*, July 26, 1790, p. 1; David Stone, Address to the Senate, January 13, 1802, *Annals of Congress* 7th Cong. 1st sess., 71.
64. William Davie to James Iredell, August 2, 1797, quoted in Griffin John McRee, *The Life and Correspondence of James Iredell* (New York: Appleton, 1858), 2:335; Chase (1799) and Iredell (1792) quoted in Clare Cushman, *Courtwatchers: Eyewitness Accounts in Supreme Court History* (Lanham, MD: Rowman and Littlefield, 2111), 34, 36.
65. Frankfurter and Landis, *The Business of the Supreme Court*, 4; Theodore Sedgwick to Ephraim Williams, June 14, 1789, *DHSC*, 4:404; Alison L. LaCroix argues that the Judiciary Act was "the defining element of American federalism," *Ideological Origins of American Federalism*, 179.
66. Anti-Injunction Act of 1793, 1 Stat. 333. In Ex Parte Young 209 U.S. 123 (1908) the Supreme Court found that injunctive relief in federal court was also available when the state court was enforcing a state law that violated the Constitution.
67. See, generally, William Eskridge Jr., "All About Words: Early Understandings of the 'Judicial Power' in Statutory Interpretation, 1776–1806" *Columbia Law Review* 101 (2001), 990–1106. An entire treatise can be written about the Anti-Injunction provisions, which, like all acts of Congress prescribing federal procedure, have undergone extensive interpretation by the federal courts the acts were to constrain. See, e.g., William T. Mayton, "Ersatz Federalism Under the Anti-Injunction Statute," *Columbia Law Review* 78 (1978), 330 and after, arguing that the act was only intended to apply to the justices on circuit at the circuit courts.
68. James Madison to Edmund Pendleton, September 23, 1789, *DHSC*, 4:517.
69. Patrick T. Conley, ed., *The Bill of Rights and the States: The Colonial and Revolutionary Origins of American Liberties* (Lanham, MD: Rowman and Littlefield, 1992), xxi–xxiv; *DHFFC*, 11:825–836.
70. Edwin G. Burrows and Mike Wallace, *Gotham: A History of New York City to 1898* (New York: Oxford University Press, 1999), 300–301; Mary Stockwell, "Hamilton and Madison: The End of a Friendship," in John R. Vile et al., eds., *James Madison: Philosopher, Founder, and Statesman* (Athens: Ohio University Press, 2008), 178; William Garrott Brown, *The Life of Oliver Ellsworth* (New York: Macmillan, 1905), 226.

Chapter 2

1. Michael J. Gerhardt, *The Federal Appointments Process: A Constitutional and Historical Analysis* (Durham, NC: Duke University Press, 2000), 46–47; Maeva Marcus and Natalie Wexler, "The Judiciary Act of 1789: Political Compromise or Constitutional Interpretation?" in Marcus, ed., *Origins of the Federal Judiciary*, 30.
2. Gerhardt, *Federal Appointments Process*, 129.
3. "A Plebeian" April 17, 1788 [Melancton Smith?], *DHRC*, 17:161.
4. Henry Marchant quoted in D. Kurt Graham, *To Bring the Law Home: The Federal Judiciary in Early National Rhode Island* (DeKalb: Northern Illinois University Press, 2010), 41, 42; James E. Pfander, "Judicial Compensation and the Definition of Judicial Power in the Early Republic," *Michigan Law Review* 107 (2008), 1–50. On the end of private practices: Judiciary Act of December 18, 1812, 2 Stat. 788. Salary figures from Daniel S. Holt, *Federal Judiciary Appropriations* (Washington, D.C.: Federal Judicial Center, 2012), 1, 34, 11, and Richard A. Posner, *The Federal Courts: Challenge and Reform* (Cambridge, MA: Harvard University Press, 1996), 21, Table 1.2; and http://law.jrank.org/pages/7948/Justice-Department-History-Department.html. Were one to compare the first federal judges' salaries with Senators' in 1815, the upper house paid $1,500 dollars per year, about the same as a district judge's salary.
5. Henry J. Abraham, *Justices, Presidents, and Senators: A History of U.S. Supreme Court Appointments from Washington to Clinton* (Lanham, MD: Rowman and Littlefield, 1999), 58; Ralph Izard to Edward Rutledge, September 26, 1789, *DHSC*, 1 (part 2): 668.
6. James Wilson to George Washington, April 21, 1789, *DHSC*, 1 (part 2): 613.

7. Edward Shippen to George Washington, April 27, 1789, *DHSC*, 1 (part 2): 614; Arthur Lee to George Washington, May 21, 1789, ibid., 620. Here and after material adapted from Hoffer, Hoffer, and Hull, *The Supreme Court*, 34–41.

8. Douglas H. Ubelaker and Philip Curtin, "Human Biology of Populations in the Chesapeake Watershed," in Philip Curtin, et al., eds., *Discovering the Chesapeake: History of an Ecosystem* (Baltimore: Johns Hopkins University Press, 2000), 141–142; George Miller Sternberg, *Report on the Etiology and Prevention of Yellow Fever* (Washington, D.C.: GPO, 1890), 43.

9. Thomas Jefferson to John Jay, July 18, 1793, in Henry P. Johnson, ed., *Correspondence and Public Papers of John Jay* (New York: Putnam, 1891), 3:408; Chief Justice Jay and Associate Justices to Washington, July 20, 1793, ibid, 3:409; Jay draft of Neutrality Proclamation, April 11, 1793, ibid., 3:398–400. Note the difference between this view of mandatory consultation and the provision of Chapter III, Article II of the Massachusetts state constitution of 1780 (in many other ways a model for the federal Constitution): "Each branch of the legislature, as well as the governor and council, shall have authority to require the opinions of the justices of the supreme judicial court upon important questions of law, and upon solemn occasions." See also Russell R. Wheeler, "Extrajudicial Activities of the Early Supreme Court" *Supreme Court Review* (1973), 123–130. Statutes giving district judges the authority to appoint commissioners to take evidence and such were not extrajudicial, but directly facilitated the adjudication of cases.

10. Casey White, *John Jay: Diplomat of the American Experiment* (New York: Rosen, 2006), 12 and after; Walter Stahr, *John Jay* (London: Bloomsbury, 2005), 347 (views of slavery), 366 (retirement home).

11. James Haw, *John and Edward Rutledge of South Carolina* (Athens: University of Georgia Press, 1997), 229; Harry Downs, "Unlikely Abolitionist: William Cushing and the Struggle Against Slavery," *Journal of Supreme Court History* 29 (2005), 134.

12. James Wilson, Lectures on Law (1791), "Of the Law of Nations," in Kermit Hall and Mark David Hall, eds., *The Collected Works of James Wilson* (Indianapolis: Liberty Fund, 2007), 1:522.

13. Ellen Holmes Pearson, *Remaking Custom: Law and Identity in the Early American Republic* (Charlottesville: University of Virginia Press, 2011), 5; John Fabian Witt, *Patriots and Cosmopolitans: Hidden Histories of American Law* (Cambridge, MA: Harvard University Press, 2007), 15–82; Charles Rappeleye, *Robert Morris: Financier of the American Revolution* (New York: Simon and Schuster, 2010), 216–217, 219, 289; Samuel Johnston to James Iredell, July 28, 1798, *DHSC*, 1 (part 2), 859; Minute Book, October 25–November 3, 1798, C.C. D.S.C., NARA Atlanta.

14. Willis P. Wichard, *Justice James Iredell* (Durham: Carolina Academic Press, 2000), 189.

15. Stephen B. Presser, "The Verdict on Samuel Chase and his 'Apologist,'" in Scott Douglas Gerber, ed., *Seriatim: The Supreme Court before John Marshall* (New York: New York University Press, 2000), 260–291 (Chase reputation underappreciated by scholars); Abraham, *Justices*, 57–58.

16. William R. Casto, *The Supreme Court in the Early Republic: The Chief Justiceships of John Jay and Oliver Ellsworth* (Columbia: University of South Carolina Press, 1995), 95–97; Abraham, *Justices*, 28.

17. G. Edward White, *Law in American History, from the Colonial Years through the Civil War* (New York: Oxford University Press, 2012), 1:225.

18. Edmund Randolph to George Washington, August 5, 1792, *DHSC*, 1:586.

19. Edward Porter Alexander, *A Revolutionary Conservative: James Duane of New York* (New York: Columbia University Press, 1938), 213, 216.

20. Harvey Bartle III, *Mortals with Tremendous Responsibilities: A History of the United States District Court for the Eastern District of Pennsylvania* (Philadelphia: St. Joseph's University Press, 2011), 10–14; Stephen B. Presser, *Studies in the History of the United States Courts of the Third Circuit* (Washington, D.C.: GPO, 1982), 23.The court did not meet: *DHSC*, 8:123, n. 23

21. Mark Edward Lender, *"This Honorable Court": The United States District Court for the District of New Jersey, 1789–2000* (New Brunswick, NJ: Rutgers University Press, 2006), 22–23.

22. Harry Innes to Thomas Jefferson, August 27, 1791, quoted in Mary K. Bonsteel Tachau, *Federal Courts in the Early Republic: Kentucky, 1789–1816* (Princeton: Princeton University Press, 1978), 38.

23. Peter Graham Fish, *Federal Justice in the Mid-Atlantic South: United States Courts from Maryland to the Carolinas, 1789–1835* (Washington, D.C.: Administrative Office of the U.S. Courts, n.d.), 25; "An Act Further to Authorize the Adjournment of Circuit Courts," 1794, 1 Stat. 369; Simeon Baldwin to Uriah Tracy, May 1794, quoted in Robert A. Katzmann, *Judges and Legislators: Toward Institutional Comity* (Washington, D.C.: Brookings Institution, 1988), 51. Typically, it was the absence of the justice rather than the judge that delayed the meeting of the circuit courts. See, e.g., Augusta (Georgia) *City Gazette*, May 5, 1798: the "failure [of Justice Wilson to attend] to the numerous suitors in the court, some of whom attended from foreign countries and distant states" was regretted. *DHSC*, 3:257.

24. Ron Chernow, *Alexander Hamilton* (New York: Penguin, 2004), 674–705; George R. Lamplugh, *Politics on the Periphery: Factions and Parties in Georgia, 1783–1806* (Newark: University of Delaware Press, 1986), 105; Fletcher v. Peck, 10 U.S. 87 (1810) (state could not repeal the act enabling the sale of the lands because repeal violated the Contracts Clause of the Constitution, Art. I, sec. 10 cl. 1).

25. Nathaniel Chipman, *Sketches of the Principles of Government* (Rutland, VT: J. Lyon, 1793), 255.

26. A very fine point Russell R. Wheeler made in correspondence with the authors, and perhaps an example of checks on balances on the early judiciary?

27. July 15, 1791, Minute Book, D.C. N.H., NARA Boston; "Simeon Baldwin," Biographical Directory of the United States Congress, http://bioguide.congress.gov/scripts/biodisplay.pl?index=B000097.

28. Messinger, *Order in the Courts*, 6–9, 12, 15, 22, 27, 32, 45, 76. The end of the fee system is discussed in Nicholas Parrillo, *Against the Profit Motive: The Salary Revolution in American Government, 1780–1940* (New Haven: Yale University Press, 2013), 110, admitting that "no direct evidence" was available for some of the shifts from fees to salaries, and the whole business of fees was a "regulatory nightmare."

29. Alexander, *Duane*, 204; Tachau, *Federal Courts*, 167. Marshals remained on fees until 1896.

30. Equity Docket, 1792-1800, C.C. Pa. NARA Philadelphia. Rawle appeared (usually for the complainant) in over half of the forty cases docketed. U.S. attorneys remained on the fee system until 1896. Daveiss and Burr: Quentin Scott King, *Henry Clay and the War of 1812* (New York: Mcfarland, 2014), 42–44; Peter Charles Hoffer, *The Treason Trials of Aaron Burr* (Lawrence: University Press of Kansas, 2008), 49, 51, 52.

31. Biographical note added to William Rawle, "Inaugural Address," *Memoirs of the Historical Society of Philadelphia* (republication edition, Philadelphia: Lippincott, 1864), 1:30–31; Harison law practice: Joseph Henry Smith, ed., *The Law Practice of Alexander Hamilton: Documents and Commentary* (New York: Columbia University Press, 1980), 3:654, 684, 714 (co-counsel with Hamilton); Edward Livingston's reputation: William B. Hatcher, *Edward Livingston: Jeffersonian Republican and Jacksonian Democrat* (Baton Rouge: Louisiana State University Press, 1940), 18–25.

32. Nancy V. Baker, *Conflicting Loyalties: Law and Politics in the Attorney General's Office, 1789–1990* (Lawrence: University Press of Kansas, 1992), 24; Philip Dray, *Capitol Men: the Epic Story of Reconstruction through the Lives of the First Black Congressmen* (New York: Houghton Mifflin, 2010), 78, 87.

33. Messinger, *Order in the Courts*, 1. "Tradition of public service," see, e.g., Carla Mulford, "Benjamin Franklin and the Myths of Nationhood," in A. Robert Lee and W. M. Verhoeven, eds., *Making America, Making American Literature: Franklin to Cooper* (Rodopi: Amsterdam, 1995), 34 (Franklin public service); Eliza Hope Harrison, "Introduction," in Harrison, ed., *Best Companions: Letters of Eliza Middleton Fisher . . . 1839–1846* (Columbia: University of South Carolina Press, 2001), 3 (Henry Middleton public service). One reason why so many of these offices appeared in the same families is that these families' wealth allowed their scions to leave the farm and the foundry to get an education and enter the professions.

34. Pennsylvania Packet, February 6, 1790; *DHSC*, 1 (part 2): 691; John Jay to William Cushing, December 7, 1789, *DHSC*, 1 (part 2): 689; Jay Charge to the Grand Jury, Johnston, ed., *Papers of Jay*, 3:387; Minutes of the C.C. D. NY, April 5–12, 1790, *DHSC*, 2:23.

35. May 18, 19, 1790, Minute Book, C.C. D. S.C., NARA Atlanta; Nathaniel Pendleton to James Iredell, March 5, 1791, *DHSC*, 1 (part 2): 719; December 8, 1789, March 7, 1790, Minute Book, D.C. D. Ga, NARA Atlanta; Final Record Books, District Court, and Final Record

Books, Circuit Court, District of Rhode Island, February 1791–February 1801, NARA Boston; Neal Allen, "A Brief History of the United States District Court for the District of Maine," paper presented at a ceremony held at the court, Bangor, Maine, September 25, 1989, p. 3; ms. in possession of the authors.

36. Final Records Book, District Court and Final Records Book, Circuit Courts, District of Rhode Island, February 1791–February 1801, NARA Boston, Higginson v. Greenwood, October 26, 1791–October 25, 1793, Minute Books, 1790–1800, C.C. D. S.C., NARA Atlanta; U.S. v. Joseph Brown and others, November 1, 1794, ibid. Trickle of appeals: Dwight Henderson, *Courts for a New Nation* (Washington, D.C.: Public Affairs Press, 1971), 55–60.

37. Federal Crimes Act, April 30, 1790, 1 Stat. 112; U.S. v. Samuel Monroe, May, 1793, Criminal Case Files, 1795–1860 C.C. D. Md., NARA Atlanta; U.S. v. Ebeneezer Sanders, May 1800, Criminal Case Files, C.C. D. Md., NARA Atlanta; Fish, *Federal Justice*, 27–28; Henderson, *Courts*, 65.

38. Henderson, *Courts*, table on p. 73; Fish, *Federal Justice*, 25–27; Miscellaneous Records, 1791–1800; C.C. D. Pa., NARA Philadelphia. On Fries' co-conspirators and the Sedition Act, see, e.g., James Iredell Charge to Grand Jury, April 11, 1799, *DHSC*, 3:350.

39. Tachau, *Federal Courts*, 201; Lender, *Honorable Court*, 35; Jeffrey Morris, *Federal Justice in the Second Circuit: A History of the United States Courts in New York, Connecticut, and Vermont, 1789 to 1987* (New York: Second Circuit Historical Society, 1987), 15–16, 18–19. See, generally, Ralph Lerner, "The Supreme Court as Republican Schoolmaster," *Supreme Court Review* (1967), 129–141, on the uses and abuses of the grand jury charge.

40. Henderson, *Courts*, table at p. 87; Wharton v. Lowrey, C.C. D. Pa., October 1793 Session; U.S. v. Edmund Randolph, April 1794 Session; U.S. v. Robert Morris and State of Maryland v. Robert Morris, October 1794 Session; Schermerhorn v. Lespinasse, April 1795 Session; John Penn v. Anthony Butler, October 1796 Session; Juan Domingo de la Torre v. Marianne Alvarez et al. April 1800 Session, Equity Docket Book, 1792–1860, C.C. D. Pa., NARA Philadelphia.

41. Criminal Case Files, 1795–1825, C.C. D. Md., NARA Philadelphia; Answer to a Bill in Chancery, LeRoy v. Thompson, C.C. N.Y., Egbert Benson papers, Box 4, New-York Historical Society, n.d.

42. Charles G. Geyh, *Judicial Disqualification: An Analysis of Federal Law*, 2nd ed. (Washington, D.C.: Federal Judicial Center, 2010), 5; Act of May 8, 1792, 1 Stat. 178–179.

43. *DHSC*, 8:280–290; Rutherford v. Fisher, 4 U.S. 22 (1800).

44. Hayburn's Case, 2 U.S. 409, 410, 411 (1792) (Wilson, J.) 2 U.S. at 414 (Jay, J.). Congress made other provisions for the veterans. Note that Jay was here sitting as a judge of the circuit court, not as the chief justice of the U.S. Supreme Court.

45. Maeva Marcus and Robert Teir, "*Hayburn's Case*: A Misinterpretation of Precedent," *Wisconsin Law Review* 1987; 527–546. Marcus and Teir added that no petitioner had come to the circuit courts in New York or North Carolina, thus the letters to Washington from those courts were advisory opinions (534). Actually, they were not opinions because there was no case or controversy (yet) for those courts to decide.

46. 2 U.S. at 415 (Jay, J.); James Kent, *Commentaries on American Law*, 2nd ed. (New York: Halstead, 1832), 1:451. (He also hinted, again mistakenly, that they agreed to hear the petitions in their judicial capacity).

47. Richard G. Miller, "The Federal City," in Weigley, Wainwright, and Wolf, eds., *Philadelphia: A 300 Year History*, 172–173.

48. 2 U.S. at 415 (Jay, J.); "Note," *DHSC* 6: 35–38; Randolph to Madison, August 12, 1792, *DHSC* 6:67–68, Mashaw, "Recovering American Administrative Law," 1331–1333; Wheeler, "Extrajudicial," 138.

49. John V. Orth, *The Judicial Power of the United States: The Eleventh Amendment in American History* (New York: Oxford University Press, 1987), 12–20.

50. Chisholm v. Georgia 2 U.S. 419, 474 (1793) (Jay, C.J.).

51. 2 U.S. at 475 (Iredell, J.).

52. *Augusta Chronicle*, November 19, 1793; Orth, *The Judicial Power of the United States*, 23–25 and after.

53. Jack P. Greene, "State and National Identities in the Era of the American Revolution," in Don H. Doyle and Marco Pamplona, eds., *Nationalism in the New World* (Athens: University of

Georgia Press, 2006), 61–79; Sam Haselby, *The Origins of American Religious Nationalism* (New York: Oxford University Press, 2015), 3; David Waldstreicher, *In the Midst of Perpetual Fetes: The Making of American Nationalism, 1776–1820* (Chapel Hill: University of North Carolina Press, 1997), 352.

54. See e.g. Robert S. Levine, *Dislocating Race and Nation: Episodes in Nineteenth-Century American Literary Nationalism* (Chapel Hill: University of North Carolina Press, 2009), 67; Merrill Jensen, *The Articles of Confederation: An Interpretation of the Social-constitutional History of the American Revolution 1774–1781* (Madison: University of Wisconsin Press, 1940), 163–164; early sectionalism: George William Van Cleve, *A Slaveholders' Union: Slavery, Politics, and the Constitution in the Early American Republic* (Chicago: University of Chicago Press, 2010), 270; Paul Finkelman, *Slavery and the Founders: Race and Liberty in the Age of Jefferson*, 2nd ed. (Armonk, NY: Sharpe, 2001), 108.

55. George Washington, "Fourth Annual Message," November 6, 1792, in James D, Richardson, ed., *A Compilation of the Messages and Papers of the Presidents* (Washington, D.C. 1902), 1:127.

56. Washington, "Proclamation," August 11, 1794, in Richardson, *Messages of the Presidents*, 1:161; May 1795 Criminal Case Files, C.C. D. Pa., NARA Philadelphia.

57. Rawle, in U.S. v. Mitchell, 2 U.S. 348 (1795); Tilghman, in ibid.; Rawle, *A View of the Constitution of the United States of America*, 2nd ed. (Philadelphia: Nicklin, 1829), 141.

58. William Paterson, "Bench notes on the Whiskey Rebellion trial, United States v. John Barnet," May 29, 1795, Gilder Lehrman collections, GLC01114.

59. Thomas Slaughter, *The Whiskey Rebellion: Frontier Epilogue to the American Revolution* (New York: Oxford University Press, 1988), 78, 216.

60. *Gazette of the United States*, April 6, 1795.

61. U.S. v. Worrall, 2 U.S. 384, 391, 394 (1798) (Chase, J.).

62. "An Act for the Punishment of Certain Crimes Against the United States" (Sedition Act) July 14, 1798, 1 Stat. 596–597; Paterson, Address to the Grand Jury, Rutland session, 1798, quoted in John E. O'Connor, *William Paterson: Lawyer and Statesman, 1745–1806* (New Brunswick, NJ: Rutgers University Press, 1986), 245.

63. Thomas Cooper, *An Account of the Trial of Thomas Cooper, of Northumberland, on a Charge of Libel against the President of the United States* (Philadelphia: J. Bioren, 1800), 47; Peter Charles Hoffer, *The Free Press Crisis of 1800: Thomas Cooper's Trial for Seditious Libel* (Lawrence: University Press of Kansas, 2011), 89–112.

64. James Callender, *The Prospect Before Us* (Richmond: Pleasants and Lyon, 1800), 30; James Morton Smith, *Freedom's Fetters: The Alien and Sedition Laws and American Civil Liberties* (Ithaca, NY: Cornell University Press, 1956), 334–358.

65. *Trial of James Callender, for Sedition* (Richmond, 1804), 53; Paul D. Newman, *Fries's Rebellion: The Enduring Struggle for the American Revolution* (Philadelphia: University of Pennsylvania Press, 2004), 177.

66. A Citizen, "Federal Judiciary No. 1," *Washington Federalist*, January 26, 1801.

67. Kathryn Turner, "Federalist Policy and the Judiciary Act of 1801," *William and Mary Quarterly* 3rd ser. 22 (1965), 3, 6, 9 (the Act was "not occasioned by the Republican victory in 1800"). Note that Federalists like Hamilton, Fisher Ames, and Robert Goodloe Harper continued to practice in state courts. See, e.g., "Opinions on the Disposition of the Estate in New York of a Foreign Intestate," (1795–1802)," in Julius W. Goebel and Joseph Henry Smith, eds., *The Law Practice of Alexander Hamilton* (New York: Columbia University Press, 1980), 4:539–543; Ron Chernow, *Alexander Hamilton* (New York: Penguin, 2004), 509.

68. Judiciary Act of 1801, 2 Stat. 89. Erwin Surrency, "The Judiciary Act of 1801," *American Journal of Legal History* 2 (1958), 63; The issue of relative convenience of federal and state courts refused to die. As late as 1890, in the debate over the Sherman Antitrust Act, Senator John Reagan of Texas, a Democrat and former Confederate postmaster, moved to amend "circuit courts in the district" to read "court of the United States or of any state of competent jurisdiction." His reasons were inconvenience and expense to "men of ordinary means," but one suspects that he thought federal courts would be less friendly to such suits than state courts. April 8, 1890, 56th Cong., 1st sess., *Congressional Record*, 3146.

69. Summary of arguments on Judiciary Bill, January 5, 1801, 6th Cong. 3rd Sess., *Annals of Congress*, 880; *Aurora* June 3, 1800.

70. Robert Goodloe Harper to his constituents, February 26, 1801, *DHSC,* 4:715–16.
71. Gouverneur Morris, Address to the Senate, January 8th 1802, 7th Cong. 1st Sess., *Annals of Congress,* 38. Note that Congress once again gave the federal courts jurisdiction "arising under" federal law in 1872.
72. Surrency, "The Judiciary Act of 1801," 54–55 n. 4; Crowe, *Building the Judiciary,* 67–69; Richard Ellis, *The Jeffersonian Crisis: Courts and Politics in the Young Republic* (New York: Oxford University Press, 1971), 40. James L. Roark et al., *The American Promise* (New York: Bedford, 2012), 293, reports the number of commissions.
73. Jeffrey Brandon Morris, *Calmly to Poise the Scales of Justice: A History of the Courts of the District of Columbia Circuit* (Durham: Carolina Academic Press, 2001), 3–7; William F. Carne, "Life and Times of William Cranch," *Records of the Columbia Historical Society,* December 1901, 298; On the D.C. Circuit's perambulation: Matthew F. Maguire, *An Anecdotal History of the United States District Court for the District of Columbia, 1801–1976* (Washington, D.C.: District Court for the District of Columbia, 1976), 19–20; On longevity: Madison appointee James Sewell Morsell was next, on the D.C. court from 1815 to 1863, followed by President James Monroe appointee Willard Hall, on the Delaware District Court from 1823 to 1871.

Chapter 3

1. White, *Law in American History,* 1: 207–208 (lower federal courts withstand the challenge).
2. Gordon S. Wood, *Empire of Liberty, A History of the Early Republic, 1789–1815* (New York: Oxford University Press, 2011), 276–314, 433–468.
3. White, *Law in American History,* 1: 193.
4. Hoffer, Hoffer, and Hull, *The Supreme Court,* 51; "Honors to Judge Marshall," *Niles Weekly Register,* July 18, 1835; Thomas Hart Benton, *Thirty Years View: Or, A History of the Workings of the American Government, from 1820 to 1850* (New York: Appleton, 1854), 2: 681; *The Papers of John Marshall,* ed. Herbert A. Johnson (Chapel Hill: University of North Carolina Press, 1977), 2:161–178; R. Kent Newmyer, *John Marshall and the Heroic Age of the Supreme Court* (Baton Rouge: Louisiana State University Press, 2001), 407.
5. George Lee Haskins and Herbert A. Johnson, *Foundations of Power: John Marshall, 1801–1815, Oliver Wendell Holmes Devise History of the Supreme Court of the United States,* Vol. 2 (New York: Macmillan, 1981), 382–389.
6. Judiciary Act of 1802, "An Act to amend the Judicial System of the United States," 2 Stat. 156, April 29, 1802.
7. Richard E. Ellis, *The Jeffersonian Crisis: Courts and Politics in the Young Republic* (New York: Oxford University Press, 1971), 45–65; Herbert A. Johnson, *The Chief Justiceship of John Marshall, 1801–1835* (Columbia: University of South Carolina Press, 1997), 56–57; Stuart v. Laird, 5 U.S. 299 (1803).
8. Hoffer and Hull, *Impeachment in America,* 208–219.
9. Caesar Rodney, February 26, 1805, Impeachment trial of Samuel Chase, *Annals of Congress,* 8th Cong., 2d sess., 597; Hoffer and Hull, *Impeachment,* 233–255.
10. Norman Risjord, *Jefferson's America, 1760–1840* (Lanham, MD: Rowman and Littlefield, 2010), 343, 344; Jeremy D. Bailey, *Thomas Jefferson and Executive Power* (New York: Cambridge University Press, 2007), 151, 155 (Jefferson adopted the spoils system).
11. [John Quincy Adams], *A Report of the Secretary of State, Together With the Causes Depending in the Courts of the United States* May, 12, 1820 (Washington, D.C.: Gales and Seaton, 1820), 3–15; Roberta Sue Alexander, *A Place of Recourse: A History of the U.S. District Court for the Southern District of Ohio, 1803–2003* (Athens: Ohio University Press, 2005), 9.
12. David P. Currie, *The Constitution in the Supreme Court: The First Hundred Years, 1789–1888* (Chicago: University of Chicago Press, 1992), 63.
13. Lender, *"This Honorable Court,"* 23–24; Noble E. Cunningham, Jr., *The Process of Government under Jefferson* (Princeton: Princeton University Press, 1978), 184, Jefferson quoted at 183. (The South Carolina post did not become vacant until 1812, however.)
14. Leonard D. White, *The Jeffersonians in Power: A Study in Administrative History, 1801–1829* (New York: Free Press, 1965), 126–127; An Act establishing Circuit Courts, and abridging the jurisdiction of the district courts in the districts of Kentucky, Tennessee, and Ohio February

24, 1807, 2 Stat. 420. On Jefferson's idealization of western settlement, H. W. Brands, "The Golden Death of Jefferson's Dream," in Sanford Levinson and Bartholomew H. Sparrow, eds., *The Louisiana Purchase and American Expansion, 1803–1898* (Lanham, MD: Rowman and Littlefield, 2005), 139–142.

15. For example, William Johnson had no hesitation about deploying judicial review. See Thomas C. Grey, "The Original Understanding and the Unwritten Constitution," in Leslie Ann Boldt-Irons, ed., *The Constitution and the Regulation of Society* (Albany: SUNY Press, 1995), 168. Nor did Brockholst Livingston dissent from Marshall's nationalist opinions; Jean Edward Smith, *John Marshall: Definer of a Nation* (New York: Henry Holt, 1996), 350–351.

16. Charles Tait, Charge to the Grand Jury, June, 1822, (Mobile) *Commercial Register*, June 6, 1822, p. 3; Niles quoted in Paul M. Pruitt Jr. and David I. Durham, "Charles Tait, A Biographical Sketch," in Pruitt, Durham, and Sally E. Hadden, eds., *Traveling the Beaten Trail: Charles Tait's Charges to Federal Grand Juries, 1822–1825* (Tuscaloosa: University of Alabama Law School, 2013), 9.

17. Leonard D. White, *The Jacksonians: A Study in Administrative History, 1829–1861* (New York: Macmillan, 1954), 143–162; Sheldon Goldman, *Picking Federal Judges: Lower Court Selection from Roosevelt through Reagan* (New Haven: Yale University Press, 1999), 7.

18. Henry Marie Brackenridge, *Recollections of Persons and Places in the West* (Philadelphia: Lippincott, 1868), 327; Kermit Hall, *The Politics of Justice: Lower Federal Judicial Selection and the Second Party System, 1829–1861* (Lincoln: University of Nebraska Press, 1979), 7–9; Hall and Eric W. Rise, *From Local Courts to National Tribunals: The Federal District Courts of Florida, 1821–1990* (Brooklyn, NY: Carlson, 1991), 5–13.

19. David W. Brady, *Critical Elections and Congressional Policy Making* (Palo Alto: Stanford University Press, 1991), 20–21; David Hackett Fischer, *The Revolution of American Conservatism: The Federalist Party in the Era of American Democracy* (New York: Harper, 1965), explains the transit of Federalists like John Quincy Adams and Daniel Webster to the Republican Party.

20. William E. Nelson, *Marbury v. Madison: The Origins and Legacy of Judicial Review* (Lawrence: University Press of Kansas, 2000), 71 (taking the court out of politics). But see the argument for "A full scale war over the courts" in these years: Jed Handelsman Shugerman, *The People's Courts: Pursuing Judicial Independence in America* (Cambridge, MA: Harvard University Press, 2012), 34.

21. G. Edward White, *The Marshall Court and Cultural Change, Oliver Wendell Holmes Devise History of the Supreme Court*, Vol. 3 (New York: Cambridge University Press, 2009), 179–180. There is a large and growing literature that downgrades the significance and the originality of *Marbury*'s claims and the scope of its version of judicial review. See, e.g. Jack Rakove, "The Origins of Judicial Review: A Plea for New Contexts," *Stanford Law Review* 49 (1997), 1039–1040; Robert Lowery Clinton, *Marbury v. Madison and Judicial Review* (1989), passim; Michael J. Klarman, "How Great Were the 'Great' Marshall Court Decisions?" *Virginia Law Review* 87 (2001), 1111, 1113.

22. A fire in the Capitol in 1898 "destroyed many of the Supreme Court's original jurisdiction case files." Jonathan W. White, *Guide to Research in Federal Judicial History* (Washington, D.C.: Federal Judicial Center, 2010), 45. The docket books still exist in RG 267, in the National Archives. After a "flurry" of suits involving citizens of one state suing another state were ended by the adoption of the Eleventh Amendment, only a handful of original jurisdiction suits graced the early Supreme Courts' dockets. *DHSC*, 6:4.

23. Marbury v. Madison, 5 U.S. 137, 177 (1803) (Marshall C.J.).

24. 5 U.S. 170 (Marshall, C.J.). The "abstention doctrine" in Marshall's dictum here is prudential, that is, judge-made law. Abstention shifted or left cases in the state courts, refused to hear cases that were moot, unripe, did not present a matter that the courts could resolve, or were brought by parties having no standing to sue in the first place, as well as abstaining in pending state criminal cases–except when states act in bad faith, when they violate the federal Constitution, and "other unusual situations calling for federal intervention" (Younger v. Harris, 401 U.S. 37, 53 [1971] [Black, J.]). The underlying question is whether courts have discretion to exercise the full extent of jurisdiction granted them by Congress. See, e.g., Martin H. Redish, "Abstention, Separation of Powers, and the Limits of the Judicial Function," *Yale Law Journal* 94 (1985), 78 and after.

25. The story of the trial is told in Peter Charles Hoffer, *The Treason Trials of Aaron Burr* (Lawrence: University Press of Kansas, 2008), 146–171. Burr was acquitted on charges of treason but a better case could have been made for conspiracy to commit a federal crime. The lapsed Sedition Act had provisions against conspiracy, but the Federal Crimes Act of 1790, under which Burr was indicted, did not.

26. T. Carpenter, comp., *The Trial of Col. Aaron Burr on an Indictment of Treason* (Washington, D.C.: Westcott, 1807), 129.

27. Carpenter, *The Trial of Burr*, 134; David Robertson, *Reports of the Trials of Colonel Aaron Burr . . .* (Philadelphia: Hopkins and Earle, 1808), 1: 254.

28. Edward Kaplan, *The Bank of the United States and the American Economy* (Santa Barbara, CA: ABC-CLIO, 1999), 67–70.

29. Quotations from Mark R. Killenbeck, *McCulloch v. Maryland: Securing a Nation* (Lawrence: University Press of Kansas, 2006), 122 and after, and the headnotes to McCulloch v. Maryland 17 U.S. 316 (1821).

30. McCulloch v. Maryland 17 U.S. 316, 431–434 (1819) (Marshall C.J.).

31. Cohens v. Virginia 19 U.S. 262 (1821) (the U.S. Supreme Court is the final authority on the constitutionality of state court criminal prosecutions); Letters of Algernon Sydney, *Richmond Enquirer*, May 25, 1821; *Debates on the Federal Judiciary: A Documentary History* (Washington, D.C.: Federal Judicial Center, 2013), 1:181–198.

32. Osborn v. Bank of the United States, 22 U.S. 738, 818, 819 (1824) (Marshall, C.J.); Bank of the United States v. Planters Bank, 22 U.S. 904, 905 (1824) (Marshall, C.J.). A telling point made to the authors by Michael Wells is that Marshall found that Congress could grant federal jurisdiction any time there was, in Marshall's words, an "ingredient"—federal issue—in the case. This was an open door to federal courts' jurisdiction whenever a federal issue was raised.

33. Maxwell Bloomfield, "Supreme Court Buildings," in Hall et al., eds., *Oxford Companion*, 100–102.

34. Bankruptcy Act of 1800 2 Stat. 19; Bruce Mann, *Republic of Debtors: Bankruptcy in the Age of American Independence* (Cambridge, MA: Harvard University Press, 2003), 2; Law and Appellate Records, Act of 1800 Bankruptcy Case Files of the U.S. District Court for the District of Maryland, 1800–1803, NARA Atlanta; Law and Appellate Records, Act of 1800 Bankruptcy Case Files of the U.S. District Court for the District of Maryland, 1800–1803, NARA New York City; Act of 1800 Bankruptcy Records of the U.S. District Court for the Eastern District of Pennsylvania, 1800–1806, NARA Philadelphia.

35. March 28th, 1809, Minute Book, D.C. D. S.C., NARA Atlanta.

36. At first, these were called "special courts" in the records. See, e.g., John Percival et al. (U.S. Gunboat number 57) v. *Charles*, October 30, 1812, Prize Cases, District Court of New York, 1812–1816, D.C. D.. NY, NARA New York City; An Act Concerning Letters of Marque, Prizes, and Prize Goods, June 26, 1812, 1 Stats. 759–760. On the commissioners, see http://www.fjc.gov/history/home.nsf/page/admin_03_02.html. The "Letters of Marque and Reprisal" Act of 1812 also created a cottage industry in the buying and selling of the documents because they were issued to the ship, not its owner or captain. See Donald A. Petrie, *The Prize Game: Lawful Looting on the High Seas in the Days of Fighting Sail* (Annapolis: Naval Institute Press, 1999), 68 and David Head, *Privateers of the Americas: Spanish American Privateering from the United States in the Early Republic* (Athens: University of Georgia Press, 2015), 54–58.

37. The Schooner Adeline and Cargo, 13 U.S. 244 (1815).

38. File papers: John Cazeaux et al., Owners of the Brig *Expedition* v. Schooner *Adeline*, May–December 1814, Prize Cases, 1812–1816, D.C. S. D. NY, NARA New York City; 13 U.S. at 284, 285 (Story J.). What is notable about Story's short opinion is that he insisted American salvage law was bound by the statutes of Congress and American precedent, not by foreign (French) laws, international law, or English precedent. It is an important case for "conflict of laws" as much as for admiralty.

39. U.S. v. Jones, 26 F. Cas 653 (C.C. D. Pa 1813); U.S. v. Clark, 25 F. Cas 441 (C.C. D. Mass 1813); John Quincy Adams] *Statement of Convictions, Executions, and Pardons of The Government of the United States . . .* February 26, 1829, 20th Cong. 2nd sess., HR Doc. 146.

40. The Wilson v. U.S., 30 F. Cas. 239, 243 (C.C. D. Va., 1820) (Marshall, J.). A filibusterer (not to be confused with a fillibusterer, who occupies a legislature with delaying oratory) was a military and political freebooter.

41. Kevin Arlyck, "Plaintiffs v. Privateers: Litigation and Foreign Affairs in the Federal Courts, 1816–1822," *Law and History Review* 30 (2012), 247.

42. Adams, *Statement of Convictions.*

43. U.S. v. Furlong, 18 U.S. 184 (1820); Jeffrey Orenstein, "Joseph Almeida, Portrait of a Privateer, Pirate, and Plaintiff," *Green Bag* 2nd 10 (2007), 309; Ellsworth to Oliver Wolcott, October 16, 1800, quoted in William Garrott Brown, *The Life of Oliver Ellsworth* (New York: Macmillan, 1905), 304.

44. [John Quincy Adams], Message from the President of the United States Transmitting (Pursuant to a Resolution of the Senate, of the 18th January, 1819) A Report from the Secretary of State Together with the Returns of Causes Depending in the Courts of the United States, S. Doc. No. 134, 16th Cong., 1st Sess., 1820.

45. Adams, Returns of Causes, 3–15.

46. Adams, Returns of Causes, 3–15.

47. Adams, Returns of Causes, 3–15.

48. Adams, *Statement of Convictions* passim; Criminal Case Files, 1801–1840, C.C. E.D. Pa., NARA Philadelphia; Stephen Mihm, *A Nation of Counterfeiters: Capitalists, Con Men, and the Making of the United States* (Cambridge, MA: Harvard University Press, 2007), 114–115.

49. Process Act of May 8, 1792, 1 Stats. 36, 277. The Judiciary Act of August 23, 1842, 5 Stat. 516 restated the presumption that depositions would be taken, though oral testimony in court was permissible at the judge's discretion. This was for many years a complaint against requiring two separate kinds of filings, until the common law and equity dockets with joined with the promulgation of the Federal Rules of Civil Procedure in 1938. Then complaints centered on the time spent in discovery.

50. Alexander v. Pendleton, 12 U.S. 462, 468 (1814) (Marshall, C.J.)

51. Adams, Return of Causes, 22–25.

52. Lawrence H. Larsen, *Federal Justice in Western Missouri: The Judges, the Cases, The Times* (Columbia: University of Missouri Press, 1994), 10, 13; A Citizen [Luke Lawless], *St. Louis Inquirer*, 1826, quoted in Arthur J. Stansbury, ed., *Report of the Trial of James H. Peck . . .* (Boston: Hilliard, 1833), 50. Claims all along the Mississippi in the Louisiana, Mississippi, and Arkansas federal courts were hotly contested "Public Lands Acquired by Treaty" [DeBow's] *Commercial Review* (February 1848) 5:16, 116.

53. Stansbury, ed., *Trial of Peck*, 3; George McDuffie, December 21, 1830, *Register of Debates in Congress*, 21st Cong., 2d sess., 17–18; Act of March 2, 1831, 4 Stat. 488 ("criminal contempt may be punished summarily if the judge certifies that he saw or heard the conduct constituting the contempt and that it was committed in the actual presence of the court"). After the Peck case came the impeachment and conviction of federal district judge West Humphreys in 1862 (for abandoning his court and serving the confederacy); Mark Delahay, who resigned before trial in 1873 for incapacity; Charles Swayne acquitted in 1904 for misuse of power; Robert Archbald convicted in 1913 for peculation; George Washington English for abuse of power in 1926 and resigned before trial; Harold Louderback acquitted for misconduct and partisanship in 1933; Halsted Ritter convicted for practicing law while sitting as a judge in 1936; Harry Claiborne convicted for tax evasion in 1986; Alcee Hastings convicted for perjury in 1988; Walter Nixon convicted for perjury in 1989; Samuel Kent for sexual misconduct toward personnel under his supervision, resigned in 2009; and Thomas Porteous, convicted for corruption in 2010. http://www.fjc.gov/history/home.nsf/page/judges_impeachments.html. On Congress and the impeachment power, see Geyh, *When Courts and Congress Collide*, 170.

54. "A wolf by the ear," Thomas Jefferson to John Holmes, April 22, 1820, Jefferson Papers, Library of Congress. The correspondence was occasioned by the Missouri Compromise controversy.

55. Arthur Zilversmit, *The First Emancipation: The Abolition of Slavery in the North* (Chicago: University of Chicago, 1967); Gary John Kornblith, *Slavery and Sectional Strife in the Early American Republic, 1776–1821* (Lanham, MD: Rowman and Littlefield, 2007), 24–27; Adam Rothman, *Slave Country: American Expansion and the Origins of the Deep South* (Cambridge, MA: Harvard University Press, 2005), 26–27.

56. U.S. v. The Kitty 26 F. Cas. 791, 792 (D.C. S.C. 1808) (Bee, J.). "Bee to South Carolina Senate Delegation supporting increased pay for federal judges handling admiralty cases," February 3, 1800, Thomas Bee Papers, Columbiana Collection, University of South Carolina Library, Columbia, SC.
57. Alexander, *A Place of Recourse*, 14–15.
58. In Re Susan, 23 F. Cas. 444, 445 (C.C.D. Ind. 1818) (Parke, J.)
59. Joseph Story, "Report of the Commissioners [on the codification of Massachusetts law], 1837, *Miscellaneous Writings of Joseph Story* (Boston: Little, Brown, 1852), 3:713.
60. Joseph Story, *Commentaries on the Constitution of the United States* (Boston: Hilliard, Gray, 1833), 1:2; Hoffer, *For Ourselves and Our Posterity*, 122–125.
61. Robert M. Cover, *Justice Accused: Antislavery and the Judicial Process* (New Haven: Yale University Press, 1975), 201; Robert Pierce Forbes, *The Missouri Compromise and Its Aftermath: Slavery and the Meaning of America* (Chapel Hill: University of North Carolina Press, 2007), 94–95 (threat of disunion taken seriously in North).
62. R. Kent Newmyer, *Supreme Court Justice Joseph Story: Statesman of the Old Republic* (Chapel Hill: University of North Carolina Press, 1986), 353; Story, *Commentaries* 3: 677; Hoffer, *For Ourselves and Our Posterity*, 124–126.
63. Steven Hahn, *The Political Worlds of Slavery and Freedom* (Cambridge, MA: Harvard University Press, 2009), 13.

Chapter 4

1. Tony A. Freyer, "Negotiable Instruments and the Federal Courts in Antebellum American Business," *Business History Review* 50 (1976), 435–455; Crowe, *Building the National Judiciary*, 78; David Brion Davis, "Introduction" to "Joseph Story, Two Versions of Law for the Frontier," in Davis, ed., *Antebellum American Culture* (State College: Pennsylvania State University Press, 1979), 147; David M. Potter, *The Impending Crisis: America Before the Civil War, 1848–1861* (New York: HarperCollins, 1979), 294.
2. See, e.g., Peter Bargdolio, *Reconstructing the Household: Families, Sex, and the Law in the Nineteenth Century South* (Chapel Hill: University of North Carolina Press, 1998), 220; Brian R. Dirck, *Lincoln the Lawyer* (Urbana: University of Illinois Press, 2008), 36. Figures for state judicial experience of antebellum federal lawyers from http://www.fjc.gov/history/home.nsf/page/judges.html.
3. On legal education and professionalization: see, e.g., Alfred Konefsky and Michael H. Hoeflich, *The Gladsome Light of Jurisprudence: Learning the Law in England and the United States in the 18th and 19th Centuries* (New York: Praeger, 1988); Robert Stevens, *Law School: Legal Education in America from the 1850s to the 1980s* (Chapel Hill: University of North Carolina Press, 1985), 3–50; Thomas Hunter, "The Institutionalization of Legal Education in North Carolina," in Steve Sheppard, ed., *History of Legal Education in the United States* (Ipswich, MA: Salem Press, 1999), 1:409–411. On the law reports, see Erwin Surrency, "Law Reports in the United States," *American Journal of Legal History* 25 (1981), 48–66.
4. See, e.g., Ronald J. Krotoszynski, *Reclaiming the Petition Clause: Seditious Libel, "Offensive" Protest, and the Right to Petition the Government for a Redress of Grievances* (New Haven: Yale University Press, 2012), 119–120.
5. James G. Randall, "The Blundering Generation," *Mississippi Valley Historical Review* 27 (1940), 3–27; but see Philip S. Paludan, "A Crisis of Law and Order," in Kenneth L. Stampp, ed., *The Causes of the Civil War*, rev. ed. (New York: Simon and Schuster, 1991), 79–84.
6. See, e.g., Michael A. Morrison, *Slavery and the American West: The Eclipse of Manifest Destiny and the Coming of the Civil War* (Chapel Hill: University of North Carolina Press, 1997), 219–251.
7. Abraham Lincoln, First Annual Message, December 3, 1861; James Buchanan, Debate on the Judiciary Act, January 9, 1826, House of Representatives, 19th Cong. 1st Sess., *Register of Debates* 2:916. On the debates Congress, see Geyh, *When Courts and Congress Collide*, 59–65. Geyh cites Buchanan's long speech to a somewhat different purpose on page 60. Daniel Webster to Joseph Story, December 26, 1826, Fletcher Webster, ed., *Private Correspondence of Daniel Webster* (Boston: Little, Brown, 1857), 1:413; Newmyer, *Story*, 317. On the debates in Congress on the circuits, see *Debates on the Federal Judiciary* 1:211–224.

8. Timothy S. Huebner, "Judicial Independence in an Age of Democracy, Sectionalism, and War," in Theodore Brown, ed., *A History of the Tennessee Supreme Court* (Knoxville: University of Tennessee Press, 2002), 63.

9. Buchanan, 19th Cong. 1st Sess. *Register of Debates (in Congress)*, 917.

10. Abraham, *Justices, Presidents, and Senators*, 76–83; "An Act supplementary to the act entitled 'An Act to amend the judicial system of the United States,'" 5 Stat. 176. March 3, 1837; here and after Hoffer, Hoffer, and Hull, *Supreme Court*, 83–88.

11. "Federal Circuit Courts," *Niles Weekly Register*, April 18, 1835; Judiciary Act of March 3, 1837.

12. Russell Wheeler and Cynthia Harrison, *Creating the Federal Judicial System* (Washington, D.C.: Federal Judicial Center, 1994), 9–22; "Establishment of the Eighth and Ninth Circuits," FJC History of the Federal Judiciary, http://www.fjc.gov/history/home.nsf/page/landmark_06.html.

13. For Barbour's views of federalism, see Barbour as counsel for the State of Virginia, in Cohens v. Virginia, 19 U.S. 264 (1821).

14. Tony Freyer and Timothy Dixon, *Democracy and Judicial Independence: A History of the Federal Courts of Alabama, 1820–1995* (Brooklyn, N.: Carlson, 1995), 11–12.

15. "An Act to establish a Circuit Court of the United States in and for the State of California, March 2, 1855," 10 Stat. 631.

16. "Landmark Judicial Legislation" the California Circuit, http://www.fjc.gov/history/home.nsf/page/landmark_07.html.

17. John Forsyth, "Report of the Secretary of State to the Senate, January 5, 1839," Cong. Globe, Senate, 25th Cong., 3rd Sess., at 50.

18. Bruce Mann, *Republic of Debtors: Bankruptcy in the Age of American Independence* (Cambridge, MA: Harvard University Press, 2003), 243–249; *Papers of Daniel Webster*, ed. Harold D. Moser (Hanover, NH: University Press of New England, 1982), 73, 89.

19. Bankruptcy Act of 1841, 5 Stat. 440.

20. D.C. N.D. Ga, Bankruptcy petitions, NARA Atlanta; Edward J. Balleisen, *Navigating Failure: Bankruptcy and Commercial Society in Antebellum America* (Chapel Hill: University of North Carolina Press, 2000), 102, 111.

21. Yonatan Eyal, *The Young America Movement and the Transformation of the Democratic Party, 1828–1861* (New York: Cambridge University Press, 2007), 72, 114; Allan G. Bogue, "An Agricultural Empire," in Clyde A. Miller II, Carol A. O'Connor, and Martha A. Sandweiss, eds., *Oxford History of the American West* (New York: Oxford University Press, 1994), 285.

22. Docket Book, 1857–1858 Circuit Court for the Southern District of New York, NARA New York City; C.C. E.D. Mo., Index to Equity and Law Cases, 1857–1858, Kansas City NARA; Wayne V. McIntosh, *The Appeal of Civil Law: A Political Economic Analysis of Litigation* (Urbana: University of Illinois Press, 1990), 32–33.

23. Jacob Thompson, "Letter from the Secretary of the Interior, Transmitting a Tabular Statement, Showing the Number of Suits on the Dockets … of the Respective United States Courts Since January 1, 1856," February 22, 1858, 35th Cong, 1st Sess., Executive Doc. No. 69. Circuit Court Minute Book, September 11, 1857–November 23, 1857 C.C. N.D. Ca. NARA San Francisco.

24. Docket Book, 1857–1858, C.C. N.D. Ga., NARA Atlanta.

25. U.S. v. Agostin Haraszthy; September 16–November 23, 1857, C.C. N. D. Ca., NARA San Francisco; Brian McGinty, *Strong Wine: The Life and Legend of Agoston Haraszthy* (Palo Alto: Stanford University Press, 1998), 277–289.

26. Don E. Fehrenbacher, *Dred Scott* (New York: Oxford University Press, 1978), 278; Richard Caham, *A Court That Shaped America: Chicago's Federal District Court from Abe Lincoln to Abbie Hoffman* (Evanston, IL: Northwestern University Press, 2002), 13; Richard Cahan, Pia Hinckle, and Jessica Boyer Ocken, *The Court that Tamed the West: From the Gold Rush to the Tech Boom* (Berkeley, CA: Heyday, 2013), 3; "The Federal Building Program," http://www.nps.gov/nr/twhp/wwwlps/lessons/136gsa/136facts1.htm.

27. Swift v. Tyson, 41 U.S. 1 (1842).

28. Michael Williams, *Americans and Their Forests: A Historical Geography* (New York: Cambridge University Press, 1992), 133–136.

29. Alan Taylor, *Liberty Men and Great Proprietors: The Revolutionary Settlement on the Maine Frontier, 1760–1820* (Chapel Hill: University of North Carolina Press, 1990), 109.

30. 41 U.S. 1, 2 (1842); Tony Freyer, *Harmony and Dissonance: The Swift and Erie Cases in American Federalism* (New York: New York University Press, 1981), 1–43.

31. 41 U.S. 38, 39, 40, 41 (1842) (Story, J.). Note that Swift did not impose federal law on the states in similar fact patterns—their courts were still free to find their own judgments on state law grounds.

32. Don Faber *The Boy Governor: Stevens T. Mason and the Birth Of Michigan Politics* (Ann Arbor: University of Michigan Press, 2012), 65. On the peculiar pecuniary mores of the age, see Mark W. Summers, *The Plundering Generation* (New York: Oxford University Press, 1988). Land sale fraud was a favorite of the schemers.

33. Oliver v. Piatt, 44 U.S. 333 (1845).

34. Lewis v. Baird, 15 F. Cas. 457, 458 (C.C. D Ohio 1842) (Leavitt, J.).

35. Hugh Dunlop and Wife v. John R. Shepley and others, March 1849, C.C. D. Mo., Law and Equity Record, March 1849; Park v. Jourdan, C.C. E.D. Mo., Equity Rule Book, October 3, 1860, 185; Goodrich patent injunctions, D.C. E.D. Mo., October 5, 1859—April 25, 1860, Equity Rule Book, pp., 143–147, 176, 207–208, all Kansas City NARA.

36. Robert E. May, *Manifest Destiny's Underworld: Filibustering in Antebellum America* (Chapel Hill: University of North Carolina Press, 2004), 121, 135, 180–181; U.S. v. Quitman, 27 F. Cas 680, 684 (C.C. D. La., 1854) (Campbell, J.). An ominous note for those who read omens in the language of opinions: Campbell referred to the "confederacy" instead of the Union or the nation. After Alabama, his home state, seceded, and Lincoln called for volunteers to put down the rebellion, Campbell resigned his place on the Supreme Court and took a position as assistant secretary of war in the Confederate cabinet.

37. The decision of the circuit court was reported in Bank of Augusta v. Earle, 38 U.S. 519, 522 (1839).

38. Howard Bodenhorn, *A History of Banking in Antebellum America: Financial Markets and Economic Development in an Era of Nation-Building* (New York: Cambridge University Press, 2000), 204–205; Bank of Augusta v. Earle, 38 U.S. 516, 586, 597 (1839) (Taney, J.).

39. Justice Nelson quoted in Hendrik Hartog, *Man and Wife in America: A History* (Cambridge, MA: Harvard University Press, 2000), 80; Mihm, *A Nation of Counterfeiters*, 133, 140, 173, 358.

40. Rothman, *Slave Country*, 51–56, 165–216.

41. On the rise of abolitionism generally, and immediatism in particular, see Timothy Patrick McCarthy, John Stauffer, Martin Duberman, and Michael Fellman, eds., *Prophets of Protest: Reconsidering the History of American Abolitionism* (New York: New Press, 2006). The subject remains one of the most controversial in historical scholarship.

42. U.S. v. Robert Baker, Antonio Evaristo, and Jason Pendleton, April 1845, C.C. D. MD, NARA Atlanta; Justice Wayne, Charge to the Grand Jury, C.C. D. Ga, 30 F. Cas. 1026 (C.C. D. Ga. 1859).

43. Polydore v. Prince, 19 F. Cas. 950, 951, 952, 955 (D.C. D. Maine) (1837); Charles P. Mattocks, "In Memoriam, Edward Fox," *Reports of Judgments of Hon. Edward Fox: United States District judge for Maine District First Circuit*, ed. Thomas Haskell (Portland, ME: 1888), 2:559–560. The precedent was an English one. In *Somerset v. Stewart* (K.B., 1772) Somerset, a somewhat reluctant William Murray, Lord Chief Justice Mansfield, found that slavery could only exist where positive law enabled it. There was no such law in England, so Stewart could not imprison his slave Somerset with the intent of carrying him back to slavery in the West Indies. Somerset v. Stewart, 98 ER 499 (1772) (Mansfield, L.C.J.); H. Robert Baker, *Prigg v. Pennsylvania: Slavery, the Supreme Court, and the Ambivalent Constitution* (Lawrence: University Press of Kansas, 2012), 19–21.

44. Charles W. Shields, *Address at the Funeral of the Hon. John K. Kane, at Fern-Rock, Philadelphia, February 24, 1858* (Philadelphia, 1858); David W. Brown, ed., *Passmore Williamson vs. John K. Kane: Action for False Imprisonment, before the Court of Common Pleas of Delaware County* (Philadelphia: Merrihew & Thompson, 1857), passim.

45. Frederick Douglas, "Speech to the American Anti-Slavery Society, January, 1842," quoted in Patrick S. Washburn, *The African American Newspaper: Voice of Freedom* (Evanston, IL: Northwestern University Press, 2007), 28; Fugitive Slave Act, 9 Stat. 462, September 18, 1850; Don E. Fehrenbacher, *The Slaveholding Republic: An Account of the United States*

Government's Relations to Slavery (New York: Oxford University Press, 2002), 231, 418, n.2; U.S. v. Amy, 24 F. Cas. 792, 802 (C.C. D. Va., 1859) (Taney, J.)

46. Timothy S. Huebner, *The Taney Court: Justices, Rulings, and Legacy* (Santa Barbara, CA: ABC-CLIO, 2003), 34, 175–176; James F. Simon, *Lincoln and Chief Justice Taney: Slavery, Secession, and the President's War Powers* (New York: Simon and Schuster, 2007), 9.

47. Bernard Christian Steiner, *Life of Roger Brooke Taney: Chief Justice of the United States Supreme Court* (Philadelphia: Williams and Wilkins, 1922), 201–203, David P. Currie, *The Constitution in the Supreme Court: The First Hundred Years, 1789–1888* (Chicago: University of Chicago Press, 1992), 209;

48. Williamjames Hull Hoffer, *The Caning of Charles Sumner: Honor, Idealism, and the Origins of the Civil War* (Baltimore: Johns Hopkins University Press, 2010), 66–95.

49. John W. Barber, *A History of the Amistad Captives . . . Also an Account of the Trials . . .* (New Haven, CT: Barber, 1840), 6.

50. The legal story is told in Howard Jones, *Mutiny on the Amistad* (New York: Oxford University Press, 1988), and Bruce A. Ragsdale, "'Incited by the Love of Liberty' The *Amistad* Captives and the Federal Courts," *Prologue* 35 (2003), http://www.archives.gov/publications/prologue/2003/spring/amistad-2.html.

51. See, generally, William L. Miller, *Arguing about Slavery: John Quincy Adams and the Great Battle in The United States Congress* (New York: Knopf, 1996), 145 and after.

52. Roger Baldwin, Counsel for Appellants in error, "Prior History," 61 U.S. v. Claimants of Schooner Amistad, 40 U.S. 518 (1841).

53. 40 U.S. at 593 (Story, J.).

54. See, generally, Baker, *Prigg v. Pennsylvania*, 140 and after, and Paul Finkelman, "Story Telling on the Supreme Court: *Prigg v. Pennsylvania* and Justice Story's Judicial Nationalism," *Supreme Court Review* (1994) 247–293. On slave catchers, John Hope Franklin and Loren Schweninger, *Runaway Slaves, Rebels on the Plantation* (New York: Oxford University Press, 2000), 156–160.

55. Story to Ezekiel Bacon, quoted in Newmyer, *Story*, 377; Prigg v. Pennsylvania, 41 U.S. 539, 610 (1842) (Story, J.).

56. Quoted in Michael W. McConnell, "Joseph Story" in Vile, *Great American Judges* 1:732.

57. McLean quoted in John Craig Hammond, *Slavery, Freedom, and Expansion in the Early American West* (Charlottesville: University Press of Virginia, 2007), 144.

58. McLean to the Reverend Jonah Wald, Nov. 10, 1850, quoted in Robert Cover, *Justice Accused* (New Haven: Yale University Press, 1977), 249; Francis P. Weisenburger, *The Life of John McLean, A Politician on the United States Supreme Court* (Columbus: Ohio State University Press, 1937), 188–210.

59. Jones v. Van Zandt, 46 U.S. 215 (1847).

60. Strader v. Graham, 51 U.S. 82, 93–94 (1851) (Taney C.J.). Were the men who aided the slaves abolitionists? Surely they were.

61. Earl Maltz, *Fugitive Slave on Trial: The Anthony Burns Case and Abolitionist Outrage* (Lawrence: University Press of Kansas, 2010), 57.

62. William Seward, "On the Irrepressible Conflict," delivered at Rochester, NY, October 25, 1858; Abraham Lincoln, "House Divided Speech," delivered at Springfield, IL, on June 18, 1858.

63. Don E. Fehrenbacher, *The Dred Scott Case: Its Significance in American Law and Politics* (New York: Oxford University Press, 1978), 259–260.

64. Dred Scott v. Sandford, U.S. Circuit Court for the Eastern District of Missouri (1854), November 2, Nov. 16, 1853; April 25, 1854. Equity and Law Final Record Books, 1831–1915, pp. 506–514. The abstract of the proceedings was copied into the Final Record because the case papers were sent to the Supreme Court after the appeal.

65. Luther v. Borden, 48 U.S. 1 (1849). Buchanan wrote to Catron on February 3, 1857, and Catron replied on the 10th. The subject of the correspondence was the Dred Scott case. Fehrenbacher, *Dred Scott*, 307. Paul Finkelman, *Dred Scott v. Sandford: A Brief History with Documents* (New York: Bedford, 1997), 46, mentions the chat.

66. Buchanan referred to the case in his inaugural address, hinting that the Court was the proper branch of the federal government to settle the question once and for all. Jean

Baker, *James Buchanan: The American Presidents Series: The 15th President, 1857–1861* (New York: Macmillan, 2004), 83.

67. Charles Evans Hughes, *The Supreme Court of the United States* (New York: Columbia University Press, 1928), 50; Weisenburger, *McLean,* 207.

68. 60 U.S. at 407 (Taney, C.J.).

69. Rayman L. Solomon, *History of the Seventh Circuit, 1891–1941* (Washington, D.C.: Bicentennial Committee of the Judicial Conference, 1987), 3; C.C. D. Mo. Law Record Book B, p. 241 (April 3, 1854, court opens with Judge Wells presiding in the absence of Justice Catron); Dred Scott v. Sandford 60 U.S. 393, 518 (1857) (Catron, J.)

70. Michael J. McManus, *Political Abolitionism in Wisconsin, 1840–1861* (Kent, OH: Kent State University Press, 1998), 128 and after.

71. McManus, *Wisconsin,* 86–88; Paul Finkelman, *An Imperfect Union: Slavery, Federalism, and Comity* (Chapel Hill: University of North Carolina Press, 1981), 336–338.

72. Ableman v. Booth, 11 Wisc. 498, 509, 510, 511, 512 (1859) (Dixon C.J.).

73. Ableman v. Booth, 62 U.S. 506, 515, 516 (1859) (Taney, C.J.).

74. If John Brown and his crew were acting not against the United States, but against individual slave owners and even slavery itself, the precedent of *Hanway* would apply. U.S. v. Hanway, 26 F. Cas. 105, 126, 128 (C.C. E.D. Pa. 1851) (Grier, J.): "The court feel bound to say, that they do not think the transaction with which the prisoner is charged with being connected, rises to the dignity of treason or a levying of war. Not because the numbers of force was insufficient. But (1) for want of any proof of previous conspiracy to make a general and public resistance to any law of the United States; (2) because there is no evidence that any person concerned in the transaction knew there were such acts of congress, as those with which they are charged with conspiring to resist by force and arms, or had any other intention than to protect one another from what they termed 'kidnappers' [by which slang term they probably included not only actual kidnappers, but all masters and owners seeking to recapture their slaves], and the officers and agents assisting therein." Paul Finkelman, "The Treason Trial of Castner Hanway," in Michal Belknap, ed., *American Political Trials* (Westport, CT: Greenwood, 1981), 77–102.

75. Brian McGinty, *Trial of John Brown* (Cambridge, MA: Harvard University Press, 2009), 72, 76, 282; quotations from *The Life, Trial, and Execution of Captain John Brown . . .* (New York: De Witt, 1859), archived at www.yale.edu/lawweb/avalon/treatise/john_brown/john_brown. htm.

76. Abraham Lincoln, First Inaugural Address, March 4, 1861, *Collected Works of Abraham Lincoln,* ed. Roy P. Basler (New Brunswick, NJ: Rutgers University Press, 1953), 4: 268.

77. See Don E. Fehrenbacher (completed by Ward M. McAfee), *The Slaveholding Republic* (New York: Oxford University Press, 2001), 247–248, and Charles B. Dew, *Apostles of Disunion: Southern Secession Commissioners and the Causes of the Civil War* (Charlottesville: University Press of Virginia, 1971), passim.

Part II

1. Eric Foner, *The Fiery Trial: Abraham Lincoln and American Slavery* (New York: Norton, 2010), 176–183, 206–247, 258–259; Foner, *A Short History of Reconstruction* (New York: Harper, 1990), 30–31 and after. But see Mark Wahlgren Summers, *The Ordeal of the Reunion: A New History of Reconstruction* (Chapel Hill: University of North Carolina Press, 2014), arguing that most northerners had little interest in aiding the freedmen or redressing the wrongs that slavery wrought once it was ended.

2. Benjamin Nathan Cardozo, *The Nature of the Judicial Process* (New Haven: Yale University Press, 1922), 103, 108; Robert Keeton, *Judging* (St. Paul: West, 1990), 2.

3. Alfred D. Chandler, Jr., *Scale and Scope: The Dynamics of Industrial Capitalism* (Cambridge: Belknap Press of Harvard University Press, 1990), 14–30; Robert Wiebe, *The Search for Order, 1877–1920* (New York: Hill and Wang, 1967), 181–182.

4. Lynn Dumenil, *The Modern Temper: American Culture and Society in the 1920s* (New York: Macmillan, 1995), 10 and after; Estelle Freedman, *No Turning Back: The History of Feminism and the Future of Women* (New York: Random House, 2007), 81–83.

5. Herbert Hovenkamp, *The Opening of American Law: Neoclassical Legal Though, 1870–1970* (New York: Oxford University Press, 2014), 6; Laura Kalman, *Legal Realism at Yale: 1927–1960* (Chapel Hill: University of North Carolina Press, 1986), 98–144; N. E. H. Hull, "Restatement and Reform: A New Perspective on the Origins of the American Law Institute" *Law and History Review* 8 (1990), 55–96.

Chapter 5

1. Lincoln, "First Inaugural Address," in Roy P. Basler, ed., *The Collected Works of Abraham Lincoln* (New Brunswick, NJ: Rutgers University Press, 1953), 4:269–271.
2. See, e.g., Texas v. White, 131 U.S. 95 (1870); Harold Hyman, *The Reconstruction Justice of Salmon P. Chase: In Re Turner and Texas v. White* (Lawrence: University Press of Kansas, 1997).
3. Daniel W. Hamilton, "A New Right to Property: Civil War Confiscation in the Reconstruction Supreme Court," *Journal of Supreme Court History* 29 (2004), 255.
4. The source for this data is FJC, "Biographical Dictionary of Federal Judges, 1789–Present," http://www.fjc.gov/history/home.nsf/page/judges.html. Kentucky unionists included a number of strong states' rights advocates, but in general the state's leaders did not favor secession. Lowell H. Harrison, *The Civil War in Kentucky* (Lexington: University of Kentucky Press, 1975), 8 and after.
5. William Hamilton Bryson, *Legal Education in Virginia, 1779–1979: A Bibliographical Approach* (Charlottesville: University Press of Virginia, 1982), 36 and after.
6. John Campbell to his mother, March 6, 1861, John Campbell Papers, Alabama Department of Archives and History; "Judge McGrath Resigns," *Richmond Daily Dispatch*, November 10, 1860; Roy Temple House, "Our Legal Centenaries," *Green Bag* 26 (1914), 11.
7. Asa Biggs, *Autobiography of Asa Biggs*, ed. R. D. W. Connor (Raleigh: North Carolina Historical Society, 1915), 24.
8. Biggs, *Autobiography*, 26, 29.
9. "High Treason," *New York Times*, January 15, 1861, p. 8.
10. Treat quoted and Catron paraphrased in Larsen, *Federal Justice in Western Missouri*, 43–44; Treat's habeas corpus dispute: David Mayer Silver, *Lincoln's Supreme Court* (Urbana: University of Illinois Press, 1956), 34. Catron: A. E. Keir Nash, "John Catron" in Urofsky, ed., *The Supreme Court Justices: A Biographical Dictionary* (New York: Routledge, 1994), 98–99.
11. Joanne Webb Chiles Eakin and Annette W. Curtis, *The Little Gods: Union Provost Marshals in Missouri, 1861–1865* (Independence, MO: Two Trails, 2002), 8–9; Jeremy Neely, *The Border Between Them: Violence and Reconciliation on the Kansas Missouri Line* (Columbia: University of Missouri Press, 2007), 116–117, 121; C.C. E.D. Mo., Law and Equity Index, 1860–1865; U.S. v. John Rucker, Joseph Richards, and twenty-four others, grand jury indictments in case file No. 49, September 1862, D.C. W.D. Mo., Criminal Case Files, volume 2, NARA Kansas City.
12. Brian McGinty, *Lincoln and the Court* (Cambridge, MA: Harvard University Press, 2008), 71. Throughout the war the military courts in the border states and southern portions of some of the midwestern states had a difficult relationship with the federal trial courts. Military commanders in Missouri and southern Indiana, for example, acted swiftly to bring suspected Confederate agents to trial under martial law when the federal courts were open and operating. See, e.g., the discussion of *Ex Parte Milligan* (1866) in Jonathan Lurie, *The Supreme Court and Military Justice* (Los Angeles: Sage, 2013), 10–25.
13. Ex parte Merryman 17 F. Cas. 144, 147 (C.C.D. Md. 1861) (Taney J.). Taney exchanged written opinions with Judge Treat, both men finding the other's views correct. Silver, *Lincoln's Court*, 34.
14. 17 F. Cas. at 148.
15. Harold M. Hyman, *A More Perfect Union: The Impact of the Civil War and Reconstruction on the Constitution* (New York: Knopf, 1973), 83–98. Union military presence ensured that Maryland would remain in the Union: Jonathan White, *Abraham Lincoln and Treason in the Civil War: The Trials of John Merryman* (Baton Rouge: Louisiana State University Press, 2011), 108. The other cases are U.S. v. Grenier 26 F. Cas. No. 15262 (1861) (suspected plotter released on bond); Ex Parte Benedict 3 F. Cas 159 (N.D. N.Y 1862) (district judge removal of five men from custody in Buffalo fort to Erie county jail, citing Merryman).

16. U.S. v. Hoxie 26 F. Cas. 397, 402 (C.C. D. Vt.1808) (Livingston, J.).
17. Morris, *District of Columbia Circuit* 37; Erwin C. Surrency, *History of the Federal Courts*, 2nd ed. (Dobbs Ferry, NY: Oceana, 2002), 430–431; Jonathan W. White, "Sweltering with Treason: The Civil War Trials of William Matthew Merrick," *Prologue* 39 (2007), 26–36.
18. Mrs. John A. Logan, *Thirty Years in Washington, or, Life and Scenes in Our National Capital* (Washington, D.C.: Worthington, 1901), 413. She called Taney "the man who hastened the Civil War." "Death of Chief Justice Taney," *New York Times* October 14, 1864; Huebner, *Taney Court*, 175–176. Over time, Taney's reputation has indeed improved and Sumner, in life never respected by his political opponents, remains a controversial figure. See, e.g., Heubner, "The Disputed Reputation of Roger B. Taney," in Finkelman, ed., *Supreme Court*, 249–256, and Louis Ruchames, "Charles Sumner and American Historiography," *Journal of Negro History* 38 (1953), 139–160.
19. William L. Richter, *Historical Dictionary of the Civil War and Reconstruction* (Lanham, MD: Scarecrow, 2011), 320.
20. July 2, 1862, 12 Stats. 128.
21. "An Act to Confiscate Property used for Insurrectionary Purposes," August 6, 1861, 12 Stat. 319.
22. "An Act to suppress Insurrection, to punish Treason and Rebellion, to seize and confiscate the Property of Rebels, and for other Purposes," July 17, 1862, 12 Stat. 589.
23. Stephen C. Neff, *Justice in Blue and Gray: A Legal History of the Civil War* (Cambridge, MA: Harvard University Press, 2010), 34. The growth of the federal bureaucracy during the war years was immense, but most of it related directly to the prosecution of the war. Richard F. Selcer, *Civil War America, 1850–1876* (New York: Infobase, 2006), 216. No new judgeships were created until the Judiciary Act of 1869 provided for additional circuit court judges.
24. See, e.g., U.S. v. Schooner George Darby 25 F. Cas. 1284 (D.C. S.D. N.Y., 1864).
25. The insurance cases were especially vexing to the families of southern men who had taken out the insurance from northern companies before the war and died during it. See David Thompson, "Clerical Concoctions and Ministerial Machinations, The Faith-Filled Pursuit of the Thirteenth Amendment." Third Biennial UnCivil War Conference, Athens, Ga., October 22, 2013. Cited with permission of the author.
26. U.S. v. 129 Packages, 27 F. Cas. 284 (D.C. E.D. Mo., 1864); McCall's Case, 15 F. Cas. 1225 (D.C. E.D. Pa., 1863).
27. Roberta Sue Alexander, "The Willson Era," in Alexander and Paul Finkelman, eds., *Justice and Legal Change on the Shores of Lake Erie: A History of the United State District Court for the Northern District of Ohio* (Athens: Ohio University Press, 2012), 29.
28. John Syrett, *Confiscation Acts: Failing to Reconstruct the South* (New York: Fordham University Press, 2005), 103, 137; Allen C. Guelzo, *Abraham Lincoln, "Redeemer" President* (Grand Rapids, MI: Eerdmans, 2002), 347.Was the emancipation an unconstitutional exercise of his presidential powers? Former Supreme Court Justice Curtis thought so and published a pamphlet attacking it. See Benjamin Robbins Curtis, *Executive Power* (Boston: Little, Brown, 1862); Stuart Streicher, *Justice Curtis in the Civil War Era: At the Crossroads of American Constitutionalism* (Charlottesville: University of Virginia Press, 2005), 156–162. Bear in mind that Curtis was a Whig, and one of the tenets of the Whig Party was opposition to the overextension of executive power.
29. Abandoned and Captured Property Act, March 12, 1863, 12 Stats. 820. On Lincoln's faith in the Unionism of many southerners, see Sean Wilentz, *The Rise of American Democracy: Jefferson to Lincoln* (New York: Norton, 2005), 783–784, and James M. McPherson, *Battle Cry of Freedom: The Civil War Era* (New York: Oxford University Press, 2003), 239.
30. Abraham Lincoln, Amnesty Proclamation, December 8, 1863, 13 Stat. 737; Amnesty Act of 1872, According to the Act, Congress could restore the rights of those excluded in the Act by a two-thirds vote.
31. David Luis-Brown, *Waves of Decolonization: Discourses of Race and Hemispheric Citizenship in Cuba, Mexico, and the United States* (Durham, NC: Duke University Press, 2008), 48–49, David J. Weber, *Foreigners in their Native Land: Historical Roots of the Mexican Americans* (Albuquerque: University of New Mexico Press, 2003), 159–160; Hyman, *A More Perfect Union*, 227; J.P. Usher, "Report of the Secretary of the Interior" December 6, 1864, 38th

Cong. 2nd Sess., Ex Doc. No. 1; Chase, Diary entry, March 20, 1865, quoted in John Niven, *Salmon P. Chase: A Biography* (New York: Oxford University Press, 1995), 390.

32. A. F. Warburton, *Trial of the officers and crew of the privateer Savannah, on the charge of piracy, in the United States Circuit Court for the Southern District of New York, Hon. Judges Nelson and Shipman, presiding* (Washington, D.C.: GPO, 1862); Mark A. Weitz, *The Confederacy on Trial: The Piracy and Sequestration Cases of 1861* (Lawrence: University Press of Kansas, 2005), are the sources for the two cases. *Savannah* case: U.S. v. Baker et al., 24 F. Cas. 962 (C.C. S.D. NY, 1861); *Enchantress* case: U.S. v. Smith, 27 F. Cas. 1134 (C.C.E. D. Pa 1861).

33. Stacy Pratt McDermott, *The Jury in Lincoln's America* (Athens: Ohio University Press, 2012), 49–50.

34. Brig Amy Warwick, 67 U.S. 635 (1863).

35. http://www.fjc.gov/servlet/nFsearch; William A. Link, *Roots of Secession: Slavery and Politics in Antebellum Virginia* (Chapel Hill: University of North Carolina Press, 2005), 164–168; "Judge Busteed and the United States Authorities," *New York Times*, December 10, 1865, p. 3; Gerardo Del Guercio, "Alabama," in Richard Zuczek, ed., *Encyclopedia of the Reconstruction Era, A–L* (Westport, CT: Greenwood, 2006), 32–33; Charles Lane, "Edward Henry Durrell, A Study in Reputation," *Green Bag* 2nd ser. 13 (2010), 153–168; Michael W. Fitzgerald, *Urban Emancipation: Popular Politics in Reconstruction Mobile, 1860–1890* (Baton Rouge: Louisiana State University Press, 2002), 99–100.

36. This and the subsequent paragraphs on Lincoln's Court from Hoffer, Hoffer, and Hull, *The Supreme Court*, 103–106.

37. Michael A. Ross, *Justice of Shattered Dreams: Samuel Freeman Miller and the Supreme Court During the Civil War Era* (Baton Rouge: Louisiana State University Press, 2003), 3, 184.

38. Elizur Southworth, *A Memorial Address on the Life and Character of David Davis* (Litchfield, IL: 1887), 3.

39. Paul Kens, *Justice Stephen Field Shaping Liberty from the Gold Rush to the Gilded Age* (Lawrence: University Press of Kansas, 1997), 2, 70–92.

40. Doris Kearns Goodwin, *Team of Rivals: The Political Genius of Abraham Lincoln* (New York: Simon and Schuster, 2005), 10, 21, and after; Niven, *Chase*, 374–375 and after.

41. Niven, *Chase*, 385–386; C. Ellen Connally, "The Use of the Fourteenth Amendment by Salmon P. Chase in the Trial of Jefferson Davis," *Akron Law Review* 42 (2009), 1165–1200; William C. Davis, *Jefferson Davis: The Man and His Hour* (Baton Rouge: Louisiana State University Press, 1996), 642–657.

42. David C. Frederick, *Rugged Justice: The Ninth Circuit Court of Appeals and the American West, 1891–1941* (Berkeley: University of California Press, 1994), 13; Cahan, Hinckle, and Ocken, *Court that Tamed the West*, 119–120; Oscar Tully Schuck, "Ogden Hoffman," *History of the Bench and Bar of California* (Los Angeles: Commercial, 1901), 472–473; Christian G. Fritz, *Federal Justice in California: The Court of Ogden Hoffman* (Lincoln: University of Nebraska Press, 1991), 28, 48, 255–263 (tables and charts of cases); Minute Book, C.C. N.D. Calif., January 3–May 1, 1865, NARA San Francisco; Kens, *Justice Stephen Field*, 98, 284.

43. Willie Lee Rose, *Rehearsal for Reconstruction: The Port Royal Experiment* (New York: Oxford University Press, 1976), 21 and after; Eric Foner, *Reconstruction: America's Unfinished Revolution, 1863–1877* (New York: Harper, 1988), 35–36.

44. Robert V. Remini, *A Short History of the United States* (New York: HarperCollins, 2009), 152.

45. Hans L. Trefousse, *Andrew Johnson: A Biography* (New York: Norton, 2007), 230.

46. Trefousse, *Johnson*, 218–228; http://www.fjc.gov/servlet/nFsearch.

47. Civil Rights Act of 1866, April 9, 1866, 14 Stat. 27. Portions of the Act are still part of the U.S. Code at 42 U.S.C. sec. 1981. See, e.g., Otis H. Stephens Jr. and John M. Scheb II, *American Constitutional Law* (Boston: Wadsworth, 2011), 2:486; Michael J. Klarman, *From Jim Crow to Civil Rights: The Supreme Court and the Struggle for Racial Equality* (New York: Oxford University Press, 2004), 19.

48. Kermit Hall, "Judiciary Act of 1866," in Hall et al., eds., *Oxford Companion*, 475; FJC, "Landmark Judicial Legislation"; "An Act to fix the Number of Judges of the Supreme Court of the United States, and to change certain Judicial Circuits," 14 Stat. 209, July 23, 1866; http://www.fjc.gov/history/home.nsf/page/landmark_09.html. Maps of the 1866 judicial circuits in Wheeler and Harrison, *History of the Federal Courts*.

49. Joseph P. Bradley, *Miscellaneous Writings of Joseph P. Bradley* ed. Charles Bradley (Newark, NJ: Hardham, 1902), 91; Kenneth W. Mack, "Civil Disobedience, State Action, and Lawmaking Outside the Courts: Robert Bell's Encounter with American Law," *Journal of Supreme Court History* 39 (2014), 352–353.

50. Melvin I. Urofsky, *The Supreme Court Justices: A Biographical Dictionary* (London: Taylor and Francis, 1994), 445; Marian C. McKenna, "Ward Hunt," in Hall et al., eds., *Oxford Companion*, 417; U.S. v. Anthony, 24 F. Cas. 829, 832 (1873) (Hunt, J.); U.S. v. Taylor, 11 F. 470, 471 (C.C. D. Kans. 1882) (McCrary, J.). On Hunt and the Anthony Trial, see N. E. H. Hull, *The Woman Who Dared to Vote: The Trial of Susan B. Anthony* (Lawrence: University Press of Kansas, 2012), 114–178.

51. John V. Orth, "Morrison R. Waite," in Hall et al., eds., *Oxford Companion*, 906–907; Donald Grier Stephenson Jr., "The Waite Court," in Paul Finkelman, ed., *The Supreme Court: Controversies, Cases, and Characters from John Jay to John Roberts* (Santa Barbara, CA: ABC-CLIO, 2014), 319.

52. Separable Controversies Act of 1866, Ch. 288, 14 Stat. 306; Note, "Separation of Causes in Removal Proceedings," *Harvard Law Review* 41 (1928), 1048–1050; Local Prejudice Act of 1867, Ch. 196, 14 Stat. 558; "Northern Claims in Southern Courts," *New York Times* January 7, 1866, p. 4.

53. Habeas Corpus Act of 1867, Ch. 28, 14 Stat. 385; Prejudice and Local Interest Act of 1867, 14 Stat. 558; William M. Wiecek, "The Reconstruction of Federal Judicial Power," in Lawrence M. Friedman and Harry N. Scheiber, eds., *American Law and the Constitutional Order: Historical Perspectives* (Cambridge, MA: Harvard University Press, 1988), 240.

54. See, e.g., Bruce Ackerman, *We the People*, Vol. 2: *Transformations* (Cambridge, MA: Harvard University Press, 2000), 121 (claiming that the Fourteenth Amendment was the centerpiece of a new and revolutionary constitutionalism). But see William E. Nelson, *The Fourteenth Amendment: From Political Principle to Judicial Doctrine* (Cambridge, MA: Harvard University Press, 1988), 7 and after (ambiguities of the amendment prevented its fuller explication), and Hyman, *A More Perfect Union*, 438–440 (Republicans did not intend the amendment to restructure federalism fundamentally).

55. The politics of the Act, as opposed to its efficacy, are the subject of some debate among historians. Compare Kermit Hall, "Judiciary Act of 1869," in Hall et al., eds., *Oxford Companion*, 548 (efficiency the primary motive for the enactment), with Crowe, *Building the Judiciary*, 159 (politics the primary consideration).

56. Judiciary Act of 1869, 16 Stat. 44; Frankfurter and Landis, *Business*, 69–77.

57. Solomon, *Seventh Circuit*, 4–5, 6, 7–9, 11.

58. Conformity Act of 1872, 17 Stat. 196, 197. But see E.W. Hinton, "Court Rules for the Regulation of Procedure in the Federal Courts," *ABA Journal* 13 (1927), 8 (arguing for a uniform federal system of rules in civil and criminal cases).

59. Cong. Globe, Senate 42nd Cong. 2nd Sess. (April 17, 1872), 2488–2490.

60. Jurisdiction and Removal Act of 1875, 18 Stat. 470; Civil Rights Act of 1875, 18 Stat. 335–337; Osborn v. Bank of the United States, 22 U.S. 738 (1824). The Act prefigured the Civil Rights Act of 1964: J. Morgan Kousser, "What Light Does the Civil Rights Act of 1875 throw on the Civil Rights Act of 1964?" in Bernard Grofman, *Legacies of the Civil Rights Act of 1964* (Charlottesville: University of Virginia Press, 2000), 33–42.

61. The "parity question," that is, whether state courts and their judges match federal courts and their judges in expertise and competence, is fully explored in Bert Neuborne, "The Myth of Parity," *Harvard Law Review* 90 (1977), 1105 and after, but debate continues.

62. Greg H. Williams, *Civil War Suits in the U.S. Court of Claims* (Jefferson, NC: McFarland, 2006), 11, 181. The old court ended its life in 1982. http://www.fjc.gov/history/home.nsf/page/courts_special_coc.html. Some of its business and all of its bench was transferred to the U.S. Court of Appeals for the Federal Circuit. A new U.S. Court of Federal Claims has a bench of sixteen judges nominated by the president and confirmed by the Senate who sit for fifteen-year terms and hear cases of money claims against the United States. http://www.fjc.gov/history/home.nsf/page/courts_special_cfc.html.

63. Marion T. Bennett, *The United States Court of Claims: A History, Part I: The Judges* (Washington, D.C.: Judicial Conference of the United States, 1976), 33.

64. Lincoln, executive order, October 20, 1862, quoted in Mechanics and Traders Bank v. Union Bank, 89 U.S. 276 (1874).
65. 89 U.S. at 295 (Strong, J.).
66. Minute Books, D.C. N.D. Ga, 1849–1862, 1867–1871, NARA Atlanta.
67. Elizabeth Lee Thompson, *The Reconstruction of Southern Debtors: Bankruptcy after the Civil War* (Athens: University of Georgia Press, 2004), 95, 143; William M. Wiecek, "The Reconstruction of Federal Judicial Power, 1863–1875," *American Journal of Legal History* 13 (1969), 334; Bankruptcy petitions, D.C. N.D. Ga, 1867–1868, NARA Atlanta; Bankruptcy Dockets, D.C. E.D. Mo., June 1867–June 1868, Kansas City NARA.
68. Docket Books, C.C. D. Mass., 1857–1870, NARA Boston; Thompson, *Southern Debtors*, 143.
69. Baker, *Conflicting Loyalties*, 64; Jed Shugerman, "The Creation of the Department of Justice: Professionalization Without Civil Rights or Civil Service," *Stanford Law Review* 66 (2014), 123; Williamjames Hull Hoffer, *To Enlarge the Machinery of Government: Congressional Debates and the Growth of the American State, 1859–1891* (Baltimore: Johns Hopkins University Press, 2007), 105.
70. *California Reports*, 16 (July/October terms, 1860), 50 (July/October terms 1875); *Illinois Reports*, 40 (1863–1866), 59 (1871); *Indiana Reports*, 14–15 (1860), 33–34 (1870–1871); *Kansas Reports*, 3 (1866), 9–10 (1872), 16 (1876); *Alabama Reports*, 35–36 (Book 27) (June 1859/January 1860 sessions), 55–56 (Book 37) (December 1876 session); *Mississippi Reports*, 36–37 (Book 18) (1858–1859), 52–53 (Book 26) (1876); *North Carolina Reports*, 52 (1859–1860), 74–75 (1876). These are representative of the other states' Supreme Court reporters.
71. Charles Fairman, *The Oliver Wendell Holmes Device History of the Supreme Court of the United States: Vol. 6: Reconstruction and Reunion, 1864–1888, Part I* (New York: Macmillan, 1971), 456.
72. The political question doctrine in Luther v. Borden 48 U.S. 1 (1849) was revisited in Baker v. Carr, 369 U.S. 186 (1962). The issue of "jurisdiction stripping" is one that directly pits Congress against the federal courts. See, Gerald Gunther, "Congressional Power to Curtail Federal Court Jurisdiction: An Opinionated Guide to the Ongoing Debate," *Stanford Law Review* 36 (1984), 895–922; James E. Pfander, "Federal Supremacy, State Court Inferiority, and the Constitutionality of Jurisdiction-Stripping Legislation," *Northwestern University Law Review* 101 (2007), 237–238.
73. Ex Parte McCardle, 74 U.S. 506, 515 (1868) (Chase, C.J.); Stanley I. Kutler, "Ex Parte McCardle: Judicial Impotency? The Supreme Court and Reconstruction Reconsidered," *American Historical Review* 72 (1967), 845.
74. U.S. v. Klein, 80 U.S. 128 (1871); Amanda L. Tyler, "The Story of *Klein*," in Vicki C. Jackson and Judith Resnik, eds., *Federal Courts Stories* (New York: Foundation Press, 2010), 92–94; Gunther, "Congressional Power," 904–906.
75. 80 U.S. 120,137, 141, 147, 148 (Chase, C.J.).
76. Vannevar v. Bryant, 88 U.S. 41 (1874); June 11, 1874, June 12, 1874, Senate, 43rd Cong., 1st Sess., *Congressional Record*, 4870, 4898; "The Jurisdiction and Removal Act of 1875," 18 Stat. 470.
77. See, e.g., F. Andrew Hessick III, "The Common Law of Federal Question Jurisdiction," *Alabama Law Review* 60 (2009), 897–898.
78. Barbara Young Welke, *Recasting American Liberty: Gender, Race, Law and the Railroad Revolution, 1865–1920* (New York: Cambridge University Press, 2001), 337; Morton J. Horwitz, *The Transformation of American Law, The Crisis of Legal Orthodoxy, 1870–1960* (New York: Oxford University Press, 1992), 11–12.
79. 16 Stat. 140 (1870).
80. April 20, 1871, 17 Stat. 13. Peter Charles Hoffer, *For Ourselves and Our Posterity: The Preamble to the Constitution in American History* (New York: Oxford University Press, 2012), argues that the Preamble's General Welfare Clause might also be the basis for such legislation.
81. Kermit L. Hall, "Political Power and Constitutional Legitimacy: The South Carolina Ku Klux Klan Trials, 1871–1872," *Emory Law Journal* 33 (1984), 909–932; Lou Falkner Williams, *The Great South Carolina Ku Klux Klan Trials, 1871–1872* (Athens, GA: University of Georgia Press, 2004), 39 and after.

82. United States v. Crosby, 25 F. Cas. 701 (C.C. D. S.C., 1871) (Bond, J.)
83. See Michael Les Benedict, *The Fruits of Victory: Alternatives in Restoring the Union, 1865–1877* (Philadelphia: Lippincott, 1975), 143–144.
84. U.S. v. Cruikshank, 25 F. Cas. 707, 710 (C.C. D. La. 1874) (Bradley, J.).
85. U.S. v. Cruikshank 92 U.S. 542, 559 (1875) (Waite, C.J.). One reading of the case suggests that it should be regarded as the foundation of all judicial restraint in civil rights matters and the demise of Reconstruction. See James Grey Pope, "Snubbed Landmark: Why *United States v. Cruikshank* (1876) Belongs at the Heart of the American Constitutional Canon," *Harvard Civil Rights-Civil Liberties Law Review* 49 (2014), 428–441. A looser reading of the intent of the amendment would have supplanted state-action limitations with broad due process protection (for example that Cruikshank and his crew had violated the right of their victims to peacefully assemble under the First Amendment) of civil rights. See Pamela Brandwein, *Reconstructing Reconstruction: The Supreme Court and the Production of Historical Truth* (Durham, NC: Duke University Press, 1999), 78–81. A critical assessment of the Court's performance is Edward A. Purcell Jr., "The Particularly Dubious Case of *Hans v. Louisiana*: An Essay on Law, Race, History and 'Federal Courts,'" *North Carolina Law Review* 81 (2003), 1979–1984.
86. Foner, *Reconstruction*, 512 and after; Hans Trefousse, *Rutherford B. Hayes* (New York: Times Books, 2002), 85 and after.
87. For a table of district and circuit court caseloads, see http://www.fjc.gov/history/caseload.nsf/page/caseloads_main_page. On the railroads removal and their lawyers, see, Edward A. Purcell, Jr., *Litigation and Inequality: Federal Diversity Jurisdiction in Industrial America, 1870–1958* (New York: Oxford University Press, 1992), 53 and William G. Thomas, *Lawyering for the Railroad: Business, Law, and Power in the New South* (Baton Rouge: Louisiana State University Press, 1999), 37–38.
88. Mark Twain and Charles Dudley Warner, *The Gilded Age: A Tale of Today* (Hartford, CT: American Publishing Company, 1873); Kunal M. Parker, *Common Law, History, and Democracy in America, 1790–1900: Legal Thought Before Modernism* (New York: Cambridge University Press, 2011), 205, 207; Harold M. Hyman and William M. Wiecek, *Equal Justice Under Law: Constitutional Development, 1835–1875* (New York: Harper and Row, 1982), 514.

Chapter 6

1. Vincent P. De Santis, *The Shaping of Modern America, 1877–1920*, 3rd ed. (Wheeling, IL: Harlan Davidson, 2000), 96–106; Mark Wahlgren Summers, *The Gilded Age or, The Hazard of New Functions* (Upper Saddle River, NJ: Prentice-Hall, 1997), 247; Roger Daniels, "The Immigrant Experience in the Gilded Age," in Charles William Calhoun, ed., *The Gilded Age: Perspectives on the Origins of Modern America* (Lanham, MD: Rowman and Littelfield, 2007), 76. Conventional dating of the Gilded Age, from the period immediately after Reconstruction to sometime in the middle of the 1890s, is somewhat imprecise: Elisabeth Israels Perry and Karen Manners Smith, *The Gilded Age and Progressive Era* (New York: Oxford University Press, 2006), 6.
2. Alfred D. Chandler, *The Visible Hand: The Managerial Revolution in American Business* (Cambridge, MA: Harvard University Press, 1977), 171, 177, 178, 333; Douglas A. Irwin, "Explaining America's Surge in Manufactured Exports, 1880–1913," National Bureau of Economic Research Working Papers, 2001, p.4.
3. See, e.g., Levy, *Freaks of Fortune*, 104, 233, 242–255.
4. Edwin G. Burrows and Mike Wallace, *Gotham: A History of New York City to 1898* (New York: Oxford University Press, 1999), 1081.
5. Edward Purcell, "The Action Was Outside the Courts," in Willibald Steinmetz, ed., *Private Law and Social Inequality in the Industrial Age* (London: Oxford University Press, 2000), 508–534; Kenneth D. Ackerman, *The Gold Ring: Jim Fisk, Jay Gould, and Black Friday, 1869* (New York: Dodd, Mead, 1988), 25–26; Philip C. Jessup, *Elihu Root* (New York: Dodd, Mead, 1938), 184; Burrows and Wallace, *Gotham*, 1045.
6. Morris, *Second Circuit*, 71; Samuel C. Duberstein, *A History of the United States Court for the Eastern District of New York* (New York: Federal Bar Association of New York, 1965),

13–14, 16; Stanley I. Kutler, "Congress and the Supreme Court: The Game of Numbers and Circuits," in Kutler, *Judicial Power and Reconstruction Politics* (Chicago: University of Chicago Press, 1968), 48–63.

7. Samuel Blatchford, *A Century of Patent Law* (Washington, D.C.: 1891), 12.

8. O'Reilly v. Morse, 56 U.S. 62 (1854).

9. Thomas P. Hughes, *American Genesis: A Century of Invention and Technological Enthusiasm, 1870–1970* (Chicago: University of Chicago Press, 2004), 151; James Willard Hurst, *Law and the Conditions of Freedom in the Nineteenth-Century United States* (Madison: University of Wisconsin Press, 1956), 75; Richard John, *Network Nation: Inventing America's Telecommunications* (Cambridge, MA: Harvard University Press, 2010), 23, 238.

10. American Bell Tel. Co. v. People's Tel. Co., 22 F. 309, 311, 314 (C.C. S.D, NY, 1884) (Wallace, J.).

11. 22 F. 309, 320.

12. Morris, *District of Columbia Circuit*, 45–50; Charles E. Rosenberg, *The Trial of the Assassin Guiteau: Psychiatry and the Law in the Gilded Age* (Chicago: University of Chicago Press, 1995), passim.

13. Francis Wharton, "Note," Guiteau's Case, 10 F. 161, 196 (C.C. D.C. 1882).

14. Guiteau's Case, 10 F. 161, 162, 165 (C.C. S.D. NY, 1882) (Cox, J.).

15. David Gardner Chardavoyne, *United States District Court for the Eastern District of Michigan: People, Law, and Politics* (Detroit: Wayne State University Press, 2012), 126–127; Judith Resnik and Dennis Curtis, *Representing Justice: Invention, Controversy, and Rights in City-States and Democratic Courtrooms* (New Haven: Yale University Press, 2011), 143–145; Antoinette Lee, *Architects to the Nation: The Rise and Decline of the Supervising Architect's Office* (New York: Oxford University Press, 2000), 71–73, 92–94, 111–113; Daniel Bluestone, *Constructing Chicago* (New Haven: Yale University Press, 1993), 174.

16. Samuel Chipman Parks, *The Great Trial of the Nineteenth Century* (Kansas City, MO: Hudson-Kimberly, 1900), 1–7, 8–10, 14, 17; Lawrence Friedman, *History of American Law*, rev. ed. (New York: Simon and Schuster, 2010), 375. The *Great Trial* anticipated Stephen Vincent Benet's "The Devil and Daniel Webster" in bringing back to life a pantheon of legal giants to hear and decide a law case.

17. Some hints of immense and telling influence of the Civil War on this generation of jurists can be found in the dream in Parks's *Great Trial*, as well as (less dramatically), David Blight, *Race and Reunion: The Civil War in American Memory* (Cambridge, MA: Harvard University Press, 2009), 3 (healing and justice) 308 ("the hell of war"); G. Edward White, *Justice Oliver Wendell Holmes: Law and the Inner Self* (New York: Oxford University Press, 1993), "duty" "bravery" "fatalism," 74; "survival," 79.

18. Jacob Cox to George Frisbie Hoar, November 6, 1896, quoted in Hoar, *The Charge of Packing the Court Against President Grant and Attorney General Hoar, Refuted* (Worchester, MA: Charles Hamilton, 1896), 26; Foner, *Reconstruction*, 294–297 (mixed motives of carpetbaggers); Ted Tunnell, *Edge of the Sword: The Ordeal of Carpetbagger Marshall H. Twitchell in the Civil War and Reconstruction* (Baton Rouge: Louisiana State University Press, 2004), 2–3 (vindictive view of carpetbaggers by southern "Redeemers"). The record books of the Circuit Court for the Northern District of Georgia in 1865 and 1866 contain the signatures of those members of the bar who took the oath of allegiance in order to practice in the federal courts. They included leading former Confederate figures.

19. [Asher Hinds], *Precedents of the U.S. House of Representatives* (Washington, D.C., 1907), 3:949–977.

20. Miller's account quoted in Charles Fairman, *Mr. Justice Miller and the Supreme Court, 1862–1890* (Cambridge, MA: Harvard University Press, 1939), 391; http://www.fjc.gov/history/caseload.nsf/page/caseloads_main_page.

21. David N. Atkinson, *Leaving the Bench: Supreme Court Justices at the End* (Lawrence: University Press of Kansas, 1999), 61.

22. Linda Przybyszewski, *The Republic According to John Marshall Harlan* (Chapel Hill: University of North Carolina Press, 1999), 41–42; Loren P. Beth, *John Marshall Harlan: The Last Whig Justice* (Lexington: University of Kentucky Press, 1992) 113.

23. John V. Orth, "John Marshall Harlan," in Kermit Hall et al., eds., *Oxford Companion to American Law*, 2nd ed. (New York: Oxford University Press, 1992), 421.
24. Foner, *Reconstruction*, 569 and after.
25. Michael Les Benedict, *The Blessings of Liberty: A Concise History of the Constitution of the United States*, 2nd ed. (Stamford, CT: Cengage, 2005), 200–201.
26. Jerrold M. Packard, *American Nightmare: The History of Jim Crow* (New York: Macmillan, 2003), 56 and after.
27. Civil Rights Cases 109 U.S. 3, 21, 24 (1883) (Bradley, J.).
28. 109 U.S. at 33, 38, 53 (Harlan, J.)
29. See, e.g., Pamela Brandwein, *Rethinking the Judicial Settlement of Reconstruction* (New York: Cambridge University Press, 2011) (Supreme Court not always unfriendly to civil rights claims); Blair L. M. Kelly, *Right to Ride: Streetcar Boycotts and African American Citizenship in the Era of Plessy v. Ferguson* (Chapel Hill: University of North Carolina Press, 2010), 31–50 (cases in lower courts).
30. Joseph A. Fry, *John Tyler Morgan and the Search for Southern Autonomy* (Knoxville: University of Tennessee Press, 1992), 23–39, 128–149.
31. The story of the plaintiffs and their counsel is told in Williamjames Hull Hoffer, *Plessy v. Ferguson: Race and Inequality in Jim Crow America* (Lawrence: University Press of Kansas, 2011), 8–68.
32. 163 U.S. 537, 544, 551 (1896) (Brown, J.); George Frederickson, *White Supremacy: A Comparative Study of American and South African History* (New York: Oxford University Press, 1981), 197–198.
33. 163 U.S. at 551–552 (Brown, J.).
34. 163 U.S. at 555, 559 (Harlan, J.).
35. Martha Lamb, "Chief Justice Morrison Remick Waite," *Magazine of American History* 20 (July 1888), 2.
36. William Strong, "Needs of the Supreme Court," *North American Review*, May 1881, 447.
37. Crowe, *Building the Judiciary*, 178–179; Judiciary Act of 1887, 24 Stat. 442, U.S. Statutes at Large 24, 49th Cong., 2d Sess. (1887), 552; Daniel Holt, *Debates on the Federal Judiciary: A Documentary History Volume II: 1875–1939* (Federal Judicial Center, 2013), 18.
38. The text following is derived from Hoffer, *To Enlarge the Machinery of Government*, 178–186.
39. Cong. Rec., 51st Cong., 1st Sess. [hereafter 21 C.R.], 3398. On Cannon, see Blair Bolles, *Tyrant from Illinois: Uncle Joe Cannon's Experiment with Personal Power* (New York: W. W. Norton & Company, 1951), 3–33.
40. After the legislation passed, continuing opposition to it may have been governed by more practical reasons. The Act had the effect of increasing delays and expenses for litigants in the West and South, where the circuits were so large and the number of judges holding courts of appeal, at first, was relatively small. Purcell, *Litigation and Inequality*, 56–57. The fact remains that the opposition in Congress was led by former confederates.
41. 21 C.R., 3402–3; Lee J. Alston and Joseph P. Ferrie, *Southern Paternalism and the American Welfare State: Economics, Politics, and Institutions in the South, 1865–1965* (Cambridge, UK: Cambridge University Press, 1999).
42. 21 C.R., 3399.
43. 21 C.R. 3410–11.
44. Chester L. Barrows, *William M. Evarts: Lawyer, Diplomat, Statesman* (Chapel Hill: University of North Carolina Press, 1941), 3–16, 28, 46–49, 56–58, 169, 174–175, 183–185, 253.
45. Barrows, *Evarts*, 435, 467, 473–474.
46. 21 C.R., 10217, 10219–10220, 10223.
47. 21 C.R. 10224, 10225.
48. 21 C.R. 10284–10305, 10306, 10308.
49. 21 C.R. 10311–10316, 10364–10365; 22 C.R. 3586.
50. "Evarts Act" Judiciary Act of 1891 March 3, 1891, 26 Stat. 826. Only the Second Circuit Court of Appeals had three circuit judge panels in 1891. Other circuits' courts of appeal panels were composed of a circuit court of appeals judge and district judges or circuit trial court judges. By 1922, all the circuits had enough courts of appeal judges to fully staff their panels.

51. District Court for the Eastern District of Illinois, Criminal Docket Book, 1908, p.254, RG 21 NARA Chicago; Eastern District, Pennsylvania, Circuit Court Docket Books, 1891–1911, RG 21 NARA Philadelphia.

52. U.S. v. Certain Tract of Land in Cumberland and Adams County, PA, 67 F. 869, 871 (C.C. E.D. Pa. 1895) (Dallas, J.); 67 F. 873 (Butler, J.); U.S. v. Gettysburg Electric Railway Co., 160 U.S. 668, 682 (1896) (Peckham, J.)

53. Figures from http://www.fjc.gov/history/caseload.nsf/page/caseloads_civil_US; http://www.fjc.gov/history/caseload.nsf/page/caseloads_private_civil. The Act also ended the variable salary system for the district judges. Henceforth they all had the same salary.

54. "Act of the Suppression of Trade in, and Circulation of, Obscene Literature and Articles of Immoral Use" (Comstock Act) of 1873, 17 Stat. 598; Minute Books 97–145 (1891–1911), District Court for the Eastern District of Pennsylvania, RG 21, NARA Philadelphia: District Court for the Southern District of New York, Minute Book, 1886, RG 21 NARA New York. On Comstock Act prosecutions, see John D'Emiloio and Estelle B. Freedman, *Intimate Matters: A History of Sexuality in America*, 3rd ed. (Chicago: University of Chicago Press, 2012), 160.

55. Skeel, *Debt's Dominion*, 57–60; Stephen J. Lubben, "Railroad Receiverships and Modern Bankruptcy Theory," *Cornell Law Review* 89 (2003–2004), 1420–1475; Albert J. Churella, *The Pennsylvania Railroad, I: Building an Empire, 1846–1917* (Philadelphia: University of Pennsylvania Press, 2012), 529, 647; Brands, *American Colossus*, 513–514.

56. Van Siclen v. Bartol et al., 95 F 793 (E.D. Pa. 1899); Platt v. Philadelphia and R.R. Company, 84 F 535 (3rd Cir. 1898); Mercantile Trust Co. v. Baltimore and Ohio R.R., 79 F. 389 (E.D. Pa. 1897).

57. Grand jury returns, 1891–1916, Western District of Texas Circuit Court, RG 21 NARA Ft. Worth; The Three Friends, 166 U.S. 1 (1897) (neutrality law prohibits U.S. private citizens taking part in a rebellion in a foreign country with which the U.S. has friendly relations); Elliott Young, *Catarino Garza's Revolution on the Texas-Mexico Border* (Durham, NC: Duke University Press, 2004), 177–179.

58. Morris, *Second Circuit*, 98–107, Records of the Second Circuit Court of Appeals, Minute Books, 1892–1911, RG 276.3 NARA New York; Records of the Third Circuit Court of Appeals, Minute Books, 1892–1911, RG 276.4 NARA Philadelphia; Docket Book, Seventh Circuit Court of Appeals, 1891–1911, RG 276.7 NARA Chicago.

59. Records of the Fourth Circuit Court of Appeals, Minute Books, 1892–1911, RG 276.5 NARA Philadelphia; Judiciary Act of February 9, 1893, 27 Stat. 434; Records of the D.C. Circuit Court of Appeals, Docket Books, RG 276.12, National Archives, Washington, D.C.

60. See FJC "History of the Federal Courts" website, U.S. Courts of Appeal caseload, http://www.fjc.gov/history/caseload.nsf/page/caseloads_courts_of_appeals; Lawrence Friedman, *History of American Law*, rev. ed. (New York: Simon and Schuster, 2010), 387.

61. Here and after, "Judges of United States Courts, Federal Judicial Center website, http://www.fjc.gov/history/home.nsf/page/judges.html.

62. Louis Galambos, "The Emerging Organizational Synthesis in Modern American History," *The Business History Review* 44(3) (Autumn, 1970): 279–290; Morton Keller, *America's Three Regimes: A New Political History* (New York: Oxford University Press, 2007), 135–136; Daniel Rodgers, *Atlantic Crossings: Social Politics in a Progressive Age* (Cambridge: Belknap Press of Harvard University Press, 1998), 260–261; Lawrence Friedman, *A History of America Law*, 3rd. ed. (New York: Simon and Schuster, 2005), 497–498; Marc Galanter, *Tournament of Lawyers: The Transformation of the Big Law Firm* (Chicago: University of Chicago Press, 1994), 8–9.

63. See, e.g, Daun van Ee, *David Dudley Field and the Reconstruction of the Law* (New York: Garland, 1986), 212–263; Robert T. Swaine, *The Cravath Firm And Its Predecessors: 1819–1947* (New York, privately printed, 1946), 313.

64. On the backward-looking ideas of the Gilded Age justices, see Herbert Hovenkamp, *Enterprise and American Law, 1836–1937* (Cambridge, MA: Harvard University Press, 1991), 171–172. On the Fuller Court, see Owen Fiss, *Troubled Beginnings of the Modern States, 1896–1910, History of the United States Supreme Court Volume VIII* (New York: Macmillan, 1993), 27 and after; James W. Ely, Jr., "Melville W. Fuller," in Roger K. Newman, ed. *Yale Biographical*

Dictionary of American Law (New Haven: Yale University Press, 2009), 211–212; John V. Orth, "Melville Weston Fuller," in Hall et al., eds., *Oxford Companion*, 320–321. Here and after, material adapted from Hoffer, Hoffer, and Hull, *Supreme Court*, 161–167.

65. Budd v. New York, 143 U.S. 517, 552 (1892) (Brewer, J.); Owen Fiss, "Stephen J. Brewer," in Hall et al., eds., *Oxford Companion*, 89–91; Michael J. Brodhead, *David J. Brewer: The Life of a Supreme Court Justice, 1837–1910* (Carbondale: Southern Illinois University Press, 1994), 43–45; Ames v. Union Pacific Railroad, 64 F. 165, 173, 175 (C.C.D. Neb. 1894) (Brewer, J.).

66. Francis Helminski, "Henry Billings Brown," in Hall, et al., eds., *Oxford Companion*, 92–93; James W. Ely, *The Fuller Court: Justices, Rulings, and Legacy* (Santa Barbara, CA: ABC-CLIO, 2003), 81–83; Richard Y. Funston, "Edward Douglas White," in Hall et al., eds, *Oxford Companion*, 927–928; Robert Baker Highsaw, *Edward Douglass White: Defender of the Conservative Faith* (Baton Rouge: Louisiana State University Press, 1981), 50–51.

67. Paul Kens, "Rufus Wheeler Peckham," in Hall et al., eds., *Oxford Companion*, 626–627; Maxwell v. Dow, 176 U.S. 581, 605 (1900) (Peckham, J.).

68. David Nasaw, *Andrew Carnegie* (New York: Penguin, 2007), 333; Ron Chernow, *Titan: The Life of John D. Rockefeller Sr.* (New York: Random House, 1998), 153, 179; Morton Horwitz, *The Transformation of American Law, 1870–1960, The Crisis of Legal Orthodoxy* (New York: Oxford University Press, 1992), 80.

69. Sherman Antitrust Act July 2, 1890, ch. 647, 26 Stat. 209; William Letwin, *Law and Economic Policy in America: The Evolution of the Sherman Antitrust Act* (Chicago: University of Chicago Press, 1981), 10–11, 15–17 and after.

70. U.S. v. Jellico Mountain Coke, 43 F. 898 (C.C. M.D. Tenn., 1891); U.S. v. Trans-Missouri Freight Association, 53 F. 440 (C.C., D. Kans., 1892); U.S. v. E.C. Knight 156 U.S. 1 (1895); U.S. v. Workingman's Amalgamated Council of New Orleans, 54 F. 994 (C.C. E.D. La., 1893). Cases from *Federal Anti-Trust Decisions*, ed. James A. Finch by direction of U.S. Attorney General (Washington, D.C.: GPO, 1907), 2v. In more modern times, the federal government files on average forty to forty-five antitrust suits a year, "Antitrust Enforcement," Department of Justice archives online, Report of the Attorney General, for 1994, 1995, 1996, and 1997; on the coming of government management of the economy through antitrust, see Dexter Merriam Keezer and Stacy May, *The Public Control of Business: A Study of Antitrust Law Enforcement* (New York: Harper and Row, 1930), 40–84; Michael French, *U.S. Economic History Since 1945* (Manchester, UK: University of Manchester Press, 1997), 141; Seymour E. Harris, *American Economic History* (Hopkins, MN: Beard, 2002), 361.

71. U.S. v. E.C. Knight, 60 F. 306, 309 (1894) (Butler, J.); U.S. v. E.C. Knight 156 U.S. 1, 10, 11, 12, 13 (1895) (Fuller, C.J.).

72. Scott B. McDonald and Albert L. Gastman, *A History of Credit and Power in the Western World* (New York: Transaction, 2001), 201.

73. Herbert Hovenkamp, *The Opening of American Law: Neoclassical Legal Thought, 1870–1970* (New York: Oxford University Press, 2014), 76–90; Paul Kens, *Lochner v. New York: Economic Regulation on Trial* (Lawrence: University Press of Kansas, 1998), 109.

74. Fiss, *Troubled Beginnings*, 97; William Wiecek, *The Lost World of Classical Legal Thought: Law and Ideology in America, 1883–1937* (New York: Oxford University Press, 1998), 177–179.

Chapter 7

1. William G. Ross, *A Muted Fury: Populists, Progressives, and Labor Unions Confront the Courts, 1897–1937* (Princeton: Princeton University Press, 2014), 10.

2. Ross, *A Muted Fury*, 28; Matthews quoted in "Federal Courts to be Defied," *New York Times*, July 25, 1896, p. 4; William Jennings Bryan, "Cross of Gold Speech," July 9, 1896, Democratic National Convention, excerpted in Richard Franklin Bensel, *Passion and Preferences: William Jennings Bryan and the 1896 Democratic Convention* (New York: Cambridge University Press, 2007), 227–228.

3. "Little brown brother": Leon Wolf, *Little Brown Brother: How the U.S. Purchased and Pacified the Philippines at the Century's Turn* (New York: Doubleday, 1961), 108; Richard Hofstadter, *The Age of Reform* (New York: Random House, 1955), 5; Walter Nugent, *Progressivism: A Very Short Introduction* (New York: Oxford University Press, 2009), 54; Alan Dawley, *Changing*

the World: American Progressives in War and Revolution (Princeton: Princeton University Press, 2003), 20–22; Samuel P, Hays, *The Response to Industrialism, 1885–1914*, rev ed. (Chicago: University of Chicago Press, 1994), 94–98.

4. Edward Purcell, *Brandeis and the Progressive Constitution: Erie, Judicial Power, and the Politics of Federal Courts in Twentieth-Century America* (New Haven: Yale University Press, 2000), 20.

5. In restraining orders and preliminary injunctions the ex parte injunction may be issued when one of the parties is not present. The ex parte injunction is not a permanent injunction. It is used as a temporary measure to prevent an irreversible injury while the litigation is proceeding. Edward Re, *Cases and Materials on Remedies* (Mineola, NY: Foundation, 1982), 231.

6. Sheldon quoted in "Raps the Federal Courts" *New York Times* September 13, 1907, p. 6; Theodore Roosevelt, Message to Congress, December 3, 1906, Cong. Rec., 59th Cong., 2d Sess., 1906, 41, pt. 1: 22. Here and after, authors owe a debt to Dan Holt, *Debates on the Federal Judiciary: A Documentary History Volume II: 1875–1939* (Federal Judicial Center, 2013).

7. In Re Debs, 158 U.S. 564 (1895); David Ray Papke, *The Pullman Case: The Clash of Labor and Capital in Industrial America* (Lawrence: University Press of Kansas, 1999), 38–58; Felix Frankfurter and Nathan Greene, *The Labor Injunction* (New York: Macmillan, 1930), 49; Toledo Railway v. Pennsylvania Company, 54 F. 730, 738 (6th Cir. 1893) (Taft, J.). The "free labor" doctrine established in the states courts in the 1830s and 1840s held that a man could walk away from a job and not be penalized for withholding his labor—the old English Statute of Artificers rule that a man was bound to finish a job had been abandoned by most state courts when Taft wrote. Contractual relations did not reintroduce servitude. See Robert J. Steinfeld, *The Invention of Free Labor: The Employment Relation in English and American Law and Culture, 1350–1870* (Chapel Hill: University of North Carolina Press, 1991), 186–187.

8. Thomas Spelling, Testimony, House of Representatives, Committee on the Judiciary, Hearings on the So-called Anti-injunction bills, and all labor bills, 60th Cong., 1st Sess., 1908, Cong. Rec., p. 13. On the industrial unions' travails in the Progressive Era, see, e.g., Melvyn Dubofsky, *The State and Labor in Modern America* (Chapel Hill: University of North Carolina Press, 1994), 37–60.

9. Judiciary Act of February 11, 1903, 32 Stat. 823; Judiciary Act of June 29, 1906, 34 Stat. 592; Three-judge Court Act of June 18, 1910, 36 Stat. 557; Ex Parte Young, 209 U.S. 123 (1908); David P. Currie, "The Three-Judge District Court in Constitutional Litigation," *University of Chicago Law Review* 32 (1964), 1–8 (Overman quoted on page 7); Three-judge Court Act of June Committee on the Federal Courts, "A Proposal to Reform the Federal Three-judge Court System," *Record of the Association of the Bar of the City of New York* 30 (1975), 562; Ely, *Fuller Court*, 175; Neal R. Pierce, *The Great Plains States of America: People, Politics and Power in the Nine Great Plains States* (New York: Norton, 1973), 114.

10. Ross, *A Muted Fury*, 3, noting that the courts "can never be apolitical" and then documenting the progressive assault. But Ross concluded that the assault was never as dangerous to judicial independence as its heated rhetoric suggested, and it never did dent the courts' view of the labor injunction. Other students of the injunction see a brief "liberalization" between 1907 and 1917; Note, "Employer Interference with Lawful Union Activity," *Columbia Law Review* 37 (1937), 816. The Clayton Antitrust Act of 1914, 38 Stat. 730, sec. 6 and 20. But see, e.g., Duplex Printing v. Deering, 254 U.S. 443 (1921), in which a union activity could be enjoined as a conspiracy against trade if it involved a "secondary boycott."

11. Louis L. Gould, *Theodore Roosevelt* (New York: Oxford University Press, 2012), 39; Gould, *The William Howard Taft Presidency* (Lawrence: University Press of Kansas, 2009), 25, 98; Theodore Roosevelt, *Theodore Roosevelt: An Autobiography* (New York: Macmillan, 1913), 89–90.

12. Lochner v. New York, 198 U.S. 45 (1905); Kens, *Lochner*, 89–91. There is something of a cottage industry of scholarly commentary on *Lochner*. Some believe its contribution is jurisprudential—the attempt to define the difference between public and private interest. A very fine review of the literature is David Bernstein, *Rehabilitating Lochner: Defending Individual Rights Against Progressive Reform* (Chicago: University of Chicago Press, 2011), 132–134, nn. 1–6.

13. 198 U.S. at 52, 56 (Peckham, J.).

14. 198 U.S. at 66, 69, 70, 71 (Harlan, J.). The mini-brief was itself precedent for the so-called Brandeis Brief in Muller v. Oregon, 208 U.S. 412 (1908).
15. 198 U.S. at 75 (Holmes, J.).
16. Editorial, "Are the Federal Courts Unworthy of Confidence?" *New York Times*, February 22, 1906, p.6; Wallace quoted in *Washington Post*, January 12, 1907, p. 6; Miller, *Direct Democracy*, 43. But by 1912 the *Times* had returned to its strong support of the federal courts; Miller, *Direct Democracy*, 195. To be sure, the Fourteenth Amendment had moved the goal line, but the issue of judicial federalism was the same.
17. Fiss, *Troubled Beginnings*, 51–221; N. E. H. Hull, *Roscoe Pound and Karl Llewellyn, Searching for an American Jurisprudence* (Chicago: University of Chicago Press, 1998), 58–65.
18. Walter Clark, "The Election of Federal Judges by the People," *The Arena*, November 1904, 457–458.
19. Robert L. Owen, "Judicial Recall, Address Before the Bar Association of Muskogee, Oklahoma," Cong. Rec., 62d Cong., 2d Sess., S. Doc. 249, 1912, 6–8; James Manahan, "The Recall of Judges, Address Before Minnesota State Bar Association," Cong. Rec., 62d Cong., 2d Sess., S. Doc. 941, 1912, 13.
20. Thomas Goebel, *Government by the People: Direct Democracy in America, 1890–1940* (Chapel Hill: University of North Carolina Press, 2003), 64; Theodore Roosevelt, "The Right of the People to Review Judge- Made Law," *Outlook*, August 8, 1914, 847.
21. "The Federal District Judgeship," *New York Times*, July 18, 1901, p. 6; George Sutherland, "The Law and the People," Address to Pennsylvania Society, New York, December 13, 1913, S. Doc. 328, 63d Cong., 2d Sess., 1913, 5–8.
22. Ezra Ripley Thayer, "Recall of Judicial Decisions," *Legal Bibliography* (March 1913), 6; Robert LaFollette, Speech before the Annual Convention of the American Federation of Labor, June 14, 1922, *Report of the Proceedings of the 42nd Annual Convention of the American Federation of Labor* (Washington, D.C.: Law Reporter, 1922), 234.
23. Russell Freedman, *Kids at Work: Lewis Hine and the Crusade Against Child Labor* (Boston: Houghton Mifflin Harcourt, 1998), 71–90.
24. Hugh D. Hindman, *Child Labor: An American History* (Sharpe, 2003), 64–69; Bryant Simon, *A Fabric of Defeat: The Politics of South Carolina Millhands, 1910–1948* (Chapel Hill: University of North Carolina Press, 1998), 4 (exclusion of black millhands).
25. Hammer v. Dagenhart, 247 U.S. 251, 268 (1918) (Day, J.) A summary of the voluminous secondary literature on the case is Logan E. Sawyer III, "Creating Hammer v. Dagenhart," *William and Mary Bill of Rights Journal* 21 (2012), 67–123.
26. 247 U.S. at 276 (Day, J.).
27. 247 U.S. 281, 279 (Holmes, J.).
28. Rayman Solomon, "The Politics of Appointment and the Federal Courts' Role in Regulating America: U.S. Courts of Appeal Judgeships from T.R. to F.D.R," *American Bar Foundation Research Journal* 9 (1984), 285–343.
29. Theodore Roosevelt to Mark Sullivan, May 13, 1907, quoted in Solomon, "Appointment," at pages 305–306; "More liberal" quoted at 311.
30. Alice Fleetwood Bartee, "Edward Terry Sanford," in Hall et al., eds., *Oxford Companion*, 754–755; William Crawford Green, "Willis Van Devanter," in ibid., 894–895.
31. G. Edward White, *Justice Oliver Wendell Holmes: Law and the Inner Self* (New York: Oxford University Press, 1994), 254 (judging as minimalist work), 299–330 (appointment to the Supreme Court), 589–607 (bibliographical essay).
32. Alice Fleetwood Bartee, "William Rufus Day," in Hall et al., eds., *Oxford Companion*, 220–221; John R. Vile, "William Henry Moody," in ibid., 559–560. Of Moody's colleagues Taft was even less impressed. He wrote to a private correspondent in 1909, "the chief [Fuller] is almost senile, Harlan does no work, Brewer is so deaf he that he cannot hear . . . Brewer and Harlan sleep almost through all the arguments." Taft quoted in Henry F. Pringle, *The Life and Times of William Howard Taft* (New York: Farrar and Rinehart, 1939), 1:529–530. Taft was being a little unfair—Harlan had lost none of his analytical powers and Fuller was as able as ever.
33. Solomon, "Appointment," 304–306, 311–312; Morris, *Second Circuit*, 73. Is there a particularly Jewish social conscience that would make a federal judge more sensitive to the rights of

other minorities? Some of the leading defenders of minority rights on the federal bench—David Bazelon, Louis Brandeis, Abe Fortas, Ruth Bader Ginsburg, and Arthur Goldberg, to name a few—were Jewish. But other Jewish jurists, for example, Felix Frankfurter, were not always on the side of minorities. Would the experience of anti-Semitism pervasive in American life have made Jewish judges more sensitive to the plight of other minorities? See, e.g., Robert A. Burt, "On the Bench," in Louis Maisel et al., eds., *Jews in American Politics* (Lanham, MD: Rowman and Litttlefield, 2001), 73, and Burt, *Two Jewish Justices: Outcasts in the Promised Land* (Berkeley: University of California Press, 1989), 35.

34. Klaus M. Naske, *A History of the Alaska Federal Courts System, 1884–1959*, (Fairbanks: University of Alaska, 1985), 78–111; "Arthur H. Noyes," in Hugh J. McGrath, *History of the Great Northwest and Its Men of Progress: A Select List of Biographical Sketches and Portraits of the Leaders in Business, Professional and Official Life* (Minneapolis: Minneapolis Journal, 1901), 516–517; Stephen C. Levi, *Boom and Bust in the Alaska Goldfields: A Multicultural Adventure* (Westport, CT: Greenwood, 2008), 106–109; In re Noyes, 121 Fed. 209 (9th Cir., 1902); *San Francisco Call*, November 10, 1901, p. 21; Theodore Roosevelt to Arthur Noyes, February 24, 1902, Roosevelt Papers, Library of Congress.

35. *Proceedings of the House of Representatives and the United States Senate in the Trial of Impeachment of Robert W. Archbald*, 3v. (Washington, D.C.: U.S. House of Representatives, 1913), 1686–1693.

36. Finkelman, *Supreme Court*, 524; Frankfurter and Landis, *Business of the Federal Courts*, 165–174; George E. Dix, "Death of the Commerce Court: A Study in Institutional Weakness," *American Journal of Legal History* 8 (1964), 238–260.

37. Dix, "Commerce Court"; Harry Barnard, *The Forging of an American Jew: The Life and Times of Judge Julian W. Mack* (New York: Herzl, 1974), 113–114; Elizabeth J. Clapp, *Mothers of All Children: Women Reformers and the Rise of Juvenile Courts in Progressive Era America* (State College: Pennsylvania State University Press, 2010), 180–181.

38. John Reed, a radical New Yorker who would later report on the Bolshevik Revolution in Russia, described Landis in the 1918 trial, quoted in David Pietrusza, *Judge and Jury: The Life and Times of Judge Kenesaw Mountain Landis* (South Bend, IN: Diamond, 1998), 122.

39. Solomon, "Appointment" 328–335; Goldman, *Picking Federal Judges*, 9.

40. Michael J. Gerhardt, *The Federal Appointments Process: A Constitutional and Historical Analysis* (Durham, NC: Duke University Press, 2003), 100; Gerald Gunther, *Learned Hand, The Man and the Judge* (New York: Harvard University Press, 1994), 193 and after.

41. Highsaw, *White*, 57–60; Abraham, *Justices*, 134.

42. Del Dickson, "A Brief History of the Conference," in Dickson, ed., *The Supreme Court in Conference (1940–1985): The Private Discussion behind Nearly 300 Court Decisions* (New York: Oxford University Press, 2001), 68–69; Hoffer, Hoffer, and Hull, *Supreme Court*, 192–196.

43. Bickel and Schmidt, *The Judiciary and Responsible Justice*, 86–199; Clare Cushman, "The 'Lost' Clerks of the White Court Era," in Cushman and Todd C. Peppers, eds., *Courtiers & Kings: More Stories by Law Clerks About Their Justices* (Charlottesville: University of Virginia Press, 2015).

44. Todd C. Peppers, "Birth of an Institution: Horace Gray and the Lost Law Clerks," in Peppers and Artemus Ward, eds., *In Chambers: Stories of Supreme Court Clerks and their Justices* (Charlottesville: University of Virginia Press, 2012), 10–43; Peppers, *Courtiers of the Marble Palace: The Rise and Influence of the Supreme Court Law Clerk* (Palo Alto: Stanford University Press, 2006), 83; Artemus Ward and David L. Weiden, *Sorcerers' Apprentices: 100 Years of Law Clerks at the United States Supreme Court* (New York: New York University Press, 2006), 34–35.

45. The discussion of the need question was particularly important during the Great Depression. See *Law Clerks to United States District Judges: Hearing Before a Subcommittee, Seventy-fourth Congress, First Session, on S. 2643, a Bill to Amend Section 118 of the Judicial Code to Provide for the Appointment of Law Clerks to United States District Court Judges*. August 1, 1935 (Washington, D.C.: GPO, 1935).

46. John W. Winkle III, "Joseph Rucker Lamar," in Hall et al., eds., *Oxford Companion*, 493–494.

47. William Crawford Green, "Willis Van Devanter," in Hall et al., eds., *Oxford Companion*, 894–895.

48. Bickel and Schmidt, *The Judiciary and Responsible Government*, 25–32; Charles Evans Hughes, *The Supreme Court of the United States* (New York: Columbia University Press, 1928), 18–19; Robert F. Wesser, *Charles Evans Hughes: Politics and Reform in New York, 1890–1910* (Ithaca, NY: Cornell University Press, 2009), 290–291.

49. Solomon, "Appointment," 314–327; Arthur S. Link, *Woodrow Wilson and the Progressive Era* (New York: Harper, 1954), 25–53; Ronald J. Pestritto, *Woodrow Wilson and the Roots of Modern Liberalism* (Lanham, MD: Rowman and Littlefield, 2005), 70 and after; Sheldon Goldman, *Picking Federal Judges: Lower Court Selection from Roosevelt Through Reagan* (New Haven: Yale University Press, 1997), 9; Morris, *Second Circuit*, 133–134.

50. John Knox, *The Forgotten Memoir of John Knox: A Year in the Life of a Supreme Court Clerk in FDR's Washington* (Chicago: University of Chicago Press, 2002); Link, *Wilson*, 64–65; Paul M. Pruitt, *Taming Alabama: Lawyers and Reformers, 1804–1929* (Tuscaloosa: University of Alabama Press, 2010), xii; Alexander M. Bickel and Benno C. Schmidt, *The Judiciary and Responsible Government, 1910–1921: History of the United States Supreme Court*, vol. 9 (New York: Macmillan, 1984), 342–357.

51. Henry F. Pringle, *The Life and Times of William Howard Taft* (New York: Farrar, 1939), 2:952; Bickel and Schmidt, *The Judiciary and Responsible Government*, 4; Melvin Urofsky, *Louis D. Brandeis, A Life* (New York: Pantheon, 2009), 430–459; Alpheus T. Mason, *Brandeis: A Free Man's Life* (New York: Viking, 1946), 153.

52. Woodrow Wilson, *The New Freedom* (Garden City, NY: Doubleday, 1913), 8; Louis D. Brandeis, *Other People's Money, and How the Banks Use It* (Boston: Stokes, 1914), 19.

53. Urofsky, *Brandeis, A Life*, 437–458.

54. Woodrow Wilson to Senator Charles A. Culbertson, Senate Judiciary Committee, May 5, 1916 in Arthur Link, ed., *Papers of Woodrow Wilson* (Princeton: Princeton University Press, 1981), 36:609; Abraham, *Justices*, 142.

55. Henry J. Abraham, *Justices, Presidents, and Senators: A History of the U.S. Supreme Court Appointments from Washington to Bush II* (Lanham, MD: Rowman and Littlefield, 2008), 374.

56. Richard Schickel, *D.W. Griffth: An American Life* (New York: Proscenium, 1984), 270; Joel Williamson, *The Crucible of Race: Black-White Relations in the American South since Emancipation* (New York: Oxford University Press, 1984), 368 and after; James M. McPherson, *The Abolitionist Legacy: From Reconstruction to the NAACP* (Princeton: Princeton University Press, 1995), 386–390.

57. Franklin v. South Carolina, 218 U.S. 161, 164–165, 168 (1910) (Day, J.).

58. The "incorporation doctrine" is the subject of a good deal of academic and jurisprudential scholarship. Compare Akhil Reed Amar, *The Bill of Rights: Creation and Reconstruction* (New Haven: Yale University Press, 2008), 222–223, defending broad incorporation; with Robert Bork, *The Tempting of America* (New York: Simon and Schuster, 2009), 93–94, the dangers of too loose incorporation.

59. Leonard Dinnerstein, *The Leo Frank Case*, rev. ed. (Athens: University of Georgia Press, 2008).

60. Frank v. Magnum, 237 U.S. 309, 326, 329 (1915) (Pitney, J.).

61. 237 U.S. at 346, 347 (Holmes, J.); Dinnerstein, *Frank*, xiii.

62. Hofstadter, *Age of Reform*, 61, 77–78, 182; Bailey v. Alabama, 219 U.S. 219 (1911).

63. Federal Peonage Abolition Act of 1867, 14 Stat. 546; Aviam Soifer, "Federal Protection, Paternalism, and the Virtually Forgotten Prohibition of Voluntary Peonage," *Columbia Law Review* 112 (2012), 1607–1639; Steinfeld, *The Invention of Free Labor*, 183–184; 219 U.S. at 228 (quoting the Alabama statute).

64. Freyer and Dixon, *Democracy and Judicial Independence*, 118–122.

65. 219 U.S. at 228. Here and after material adapted from Hoffer, Hoffer, and Hull, *Supreme Court*, 204–205.

66. 219 U.S. at 236, 244 (1911) (Hughes, J.).

67. Robert H. Zieger, *America's Great War: World War I and the American Experience* (Lanham, MD: Rowman and Littlefield, 2007), 7–17; 59–62, 70–72, 74.

68. David Rabban, *Free Speech in its Forgotten Years, 1870–1920* (New York: Cambridge University Press, 1999) 249; David M. Kennedy, *Over Here: The First World War and American Society*, 25th anniversary ed. (New York: Oxford University Press, 2004), 23 and after. Here and after material adapted from Hoffer, Hoffer, and Hull, *Supreme Court*, 208–216.

69. Espionage Act of 1917, 40 Stat. 217; Sedition Act of 1918, 40 Stat. 553.
70. Gunther, *Learned Hand*, 149–156.
71. Masses Publication Company v. Patten, 244 F. 535, 538, 540, 543 (1917) (Hand, J.).
72. Schenck v. U.S. 249 U.S. 47, 52 (1919) (Holmes, J.); Rabban, *Free Speech*, 280–285.
73. Richard Polenberg, *Fighting Faiths: The Abrams Case, The Supreme Court, and Free Speech* (Ithaca, NY: Cornell University Press, 1998), 95–102, 218–228.
74. Judge Clayton's charge to the jury quoted in Polenberg, *Fighting Faiths*, 135, 136; his tirade at the end of the trial is quoted at ibid., 142–145.
75. Abrams v. U.S., 250 U.S. 616, 620–621 (1920) (Clarke, J.).
76. 260 U.S. at 626, 628, 630 (Holmes, J.)
77. 260 U.S. at 620 (Holmes, J.).
78. Anarchist Exclusion (Dillingham-Hardwick) Act of October 16, 1918, ch. 186, 40 Stat. 1012. On Palmer and the raids, Christopher M. Finan, *From the Palmer Raids to the Patriot Act: A History of the Fight for Free Speech in America* (Boston: Beacon, 2007), 24–37. In fact there had been eight bombing incidents, all the work of radical anarchists. Socialists and communists were not involved in the violence.
79. Robert K. Murray, *Red Scare: A Study in National Hysteria, 1919–1920* (Minneapolis: University of Minnesota Press, 1955), 178; Kane resignation letter, January 31, 1920, in *The Survey* 43 (1919–1920) 501. Post's role was the subject of his own *The Deportations Delirium of Nineteen-Twenty, A Personal Narrative* (New York, 1923), 148–149 and after.
80. National Popular Government League, *To the American People: A Report of the Illegal Practices of the United States Department of Justice* (Washington, D.C.: National Popular Government League, 1920), 9; Murray, *Red Scare*, 225.
81. Colyer v. Skeffington, 265 F. 17, 20, 21 (D.C. D. Mass. 1920) (Anderson, J.). Anderson was also ahead of his times in civil rights jurisprudence: Alan Rogers, "George W. Anderson and Civil Rights in the 1920s," *The Historian* 54 (2007), 289–304.
82. 265 F. at 22.
83. 265 F. at 23.
84. 265 F. at 23, 24.
85. 265 F. at 44, 63, 65, 67–68; Skeffington v. Katzeff, 277 F. 129 (1st Cir 1922). The *Colyer* decision was widely reported, Murray, *Red Scare*, 250, but it was the exception that proved (tested) the rule. See, e.g., Edward Purcell, "Reconsidering the Frankfurtian Paradigm: Reflections on Histories of the Lower Federal Courts," *Law and Social Inquiry* 24 (1999), 711. Deer Island was already infamous—the site where "friendly" Christian Indians were rounded up and held during King Philip's War in 1675–1676. There many men, women, and children suffered through the winter and died of malnutrition and disease. James David Drake, *King Philip's War: Civil War in New England, 1675–1676* (Amherst: University of Massachusetts Press, 1999), 103.
86. Bickel and Schmidt, *The Judiciary and Responsible Government*, 990.

Chapter 8

1. Warren G. Harding, Address in Boston, May 14, 1920; John W. Dean, *Warren G. Harding: The American Presidents Series: The 29th President, 1921–1923* (New York: Times Books, 2004), 57.
2. Wyn Craig Wade, *The Fiery Cross: The Ku Klux Klan in America* (New York: Oxford University Press, 1998), 172, 181–182; Pericles Lewis, *The Cambridge Introduction to Modernism* (New York: Cambridge University Press, 2007), 117–120; James R. Mellow, *Charmed Circle: Gertrude Stein and Company* (New York: Macmillan, 2003), 273.
3. Colin Gordon, *New Deals: Business, Labor, and Politics in America, 1920–1935* (New York: Cambridge University Press, 1994), 123.
4. Sinclair Lewis, *Main Street* (New York: Harcourt Brace, 1920), 1; Thorstein Veblen, *The Theory of the Leisure Class: An Economic Study of Institutions* (New York: Macmillan, 1912), 91; Frederick Lewis Allen, *Only Yesterday: An Informal History of the 1920s* (New York: Wiley, 1931), 125–126. Ben Yagoda, *Will Rogers: A Biography* (Norman: University of Oklahoma Press, 2000), 216.
5. William Howard Taft to George Sutherland, September 10, 1922, George Sutherland Papers, Library of Congress.

6. Jonathan Lurie, *William Howard Taft: The Travails of a Progressive Conservative* (New York: Cambridge University Press, 2012), 195; Louis Gould, *The William Howard Taft Presidency* (Lawrence: University Press of Kansas, 2009), 100; here and after material adapted from Hoffer, Hoffer, and Hull, *Supreme Court*, 219–221.

7. Peter G. Renstrom, *The Taft Court: Justices, Rulings, and Legacy* (Santa Barbara, CA: ABC-CLIO, 2003), 189.

8. Bernard Schwartz, *A History of the Supreme Court* (New York: Oxford University Press, 1993), 225–226; William H. Rehnquist, *The Supreme Court* (New York: Random House, 2002), 229.

9. Hadley Arkes, *The Return of George Sutherland: Restoring a Jurisprudence of Natural Rights* (Princeton: Princeton University Press, 1997), 41–43; Professor and Judge Thomas Cooley's *A Treatise on the Constitutional Limitations Which Rest Upon the Legislative Power of the States of the American Union* (Boston: Little, Brown, 1868), iv, argued that the framers had wisely limited the legislative powers; these included the right to enjoy private property (357–358); the preservation of public morals fell within the legislative powers of the states (596), however.

10. Timothy L. Hall, "Pierce Butler," *Supreme Court Justices: A Biographical Dictionary* (New York: Infobase, 2001), 284–284; David Joseph Danelski, *A Supreme Court Justice is Appointed* (New York: Random House, 1964), 56–72, 130–131; Taft to Harding, December 4, 1922, quoted in ibid., 132.

11. Alpheus T. Mason, *Harland Fiske Stone: Pillar of the Law* (New York: Viking, 1956), 184 and after.

12. David E. Kyvig, *Repealing National Prohibition* (Kent: Kent State University Press, 2000), 2–15.

13. Chief Justice Taft, "To the Circuit Judges and District Judges of the United States, June 16, 1925" enclosing recommendations from the Council of the Conference, p. 12, file:///C:/Users/N.%20E.%20H.%20Hull/Downloads/1925-06_0.pdf; Volstead Act (National Prohibition Act) of October 28, 1919, 41 Stat. 305; Crowe, *Building the Judiciary*, 199; Mason, *Taft*, 108. On Taft and the Volstead Act, see Robert Post, "Federalism, Positive Law, and the Emergence of the American Administrative State: Prohibition in the Taft Court Era," *William and Mary Law Review* 48 (2006–2007), 6–7, 10.

14. http://www.fjc.gov/history/caseload.nsf/page/caseloads_main_page; "Report of the Conference of Senior Circuit Judges, June 9, 1925," p. 12; U.S. Treasury Department, Bureau of Industrial Alcohol; *Statistics Concerning Intoxicating Liquors*, December, 1930.

15. U.S. Treasury Department, Bureau of Industrial Alcohol; *Statistics Concerning Intoxicating Liquors*, December, 1930; Patridge quote in Cahan, Hinckle, and Ocken, *The Court that Tamed the West*, 184; Herbert Hoover, Inaugural Address, March 4, 1929, http://www.inaugural.senate.gov/swearing-in/address/address-by-herbert-hoover-1929.

16. Capone v. U.S. 56 F. 2d 927, 931 (D.C. N.D. Ill. 1932) (Sparks, J.); Robert B. Grant and Joseph Katz, *The Great Trials of the 1920s: The Watershed Decade in America's Courtrooms* (Rockeville Center, NY: Sarpedon, 1998), 98–120.

17. "Chronological History of Authorized Judgeships, All Judgeships, 1789 to Present," p. 5 http://www.uscourts.gov/JudgesAndJudgeships/Viewer.aspx?doc=/uscourts/JudgesJudgeships/docs/all-judgeships.pdf.

18. William Howard Taft, "Possible and Needed Reforms in the Administration of Civil Justice in the Federal Courts," *Annual Report of the American Bar Association* 45 (1922), 252–253; Russell R. Wheeler and Donald W. Jackson, "Judicial Councils and Policy Planning: Continuous Study and Discontinuous Institutions," *Justice System Journal* 2 (1976), 127–128. Taft's comments were double edged—a promise of help for the beleaguered judge and a veiled threat against the sluggardly judge.

19. David S. Myers, "Organization of the Judicial Conference," *American Bar Association Journal* 57 (1971), 598; Alan Brinkley, *Liberalism and its Discontents* (Cambridge, MA: Harvard University Press, 1998), 113; Judiciary Act of 1922, September 14, 1922, 42 Stat. 837; Peter G. Fish, *The Politics of Federal Judicial Administration* (Princeton: Princeton University Press, 1973), 206; Fish, "William Howard Taft and Charles Evans Hughes, Conservative Politicians as Chief Judicial Reformers," *Supreme Court Review* (1975), 140. On the organizational synthesis, see Louis Galambos, "The Emerging Organizational Synthesis in Modern American History," 279–290; Keller, *America's Three Regimes*, 135–136.

20. Judiciary Act of 1922; 42 Stat. 837. On New York, see, e.g. Ira Rosenwaike, *Population History of New York City* (Syracuse: Syracuse University Press, 1972), 92–94.

21. John K. Shields, Speech in the U.S. Senate, March 22, 1922, Cong. Rec. 67th Cong., 2d Sess., 1922, 62, 5:4855–65.

22. John C. Godbold, "Governance of the Courts and Structure of the Circuits," in Cynthia Harrison and Russell R. Wheeler, eds., *The Federal Appellate Judiciary in the Twenty-First Century* (Washington, D.C.: FJC, 1989), 32; Carl McGowan, "Perspectives on Taft's Tenure as Chief Justice and Their Special Relevance Today," *University of Cincinnati Law Review* 55 (1987), 1151.

23. 9 Stat.442; Revised Statutes 1 (1875), Sec. 591–593, p. 103; 34 Stat. 1417 (1907); 38 Stat. 203 (1913). Thanks to Dan Holt for this information.

24. Taft, "Needed Reforms," 254, 263.

25. Fallon et al., *Federal Courts*, 1448; Willis Van Devanter, testimony, December 18, 1924, 68th Cong., 2d Sess. House of Representatives, Committee on the Judiciary, *Jurisdiction of Circuit Courts of Appeals and of the Supreme Court of the United States*, p. 12.

26. Judges' Bill: "An Act To amend the Judicial Code, and to further define the jurisdiction of the circuit courts of appeals and of the Supreme Court, and for other purposes," 43 Stat. 936.

27. Felix Frankfurter, "Distribution of Judicial Power Between United States and State Courts," *Cornell Law Quarterly* 13 (1927–1928), 504–506; Jonathan Sternberg, "Deciding Not to Decide: The Judiciary Act of 1925 and the Discretionary Court," *Journal of Supreme Court History*, 33 (March 2008), 8–16.

28. On the "rule of four" for certiorari, see Joan M. Leiman, "The Rule of Four," *Columbia Law Review* 57 (1957), 981. On the impact of the Act, see Judiciary Act of 1925, http://www.fjc.gov/history/home.nsf/page/landmark_15.html. For the figures of cases disposed, see http://www.fjc.gov/history/caseload.nsf/page/caseloads_Sup_Ct_totals.

29. Wheeler and Harrison, *Creating the Federal Judicial System*, 22; Denise Bonn, "The Geographical Division of the Eighth Circuit Court of Appeals," FJC Research Paper, 1974, 16–29.

30. Thomas W. Shelton, "Reform and Uniformity of Judicial Procedure," *Central Law Journal*, February 14, 1913, 114; Edson R. Sunderland, "The Michigan Judicature Act of 1915: The Distinctions between Law and Equity Proceedings," *Michigan Law Review* 14 (1916), 273–280; Federal Law and Equity Act of 1915, 38 Stat. 956; Henry D. Clayton, "Uniform Federal Procedure," *Central Law Journal*, January 5, 1917, 7–13; Senator Thomas J. Walsh, "Reform of Federal Procedure," speech before Tri-State Bar Association at Texarkana, April 23, 1926, reprinted as S. Doc. 105, 69th Cong., 1st Sess. (1926); Stephen N. Subrin, "The New Era in American Civil Procedure," *American Bar Association Journal* 67 (1981), 1652.

31. Until 1922, one could count the number of cases resting on the first ten amendments on the fingers of two hands. After 1925, they became a regular feature of every Supreme Court session. First Amendment cases led the way. The justices of the Taft Court were not the first argue for incorporation of the Bill of Rights however. See Hurtado v. California, 110 U.S. 516, 548 (1884) (Harlan, J. diss.).

32. Meyer v. Nebraska, 262 U.S. 390, 400, 399, 401, 402 (McReynolds, J.) (1923).

33. Pierce v. Society of Sisters, 268 U.S. 510, 534, 536 (McReynolds, J.) (1925).

34. Gitlow v. New York, 268 U.S. 652, 666 (1925) (Sanford, J.); Marc Lendler, *Gitlow v. New York: Every Idea an Incitement* (Lawrence: University Press of Kansas, 2012), 107–115.

35. John Crittenden Duval, *Early Times in Texas, or, the Adventures of Jack Dobell* (Lincoln: University of Nebraska Press, 1986), xx; "DuVal West," http://www.tshaonline.org/handbook/online/articles/fwe31; Darlene Clark Hine, *Black Victory: The Rise and Fall of the White Primary in Texas* (Columbia: University of Missouri Press, 2003), 113–116; Charles L. Zelden, *The Battle for the Black Ballot: Smith v. Allwright and the Defeat of the Texas All-White Primary* (Lawrence: University Press of Kansas, 2004), 54–56.

36. Nixon v. Herndon, 273 U.S. 536, 540–541 (1927) (Holmes, J.).

37. Gong Lum v. Rice, 275 U.S. 78, 84 (1927) (Taft, C.J.).

38. Steve Fraser, *Every Man a Speculator: A History of Wall Street in American Life* (New York: HarperCollins, 2005), 400–425.

39. Michael E. Parrish, *The Hughes Court: Justices, Rulings, and Legacy* (Santa Barbara, CA: ABC-Clio, 2002), 90.

40. Hall, *Supreme Court Justices*, 247–251; William G. Ross, *The Chief Justiceship of Charles Evans Hughes: 1930–1941* (Columbia: University of South Carolina Press, 2007), 219–220; Lawrence Wrightsman, *Oral Arguments Before the Supreme Court: An Empirical Approach* (New York: Oxford University Press, 2008), 39.

41. Richard D. Friedman, "Owen Josephus Roberts," in Newman, ed., *Yale Biographical Dictionary*, 461–462; Peter G. Fish, "John Johnson Parker" in Newman, ed., *Yale Biographical Dictionary*, 416–417.

42. Andrew L. Kaufman, *Cardozo* (Cambridge, MA: Harvard University Press, 1998), 461–470.

43. Cardozo, *The Nature of the Judicial Process* (New Haven: Yale University Press, 1921), 27 and after; Cushman, *Courtwatchers*, 113; Kaufman, *Cardozo*, 175, 466, 569; Richard A. Posner, *Cardozo, A Study in Reputation* (Chicago: University of Chicago Press, 1990), 107.

44. Taft to Horace Taft, quoted in Alpheus Mason, *William Howard Taft, Chief Justice* (New York: Simon and Schuster, 1965), 295; Michael E. Parrish, *The Hughes Court: Justices, Rulings, and Legacy* (Santa Barbara, CA: ABC-CLIO, 2002), 90.

Part III

1. Bruce Ackerman, *We the People:* Vol. 1: *Foundations* (Cambridge, MA: Harvard University Press, 1993), 105–108.

2. Henry R. Luce, "The American Century," *Time-Life*, February 17, 1941, 64; James T. Patterson, *Grand Expectations: The United States, 1945–1974* (New York: Oxford University Press, 1996), 92, 130–131; Benn Stiel, *The Battle of Bretton Woods: John Maynard Keynes, Harry Dexter White, and the Making of a New World Order* (Princeton, NJ: Princeton University Press, 2013), 259–260; Alfred E. Eckes Jr. and Thomas Zeiler, *Globalization and the American Century* (New York: Cambridge University Press, 2003), 156–183.

3. Amy Gutman, "Introduction," *Democracy and the Welfare State* (Princeton, NJ: Princeton University Press, 1988), 3–10; Kenneth Feingold, "The United States: Federalism and it Counterfactuals," in Herbert Obinger et al., eds., *Federalism and the Welfare State: New World and European Experiences* (New York: Cambridge University Press, 2005), 161–164.

4. See, e.g., Patricia Cain, *Rainbow Rights: The Role of Lawyers and Courts in the Gay Civil Rights Movement* (Boulder, CO: Westview, 2000), 12–44; Stephen L. Wasby, "Litigation and Lobbying as Complementary Strategies for Civil Rights," in Bernard Grofman, ed., *Legacies of the Civil Rights Act of 1964* (Charlottesville: University of Virginia Press, 2000), 65–82; Leslie Friedman Goldstein, *Contemporary Cases in Women's Rights* (Madison: University of Wisconsin Press, 1994), 299–300.

5. Gunnar Myrdal, *An American Dilemma: The Negro Problem and Modern Democracy* (New York: Harper, 1944), xix; James C. Cobb, *The Brown Decision, Jim Crow, and Southern Identity* (Athens: University of Georgia Press, 2005), 21–30; Charles L. Black, Jr., *Decision According to Law* (New York: Norton, 1981), 16, but see Gerald Rosenberg, *The Hollow Hope: Can Courts Bring About Social Change* (Chicago: University of Chicago Press, 1991), 4 and after (federal courts' efforts to affect social change largely illusory).

6. The poster book for the litigation explosion was Walter K. Olson, *The Litigation Explosion: What Happened When America Unleashed the Lawsuit* (New York: Dutton, 1991). One response, suggesting that the language and the thesis of the book were driven by certainly lobbying groups is William Haltom and Michael McCann, *Distorting the Law: Politics, Media, and the Litigation Crisis* (Chicago: University of Chicago Press, 1994). On rights and litigation, compare Mary Ann Glendon, *Rights Talk: The Impoverishment of Political Discourse* (New York: Free Press, 1993), 3: decrying that "legal speech today is a good deal more morally neutral, adversarial, and rights oriented" than in past years, with Cass Sunstein, *After the Rights Revolution* (Cambridge, MA: Harvard University Press, 1990), v: extolling "the extraordinary explosion of statutory rights in the 1960s and 1970s."

7. Stephen Daniel, "Ladders and Bushes: The Problem of Caseloads and Studying Court Activities over Time," *American Bar Foundation Research Journal* (1984), 751–795; Posner, *Federal Courts*, 83–85; Marc Galanter, "Reading the Landscape of Disputes," *UCLA Law Review* 31 (1983), 71. Census figures from U.S. Department of Commerce Bureau of the Census and district court figures from http://www.fjc.gov/history/caseload.nsf/page/

caseloads_main_page. But the fact that Congress can increase or reduce the load that courts face by expanding causes of action or limiting jurisdiction may figure in this calculation.

8. John P. Parker, "Dual Sovereignty and the Federal Courts," *Northwestern Law Review* 51 (1956), 412; Purcell, *Litigation and Inequality*, 247, 291; Ellen A. Peters, "Capacity and Respect: A Perspective on the Historical Role of the State Courts in the Federal System," *New York University Law Review* 73 (1998), 1069, 1071; on "new federalism," see generally, Christopher P. Banks and John C. Blakeman, *The U.S. Supreme Court and New Federalism: From the Rehnquist to the Roberts Court* (Lanham, MD: Rowman and Littlefield, 2012), 2, 6, 8 and after (federalism cases still a staple of the Court).

9. William Campbell quoted in Dumnarski, *Federal Judges Revealed*, 143; David S. Clark, "Adjudication to Administration: A Statistical Analysis of Federal District Courts in the Twentieth Century," *Southern California Law Review* 55 (1981–1982), 65–152; Jack H. Friedenthal and Joshua E. Gardner, "Judicial Discretion to Deny Summary Judgment in the Era of Managerial Judging," *Hofstra Law Review* 31 (2002), 91–132. The classic essay is Abram Chayes, "The Role of the Judge in Public Law Litigation," *Harvard Law Review* 89 (1976), 1281–1316.

10. See, e.g., Nancy Scherer, *Scoring Points: Politicians, Activists, and the Lower Courts Appointment Process* (Palo Alto: Stanford University Press, 2005).

11. Data from Robert A. Carp, Kenneth L. Manning, and Ronald Stidham, "The Decision-Making Behavior of George W. Bush's Judicial Appointees," *Judicature* 88 (2004), 27, table 1.

12. Jeffrey Morris, *Eighth Circuit*, 189; *Picking Federal Judges*, 291 and after; Lee Epstein and Jeffrey A. Segal, *Advice and Consent: The Politics of Judicial Appointments* (New York: Oxford University Press, 2007), 52, 61, and after; Sidney M. Milkis and Emily J. Charnock, "History of the Presidency," in Michael Nelson, ed., *Guide to the Presidency and the Executive Branch* (Thousand Oaks, CA: CQ Press, 2012), 169.

Chapter 9

1. Amity Schlaes, *The Forgotten Man: A New History of the Great Depression* (New York: Harper, 2007), 85–104; Robert S. McElvaine, *The Great Depression: America, 1929–1940* (New York: Random House, 1984), 38–39; Kenneth Galbraith, *The Great Crash 1929* (New York: Time, 1954), 135–137.

2. Meridel Le Sueur, "Women on the Breadlines," *New Masses* 7 (January 1932), 5; John A. Fliter and Derek S. Hoff, *Fighting Foreclosure: The Blaisdell Case, the Contract Clause, and the Great Depression* (Lawrence: University Press of Kansas, 2012), 51–53.

3. Mikva and Dillin quoted in William Domnarski, *Federal Judges Revealed* (New York: Oxford University Press, 2009), 2, 15; Constance Baker Motley, *Equal Justice Under Law: An Autobiography* (New York: Macmillan, 1999), 15–16; Warren K. Urbom recalling his childhood in *Called to Justice: The Life of a Federal Trial Judge* (Lincoln: University of Nebraska Press, 2012), 5.

4. Franklin D. Roosevelt, Democratic National Party Convention Nomination Address, Chicago, July 2, 1932; http://newdeal.feri.org/speeches/1932b.htm; Kirstin Downey, *The Woman Behind the New Deal: The Life and Legacy of Francis Perkins* (New York: Random House, 2010), 121, 244; Jonathan Alter, *The Defining Moment: FDR's Hundred Days and the Triumph of Hope* (New York: Simon and Schuster, 2007), 93 and after.

5. The Supreme Court found the Wagner Act constitutional in 1937, but labor relations cases continued to arrive at the federal courts—indeed the law and the sequel, the Taft-Hartley Act of 1947, brought even more cases. National Labor Relations Board v. Jones and Laughlin Steel, 301 U.S. 1 (1937); Stephen Fraser, "The Labor Question," in Stephen Fraser and Gary Gerstle, eds., *The Rise and Fall of the New Deal Order, 1930–1980* (Princeton: Princeton University Press, 1989), 68; 176 cases in the Supreme Court turned on the Act.

6. Russ Immarigeon, "The Wickersham Commission," in David Levinson, ed., *Encyclopedia of Crime and Punishment* (Santa Barbara: Sage, 2002), 1:1707–1711. Statement of Newton D. Baker, January 7, 1931; Statement of Monte Lehman, January 7, 1931, Statement of Frank J. Loesch, January 7, 1931, National Commission on Law Observance and Enforcement, *Report on the Enforcement of the Prohibition Laws and the United States* (Washington, D.C.: GPO, 1931) 1: 111, 139, 149.

7. "Historical Caseloads in the Federal Courts," http://www.fjc.gov/history/caseload.nsf/page/caseloads_main_page; "Report of Criminal Cases, U.S. District Courts"; "Report of the Judicial Conference, September 29–30, 1932, 5; "Report of the Judicial Conference, September 18, 1933," 5, all on FJC website.

8. Charles E. Clark, "The Challenge for a New Federal Civil Procedure," *Journal of the American Judicature Society* 19 (1935), 8. Attorney General Report to the Conference, September 14, 1933, 2, 3, 4–5. On the caseloads, see http://www.fjc.gov/history/caseload.nsf/page/caseloads_main_page.

9. "Authorized Judgeships," www.uscourts.gov/judges-judgeships/authorized-judgeships. Gordon Bermant, William W. Schwarzer, Edward Sussman, and Russell R. Wheeler, *Imposing a Moratorium on the Number of Federal Judges* (Washington, D.C.: Federal Judicial Center, 1993), 45 table 96. Note that birth rate in the United States dropped from 25.1 per thousand in 1925 to 18.7 in 1935. In 1920, immigrants made up a little over 13 percent of the nation's population. By 1940, this number had shrunk to 9 percent.

10. John Henry Schlegel, *American Legal Realism and Empirical Social Science* (Chapel Hill: University of North Carolina Press, 1995), 88–89; Kalman, *Legal Realism at Yale, 1927–1960*, 31. Not every realist was on board. Felix Frankfurter and Thurmond Arnold agreed that the study was hurried and should not be published as it was. Frankfurter was not an advocate of expanding the scope of federal jurisdiction. See Arnold to Frankfurter, April 5, 1933. Frankfurter Papers, Library of Congress; Thomas Thatcher to Frankfurter, May 9, 1927, Frankfurter Papers, Library of Congress.

11. Arnold to Frankfurter, April 5, 1933, Frankfurter Papers, Library of Congress; American Law Institute, *Study of the Business of the Federal Courts, Part II, Civil Cases* (Philadelphia: ALI, 1934), 49, 17, 18, 19.

12. National Bankruptcy Act of 1898, 30 Stat. 544; Bankruptcy Act of 1938, 52 Stat. 840–842. Martin A. Frey and Sidney K. Swinson, *An Introduction to Bankruptcy Law* (Clifton Park, NY: Cengage, 2012), 4; David A. Skeel, *Debt's Dominion: A History of Bankruptcy Law in America* (Princeton: Princeton University Press, 2001), 76, 80, 86–89. An Act of Congress in 1978 with a somewhat troubled history made these hearings into quasi-judicial proceedings and gave the referees judge-like powers, but after the Supreme Court decided that the Congress had overstepped in giving such powers to individuals who were not Article III judges, Congress passed the Bankruptcy Amendments and Federal Judgeship Act of 1984, providing for referral of bankruptcy cases to bankruptcy judges appointed for terms by courts of appeal judges, with district courts hearing challenges to the findings of the bankruptcy court judges. See Kenneth N. Klee, "Legislative History of the New Bankruptcy Law," *DePaul Law Review* 28 (1979), 941–960; "Bankruptcy Courts," http://www.fjc.gov/history/home.nsf/page/courts_special_bank.html.

13. http://www.fjc.gov/history/courthouses.nsf; Lender, *This Honorable Court*, 166–170; Cahan, Hinckle, and Ocken, *Court that Tamed the West*, 208; Robert A. M. Stern, "Introduction," in Barbara S. Christen and Steven Flanders, eds., *Cass Gilbert, Life and Work: Architect of the Public Domain* (New York: Norton, 2001), 9–11; Judith Resnik, "Building the Federal Judiciary (Literally and Legally) The Monuments of Chief Justices Taft, Warren, and Rehnquist," *Indiana Law Journal* 87 (2012), 860–864; Resnik and Dennis Curtis, "Inventing Democratic Courts: A New and Iconic Supreme Court," *Journal of Supreme Court History* 38 (2013), 231–233.

14. Bankruptcy cases: http://www.fjc.gov/history/caseload.nsf/page/caseloads_bankruptcy; Lender, *This Honorable Court*, 176–177; Jerry L. Mashaw, "Federal Administration and Administrative Law in the Gilded Age," *Yale Law Journal* 119 (2010), 1367 and after.

15. Charles L. Zelden, *Justice Lies in the District: The U.S. District Court, Southern District of Texas, 1902–1960* (College Station: Texas A&M Press, 1993), 99–121.

16. Larsen, *Federal Justice in Western Missouri*, 154–157.

17. http://www.fjc.gov/history/caseload.nsf/page/caseloads_main_page; Figure 1, "Population, Appellate Judgeships, and Appeals Commenced, 1890–1989," in Harrison and Wheeler, eds., *The Federal Appellate Judiciary*, 253; Irving Kaufman, "Second Circuit." 201; Byron R. White, "Enlarging the Capacity of the Supreme Court." in Wheeler and Harrison, eds., *The Federal Appellate Judiciary*, 145; Gordon Bermant, William W. Schwarzer, Edward Sussman, and Russell

Wheeler, *Imposing a Moratorium on the Number of Federal Judges* (Washington, D.C.: Federal Judicial Center, 1993), 53; Peter Irons, *The New Deal Lawyers* (Princeton, Princeton University Press, 1993), 264; A. Leo Levin, "Uniformity of Federal Law." in Wheeler and Harrison, eds., *The Federal Appellate Judiciary*, 133–134; circuit "view," quoting Judge Henry Friendly, at 135.

18. John C. Knox, *A Judge Comes of Age* (New York: Charles Scribner's Sons, 1940), 263; *Proceedings Had on November 3, 1939, in the United States District Court for the Southern District of New York on the One Hundred Fiftieth Anniversary of its Organization* (Boston: Merrymount, 1939), Charles Evans Hughes letter quoted on page 10; "Current Legislation," *St. John's Law Review* 8 (1933), 207; "Legislation," *Columbia Law Review* 33 (1933), 1225; Benjamin Klebaner, *American Commercial Banking: A History* (Boston: Twayne, 1990), 161; Gary Richardson and Patrick Van Horn, "Intensified Regulatory Scrutiny and Bank Distress in New York City During the Great Depression," National Bureau of Economic Research Working Paper No. 14120, June 2008, 3–5.

19. Edward A. Purcell, *Brandeis and the Progressive Constitution: Erie, the Judicial Power, and the Politics of the Federal Courts in Twentieth-Century America* (New Haven: Yale University Press, 2000), 23; Gunther, *Learned Hand*, 241–244, 444; Morris, *Second Circuit*, 133–134.

20. G. Edward White, *American Judicial Tradition: Profiles of Leading American Judges*, 3rd ed. (New York: Oxford University Press, 2007), 212–215; Gunther, *Learned Hand*, 550; Geoffrey R. Stone, *Perilous Times: Free Speech in Wartime from the Sedition Act of 1798 to the War on Terrorism* (New York: Norton, 2004), 200.

21. Roger Miner, "Augustus Noble Hand," in Newman, ed., *Yale Biographical Dictionary*, 247–248; United States v. One Package, 86 F.2d 737 (2d Cir. 1934); United States v. One Book Entitled Ulysses by James Joyce, 72 F.2d 705 (2nd Cir. 1934).

22. Jeffrey Brandon Morris, *Establishing Justice in Middle America: A History of the United State Court of Appeals for the Eighth Circuit* (Minneapolis: University of Minnesota Press, 2007), 110–111, 138–139, Justice Blackmun quotation at 111.

23. Federal Writers Project, *Los Angeles in the 1930s: The WPA Guide to the City of Angels* (Los Angeles: University of California Press, 2011), 242; William H. Mullins, *The Depression and the Urban West Coast, 1929–1933: Los Angeles, San Francisco, Seattle, and Portland* (Bloomington: University of Indiana Press, 1990), 50–51; Frederick, *Rugged Justice*, 175–177, 178–181, 185.

24. Sarah Wilson, "Florence Ellinwood Allen," in Rebecca Mae Salokar and Mary L. Volcansek, eds., *Women in Law: A Bio-Bibliographical Sourcebook* (Santa Barbara, CA: ABC-CLIO, 1996), 17–24; Jeanette E. Tuve, *First Lady of the Law: Florence Ellinwood Allen* (Lanham, MD: University Press of America, 1984), passim.

25. See, generally, Michael E. Parrish, *The Hughes Court: Justices, Rules, and Legacy* (Santa Barbara, CA: ABC-CLIO, 2002), 3 and after.

26. "Four horsemen": William Wiecek, "New Deal," in Hall et al., eds., *Oxford Companion*, 584. Cluster bloc analysis of voting, especially on the Hughes Court: John D. Sprague, *Voting Patterns of the United States Supreme Court: Cases in Federalism, 1889–1959* (Indianapolis: Bobbs Merrill, 1968), 97–98. But see Barry D. Cushman, "The Secret Lives of the Four Horsemen," *Virginia Law Review* 83 (1997), 559–584, arguing for greater diversity in their views.

27. Amazon Refining v. Railroad Commission, F. Supp 639, 644 (1934) (Bryant, J.).

28. Panama Refining Company v. Ryan, 293 U.S. 388, 415, 418 (1935) (Hughes, C.J.).

29. Schechter Poultry v. U.S. 295 U.S. 495, 528, 529, 542 (1935) (Hughes, C.J.); Adkins v. Children's Hospital, 262 U.S. 525 (1923) (minimum wage for women and children workers set by Congress ruled unconstitutional).

30. U.S. v. Butler, 197 U.S. 1 (1936); Carter v. Carter Coal Co., 298 U.S. 238; Ashton v. Cameron County Water Improvement District, 298 U.S. 513, 532 (1936) (McReynolds, J.).

31. Newspaper letters to the editor quoted in Daniel Holt, ed. *Debates on the Federal Judiciary, A Documentary History Volume II: 1875–1939* (Washington, D.C.: FJC, 2013), 222–223.

32. Charles Evans Hughes, Letter to the Senate Judiciary Committee, March 22, 1937, U.S. Senate, Committee on the Judiciary, Reorganization of the Federal Judiciary, Hearings on S. 1392, Part 3, 75th Cong., 1st Sess., 1937, 490–91; Burt Solomon, *FDR v. The Constitution: The Court-Packing Fight and the Triumph of Democracy* (New York: Bloomsbury, 2009), 20–22;

William E. Leuchtenburg, "The Origins of Franklin D. Roosevelt's Court-Packing Plan," *Supreme Court Review* (1966), 394.

33. Frederick, *Rugged Justice*, 181; William E. Leuchtenberg, *The Supreme Court Reborn: The Constitutional Revolution in the Age of Roosevelt* (New York: Oxford University Press, 1995), 113. The term was not new in law—lawyers representing clients in early prize cases were called proctors.

34. West Coast Hotel v. Parrish, 300 U.S. 379 (1937); NLRB v. Jones and Laughlin Steel, 301 U.S. 1 (1937); Stewart Machine Co. V. Davis, 301 U.S. 548 (1937), Helvering v. Davis, 301 U.S. 619 (1937).

35. Solomon, *F.D.R. vs. the Constitution*, 58–59; Barry Cushman, *Rethinking the New Deal Court: The Structure of a Constitutional Revolution* (New York: Oxford University Press, 1998), 30.

36. James Goodman, *Stories of Scottsboro* (New York: Pantheon, 1994), 161.

37. Powell v. Alabama, 287 U.S. 45, 49, 52, 58 (1932) (Sutherland, J.).

38. Norris v. Alabama, 294 U.S. 587, 588 (1935) (Hughes, C.J.).

39. 294 U.S. at 591 (Hughes, C.J.); Strauder v. West Virginia, 100 U.S. 303 (1880).

40. 294 U.S. at 594 (Hughes, C.J.).

41. U.S. v. Carolene Products, 304 U.S. 144, 147, 153 (1938) (Stone, J.); Louis J. Lusky, "Footnote Redux, A *Carolene Products* Reminiscence," *Columbia University Law Review* 82 (1982), 1093–1099.

42. 28 U.S.C. § 634 (1928), quoted in Ezra Siller, "The Origins of the Oral Deposition in the Federal Rules: Who's in Charge?" 5, Student Legal History Papers. Paper 1, http://digitalcommons.law.yale.edu/student_legal_history_papers/1.

43. See, e.g., Peter Julian, "Charles E. Clark and Simple Pleading: Against a Formalism of Generality," *Northwestern Law Review* 104 (2010), 1186–1187; Geoffrey C. Hazard Jr. And Michele Taruffo, *American Civil Procedure: An Introduction* (New Haven: Yale University Press, 1993), 25.

44. Taft 1914 statement quoted in Stephen N. Burbank, "The Rules Enabling Act of 1934," *Pennsylvania Law Review* 130 (1982), 1051–1052; William Howard Taft, "Possible and Needed Reforms in the Administration of Justice in the Federal Courts," *American Bar Association Reports* 47 (1922), 268.

45. Taft quoted in Edward A. Purcell, *Brandeis and the Progressive Constitution: Erie, the Judicial Power, and the Politics of the Federal Courts in Twentieth-Century America*, rev.ed. (New Haven: Yale University Press, 1999), 32; Burbank, "Rules Enabling Act," 1078–1095. The political spin on this tale is the present authors'.

46. Stephen N. Subrin, "Fishing Expeditions Allowed: The Historical Background of the 1938 Federal Discovery Rules," *Boston College Law Review* 39 (1998), 711–712; David Marcus, "The Federal Rules of Civil Procedure and Legal Realism as a Jurisprudence of Law Reform," *Georgia Law Review* 44 (2010), 433–510.

47. Cornell Clayton, "Homer Stille Cummings," in John R. Vile, ed., *Great American Lawyers: An Encyclopedia* (Santa Barbara, CA: ABC-CLIO, 2001), 150–155; Burbank, "Rules Enabling Act," 1015; Charles Clark and James William Moore, "New Federal Procedure—The Background," *Yale Law Journal* 44 (1935), 388; "Report of the Conference of the Senior Circuit Justices, September 27, 1934," 8.

48. Rules Enabling Act of 1934. c. 651, 48 Stat. 1064; 28 U. S. C. § 723 b, c; Sibbach v. Wilson and Co., 312 U.S. 1, 10, (Roberts, J.) (1941).

49. In May 1935, Mitchell was still trying to decide whether Clark or Sunderland should be reporter. Clark did not let his opportunity slip away but undermined Sunderland's views to Mitchell. When Mitchell agreed that Clark ought to have the job, Clark wrote to Sunderland and offered him the task of preparing the rules on discovery, just as dear to Sunderland as merger of law and equity was to Clark. Sunderland asked to prepare the rules for summary judgment, and Clark sweetened the pot with that concession and $125 per week or $500 per month to Sunderland for the project. Thereafter, Sunderland supported Clark consistently. See Clark to Mitchell, May 11, 1935; Mitchell to Clark, May 16, 1935; Sunderland to Clark, May 22, 1935; Clark to Sunderland, May 25, 1935; Mitchell to Clark, May 22, 1935; Clark to Mitchell, May 23, 1935; Mitchell to Sunderland, May 23, 1935; Clark to Mitchell, May

25, 1935; Clark to Sunderland, June 22, 1935; Sunderland to Clark, June 25, 1935; Clark to Sunderland, June 28, 1935. Clark Papers, Yale University Library, folders 40, 41, 42, box 108.

50. A stenographic record of the deliberations is preserved in the archives of the Administrative Office of the Federal Courts entitled "Proceedings of the Advisory Committee on Federal Rules of Civil Procedure," stenographic typescript, June 1935–February 1937. The passage here is from Proceedings of the Advisory Committee, November 17, 1935, 831–836.

51. See, e.g., Judith Resnik, "Failing Faith: Adjudicatory Procedure in Decline," *University of Chicago Law Review* 53 (1986), 555. For an attack on Clark and later scholars who continue to argue for the formalist/realist divide, Brian Z. Tamanaha, *Beyond the Formalist-Realist Divide: The Role of Politics in Judging* (Princeton: Princeton University Press, 2009), 3–8, 200–202, (and, frankly, just about everything in between).

52. Subrin, "Fishing Expeditions," 720–725, has excerpted comments from lawyers and judges urging caution in the framing of rules for discovery.

53. "Rules of Civil Procedure for the U.S. District Courts, Hearing before a Subcommittee of the Committee on the Judiciary," U.S. Senate, April 18, 1938, 2, 3, 4, 6, 7, 8, 11, 16, 20, 24.

54. "Rules of Civil Procedure . . ." Hearing, May 19, 1938," Part II, 28, 29, 30, 34, 35, 36, 39, 73, 74.

55. Charles E. Clark, "The New Federal Rules of Civil Procedure: The Last Phase—Underlying Philosophy Embodied in Some of the Basic Provisions of the New Procedure," *American Bar Association Journal* 12 (1937) 976, 977; Peter Charles Hoffer, "Text, Translation, Context, Conversation: Preliminary Notes for Decoding the Deliberations of the Advisory Committee that Wrote the Federal Rules of Civil Procedure," *American Journal of Legal History* 37 (1993), 414–415.

56. For a table of these acts, along with citations of hearings, see "Legislative History, Rules Enabling Act, 28 U.S.C. §§ 2071–2077," at the U.S. Courts web page, uscourts.gov/RulesAndPolicies/FederalRulemaking/Legislation/RulesEnablingAct.aspx.

57. Geoffrey C. Hazard Jr., "Discovery Vices and Trans-Substantive Virtues in the Federal Rules of Civil Procedure," *University of Pennsylvania Law Review* 137 (1989), 2238; *Federal Rules of Civil Procedure* (Chicago: Palmer Edwards, 1938), 2 v., with notes.

58. A mere sampling of a cottage industry in complaints: on the shift in lawyering, see Marc Galanter, "Mega-Law and Mega-Lawyering in the Contemporary United States," in Robert Dingwall & Phillip Lewis, eds., *The Sociology of the Professions: Lawyers, Doctors and Others* (New York: St. Martins, 1983), 152–153. On the perils of equity pleading in general, Stephen N. Subrin, "How Equity Conquered Common Law: The Federal Rules of Civil Procedure in Historical Perspective," *University of Pennsylvania Law Review* 135 (1987), 909–1002.

59. William E. Nelson, *Legalist Reformation: Law, Politics, and Ideology in New York, 1920–1980* (Chapel Hill: University of North Carolina Press, 2001), 32, argues that the FRCP evened the playing field, but Martin Redish, *Wholesale Justice: Constitutional Democracy and the Problem of the Class Action Lawsuit* (Palo Alto: Stanford University Press, 2009), 62, disagrees. The idea that the Rules imposed an unfair redistribution of private property, a penalty on wealthy individuals, although they have done no wrong, is most thoroughly argued in Richard Epstein, *Design for Liberty: Private Property, Public Administration, and the Rule of Law* (Cambridge, MA: Harvard University Press, 2011), 181.

60. On the story of how the case came to the Court, see Purcell, *Brandeis and the Progressive Constitution*, 97–105.

61. Erie Railroad v. Thompkins, 304 U.S. 64, 74, 78 (1938) (Brandeis, J.). Charles Warren, "New Light on the History of the Federal Judiciary Act of 1789," *Harvard Law Review* 37 (1923), 49, 51–52, 81–88, 108. It is not clear why Brandeis, otherwise relying on original evidence, would or should prefer law professor Charles Warren's views to Supreme Court Justice Joseph Story's, given that Story's were Supreme Court precedent on point and Warren's was a stand-alone piece of law review scholarship, subject to no refereeing save that of his own students at Harvard Law School. Perhaps Warren was simply conveniently on point? Purcell, *Brandeis and the Progressive Constitution*, 342, n.78 and 343 n.102.

62. On Rule 23, see, e.g., Stephen C. Yeazell, *From Medieval Group Litigation to the Modern Class Action* (New Haven: Yale University Press, 1987), 236–237. On Erie, see, e.g., John Hart Ely, "The Irrepressible Myth of Erie," *Harvard Law Review* 87 (1974), 693–740.

63. Fish, *The Politics of Federal Judicial Administration*, 113–114, 152.

64. http://www.uscourts.gov/FederalCourts/UnderstandingtheFederalCourts/ AdministrativeOffice.aspx; "Report of the Conference, Appendix," January 22, 1940, 141–145.

65. Geyh, *When Courts and Congress Collide*, 108. Procedural law is like a river, never the same and always in motion, its flow from the courts, its banks leveed by Congress. See, e.g., Gregory C. Sisk, "The Balkanization of Appellate Justice: The Proliferation of Local Rules in the Federal Circuits," *University of Colorado Law Review* 68 (1997), 1–61 (local variation in appellate practice rules actually encouraged by procedural reform).

66. Goldman, *Picking Federal Judges*, 17–36, Denman quotation at page 32; Wyatt Wells, "Research Note: Appointments of Catholics During the New Deal," *The Journal of the Historical Society* 13 (2013), 361–413; George Martin, *CCB: The Life of Charles Culp Burlingham, New York's First Citizen, 1858–1959* (New York: Hill and Wang, 2005), 485.

67. Roger K. Newman, *Hugo Black: A Biography* (New York: Fordham University Press, 1997), 13. Here and after, material adapted from Hoffer, Hoffer, and Hull, *Supreme Court*, 265–269.

68. Qouted in Leuchtenburg, *Supreme Court Reborn*, 187.

69. Howard Ball, *Hugo L. Black: Cold Steel Warrior* (New York: Oxford University Press, 1996), 60–61.

70. Noah Feldman, *Scorpions: The Battles and Triumphs of FDR's Great Supreme Court Justices* (New York: Twelve, 2010), 38–39; Jeff Shesol, *Supreme Power: Franklin Roosevelt vs. the Supreme Court* (New York: Norton, 2011), 51–53.

71. Melvin I. Urofsky, *Felix Frankfurter: Judicial Restraint and Individual Liberties* (Boston: Twayne, 1991), 32 and after; H. N. Hirsch, *The Enigma of Felix Frankfurter* (New York: Basic, 1981), 106, 144 (flattery); Ward and Weiden, *Sorcerers' Apprentices*, 63; Polly J. Price, *Judge Richard S. Arnold: A Legacy of Justice on the Federal Bench* (Amherst, NY: Prometheus, 2009), 42.

72. Douglas told his own story in *Go East Young Man: The Early Years, the Autobiography of William O. Douglas* (New York: Random House, 1974), and *The Court Years, 1939–1975* (New York: Random House, 1980).

73. Stephen B. Duke, "Justice Douglas and the Criminal Law," in Stephen L. Wasby, ed., *"He Shall Not Pass This Way Again": The Legacy of Justice William O. Douglas* (Pittsburgh: University of Pittsburgh Press, 1990), 133–134; James F. Simon, *Independent Journey: The Life of William O. Douglas* (New York: Harper and Row, 1980), 354; Douglas, memo to Frankfurter, May 29, 1954, in Melvin I. Urofsky, ed., *The Douglas Letters: Selections from the Private Correspondence of William O. Douglas* (Bethesda, MD: Adler and Adler, 1987), 85.

74. Sidney Fine, *Frank Murphy: The Detroit Years* (Ann Arbor: University of Michigan Press, 1975), 235–239.

75. Parrish, *The Hughes Court*, 122–124; Murphy quoted in William Wiecek, *The Birth of the Modern Constitution, The United States Supreme Court, 1941–1953* (New York: Cambridge University Press, 2006), 103.

76. Robert Jackson, in "Report of the Judicial Conference, September 14, 1940," 2.

Chapter 10

1. Jytte Klausen, "Did World War II End the New Deal?" in Sidney M. Milkis and Jerome M. Mileur, eds., *The New Deal and the Triumph of Liberalism* (Amherst: University of Massachusetts Press, 2002), 197; For the U.S. experience in World War II: Alan Brinkley, *The End of Reform: New Deal Liberalism in Recession and War* (New York: Alfred A. Knopf, 1995), 175–226; Mark Jonathan Harris, Franklin D. Mitchell, and Steven J. Schechter, eds., *The Homefront: America During World War II* (New York: G. P. Putnam's Sons, 1984), a collection of recollections; and David M. Kennedy, *Freedom from Fear: The American People in Depression and War, 1929–1945* (New York: Oxford University Press, 1999), 381–851.

2. Tom Brokaw, *The Greatest Generation* (New York: Random House, 2004), ix and after; William M. Tuttle, *"Daddy's Gone to War": The Second World War in the Lives of America's Children* (New York: Oxford University Press, 1993), 6; Emily Yellin, *Our Mothers' War: American Women at Home and at the Front During World War II* (New York: Free Press, 2004), 37–72; Michael J. Klarman, *From Jim Crow to Civil Rights: The Supreme Court and the Struggle for Racial Equality* (New York: Oxford University Press, 2004), 174–176; John Reynolds, in Domnarski, *Federal Judges Revealed*, 24–25.

3. Roger Daniels, *The Japanese American Cases: The Rule of Law in Time of War* (Lawrence: University Press of Kansas, 2013), 26; Madison, Federalist No. 48, in Rossiter, ed., *Federalist Papers*, 308; Geoffrey R. Stone, *Perilous Times*, 544; Richard W. Steele, *Free Speech in the Good War* (New York: Palgrave Macmillan, 1999), 12–13; Peter Irons, *Justice at War: The Story of the Japanese American Internment Cases*, rev. ed. (Berkeley: University of California Press, 1993), 345–346.

4. Francis Biddle, "Statement of the Attorney General," *Report of the Judicial Conference*, September 29, 1942, 2–3, 4. Biddle did not include in this category suits he pressed against labor leaders for slowing the war effort. See Nelson Lichtenstein, *Labor's War at Home: The CIO in World War II*, 3rd. ed. (Evanston, IL: Northwestern University Press, 2010), 169.

5. Judge Biggs quoted in Joseph C. Goulden, *The Benchwarmers, The Private World of the Powerful Federal Judges* (New York: Weybright and Talley, 1974), 297; Mark Gelfand, "Charles E. Wyzanski," in Newman, ed., *Yale Biographical Dictionary*, 606–607: "Charles E. Wyzanski, 80, Is Dead," *New York Times*, September 5, 1986. During the 1930s, there were some calls for term limits on federal judges, mainly from disgruntled New Dealers. See Mark C. Miller, *The View of the Courts from the Hill: Interactions Between Congress and the Federal Judiciary* (Charlottesville: University of Virginia Press, 2009), 97. These went nowhere, although they are periodically revived.

6. Thurman Arnold, *Fair Fights and Foul: A Dissenting Lawyer's Life* (New York: Harcourt, 1965), 159.

7. Jerome Frank, *Law and the Modern Mind* (New York: Transaction, 1930), 148; Robert Jerome Glennon, *The Iconoclast as Reformer: Jerome Frank's Impact on American Law* (Ithaca, NY: Cornell University Press, 1985), 187–188; J. A. Jolowicz, *On Civil Procedure* (New York: Cambridge University Press, 2000), 109–110. "Private attorney general": Associated Industries v. Ickes, 134 F. 2d 694, 700 (2nd Cir. 1943) (Frank, J.). Congress codified the concept in the Civil Rights Attorney's Fees Awards Act of 1976 but subsequent Supreme Court decisions have narrowed it.

8. Gregory Caldieera, "Robert Houghwout Jackson,." in Hall et al., eds., *Oxford Companion*, 443–445.

9. Robert H. Jackson, *The Struggle for Judicial Supremacy: A Study of a Crisis in American Power Politics* (New York: Knopf, 1941), 109. "The Constitution is not a suicide pact": Terminiello v. City of Chicago, 337 U.S. 1, 36 (1949) (Jackson, J.); Brown v. Allen, 344 U.S. 443, 540 (1953) (Jackson, J.). On the feud between Jackson and Black, see Tony Freyer, "Black-Jackson Feud," in Hall et al., eds., *Oxford Companion*, 445–446; Wiecek, *Birth of the Modern Constitution*, 413.

10. See, generally, David Robertson, *Sly and Able: A Political Biography of James F. Byrnes* (New York: Norton, 1994); on Byrnes's reading law, see Winfred B. Moore, Jr., "James F. Byrnes," in Clare Cushman, ed., *The Supreme Court Justices: Illustrated Biographies*, 3rd ed. (Los Angeles: CQ Press, 2013), 365.

11. Abraham, *Justices and Presidents*, 186–187; John M. Ferren, *Salt of the Earth, Conscience of the Court: The Story of Justice Wiley Rutledge* (Chapel Hill: University of North Carolina Press, 2004), 62, 112, 228, 305, 342.

12. Edward Moore Bennett, *Franklin D. Roosevelt and the Search for Security: American-Soviet Relations, 1933–1939* (Lanham, MD: Rowman and Littlefield, 2006), 1:75–77 and after.

13. Paul L. Murphy, *The Constitution in Crisis Times, 1918–1969* (New York: Harper and Row, 1972), 213–218. The Act is still good law, though it has been modified a number of times and since the 1950s no prosecutions have been brought under it. More recent immigration law has also superseded the registration provisions.

14. Alien Registration Act of 1940, ch. 439, 54 Stat. 670, 18 U.S.C. § 2385.

15. Michal Belknap, *Cold War Political Justice: The Smith Act, the Communist Party, and American Civil Liberties* (Westport, CT: Greenwood, 1977), discusses the entire episode.

16. Ex Parte Bridges, 49 F. Supp. 292, 297 (D.C. N.D. Cal. 1943) (Welsh, J.).

17. 49 F. Supp at 299, quoting Soon Hing v. Crowley, 113 U.S. 703, 710 (1885) (Field, J.); Bridges v. Wixon, 144 F. 2d 927, 933 (1944) (Wilbur, J.), 144 F. 2d at 939 (Healy, J.); Rebecca Hill, "The History of the Smith Act and the Hatch Act," in Robert Justin Goldstein, *Little Red*

Scares: Anti-Communism and Political Repression in the United States, 1921–1946 (Burlington, VT: Ashgate, 2014), 339.

18. Bridges v. Wixon, 326 U.S. 135, 142, 143 (1945) (Douglas, J.); 326 U.S. at 157 (Murphy, J.).
19. The case is usually regarded as part of the history of organized labor. See, e.g., Atleson, *Labor and the Wartime State*, 40 n.50.
20. Dunne v. U.S, 138 F.2d 137 (8th Cir. 1943) (Stone, J.).
21. U.S. v. McWilliams, 54 F. Supp. 791 (D.C. D.C. 1944); George Michael, *Confronting Right Wing Extremism and Terrorism in the USA* (New York: Routledge, 2004), 125–126. Michal Belknap, who has studied these cases thoroughly, believes that the delay was less a tactic than an unfortunate byproduct of so many counsel for so many defendants, many of the former serving pro bono, and not being familiar with criminal law. Belknap to the authors, January 14, 2014.
22. The plan for salvation Bell proposed appeared in his *Mankind United* published by the equally imaginative International Registration Bureau in 1934. Like the membership of the cult, the book's sales were slight. John Lofland, *Protest: Studies of Collective Behavior and Social Movements* (New Brunswick, NJ: Transaction, 1985), 249–254. The complaint was quoted in Justice Burton's dissent in *Bell v. Hood*, 327 U.S. 678, 685 (1946) (Burton, J.).
23. Bell v. Hood, 150 F.2d 96, 100 (9th Cir. 1945) (Stephens, J.); Bell v. Hood, 327 U.S. 678, 684 (1946) (Black, J.). The case returned to the Southern District of California District Court in 1947, and the court found no ground for the tort award, Bell v. Hood, 71 F. Supp. 813 (D.C. S.D. Calif., 1947).
24. Daniels, *The Japanese American Cases*, 15–27.
25. Mark S. Weiner, *Americans Without Law: The Racial Boundaries of Citizenship* (New York: New York University Press, 2006), 98–105; Irons, *Justice at War*, 3–134.
26. Irons, *Justice at War*, 152–154; Roger Daniels, *Prisoners Without Trial: Japanese Americans in World War II*, rev. ed. (New York: Hill and Wang, 2004), 49–71.
27. Korematsu v. U.S., 140 F.2d 289, 290 (9th Cir. 1943) (Wilbur, J.).
28. 140 F. 2d. at 291, 292, 295, 303 (Denman, J.)
29. Hirabayashi v. U.S. 320 U.S. 81, 102 (1943) (Stone, C.J.).
30. 321 U.S. at 110 (Murphy, J.)
31. Korematsu v. U.S. 323 U.S. 214, 218 (1944) (Black, J.); 323 U.S. at 225 (Frankfurter, J.).
32. 323 U.S. at 225, 226 (Roberts, J.), 323 U.S. at 223 (Murphy, J.), 323 U.S. at 242–243 (Jackson, J.).
33. Ex Parte Mitsuye Endo, 323 U.S. 283, 294 (1945) (Douglas, J.).
34. 323 U.S. at 297 (Douglas, J.).
35. 323 U.S. at 308 (Murphy, J.), 323 U.S. at 310 (Roberts, J.).
36. Daniels, *Japanese Cases*, 136–202.
37. Hill v. Texas, 316 U.S. 400, 403 (1942) (Stone, C.J.).
38. U.S. v. Classic, 35 F. Supp 66, 68 (D.C. E.D. La. 1940); U.S. v. Classic, 313 U.S. 299, 319 (1941) (Stone, C.J.).
39. Grovey v. Townshend, 295 U.S. 45 (1935); Smith v. Allwright, 131 F. 2d 593 (5th Cir. 1942); Smith v. Allwright, 321 U.S. 649, 663 (1944) (Reed, J.).
40. Jonathan Bryant, *How Curious a Land: Conflict & Change In Greene County, Georgia, 1850–1885* (Chapel Hill: University of North Carolina Press, 1996), 16–17, 147–148.
41. Screws v. U.S. 140 F. 2d, 662, 666, 667 (5th Cir. 1944) (Sibley, J.).
42. Screws v. U.S., 325 U.S. 91, 139 (1945) (Roberts, J.); U.S. at 101 (Douglas, J.); 325 U.S. at 129 (Rutledge, J.); 325 at 136–137 (Murphy, J.).
43. Sumners Courts Act, June 29, 1940, 76 P.L. 675; 54 Stat. 688; Federal Rules of Criminal Procedure (Washington, D.C.: U.S. House of Representatives, 2010).
44. Homer S. Cummings, "New Criminal Rules—Another Triumph of the Democratic Process," *American Bar Association Journal* 31 (1945), 236.
45. Cummings, "Criminal Rules," 237–238.
46. John Scheb and John Scheb II, *Law and the Administrative Process* (Stamford, CT: Cengage, 2004), 36–37; Joanna L. Grisinger, *The Unwieldy American State: Administrative Politics Since the New Deal* (New York: Cambridge University Press, 2012), 12.

47. Landis, *The Administrative Process,* 12 and after (expertise); G. Edward White, *The Constitution and the New Deal* (Cambridge, MA: Harvard University Press, 2000), 117–118; Reuel E. Schiller, "The Era of Deference: Courts, Expertise, and the Emergence of New Deal Administrative Law," *Michigan Law Review* 106 (2007), 430–432; Morton J. Horwitz, *The Transformation of American Law, 1870–1960: The Crisis of Legal Orthodoxy* (Cambridge, MA: Harvard University Press, 1992), 213–214; Louis Fisher, *American Constitutional Law* (New York: McGraw Hill, 1990), 2: 292–293.

48. Administrative Procedure Act of 1946, June 11, 1946, 60 Stat. 237.

49. White, *The Constitution and the New Deal,* 94–95.

50. Note, "The Administrative Procedure Act and Judicial Review of Agency Actions," *Georgetown Law Journal* 37 (1948–1949), 559, 560; Frederick F. Blachly and Miriam E. Oatman, "The Federal Administrative Procedure Act," *Georgetown Law Journal* 34 (1946), 427, 428.

51. Murphy, *The Court in Crisis Times,* 246–247; Tom Clark, "Statement of the Attorney General," *Report of the Judicial Conference,* September 24, 1945.

52. Wiecek, *The Birth of the Modern Constitution,* 399.

Chapter 11

1. Kennedy, *Freedom from Fear,* 853. The "Four Points" were elucidated in President Franklin D. Roosevelt's January 6, 1941 State of the Union address.

2. Goldman, *Picking Federal Judges,* 40–41, 348, table 9.1.

3. Morris, *Eighth Circuit,* 111–112; Truman and Collet at Key West, President Harry S. Truman Library, November 20, 1946, Accession no.: 63-1373-23.

4. William E. Nelson, *In Pursuit of Right and Justice: Edward Weinfeld as Lawyer and Judge* (New York: New York University Press, 2004), 114–124, quotation at p. 123.

5. Carl Solberg, *Hubert Humphrey: A Biography* (St. Paul: Minnesota Historical Society, 2003), 151–152.

6. Such correlations were not possible earlier in federal courts' history, when the only lawyers available for posts in the far West and the High Plains came from east of the Mississippi. Truman believed in the importance of local attachments, but supply and demand (of lawyers and court seats) in newer districts may have played a part in this statistic.

7. James L. Baughman, "Television Comes to America, 1947–1957," http://www.lib.niu.edu/1993/ihy930341.html; Truman to William M. Byrne, October 19, 1950, quoted in Goldman, *Picking Federal Judges,* 76; Abrams, *Justices and Presidents,* 241; Epstein, *Advice and Consent,* 68; Lender, *This Honorable Court,* 160–161; Kermit L. Hall and Kevin T. McGuire, *Institutions of American Democracy: The Judicial Branch* (New York: Oxford University Press, 2005), 153; Sean J. Savage, "Truman in Historical, Popular and Political Memory," in Daniel S. Margolies, ed., *A Companion to Harry S. Truman* (Chichester, UK: Blackwell, 2012), 14.

8. Chardavoyne, *Eastern District of Michigan,* 258; "The Effects of Sentencing Councils on Sentencing Disparity," FJC Staff Paper, 1981, 1–2.

9. The Durham Rule, introduced by Bazelon in Durham v. U.S., 214 F.2d 862 (C.A. D.C., 1954), found that "an accused is not criminally responsible if his unlawful act was the product of mental disease or defect."; Morris, *District of Columbia Circuit* 118; Kim Eisler, *The Last Liberal: Justice William J. Brennan, Jr. and the Decisions That Transformed America* (Washington, D.C.: Beard, 2003), 202 (Bazelon a dangerous liberal to conservatives); David M. O'Brien, *What Process Is Due?: Courts and Science-Policy Disputes* (Santa Barbara, CA: Russell Sage, 1988), 156–157 (on Bazelon and administrative agency regulation); Alan Dershowitz, *Chutzpah* (New York: Simon and Schuster, 1992), 58–59 (Bazelon an inspiring mentor).

10. Goldman, *Picking Federal Judges,* 68; Michael R. Gardner, *Harry Truman and Civil Rights: Moral Courage and Political Risks* (Carbondale: Southern Illinois Press, 2002), 152–153; Kermit Hall, "William Henry Hastie," in Vile, ed., *Great American Lawyers* (Santa Barbara, CA: ABC-CLIO, 2001), 343–349.

11. Eric A. Chiappinelli, "Harold Hitz Burton," in Hall et al., eds., *Oxford Companion,* 106–107; "Sherman Minton," in ibid., 551–552; Truman and Vinson: James E. St. Clair and Linda C. Gugin, *Chief Justice Fred M. Vinson of Kentucky, A Political Biography* (Lexington: University of Kentucky Press, 2002), 154, 190; Justice Douglas quoted in William Dumnarski, *The Great Justices,* 46–47; Noah Feldman, *Scorpions: The Battles and Triumphs of FDR's Great Supreme*

Court Justices (New York: Hachette, 2010), 298 and after. Also, here and after, material adapted from Hoffer, Hoffer, and Hull, *Supreme Court*, 307–310.

12. St. Clair and Gugin, *Vinson*, 176–178; Richard Kluger, *Simple Justice: The History of Brown v. Board of Education and Black America's Struggle for Equality* (New York: Knopf, 2011); 244; Michal Belknap, *The Vinson Court: Justices, Rulings, and Legacy* (Santa Barbara: ABC-CLIO, 2004), 35–41; Cushman, *Courtwatchers*, 175.

13. Mimi Clark Gronlund, *Supreme Court Justice Tom C. Clark: A Life of Service* (Austin: University of Texas Press, 2010), a "loving" biography by his daughter.

14. Alexander Wohl, *Father, Son, and Constitution: How Justice Tom Clark and Attorney General Ramsey Clark Shaped American Democracy* (Lawrence: University Press of Kansas, 2013), 88–93 (civil rights work), 82–154 (Vinson Court).

15. Linda C. Gugin and James E. St. Clair, *Sherman Minton: New Deal Senator, Cold War Justice* (Indianapolis: Indian Historical Society, 1997), 179, 180, 204, 210, 215, 217; N. E. H. Hull, "Sherman Minton," in Hall et al., eds., *Oxford Companion*, On changing titles of appeals courts: Judicial Code of 1948, Act of June 25, 1948, 62 Stat. 869, 985.

16. Edward McWhinny, 1957, quoted in Schick, *Learned Hand's Court*, 12.

17. Schick, *Learned Hand's Court*, 219–303 (Clark and Frank); Gunther, *Hand*, 521–535. Clark was certainly capable of pushing other judges around, playing a major role in getting a number of judges very advanced in age to step down from their posts as chief judges; Fish, *Politics of Judicial Administration*, 214–215.

18. David M. Dorsen, *Henry Friendly: Greatest Judge of His Era* (Cambridge, MA: Harvard University Press, 2012), 72–75, 89, 95, 99, 100–101, 154; Henry J. Friendly, *Benchmarks* (Chicago: University of Chicago Press, 1967); Friendly, *Federal Jurisdiction: A General View* (New York: Columbia University Press, 1973); Friendly, *The Federal Administrative Agencies: The Need for Better Definition of Standards* (Cambridge, MA: Harvard University Press, 1962).

19. Bazelon quoted in Morris, *District of Columbia Circuit*, 159; Bazelon-Burger controversy, ibid., 202–203; lack of congeniality, ibid., 323; seed bed, ibid., 363.

20. For the FDR plan for the postwar world see Elizabeth Borgwardt, *A New Deal for the World: America's Vision for Human Rights* (Cambridge: Belknap Press of Harvard University Press, 2007), 5, 78, 139 and after. The term "superpowers" originated with Professor William T. R. Fox in his book *Superpowers: The United States, Britain, and the Soviet Union—Their Responsibility for Peace* (New York: Harcourt, Brace, 1944). The term Cold War originated in an article George Orwell wrote in the *Observer* on March 10, 1946.

21. The full text of Executive Order 9835, "Prescribing Procedures for the Administration of an Employees Loyalty Program in the Executive Branch of the Government, March 21, 1947" can be found at http://teachingamericanhistory.org/library/document/executive-order-9835/.

22. Patterson, *Grand Expectations*, 187–205; Ellen Schrecker, *Many Are the Crimes: McCarthyism in America* (Boston: Little, Brown, 1998), 241 and after; George Martin, *Causes and Conflicts: A Centennial History of the Association of the Bar of the City of New York* (Boston: Houghton Mifflin, 1970), 274. See, generally, David Caute, *The Great Fear: The Anti-Communist Purge Under Truman and Eisenhower* (New York: Simon and Schuster, 1978).

23. Internal Security Act of 1950, 64 Stat. 987; Albertson v. Subversive Activities Control Board, 382 U.S. 70 (1965) (members of the Communist Party were not required to register with the control board, as it violated their right against self-incrimination).

24. William L. O'Neill, *America High: The Years of Confidence, 1945–1960* (New York: Simon and Schuster, 1989), 152; Ronald Radosh, *The Rosenberg File* (New Haven: Yale University Press, 1997), 129.

25. Allen Weinstein, *Perjury: The Hiss-Chambers Case*, 3rd ed. (Palo Alto, CA: Hoover Institution, 2013), 189–192.

26. Weinstein, *Perjury*, 437–526; G. Edward White, *Alger Hiss's Looking-Glass Wars: The Covert Life of a Soviet Spy* (New York: Oxford University Press, 2004), 75–77.

27. Radosh and Milton, *The Rosenberg File*, 1–19, 48–88.

28. It is a basic canon of the conduct of federal judges that "a judge should not initiate, permit, or consider ex parte communications or consider other communications concerning a pending or impending matter that are made outside the presence of the parties or their lawyers" (quoting the

current Judicial Conference Code of Conduct for Federal Judges, canon three). http://www. uscourts.gov/RulesAndPolicies/CodesOfConduct/CodeConductUnitedStatesJudges. aspx. A similar admonition appeared in the 1924 ABA model code for judges canon 17: "He should not permit private interviews, arguments or communications designed to influence his judicial action, where interests to be affected thereby are not represented before him, except in cases where provision is made by law for ex parte application." http://www. americanbar.org/content/dam/aba/migrated/cpr/pic/1924_canons.authcheckdam.pdf. While prosecutors have absolute immunity for misconduct in the course of their official duties, including colluding with the bench, see See Ashelman v. Pope, 793 F.2d 1072, 1078 (9th Cir. 1986), it is a nevertheless a violation of prosecutorial ethics to conspire with a judge. See Leslie E. Williams, "The Civil Regulation of Prosecutors," *Fordham Law Review* 67 (1999), 3461.

29.	Radosh and Milton, *Rosenberg File*, 275–290, 402–410, 428–430; James D. Zirin, *The Mother Court: Tales of Cases that Mattered in America's Greatest Trial Court* (Chicago: ABA, 2014), 91.

30.	Rosenberg v. United States, 346 U.S. 273, 289 (1953) (Vinson, C.J.). Douglas faced criticism too, including accusations of "grandstanding." Howard Ball, "Loyalty, Treason, and the State: An Examination of Justice William O. Douglas' Style, Substance, and Anguish," in Stephen L. Wasby, *He Shall Not Pass This Way Again: the Legacy of Justice William O. Douglas* (Pittsburgh: University of Pittsburgh Press, 1990), 24.

31.	Gerende v. Board of Supervisors of Elections of Baltimore, 341 U.S. 56 (1951); Garner v. Board of Public Works, 341 U.S. 716 (1951).

32.	New York Education Law of 1949, Section 3022, Thompson v. Wallin, 301 N.Y. 476 (1950); Marjorie Heins, *Priests of Our Democracy: The Supreme Court, Academic Freedom, and the Anti-Communist Purge* (New York: New York University Press, 2013), 76 and after; 301 N.Y. at 487, 488 (Lewis, J.).

33.	Adler v. Board of Education, 342 U.S. 485, 493 (1952) (Minton, J.); Heins, *Priests of Our Democracy*, 118–131.

34.	342 U.S. at 496–497 (Black, J.); 342 U.S. at 498 (Frankfurter, J.); 342 U.S. at 508 (Douglas, J.).

35.	Michael D. Bowen, *The Roots of Modern Conservatism: Dewey, Taft, and the Battle for the Soul of the Republican Party* (Chapel Hill: University of North Carolina Press, 2011), 49–51; James Gross, *Broken Promise: The Subversion Of U.S. Labor Relations* (Philadelphia: Temple University Press, 2010), 73–74; American Communications Association v. Douds, 339 U.S. 382 (1950).

36.	See, e.g., Michal Belknap, "Cold War in the Courtroom: The Foley Square Communist Trials," in Belknap, ed., *American Political Trials*, rev. ed. (New York: Praeger, 1994), 211 and after.

37.	J. Woodford Howard, "Harold R. Medina," in Vile, ed., *Great American Judges*, 2:512–523.

38.	United States v. Dennis, 183 F.2d 201, 212 (2nd Cir. 1950) (Hand, J.); U.S. v. Carroll Towing Co. 159 F.2d 169 (2nd Cir. 1947) (L. Hand, J.).

39.	Dennis v. U.S., 341 U.S. 494, 510 (1951) (Vinson, J.); 341 U.S. at 525, 527, 539, 540 (Frankfurter, J.); 341 U.S. at 561 (Jackson, J.).

40.	341 U.S. at 580 (Black, J.); 341 U.S. at 581, 583 (Douglas, J.).

41.	Habeas Corpus Act of 1948, 62 Stat. 967 (28 U.S.C. sec. 2241, section d.); Charles Doyle, "Federal Habeas Corpus: a Brief Legal Overview," April 26, 2006, Congressional Research Service, 7–10. On the mix of statutory, procedural, and constitutional questions see Yaekel, *Federal Courts*, 576–580.

42.	"Permissive society": Alan Petigny, *The Permissive Society: America, 1941–1965* (New York: Cambridge University Press, 2009), passim; "soft on crime": Nolan E. Jones, "Three Strikes and You're Out: A Symbolic Crime Policy," in Darnell Felix Hawkins et al., eds., *Crime Control and Social Justice: The Delicate Balance* (Westport, CT: Greenwood, 2003), 53; Robert R. Sullivan, "Neo-Liberal Criminal Justice," in Kevin Stenson and Robert R. Sullivan, eds., *Crime, Risk, and Justice* (New York: Routledge, 2012), 40.

43.	Michael Klarman, *From Jim Crow to Civil Rights: The Supreme Court and the Struggle for Racial Equality* (New York: Oxford University Press, 2004), 325 ("Not until 1959 did he declare that 'segregation is morally wrong'"); Dwight Eisenhower to James Byrnes, August 14, 1953, Eisenhower Presidential Library; James Byrnes to Dwight Eisenhower, November 20, 1953, Eisenhower Presidential Library.

44. Dwight D. Eisenhower, "Annual Message to the Congress on the State of the Union," February 2, 1953, http://www.eisenhower.archives.gov/all_about_ike/speeches/1953_state_of_the_union.pdf.

45. Mary Dudziak, *Cold War Civil Rights: Race and the Image of American Democracy* (Princeton: Princeton University Press, 2011), 27 and after.

46. Mark Tushnet, *The NAACP's Legal Strategy Against Segregated Education, 1925–1950* (Chapel Hill: University of North Carolina Press, 1987), 105–137.

47. Jack Greenberg, *Crusaders in the Courts: How a Dedicated Band of Lawyers Fought for Civil Rights in the Courts* (New York: Basic, 1994), 107.

48. Tushnet, *NAACP's Legal Strategy against Segregated Education,* 47–48; Genna Rae McNeil, *Groundwork: Charles Hamilton Houston and the Struggle for Civil Rights* (Philadelphia: University of Pennsylvania Press, 1983), 151–193.

49. Henderson v. Interstate Commerce Com., 80 F. Supp. 32, 37 (D.C. D. Md. 1948) (Coleman, J.); Larry S. Gibson, *Young Thurgood: The Making of a Supreme Court Justice* (Amherst, NY: Prometheus, 2012), 172–183. For the Supreme Court cases: see, e.g., Bob-Lo Excursion Co. v. Michigan, 333 U.S. 28 (1948) (segregated ferries); Henderson v. United States, 339 U.S. 816 (1950) (segregated dining cars); Shelley v. Kraemer, 334 U.S. 1 (1948) (racially discriminatory housing covenants); Hurd v. Hodge, 334 U.S. 24 (1948) (discrimination in housing sales); Barrows v. Jackson, 346 U.S. 249 (1953) (racially discriminatory covenant); Brotherhood of Railroad Trainmen v. Howard, 343 U.S. 768 (1952) (racially discriminatory conduct of union).

50. Sipuel v. Board of Regents, 199 Okla. 36, 45 (1947) (Welch, J.); Sipuel v. Board of Regents of Univ. of Okla., 332 U.S. 631, 633 (1948) (per curiam).

51. Fisher v. Hurst, 333 U.S. 147, 152 (1948) (Rutledge, J.); Fowler V. Harper, *Justice Rutledge and the Bright Constellation* (Indianapolis: Bobbs-Merrill, 1965), 332; Kramer, *Jim Crow to Civil Rights,* 205–206.

52. McLaurin v. Board of Regents, 339 U.S. 637 (1950).

53. On the choice of precedents, see Richard A. Posner, *How Judges Think* (Cambridge, MA: Harvard University Press, 2008), 45.

54. Brown v. Board of Educ., 98 F. Supp. 797, 798 (D.C. D. Kans. 1951) (Huxman, J.); Kluger, *Simple Justice* 424.

55. Briggs v. Elliott, 98 F. Supp. 529, 531, 532 (D.C. E.D. S.C., 1951) (Parker, J.). On Parker's "venerable dictum of restraint" after *Brown* that the decision merely barred state mandated segregation rather than contemplating unitary school systems, see J. Harvie Wilkinson, *From Brown to Bakke: The Supreme Court and School Integration: 1954–1978* (New York: Oxford University Press, 1981), 113, 81–82. Note that deference to states when it came to their peacekeeping role (and claims of its importance by judges) was not confined to segregation cases. As Justice Reed wrote in Brown v. Allen, 344 U.S. 443, 487 (1953) (Reed, J.), denying relief to a black convict in North Carolina whose confession was coerced and from whose jury persons of color were systematically excluded, "the states are the real guardians of peace and order within their boundaries" and state supreme court findings must be given deference by the federal courts.

56. Kluger, *Simple Justice,* 141–144; John J. Parker, "The Federal Jurisdiction and Recent Attacks Upon It," Address to the Georgia Bar Association, June 8, 1932, *American Bar Association Journal* 18 (1932), 433. The U.S. Supreme Court found the grandfather clauses violated the Fifteenth Amendment in Guinn v. U.S. 238 U.S. 347 (1915). The failed nomination of Parker is discussed in Stephen W. Stathis, *Landmark Debates in Congress* (Washington, D.C: CQ Press, 2008), 303–310.

57. Christopher W. Schmidt, "J. Waties Waring," in Newman, ed., *Yale Biographical Dictionary,* 570–571; Tinsley E. Yarbrough, *A Passion for Justice: J. Waties Waring and Civil Rights* (New York: Oxford University Press, 1987), 195–197; 98 F. Supp, at 540 (Waring, J.).

58. Davis v. County Sch. Bd., 103 F. Supp. 337, 338, 339 (D.C. E.D. Va., 1952) (Bryan, J.).

59. Kluger, *Simple Justice,* 423 and after.

60. "Deeply regretted" in Earl Warren, *Memoirs of Earl Warren* (New York: Doubleday, 1977), 146; and California politics: G. Edward White, *Earl Warren: A Public Life* (New York: Oxford University Press, 1982), 26–128; leadership role and reputation: Bernard Schwartz, *Super*

Chief : Earl Warren and His Supreme Court, A Judicial Biography (New York: New York University Press, 1983), passim, and Schwartz, *Decision: How the Supreme Court Decides Cases* (New York: Oxford University Press, 1997), 88–95.

61. Kluger, *Simple Justice*, 668–676; Klarman, *Jim Crow to Civil Rights*, 290–311; James T. Patterson, *Brown v. Board of Education: A Civil Rights Milestone and its Troubled Legacy* (New York: Oxford University Press, 2001), 46–69.

62. Patterson, *Brown*, 56.

63. Kluger, *Simple Justice*, 617.

64. Warren lobbying: Kluger, *Simple Justice*, 699–702. Brown v. Board of Education, 347 U.S. 483, 493 (1954) (Warren, C.J.).

65. 347 U.S. at 493.

66. 347 U.S. at 494.

67. 347 U.S. at 495 (Warren, C.J.).

68. Bolling v. Sharpe, 347 U.S. 497 (1954).

69. Jack M. Balkin, "Rewriting *Brown*," in Balkin, ed., *What Brown v. Board of Education Should Have Said: The Nation's Top Legal Experts Rewrite America's Landmark Civil Rights Decision* (New York: New York University Press, 2002), 50–52.

70. Thus the Court did not resurrect Justice John Marshal Harlan's dissent in *Plessy*, which, prescient for its time, was still ahead of the Court's jurisprudence in 1954.

71. Klarman, *From Jim Crow to Civil Rights*, 312–320; Patterson, *Brown*, 78–85; John T. Fassett, *New Deal Justice: The Life of Stanley Reed of Kentucky* (New York: Vintage, 1994), 550–575.

72. 347 U.S. at 495 (Warren, C.J.).

Chapter 12

1. Robert J. Cottrol, Raymond T. Diamond, and Leland B. Ware, *Brown v. Board of Education: Caste, Culture, and the Constitution* (Lawrence: University Press of Kansas, 2004), 183–232; James T. Patterson, *Grand Expectations: The United States, 1945–1974* (New York: Oxford University Press, 1996), 287–291, 299–310,444, 487–505, 568–579, 593–636.

2. U.S. Courts, "Over Two Decades, Civil Rights Cases Rise 27 Percent," Judiciary News, June 9, 2014, http://www.uscourts.gov/news/2014/06/09/over-two-decades-civil-rights-cases-rise-27-percent.

3. The involvement of federal courts in civil rights enforcement dates to the first Civil Rights Acts of the Reconstruction Era. See, e.g., Robert Kaczorowski, *The Politics of Judicial Interpretation: The Federal Courts, Department of Justice, and Civil Rights, 1866–1876* (New York: Fordham University Press, 2005).

4. Klarman, *Jim Crow*, 347–349; Patterson, *Brown*, 70–85. Just how many, or to what extent, white southerners opposed desegregation is a still unanswered question. Certainly massive resistance was "a particularly obnoxious species of popular constitutionalism," something akin to the popular defense of slavery in the later antebellum years of the South. Mark Golub, "Remembering Massive Resistance to School Desegregation," *Law and History Review* 31 (2013), 495. "Full compliance would not and did not come until [white] southerners had themselves assumed responsibility for controlling and punishing racist violence," Michal R. Belknap, *Federal Law and Southern Order: Racial Violence and Constitutional Conflict in the Post-Brown South* (Athens: University of Georgia Press, 1987), 228.

5. Jackson (Mississippi) *Daily News* May 18, 1954; Southern Manifesto on Integration, March 12, 1956, 84th Cong. 2nd Sess. *Congressional Record*, v. 102, part 4, pp. 4459–4460; Numan V. Bartley, *The New South, 1945–1980* (Baton Rouge: Louisiana State University Press, 1995), 198. Although the signers were overwhelmingly Democrats, two Republican Virginia congressmen, Joel Broyhill and Richard Poff, also signed.

6. Patterson, *Brown*, 117; Klarman, *Civil Rights*, 160; Kluger, *Simple Justice*, 734–735.

7. Brown v. Board of Education, 349 U.S. 294, 298, 300 (1955) (Warren C.J.); Earl Warren, *The Memoirs of Earl Warren* (New York: Doubleday, 1977), 299; Russell L. Weaver et al., *Inside Constitutional Law: What Matters and Why* (New York: Aspen, 2009), 234 and after.

8. Gibson v. Board of Public Instruction, 246 F.2d 913, 915 (5th Cir. 1957); Gibson v. Board of Public Instruction, 170 F. Supp. 454, 457 (D.C. S.D. Fla. 1958) (Lieb, J.); Gibson v. Board of Public Instruction, 272 F.2d 763 (5th Cir. 1959). On the judge who refuses to follow the

dictates of the higher court, see, e.g., Jeffrey Brand-Ballard, *The Limits of Legality: The Ethics of Lawless Judging* (New York: Oxford University Press, 2010), 3–11. In this case, one cannot presume that Lieb misunderstood the precedent. He simply thought it wrong and refused to follow it.

9. Thomas Tobin, "Where Are They Now?" *St. Petersburg, Tampa Bay Times*, May 21, 2003, sptimes.com/2003/05/21/Tampabay/Where_are_they_now.shtml.

10. Quotations in Charles Zelden, *Thurgood Marshall: Race, Rights, and the Struggle for a More Perfect Union* (New York: Routledge, 2013), 98–99.

11. Hall v. West, 335 F. 2d 481, 484 (5th Cir. 1964) (Wisdom, J.); Hall v. St. Helena Parish School Board, 233 F. Supp. 136 (D.C. E.D. La. 1964) (West, J.).

12. Earl Benjamin Bush et al., Plaintiffs v. Orleans Parish School Board et al., Defendants, 138 F. Supp. 337, 340, 341 (E.D. La. 1956) (Wright, J.); Patricia Wald, "J. Skelly Wright," in Newman, ed., *Yale Biographical Dictionary*, 605–606; Arthur S. Miller, *A Capacity for Outrage: The Judicial Odyssey of J. Skelly Wright* (Westport, CT: Greenwood, 1984), 71 and after.

13. Freyer and Dixon, *Democracy and Judicial Independence*, 215–242; Jack Bass, *Taming the Storm: The Life and Times of Judge Frank M. Johnson, Jr., and the South's Fight over Civil Rights* (Athens: University of Georgia Press, 2002), 52–53; Tinsley E. Yarbrough, *Judge Frank Johnson and Human Rights in Alabama* (Tuscaloosa: University of Alabama Press, 1981), 49.

14. Anne Emanuel, *Elbert Parr Tuttle: Chief Jurist of the Civil Rights Revolution* (Athens: University of Georgia Press, 2011), 153, 158.

15. Civil Rights Cases 109 U.S. 3 (1883); Heart of Atlanta Motel, Inc. v. United States, 231 F. Supp. 393, 395, 396 (D.C. N.D. Ga. 1964) (Tuttle, J.). The Supreme Court upheld the panel in Heart of Atlanta Motel, Inc. v. U.S. 379 U.S. 241 (1964).

16. This point is not limited to civil rights litigation, although it provided the most numerous examples of what may be called district court nullification. See, e.g., Chad Westerland, Jeffrey A. Segal, Lee Epstein, Charles M. Cameron, and Scott Comparato, "Strategic Defiance and Compliance in the U.S. Courts of Appeals," *American Journal of Political Science*, 54 (2010), 891–905; Charles A. Johnson, "Law, Politics, and Judicial Decision Making: Lower Federal Court Uses of Supreme Court Decisions," *Law and Society Review* 21 (1987), 325–340.

17. Robert A. Pratt, *The Color of Their Skin: Education and Race in Richmond, Virginia, 1953–1989* (Charlottesville: University of Virginia Press, 1993), 34–36; James E. Ryan, *Five Miles Away; A World Apart: One City, Two Schools, and the Story of Educational Opportunity in Modern America* (New York: Oxford University Press, 2010), 47–48; J. Lindsay Almond Jr., Oral History Interview, February 7, 1968, transcript in John F. Kennedy Oral History Program, p. 4; Matthew D. Lassiter and Andrew B. Lewis, "Massive Resistance Revisited: Virginia's White Moderates and the Byrd Organization," in Lassiter and Lewis, ed., *The Moderates' Dilemma: Massive Resistance to School Desegregation in Virginia* (Charlottesville: University of Virginia Press, 1998), 6–9; Green v. County School Board of New Kent County, 382 F. 2d 338 (4th Cir. 1967); Green v. County School Board of New Kent County, 391 U.S. 430 (1968).

18. Harvey C. Couch, *A History of the Fifth Circuit, 1891–1981* (Washington, D.C.: Judicial Conference of the U.S. Courts, 1984), 148–149; Deborah J. Barrow and Thomas G. Walker, *A Court Divided: The Fifth Circuit Court of Appeals and the Politics of Judicial Reform* (New Haven: Yale University Press, 1988), 55–61, 123, 224–251; Harrison and Wheeler, *Creating the Federal Judiciary*, 26.

19. Morris, *Eighth Circuit*, 62–169; Michael Molyneux, "Ronald Davies, 91, Who Issued Little Rock Order, Is Dead," *New York Times*, April 21, 1996.

20. Tony Freyer, *Little Rock on Trial, Cooper v. Aaron and School Desegregation* (Lawrence: University Press of Kansas, 2007), 133, 144–146; Cooper v. Aaron, 163 F. Supp. 13 (D.C. E.D. Ark. 1958); 257 F. 2d 33, 37, 39 (8th Cir. 1958) (Matthes, J.); 257 F. 2d at 41 (Gardner, J.).

21. 358 U.S. 1 (1958); Freyer, *Little Rock*, 210–211.

22. Maurice Isserman and Michael Kazin, *America Divided: The Civil War of the 1960s*, 2nd. ed. (New York: Oxford University Press, 2004), 30–32; Patterson, *Grand Expectations*, 400–405.

23. Donnie Williams and Wayne Greenhaw, *The Thunder of Angels: The Montgomery Bus Boycott and the People Who Broke the Back of Jim Crow* (Chicago: Chicago Review Press, 2006), 212–221; Browder v. Gayle, 141 F. Supp 707, 713, 717 (D.C. M.D. Ala. 1956) (Rives, J.).

24. Barrow and Walker, *A Court Divided*, 15–16.
25. 141 F. Supp at 718, 720, 721 (Lynne, J.); Douglas Martin, "Seybourn Lynne, 93; Ruled in Civil Rights Case," *New York Times*, January 12, 2000.
26. Isserman and Kazin, *America Divided*, 33–34.
27. Raymond Arsenault, *Freedom Riders: 1961 and the Struggle for Racial Justice* (New York: Oxford University Press, 2006), 367 (denial of habeas corpus relief), 507 (general inaction of federal courts); Isserman and Kazin, *America Divided*, 34–35; Patterson, *Grand Expectations*, 468–471.
28. Meredith v. Fair, 199 F. Supp. 754, 757 (D.C. S.D. Miss., 1961) (Mize, J.).
29. Meredith v. Fair, 305 F.2d 343, 344 (5th Cir.) (Wisdom, J.).
30. John M. Spivack, "Richard Taylor Rives and Benjamin F. Cameron: The Varieties of Southern Judges," *Southern Studies* 1 (1990): 225–41; John W. Dean, *The Rehnquist Choice: The Untold Story of the Nixon Appointment That Redefined the Supreme Court* (New York: Simon and Schuster, 2002), 20; Morton L. Wallerstein, *The Public Career of Simon E. Sobeloff* (Boston: Marlborough House, 1975), passim; Sanford J. Rosen, "Judge Sobeloff's Public School Race Decisions," *Maryland Law Review* 34 (1974), 498–531.
31. Nicholas Andrew Bryant, *The Bystander: John F. Kennedy and the Struggle for Black Equality* (New York: Basic Books, 2006), 116 and after (need for black votes), 120 and after (civil rights bills in the Senate), 174 and after (civil rights as Kennedy policy).
32. Cahan, *The Court that Shaped America*, 144. Of course, Parsons had—had to have—the support of the Daley machine and Senator Paul Douglas. Every federal judgeship in the Northern District of Illinois had their stamp of approval in these years. Goulden, *Benchwarmers*, 119–120.
33. Goldman, *Picking Federal Judges*, 129–130, 183–184.
34. Dumnarski, *Federal Judges Revealed*, 117–118; Howard Ball, *A Defiant Life: Thurgood Marshall and the Persistence of Racism in America* (New York: Crown, 1999), 57–65, 115–140; Kluger, *Simple Justice*, 173–238; Mark Tushnet, *Making Constitutional Law: Thurgood Marshall and the Supreme Court* (New York: Oxford University Press, 1997), 11–12 (2nd Circuit confirmation), 18–19 (solicitor general); *Supreme Justice: The Writings and Speeches of Thurgood Marshall* (Philadelphia: University of Pennsylvania Press, 2003), 147.
35. A. Leon Higginbotham, *Shades of Freedom: Racial Politics and Presumptions of the American Legal Process* (New York: Oxford University Press, 1996), 3–17.
36. Motley, *Equal Justice Under Law: An Autobiography*, 215–216; Tushnet, *Making Civil Rights Law*, 72 and after.
37. David A. Nichols, *A Matter of Justice: Eisenhower and the Beginning of the Civil Rights Revolution* (New York: Simon and Schuster, 2007), 100–108; Ted Sorensen, *Kennedy* (New York: Harper and Row, 1965), 273; Robert A. Caro, *The Passage of Power: The Years of Lyndon Johnson* (New York: Knopf, 2012), 443; Harry N. Schieber, "Introduction," in Schieber, ed., *Earl Warren and the Warren Court: The Legacy in American and Foreign Law* (Lanham, MD: Lexington, 2007), 11,14–16. The question of influence is a complex one, and in Warren's case, might invite "broad and vapid generalizations." G. Edward White, "Earl Warren's Influence on the Warren Court," in Tushnet, ed., *Earl Warren*, 37, 40, 41; Kermit A. Hall, "The Warren Court in Historical Perspective," in Bernard Schwartz, ed., *The Warren Court, A Retrospective* (New York: Oxford University Press, 1996), 296. As well, here and after, material adapted from Hoffer, Hoffer, and Hull, *Supreme Court*, 335–340.
38. Tinsley E. Yarbrough, *John Marshall Harlan: Great Dissenter of the Warren Court* (New York: Oxford University Press, 1992), 92, 95–105.
39. "Frankfurter without the mustard" quoted in David J. Garrow, *Liberty and Sexuality: The Right to Privacy and the Making of Roe v. Wade* (New York: Scribner's, 1994), 184. Harlan was an exponent of the "legal process" school of constitutional adjudication best seen in the Harvard Law School Professors Henry Hart and Albert Sacks' case book on the legal process, and Hart and Herbert Wechsler's case book *The Federal Courts and the Federal System* (1953). On the influence of Frankfurter on Harlan, see Charles Nesson, "The Harlan-Frankfurter Connection: An Aspect of Justice Harlan's Education," *New York University Law Review* 36 (1991), 179–198.
40. John Chancellor, "Forward," in Herbert Brownell, *Advising Ike: The Memoirs of Attorney General Herbert Brownell* (Lawrence: University Press of Kansas, 1993), xiv; Seth Stern and

Stephen Wermiel, *Justice Brennan, Liberal Champion* (New York: Houghton Mifflin, 2010), 71–72, and after.

41. Kim Isaac Eisler, *The Last Liberal: Justice William J. Brennan, Jr. and the Decisions That Transformed America* (Santa Ana, CA: Beard, 2003), 167; Bradley C. S. Watson, "Progressivism and the Decline of the Rule of Law," in Anthony Arthur Peacock, ed., *Freedom and the Rule of Law* (Lanham, MD: Rowman and Littlefield, 2010), 182; Ruth Bader Ginsburg, "Closing Remarks for Symposium on Justice Brennan and the 'Living Constitution,'" *California Law Review* 95 (2007), 2017–2022.

42. Clare Cushman, Supreme Court Clerks, 499–523: "Memories of Clerking for Potter Stewart, by Monroe E. Price, with Thomas Kauper, Alan R. Novak, Steven M. Umin, Thomas D. Rowe Jr., David M. Schulte, Frederick T. Davis, and Daniel R. Fischel," ms. in possession of the author; Sidney M. Milkis, "Lyndon Johnson, The Great Society, and the 'Twilight' of the Modern Presidency," in Milkis and Jerome M. Milieur, eds., *The Great Society and the High Tide of Liberalism* (Amherst: University of Massachusetts Press, 2005), 16–28 (Johnson and the Civil Rights Movement); Douglas Charles Rossinow, *Visions of Progress: The Left-liberal Tradition in America* (Philadelphia: University of Pennsylvania Press, 2008), 239.

43. Here and after material adapted from Hoffer, Hoffer, and Hull, *Supreme Court*, 341–346.

44. Dennis Hutchinson, *The Man Who Once Was Whizzer White: A Portrait of Justice Byron R. White* (New York: Free Press, 1998), 309 and after (appointment), 382 and after (judicial philosophy), 397 (deference).

45. Escobedo v. Illinois, 378 U.S. 478 (1964); Griswold v. Connecticut, 381 U.S. 479 (1965); David L. Stebenne, *Arthur J. Goldberg: New Deal Liberal* (New York: Oxford University Press, 1996), 317.

46. Stebenne, *Goldberg*, 360–363; Laura Kalman, *Abe Fortas, A Biography* (New Haven: Yale University Press, 1990), 243–245.

47. Kalman, *Fortas*, 19–20 and after.

48. Gideon v. Wainwright, 372 U.S. (1963); Del Dickson, ed., "Headnote to Gideon v. Wainwright," in *The Supreme Court in Conference (1940–1985): The Private Discussions Behind Nearly 300 Supreme Court Decisions* (New York: Oxford University Press, 2001), 502; Anthony Lewis, *Gideon's Trumpet* (New York: Knopf, 1964), 178–183, 189–190.

49. In re Gault, 387 U.S. 1 (1967), David S. Tanenhaus, *The Constitutional Rights of Children: In re Gault and Juvenile Justice* (Lawrence: University Press of Kansas, 2011), 82–92; Tinker v. Des Moines, 393 U.S. 503 (1969); John W. Johnson, *The Struggle for Student Rights: Tinker v. Des Moines and the 1960s* (Lawrence: University Press of Kansas, 1997), 170–174.

50. David N. Atkinson, *Leaving the Bench: Supreme Court Justices at the End* (Lawrence: University Press of Kansas, 1999), 8, 179–180.

51. Colegrove v. Green, 328 U.S. 549 (1946); Zelden, *Battle for the Black Ballot*, 109–132; Terry v. Adams, 345 U.S. 461 (1953). The Voting Rights Act of 1965 confirmed these holdings until the Supreme Court found Congress lacked a sufficient basis for continuing federal court supervision with some exceptions in Shelby County v. Holder, 571 U.S. 193 (2013).

52. Baker v. Carr, 369 U.S. 186 (1962) (Brennan, J.). For "political thicket," see 328 U.S. at 556 (Frankfurter, J.).

53. Gray v. Sanders, 372 U.S. 368, 381 (1963) (Douglas, J.).

54. Sims v. Frink, 208 F. Supp. 431432, 437 (D.C. M.D. Ala., 1962) (per curiam).

55. Lucas v. Forty-Fourth General Assembly, 377 U.S. 713, 738 (1964) (Warren, C.J.); Reynolds v. Sims, 377 U.S. 533, 566, 580 (1964) (Warren, C.J.).

56. Germano v. Kerner, 241 F. Supp. 715, 717, 720 (D.C. N.D. Ill. 1964) (Campbell, J.); Scott v. Germano, 381 U.S. 407, 409 (1965) (per curiam).

57. Carl Auerbach, "Commentary," in Nelson Polsby, ed., *Reapportionment in the 1970s* (Berkeley: University of California Press, 1971), 74–75;

58. Voting Rights Act of 1965, 79 Stat. 437 42 U.S.C. §§ 1973–1973bb-1; South Carolina v. Katzenbach, 383 U. S. 301 (1966); Allen v. State Board of Elections, 393 U.S. 544, 569 (1969) (Warren, C.J.). Note that as in the first desegregation cases, the Supreme Court had to reverse the judgment of the district court for the state defendant, compare Allen v. State Board of Elections, 268 F. Supp. 218 (C.C. E.D. Va. 1967) with 393 U.S. 572. Section 5 was renewed and amended by Congress four times, a twenty-five-year extension signed into law

by President George W. Bush in 2006. But in 2013 the Supreme Court in *Shelby County v. Holder* (2013) substantially revised *Allen*, striking down Section 4(b) of the Act, which contained the conditions determining Section 5 preclearance. Other sections of the Act regarding poll taxes, literacy tests, coercion by any person, refusal to count the vote of a qualified voter, and providing for language assistance to qualified voters remained in place. Shelby County v. Holder, 570 U.S. 193 (2013).

59. Criminal Justice Act of 1964, Public Law 88 -455, 78 Stat. 522, 1970 amendment at 84 Stat 916, PL 91–447, codified at 18 U.S.C. Sec. 3006A; Bail Reform Act of 1966 Public Law 89–465, 80 STAT 214, substantially revised by the Bail Reform Act of 1984; 98 Stat 1976, PL 98–473, codified at 18 U.S.C. Sec. 3142, Patricia M. Wald and Daniel J. Freed, "The Bail Reform Act of 1966: A Practitioner's Primer," *A.B.A. Journal* 52 (1966) 940.

60. Federal Magistrates Act, PL 90–1107, 82 Stat. 1107, codified at 28 U.S.C. Sec. 6631 et seq, the Federal Magistrates Act at the Federal Judicial Center history site, under Landmark Judicial Legislation at http://www.fjc.gov/history/home.nsf/page/landmark_19.htm. Judicial Panel on Multidistrict Litigation created in April 1968, 82 Stat. Sec. 109, P.L. 90–296, codified at 28 USC § 1407; the Judicial Panel on Multi-district Litigation, at the Federal Judicial Center history site, under Courts of Special Jurisdiction at http://www.fjc.gov/history/home.nsf/page/courts_special_jpml.html.

61. Federal Judicial Center created by 81 Stat. 670, codified at 28 U.S.C. Sec. 620 et seq, Russell Wheeler, "Empirical Research and the Politics of Judicial Administration: Creating the Federal Judicial Center," *Law and Contemporary Problems* (1988), 31; a general description of the FJC appears at its website, http://www.fjc.gov/. This paragraph is the work of Russell Wheeler, edited by the authors.

62. Kalman, *Fortas*, 359–367. The attack on Fortas was orchestrated by those opposed to his jurisprudence rather than those offended by his personal conduct. It began before the revelations of fiscal improprieties. Laura Kalman, "The Long Reach of the 1960s: Confirmation Struggles and the Making of the Modern Supreme Court," Plenary Lecture, Annual Meeting of the American Society for Legal History, Washington D.C., October 31, 2015.

63. Smoke in chambers: Joyce Hens Green, "Oral History of Honorable Joyce Hens Green," December 2, 1999, Historical Society of D.C., Oral History Collection, 110; generally: William L. O'Neill, *Coming Apart: An Informal History of America in the 1960s* (New York: Quadrangle, 1971), 360–392.

64. Bruce Ragsdale, "The Chicago Seven: 1960s Radicalism in the Courts," Federal Judicial Center, 2008, 3; *Report of the National Commission on the Causes and Prevention of Violence*, [Walker Report] (December 1968), quoted in Frank Kusch, *Battleground Chicago: The Police and the 1968 Democratic National Convention* (Chicago: University of Chicago Press, 2008), 120.

65. "Judge Julius Hoffman, 87, Dies," *New York Times*, July 2, 1983; Rick Perlstein, *Nixonland: The Rise of a President and the Fracturing of America* (New York: Simon and Schuster, 2010), 447–457. Caveat lector: Perlstein, a journalist, had little sympathy for Hoffman's dilemma.

66. Ragsdale, "Chicago Seven" 4, 8.

67. United States v. Dellinger, 472 F.2d 340, 390, 375, 386, 387, 389 (7th Cir. 1972) (Fairchild, J.); Cahan, *Court That Shaped a Nation*, 178–179.

68. Green, "Oral History of Honorable Joyce Hens Green," December 2, 1999, 121; Ragdale, "Chicago Seven," passim; In Re David Dellinger et al. 370 F. Supp. 1304, 1321 (N.D. Ill. 1973) (Gignoux, J.).

69. Neal Devins, "Congress and Judicial Supremacy," in Bruce Peabody, ed., *The Politics of Judicial Independence* (Baltimore: Johns Hopkins University Press, 2011), 52; Goulden, *Benchwarmers*, 123; Cahan, *Court That Shaped America*, 179; White, *Warren*, 308, 311, 319; Warren, *A Republic, If You Can Keep It* (New York: Quadrangle, 1972), 84.

Chapter 13

1. Pew Research Center, "Deconstructing Distrust: How Americans View Government," 23 (Washington, D.C.: Pew Research Center, 1998) (sharpest decline between 1964

and 1974); Richard M. Nixon, "First Inaugural Address," January 20, 1969, http://ava-lon.law.yale.edu/20th_century/nixon1.asp; William O. Douglas, *Points of Rebellion* (New York: Random House, 1970), 6; Arthur Selwyn Miller, "Public Confidence in the Judiciary, Some Notes and Reflections," *Law and Contemporary Problems* (1970), 86; Lloyd Gardner, "The Last Casualty? Richard Nixon and the End of the Vietnam War, 1969–1975," in Marylyn B. Young and Robert Buzzanco, eds., *A Companion to the Vietnam War* (Malden, MA: Blackwell, 2008), 239; Peter Braunstein and Michael William Doyle, "Introduction," in Braunstein and Doyle, eds., *Imagine Nation: The American Counterculture of the 1960s and 70s* (New York: Routledge, 2013), 5–23.

2. Steven W. Hayes and James W. Douglas, "Judicial Administration: Modernizing the Third Branch," in Jack Rabin et al., eds., *Handbook of Public Administration* 3rd ed. (Boca Raton, FL: Taylor & Francis, 2007), 1003; Grant Gilmore, *The Ages of American Law*, 2nd ed. (New Haven: Yale University Press, 2014), 88, Warren E. Burger, "The State of the Federal Judiciary," *American Bar Association Journal* 57 (1971), 855; Earl M. Maltz, *The Chief Justiceship of Warren Burger, 1969–1986* (Columbia: University of South Carolina Press, 2000), 32, 64; Thomas R. Hensley, Kathleen Hale, and Carl Snook, *The Rehnquist Court: Justices, Rulings, and Legacy* (Santa Barbara, CA: ABC-CLIO, 2006), 161, 162.

3. Goldman, *Picking Federal Judges*, 197.

4. Goldman, *Picking Federal Judges*, 198–224, Nixon quote at 198; Kevin J. McMahon, *Nixon's Court: His Challenge to Judicial Liberalism and Its Consequences* (Chicago: University of Chicago Press, 2011), 65–67, 73–75; Kevin Lyles, *The Gatekeepers: Federal District Courts in the Political Process* (Westport, CT: Praeger, 1997), 98–99; Cornell W. Clayton, *The Politics of Justice: The Attorney General and the Making of Legal Policy* (Armonk NY: M.E. Sharpe, 1992), 140.

5. Opinion of Chief Justice Burger is divided more according to the jurisprudential preferences of observers than Burger's own jurisprudence, which was conservative but pragmatic. See, e.g., Robert Henry, "The Players and the Play," in Bernard Schwartz, ed., *The Burger Court: Counter-Revolution or Confirmation?* (New York: Oxford University Press, 1998), 28. A frankly admiring appraisal of Warren Burger's qualities came from the deputy attorney general at the time, Richard Kleindienst. See his *Justice: The Memoirs of an Attorney General* (Ottawa, IL: Jameson, 1985), 113–115. Bernard Schwartz is also generally complimentary in *the Unpublished Opinions of the Burger Court* (New York: Oxford University Press, 1988), 4–7. Here and after material adapted from Hoffer, Hoffer, and Hull, *Supreme Court*, 370–378.

6. Editorial, "Needed: Court Managers," *American Bar Association Journal* 57 (April 1971), 342; NCSC Mission and History, http://www.ncsc.org/About-us/Mission-and-history.aspx; Russell R. Wheeler and Donald W. Jackson, "Judicial Councils and Policy Planning: Continuous Study and Discontinuous Institutions," *The Justice System Journal* 2 (1976), 129; "Warren Burger Leaves Imprint on the Judiciary," *The Third Branch*, July 1995, http://www.uscourts. gov/News/TheThirdBranch/95-07-01/Warren_Burger_Leaves_Imprint_on_the_Judiciary. aspx; Bernard Schwartz, *The History of the Supreme Court* (New York: Oxford University Press, 1995), 313.

7. On the effort to effectuate the proposal of the Commission on Revision of the Federal Court Appellate System, see Senate Report on the Commission, Report 93–742, 93rd Cong. 2nd Sess., p. 4 (conflicts of circuits). Carl Tobias, "Warren Burger and the Administration of Justice," *Villanova Law Review* 41 (1996), 505–515. The Circuit Executive Act of 1971 84 Stat. 1907 provided for an officer to handle the financial, personnel, and other nonjudicial business of the circuit. The Federal Courts Improvement Act of 1982, 96 Stat. 25, merged the U.S. Court of Customs and Patent Appeals and the U.S. Court of Claims to form the U.S. Court of Appeals for the Federal Circuit. Of the twelve judgeships authorized for the Federal Circuit, five were from the U.S. Court of Customs and Patent Appeals and seven from the U.S. Court of Claims.

8. Schwartz, *Supreme Court*, 313; Earl M. Maltz, *The Chief Justiceship of Warren Burger* (Columbia: University of South Carolina Press, 2000), 10–12; Mark V. Tushnet, "The Warren Court as History: An Interpretation," in Tushnet, ed., *The Warren Court in Historical and Political Perspective* (Charlottesville: University of Virginia Press, 1993), 31–32.

9. Richard M. Nixon, *RN: The Memoirs of Richard Nixon* (New York: Grosset and Dunlap, 1978), 420.

10. McMahon, *Nixon's Court*, 70, 117–118; David Alistair Yalof, *Pursuit of Justices: Presidential Politics and the Selection of Supreme Court Nominees* (Chicago: University of Chicago Press, 2001), 105–112; Epstein and Segal, *Advice and Consent*, 55–56; Domnarski, *Federal Judges Revealed*, 112, here and after, text from Hoffer, Hoffer, and Hull, *Supreme Court*, 370–376.

11. Linda Greenhouse, *Becoming Justice Blackmun* (New York: Macmillan, 2006), 186, 235 (transformation from conservative to liberal).

12. A "hard line moderate" whose views were moderated by necessity and practicality. John Calvin Jeffries, *Justice Lewis F. Powell, Jr.* (New York: Fordham University Press, 2001), 169, 366.

13. John A. Jenkins, *The Partisan: The Life of William Rehnquist* (New York: PublicAffairs, 2012), 37 and after (Rehnquist believed that the Fourteenth Amendment should be interpreted narrowly).

14. Jenkins, *Rehnquist*, 84; John W. Dean, *The Rehnquist Choice: The Untold Story of the Nixon Appointment That Redefined the Supreme Court* (New York: Simon and Schuster, 2002), 270–278; David L. Hudson Jr., *The Rehnquist Court: Understanding Its Impact and Legacy* (Westport, CT: Praeger, 2007), 23.

15. See, generally, Stanley Kutler, *The Wars of Watergate: The Last Crisis of Richard Nixon* (New York: Norton, 1992), 200 and after.

16. Roger K. Newman, "John J. Sirica," *Yale Biographical Dictionary*, 498; U.S. v. Liddy, 509 F. 2d. 428, 442 (D.C. Cir. 1974) (Leventhal, J.). For Sirica's account of the trials, see John Sirica, *To Set the Record Straight: The Break-In, the Tapes, the Conspirators, the Pardon* (New York: Norton, 1979).

17. Kutler, *Watergate*, 369.

18. In re Subpoena to Nixon, 360 F. Supp. 1, 9 (D.C. D.C. 1973) (Sirica, J.); United States v. Nixon, 418 U.S. 683, 716 (1974) (Burger, C.J); Kutler, *Watergate*, 547, 548, 562–563. On Marshall, Jefferson, Burr, and the order to provide documentary evidence in Burr's treason trial, see Hoffer, *The Treason Trials of Aaron Burr*, 135–141.

19. Bill Barnhart, Eugene F. Schlickman, and Gene Schlickman, *John Paul Stevens: An Independent Life* (DeKalb: Northern Illinois University Press, 2010), 20 and after (liberal jurisprudence).

20. Goldman, *Picking Federal Judges*, 244–245; Goldman, "Carter's Judicial Appointments: A Lasting Legacy," *Judicature* 64 (1980), 344–355. Laura Kalman has reviewed the Bell correspondence in the Carter Library and found abundant evidence that Bell's say so had a good deal to do with Carter choices. Letter to the authors, November 15, 2014.

21. Federal District and Circuit Judges Act of 1978, 98 Stat 1629–1634; Jack Bass, *Taming the Storm: The Life and Times of Judge Frank M. Johnson, Jr. and the South's Fight over Civil Rights* (New York: Anchor, 1993), 395; Arthur Alarcón, oral history, 1991, Ninth Circuit Historical Society, in Domnarski, *Federal Judges Revealed*, 120; Hon. Carolyn Dineen King, ABA Women Trailblazers in the Law, oral history, July 19, 2010, americanbar.org/content/dam/aba/directories/women_trailblazers/king_interview_1.authcheckdam.pdf, quotations from pages 8 and 47.

22. Morris, *Calmly to Poise the Scales of Justice*, 319–320; "Jimmy Carter," *New Georgia Encyclopedia*, http://www.georgiaencyclopedia.org/articles/government-politics/jimmy-carter-b-1924.

23. Isaac Unah, *The Supreme Court in American Politics* (New York: Macmillan, 2010), 59.

24. Sandra Day O'Connor, *Lazy B: Growing Up on a Cattle Ranch in the American Southwest* (New York: Random House, 2003), 317.

25. Ann McFeatters, *Sandra Day O'Connor: Justice in the Balance* (Albuquerque: University of New Mexico Press, 2005), 116, 205; Nancy Maveety, *Justice Sandra Day O'Connor: Strategist on the Supreme Court* (Lanham, MD: Rowman and Littlefield, 1996), 21–22; A full list of the many, often contradictory, assays of O'Connor's jurisprudence appears in G. Edward White, *The American Judicial Tradition: Profiles of Leading American Judges*, 3rd rev. ed. (New York: Oxford University Press, 2006), 577–578.

26. Richard A Posner, *Public Intellectuals: A Study of Decline* (Cambridge, MA: Harvard University Press, 2001), 364 (search for conservative legal academics for judicial posts); Rebecca Love Kourlis and Russell R. Wheeler, "Options for Federal Judicial Screening Committees," September 13, 2011 (Washington, D.C.: Brookings Institution); Kevin L. Lyles, *The Gatekeepers: Federal District Courts in the Political Process* (Westport, CT: Greenwood, 1997), 138 (discarding the merit panels); Goldman, *Picking Federal Judges*, 285–345 (Reagan appointments), quotation on page 292; Dawn E. Johnsen, "Should Ideology Matter in

Selecting Federal Judges? Ground Rules for the Debate," *Cardozo Law Review* 26 (2005), 466 (greater uniformity of views in Reagan administration).

27. On Bork's ideology and the politics of the Meese Department of Justice, see Robert H. Bork, *A Time to Speak: Selected Writings and Arguments* (Wilmington, DE: Intercollegiate Studies Institute, 2008), passim, and John Massaro, *Supremely Political: The Role of Ideology and Presidential Management in Unsuccessful Supreme Court Nominations* (Albany: SUNY Press, 1990), 162–171.

28. "Interview of Robert H. Bork, March 13, 1992," final approved transcript, Historical Society of the District of Columbia Federal Courts, Oral History Collection.

29. Goldman, *Picking Federal Judges*, 300–312; Ethan Bronner, *Battle for Justice: How the Bork Nomination Shook America* (New York: Norton, 1989), 270–272, Bork quoted at 341. Law professor Ronald Dworkin was a leading critic, see his "From Bork to Kennedy," *New York Review of Books*, December 17, 1987, 36, and Nina Totenberg, "Robert Bork's Supreme Court Nomination 'Changed Everything, Maybe Forever.'" NPR, December 19, 2012; David W. Neubauer and Stephen Scott Meinhold, *Judicial Process: Law, Courts, and Politics in the United States,* 6th ed. (Boston: Wadsworth, 2013), 56–57. See a reply in Robert H. Bork, *The Tempting of America* (New York: Free Press, 1989), 75, 76.

30. Richard Posner, *Reflections on Judging* (Cambridge, MA: Harvard University Press, 2013), 1–17, 149–150. Note that on the latter page, Posner cites Judge Wilkinson's views on judicial restraint. Posner's *Federal Courts* is much cited in the present volume.

31. Goldman, *Picking Federal Judges*, 325–326; Lawrence Baum, *Judges and Their Audiences: A Perspective on Judicial Behavior* (Princeton: Princeton University Press, 2005), 1–2; J. Harvie Wilkinson III, *Cosmic Constitutional Theory: Why Americans Are Losing Their Inalienable Right to Self-Governance* (New York: Oxford, 2012), 4, 15, and after; Elizabeth Bumiller, "An Interview By, Not With, the President" *New York Times,* July 21, 2005.

32. Joan Biskupic, *American Original: The Life and Constitution of Supreme Court Justice Antonin Scalia* (New York: Farrar, Strauss, and Giroux, 2009), 11–65; here and after, Hoffer, Hoffer, and Hull, *Supreme Court*, 409–410.

33. Richard A. Brisbin, *Justice Antonin Scalia and the Conservative Revival* (Baltimore: Johns Hopkins University Press, 1998), 34–41. Scalia's account of his reading of law, particularly constitutional text, is amply conveyed in his condemnation of the courts' adventurism in social reform and "judicial overreaching." See, e.g., Ralph Rossum, *Antonin Scalia's Jurisprudence: Text and Tradition* (Lawrence: University Press of Kansas, 2009), 179.

34. See, e.g., Bruce Allen Murphy, *Scalia: A Court of One* (New York: Simon and Schuster, 2014), 244 (plain meaning); Brisbin, *Scalia and the Conservative*, 117–119 (legislative intent).

35. [35] William Rehnquist, *The Supreme Court*, 2nd ed. (New York: Knopf, Doubleday, 2007), 267.

36. Helen J. Knowles, *The Tie Goes to Freedom: Justice Anthony M. Kennedy on Liberty* (Lanham, MD: Rowman and Littlefield, 2009), 3.

37. See, e.g., Tom S. Clark, *The Limits of Judicial Independence* (New York: Cambridge University Press, 2010), 27–28.

38. E. Donald Elliott, "Managerial Judging and the Evolution of Procedure," *University of Chicago Law Review* 53 (1986), 309. On balance of equity see Hoffer, *Law's Conscience* 152–174, 180–198 (connection between nuisance suits and desegregation); on managerial responsibilities at the district court level after the conclusion of a trial, see Steven Harmon Wilson, *The Rise of Judicial Management in the U.S. District Court, Southern District of Texas, 1955–2000* (Athens: University of Georgia Press, 2002), 327–345. Note that this kind of managerial judging is different from pretrial management of discovery and other motions.

39. Green v. New Kent County 391 U.S. 430 (1968) (freedom of choice plans not acceptable step toward genuine desegregation); Bernard Schwartz, *Swann's Way: The School Busing Case and the Supreme Court* (New York: Oxford University Press, 1986), 3–4, 14–18, 19; Davison M. Douglas, *Reading, Writing, and Race: The Desegregation of the Charlotte Schools* (Chapel Hill: University of North Carolina Press, 1994), 245–246; Swann v. Charlotte-Mecklenburg Board of Education, 402 U.S. 1 (1970) (unanimous court finds extensive busing acceptable way to end majority minority schools); Wilson, *Southern District of Texas, 1955–2000*, 193.

40. Thomas Sugrue, *The Origins of the Urban Crisis: Race and Inequality in Post-war Detroit* (Princeton: Princeton University Press, 1996), 63–86; Joyce A. Baugh, *The Detroit School*

Busing Case: Milliken v. Bradley and the Controversy over Desegregation (Lawrence: University Press of Kansas, 2011), 88–118, 127–130; Bradley v. Milliken, 338 F. Supp. 582, 586–587 (D.C. E.D. Mich., 1971) (Roth, J.); Milliken v. Bradley, 418 U.S. 717 (1974) (de jure state segregation can only be proven when there is evidence of prior or present intent to impermissibly segregate).

41. Kelley v. Board of Education of the City of Nashville, 159 F. Supp. 272 (D.C. M.D. Tenn. 1958); Richard A. Pride and J. David Woodard, *The Burden of Busing: The Politics of Desegregation in Nashville, Tennessee* (Knoxville: University of Tennessee Press, 1985), 54–65, 71, 168.

42. J. Anthony Lukas, *Common Ground: A Turbulent Decade in the Lies of Three American Families* (New York: Knopf, 1985), 222–251; Morgan v. Hennigan 379 F. Supp, 410, 416 (D.C. D. Mass., 1974) (Garrity, J.).

43. Baugh, *Detroit School Busing Case*, 88–90, 114–116; Lukacs, *Common Ground*, 251.

44. Jack Bass, *Unlikely Heroes* (New York: Simon and Schuster, 1981), 19; Little Rock Sch. Dist. v. Pulaski County Special Sch. Dist., 740 F. Supp. 632, 633, 636 (D.C. E.D. Ark. 1990) (Woods, J.)

45. *Federal Rules of Civil Procedure, with Forms, December 1, 2014, Printed for the Use of the Judiciary Committee of the House of Representatives* (Washington, D.C.: GPO, 2014), is a 170-page document, in which pages 26–29 trace the evolution of Rule 23 for class actions. The key amendments came on Feb. 28, 1966, eff. July 1, 1966; which made class-action suits easier, and Mar. 2, 1987, eff. Aug. 1, 1987; Apr. 24, 1998, eff. Dec. 1, 1998, which made class actions harder (because of the notification and opt out provisions).

46. Stephen C. Yeazell, *From Medieval Group Litigation to the Modern Class Action* (New Haven: Yale University Press, 1987); 238–266; Brian Anderson and Andrew Trask, *The Class Action Playbook* (New York: Oxford University Press, 2012), 70. Aaron B. Lauchheimer, "A Classless Act," in Daniel Sherwyn and Samuel Estreicher, eds., *Employment Class and Collective Actions* (Frederick, MD: Aspen, 2009), 333.

47. On modern rules, see, e.g., Federal Judicial Center, *Manual for Complex Litigation*, 4th ed. (St. Paul: Thompson, West, 2004). Class-action law does not provide for the "opt-in"—that would be joinder or interpleader. Still, the absence of the opt-in, along with the difficulties of opt-out, concern some students of class action. See, e.g., Martin H. Redish, *Wholesale Justice: Constitutional Democracy and the Problem of the Class Action Law Suit* (Palo Alto, CA: Stanford University Press, 2009), 218–219, 231.

48. In Re A.H. Robins Co., 880 F. 2d. 709 (4th Cir. 1989).

49. Richard B. Sobol, *Bending the Law: The Story of the Dalkon Shield Bankruptcy* (Chicago: University of Chicago Press, 1993), 12–14. Note that only one in twenty mass tort filings went to federal courts in this period; state courts handled the great bulk of these claims. By far the largest number of federal cases involved product liability, and even these, while growing substantially, represented a shrinking portion of the federal civil docket over these years. William Haltom and Michael McCann, *Distorting the Law: Politics, Media, and the Litigation Crisis* (Chicago: University of Chicago Press, 2004), 87–88.

50. Sobol, *Dalkon*, 15–45; similar problems of proving individuals belonged in the class, that an individual's malady was caused by the product, and that the fund was sufficient to pay off the damages plagued the Agent Orange cases. See Peter H. Schuck, *Agent Orange on Trial: Mass Toxic Disasters in the Courts* rev. ed. (Cambridge, MA: Harvard University Press, 1987), 7 (Agent Orange first mass toxic suit certified as class action), 46 (novelty of the trust fund relief idea), 300–301 (problems on appeal with proximate cause).

51. Sobol, *Dalkon*, 218; In Re A.H. Robins Co., 880 F. 2d. 709, 711, 712, 724, 740 (4th Cir. 1989) (Russell, J.).

52. Augustus B. Cochran, *Sexual Harassment and the Law: The Mechelle Vinson Case* (Lawrence: University Press of Kansas, 2004), 18–24; Flora Davis, *Moving the Mountain: The Women's Movement in America Since 1960* (Urbana: University of Illinois Press, 1999), 66–67; Ruth Rosen, *The World Split Open: How the Modern Women's Movement Changed America* rev. ed (New York: Penguin, 2006), 74–89.

53. Guido Calabresi, *A Common Law for the Age of Statutes* (Cambridge, MA: Harvard University Press, 1982), 178.

54. Susan Ehrlich Martin and Nancy C. Jurik, *Doing Justice, Doing Gender* (Thousand Oaks, CA: Sage, 2006), 110; Marilyn Tucker and Georgia A. Niedzielko, "Options and Obstacles: A Survey of the Studies of the Careers of Women Lawyers," American Bar Association Commission on Women in the Profession, July 1994, 16; Cynthia Fuchs Epstein, *Women in Law* (Urbana: University of Illinois Press, 1993), 52, 194, 200; Karen Berger Morello, *The Invisible Bar: The Woman Lawyer in America, 1638 to the Present* (New York: Random House, 1986), 101; Lani Guinier, "Becoming Gentlemen: Women's Experiences at One Ivy League Law School," in Guinier et al., *Becoming Gentlemen: Women, Law School, and Institutional Change* (Boston: Beacon: 1997), 28; Deborah S. Katz, "Perspectives on Women in Public Sector Law," in Shimon Shetreet, ed., *Women in Law* (London: Kluwer, 1998), 75–77. Elena Kagan quoted in Adam Liptak, "Kagan Says Her Path to Supreme Court Was Made Smoother by Ginsburg's," *New York Times*, February 10, 2014.

55. Carmen Bredeson, *Ruth Bader Ginsburg: Supreme Court Justice* (Springfield, NJ: Enslow, 1995), 50–51.

56. Amy Leigh Campbell, *Raising the Bar: Ruth Bader Ginsburg and the ACLU Women's Rights Project* (Bloomington, IN: Xlibris, 2004), 25–87; Reed v. Reed, 404 U.S. 71 (1971); Phillips v. Martin Marietta Corp., 400 U.S. 542 (1971); Frontiero v. Richardson, 411 U.S. 677 (1973). The cases are included in Clare Cushman, ed., *Supreme Court Decisions and Women's Rights: Milestones to Equality* (New York: CQ Press, 2000, 2010).

57. Cleveland Board of Education v. LaFleur, 414 U.S. 632 (1974); Corning Glass Works v. Brennan, 417 U.S. 188 (1974); Weinberger v. Wiesenfeld, 420 U.S. 636 (1975); Craig v. Boren, 429 U.S. 190, 197 (1976) (Brennan, J.).

58. Roe v. Wade 314 F. Supp 1217 (D.C. N.D Tex. 1970) and Doe v. Bolton 319 F. Supp 1048 (D.C. N.D. Ga. 1970). This and the following from N. E. H. Hull and Peter Charles Hoffer, *Roe v. Wade: The Abortion Rights Controversy in American History*, 2nd ed. (Lawrence: University Press of Kansas, 2010), 135–179.

59. 314 F. Supp. at 1221; Goldberg was an intellectual on the bench. He loved discussing the law with his clerks and genuinely valued their ideas. Judge Diane Wood, in "Interviews with United States Court of Appeals Judges: Chief Judge Diane P. Wood," *Scribes Journal of Legal Writing* 15 (2013), 99, 100.

60. Roe v. Wade 410 U.S. 113, 154, 162, 164, 165 (1973) (Blackmun, J.).

61. 410 U.S. at 165 (Blackmun, J.); 410 U.S. at 170 (Stewart, J.).

62. 410 U.S. at 222 (White, J.); 410 U.S. at 171, 172, 177 (Rehnquist, J.).

63. Hull and Hoffer, *Roe v. Wade*, 272 and after. "Ripe for attack" (among jurists generally supportive of women's rights, see, e.g., John Hart Ely, "The Wages of Crying Wolf: A Comment on *Roe v. Wade*," *Yale Law Journal* 82 (1973), 926–927 (should have been left to states' elected bodies); Ruth Bader Ginsburg, "Some Thoughts on Autonomy and Equality in Relation to Roe v. Wade," *North Carolina Law Review* 63 (1985), 376–377 (decision should have been based on the gender question and the Equal Protection Clause).

64. Lawrence Friedman, "The Litigation Revolution," in Michael Grossberg and Christopher Tomlins, eds., *The Cambridge History of Law in America*: Vol. 3, *The Twentieth Century and After* (New York: Cambridge University Press, 2008), 179–180; Michael Willrich, "Criminal Justice in the United States," in ibid., 3:225; Curtis Marez, *Drug Wars: The Political Economy of Narcotics* (Minneapolis: University of Minnesota Press, 2004) 107 (criminalization of marijuana in the U.S. related to anti-Mexican immigration movement of the 1930s); Kathleen Frydl, *The Drug Wars in America, 1940–1973* (New York: Cambridge University Press, 2013).

65. Comprehensive Drug Abuse, Prevention, and Control Act of 1970, 84 Stat. 1236; United States v. Stephenson, 490 F. Supp. 625 (D.C. E.D Mich. 1979); "DEA History," www.justice.gov/dea/about/history.shtml; Racketeer Influenced and Corrupt Organizations Act of 1970, 84 Stat. 922.

66. Filing data compiled from AO tables C (civil) and D (criminal), "Detailed Statistical Tables," in *Report of the Director of the Administrative Office of the United States Courts* and is successor *Judicial Business of United States Courts* by Russell Wheeler (ms in his possession); Federal Bureau of Prisons, http://www.bop.gov/news/quick.jsp#2 (2013 breakdown); Elliott Currie, *Crime and Punishment in America* (New York: Macmillan, 2013), 15–16 and after;

Lawrence Friedman, *Crime and Punishment In American History* (New York: Basic Books, 1994), 356–357.

67. "Distribution" of cases: Lawrence Friedman, "The Litigation Explosion," in Grossberg and Tomlins, eds., *Cambridge History of Law in America:* Vol. 3, *The Twentieth Century and After*, 178–179; case figures: "Federal Courts Caseloads," http://www.fjc.gov/history/caseload.nsf/page/caseloads_civil_us; http://www.fjc.gov/history/caseload.nsf/page/caseloads_private_civil.

68. Posner, *Federal Courts* (1996), table 1.1.

69. This paragraph and the next two are based on FJC History website, http://www.fjc.gov/history/home.nsf/page/admin_03_11.html.

70. *Proceedings of the Judicial Conference*, September 1981, p. 71 and March 1999, p. 22; Laural Hooper, Dean Miletich, and Angela Levy, *Case Management Procedures in the Federal Courts of Appeals*, 2d ed. (Washington, D.C.: Federal Judicial Center, 2011), 11–12; Donna Stienstra, Jared Bataillon, and Jason A. Cantone, *Assistance to Pro Se Litigants in District Courts* (Washington, D.C.: Federal Judicial Center, 2011), 11–13. The text of the previous paragraph, edited and amended by the authors, is the original work of John S. Cooke, who thanks Daniel Holt for assistance.

71. The Federal Magistrates Act: "An Act to abolish the office of United States commissioner, to establish in place thereof within the judicial branch of the Government the office of United States magistrate, and for other purposes." 82 Stat. 1107; Judicial Improvements Act of 1990 (104 Stat. 5089).

72. Federal Magistrates Act of 1979, 93 Stat. 643; Irving R. Kauffman, "The Judicial Crisis, Court Delay and the Para-Judge," *Judicature* 54, no. 4 (Nov 1970): 145–148. *Proceedings of the Judicial Conference*, March 1975, p. 30. Checklist reprinted in U.S. Senate, Committee on the Judiciary, "Jurisdiction of United States Magistrates, Hearings on S. 1283," July 16, 1975, p. 22; Philip Pro, "United States Magistrate Judges: Present but Unaccounted For," unpublished M.A. thesis, Duke University, 2014, 4–5, 10, 12–13, 15, 22, 24, 44–45; Tim A. Baker, "The Expanding Role of Magistrate Judges in the Federal Courts," *Valparaiso University Law Review* 661 (2005), 665, 669–670.

73. Edward A. Tamm and Paul C. Reardon, "Warren E. Burger and the Administration of Justice," *Brigham Young Law Review* (1981) 447–552; Burger quoted at 463.

74. Hon. J. Harvie Wilkinson to the authors, October 25, 2013.

75. "Bankruptcy Cases," http://www.fjc.gov/history/caseload.nsf/page/caseloads_bankruptcy.

76. An Act to establish an Uniform Law on the Subject of Bankruptcies." Excerpt: "Title II— Amendments to Title 28 of the United States Code and to the Federal Rules of Evidence" 92 Stat. 2657 November 6, 1978. This paragraph and next three are based on "Bankruptcy Jurisdiction in the Federal Courts," http://www.fjc.gov/history/home.nsf/page/jurisdiction_bankruptcy.html.

77. Northern Pipeline Construction Co. v. Marathon Pipeline Co., 458 U.S. 50 (1982); Malia Reddick and Natalie Knowlton, *A Credit to the Courts: The Selection, Appointment and Reappointment Process for Bankruptcy Judges* (2013), http://iaals.du.edu/images/wygwam/documents/publications/A_Credit_to_the_Courts.pdf; http://www.uscourts.gov/Statistics/JudicialBusiness/2014/status-bankruptcy-judgeships.aspx.

78. Stern v. Marshall, 564 U.S. 2 (2011).

79. Owen Fiss, "The Bureaucratization of the Judiciary," *Yale Law Journal*, 92 (1983), 1442 and after; Alvin Rubin, "Bureaucratization of the Federal Courts: The Tension between Justice and Efficiency," *Notre Dame Law Review*, 55 (1980), 648 and after; Albert Yoon, "Federal Law Clerks and the Institutional Design of the Federal Judiciary," *Marquette Law Review*, 98 (2014), 131 and after; Todd C. Peppers, "Symposium: Judicial Assistants of 'Junior Judges'— The Hiring, Utilization, and Influence of Law Clerks," *Marquette Law Review* 98 (2014), 1–12.

Afterword

* The views expressed here are those of these authors.

1. United States Census Bureau, "State & County Quick Facts," Table, http://www.census.gov/qfd/states/00000.

THE FEDERAL JUDICIAL CENTER

THURGOOD MARSHALL FEDERAL JUDICIARY BUILDING
ONE COLUMBUS CIRCLE, N.E.
WASHINGTON, DC 20002-8003

TEL.: 202-502-4160
FAX: 202-502-4099
jfogel@fjc.gov

JUDGE JEREMY D. FOGEL
DIRECTOR

March 8, 2016

To: All United States Judges

From: Jeremy Fogel

I am pleased to provide to you this copy of *The Federal Courts: An Essential History*, produced by the Supreme Court Historical Society and the Federal Judicial Center. Written for a wide audience, the book traces the development of the federal courts from their modest beginnings to the present and illuminates their role in American government and society. It is a history in which we as judges can take great pride.

I hope that you will enjoy the book.

Sincerely,

Jeremy Fogel
United States District Judge
Director, Federal Judicial Center

2. Pew Research Center, "Political Polarization in the American Public: How Increasing Ideological Uniformity and Partisan Antipathy Affect Politics, Compromise and Everyday Life," June 12, 2014, http://www.people-press.org/2014/06/12/political-polarization-in-the-american-public/.

3. Demographic and employment data from the Federal Judicial Center's Biographical Directory of Federal Judges, http://www.fjc.gov/history/home.nsf/page/judges.html; Chief Justices' *Year-End Reports on the Federal Judiciary* 2006, at 8, http://www.supremecourt.gov/publicinfo/year-end/year-endreports.aspx.

4. http://www.supremecourt.gov/publicinfo/year-end/year-endreports.aspx.

5. Nomination and confirmation data from Denis Steven Rutkus and Mitchel A. Sollenberg, "Judicial Nomination Statistics: U.S. District and Circuit Courts, 1977-2003," Tables 2(b) and 4(b), February 23, 2004, Congressional Research Service RL 31635. Federal Judicial Center, Biographical Directory of Federal Judges, at http://www.fjc.gov/history/home.nsf/page/judges.html, along with data maintained by Russell Wheeler. Median days for Reagan and H. W. Bush appointees are from the successful nomination; time for Clinton, W. Bush, and Obama appointees are from the initial nomination, reflecting the vastly increased incidence of resubmitted nominations in those years.

6. "Senators Compromise on Filibusters," CNN, May 24, 2005, http://www.cnn.com/2005/POLITICS/05/24/filibuster.fight/. Paul Kane, "Reid, Democrats Trigger 'Nuclear' Option; Eliminate most Filibusters on Nominees," *Washington Post*, Nov. 21, 2013, http://www.washingtonpost.com/politics/senate-poised-to-limit-filibusters-in-party-line-vote-that-would-alter-centuries-of-precedent/2013/11/21/d065cfe8-52b6-11e3-9fe0-fd2ca728e67c_story.html.

7. *Annual Report of the Director of the Administrative Office of the United States Courts* (1987), http://www.uscourts.gov/statistics-reports/annual-report-2014, and *Judicial Business of the United States Courts* (2014) various tables, http://www.uscourts.gov/statistics-reports/judicial-business-2014. See also note 15.

8. See http://www.uscourts.gov/judges-judgeships/authorized-judgeships. William H. Rehnquist, "Seen in a Glass Darkly: The Future of the Federal Courts," *Wisconsin Law Review* 1 (1993); Gordon Bermant et al., "Imposing a Moratorium on the Number of Federal Judges: Analysis of Arguments and Implications," (Washington, D.C.: Federal Judicial Center, 1993); *Authorized Judgeships—From 1789 to the Present*, http://www.uscourts.gov/judges-judgeships/authorized-judgeships. As of June 2015, the Judicial Conference was recommending the creation of seventy-three new judgeships.

9. Thomas E. Willging and Emery G. Lee III, "From Class Actions to Multidistrict Consolidations: Aggregate Mass-Tort Litigation After *Ortiz*," *University of Kansas Law Review* 58, no. 4 (May 2010), 775–807; Administrative Office of United States Courts, *Judicial Business of the United States* (1987, 2014), http://www.uscourts.gov/statistics-reports/judicial-business-1987; Patricia Lombard and Carol Krafka, et al., *2003–2004 District Court Case-Weighting Study* (Washington, D.C.: Federal Judicial Center, 2005), Appendix Y; Federal Rule of Evidence 502, Advisory Committee Notes (Explanatory Note, Revised Nov. 28, 2007); Steven S. Gensler, Lee H. Rosenthal, "Four Years After Duke: Where Do We Stand on Calibrating the Pretrial Process?" *Lewis & Clark Law Review* 18, no. 3 (2014), 643–672; "Symposium on the Challenges of Electronic Evidence," *Fordham Law Review* 83, no. 3 (Dec. 2014), 1163–1285.

10. For proposals and responses about the FISC, compare *Liberty and Security in a Changing World, Report and Recommendations of the President's Review Group on Intelligence and Communications Technologies*, Dec. 2013, https://www.whitehouse.gov/sites/default/files/docs/2013-12-12_rg_final_report.pdf and Letter from Judge John D. Bates to Senator Diane Feinstein, January 13, 2014, enclosing "Comments of the Judiciary on Proposals Regarding the Foreign Intelligence Surveillance Act," http://fas.org/irp/news/2014/01/bates.pdf. For debate over the FISC's composition, see Russell Wheeler, "The Changing Composition of the Foreign Intelligence Surveillance Court and What If Anything To Do About It," Lawfare Research Paper Series, Vol. 2, June 2014, with basic data updated as of April 16, 2015, http://www.brookings.edu/blogs/fixgov/posts/2015/04/16-fisc-judges-wheeler; USA Freedom Act of 2015, Public Law 114–23, *U.S. Statutes at Large* 129 (2015), 268.

11. *Report of the Federal Courts Study Committee* (Washington, D.C.: Federal Judicial Center, April 2, 1990), 4; Richard Posner, *The Federal Courts: Crisis and Reform* (Cambridge, MA: Harvard University Press, 1985). See also Erwin Chemerinsky and Larry Kramer, "Defining the Role of the Federal Courts," *Brigham Young University Law Review*, no. 1 (1990), 67. Not all judges ascribed to the crisis idea, as described, for example, in Jack M. Beermann, "Crisis? What Crisis?" *Northwestern University Law Review* 80, no. 5 (1986), 1383–1406; *Long Range Plan for the Federal Courts* (Washington, D.C.: Judicial Conference of the United States, 1995), vii, 14; *Commission on Structural Alternatives for the Federal Courts of Appeals, Final Report*, Dec. 18, 1998.

12. *Report of the National Commission on Judicial Discipline and Removal* (Washington, D.C.: GPO, 1993); Judicial Conduct and Disability Act Study Committee, *Implementation of the Judicial Conduct and Disability Act of 1980, A Report to the Chief Justice* (Washington, D.C.: GPO, 2006).

13. Brookings Task Force on Civil Justice Reform, *Justice for All, Reducing Cost and Delay in Civil Litigation* (Washington, D.C.: Brookings Institution, 1989); *Judicial Conference of the United States, Rules for Judicial-Conduct and Judicial-Disability Act Proceedings*, adopted March 11, 2008, http://www.uscourts.gov/judges-judgeships/judicial-conduct-disability. Civil Justice Reform Act and Judicial Improvements Act of 1990, Public Law 101–650, *U.S. Statutes at Large* 104 (1990), 5089. The reporting requirement is codified at 28 U.S.C. § 476. See, for an example of a report, Administrative Office of the United States Courts, *Civil Justice Reform Act Report*, http://www.uscourts.gov/statistics-reports/september-2014-civil-justice-reform-act. See also Jeffrey J. Connaughton, "Judicial Accountability and the CJRA," *University of Alabama Law Review* 49, no. 1 (Fall 1997), 251–260.

14. Henry J. Friendly, "Averting the Flood by Lessening the Flow," *Cornell Law Review* 59, no. 4 (April 1974): 634–657. William W. Schwarzer and Russell R. Wheeler, "On the Federalization of the *Administration* of Civil and Criminal Justice," *Stetson Law Review* 23, no. 3 (Summer 1994), 651–700; Martin H. Redish, "Reassessing the Allocation of Judicial Business Between State and Federal Courts: Federal Jurisdiction and 'The Martian Chronicles,'" *University of Virginia Law Review* 78, no. 8 (November 1992), 1769–1832; William P. Marshall, "Federalization: A Critical Overview," *DePaul Law Review* 44, no. 3 (Spring 1995), 719–754. The Violent Crime and Law Enforcement Act of 1994, Public Law 103–322, *U.S. Statutes at Large* 108 (1994), 1796, was a major contributor to the federalization of criminal law. See statement of Stephen J. Markman in House Judiciary Committee, Subcommittee on Courts, Civil Liberties, and the Administration of Justice, Court Reform and Access to Justice Act, Hearings on HR 3152, October 14, 1987, 100th Cong., 2nd Sess., 256–261. See also *Long Range Plan for the Federal Courts*, 28, 37, see note 11.

15. Justin J. Wert, *Habeas Corpus in America* (Lawrence: University Press of Kansas, 2011), chapters 4 and 5; Administrative Office of United States Courts, *Judicial Business of the United States Courts*, 2000, http://www.uscourts.gov/statistics-reports/judicial-business-2000], Table C-2A; The federal prison population grew from 24,640 in 1980 to 49,378 in 1987 to 145,125 in 2000 and to 214,149 in 2014. See Federal Bureau of Prisons, statistics, http://www.bop.gov/about/statistics/population_statistics.jsp. Prisoner civil rights cases exceeded 32,000 in 2014; habeas cases increased from 16,429 in 1996 to 19,350 in 2014. Administrative Office of United States Courts, *Judicial Business of the United States* 1997, 2014 http://www.uscourts.gov/statistics-reports/judicial-business-1997; http://www.uscourts.gov/statistics-reports/judicial-business-2004, Table C-2A.

16. John W. Avery, "Securities Litigation Reform: The Long and Winding Road to the Private Securities Litigation Reform Act of 1995," *Business Lawyer* 51, no. 2 (1996): 335–378. Bankruptcy Abuse Prevention and Consumer Protection Act of 2005, Public Law 109–8, *U.S. Statutes at Large* 119 (2005), 23; Administrative Office of United States Courts, *Judicial Business of the United States Courts*, 2005,2014, http://www.uscourts.gov/statistics-reports/judicial-business-2005; http://www.uscourts.gov/statistics-reports/judicial-business-2014, Table F.

17. Erwin Chemerinsky, *Federal Jurisdiction* 6th ed. (New York: Walters and Kluwer Law and Business, 2012), 317; Emery G. Lee, III and Thomas Willging, *The Impact of the Class Action Fairness Act of 2005 on the Federal Courts* (Washington, D.C.: Federal Judicial Center, 2008).

18. Andrew von Hirsch, Kay Knapp, and Michael Tonry, *The Sentencing Commission and Its Guidelines* (Lebanon, NH: University Press of New England, 1987); U.S. Senate, Committee on the Judiciary, Subcommittee on Criminal Law, *Comprehensive Crime Control Act of 1983: Hearings on S. 829*, 98th Cong., 1st Sess., May 1983, 37 (Statements of Senator Strom Thurmond and Senator Edward Kennedy); U.S. Sentencing Commission, *Supplementary Report on the Initial Sentencing Guidelines and Policy Statements* (Washington, D.C.: U.S. Sentencing Commission, 1987); Kate Stith and Jose A. Cabranes, *Fear of Judging: Sentencing Guidelines in the Federal Courts* (Chicago: University of Chicago Press, 1998), 35–77.

19. Molly Johnson and Scott Gilbert, *The U.S. Sentencing Guidelines, Results of the Federal Judicial Center's 1996 Survey* (Washington, D.C.: Federal Judicial Center, 1997); examples of judicial criticism include Jose Cabranes, "Sentencing Guidelines: A Dismal Failure," *New York Law Journal* 207 (1992), 1; and Marvin Frankel, "Sentencing Guidelines: A Need for Creative Collaboration," *Yale Law Journal* 101, no. 8 (June 1992), 2043–2052; Paul G. Cassell, "Too Severe?: A Defense of the Federal Sentencing Guidelines (and a Critique of Federal Mandatory Minimums)," *Stanford Law Review* 56, no. 5 (April 2004), 1017–1048.

20. United States v. Booker, 543 U.S. 220 (2005); United States Sentencing Commission, *Report on the Continuing Impact of Booker on Federal Sentencing* (Washington, D.C.: U.S. Sentencing Commission, 2012), 58.

21. See note 15. Among those questioning incarceration policies toward the end of the period were Senators Richard Durbin (D-Ill.) and Mike Lee (R-Utah). See http://www.lee.senate. gov/public/index.cfm/2015/2/lee-durbin-introduce-smarter-sentencing-act-of-2015.

22. PROTECT Act of 2003, Public Law 108–21, *U.S. Statutes at Large* 117 (2003), 650; Reports of the *Proceedings of the Judicial Conference of the United States* Sept. 23., 18, http://www. uscourts.gov/about-federal-courts/reports-proceedings-judicial-conference-us. William H. Rehnquist, "2003 Year-End Report on the Federal Judiciary," www.supremecourt.gov.

23. Sensenbrenner Remarks before the U.S. Judicial Conference Regarding Congressional Oversight Responsibility of the Judiciary, March 17, 2004, available at http://www.tulane-link.com/tulanelink/judicialoversight_box.htm. *Implementation of the Judicial Conduct and Disability Act: A Report to the Chief Justice,* Sept. 2006, http://www.fjc.gov/public/pdf.nsf/lookup/breyer06.pdf/$file/breyer06.pdf.

24. Todd Gillman, "GOP Group Plans to Turn up Scrutiny on Federal Judges," *Dallas Morning News*, July 27, 2003. Generally, Charles Gardner Geyh, *When Courts and Congress Collide: The Struggle for Control of America's Judicial System* (Ann Arbor: University of Michigan Press, 2006).

25. Federal Judicial Center, *Federal Judiciary Appropriations, 1792–2010*, comp. Daniel S. Holt, 2012, http://www.fjc.gov/public/pdf.nsf/lookup/Appropriations.pdf/$file/Appropriations. pdf; Budget Control Act of 2011, Public Law 112–25, *U.S. Statutes at Large* 125 (2011), 240.

26. Administrative Office of the U.S. Courts, *Annual Report of the Director* (Washington, D.C.: Administrative Office of the U.S. Courts, 1971), 97; ibid., 1987, 50; Administrative Office of the U.S. Courts, *The Judiciary Fair Employment Practices Annual Report* (Washington, D.C.: Administrative Office of the U.S. Courts, 2013), 8; *Federal Judiciary Appropriations.* The 2015 appropriation figure does not include most judicial salaries.

27. Judicial Conference of the United States, Records of the Committee on Court Administration and Case Management; William W. Schwarzer and Alan Hirsch, *The Elements of Case Management: A Pocket Guide for Judges,* (Washington, D.C.: Federal Judicial Center, 2006); *Alternative Dispute Resolution Act of 1998*, Public Law 105–315, *U.S. Statutes at Large* 112 (1998), 2993; Judicial Conference of the United States, *Long Range Plan for the Federal Courts* (Washington, D.C.: Judicial Conference of the United States, 1995), 70, http://www. uscourts.gov/statistics-reports/publications/long-range-plan-federal-courts.

28. Judicial Conference of the United States, *Strategic Plan for the Federal Judiciary* (Washington, D.C.: Judicial Conference of the United States, 2010), http://www.uscourts.gov/statistics-reports/publications/strategic-plan-federal-judiciary. For state court efforts to lure business back from alternative forums, see Nancy A. Welsh, "Mandatory Predispute Consumer Arbitration, Structural Bias, and Incentivizing Procedural Safeguards," *Southwestern Law Review* 42, no. 1 (2012), 187, 194–95, n. 41; Federal Arbitration Act of 1925, Public Law

68–401, *U.S. Statutes at Large* 43 (1923–25), 883; Arbitration Fairness Act of 2015, HR 2087, S1133, 114th Cong., 1st sess. (April 29, 2015), Section 2 ("Findings").

29. "Vanishing Trial Symposium," *Journal of Empirical Legal Studies* 1, no. 3 (2004), 459–981; Administrative Office of the U.S. Courts, *Judicial Business of the United States Courts* (Washington, D.C.: Administrative Office of the U.S. Courts, various years).

30. Compare Judith Resnik, "The Role of the Judge in the Twenty-First Century: Whither and Whether Adjudication?" *Boston University Law Review* 86, no. 5 (2006), 1101 and D. Brock Hornby, "The Business of the U.S. District Courts," *The Green Bag* 10, no. 4 (2007), 453.

31. Administrative Office of the U.S. Courts, *Annual Report of the Director* (Washington D.C. 1987), Tables B, C, D-1; Administrative Office of the U.S. Courts, *Judicial Business of the United States Courts*, 2005, Tables B, C, D-13, http://www.uscourts.gov/statistics-reports/judicial-business-2005; *Judicial Business of the United States Courts*, 2014, Tables B, C, D-13, http://www.uscourts.gov/statistics-reports/judicial-business-2014; Administrative Office of the U.S. Courts, *Authorized Judgeships—From 1789 to Present*, http://www.uscourts.gov/judges-judgeships/authorized-judgeships.

32. Federal Judicial Center, *Supreme Court of the United States, Method of Disposition, 1970–2013*, http://www.fjc.gov/history/caseload.nsf/page/caseloads_Sup_Ct_methods_of_disposition_2.

33. Federal Judicial Center, *Supreme Court of the United States, Caseload, 1878–2013*, http://www.fjc.gov/history/caseload.nsf/page/caseloads_Sup_Ct_totals; and statistics gathered from *The Journal of the Supreme Court of the United States*, http://www.supremecourt.gov/orders/journal.aspx.

34. SCOTUSblog Stat Pack, October term 2013, http://sblog.s3.amazonaws.com/wp-content/uploads/2014/07/SCOTUSblog_votesplit_OT13.pdf.

35. R. Reeves Anderson and Anthony J. Franze, "Commentary: The Court's Increasing Reliance on Amicus Curiae in the Past Term," *National Law Journal*, August 24, 2011. A count of such briefs in the 2014–2015 term as listed in SCOTUSblog's "Merits Cases" revealed only one orally argued case with no such briefs (http://www.scotusblog.com/case-files/terms/ot2014/. See also Joseph D. Kearney and Thomas W. Merrill, "The Influence of Amicus Curiae Briefs on the Supreme Court," *University of Pennsylvania Law Review* 148, no. 3 (2000), 743.

36. Ninia Baehr, *Abortion Without Apology: A Radical History for the 1990s* (Boston: South End Press, 1990), 6 (late 1980s); Melody Rose, *Abortion: A Documentary and Reference Guide* (Santa Barbara, CA: ABC-CLIO, 2008), 171–172 (1990s); Scott H. Ainsworth and Todd E. Hall, *Abortion Politics in Congress: Strategic Instrumentalism and Policy Change* (New York: Cambridge University Press, 2010), 60, 199–200 (abortion politics in Congress); David Karol, *Party Position Change in American Politics: Coalition Management* (New York: Cambridge University Press, 2009), 69–74 (presidential candidates' views on abortion); William V. D'Antonio, Steven A. Tuch, and Josiah R. Baker, *Religion, Politics, and Polarization: How Religiopolitical Conflict Is Changing Congress and American Democracy* (Lanham, MD: Rowman and Littlefield, 2008), 115; N. E. H. Hull and Peter Charles Hoffer, *Roe v. Wade*, 222–271. Key cases: Webster v. Reproductive Health Services, 492 U.S. 490 (1989); Planned Parenthood v. Casey, 505 U.S. 833 (1992); Stenberg v. Carhart, 530 U.S. 914 (2000).

37. Obergefell v. Hodges, 576 U.S. ___ (June 26, 2015); *United States v. Windsor*, 570 U.S. ___ (2013); Lawrence v. Texas, 539 U.S. 588 (2003); Bowers v. Hardwick, 479 U.S. 186 (1986).

38. District of Columbia v. Heller, 554 U.S. 570 (2008); see also McDonald v. Chicago, 561 U.S. 742 (2010), holding that the Second Amendment right applies to states and the federal government.

39. Bush v. Gore, 531 U.S. 98, 118 (2000); William Kristol, "A President by Judicial Fiat," in E. J. Dionne and William Kristol, eds., *Bush v. Gore: The Court Cases and the Commentary* (Washington, D.C.: Brookings Institution Press, 2010), 253–254; (*Bush v. Gore* widely seen as proof of political partisanship on the Court); Richard A. Posner, *Breaking the Deadlock: The 2000 Election, the Constitution, and the Courts* (Princeton: Princeton University Press, 2001), 219 (alternative ways of seeing the outcome). There are not only dozens of books and hundreds of articles, from within and without the legal community, on the case, there are also articles that collect references to all the other articles. See, e.g., Richard L. Hasen, "A Critical

Guide to *Bush v. Gore* Scholarship," *Annual Review of Political Science* 7 (2004), 297–313. Aside from its effect on the 2000 election, *Bush v. Gore* encouraged litigation over elections in later years. See Richard L. Hasen, "What to Expect When You're Electing: Federal Courts and the Political Thicket in 2012," *The Federal Lawyer,* June 2012, 34.

40. Citizens United v. Federal Election Commission, 558 U.S. 310 (2010); McCutcheon v. Federal Election Commission, 572 U.S. ____ (2014); see also Arizona Free Enterprise Club's Freedom Club PAC v. Bennett, 564 U.S. ____ (2011); Vieth v. Jubelirer, 541 U.S. 267 (2004); Alabama Legislative Black Caucus v. Alabama, 135 S. Ct. 1257 (2015); Shelby County v. Holder, 570 U.S. ____ (2013); Crawford v. Marion County Election Board, 553 U.S. 181 (2008). See also Richard Pildes, "The Constitutionalization of Democratic Politics," *Harvard Law Review* 118, no. 1 (November 2004): 29–154; Richard L. Hasen, "Introduction: Election Law at Puberty," *Loyola Law Review* 32, no. 4 (June 1999): 1095–1104. In Arizona State Legislature v. Arizona Independent Redistricting Commission, 576 U.S. ____ (June 29, 2015), the Court held that Arizona's establishment of a redistricting commission independent of its legislature did not violate Article I, § 4, cl. 5 of the Constitution, which says that the "Times, Places, and Manner of holding Elections for" the U.S. Congress "shall be prescribed in each State by the Legislature thereof."

41. Regents of the University of California v. Bakke, 438 U.S. 265 (1978); Gratz et al. v. Bollinger, 539 U.S. 244 (2003); Grutter v. Bollinger, 539 U.S. 306 (2003); Fisher v. University of Texas, 570 U.S. ____ (2013); Schuette v. BAMN, 572 U.S. ____ (2014). On *Bakke,* see Howard Ball, *The Bakke Case: Race, Education, and Affirmative Action* (Lawrence: University Press of Kansas, 2000), 107–140 (a divided Court permits non-quota consideration of race). On *Gratz* and *Grutter,* see Barbara A. Perry, *The Michigan Affirmative Action Cases* (Lawrence: University Press of Kansas, 2007), 135–156 (diversity a compelling state interest when prior discrimination evident).

42. Authorization for the Use of Military Force Act of 2001, Public Law 107–40, *U.S. Statutes at Large* 115 (2001). 224; Uniting and Strengthening America by Providing Appropriate Tools Required to Intercept and Obstruct Terrorism Act of 2001, Public Law 107–56, *U.S. Statutes at Large* 115 (2001), 272; amended in 2005 as U.S.A. Patriot Improvement and Reauthorization Act; and in 2011 as Patriot Sunsets Extension Act. See, generally, Terry H. Anderson, *Bush's Wars* (New York: Oxford University Press, 2011) and Susan N. Herman, *Taking Liberties: The War on Terror and the Erosion of American Democracy* (New York: Oxford University Press, 2011), 132 and after.

43. Hamdi v. Rumsfeld, 542 U.S. 507 (2004); Rasul v. Bush, 542 U.S. 466 (2004); Hamdan v. Rumsfeld, 548 U.S. 557 (2006); Boumediene v. Bush, 553 U.S. 723 (2008).

44. Patient Protection and Affordable Care Act, Public Law 111–148, *U.S. Statutes at Large* (2010), 119; National Federation of Independent Business v. Sebelius, 567 U.S. ____, 132 S. Ct. 2566 (2012); King v. Burwell, 576 U.S. ____ (June 25, 2015).

Conclusion

1. Lewis Powell, "Preface" in Gunther, *Hand,* xiii; Gunther, *Hand,* xiv, 664.

2. See, e.g., Peter Charles Hoffer, *The Historians' Paradox: The Study of History in Our Time* (New York: New York University Press, 2008), 9–11 (the question of objectivity), and Hoffer, *Clio Among the Muses: Essays on History and the Humanities* (New York: New York University Press, 2013), 152–154 (value added by historical judgment).

3. Hon. Judge Diane Wood to the authors, October 22, 2013.

4. Figures from the Office of Management of the Budget, courtesy of Russell Wheeler, correspondence with the authors, October 22, 2013; Thomas F. Hogan, Director's Message, Administrative Office of the United States Courts Annual Report for 2012, uscourts.gov/FederalCourts/UnderstandingtheFederalCourts/AdministrativeOffice/ DirectorAnnualReport/annual-report-2012/director-message.aspx; Chief Justice John G. Roberts, Jr., *2012 Year-End Report on the Federal Judiciary,* http://www.supremecourt.gov/ publicinfo/year-end/2012year-endreport.pdf.

5. Fred Anderson and Andrew Cayton, *The Dominion of War: Empire and Liberty in North America, 1500–2000* (New York: Viking, 2004), 420 (war fought in the name of freedom

was also war waged for the purpose of empire). Not all historians condemn our fascination with war: "After four decades of study what impresses me most is how far superior democracy is to all other forms of government in making war." Stephen E. Ambrose, *Americans at War* (Jackson: University Press of Mississippi, 1997), x.

6. See, generally, Stephen Breyer, *The Court and the World: American Law and the New Global Realities* (New York: Knopf, 2015), 89–246. The historical component of this is a very complicated subject matter, growing in scholarship by leaps and bounds, which cannot be more than touched upon here. The quotation from David Golove, "The Supreme Court, The War on Terror, and the American Just War Constitutional Tradition," in David L. Sloss, Michael D. Ramsey, and William S. Dodge, eds., *International Law in the U.S. Supreme Court: Continuity and Change* (New York: Cambridge University Press, 2001), 564. For more politically oriented accounts, see Kenneth Roth, "The Law of War in the War on Terror," *Foreign Affairs* 83 (January/February 2004), 1–12, and Jordan J. Paust, *Beyond the Law: The Bush Administration's Unlawful Responses in the "War" on Terror* (New York: Cambridge University Press, 2007), 118–128.

7. But see Posner, *Federal Courts,* 282 (readjusting the balance between state and federal courts).

8. See, e.g., Terri Perretti, "Does Judicial Independence Exist," in Stephen Burbank and Barry Friedman, eds., *Judicial Independence at the Crossroads: An Interdisciplinary Approach* (Thousand Oaks, CA: Sage, 2002), 111.

9. Barrow and Walker, *Court Divided,* ix; Mark C. Miller, *The View of the Courts from the Hill: Interactions Between Congress and the Federal Judiciary* (Charlottesville: University of Virginia Press, 2009), 88.

10. Lucas A. Powe Jr., *The Supreme Court and the American Elite, 1789–2008,* (Cambridge, MA: Harvard University Press, 2009), 350.

BIBLIOGRAPHICAL NOTE

Any essay on the history of the federal courts confronts a problem of sources—not too few or too difficult to find but the reverse. Just as the authors of this book had to select a few among almost too many stories to tell, so here we have to restrict the number of sources we include to those few that are essential reading. All the secondary scholarly sources we used in the book are cited in the endnotes, but we declined, again for reasons of clarity and conciseness, to engage in extensive source criticism there. Nor did we find a need to reinvent the wheel with string citations of cases on point.

For the book's notes we adopted a version of citation style based on the Chicago University Press's *Manual of Style* that Kate Turabian introduced rather than th *Blue Book* style used in law reviews. Lay readers are more familiar with the former than the latter.

For the historian, primary sources are evidence of events, people, and ideas from the period under study. They may be in print or digitized (for example the opinions of the judges and justices of the federal courts) or in manuscript (for example the private correspondence or other writings of the judges and justices). One could write history without looking at primary sources, relying on other historians' research on them, but that is not best practice.

In a history of any court the most important primary sources are the documents that the court creates and those submitted to the court in the process of litigation or prosecution of cases. Records for the Article III district and the old circuit federal courts comprise National Archives Record Group (RG) 21. Records of the courts of appeals are (RG) 276. The Supreme Court's records comprise (RG) 267. While the records for the courts of the District of Columbia can be accessed at the National Archives in Washington, DC, those for the other district, circuit, and appeals courts are archived at the regional National Archives and Records Administration (NARA) facilities throughout the country. The old naming scheme for these regional offices, for example Southeastern Region at Atlanta, has been changed (in 2010) to "NARA at" the city in which the facility exists. Not all of these facilities include RG 21 records. Researchers should contact the archivist or check the online guides to collections at any particular regional archive.

Manuscript records include court minute books, dockets (judges dockets, clerks dockets, motions dockets and judgment dockets, grand jury dockets), criminal case files, lists of grand and petty jurors, federal attorney's proposed rules, and the personnel of the court itself. Names of those attorneys permitted to practice in it appear as well. File papers (depositions, affidavits, other evidence, and records of testimony at trial) are created by the parties to lawsuits or equitable complaints and sometimes copied into the court records by the court clerk. Orders of the court (summonses, subpoenas, and writs including those issued by the court and those sought by parties) are listed in the minute books or other variously named bound journals. The array and quality of these surviving records depended on the ability and care of the court's clerk, and this too varies considerably from court to court. This concession to long-established local autonomy can be seen in every one of the depositories: each of the circuits had its own rules for filing, for fees, and the like. The record books of the courts thus demonstrate a bizarre and sometimes bewildering variety docket- and minute-recording systems, sometimes in account book size ledgers, sometimes in much smaller unlined volumes, sometimes numbered consecutively, sometimes arranged alphabetically. The entries display a variety of forms and formats. Before the introduction of the typewriter, the clerk's hand, long the best calligraphy in America, might be large or small, include just the parties' names or add the counsel, might or might not state the legal category of the suit or the grounds for federal prosecution. The clerks of the Northern District of Illinois did not keep minute books. Instead, they had separate books for entry of cases, judgment rolls, and other orders of the courts. The record books of the Third Circuit Court of Appeals from 1891 to 1917 bear little more than facial resemblance to the record books of the Fourth Circuit Court of Appeals for the same years. The docket books were different sizes, the entries in the former were arrayed differently from the entries in the latter, and the indexes to the two were differently designed. The only sure uniformity was that some books would stop in the middle of the year, leave an empty page, and add, sometimes at the end, bits of information that seemed to float in a kind of notarial ether. The clerk could have explained the system but did not bother to do so in the records. Some records simply have not survived, for example grand jury indictments are missing from the records in some regional NARAs. In all, doing research in the manuscript records is not for the fainthearted. Clerks also kept records of the administrative side of the court, the collection and disbursement of funds, for example, citizenship oaths, as well as loyalty oaths and amnesty oaths during the Civil War. On the clerks, see Scott Messinger, *Order in the Courts: A History of the Federal Court Clerk's Office* (Washington, D.C.: Federal Judicial Center, 2002).

As federal courts were both law and equity courts, the records include both types of adjudication, kept on separate dockets until 1938's Federal Rules of Civil Procedure merged the two and ended the writ pleading system, some 800 years after it was introduced in the king's courts in England. One can find criminal cases, admiralty cases, and bankruptcy cases, the latter until separate courts for bankruptcy were established in 1978. After 1978, bankruptcy records appear in RG 578. The Court of Claims early records are RG 123. The Court became the U. S. Court of Federal Claims in 1982. Its records are RG 502.

The manuscript district court records include jury verdicts and orders of judges. The records of the courts of appeals record outcome, but one has to look elsewhere for the opinions of their judges accompanying their rulings and decisions. In a common law system like ours, the opinions of majority of the courts of appeals become "precedent"—law governing similar cases in that circuit. Although much of our law is now statute brought together in codes (for example the U.S. Statutes, later the U.S. Code annotated), courts have to interpret the meaning of the language in the statute and apply it to particular cases.

Appeals courts' interpretations of that sort become precedent for later cases under that statute. Federal judges' opinions can be found in published (print) versions prepared by the "reporters" for the courts and on Lexis and Westlaw websites. These are proprietary subscription sites, but state law school libraries have access to them and most are open to the public. Most Supreme Court and some lower courts of appeal opinions can also be found online at Oyez and other nonproprietary sites.

The West Publication company began to collect and publish the state supreme courts' opinions from the 1870s, and from 1880 the West *Federal Reporter* printed opinions from the lower federal courts in (F. and F. 2d). From 1894 to 1897 West collected and published federal cases from the beginning of the federal courts to 1880 in a special 30-volume edition (F. Cas.). Starting in the 1930s, West brought out the reports of the courts of claims and district courts (Fed Supp and Fed Supp 2d). The *U.S. Reports* (for the Supreme Court) began with the reports Alexander James Dallas published, and thereafter the Supreme Court selected a publisher. In one infamous episode, when Court reporter Richard Peters condensed the reports of his predecessor, Henry Wheaton, Wheaton sued and lost. He did not have copyright to the Court's opinions. They were then, and remain, "in the public domain." (Peters was fired in 1843 for malfeasance.) The records of the Supreme Court include the appellate cases and the cases in which the Supreme Court had original jurisdiction. The personal records of the justices can be found in the Library of Congress manuscript collections and other archives around the United States. The FJC biographical directory of federal judges lists the location of all known Supreme Court justices manuscript collections. Finally, a series of maps derived from Cynthia Harrison and Russell R. Wheeler and

Harrison's history of the creation of the federal judicial system illustrates the changing federal circuits. See http://www.fjc.gov/history/home.nsf/page/index.html to navigate to these web pages.

The Judicial Conference of the United States (1922–present) has become another policy-making body for the federal judiciary (along with Congress and the Supreme Court). As presently constituted, it includes chief judges in the circuits and districts and the chief judge of the Court of International Trade. Its records appear in RG 269, and its yearly *Report of the Proceedings* has since 1922 summarized its recommendations. See http://www.uscourts.gov/FederalCourts/JudicialConference/Proceedings.aspx.

The Administrative Office of the United States Courts (1939–present) succeeded the Department of Justice handling day-to -ay administrative matters for the federal courts. Its records are collected in RG 116. Its yearly *Report of the Director* summarizes its activities. From 2003, these are online at http://www.uscourts.gov/annualreport.aspx. The records of the attorney general of the United States and the Department of Justice comprise RG 60.

Other records pertaining to the federal courts include the texts of the Judiciary Acts and other statutes of Congress bearing on the courts, the debates in Congress and the records of the House Judiciary Committee (from 1813) and the Senate Judiciary Committee (from 1816), their hearings, and the Senate judiciary confirmation hearings are available in federal document depositories part of the Federal Depository Library program. The published records of the Congress, the Annals, the Globe, and the Congressional Record, along with publication of the committee hearings, are deposited in government documents departments of libraries throughout the country. See http://catalog.gpo.gov/fdlpdir/FDLPdir.jsp for a list of these depositories. They are open to the public.

Jonathan W. White of the History Office of the Federal Judicial Center has compiled the authoritative *Guide to Research in Federal Judicial History* (Washington, D.C.: Federal Judicial Center, 2010). The authors found his work of inestimable aid. The History Office of the FJC has also prepared annotated lists and descriptive chronologies on the history of the federal courts and biographical information on the judges and justices of the federal courts. These can be found online at "History of the Federal Judiciary" http://www.fjc.gov/history/home.nsf/page/index.html.

Unless otherwise noted, statistical information, including caseloads by type of case and by court, in this book are found at the Federal Judicial Center website, http://www.fjc.gov/history/caseload.nsf/page/caseloads_main_page; and at the Administrative Office of United States Courts, Annual Report of the Director website; and the Department of Justice, Bureau of Justice Statistics Sourcebook of Criminal Justice Statistics, 1995.

The website for the federal courts, uscourts.gov, and the History Office of the Federal Judicial Center have created electronic data bases for the courts and the bench of the federal judicial system. Each year, more state and federal judges' opinions, law review articles, and other secondary sources are available on HeinOnline. These and data bases of American imprints, newspapers, and journal and magazine articles from ProQuest, Epsco, J-Stor, and Project Muse are readily available from research libraries. The Library of Congress's "A Century of Lawmaking" has a searchable documentary data base, including the entire text of the congressional Annals, Globe, and Record through the year 1876. Amazon, Google, and other websites have scanned parts of or wholes of older books on judges into their accessible data bases.

INDEX